Communications in Computer and Information Science 465

Giedre Dregvaite   Robertas Damasevicius (Eds.)

Information and Software Technologies

20th International Conference, ICIST 2014
Druskininkai, Lithuania, October 9-10, 2014
Proceedings

 Springer

Volume Editors

Giedre Dregvaite
Kaunas University of Technology
Studentu g. 50-409a
51368 Kaunas, Lithuania
E-mail: giedre.dregvaite@ktu.lt

Robertas Damasevicius
Kaunas University of Technology
Studentu g. 50-409a
51368 Kaunas, Lithuania
E-mail: robertas.damasevicius@ktu.lt

ISSN 1865-0929   e-ISSN 1865-0937
ISBN 978-3-319-11957-1   e-ISBN 978-3-319-11958-8
DOI 10.1007/978-3-319-11958-8
Springer Cham Heidelberg New York Dordrecht London

Library of Congress Control Number: Applied for

Typesetting: Camera-ready by author, data conversion by Scientific Publishing Services, Chennai, India

Printed on acid-free paper

Springer is part of Springer Science+Business Media (www.springer.com)

Preface

We are glad to introduce to scholars and researchers the selection of papers presented during the International Conference on Information and Software Technologies – ICIST 2014. This year the International Conference on Information and Software Technologies – ICIST formerly known as the IT Conference is celebrating its 20th anniversary and welcoming scholars from all over the world.

In 2012 the proceedings of the conference published by Springer for the first time marked a new qualitative step. This issue of *Communications in Computer and Information Science* series signifies our continuing cooperation.

Despite the venue of the conference being changed from the second largest city Kaunas to one of the resorts of Lithuania, Druskininkai, the organizers of the conference still aim to develop a bind between researchers and industry representatives in promotion and application of new supporting information technology means. Moreover, the scope and topics of the conference were also reconsidered to rely on developing fields of information technology the most. Therefore, the topics this year were modified to encourage the submission of papers in the fields of information systems, business intelligence for information and software systems, software engineering, and IT applications. These themes have definitely become indistinguishable objects of discussion of society encouraging researchers to develop interdisciplinary approaches and employ multivariate ways of thinking and analysis. On the other hand, scientific innovation is no longer an issue of academia only, hence the attempt to integrate science into business is also of importance. As a result participants of the conference were encouraged to take part in both research sessions and industrial tutorials on IT security issues discussed by well-known practitioners. The event was co-located with the conference for the 5th year in a row.

There were 68 submissions this year, and 34 papers were selected for this publication. The composition of the Program Committee also changed this year which also reflects the growing attention aimed at improving the quality of the papers submitted and a part of them accepted for publication afterwards. The papers were reviewed and selected by the Program Committee consisting of 83 reviewers (supported by 25 additional reviewers) representing more than 50 academic institutions and companies from 28 countries. Each submission was reviewed following the double-blind process by at least two reviewers, while borderline papers were evaluated by three or more reviewers.

Finally, we would like to express our gratitude to the Lithuanian State Science and Studies Foundation and the Faculty of Informatics of Kaunas University of Technology whose support has made this event and this book possible.

July 2014

Giedre Dregvaite
Robertas Damasevicius

Organization

The 20th International Conference on Information and Software Technologies (ICIST 2014) was organized by Kaunas University of Technology and took place in Druskininkai, Lithuania (October 9–10, 2014).

General Chair

Eduardas Bareisa   Kaunas University of Technology, Lithuania

Local Organizing Committee

Giedre Dregvaite (*Chair*)	Kaunas University of Technology, Lithuania
Rita Butkiene (*Co-chair*)	Kaunas University of Technology, Lithuania
Gintare Dzindzeletaite	Kaunas University of Technology, Lithuania
Gintare Krisciuniene	Kaunas University of Technology, Lithuania
Ignas Martisius	Kaunas University of Technology, Lithuania
Kestutis Valincius	Kaunas University of Technology, Lithuania
Kestutis Jankauskas	Kaunas University of Technology, Lithuania
Agne Paulauskaite-Taraseviciene	Kaunas University of Technology, Lithuania
Ingrida Lagzdinyte-Budnike	Kaunas University of Technology, Lithuania

Program Committee

Lina Nemuraite	Kaunas University of Technology, Lithuania
Olga Kurasova	Vilnius University, Lithuania
Jurgita Kapociute-Dzikiene	Vytautas Magnus University, Lithuania
Yuh-Min Tseng	National Changhua University of Education, Taiwan
Irene Krebs	University of Technology Cottbus, Germany
Sevinc Gulsecen	Istanbul University, Turkey
Jörg Becker	University of Münster, Germany
Moacyr Martucci	University of Sao Paulo, Brasil
Constantine Filote	Stefan cel Mare University of Suceava, Romania
Albertas Caplinskas	Vilnius University, Lithuania
Jose Luis Herrero Agustin	University of Extremadura, Spain
Massimo Tivoli	University of L'Aquila, Italy
Vladimir Hahanov	Kharkov National University of Radio Electronics, Ukraine

Yuko Murayama	Iwate Prefectural University, Japan
Michael Pantazoglou	National and Kapodistrian University of Athens, Greece
Ivana Podnar Žarko	University of Zagreb, Croatia
Graziano Pravadelli	University of Verona, Italy
Saulius Gudas	Vilnius University, Lithuania
Christian Reimann	Dortmund University of Applied Sciences and Arts, Germany
Marite Kirikova	Riga Technical University, Latvia
Mirjana Ivanovic	University of Novi Sad, Serbia
Alvydas Jaliniauskas	SubscriberMail, A Harland Clarke Company, USA
Raimundas Jasinevicius	Kaunas University of Technology, Lithuania
Willy Picard	Poznań University of Economics, Poland
Marisa Gil	Polytechnic University of Catalonia, Spain
Achim Schmidtmann	Dortmund University of Applied Sciences and Arts, Germany
Mehmet Aksit	University of Twente, The Netherlands
Sanda Martinčić-Ipšić	University of Rijeka, Croatia
José Raúl Romero	University of Córdoba, Spain
Milena Krumova	Technical University of Sofia, Bulgaria
Damjan Vavpotič	University of Ljubljana, Slovenia
Roberto Giacobazzi	University of Verona, Italy
Sandro Leuchter	Rhine-Waal University of Applied Sciences, Germany
Zheying Zhang	University of Tampere, Finland
Martin Gaedke	Technical University of Chemnitz, Germany
Yiwei Gong	Nyenrode Business University, The Netherlands
John Gammack	College of Technological Innovation, United Arab Emirates
Paulo Rupino Cunha	University of Coimbra, Portugal
Jyrki Nummenmaa	University of Tampere, Finland
Matjaž Debevc	University of Maribor, Slovenia
Björn W. Schuller	University of Passau, Germany
Nuno Castela	Polytechnic Institute of Castelo Branco, Portugal
Algirdas Pakstas	London Metropolitan University, UK
Marcin Paprzycki	Systems Research Institute, Polish Academy of Science, Poland
Stefano Squartini	Polytechnic University of Marche, Italy
Henrikas Pranevicius	Kaunas University of Technology, Lithuania
Janis Grabis	Riga Technical University, Latvia
Marite Kirikova	Riga Technical University, Latvia
Ana Paula Neves Ferreira da Silva	University of Coimbra, Portugal

Tor-Morten Grønli	Brunel University, Norway
Christophoros Nikou	University of Ioannina, Greece
Elena Sánchez Nielsen	University of San Fernando de la Laguna, Spain
Vira Shendryk	Sumy State University, Ukraine
André Schekelmann	Niederrhein University of Applied Science, Germany
Gert Jervan	Tallinn University of Technology, Estonia
Oleg Zabolotnyi	Lutsk National Technical University, Ukraine
Harri Oinas-Kukkonen	University of Oulu, Finland
Virgilijus Sakalauskas	Vilnius University, Lithuania
Dalia Kriksciuniene	Vilnius University, Lithuania
Audrius Lopata	Vilnius University, Lithuania
Aleksandras Targamadze	Kaunas University of Technology, Lithuania
Laimutis Telksnys	Vilnius University, Lithuania
Peter Thanisch	University of Tampere, Finland
Babis Theodoulidis	University of Manchester, UK
Lovro Šubelj	University of Ljubljana, Slovenia
Kestutis Driaunys	Vilnius University, Lithuania
Karin Harbusch	University of Koblenz-Landau, Germany
Arthur Caetano	University of Lisbon, Portugal
Joao Manuel R.S. Tavares	University of Porto, Portugal
Winfried Lamersdorf	University of Hamburg, Germany
Ernest Teniente	Polytechnic University of Catalonia, Spain
Marco Bajec	University of Ljubljana, Slovenia
Zakaria Maamar	Zayed University, United Arab Emirates
Juan Manuel Vara Mesa	University of Rey Juan Carlos, Spain
Kari Smolander	Lappeenranta University of Technology, Finland
Alexander Maedche	University of Mannheim, Germany
Ljupcho Antovski	University Ss. Cyril and Methodius, Macedonia
Pavel Kordik	Czech Technical University, Czech Republic
Olegas Vasilecas	Vilnius Gediminas Technical University, Lithuania
Radu Adrian Vasiu	Politehnica University of Timisoara, Romania
Darius Birvinskas	Kaunas University of Technology, Lithuania
Rimantas Butleris	Kaunas University of Technology, Lithuania
Tomas Krilavicius	Vytautas Magnus University, Lithuania
Lucio Tommaso de Paolis	University del Salento, Italy
Eduard Babkin	National Research University, Russia

Additional Reviewers

Robertas Damasevicius	Kaunas University of Technology, Lithuania
Tomas Blazauskas	Kaunas University of Technology, Lithuania
Kaspars Sudars	Institute of Electronics and Computer Science, Latvia

Janis Stirna	Stockholm University, Sweden
Virginija Limanauskiene	Kaunas University of Technology, Lithuania
Daina Gudoniene	Kaunas University of Technology, Lithuania
Tomas Skersys	Kaunas University of Technology, Lithuania
Vytautas Stuikys	Kaunas University of Technology, Lithuania
Alfonsas Misevicius	Kaunas University of Technology, Lithuania
Antanas Lenkevicius	Kaunas University of Technology, Lithuania
Ints Mednieks	Institute of Electronics and Computer Science, Latvia
Vacius Jusas	Kaunas University of Technology, Lithuania
Jonas Valantinas	Kaunas University of Technology, Lithuania
Lina Ceponiene	Kaunas University of Technology, Lithuania
Raimundas Matulevicius	University of Tartu, Estonia
Rimantas Barauskas	Kaunas University of Technology, Lithuania
Rita Butkiene	Kaunas University of Technology, Lithuania
Bronius Paradauskas	Kaunas University of Technology, Lithuania
Agnius Liutkevicius	Kaunas University of Technology, Lithuania
Stasys Maciulevicius	Kaunas University of Technology, Lithuania
Germanas Budnikas	Kaunas University of Technology, Lithuania
Algimantas Venckauskas	Kaunas University of Technology, Lithuania
Jevgenijus Toldinas	Kaunas University of Technology, Lithuania
Armantas Ostreika	Kaunas University of Technology, Lithuania
Cahit Gungor	University of Cukurova, Turkey
Ka Lok Man	Xi'an Jiaotong-Liverpool University, China

Co-editors

Giedre Dregvaite	Kaunas University of Technology, Lithuania
Robertas Damasevicius	Kaunas University of Technology, Lithuania

Table of Contents

Information Systems

Business Intelligence for Information and Software Systems

Software Engineering

Information Technology Applications

Information System for Monitoring
and Forecast of Building Heat Consumption

Yuliia Parfenenko, Vira Shendryk, Victor Nenja, and Svitlana Vashchenko

Sumy State University, Sumy, Ukraine
{yuliya_p,ve-shen,sveta}@opm.sumdu.edu.ua

Abstract. In this paper an implementation of a web-based monitoring system, which introduces the components and principles of this monitoring system, and provides the model of heat consumption prediction is presented. The general architecture of the information system is described.

The data collection subsystem comprises monitoring devices such as digital sensors and a data collection terminal. This allows providing relevant information about the status of the heating supply system for monitoring in real-time. The HeatCAM system (web-based information system for monitoring and prediction of building heat consumption) was implemented to provide analysis of current state of heating in buildings and short-term prediction of the required amount of heat under certain climatic conditions.

Keywords: Monitoring, forecast, public sector, system, data collection, heating, consumption, energy saving.

1   Introduction

Traditionally district heating plays an important role in covering the heat demand in Ukraine. It is normally delivered to satisfy heat requirements in cities for heating and hot water in residential, commercial, and public buildings. According to the Department of Statistics of Ukraine, thermal energy consumption is growing from year to year all over the country and in particular in the public sector. At the same time, the cost of heat and hot water production is growing due to increases in fuel prices.

Ukraine can't completely eliminate the use of fossil fuels and replace them with electricity or renewable energy sources as these are not cost effective for the production of heat energy in large scale. There are also important ecological aspects, because increasing of energy usage in general has mostly negative environmental impact.

Fuel combustion, which is used to generate heat energy for centralized district heating, releases huge amount of carbon dioxide into the atmosphere. This greenhouse gas emission is the main cause of increasing global warming.

Therefore the heating process must be economical in its realization but satisfy consumers' demand. Thus provision of the economical use of power resources is a prerequisite for sustainable development of every country.

The central heating in Ukraine is based on the following principle. The hot water which used as the heat carrier is supplied by the heat generation company.

G. Dregvaite and R. Damasevicius (Eds.): ICIST 2014, CCIS 465, pp. 1–11, 2014.

The transfer of heat and hot water to the end consumer is carried via the municipal heat distribution systems. These systems will be called District Heating systems (DH systems). The main goal of such systems is providing of the indoor comfort of buildings according to changing outdoor temperature.

There are two basic approaches to improve energy efficiency in the public sector. The first is equipment of buildings with energy-saving elements and structures (replacement of windows, wall insulation and so on). The second includes control of the heat energy amount and the monitoring of energy consumption.

The public sector buildings require real-time heat consumption monitoring. Accurate and efficient monitoring is one of the most important requirements for energy saving. A peculiarity of the public sector buildings against private buildings is that they work according to a fixed schedule. The effective regulation of heat distribution in days off is one of the ways of energy saving in public sector. The accumulation of heating information for public sector buildings is essential for the effective control of their thermal energy consumption, future consumption prediction, identification of the reasons of inefficient energy use and ways to implement energy saving measures.

Monitoring is the regular collection of information on energy use. Its purpose is to establish a basis of management control, to determine deviation of energy consumption from an established pattern. The monitoring data is the basis for taking management action where it is necessary.

To improve energy saving in public sector we propose the HeatCAM system providing data collection, processing and analysis of the heat delivery and distribution system (HDDS) as a tool of realization of effective energy management strategy of each institution (school, university, hospital etc.). Thus it is possible to achieve heat energy savings.

This paper is organized as follows. Section 2 describes related works on monitoring systems and approaches of heat consumption prediction. Section 3 presents the architectural consideration for the design of system for monitoring and prediction of heat consumption. The conclusions are presented in Section 4.

2   Related Work

Initially information technologies used to calculate the parameters of heating network. Implementation of artificial intelligence technologies and widespread usage of web applications caused new possibilities for real-time access to information about the current state of a heating system and data processing. Current research in computer science concerning district heating is directed to the development of monitoring systems with high efficiency of data presentation. In [4] is described an integrated architecture of monitoring power system combines two systems typical for power industry: the energy producing/delivery system and the information system. Supervisory control and data acquisition level in this system based on SCADA system performs tasks that are typical for a power dispatch unit – acquisition data to the databases, visualization of the process status, as well as detection and reporting of emergency conditions. Another approach to organizing of monitoring system architecture presented by

Fredrik Wernstedt [17] lies in investigation into the use of multi-agent systems for automatic distributed control of district heating systems. In [3] the authors proposed a system for monitoring the heating network using wireless technology ZigBee. The main disadvantage of such wireless sensors networks as ZigBee, Bluetooth is that distance between sensors and the base station is limited to about 1500 m. GPS is the only satellite system with sufficient availability and accuracy for most distributed monitoring and control applications in distribution systems. Therefore should be used the monitoring technique based on GPS network for monitoring data acquisition in district heating system [13].

In paper [8] the main components and functions of computer heating monitoring system are presented. The typical monitoring system can provide a real-time monitoring of heat supply, indoor and outdoor temperature, save and print the monitoring data. However, the effective regulation of the heating system requires analysis of monitoring data. In addition it should be considered that demand for heat significantly depended on ambient temperature. There is a need to predict heat demand of a consumer to optimize heat supply. A number of papers have been published dealing with problem of short term heat consumption forecasting. In general forecasting methods may be classified into two categories: statistical approaches and artificial intelligence based techniques. The goal of and the requirements for demand prediction in heating system is presented in [6]. Several studies in heat supply forecast are based on the Box-Jenkins method for the correlation analysis of time series (ARIMA models) [2, 5].

A number of heat demand forecasting has been performed with artificial neural networks [1, 7, 16]. The quality of forecasting depends on the number of data of heat supply in specific weather conditions. Thus a combination of online monitoring heat consumption and short-term forecasting in a single information system is an efficient tool for making decision of heat supply regulation. Let's consider the examples of information systems for monitoring consumption of heat energy which are used in Ukraine. The MiCON system [10] provides an ability of remote monitoring of sensors and heat meters using data transmission technology GSM. The Teplocom system [15] and its software "SEMPAL Device Manager" possess similar functionality [14]. They are based on a closed data transmission protocol for data collection. Also these systems require a separate dedicated server for the database and are intended for a particular type of a heat meter. Such systems cannot be applied as a universal monitoring tool because there is no possibility to customize them for each monitoring object.

3   The «HeatCAM» Monitoring System

3.1   System Architecture

The proposed information system is directly linked to monitoring and forecasting of heat consumption. It can also help in processing specific information for decision-making on heat consumption regulation.

The «HeatCAM» information system, which is described in this paper, uses an open protocol for interaction between the server and each heat meter. It can be applied to all types of heat meters with digital output. The advantage of this system may be its ability to apply its own software for data collection and monitoring. Thus, the proposed system is flexible due to the expandable functions of its modules. Fig. 1 gives the overview of the architecture of the «HeatCAM» system.

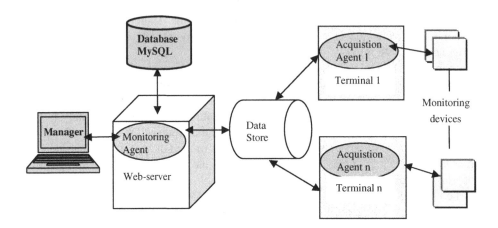

Fig. 1. The «HeatCAM» System Architecture

The information system «HeatCAM» is organized in combination three-tier architecture with software agent's technology. For data acquisition from distributed monitoring devices we use the approach described in [9], according to which software entities with its own actions can be considered as software agents.

The acquisition agent is a software component, which is written in C++ and installed on every terminal. Every acquisition agent works autonomously from each other and collects data from one monitored object. It collects data from monitoring devices (thermal and pressure sensors, digital heat meters) and places them in a temporary data store. Every acquisition agent performs its main task during certain time intervals (as a rule, an hour). The temporary data store can be implemented as a file that contains records of monitoring data. The elements of such record are the monitoring time; date, the number of acquisition agent and the data which are transferred by the acquisition agent.

Therefore the monitoring of distributed objects is possible. To add a new monitored object in "HeatCAM" system it is necessary to equip it with sensors and connect it to the terminal. Possible failures in work of one of the terminals should not impact on functioning of the monitoring system as a whole.

The web HTTP server Apache runs PHP scripts which are realized the functionality of monitoring agent, data representation and short-term forecasting.

The monitoring agent resides on a web-server. It parses temporary data store in a certain time interval matched to the interval data acquisition. Then it performs data validation and places them into MySQL database. The data storage mechanism is realized by InnoDB storage engine. To ensure data integrity the transactions mechanism is used.

Thus the "HeatCAM" system is based on autonomous components for data acquisition, which are working independently and provide data transmission into a data store.

The HeatCAM system is equipped with the hardware components which are incorporated into the Data Collection Subsystem (Fig. 2).

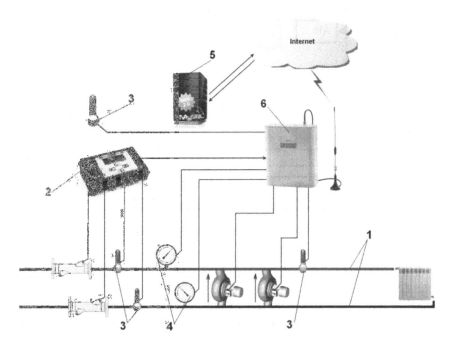

Fig. 2. The Data Collection Subsystem

Fig. 2 describes the connection structure of the monitoring components where 1 – a section of the heating network; 2 – a heat meter; 3 – thermal sensors; 4 – pressure sensors; 5 – a server of system; 6 – a modem.

A heat meter with digital output must be mounted on the incoming heating pipeline of the building. Sections with forward and reverse pipes must be equipped with pressure and thermal sensors. Some sensors are designed to control the temperature in the heated indoors and others to monitor ambient temperature.

The heat meters, thermal and pressure sensors are connected to the terminals. Every terminal is equipped with GSM modem. It transmits collected data to a web-server through GPRS [12]. After the data have been transmitted to the base station of the mobile operator, they are transmitted over the Internet to the temporary data store. The acquisition agent that is installed on each terminal is responsible for data collection. The main components of the terminal are shown in Fig. 3.

The basis of the terminal is a single-chip microcontroller (MC). Pinouts are configured in the mode of the analog-to-digital converter (ADC). Digital thermal sensors (t_0 ... t_n) are connected to the terminal by a single-wire bus (1-Wire). This method allows for simultaneous connection of 50 thermal sensors at a distance up to 300 meters.

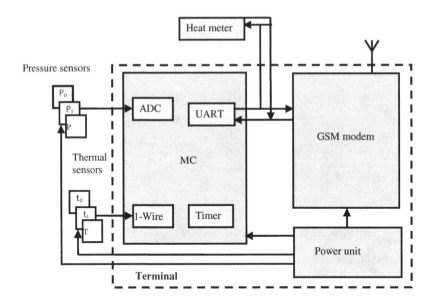

Fig. 3. The Data Collection Terminal Block Diagram

The heat meter is connected to the terminal via protocol RS-232 with three conductors. The GSM-modem is connected to pinouts 2 and 3 of the MC using the UART protocol.

The acquisition agent manages the functions of the microcontroller. This program converts the readings from the meter to a form compatible with the COM port and transmits this data to the web-server in one minute intervals [11]. Data verification script on the web-server validates the data acquisition and enters them into the database. The program also performs records of all actions taken (log generation) into the log file.

3.2   Main Features of the HeatCAM

Access to the HeatCAM system is limited. Therefore, each user must be authorized. There is a defined a list of persons which have received a login and a password to allow access to the system. The categories of users are listed as follows:

— a system administrator has full rights for data access, giving user rights to all categories of users and creating database backups;
— an engineer or energy auditor performs analysis of forecast data of the heating consumption and on the basis of this information makes decisions about heat-supply regulation. It also allows him to identify control devices failures;
— an accountant has access to accounts for heat supply services which are formed on the basis of current heat energy consumption;
— an operator has access to the monitoring data and can add new data in the case of absence of the monitoring devices in the building.

The functionality of the HeatCAM system is illustrated in the form of a tree chart in Fig. 4.

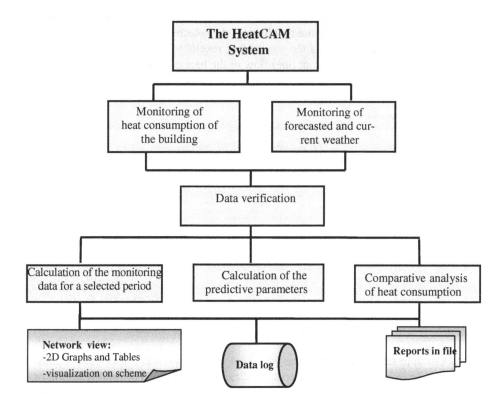

Fig. 4. The Functionality of the HeatCAM

Monitoring of weather conditions consists of weather forecast data for every three hours of a particular day of the week. The source of weather forecast is the web-site www.gismeteo.ua which allows for accessing the information over HTTP by addressing a server four times a day. The monitoring heat consumption data, are collected from heating meters and sensors are represented by set $S = \{date, T_1, T_2, T_3, q_{f,} A, n\}$, where date – the monitoring date; T_1 – a forward heat carrier temperature, ° C; T_2 – a return heat carrier temperature, ° C; T_3 – a heat carrier temperature after mixing, ° C; q_f – an instantaneous heat output, Gcal / h; v – a heat carrier flow, m^3 / h; A – amount of heat energy, Gcal; n –a reference number for the recorded object.

These data are passed from the acquisition agent to the monitoring agent and placed in the database. Further processing of monitoring data lies in the comparative analysis of heat consumption for different periods.

3.3   The Network View Representation of the Monitoring Results

The web presentation level of the HeatCAM system provides an ability to view moni-tored data for ambient weather conditions, together with the current and calculated parameters of the heating in definite building for the selected period.

As an example, Fig. 5 depicts the monitoring results of the temperature of direct (the top line) and return (the bottom line) flow of the heat carrier for 5 days of January 2014.

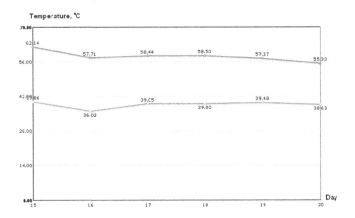

Fig. 5. Graphical Representation of the Monitoring Data

In addition to temperature data, the web page also can present information regard-ing changes in instantaneous heat output and heat consumption. The representation of the monitoring data on the web-page in the form of tables and diagrams is supple-mented with the interactive interface, which displays the current data on the user's web page. The example of the monitoring data is shown in Fig. 6.

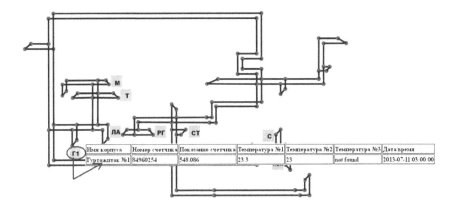

Fig. 6. Graph Representation of the Heating Network

Location of metering devices is marked as squares. The information about the parameters of the heat network such as length and diameter of pipe on this scheme is hidden. To view the monitoring information, it is necessary to click with the cursor on the square with the name of the building inside. Then the monitoring parameters for a selected building will be displayed as a table.

Visualization of the monitoring data is implemented by using scalable vector graphics SVG. The interactivity of data changing of the heating diagram is provided by using this technique. The current parameters of the heating are displayed when selecting a particular monitoring object on the scheme. The information displayed on the scheme is extracted by a JSON request. An additional feature of the data visualization subsystem is a convenient data control interface. If the parameters are outside the region of admissibility, the icon color of the monitoring object on the diagram will change. Thus the presentation of real-time data monitoring facilitates a timely reaction to the changes in the heating mode.

3.4 Forecasting

Neural networks can be used by energy managers and can help in making decisions of heat supply regulation. The architecture of the proposed neural network used in this study is the nonlinear autoregressive neural network architecture (NARX) with 16 hidden nodes and one output node. Forecast is based on the previous values of the forecast variable and exogenous inputs.

The prediction subsystem had been implemented into existing architecture of the HeatCAM system. It was tested for heat demand forecast for the one building of public sector. Whole data set for neural network consist of measured values for past 3 years. Fig.7 illustrates results of testing.

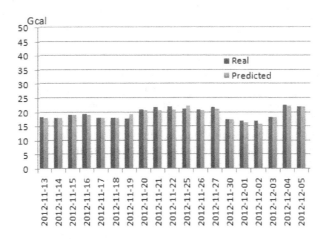

Fig. 7. Test of Heat Demand Prediction

Networks inputs X (t) are weather variables (measured air temperatures, humidity, wind speed, wind direction, precipitation) and amount of heat demand. Networks output Y (t) is predicted heat demand amount.

Training of neural network is done on basis of 70% of the testing, 20% of the validation and 10% of the training data samples. We take a number of time periods, called latency period, which are accounted for forecasting d = 7. The neural network is trained by the Levenberg-Marquardt algorithm.

When the neural network was trained and tested the overall predictive accuracy obtained was 96 %.

4   Conclusion

The problem of energy saving in buildings of public sector nowadays is an actual. The existing monitoring systems as a rule use a closed data transmission protocol require a separate dedicated server for the database and focus on a particular type of a heat meter. It is difficult to expand the functionality of such systems because their software codes are closed.

In addressing this problem architecture of information system for monitoring and prediction of heat consumption is proposed. The architecture integrates data collection subsystem, subsystem of heat consumption data forecasting and a web-based interface for graphical data presentation and reporting. The basis of the data acquisition subsystem is the terminal where the acquisition agent is installed. This agent provides data collection and places them in a temporary data store. The monitoring agent keeps track of the data in temporary data store, checks it on mistakes and places them into the database.

Data presentation of the information system «HeatCAM» is implemented as a web resource, which is located on the Internet for the authorized access. Furthermore the current monitoring data are displayed on a heating scheme and updated by the user's request. Forecasting of the building heat consumption is performed using of artificial neural networks.

The forecasting accuracy is more than 90 %. Thus the proposed system is an efficient tool to support energy saving in heat consumption of public sector buildings. The system's advantage lies in combination of data acquisition, fast data manipulation via web interface and short-term heat consumption data forecasting. The architecture of "HeatCAM" enables its expanding with the addition of software components. So the system is flexible, its functionality may be supplemented. Also another advantage of proposed system is its scalability. It should be easily to apply this system for monitoring of different number of metering devices.

References

1. Buhari, M.: Short-term load forecasting using artificial neural network. In: Proceedings of the IMECS 2012, Hong Kong, vol. 1 (2012)
2. Chramcov, B., Baláte, J., Princ, M.: Heat demand forecasting for concrete district heating system. International Journal of Mathematical Models and Methods in Applied Sciences 4(4), 231–239 (2010)

3. Finogeev, G., Diltman, V.B., Maslov, A.A., Finogeev, A.A.: Sistema udalennogo monito-ringa i upravlenija setjami teplosnabzhenija na baze sensornyh setej (Operational system for remote monitoring and control of heating systems based on wireless sensor networks). Applied Informatics 3(33), 83–93 (2011) (in Russian)
4. Grega, W.: Information technologies supporting control and monitoring of power system. Przeglad Elektrotechniczny 5a, 193–197 (2012)
5. Grosswindhager, S., Voigt, A., Kozek, M.: Online short-term forecast of system heat load in district heating networks. In: Proceedings of the 31st International Symposium on Fore-casting, Prag, Czech Republic (2011)
6. Grzenda, M.: Consumer-oriented heat consumption prediction. Control and Cybernetics, Systems Research Institute, Polish Academy of Sciences 41(1), 213–240 (2012)
7. Grzenda, M., Macukow, B.: Demand prediction with multi-stage neural processing. Ad-vances in Natural Computation and Data Mining, 131–141 (2006)
8. Hongbing, C.: Development of a computer heating monitoring system and its applications. In: Proceedings of the Sixth International Conference for Enhanced Building Operations, Shenzhen, China (2006)
9. Katehakis, D.G., Chalkiadakis, G., Tsiknakis, M.N., Orphanoudakis, S.C.: A distributed, agent-based architecture for the acquisition, management, archiving and display of real-time monitoring data in the intensive care unit. http://www.ics.forth.gr/tech-reports/1999/1999.TR261.IntensiveCare_CORBA_SoftwareAgents_real-time-ICU-monitoring.ps.gz (accessed April 20, 2014)
10. MiCON Systems homepage, http://www.micon.com (accessed April 20, 2014)
11. Okopnyi, R., Nenja, V.: The author's certificate of Ukraine on computer program The data acquisition subsystem Heat Data Collector, No 47753, (January 21, 2013)
12. Parfenenko, Y., Okopnyi, R., Nenja, V.: Rozrobka instrumental'nyh zasobiv kontrolju tep-lozabezpechennja budivel' (Creation of control instruments for buildings' heating). The Journal of the National Technical University NTU KPI, Series Information Systems and Networks. 34, 93–97 (2012) (in Ukrainian)
13. Peulic, A., Dragicevic, S., Snezana, M., Jovanovic, Z., Krneta, R.: Flexible GPS/GPRS based system for parameters monitoring in the district heating system. International Jour-nal of Computers Communications & Control 8(1), 105–110 (2013)
14. Sempal Meters homepage, http://www.sempal.com (accessed April 20, 2014)
15. Teplocom information-measuring system homepage,
   http://www.teplocom.spb.ru (accessed April 20, 2014)
16. Voronovskiy, G.K.: Usovershenstvovanie praktiki operativnogo upravlenija krupnymi teplofikacionnymi sistemami v novyh jekonomicheskih uslovijah (Improvement of Opera-tional Management Practices in Large Heating Systems in the New Economy). Kharkiv (2002) (in Russian)
17. Wernstedt, F.: Multi-agent systems for distributed control of district heating systems. Dissertation, Blekinge Institute of Technology, Sweden (2005)

The Features of the Smart MicroGrid as the Object of Information Modeling

Olha Shulyma, Vira Shendryk, Iryna Baranova, and Anna Marchenko

Sumy State University, Sumy, Ukraine
{o.shulym,ve-shen,gloria,nenja_av}opm.sumdu.edu.ua

Abstract. This paper describes the features of Smart MicroGrid and explains the of prior building appropriate information model of this system. It was determined information power system evaluation techniques and existing methods that can be applied in information system with simulation tools classification. This paper compares different tools for modeling, which are based on using renewable energy sources. The system has to combine basic points: evaluation energy sources in region, their calculation, gives recommendation for building energy smart grid in micro grid level and modelling her work. Our goal is definition of existing approaches, which can be used in future system.

Keywords: Renewable Energy Sources, Distributed Generation, MicroGrid, Smart Grid Simulation, Decision Support System.

1 Introduction

There are two rapidly growing Renewable Energy Sources (RES) in Ukraine: wind and solar energy, which can be used as renewable distributed generated sources in MicroGrid (MG). A well-planned MG combining the large amount of RES will be able to dramatically reduce the overall cost and will make the power system more reliable and flexible. Such hybrid system reduces the energy storage requirements compared to systems comprising only one single renewable energy source.

The optimal sizing of hybrid system plays a pivotal role to use solar and wind energy resources more efficiently and economically. The large number of small-scale components with their own characteristics is a big challenge for MicroGrid modeling and planning. System is characterized by rapidly changing operating modes and configurations. The hybrid system can be reconfigured periodically; some RES may be unobtainable and units can be disconnected; storage units may have discharging or charging mode. With these cases in the hybrid system the chaos level will increase dramatically. Although this dynamic features increase the flexibility, it also causes problems from point of energy management. Subsequently, the associated analytics is quite complex.

This paper will be intended for researchers, practitioners in the field, engineers and scientists are involved in the design and development of the information modeling of smart MicroGrid with using renewable energy sources.

G. Dregvaite and R. Damasevicius (Eds.): ICIST 2014, CCIS 465, pp. 12–23, 2014.
© Springer International Publishing Switzerland 2014

The paper will adopt an interdisciplinary approach to determine technical features of grid with descriptive component and to determine existing techniques to determine theoretical and practical approaches in information modelling, in order to be the targeted for multiple audiences.

2   Definition the Goal

The main goal of this study is to outline the structure of MG as the object of study and the determination of the approaches of MG prior assessment. For achieving this goal will be doing next steps:

— determinations MG's features with the study of existing standards, methodologies and projects;
— the schema building of MG's structure on the macro level for the further informational modeling;
— the tasks determination for the information assessment of MG;
— the study of the approaches of information modeling the Smart MG and tools for these tasks.

3   The Main Concept of Smart MicroGrid

There is no one common definition of Smart Grid. According to [27] Smart Grid is an electricity network that can intelligently integrate the actions of all users connected to it - generators, consumers and those that do both - in order to efficiently deliver sustainable, economic and secure electricity supplies. IEEE4 defines the Smart Grid as the concept of a fully integrated, self-regulating and self-healing power grid, which has a network topology and includes all sources of generation, transmission and distribution networks and all types of electricity consumers, managed unified network of information and control devices and systems in real-time [28].

According to [26] distinguish the key features of Smart Grid: Self-healing, Incorporates and empower the user, Tolerates security attack, Offers power quality enhancement, Accommodates various generation sources, Fully supports energy market, Optimizes asset utilization and reduces the expenses for system operations and maintenance.

Thus, the key idea of a Smart MicroGrid is integrating and coordinating operations of all grid consumers, they can be large power plants or small production units and active or passive households in friendly way with environmental and efficient point of view. This is caused by introducing the big part of interconnections in the power grid and more intelligence for automatic decision with measurements from the power grid. Consumers and active households can make decisions based on the actual electricity price. The main benefits of smart power grids can be broken into three parts [6]:

— Lower environmental impacts.
— Higher reliability. It will be able to automatically respond and prevent faults in the grid [18].
— Lower operational cost or economy. End consumers will have the opportunity to coordinate the peak consumption and sell RES produced electricity.

The transfer from non-renewable electricity production puts new keys on the grid. RES such as solar panels and wind turbines can be distributed around local territory and produce electricity nearly to the end consumers. This causes new issues, due to being wind and solar power stochastic energy sources, thus it is hard to predict when electricity will be generated. The grid must be able to address locally the overproduction of electricity. The main objective is to provide 24 h grid quality power in remote communities.

Next step should be related to defining the architecture of MG based on supporting main concept of Smart MicroGrid: achieving stable reliability with lower environmental impacts and operational cost to harmonize consumption with generation.

4   The Defining Features of Smart Microgrid Architecture for Further Modelling

Firstly, it should be pointed, that MG is a small grid which is operated as the part of a large power grid or independently, and can manages their own energy conversion, storage and recycling. The MG consists of smaller power sources, which typically generate from 1kW to 1MW and they are located near to the consumers to provide the electrical energy. The typically MG includes distributed energy resource (DER) units with both distributed generation (DG) and distributed storage (DS) units and the different types of the end consumers of electricity [16]. The DER is the source of electric power that is not directly connected to a bulk power transmission system [9].

Presented below is a list of possible logical systems reflects the capabilities of the power system based on the concept of Smart Grid: Distributed Monitoring and Control System, Distributed System Monitoring Substation Automatic System Shutdown, Distributed Monitoring System for the Generation, Automatic Measurement of the Running Processes, Measurement Control System, Distributed Forecasting System; Operating Management System Smart [14].

Despite that, according to IEEE Guide for Smart Grid Interoperability of Energy Technology and Information Technology Operation with the Electric Power System (EPS), End-Use Applications, and Loads [9] there are next domains of power systems architecture: Bulk generation, Transmission, Distribution, Customer, Control and Operations, Market and Service Providers domains. The each of these domains plays a role in the operation of the electrical power systems and consists of different entities, which are connected by special interfaces.

It is planned to build a simulation model of small distributed power system in macro level, consisting of an array of buildings are equipped with solar panels, joint wind turbines and energy storage bank, and also the ability to connect to an external power grid. At this stage it is just an idea with no real research object, which holds the concept, that each smart unit has appropriate System Controller, which gathers information from the house's grid without a break [1]. The System Controller makes decisions using this information to be sure in not violated of internal grid conditions and using in an effective way the micro generation units. A schematic idea of the interactions in Smart MG is presented in figure 1 [19]. On this schema use next reductions: AC – alternating current; DC – direct current.

The connecting such smart houses to the medium voltage local grid is operated by system controller, which on this level controls the number of generators, the battery and the number of houses. The main goal of the creating controller design is to prove the properly work of the system in both islanding mode and grid-connected mode [8].

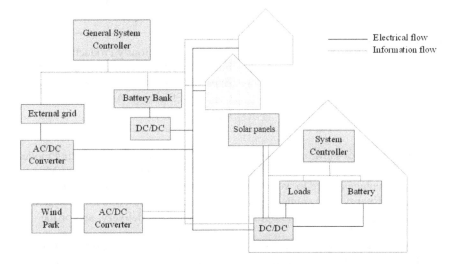

Fig. 1. A schematic idea of smart MicroGrid

As it is clearly illustrated on the figure 1, there are two flows: electrical and information; the last is directly linked with controllers. According to main idea about system stable reliability, firstly, it's important to build adequate distribution between sources based on electrical flow, information flow is not considered. For this task is planned to use prior information modeling.

5   The Information Energy System of MicroGrid

The models are important for almost all engineering activities. They are used in the design and the analysis of new and existing systems and they are an increasingly important ingredient in all static and, above all, dynamic systems.

A Smart Grid simulation study may involve the elements of different types. The type of models and simulation analyses to be applied depends in part on the advanced timeframe which system performance have to be studied. In general, planning time frames are typically dictated by the duration of time required to plan, purchase, and install new system assets. In the Table 1 are proposed the general set of timeframes for power system operations and planning, it was conditionally indicated general features for future information energy system.

Table 1. The Features of Information System depend on Timeframe

	Timeframes	Main tasks
Real-time operations and operations planning	<1 year	Reliability, the Hourly Production Forecast from RES.
Short-term planning	1-3 year	Reliability, the Hourly Production Forecast from RES, Economics, Capacity Efficiency.
Long-term planning	3-10 year	Reliability, the Hourly Production Forecast from RES, Asset Management, Expansion Planning, Economics, Capacity Efficiency, Accounting for Equipment Replacement.

As common point of view, it can be mentioned, that the aim of the building models and further Decision Support System for Energy Management System (DSEMS) are related to give manage advice to work with sources and loads in the MicroGrid.

In the whole Energy Management System (EMS) can be describe as the system of tools used to monitor, control, and optimize the generation, delivery, and/or the consumption of energy [9].

The power production should share among the DER units and external grid. Therefore, the DSEMS should recommend power references and appropriate control signals to the renewable energy units and controllable loads.

The planning system design for energy sharing can be consist of systems, which operates information about energy harvesting and consumption prediction algorithms for predicting future energy information. Then, with the predicted energy information, can be described energy sharing among units and scheduling energy transmissions. So such information system will be consisted of next subsystems (Table 2), which will be operated long-term energy control and short-term power management points.

Table 2. The Subsystem of Information System

Subsystem	Description
Renewable Energy Prediction	It can be forecasted weather condition to predict energy from RES every hour for the next 24 hours.
Energy Consumption Prediction	To predict the home's energy consumption, can be used a model based on exploiting the diurnal nature of home consumption, while it also adapts to seasonal variations.
Energy Transmission Scheduling	The basic idea of transmission scheduling is to have transmissions executed simultaneously only, if those transmissions do not cause transmission chaos. Generally, transmissions with one supplier do not cause transmission chaos because demanders cannot fetch energy from other homes and

Table 2. (*continued*)

	energy transmission flow can be controlled. Transmissions with one demander also do not cause transmission chaos. Thus, our solution is to combine the transmissions that share the same supplier or demander.
Energy Sharing	There can be used energy matching algorithm and transmission scheduling algorithm.

According to the classification of tasks, which are put in DSEMS and idea about the macro level presentation of MG, it can be concluded, that future Decision Support System (DSS) will be used for short-term planning and will give recommendations for energy supply based on hourly production forecast from RES (the common structure are presented on a figure 2). For these complex tasks can be used different approaches to achieve optimal solution in real-time.

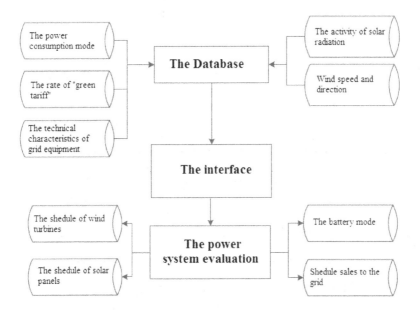

Fig. 2. A schematic idea of DSEMS

6   The Current State in Modeling, Optimization and Simulation Researches

Researchers have tried developing integrated energy models linking both commercial and renewable energy sources. A worldwide research and development using modeling, optimization and simulation tools in the field of renewable energy resources and systems is carried out during the last two decades. The different types of models are presented in the Table 3.

Table 3. Modeling, Optimization and Simulation Research Review

Author(s)	The Main Idea	Reference
Ramachandra, T.V.	A tool for resource planning and management, which uses a Multi-Criteria Decision Analysis, and the method NAIADE to find a compromise solution in the fuzzy decision-making environment. The approach was used to determine the optimal use of wind turbines in the island of Salina (Aeolian Islands, Italy).	[24]
Iyad. M., et al	In this paper is described an approach to building DSS, that uses software HOMER, as a way of calculating and determining the best design MicroGrid. The using of an integrated system is proposed, that uses solar and wind energy are calculated every hour. As emergency funds for isolated areas electricity supply offered a diesel generator and a battery. The basis of the selection of the final set put function to minimize costs, which takes into account the life cycle cost of the installation.	[20]
Dagdougui, H., et al	It was constructed a system of distributed energy management in buildings in real-time Capo Vado (Liguria Region), which allows to determine the optimal flow of energy in the building and is characterized by a combination of renewable resources. Solar collector, photovoltaic modules, one device for converting biomass, wind turbine and a battery are used for calculations. DSS allows you to determine the time of the greatest generation of energy from different sources.	[5]
Tiba, C., et al	The methodology is developed for the definition of the better localities for using new energy systems but without performing grid studies.	[32]
Lejeune, P., et al	The DSS is developed for regional planners to analyze the many wind energy projects for private investors in Belgium.	[13]
Lazarou, S., et al	The DSS using GIS assists to define a preferred installation location for the construction of RES, to search for potential sites for RES installations and then to analyze the behavior of the grid and distributed generation systems, but system doesn't use idea of smart grid.	[11]
Azadeh, A., et al	The model of agent based simulation, Ant Colony Optimization algorithm is used to compare three available strategies of clearing electricity markets, uniform, pay-as-bid, generalized Vickrey rules.	[3]
J.M. Yusta et al.	A mathematical optimization model development is presented to simulate electricity demand of a machining process and to find the optimum production schedule that increase profit considering the hourly variations.	[34]

Table 3. (*continued*)

H. Siahkali and M. Vakilian	Development of a new approach for solving the generation scheduling problem considering the reserve load balance, requirement and wind power availability constraints using particle swarm optimization method applied to a 12-unit test system.	[29]
Louit, D., et al.	A simple model to determine the optimal major maintenance actions interval based on a relative time and the combination of data from different sections of a grid.	[12]

7   Approaches and Tools for Building Smart MicroGrid

For power system evaluation techniques are used two main categories: analytical and simulation methods (Table 4). Analytical techniques represent the system by analytical models and using mathematical solutions to calculate the reliability indices. Simulation methods, such as Monte Carlo simulation, estimate the reliability by simulating the actual processes and random the behaviors of the system [7].

The hybrid solar–wind system design is mainly dependent on the performance of individual components. In order to predict the system's performance, individual components should be modeled first and then their combination can be evaluated to meet the demand reliability.

Table 4. Simulation Modelling of Hybrid Solar–Wind System Components

Modelling of Solar System	Modelling of Wind Energy System	Modelling of Battery Storage System
1. Analysis of the environmental factors that influence the solar module/array's performance. 2. For engineering application, are used the simplified simulation models, which can predict the time series or average performance of a solar array under variable climatic conditions.	1. The hour-by-hour simulation determines the long-term performance of wind energy systems. 2. Models with the effect of instantaneous variations of wind speed.	1. Models tend to be used to assess the theoretical performance of battery designs. 2. Developing an electrical circuit that is designed to be functionally equivalent to the battery. 3. Modelling based on the state of charge counting. 4. Modelling based on the state of voltage counting. 5. Empirical models.

An optimum combination for hybrid system can make the best compromise between the two considered objectives: power reliability and system cost, for these tasks can be used different criteria (Table 5).

Table 5. Hybrid Solar–Wind System Optimizations

Power Reliability Analysis	System Cost Analysis
1. The loss of power supply probability method. 2. Loss of Load Probability. 3. System Performance Level.	1. Net Present Cost. 2. Levelised Cost of Energy. 3. Life-cycle cost.

It should be considered that there will be used hybrid modelling approaches combining the main elements from simulation and optimization modelling categories. There can be used main approaches:

— The Agent-Based Modeling (ABM).

The basic point is that the system consists of some subsystems, which are called agents [3]. Agents are characterized by the ability to cooperate, autonomously act and the ability to learn. Combinations of these characteristics depend on the agent's functions.

— Simulators for Dynamic Models and Networks (SDM&N).

According to fact, that it can planned to build system with short-term planning, it was compared features of software to main tasks of this predictions, which are presented on the Table 6. In the table are used next reductions: R – realized; NR – not realized; NFR – not fully realized. NFR means, that there is present only the idea of tasks or a basic implementation.

Table 6. The Comparison Review of Software

Software	Approaches for Building Smart Microgrid	Building Simulation Models	Building Optimization Models	Reliability	The Hourly Production Forecast from RES	Economics	Capacity Efficiency	User Friendly Interface
REPAST [25]	ABM SDM&N	R	R	NFR	NFR	R	NFR	R

Table 6. (*continued*)

NetLogo [33]	ABM, SDM&N	R	NFR	NFR	NFR	R	NFR	R
JADE [10]	ABM	R	NFR	NFR	NFR	NFR	NFR	NFR
Cormas [4]	ABM	R	R	NFR	R	NR	NR	NR
AnyLogic [2]	ABM, SDM&N	R	R	R	R	R	R	R
NEPLAN [21]	SDM&N	R	NFR	NFR	R	R	R	NR
MATLAB [15]/ Simulink [30]	ABM, SDM&N	R	R	R	R	R	R	R
PSS NETOMAC & SINCAL [23]	SDM&N	R	R	R	R	NR	NFR	R
VTB [17]	SDM&N	R	NR	R	NR	NR	NFR	NFR
NS-3 [31]	SDM&N	R	NR	R	NR	NR	NR	NR
OPNET [22]	SDM&N	R	R	R	NR	NR	NR	R
OMNeT++ [35]	SDM&N	R	NFR	R	NFR	NR	NR	R

What is more, it can be mentioned, that for increasing functionality it can be composed different ABM and SDM&N software. Thus, it was decided for posed problem, use Matlab&Simulink with AnyLogic, as only two packages satisfies completely the requirements. It also should be mentioned, that Matlab is considered more as SDM&N and AnyLogic as ABM.

8   Conclusions

According to the analysis of existing standards it was determined the structure of Smart MG on the macro level, thus the future structure will be consist of the array of buildings are equipped with solar panels, joint wind turbines and energy storage bank and also the ability to connect to an external power grid. What is more, there are two flows in system: electrical and information, which are combined for achieving the suitable reliability level of load power supply it is necessary to do the prior information assessment of MG based on creation complex DSS to giving advice for short-term planning with hourly production forecast from RES.

According to the analysis of existing methods that can be applied in information system and the tasks of the information simulation, it can be concluded that there are many the disparate ways of solving problems. Thus, further study is aimed to simulate Smart MG with the different parameters of RES for achieving the optimum combination based on supporting stable reliability with lower environmental impacts and operational cost.

References

1. Active distributed power systems functional structures for real-time operation of sustainable energy systems, `http://lup.lub.lu.se/luur/download?func=downloadFile&recordOId=25752&fileOId=26626`
2. AnyLogic Overview, `http://www.anylogic.ru/overview`
3. Azadeh, A., Skandari, M.R., Maleki-Shoja, B.: An integrated ant colony optimization approach to compare strategies of clearing market in electricity markets: agent-based simulation. Energy Policy 38, 6307–6319 (2010)
4. Cormas, Cormas: Natural resources and agent-based simulations (2004), `http://cormas.cirad.fr/indexeng.htm`
5. Dagdougui, H., Minciardi, R., Ouammi, A., Robba, M., Sacile, R.: A dynamic optimization model for smart micro-grid: integration of a mix of renewable resources for a green building. In: The International Congress on Environmental Modelling and Software, pp. 234–242 (2010)
6. Enerbäck, J., Nalin Nilsson, O.: Modelling and simulation of Smart Grids using Dymola/Modelica, `https://www.iea.lth.se/publications/MS-Theses/Full%20document/5313_full_document.pdf`
7. Fang, L.-B., Cai, J.-D.: Reliability assessment of microgrid using sequential monte carlo simulation. Journal of Electronic Science and Technology 9, 31–34 (2011)
8. Guo, F., Herrera, L., Murawski, R., Inoa, E., Wang, C.-L., Beauchamp, P., Ekici, E., Wang, J.: Comprehensive Real-Time Simulation of the Smart Grid. IEEE Transactions on Industry Applications 49, 899–908 (2013)
9. IEEE Guide for Smart Grid Interoperability of Energy Technology and Information Technology Operation with the Electric Power System (EPS), End-Use Applications, and Loads. IEEE Standard 2030-2011 (2011)
10. Java agent development framework (JADE), `http://jade.tilab.com/`
11. Lazarou, S., Oikonomou, D.S., Ekonomou, L.: A platform for planning and evaluating distributed generation connected to the hellenic electric distribution grid. In: The 11th WSEAS International Conference on Circuits, Systems, Electronics, Control & Signal Processing, pp. 80–86 (2012)
12. Lejeune, P., Feltz, C.: Development of a decision support system for setting up a wind energy policy across the Walloon Region (southern Belgium). Renewable Energy 33, 2416–2422 (2008)
13. Louit, D., Pascual, R., Banjevic, D.: Optimal interval for major maintenance actions in electricity distribution networks. The International Journal of Electrical Power & Energy Systems 31, 396–401 (2009)

14. Massel, L.V., Bakhvalov, K.S.: Open integrated environment InterPSS as a basis of Smart Grid IT-Infrastructure, Vestnik ISTU, 7, 10-15 (2012)
15. Matlab, http://www.mathworks.co.uk/
16. Menniti, D., Pinnarelli, A., Sorrentino, N.: A method to improve microgrid reliability by optimal sizing PV/wind plants and storage systems. In: The 20th International Conference on Electricity Distribution, pp. 1–4 (2009)
17. Monti, A., Ponci, F., Smith, A., Liu, R.: A design approach for digital controllers using reconfigurable network-based measurement. In: The International Instrumentation and Measurement Technology Conference, pp. 1073–1081 (2009)
18. Moslehi, K., Kumar, R.: Smart grid - a reliability perspective. IEEE Transactions on Smart Grid 1, 57–64 (2010)
19. M.M., Allerding, F., Schmeck, H.: Integration of electric vehicles in smart homes - an ICT-based solution for V2G scenarios. In: The 2012 IEEE PES Innovative Smart Grid Technologies, pp. 1–8 (2012)
20. Muslih, I.M., Abdellatif, Y.: Hybrid micro-power energy station; design and optimization by using HOMER modeling software. In: The 2011 International Conference on Modeling, Simulation and Visualization Methods, pp. 183–193 (2011)
21. NEPLAN desktop overview, http://www.neplan.ch
22. Network Simulation (OPNET Modeler Suite),
http://www.riverbed.com/products-solutions/products/
network-planning-simulation/Network-Simulation.html
23. PSS Product Suite, http://www.energy.siemens.com/fi/en/services/
power-transmission-distribution/power-technologies-
international/software-solutions/
24. Ramachandra, T.V.: RIEP: Regional integrated energy plan. Renewable and Sustainable Energy Reviews 13, 285–317 (2009)
25. Repast 3 Overview, http://repast.sourceforge.net/
26. Roncero, J.R.: Integration is key to smart grid management. In: The IET-CIRED Seminar Smartgrids for Distribution, pp. 1–4 (2008)
27. SmartGrids Strategic Deployment Document finalized,
http://www.smartgrids.eu
28. Smart Power Grids — Talking about a Revolution,
http://www.ieee.org/about/technologies/emerging/
emerging_tech_smart_grids.pdf
29. Siahkali, H., Vakilian, M.: Electricity generation scheduling with large-scale wind farms using particle swarm optimization. The Electric Power Systems Research 79, 826–836 (2009)
30. Simulink, http://www.mathworks.com/products/simulink/
31. Tiba, C., Candeias, A.L.B., Fraidenraich, N., de Barbosa, E.M., de Carvalho Neto, P.B., de Melo Filho, J.B.: A GIS-based decision support tool for renewable energy management and planning in semi-arid rural environments of northeast of Brazil. Renewable Energy 35, 2921–2932 (2010)
32. The NS-3 Consortium, http://www.nsnam.org/
33. Tisue, S., Wilensky, U.: NetLogo: A simple environment for modeling complexity. In: The International Conference on Complex Systems, pp. 1–10 (2004)
34. Varga, A., Hornig, R.: An overview of the OMNET++ simulation environment. In: The Simutools, pp. 60–70 (2008)
35. Yusta, J.M., Torres, F., Khodr, H.M.: Optimal methodology for a machining process scheduling in spot electricity markets. The Energy Conversion and Management 51, 2647–2654 (2010)

Information Systems Requirements Specification and Usage in Test Case Generation

Neringa Sipavičienė[1], Kristina Smilgytė[1,2], and Rimantas Butleris[1,2]

[1] Kaunas University of Technology, Department of Information Systems,
Studentu St. 50-309, LT-51368, Kaunas, Lithuania
{neringa.sipaviciene,kristina.smilgyte}@ktu.edu
[2] Kaunas University of Technology, Centre of Information Systems Design Technologies,
Studentu St. 50-313a, LT-51368, Kaunas, Lithuania
rimantas.butleris@ktu.lt

Abstract. The considerable attention implementing information systems test should be paid to the development test of the specified requirements. The paper discusses the possibility and the importance of the functional test case generation using artifacts obtained during the analysis of requirements in test process. Based on requirements description formats and test case generation methods of analysis the use case and activity diagrams are suggested to use for this purpose. This paper presents the methodology and practical evaluation of the description of requirements and their use in generating test cases. This decision is relevant for the information system analytics and testers, test managers and others involved in test process.

Keywords: software testing, software requirements, functional test case generation, Microsoft Test Manager, use case diagram, activity diagram.

1 Introduction

Every day we are dealing with information systems (banking, patient registration, e-commerce, public services, etc.) or software controlling various devices (mobile phones, computers, industrial machines, traffic control systems, etc.). Strong dependence on software requires big investments in quality assurance activities in order to ensure reliability of information system work.

During test process the popular "black-box", sometimes called "specification-based" method is used to check whether system is in accordance with the requirements defined during the stage of analysis or not. Requirements play an important role in test activity therefore the demand to find ways to enhance the integrity of requirements and testing due to the testing process efficiency (i.e. better quality, requiring less resource) increases.

Planning and performing test activities the following problems occur:

- Artifacts created in the analysis of requirements stage little or completely cannot be reused therefore the great manual work is required thus demotivating testers;

G. Dregvaite and R. Damasevicius (Eds.): ICIST 2014, CCIS 465, pp. 24–34, 2014.
© Springer International Publishing Switzerland 2014

- Changes in requirements are common and hard to be traced;
- Concerning time and the lack of human resources all potential tests are impossible to accomplish so the opportunity to select test suits based on certain criteria (risk, priority) is necessary.
- The variety of different requirements presentation and processing methods encumbers the choice of strategy, tests scenario and data preparation.

These problems are widely discussed in literature. According to the paper's [14] author, the automated development of test cases in accordance with artifacts used in an early stage of information system development reduces efforts necessary for test activities and increases efficiency. There are diverse test case generation methods which enable the usage of various UML diagrams: use case and sequence diagrams [5]; activity and sequence diagrams [12]; only use case diagrams [14]; class, sequence diagrams and OCL (Object Constraint language) constraints [16], etc. Some of these methods solve not only the problem of artifacts use in test case generation, but deal selecting which test cases to perform with reference to objective criteria [5], [14].

The solution presented in this paper enables the total use of use cases defined in a stage of analysis for automated test case generation saving links not only with the use case based of which test cases were generated, but with the requirement itself. The list of new and modified test cases is given to tester if any changes or new test cases occur; it is suggested to generate the new or changed test cases. The values (these values are inherited from the use case if information is indicated) of risk or priority parameters can be defined for test cases in order to select and perform the actual test case set in current moment.

The paper is structured as follows. The review of related work is presented in second part of the paper. The possible formats of requirements are reviewed in the third part. The fourth part of the paper introduces the method of requirements' description and their usage in test case generation. The results of method application are reviewed in the fifth part. The work conclusions are presented in the sixth part of the paper.

2   Related Work

Analysis of literature shows that there are many methods of test case generation and prioritization. The methodology of test case objective selection and automated generation called Cow_Suite is one of them. It gives an opportunity to generate and plan test sets based on UML (Unified Modeling Language) in an early stage of system analysis and modeling [5] using use case and sequence diagrams. The next method [14] solving the same problems composes two processes:

- Priority allotment to requirements – the most important test cases that require generation are selected using priorities;
- Test case generation – test scenarios are generating by using UML use case diagrams and Heuman's algorithm [15].

Also, test cases can be generated using activity-sequence combined diagram [12] composed of activity and sequence diagrams formed by "Rational Rose" software or using class and sequence diagrams and OCL constrains [16].

3   Requirements Description Formats

Ordinarily, requirements are described in a natural or in a special formed language for scenarios descriptions (eg. ScenarioML); also requirements are defined by using diagrams (UML, SysML).

UML is standardized modeling language widely used in a process of software development. This language enables describing and mapping systems or their parts using models [17].

SysML (System Modeling Language) is UML 2.0 extension used in that case when there is a shortage of given UML possibilities to achieve desirable goals. SysML enables performing systems' specification, analysis, design, verification and validation [18].

The information concerning commonly mentioned requirements' description formats in literature sources is given below.

Natural Language
Describing needs and requirements in a natural language the following problems occur: inevitable uncertainties, ambiguities, and the lack of significant information. Sentences become complicated because of the described conditions and terms which define several objects, events and/or activities [8]. The information systems development requires more accuracy, formality and simplicity than natural language provides [8].

Use Case Description
Use case is the interfaces between system and one or more external actors sequence description which results the value for at least one actor [2].

Normally use cases are described in a structured textual form using use case patterns. The following information can be filled up: title, description, actor, pre-conditions, post-conditions, main success scenario, extensions, etc.

Use Case Diagram
Use case diagram has two main elements: actors and use case (process) [17]. This diagram shows the interaction between actor and test cases, i.e. use case diagram describes the functionality of the system.

Activity Diagram
Activity diagrams illustrate the work process: the sequence of activities, show which activities happen in parallel and present alternative ways. UML activity diagram is appropriate for modeling computers and organized processes [6].

Activity diagrams can represent business rules, use cases, parallel activities, and processes with decision points or alternative ways to perform them.

Sequence Diagram
Sequence diagram is dynamic UML diagram describing the sequence of object interaction for each use case. Sequence diagram defines the sequence of events. Performing use case the sequence diagram illustrates the link between several actors and system because

the interface and messages between actors and information system objects are seen [2]. This type of diagrams captures the important aspects of objects' interfaces and can be used defining testing objectives which should be achieved during test [3].

Sequence diagrams can be used not only describing use cases, but also test cases. UML Testing profile (UML-TP) can be used for this purpose. This is UML extension which uses UML language defining test cases, documentation and development [4].

State Machines

State diagram describes object's behavior. It is a graphic description of object's state sequences, events influencing state changes and actions which are initiated by varied state [17]. State diagram gives an opportunity to describe business rules and constrains unambiguously.

Collaboration Diagram

Collaboration diagram defines the structure and behavior of the system, i.e. describes what requirements should the system objects meet and what relations should be between them in order to achieve the particular task [11]. Also, the collaboration diagram describes systems constrains [11]. UML collaboration diagrams can be significant during testing because they present the links between system's functions and how manipulate them automatically [11].

SysML Requirements Diagram

The main aim of the requirements diagram is to present requirements structurally and visually. Requirements diagram fixes the hierarchy and sources of requirements [7], so there is an opportunity for a modeler to link the requirement with the model element which meets and verifies the requirement. The model of requirements describes textual requirements and their correlation with the specification, models of analysis, design and others. The requirement describes behavior, structure and/or characteristics, which have to be fulfilled by system, component or other model element [9]. The diagram of requirements is like a bridge between typical management tools of requirements and system models [7].

ScenarioML

ScenarioML is the language describing scenarios. It uses recursively defined events, ontologies, references and combination of scenario parameters in order to make scenarios more definite, more valuable and more effective [2]. Artefacts created by ScenarioML are defined by XML format, so the possibility to use them in other software tools (e.g. test management tools) emerges.

Business Action Language (BAL)

BAL is the language to describe business rules and composes of the followings: definitions – business rules variables are described; if – the conditions of business rules are described; then – the actions when the condition is met are defined; else - the actions when the condition is not met are described.

4   The Method of Requirements' Description and Their Usage in Test Case Generation

The method idea: analyst structurally describes requirements, use cases are described using use case and activity diagrams, whereas tester calls test case generator which generates test case in accordance with the early drawn diagrams given them traceability, i.e. saving the link between the generated test case and an appropriate use case. Test case generator gives a list of all changed or new use cases suggesting generating/regenerating test cases.

The diagram of method activity is given in Fig. 1 1-3 steps should be performed by system analyst, while 4th step by system tester.

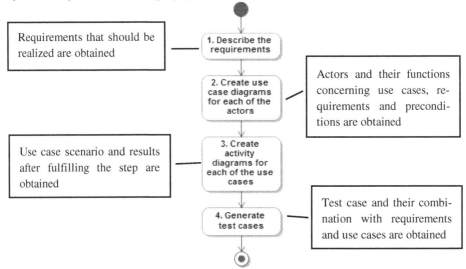

Fig. 1. Method activity diagram

The description of requirements should process in the following sequence:

1. Analyst describes the requirements (e.g. "R-100 The possibility controlling analysis and their information should be in a system");
2. Analyst creates use case diagrams for each of the actors defining (if necessary) preconditions (e.g. entity states) next to use case in order to pursue them. Thus, the information is obtained:
   (a) what functions are performed by each actor in the system;
   (b) related use cases;
   (c) what preconditions should be in order to perform an appropriate use case.
3. Analyst creates activity diagrams for each of the use cases:
   (a) draws activity diagram – the use case scenario is obtained;
   (b) other information (requirement, which is "covered" by use case, priority, risk) describing use case is presented in a window of use case parameters. Generated test cases are going to be "inherited" by this information.
4. Tester generates test cases.

Generated test case inherits classifier "Risk" and "Priority" values from the use case. It enables the selection of test cases which have to be performed most frequently (according to parameter "Risk") because they are appropriate for checking the most critical functions of system and firstly (according to parameter "Priority").

The algorithm of test case generation, test case generation rules and realization example is presented below.

Test Case Generation Algorithm

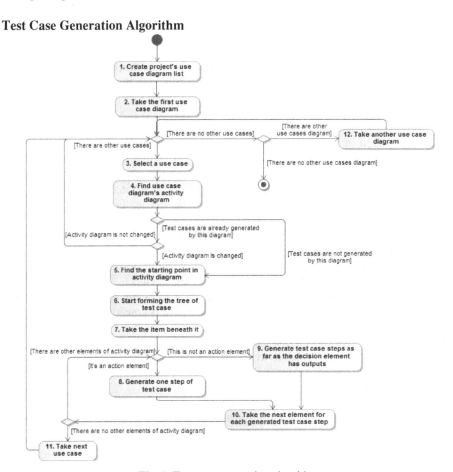

Fig. 2. Test case generation algorithm

Test Case Generation Rules:

1. In activity diagram, describing use case scenario through the branch "Yes" the main scenario is developed, while through others – alternative scenarios.
2. Firstly, the test case is generated according to the main use case scenario and then use cases for alternative use case scenarios are generated in order to be tested.
3. Generated test case title coincides with the use case title according to which the test case was generated. When test case is generated in order to check the alternative use

case scenario, in the end of its title the insertion "(decision_element_title – branch_title)" is entered. If there are several decision elements their titles and branch values in the title of test case are separated by semicolon (e.g. decision_element_title1 – branch_title; decision_element_title2 – branch_title).

4. If there is aggregation link <<include>> in the use case diagram between use cases "A" and "B", according to use case "A" generated test cases will be linked to the generated test cases according to use case "B" (Work Item type "Team Foundation Server" – "Test Case", tab "All links", link type "Predecessor") since "A" could not be performed without performing "B".

5. If in the use case diagram between use cases "A" and "B" is link <<extend>> according to use case "A" and "B" generated test cases the preconditions will not be entered since "A" and "B" can be processed irrespectively but these test cases will be also linked (Work Item type "Team Foundation Server" – "Test Case", tab "All links", link type "Related").

6. If preconditions were indicated in the use case parameters (in use case diagram) they are entered in generated test cases as preconditions (Work Item type "Team Foundation Server" – "Test Case", tab "Summary").

7. If in the use case scenario describing activity diagram the step parameter value "Expected_result is pointed it is being entered in the generated test case as an expected result of respective step (Work Item type "Team Foundation Server" – "Test Case", tab "Steps", field "Expected Result").

8. Only use cases with the value "True" of the parameter "Is_Final" are processing in test case generation.

9. Generated test cases are entered into "Team Foundation Server" according to test case title in ascending order (e.g. UC 1; UC 1.1; UC 2, etc.).

10. If any changes in the activity diagram describing use case were made it is suggested to regenerate relative test cases. The use case is considered changed if any of these conditions are satisfied:
    (a) The title of action or decision element change;
    (b) Arrow "to" or "from" relative to the element of action or decision change.

11. The earlier made test case information is renewed but not newly made while generating use case.

12. Generating test case for verifying the main use case scenario is automatically related to test cases for verifying alternative use case scenarios (Work Item type "Team Foundation Server" – "Test Case", tab "All links", link type "Child").

Necessary Environment for Realization

The programming tool "Microsoft Visual Studio 2010" was chosen for realization of developed method. DSL (Domain Specific Language) enables the creation functionality of UML diagrams (analyst's workplace). Test case generator (tester's workplace) was created as the plugin of "Microsoft Visual Studio". Therefore, both requirements' description using models and test case generation proceed in the environment of "Microsoft Visual Studio". Models (diagrams) and generated test cases are saved in the team work platform "Team Foundation Server 2010" which secures an access for general information to all the team members of the project and the versioning of the entire project's information. All the tools giving the access to protected data (e.g. "Microsoft Visual Studio", "Team System Web Access") of "Team Foundation server" can be used working with generated test cases, however, the usage of test management system "Microsoft Test Manager" would be the most purposive in order to administrate test plans, run test cases, monitor testing progress, results and get test reports automatically. Diagram of introduced decision context is presented in Fig. 3.

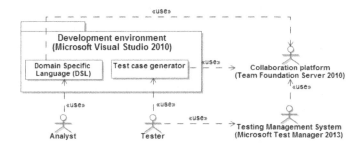

Fig. 3. Decision context diagram

5 The Results of Method's Application in Practice

In order to ascertain whether the method is applicable in practice and gives expected benefit or not the experiment was performed. This following scenario was chosen for method's application:

1 Step. Draw use case diagram (Fig. 4);

2 Step. Describe use cases "UC 2", "UC 2.1" (there is an alternative scenario too), "UC 2.2", "UC 2.3" (there is an alternative scenario too), "UC 2.4", "UC 2.5", "UC3" and "UC 4";

3 Step. Create test cases for earlier described use cases in order to test them;

4 Step. Change the "UC 2.3","UC 2.4","UC 2.5" information in use case description (2 scenario step);

5 Step. Change the information of test cases developed for use cases "UC 2.3","UC 2.4","UC 2.5";

6 Step. Complement the use case record with the description of "UC 1" and "UC 1.1";

7 Step. Create test cases appropriate for verifying the newly developed use cases "UC 1" (there is alternative scenario too) and "UC 1.1".

Scenario was accomplished both manually and automatically. Implementing the scenario manually, use case diagram was drawn using "MagicDraw" tool. Use case scenarios were described by text using "Microsoft Word" tool. Test cases are entered into "Team Foundation Server" using "Microsoft Test Manager" tool.

Implementing the scenario automatically all the scenario steps were performed using tools described in method (Section 4). For example, "Magic Draw" is changed to "Microsoft Visual Studio" using DSL and "Microsoft Word" is changed to activity diagram according to which use case and test case scenarios can be generated later.

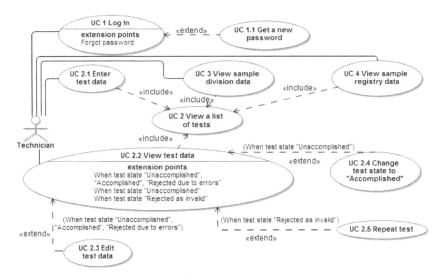

Fig. 4. Example of use case diagram

The results of experiment are presented in Table 1.

Table 1. Experiment's results

Step	Action	Duration	
		Manual process	Automated process
1.	Use case diagram	11 m	10 m
2.	Use case description	40 m	27 m
3.	Test case preparation	23 m	~ 7 s
4.	Use case description renewal	1 m	3 m
5.	Test case renewal	1 m	~ 7 s
6.	Use case description complement with new use cases	5 m	5 m
7.	New test case preparation	2 m	~ 7 s

In both cases similar time period needed for drawing use case diagrams, whereas use case description automatically lasted considerably shorter time. The test case preparation in automatic manner is superior to manual way. The changing of the use case description automatically lasts longer since correcting described use cases manually because of necessity to remove arrows and add new elements as in the use case description using activity diagram.

The use case description's addition with new use cases continued the same time in both cases. It might be determined by the factor that between two use cases one which contained alternative scenario.

The aim of creating the method is to find such a solution that would reduce testers' work but not burden analysts with extra work. The results of experiment show that the strain of analysts remains almost the same or even less in the case of automated process; whereas the advantage of automated process for testers is obvious.

6   Conclusions and Future Works

The review of test case generation methods revealed the existence of various solutions which let using use cases described in various formats for test case generation. Some of them give the solutions how to select the optimal test case set of great pack of generated test cases. The solution presented in this paper not only lets the test case generation using use case and activity diagrams, but also gives an opportunity regenerate test cases for modified use cases and generate test cases for newly developed use cases. It is also developed by fully using "Team Foundation Server" links such as related, child, and predecessor which are mentioned describing test case generation rules. The information about the need to generate/regenerate test cases is given to tester when the test case generator is called. This method secures that test follows in accordance with the test cases of the newest version.

This solution can be applied for test entity (document, analysis, audit, etc.) states too. Describing the variation of entity states using activity diagram the test cases can be generated in order to verify whether entity passes from one state to another or not.

The future plans are to expand this method and use it for generation of test cases appropriate for verifying particular limitations (e.g. minimal and maximum value of entity parameter). Also, the experiment is planned in order to evaluate its efficiency.

Acknowledgements. The work described in this paper has been carried out within the project VP1-3.1-ŠMM-10-V-02-008 „Integration of Business Processes and Business Rules on the Base of Business Semantics".

References

1. Westfall, L.: Software Requirements Engineering: What, Why, Who, When, and How. Westfall Team (2006), http://www.westfallteam.com (accessed on December 5, 2012)
2. Alspaugh, T.A., Sim, S.E., Winbladh, K., Diallo, M.H., Naslavsky, L., Ziv, H., Richardson, D.J.: The Importance of Clarity in Usable Requirements Specification Formats. ISR Technical Report UCI-ISR-06-14 (2006)
3. Rountev, A., Kagan, S., Sawin, J.: Coverage Criteria for Testing of Object Interactions in Sequence Diagrams. In: Cerioli, M. (ed.) FASE 2005. LNCS, vol. 3442, pp. 289–304. Springer, Heidelberg (2005)
4. Lamancha, B.P., Mateo, P.R., de Guzmán, I.R., Usaola, M.P., Velthius, M.P.: Automated Model-based Testing using the UML Testing Profile and QVT. In: Proceedings of the 6th International Workshop on Model-Driven Engineering, Verification and Validation (MoDeVVa 2009), pp. 6:1–6:10. ACM Press, New York (2009)
5. Basanieri, F., Bertolino, A., Marchetti, E.: The cow_Suite approach to planning and deriving test suites in UML projects. In: Jézéquel, J.-M., Hussmann, H., Cook, S. (eds.) UML 2002. LNCS, vol. 2460, pp. 383–397. Springer, Heidelberg (2002)
6. Dumas, M., Hofstede, A.H.M.: UML Activity Diagrams as a Workflow Specifica-tion Language. In: Proceedings of the 4th International Conference on The Unified Modeling Language, Modeling Languages, Concepts, and Tools, pp. 76–90. Springer, London (2001)

7. OMG, OMG Systems Modeling Language, `http://www.omgsysml.org` (accessed on December 02, 2012)
8. Boyd, N.: Using Natural Language in Software Development, `http://www.educery.com/papers/rhetoric/road/` (accessed on December 02, 2012)
9. Hause, M., Thom, F.: Modeling High Level Requirements in UML/SysML. In: Rochester 2005 Proceedings, INCOSE International Symposium (2005)
10. Help - IBM WebSphere ILOG JRules BRMS V7.1.1, `http://pic.dhe.ibm.com/infocenter/brjrules/v7r1/index.jsp?to pic=%2Fcom.ibm.websphere.ilog.jrules.doc%2FContent%2FBusines s_Rules%2FDocumentation%2F_pubskel%2FJRules%2Fps_JRules_Glob al493.html` (accessed on January 23, 2013)
11. Abdurazik, A., Offutt, J.: Using UML Collaboration Diagrams for Static Checking and Test Generation. In: Evans, A., Caskurlu, B., Selic, B. (eds.) UML 2000. LNCS, vol. 1939, pp. 383–395. Springer, Heidelberg (2000)
12. Sumalatha, V.M., Raju, G.S.V.P.: UML based Automated Test Case Generation technique using Activity-Sequence diagram. The International Journal of Computer Science & Applications (TIJCSA) 1(9), 58–71 (2012) ISSN 2278-1080
13. Meservy, T.O., Zhang, C., Lee, E.T., Dhaliwal, J.: The Business Rules Approach and Its Effect on Software Testing. IEEE Software 29(4), 60–66 (2012)
14. Kosindrdecha, N., Daengdej, J.: A Test Case Generation Processand Technique. Journal of Software Engineering 4(4), 265–287 (2010)
15. Heumann, J.: Generating Test Cases from Use Cases. Rational Software (2001)
16. Nayak, A., Samanta, D.: Automatic Test Data Synthesis using UML Sequence Diagrams. Journal of Object Technology 9(2), 115–144 (2010)
17. OMG, OMG Unified Modeling Language (UML), v2.4.1, OMG Available Specification, formal/2011-08-06 (2011)
18. OMG, OMG System Modeling Language (SysML), v1.3, OMG Available Specification, formal/2012-06-01 (2012)

Communications and Security Aspects
of Smart Grid Networks Design

Josef Horalek, Vladimir Sobeslav, Ondrej Krejcar, and Ladislav Balik

University of Hradec Kralove, Faculty of Informatics and Management,
Center for Basic and Applied Research, Rokitanskeho 62,
Hradec Kralove, 500 03, Czech Republic
{josef.horalek,vladimir.sobeslav,
ondrej.krejcar,ladislav.balik}@uhk.cz

Abstract. The article explores a global principle of communication in Smart Grid networks with a focus on specific communication infrastructure aspects. The paper is divided in two main parts. First part focuses on a description of the main concepts and control of Smart Grid network power distribution. Second part of this paper presents specific requirements regarding Smart Grid distribution flows and network elements. The paper proposes a general scheme of Smart Grid network communication infrastructure, which enables complex perspective of the given issue and its effective use. It presents different power grid management requirements in various types of regions in Czech Republic.

Keywords: Smart grid, Power automation, Energy management networks, Power distribution management, Automatic Meter Management, Power grid, Power system reliability, Renewable energy sources integration.

1   Introduction

The Smart Grid is a recent and very popular issue. It presents a wide area, which is undergoing dynamic and fast development. Therefore Smart Grid offers numerous perspectives, how its topics can be handled and this differentiation is relevant. At first, Smart Grid is a subject to energy-communicational perspective considering the large spectre of communication norms used in energetics. These include not only the family of IEC 60870, IEC 61850 or IEC 61968/61970 as treated [1] and [2].

Principles and structure of the Smart Grid networks communication offer another perspective of their use as the main component of intelligent control and management of energy networks.   Although this perspective may appear elemental and fully solved, the reality is different; due to frequent focus on local issues, such as the communication of alternative electrical energy sources with the SCADA systems [12, 14]. The possibility of Smart Grid implementation is significantly influenced by the requirements specification for network infrastructure and requirements for individual communication elements in Smart Grid networks. This point of view is accentuated in [3], where the authors focus on the analysis of the quality and meaning of the information transferred, which is highly symptomatic of Smart Grid networks.

G. Dregvaite and R. Damasevicius (Eds.): ICIST 2014, CCIS 465, pp. 35–46, 2014.

More technical Smart Grid perspective is provided in [4], where the authors correlate the connection between the IEC 61850 protocol and communication of ISO/OSI network model thanks to the application of packet analyser. The authors succeed in connecting the understanding of IEC 61850 protocol with classical understanding of network communication.

Following to these resources, another question concerning Smart Grid network particularities is in place. General architecture and standardization of Smart Grid network components is an actual topic; due to the implementation of Smart Grid networks for e.g. intelligent remote data collection from electrometers or remote optimization of electricity consumption units using Smart Grid Metering. These issues are insightfully treated, however, focusing purely on the providing of electricity, and its way from the source to the distributor. This perspective is offered in [5], which can be used generally for understanding the requirements of Smart Grid networks, if we ignore Photovoltaic System specificities. Similarly, in [6], the authors consider solely the use and optimization of Smart Grid networks in the field of wind power plants.

The authors of [7] provide a ground-breaking and comprehensive treatment of implementation and optimization of Smart Grid networks.

Furthermore, project [8] cannot be omitted, albeit it predominantly deals with practical implementation of Smart Grid networks and their reliability. It introduces calculations pointing to one of the possible approaches to reliability evaluation. This project is connected also to [9], dealing with Smart Grid network error detection.

2   Smart Grid Concept of Power Distribution

This paper presents similar approaches towards Smart Grid issues as treated in [10]. Similarly to [10] this analysis specifies the approach to the migration of the IT Technologies to the Smart Grids. The analysis focuses on the classical approach to data networks via perspective of ISO/OSI model in the process of network elements implementation into Smart Grid networks. The Smart Grid implementation and its possibilities, use and optimizations are influenced by its geographical locations and classical distribution network topology. In other words, the requirements for both Smart Grid network implementation and for individual organizational networks, as treated in the present analysis, are greatly influenced by the current situation in the Czech Republic, which resembles the conditions in similar geographical setting of distribution networks in Western and Central Europe.

The present analysis builds on the implementation and use of Smart Grid networks in a selected region of the Czech Republic in case of the most significant energy producer and distributor. Therefore the paper provides a different perspective; unlike similar analyses, it accentuates not only the horizontal perspective of Smart Grid implementation, but predominantly vertical perspective, i.e. from the distributor to various individual customers. The present regional specification is influenced by local operation of the producer, although generalised results can provide realization in the whole Europe, where citizen distribution is the same as in the Czech Republic.

3   Control of Smart Grid Network

The term Smart Grids can be defined as intelligent automatically regulated electrical networks able to transmit produced energy from any source of centralised or decentralised energy power plant to its end customer. In January 2010 the National Institute of Standards and Technology (NIST) defined the first version of Smart Grid reference model [11]. It was divided into domains describing the electrical power production, its transmission, distribution, markets, control of distribution system, service provider, and customer.

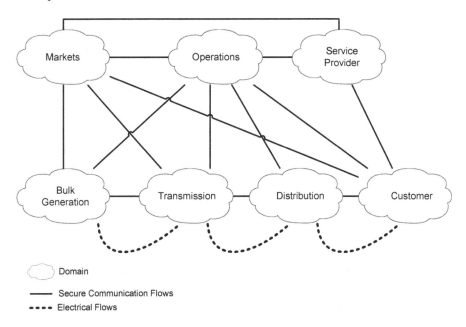

Fig. 1. Smart Grid Domains

Figure 1 represents the domains that are affected by the implementation of Smart Grid concept. This work does not cover the whole area, but deals specifically with the distribution of electric energy and its control. The significance and complexity regarding specification of individual requests for Smart Grid concept in the field of electric energy distribution and its control shall be highlighted in the comparison with the state of the art condition.

4   Smart Grid Distribution Flows

The elemental task of Smart Grid is implementation of intelligent elements for effective control of individual technological devices of distribution system, such as distribution switching stations, circuit breakers (switches), isolator switches, accumulation devices, intelligent electrometers etc. The implementation of these local systems of distribution system control will manage distribution system in order to optimize processes of local production, accumulation and consumption in the region. Local control systems will operate autonomously, including the function to control regions in island operation and black-start modes. Local control centres then must be integrated into central control system, which enables to control the region under its supervision. Detailed and aggregated data concerning consumption and other operation characteristics measured by intelligent electrometers, active elements and probes must be provided to central systems of energetic company to be processed. This enables advanced functions such as tariffication of subscribers, analysis and prediction of consumption of distribution system operation.

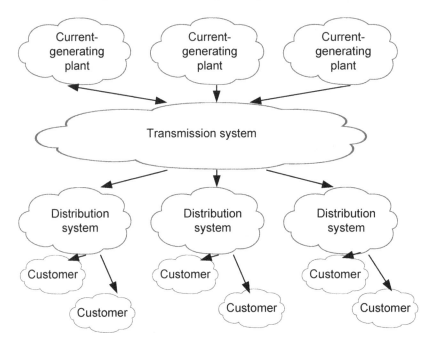

Fig. 2. Classical distribution flows

4.1   Requirements for the Power Distribution

The leading purpose of Smart Grid concept is the optimization of distribution system operation by increasing the energy system resistance, increasing of operation efficiency, balancing the peak load of the network, decreasing the influence of unpredictable sources on the network stability. This is achieved by an optimization of consumption control as far as individual consumer level with use of automated metering machines (AMM), providing detailed information to the customer concerning his consumption, optimization of the local sources and their use during the control of self-contained regions of distribution network, enabling island operation and its control, limiting the number of black-outs and minimization of the black-out impact by automated interference in network configuration (self-healing). To ensure this optimization, immediate reaction to changes in the electrical grid is vital. Majority of controlling processes and systems has to be automated on the side of electric energy distributors. Also close cooperation with central control systems (Dispatching Control System), the function of temporary autonomous operation during black-outs between region and central systems (data island) and high security of solution has to be guaranteed. Because of their complexity and high-investment, Smart Grid regions evolve gradually with great differences in the regional sizes, source possibilities, population density, consumption and balance. On the basis of these main differences it was necessary to define type regions, which can cover with their model solution the whole distribution system. The following section briefly outlines various types of regions dealing with the issues of Smart Grids.

The Region of High Population Density: the specificity of this region is small area utilization with a high population density. Due to the character of the region, the deployment of high-speed communications in combination with smart power management of customer devices (washing machines, dishwashers, etc.) is suitable. This attitude enables the creation of new value-added services. This type of region provides a great potential for Smart-City, Smart-Buildings and Smart-Homes services. This region also has the most negative energy balance on the production side. On the other hand, it is thought that an integral part of Smart Grids networks in the region is usually the central heat production (CVT).

The Region Is of Scattered Population Density: this region consists of a number of medium-sized and large cities and smaller communities. This area is usually larger than the region with high density of population, but the potential for smart power management is smaller. Utilisation of high-speed communication technologies is also more complicated according to the size of the area.   This region will be the most common in the Czech Republic.

Industrial Region: a region with a highly developed energy-intensive industry. This region is relatively small with a high power consumption, which is sufficiently optimized. The benefit of Smart Grid concept for this type of region lies mainly in the critical situations resolutions, either at the distributor or the consumer side. New Smart features can be consumer self-used, where the consumer can act as a local distributor; therefore the system can be viewed as a region within the region.

Region of Low Population Density: the specificity of this region is the lack of regional resources; the development is problematic for many reasons. Most types of the power sources are renewable, usually small hydro power and wind turbines. The development of photovoltaic energy in these kinds of regions is controversial and currently imaginable just as home roof applications. Large distances between network elements, often difficult accessibility, adverse climatic conditions and relatively little impact on the end users lead to the minor focus of Smart Grid network development of these regions.

4.2   Requirements for the Communications Infrastructure

Communication infrastructure is a key element of the entire Smart Grid network. Smart Grid concept cannot be realized without an appropriate vertical and horizontal communication infrastructure. The key prerequisite is the existence of communication link with backbone communication distribution system, as described in above structure model. With regards to common solutions and with regards to its sufficient flexibility, this place is distribution switching station 110kV/HV (high voltage). This point is the place which ensures the connections of all partial subsystems of individual layers according to their specific requirements. Inconsistent development requires integration or coexistence of other kinds of solutions different from required vertical connections on lower level (e.g. application of GSM/GPRS communication in controlling systems of switching points in the network). This communication is centre oriented; there exists a direct vertical connection between the given point and the central level. This solution rather complicates its potential use for local control of such constructed switching points. Typical division of communication infrastructure into individual network segments is depicted in the figure 2. The backbone network provides also the connection to SCADA system. MAN SG (Metropolitan Area Network Smart Grid) network is also connected to the backbone network; MAN SG provides connection between individual LAN SGs (Local Area Network Smart Grid), which represent individual local networks of Smart Grid architecture. MAN SG is typically spread on the level of one smart region, which connects individual LAN SG local networks which on the smart field level. There can be several smart fields within a smart region. Such designed hierarchical structure is highly flexible and allows easy implementation of new technologies and services.

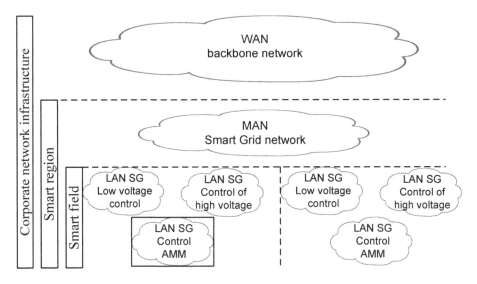

AMM - Automatic Meter Management

Fig. 3. Segments of the communications infrastructure

Regarding the requirements for communication infrastructure we may define the following levels and areas that are or can be components of communication infrastructure within Smart Grid concept:

Vertical connection between technology controlling systems and central level is applied both on the MAN SG level and LAN SG level. These connections are mostly realised in case of 110kV or HV objects; their fundamental application is essential in regions which will be controlled (DTS), but are mostly not yet controlled nowadays. If LV objects are controlled, LV increases in each given HV field.

Horizontal connection for adaptation protection functions (for example between neighbouring HV substations). In this case it is necessary to realise data networks enabling fast and reliable communication, which is achieved by using simple technology (without complicated processing of transmitted data) with minimum of intermediate elements. These requirements may be met on the LAN SG level. Similarly to the previous example (most notably in HV and LV networks) during the implementation of Smart Grid there appear cascades of protection (loops of HV or LV networks).

Vertical Connection between controlling technology systems and networks field controlling system may be defined on the LAN SG level. Parallel solution of vertical connection exists practically between the technology controlling system and central level. Each technology controlling system controlling an object, which is a part of network controlling, must have given realised communication with network controlling system. It generally concerns all levels (110 kV, HV-LV). Practically it will most frequently deal with HV selected objects and Their Affiliated LV objects.

The following figure describes the interconnection between horizontal and vertical communication types at substation level and the high-voltage to customer low-voltage transformation process in Smart Grid network topology.

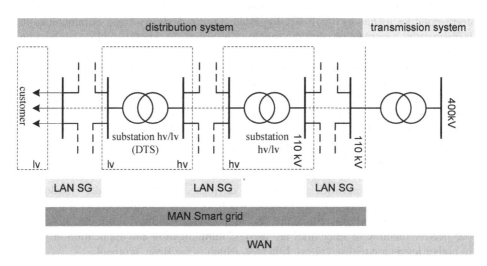

Fig. 4. The relationship between IT network and distribution system

5   Requirements for the Smart Grid Network Elements

General requirements of this type of networks can be specified on the basis of executed analysis. The use of Smart Grid network in the Czech environment is influenced by the way of construction, operation and control of distribution network. The task of Smart Grid is to ensure the function and distribution of electric energy in the HV network part and adjacent LV network in the extent described below:

HV network automation, which includes an automation of HV distribution transformation substation (HV objects part of HV/LV transformation) - DTS.

Automation of LV network in HV/LV objects of transformation (DTS) – LV DTS and isolating and circuit breaking boxes, possibly in bifurcation boxes of the LV network.

Connection and operation of local sources, both to LV network and HV network – cogeneration units, photovoltaic power plants and small water sources.

Network control (functions of monitoring, control, protection and automation) of field via thy system or subsystems of network control functions – field balance control, automation of island operation, sequence manipulation, regulation, voltage regulation in island operation mode.

Consumption monitoring and control of the filed in via cooperation of control system with AMM system (Smart Metering).

This basic set of distribution network requires a corresponding communication technology type. Each unit of energy system, which will be remotely controlled and monitored, will define a basic set of requirements on permeability, latency and reliability.

Permeability describes the speed of transmitted data from the source device to the target device. By latency we mean time which it takes for a message sent from the source device to the target device. Reliability is affected by electronic or magnetic interferences, or meteorological conditions. The aim is to have maximum permeability, low latency and high reliability. Taking into consideration investment possibilities, technical requirements and operation costs in the given locality, corresponding technology will be suggested. Figure 5 shows basic communication infrastructure organization physical topology in Smart Grid region and its connection to central systems and backbone network.

Communication link among objects may be realised both on direct or wireless lines. To support switching and routing of network frameworks and packets in each locality, switch and router might be integrated into an individual physical device. Switch will then ensure local communication within the locality (DTS) and physical communication within regional communication network between localities. Router controls communication to MAN network. Furthermore, the communication is protected by encryption and filtering. Among the network types within Smart Grid region belong LAN SG, protection and command network, and access network.

LAN SG is a network connecting devices within an object (building). Communication is managed by a central switch. In critical localities central switches can be implemented as redundant for higher accessibility. From technological perspective metallic or fiber lines are used. Communication and application protocol of higher levels are realised above Ethernet, which is the Basic protocol.

Protection network and command network are organized into circuit for communication redundancy in case of switch blackouts. This network transmits commands and GOOSE communications. The need of circular topology is defined by requirement for a very low latency (up to 4ms) communication.

Access network for Smart Grid regions connection to backbone is MAN and WAN network, through which it is connected to central systems.

On top of the physical communication infrastructure we recommend the implementation of virtual LAN networks according to IEEE 802.1Q standard. Individual virtual networks will be used for separation of individual communication types. The mutual separation of traffic in observed flow is significant for proper

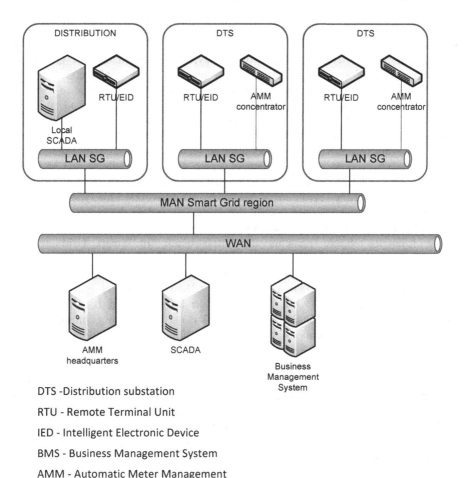

DTS -Distribution substation

RTU - Remote Terminal Unit

IED - Intelligent Electronic Device

BMS - Business Management System

AMM - Automatic Meter Management

Fig. 5. The basic communication infrastructure scheme

distribution of datagrams based on Quality of Service (QoS) parameters. It is also useful for ensuring security across the network based on different traffic types. For the same reason may be used VPN network between Layer 3 devices or Layer 2 VLAN on one broadcast domain. GOOSE protocol is used for standardized horizontal communication from IED to DTS device. These protocols are utilized in management processes in distribution networks to collect and send information between distinct distribution system elements. Also they are used in network event management systems for collecting measurement values from AMM and other devices. ICT networks act as configuration support and monitoring unit for every single intelligent device in distribution network.

As mentioned above, high reliability and low latency are key part of the infrastructure, especially considering fact that the network is also used for control commands and GOOSE communication. Optical lines, BPL (Broadband over PowerLine) and WiMAX are recommended as a lower layer technologies. The design of Smart Grid network should also contain primary and backup communication lines; preferably using different technologies. For a primary communication lines optical fibers fulfill the all demands of network safety, throughput and other Quality of Services criteria. Communication parameters and the Quality of Services (QoS) mechanisms are very important part of Smart Grid networks design, due to its direct influence on a communication performance. Utilization of BPL and WiMAX technologies is rather appropriate for backup lines, because of their security and transmission stability mechanism. In this case, use of secure VPN (preferably IPsec) tunnels is highly recommended to meet all high security standards. The Ethernet and its industry sub-versions is the fundamental protocol to be implemented in higher network communication layers. The Access Network to the Smart Grid central system and the backbone of the region are MAN and WAN networks. This type of network transfers a large amount of data over long distances including the control commands and priority settings with a higher latency tolerance.

The following figure presents the infrastructure of Smart Grid network communication concept, which has been developed in cooperation with national power distributor of Czech Republic, CEZ. This concept is built upon the well-known industrial protocols, and solutions. The IEC 61850 standard is utilized for the protection of horizontal GOOSE communication level between IED devices and various distribution substations. Control Network is used for passing commands form the parts controlled elements of the grid, collection of states and events in the distribution system, SCADA, local SCADA, RTU AMM concentrators. Data Network provides the capabilities for taking measurements and readings from meters and other active elements, probes and sensors in the distribution system. Non-critical grid network elements are not directly related to the management and operations of the distribution system, for example customer setting measurement devices [13], AMM concentrators, SCADA, RTU, BMS etc. Communication is isolated to virtual networks and interconnected via specialized security appliances for better security. ICT supervisory network is used for the configuration and monitoring of ICT equipment such as switches, routers, or a local SCADA and other computer systems or active elements of communication networks. The network management element of Smart Grid concept utilized the industrial standards IEC 60870-5 and IEC-61850-8-1 due to their better security options communication. The IEC-60870-5-101 should be used only for the incompatible equipment with the IEC-60870-5-104 standard.

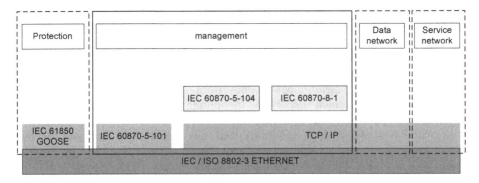

Fig. 6. Proposed Smart Grid network topology and protocols

6   Conclusion

Reliable data network is a vital component to meet aims of Smart Grid concept. Effective communication with network elements on the customer side must be ensured. The absence of standards for interoperability between data concentrator AMM and RTU units cannot provide desired outcome, i.e. management of appliances via smart electrometers. It is also caused by the fact that corresponding communication infrastructure meeting requirements of quick isolating and switching would be extremely expensive. Including the communication with smart electrometer during a blackout, when no controlling signals (to eliminate negative starting impulse) exists. Additional barrier, which prevents a massive rollout of smart electrometers is a study performed by a Ministry of Industry and Trade. Its preliminary outcomes suggest that in Czech region, the financial benefits of Smart Grid network would not reach as level as in other EU regions. Regardless a pilot projects are realized, which shows a possible future developments. Worthy of mentioning is a project BIOZE14, which in praxis shows possibilities of renewable energy sources control. Outcome of this project was up to 78% reduction of outer region energy export in a region with a high rate of renewable energy sources.

Acknowledgment. This work and contribution is supported by the project of the European Operational Programme Education for Competitiveness project CZ.1.07/2.3.00/45.0014 and by the project No. CZ. 1.07/2.2.00/28.0327 Innovation and support of doctoral study program (INDOP), financed from EU and Czech Republic funds; and by project "SP/2014/05 - Smart Solutions for Ubiquitous Computing Environments" from University of Hradec Kralove.

References

[1] Wu, J., Zhang, P., Yu, J.I.: 61968 standard-based distribution systems integration solutions and application research. In: 2nd International Conference on Energy, Environment and Sustainable Development, Jilin: EESD 2012, vol. 614-615, pp. 785–791 (2012) ISBN 978-303785551-5, ISSN 10226680

[2] Horálek, J., Soběslav, V.: Remote Control In Power Substation Automation. In: De La Cruz, P. (ed.) Recent Researches in Circuits, Systems, Communications & Computers, WSEAS, vol. 5, pp. s.110–s.117 (2011) ISBN 978-1-61804-056-5

[3] Li, W., Liu, J., Tian, W.: Study on classification of information to realize grid intelligent. In: Environment and Sustainable Development. Jilin: EESD 2012, vol. 614–615, pp. 1706-1709 (2012) ISBN 978-303785551-5, ISSN 10226680.

[4] Lee, C., Park, M., Lee, J., Joe, I.: Design and implementation of packet analyzer for IEC 61850 communication networks in smart grid. In: Kim, T.-h., Ko, D.-s., Vasilakos, T., Stoica, A., Abawajy, J. (eds.) FGIT 2012. CCIS, vol. 350, pp. 33–40. Springer, Heidelberg (2012)

[5] Sechilariu, M., Wang, B.C., Locment, F.: Building Integrated Photovoltaic System With Energy Storage and Smart Grid Communication. IEEE Transactions on Industrial Electronics 60(4), 1607–1618 (2013) ISSN: 0278-0046

[6] Chen, Y., Xu, Z., Ostergaar, J.: Islanding Control Architecture in future smart grid with both demand and wind turbine control. Electric Power Systems Research 95, 214–224 (2013) ISSN 03787796

[7] Khan, R.H., Khan, J.Y.: A comprehensive review of the application characteristics and traffic requirements of a smart grid communications network. Computer Networks (5), 1–21 (2012) ISSN 1389-1286

[8] Gudzius, S., Gecys, S., Markevicius, L.A., Miliune, R., Morkvenas, A.: The Model of Smart Grid Reliability Evaluation. Electronics and Electrical Engineering 116(10) (2011) ISSN: 2029-5731

[9] Gudzius, S., Markevicius, L.A., Morkvenas, A.: Characteristics of Fault Detection System for Smart Grid Distribution Network. Electronics and Electrical Engineering 112(6) (2011) ISSN: 2029-5731

[10] Cepa, L., Kocur, Z., Muller, Z.: Migration of the IT Technologies to the Smart Grids. Electronics and Electrical Engineering 123(7) (2012) ISSN: 2029-5731

[11] NIST Smart Grid Homepage. NIST Smart Grid . The National Institute of Standards and Technology (NIST) is an agency of the U. S. Department of Commerce., 24. 8. 2010, 29. 3. 2012 [cit. 2012-04-16], http://www.nist.gov/smartgrid/

[12] Machacek, Z., Slaby, R., Hercik, R., Koziorek, J.: Advanced system for consumption meters with recognition of video camera signal. Elektronika Ir Elektrotechnika 18(10), 57–60 (2012) ISSN: 1392-1215

[13] Penhaker, M., Darebnikova, M., Cerny, M.: Sensor Network for Measurement and Analysis on Medical Devices Quality Control. In: Yonazi, J.J., Sedoyeka, E., Ariwa, E., El-Qawasmeh, E. (eds.) ICeND 2011. CCIS, vol. 171, pp. 182–196. Springer, Heidelberg (2011)

[14] Tutsch, M., Machacek, Z., Krejcar, O., Konarik, P.: Development Methods for Low Cost Industrial Control by WinPAC Controller and Measurement Cards in Matlab Simulink. In: Proceedings of Second International Conference on Computer Engineering and Applications, ICCEA 2010, Bali Island, Indonesia, March 19-21, vol. 2, pp. 444–448 (2010), doi:10.1109/ICCEA.2010.235

Generating a Business Model through the Elicitation of Business Goals and Rules within a SPEM Approach

Carlos E. Salgado[1], Juliana Teixeira[1], Ricardo J. Machado[1], and Rita S.P. Maciel[2]

[1] Universidade do Minho, Guimarães, Portugal
[2] Universidade Federal da Bahia, Salvador, Brasil
carlos.salgado@algoritmi.uminho.pt,
juliana.teixeira@research.ccg.pt, rmac@dsi.uminho.pt,
ritasuzana@dcc.ufba.br

Abstract. Business Models play a pivotal role in organizations, especially in building bridges and enabling dialogue between business and technological worlds. Complementarily, as Use Cases are one of the most popular techniques for eliciting requirements in the design of Information Systems, Business Goals and Business Rules associate with Business Process Use Cases to compose a Business Model base structure. However, methods for relating Business Processes, Goals and Rules (PGR) are scarce, dissonant or poorly grounded. In this sense, we propose the specification of a method, within a SPEM approach, covering the elicitation of Business Goals and Rules from Process-level Use Cases, and their mapping to a Business Model representation. As a result, a tailorable method for the generation of a solution Business Model, by aligning the resulting trios (PGR) with a Business Model Canvas, is presented and demonstrated in a live project.

Keywords: Business Model, Business Goals, Business Rules, Business Use Cases, SPEM.

1 Introduction

Business Models play an ever more pivotal role in the development and continued management of Information Systems (IS). Nevertheless, recent literature review on Business Models (BM) results show that there is no agreement on what a BM is, although some emerging common themes already exist [22]. Overall, the BM artifact, as a conceptual tool that contains a set of elements and their relationships, expressing the business logic of a specific firm and the value it offers, is seen as crucial for improving the dialogue between Business and IS/IT.

Our recent work in generating a BM in ill-defined contexts, within a RUP-based approach and grounded on reference model representations, stands as a contribution inside this topic [15]. The use of Process-level Use Cases, together with Business Goals and Business Rules associated information (PGR), allows developing an activity direct-mapped BM to present to stakeholders for validation. Also, the use and adaptation of 'standard' methods and techniques to infer goals and rules requirements

G. Dregvaite and R. Damasevicius (Eds.): ICIST 2014, CCIS 465, pp. 47–58, 2014.
© Springer International Publishing Switzerland 2014

from scenarios and process-like diagrams, mapping backwardly the traditional business to process workflow, could allow for better and continuous alignment between Business and IS/IT, with improved traceability.

Accordingly, the knowledge represented in terms of goals, rules and methods can make reengineering tasks more systematic and effective [21]. Whether it involves the development of a new system or the reengineering of business processes, decisions about what goals to pursue and on selecting the appropriate strategies to achieve them are always vital. The discovery of goals and rules is part of requirements elicitation, recognized as one of the most critical activities of software development, with many prescribed methods and techniques.

However, it is virtually impossible to define a unified model for the elicitation process, due to the constantly changing needs associated to requirements activities. Even if specific methodologies, broken down into multiple steps, describe general approaches and overall principles to assist analysts in understanding needs, only the experienced analyst understands intuitively which method or technique is effective, in each circumstance, and applies it [5]. This raises issues as lack of formality and analyst dependency.

Our approach, first detailed in [14], tries to obviate to these, presenting a method to guide the analyst in the elicitation of Business Goals and Rules from Process-level Use Cases, and transforming them, in order to arrive at a Business Model representation. This later can then be presented to the involved stakeholders for review, validation and further negotiation. As the entire method follows a model-based approach, the changes agreed upon could be traced back to the original Use Cases, allowing for requirements traceability and a Business-IS/IT aligned solution.

To support this solution, a specification of the method in Software and Systems Process Engineering Meta-Model (SPEM) [12] is presented and then demonstrated in a live project. As a result, due to the SPEM features, the method is tailored and applied in the project, according to the involved teams and analysts preferences.

This document follows with background research reviews on Business Model representations and on diverse methods, techniques and guidelines for the elicitation of Business Goals and Rules, and also a synthesis on SPEM. Following, we present a specification in SPEM of our proposed method, covering the elicitation of Business Goals and Rules from Process-level Use Cases, and their mapping to a BM representation, resulting in a generated BM aligning our PGR trios with the original Use Cases. Next we apply and demonstrate it in a live project setting, instantiating the SPEM process definition, and analyze the results obtained and future work ahead. Finally, some conclusions are drawn for this paper.

2   Related Research

This section presents related research regarding Business Models representations, and Business Goals and Rules elicitation approaches. For the BM topic, it focuses solely on the Business Model Canvas (BMC) [13] and its early connection with the Balanced Scorecard (BSC) [7], mainly due to their popularity in Business-IS/IT communities.

Relating to methods and techniques for eliciting goals and rules, it falls in their associated combination of checklists and guidelines from the Rational Unified Process (RUP) [10], and in the business plans representation of the Business Motivation Model (BMM) [11]. Notwithstanding other elicitation methods and techniques associated to i*[20] or KAOS [3], this choice is due to the more complete and business oriented side of RUP and BMM, which help in defining the business requirements specification for business modeling, and promote the Business and IS/IT alignment questions that are comprised in process-oriented approaches.

Finally, a brief characterization of the SPEM specification is presented.

2.1   Business Models

The BMC, a strategic management template for developing new or documenting existing business models, currently stands out as one of the preferred tools for their generation, especially in business related audiences. The BMC is based on the Business Model Ontology proposed by [13], where the formal descriptions of the business become the building blocks for its activities. These are divided in nine different business conceptualizations, organized by four dimensions: Infrastructure, Offering, Customers and Finance. In turn, this division was based on the early work of [7] with the BSC four perspectives: Financial, Customer, Internal Business Process and Learning & Growth.

BMC and BSC are two different but complementary tools to achieve innovation, tactical directions and action plans in an existing or planned organization. While BMC determines part of the business strategy, BSC is aimed to track implementation and ensure that the organization strategy is executed. Recent research by [2], classified BMC and twenty nine other relevant literature sources on business model, with BMC obtaining interesting global results: positive on 66,7% of all the criteria analyzed, checked on all of the top-six criteria items and on 50% (six out of twelve) of the second-level ones.

2.2   Business Goals and Rules Elicitation

A recurrent question in research over Business Goals (BG) elicitation is that Use Case (UC) notation is intended for functional requirements and not non-functional requirements, which oversimplifies assumptions on the problem domain. Nowadays, in order for a software system to be of value, it should meet both functional and non-functional requirements, these last by using a goal-oriented representation [17]. In recent years, goal-oriented requirements engineering (GORE) current states and trends from the viewpoints of both academia and industry have been fully scrutinized, with results pointing for goal models to be useful for supporting the decision making process in the early requirements phase [19].

GORE is generally complementary to other approaches, well suited to analyzing requirements early in the software development cycle, especially with respect to non-functional requirements, but its analysis and evaluation also leads to many challenges [1]. A great variety of techniques for analyzing goal models have been proposed in recent years, but, on the other hand, this diversity creates a barrier for widespread adoption of such techniques, also due to the lack of guidance in literature on which one to choose [6].

Business Rules (BR) are an important artifact in the requirement elicitation process of IS and a vital part in its development cycle, as they describe ongoing policies, procedures, and constraints, which concern an organization in order to achieve its business goals and objectives [16]. Its concept has been examined from different points of view, whether as extensions of business goals, or as limitations or constraints on business activities. By structuring, organizing and expressing tactics and policies in a way that is close to business viewpoints, it helps collecting and organizing supports for the implementation of change for the associated IS [9].

It is important for software to evolve according to changes in its business environment, having BR as an integral part of the software system, its management and evolution. This improves requirements traceability in design as well as minimizes the efforts of changes, as when they are systematically identified and linked to design elements, these are easier to locate and implement [18]. Even so, the quality of software engineering projects suffers, due to the large gap between the way stakeholders present their requirements and the way analysts capture and express them, with representation of BR as one problem, and also because requirements elicitation techniques tend to be much analyst-oriented and dependant [8].

2.3   Software and Systems Process Engineering Meta-model (SPEM)

The development of artifacts in information systems, as business models are, encompasses the application of several good practices and diversified knowledge as well as, eventually, the introduction of new ideas or strategies. This results on the possibility of existence of several distinct approaches or ways for their development. In order to be able to express, establish, or organize the structure of activities inherent to the development approach, it is convenient a standard way for expressing the process structure. In this context, the SPEM 2.0, standardized by the Object Management Group (OMG), is a process engineering meta-model that provides to process engineers a conceptual framework for "modeling, documenting, presenting, managing, interchanging, and enacting development methods and processes" [12].

SPEM is used to define software and systems development processes and their components, trying to accommodate a large range of development methods and processes of different styles, but on the other hand, it does not intend to be a generic modeling language and provides only the minimal concepts needed to describe a development process. Though, for many development approaches and methods, human consumable documentation providing understandable guidance for best development practices is more important than precise models, with higher value than strict obedience to a formally defined process, as they cannot be formalized with models, but can only be captured in natural language documentation.

With SPEM 2.0, users can define Method Content, primarily expressed using work product definitions, role definitions, task definitions, and guidance, in a general direction, building up a knowledge base of development methods. This supports development practitioners in setting-up a knowledge base of intellectual capital for software and systems development that allows them to manage and deploy their content using a standardized format. Then, development teams are able to define how to apply the development methods and best practices throughout a project lifecycle, selecting and tailoring the development process as they require.

In a recent study [4], SPEM was considered the most widespread and popular language for representing development processes, with a high degree of acceptance of its metamodel, and its uses and applications. Over half of the papers collected only used SPEM as an annotation to represent certain activities in the context of the research performed in each case, while many others described extensions for improving certain deficiencies in the SPEM metamodel. Despite these weaknesses, SPEM is considered as a suitable language for representing development processes, and attending to this, we use it to describe our approach.

3 Generating a Business Model Canvas

In a previous work [15], we proposed the adaptation of standard techniques to infer goals and rules from scenarios and process-like diagrams, mapping backwardly the traditional business to process workflow, which helped in building a business motivation model and defining a strategy for the information system. With an approach based on a BMM representation and guided by a RUP-based backward transformation from process to business, it could allow for better and continuous alignment between Business and IS/IT, with improved traceability.

Following this research work, supported in the previously proposed PGR metamodel [15], we then proposed a method to guide analysts in the elicitation of goals and rules from use cases, and transforming them, in so generating a business-oriented business model for an IS [14]. This is achieved by combining the use of Business Goals and Rules elicited from Business Process Use Cases in a BSC structure, and then performing their mapping to a BMC panel.

Our proposed method, here presented in a SPEM perspective (Fig. 1), is composed by two activities ("Inferring Goals and Rules from UC" and "BSC to BMC mapping") and involves three work products ("Top-level Use Cases", "Balanced Scorecard", "Business Model Canvas"). The activities are sequentially performed in a way that an activity starts only when its predecessor activity has finished (as indicated by the «predecessor» dependencies), and use and produce (as indicated by «input» and «output» associations) artifacts.

The first activity aims to elicit and represent the PGR business-side information by following a 'standard' referential, spanning the four perspectives of the BSC, in so improving the consistency of the use cases coverage. The second activity analyses and maps each previous elicited item in an adequate section of the BMC panel, linking them to the more abstract level of business modeling, thus delivering an integrated business model canvas to present to stakeholders.

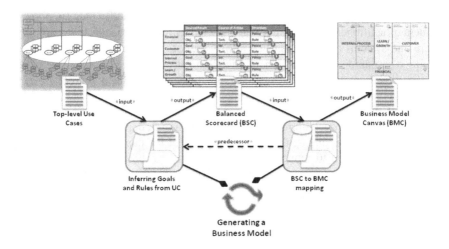

Fig. 1. SPEM diagram of our approach process

3.1   Inferring Goals and Rules from Use Cases

The first activity receives a set of Use Cases and outputs a Balanced Scorecard, being composed by two sets of three tasks each. It starts with the elicited top-level UC for the proposed IS and involves two iterations, one for each UC and another one for each BSC perspective (Financial, Customer, Internal Business Process and Learn & Growth) with the added BMM representational elements (Goal, Objective, Strategy, Tactic, Business Policy and Business Rule item).

Inside the double-iteration, there are three tasks to be performed (Fig. 2), covering the elicitation of Goals and Rules, with its associated strategies and policies, for each root UC:

1. Envision the UC associated **Goal**;
2. Determine its governing **Strategy**;
3. Associate the controlling **Business Policy**.

These are the more abstract BMM items, the ones preferable to start with due to their business nature, as they should be easier to elicit using the available business documentation. Also, depending on the project, the elicitation of these first elements could be enough for the generation of a high-level, more abstract Business Model to present to stakeholders for review.

Thereafter, in a second three tasks sequence (Fig. 2), the more concrete and specific goals and rules items should be determined:

4. a) Define a (SMART) **Objective**, associated to **Goal**;
4. b) Determine a **Tactic**, associated to **Strategy**;
4. c) Delineate a **Business Rule** item, associated to **Business Policy**.

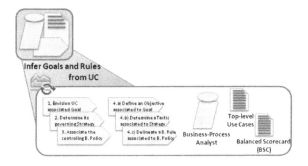

Fig. 2. SPEM Activity "Infer Goals and Rules from UC" constituents

Here, more detailed, concrete information is needed from the project documentation to be able to elicit these items. Although not all fields are mandatory, it is important to fill the most part of them, for higher system specification coverage and future implementation purposes.

All these tasks follow on the guidelines and checklists from RUP and BMM [15], for the elicitation of Business Goals and Rules, and its associated inner constituent elements. Any further knowledge of other associated techniques by the analysts involved, as well as heuristics associated to their previous experience in the specific domain of the project, are valuable to aid in these tasks. All referred tasks are to be performed by a Business-Process Analyst role.

3.2   BSC to BMC Mapping

As stated earlier, BMC stands as one of the preferred tools for the generation of business models, especially in business related audiences. Also, BMC relates its roots with BSC, an also popular strategy performance management tool.

According to the Business Model Ontology work [13], the nine elements of the BMC relate directly to the four perspectives of BSC, namely:

— Financial – Cost Structure and Revenue Streams;
— Customer – Customer Relationships, Channels and Customer Segments;
— Internal Business Process – Key Partners, Activities and Resources;
— Learn & Growth – Value Propositions.

Therefore, our proposal for the mapping of the sentences from our BSC-like structure to the BMC panel follows on this same line of thought: each sentence in BSC maps to a correspondent element in BMC. When there is a correspondence to two or three elements in BMC, any necessary decisions to choose on which specific element the sentence maps or on the separation in two or three statements, is responsibility of the analysts involved, whether based on the Business Model Ontology guidelines or on their own business heuristics.

So, the second activity receives the previous set of BSC and outputs a BMC, being composed of four tasks (Fig. 3). All referred tasks are also to be performed by a Business-Process Analyst role.

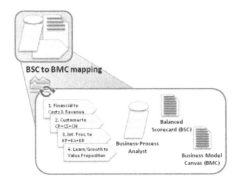

Fig. 3. SPEM Activity "BSC to BMC mapping" constituents

Surely there can be some overlaps between some elements, for example, the value proposition is closely related to any other element, especially the customer ones, so it is not impossible for mappings to occur outside elements than the ones here proposed. Other solutions in the business market propose slightly different mappings, but overall it depends on each particular case business type, and the informed or heuristic-based decisions of the analysts. All these matters should be the target for a final round of negotiations with the stakeholders, with the possibility for backtracking the changes made, back onto the Use Cases.

Several iterations of this entire process should be performed until all parts are comfortable with the obtained solution. The generation of a Business Model through the use of this first PGR step serves two purposes: on one hand it allows to communicate with the stakeholders of the project in a more business-like language, in a format that is familiar to them; on the other hand, it allows for a direct alignment and enabled traceability between the Use Cases elicited for the proposed Information System and the Business Model to be analyzed and validated by the stakeholders.

4   Demonstration Case

The demonstration project is a new job matching and e-learning, cloud based platform, sponsored by technology-leading European companies, which aims to recognize and develop talents on the skills searched by employers, in order to tackle the shortage of professionals in technical areas. Core ambition is to offer targeted online education programs to improve ICT-skills, leveraging demand/supply on the European ICT job market, for STEM engineers, preparing graduates for an industrial career and offering new skills and capabilities to empower current workforce.

Although diverse forms of information are available in the project (informal text, activity diagrams etc.), a structured description per Use Case during elicitation is not enough to generate the inputs for the Business Model as the stakeholders needed. This due, it was decided to apply our developing method in this live setting.

As described in the previous section, our proposal involves two activities which envision the filing of until twenty four (four BSC times six BMM) statements, not all mandatory, per Use Case, and a mapping to a BMC panel. At this point, the previously SPEM Method Content definitions (work product, role, and task) for each activity are tailored and applied in this project by the development analysts.

4.1   Activity "Inferring Goals and Rules from Use Cases"

Although some projects require only the generation of the high-level and abstract BM information, including only the filling of the three more abstract tasks, in this case, the developers decided to tailor the first activity of the previously defined process (Fig. 2) with the total three plus three tasks for the first activity (Fig. 4).

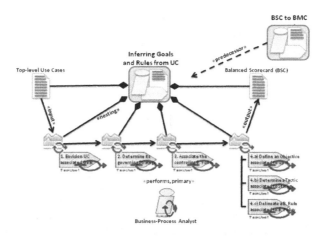

Fig. 4. Tailored development process for activity "Inferring Goals and Rules from UC"

Due to the strong business-orientation of the first three tasks, it was decided to iterate individually each one at a time, eliciting first all the goals for each top-level UC, then passing on to all the strategies and then to Business Policies. This allowed keeping the mindset about the business guidelines for each BMM item, throughout all the UC analysis. Next, the remaining three tasks were grouped and iterated sequentially, as their composition is somewhat easier to develop, highly-dependable of the previous elicited items.

This activity is itself iterated through the four dimensions of the BSC grid, which after being populated with all the elicited BMM items for all the five UC, is ready to follow as an input to the next activity.

4.2   Activity "BSC to BMC Mapping"

In this first round of execution, only the three more abstract items of each BSC perspective were considered relevant to be transposed to the BMC elements, due to this high-level positioning, and also to the shortage of information and ill-definitions of the project.

This second activity has less flexibility for tailoring, nevertheless each task can be enriched with guidance information for its execution, depending on the project characteristics. In this case the four available tasks (Fig. 3) were sequentially iterated through the BSC dimensions (Fig. 5), splitting and adapting items as needed to map in the BMC sections. This activity is itself iterated through all the BSC cards served as input from the previous activity, giving origin to a complete BMC panel.

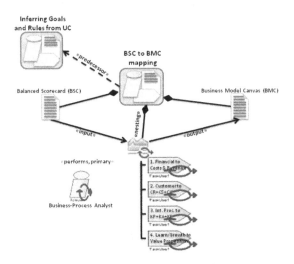

Fig. 5. Tailored development process for activity "Inferring Goals and Rules from UC"

The solution business model for this project, after the first iteration, generated by aligning the resulting trios (PGR) with the BMC, was presented to the project stakeholders. In the actual phase, they are currently analyzing the information received, which is being used as a token of discussion for the meetings adjourned.

4.3   Discussion

Our proposal for generating a Business Model through the elicitation of Business Goals and Rules from Process-level Use Cases has a dual standpoint, while it relies on 'traditional', established reference techniques and model representations; it also innovates on the organization and relationship of these to achieve a solid solution. The basis on established references strengthens the solution and the innovative organization allows for advances in research. Flexible and open solutions maintain an open door for dialogue between Business and IS/IT, leaving to the analysts the choice for using other complementary techniques at some points, as some room for negotiation with stakeholders.

The proposed method supports the effectiveness of BSC due to the individual connection to each UC and the associated elicitation of Goals and Rules elements, as they are segmented in the four BSC perspectives. Also, it allowed for negotiating the positioning of this previous information in the BMC elements and supported the business-IT dialogue, by triggering interactions from the stakeholders.

One of the purposes for the proposal of this method was to overcome the lack of data in the initial documentation and more specific inputs from stakeholders to define the business requirements. The use of mixed techniques between Business and IS/IT allowed the analysts to, simultaneously, advance in the development of the IS and communicate with stakeholders, which helped in overcoming those issues.

The solution obtained already had a positive impact in the development, sustainability and evolution of the project. The results have been promising so far, with positive feedback from involved stakeholders and research peers, but further work is needed in order to solve issues and validate the entire process.

The need for formality on the process representation, especially for the lower-level items, led us to use SPEM, and for now the only tool used to aid in this process are some spreadsheets, but as this research evolves, the development of an Eclipse-based tool is being considered. Also, for all the tasks to be performed by a person with a Business-Process Analyst profile seems too broad. In this project we observed that the first activity requires a more IS/IT-oriented profile while the second activity requires a more Business-oriented profile.

5   Conclusions

Business Models are a top concern in todays IS research, helping to link business and technological worlds, with Balanced Scorecard and Business Model Canvas as recurrent references. Also, the PGR information trio is ever more interconnected and involved in issues of requirements elicitation, process modeling and business strategy.

Our work integrates all of these topics and proposes a SPEM-tailorable method to generate an aligned Business Model for a desired Information System, based on elicitation of Use Cases and its related Business Goals and Rules.

In this paper, we present a method to support the connection between a BMC and the four perspectives of BSC, eliciting BMM Goals and Rules for each designed UC. The method is specified in SPEM, then tailored and applied in a live project to infer its adequacy. The promising results obtained point to future work for solving issues on roles and tasks, develop support tools and ensure validation of the proposal.

Acknowledgments. This work has been supported by *FCT – Fundação para a Ciência e Tecnologia* in the scope of the project: PEst-OE/EEI/UI0319/2014.

References

1. Amyot, D., et al.: Evaluating goal models within the goal-oriented requirement language. Int. J. Intell. Syst. 25(8), 841–877 (2010)
2. Burkhart, T., et al.: Analyzing the Business Model Concept-A Comprehensive Classification of Literature. In: ICIS, pp. 1–19 (2011)
3. Dardenne, A., et al.: Goal-directed acquisition. Sci. Comput. Program. 20(1), 3–50 (1993)
4. Dodero, J.M., et al.: Uses and Applications of SPEM Process Models. A Systematic Mapping Study. J. Softw. Maint. Evol. Res. Pract. 1(32), 999–1025 (2012)
5. Hickey, A., Davis, A.: A Unified Model of Requirements Elicitation. J. Manag. Inf. Syst. 20(4), 65–84 (2004)
6. Horkoff, J., Yu, E.: Analyzing Goal Models – Different Approaches and How to Choose Among Them. In: ACM Symposium on Applied Computing, pp. 675–682 (2011)

7. Kaplan, R.S., Norton, D.P.: Linking the Balanced Scorecard to Strategy. Calif. Manage. Rev. 39(1), 53–79 (1996)
8. Kapočius, K., Butleris, R.: Repository for business rules based IS requirements. Informatica 17(4), 503–518 (2006)
9. Kardasis, P., Loucopoulos, P.: A roadmap for the elicitation of business rules in information systems projects. Bus. Process Manag. J. 11(4), 316–348 (2005)
10. Kroll, P., Kruchten, P.: The rational unified process made easy: a practitioner's guide to the RUP. Addison-Wesley Professional (2003)
11. OMG: Business Motivation Model (2010)
12. OMG: Software & Systems Process Engineering Meta-Model (SPEM) Specification (2008)
13. Osterwalder, A.: The business model ontology: A proposition in a design science approach (2004)
14. Salgado, C.E., et al.: Generating a Business Model Canvas through Elicitation of Business Goals and Rules from Process-level Use Cases. In: Business Informatics Research, pp. 1–14 (2014)
15. Salgado, C.E., et al.: Using Process-level Use Case Diagrams to Infer the Business Motivation Model with a RUP-based Approach. In: Information Systems Development, pp. 1–12 (2013)
16. Shao, J., Pound, C.: Extracting business rules from information systems. BT Technol. J. 17(4), 179–186 (1999)
17. Supakkul, S., Chung, L.: A UML profile for goal-oriented and use case-driven representation of NFRs and FRs. In: Third ACIS Int. Conf. Softw. Eng. Res. Manag. Appl., pp. 112–119 (2005)
18. Wan-Kadir, W.M., Loucopoulos, P.: Relating evolving business rules to software design. J. Syst. Archit. 50(7), 367–382 (2004)
19. Yamamoto, S., et al.: Goal oriented requirements engineering: trends and issues. IEICE Trans. Inf. Syst. 89(11), 2701–2711 (2006)
20. Yu, E.S.K.: Towards modelling and reasoning support for early-phase requirements engineering. In: Proc. of 3rd IEEE Int. Symp. Requir. Eng., ISRE 1997, pp. 226–235 (1997)
21. Yu, E.S.K., Mylopoulos, J.: Using Goals, Rules, and Methods to Support Reasoning in Business Process Reengineering. Proceedings of the Twenty-Seventh Hawaii International Conference on System Sciences, pp. 234–243 (1994).
22. Zott, C., et al.: The Business Model: Recent Developments and Future Research. J. Manage. 37(4), 1019–1042 (2011)

Strategy Guided Enterprise Architecting: A Case Study

Rūta Pirta and Jānis Grabis

Dept.of Management Information Technology, Riga Technical University
Kalku 1, Riga, LV-1658, Latvia
{ruta.pirta,grabis}@rtu.lv

Abstract. Enterprises and their architecture (EA) are changing continuously, what leads to changes in enterprise information systems (IS) and its architecture. Ineffective IS change management has a particularly adverse effect on EA because of wrong architectural decisions. These decisions can lead to several problems such as poor IS performance, wrong interfaces, bad data quality, doubled data input and sub-optimal IS support to business processes. It is assumed than an enterprise IS strategy is an important source of information guiding the EA architecting and implementation of the changes. In this paper, a case study on definition of the IS strategy for a Latvian telecommunication company is presented. The goal of the case study is to identify typical practical challenges arising in EA architecting and to examine the role of the enterprise IS strategy. The results of this study will be used in further research on development of the approach for the strategic IS change control.

Keywords: Enterprise architecture, EA landscapes, IS changes, IS strategy, Case study.

1 Introduction

Nowadays the majority of enterprise business processes are executed and/or supported by information systems (IS). IS have an essential role in business process optimization and transformation in order to capture opportunities arising in a dynamic business environment. To remain competitive and to develop the business, the enterprise business processes undergo continuous improvement and changes are frequently introduced.

The changes in the enterprise business processes cause modification in enterprise IS, for example, new functionality, updated existing functionality and new interfaces. These modifications can be systematically managed following an engineering change management (ECM) process [29]. The change management and governance according to the best practices is defined and described in several international methodologies and frameworks (ITIL, COBIT, ValIT etc.). The change and its impact assessment are defined as one of the most important change management components in the before mentioned frameworks.

However, empirical observations made by the authors in Latvian enterprises and state institutions and several research works [1, 2, 3] share opinion that the IS changes and their impact frequently are not evaluated according to the best practices.

G. Dregvaite and R. Damasevicius (Eds.): ICIST 2014, CCIS 465, pp. 59–72, 2014.

For example, business value of the proposed IS changes is not estimated, which can lead to the risk that the IS changes are not cost-efficient, functional and non-functional requirements of the IS changes are not specified in the appropriate level and others. Besides that, the change management usually requires large investments. The size and complexity of IS makes the change management costly and time consuming. It has been reported that 85 to 90 percent of the software system budget goes to operation and maintenance [1].

Ineffective change management has a particularly adverse effect on enterprise architecture (EA) [15] because of wrong architectural decisions such as poor IS performance, wrong interfaces, bad data quality, doubled data input and sub-optimal IS support to business processes. According to [2]: "In many organizations, the IT landscape has evolved organically over decades". The modifications are introduced in an ad hoc manner rather than being comprehensively planned and cleanly integrated to pressure to deliver quick answers to business requirements. The strategic planning for ICT investments is thought to be a more appropriate approach for both private business and public organizations facing the challenges of rapidly evolving technologies and business environments [4].

EA and its management are topics receiving ongoing interest from academia, practitioners, standardization bodies, and tool vendors [7]. EA is used to represent the enterprise and its underlying information technology in models that can support decision making. Such EA models cover aspects from business, processes, integration, software and technology [8]. Previous investigations prove that a better governance of IT architectures and the whole organizational ICT both in large private companies and in public organizations can be ensured with the EA approach [9], [10], [11], [12], [13], [14], [16].

It is assumed than an enterprise IS strategy is an important source of information guiding the EA architecting and implementation of the changes. In order to provide empirical foundations for the study, a case study of EA architecting is conducted. It is conducted at a Latvian telecommunication company. The case study goal is to identify typical practical challenges arising in EA architecting and to examine the role of enterprise IS strategy. The results of this study will be used in further research on development of the approach for the strategic IS change control.

The rest of the paper is structured as follows. Section 2 provides brief background information and the review of related work. In Section 3, the case study design is presented. Sections 4 and 5 report the case study about creating the IS strategy at a Latvian telecommunication enterprise, including documentation of the EA and the risk analysis of the envisioned EA implementation. The paper closes with Section 5, containing conclusions and outlook for future research.

2   Background and Related Work

The IS strategy of an enterprise is defined as a *"long-term, directional plan which decides what to do with information technology"* [20]. The concept of IS strategy has been defined more than 50 years ago and initially were referred as the IS plan [22]. According to [30]: "With the development of IS Strategy, the enterprises have their great efforts on its utilization to change and improve their management and competitive situations". IS strategy research works [23], [24], [25], [26], [27] etc. are closely related to the strategic management research field and mainly focus on the techniques, tools, frameworks, and methodologies of IS strategy development. Nevertheless, there is many fundamental issues related to the IS strategy concept that remain unresolved [22].

There are three types of IS strategy: 1) IS for Efficiency IS strategy, 2) IS for Flexibility IS strategy and 3) IS for Comprehensiveness IS strategy [21]. The first of them includes the portfolio of systems supporting operational and cost efficiency, the second includes a portfolio that supports innovation and enables new market opportunities and the third encompasses characteristics of the first two. However, empirically it is observed that in practice the enterprises IS strategy includes all of the mentioned portfolios and they are interrelated in united EA. The IS strategy usually includes following main parts: 1) the existing situation definition and analysis (to fix the existing situation and ongoing initiatives); the existing situation description shows the current EA; 2) the IS development direction (to provide the IS development rules and directions); the IS development direction incudes the future EA (i.e. the ideal EA) that needs to be achieved in the defined period; 3) the IS strategy implementation plan (to show the project portfolio that needs to be performed to meet the ideal EA).

As already mentioned the IS strategy might include several EA states (the current EA landscape, the future EA landscape, sometimes also the planned EA landscape). IEEE, ArchiMate, and TOGAF define EA as a set of normative means to direct enterprise transformations. The normative means can take the shape of principles, views, or high level architecture models, whose role is to be a normative instrument during the intended transformation [17]. EA includes several dimensions/views/layers. The four views that are usually considered in literature are [4]:

1. Business Architecture (BA). BA depicts the business dimension (Business processes, service structures, organization of activities).
2. Information Architecture (IA). IA captures the information dimension of EA; high level structures of business information and, at a more detailed level, the data architecture.
3. Systems or Applications Architecture (SA/AA). SA/AA contains the systems dimension, the information systems of the enterprise. Some conventions call it the Applications Architecture or Portfolio, the latter stressing the nature of the information systems as a business asset.
4. Technology Architecture (TA). TA or the technology dimension covers the technologies and technological structures used to build the information and communication systems in the enterprise.

Other frameworks such as the Zachman framework and TOGAF include additional dimensions/views/layers, for example, people, time, motivation.

According to [4] EA is a well suited tool for interconnected planning of business strategies, models and structures, and IT architectures. EA can be analyzed in different ways and thus can support the decision making process that has to cope with an increasing number of changes, the clarification of the extent of changes and the complexity of these changes [6].

EA has been used in several approaches supporting ECM [6], [18], [19], [5]. These approaches analyze gaps between different EA states with the aim to support architectural decisions related to IS change management and implementation in EA. The term "gap analysis" is used in context of enterprise architecture as a name for the comparison between two architectures or strictly speaking two states of the same architecture. However, the proposed approaches for gap analysis mainly cover topic how to analyze different EA states, eg. how to achieve that change will be aligned with ideal future EA, so the problem: how to create the ideal EA landscape, still exists and this is the challenge.

3   Case Study Design

In this paper the empirical evidence of creating an organization's IS strategy is described. The case study includes a description of the IS strategy development project at a telecommunications company (referred as to TLO) in Latvia. The TLO core business is internet and data transmission solutions delivery throughout Latvia. The organization is established more than 15 years ago, but in the recent years it has enlarged the range of services. Because of the new services and changes in the TLO operating model, the TLO business processes also have been changed. The company realized that the existing IS support level for business was not sufficient, so the external consultants were asked to document the business needs and develop the TLO IS strategy.

The project was realized in three main stages: (1) analysis and assessment existing situation, (2) definition of IS development scenarios and (3) development of the IS strategy. The main objective of the project was to identify and to determine IS and IT governance development goals and priorities for the 3 years period. In the project the international internal transformation framework was used and a target group benchmarking was applied.

The case study aims to highlight practical drivers of EA architecting, to describe role of IS strategy in EA architecting and to identify practical challenges and risks associated with EA architecting. The results of this study will be used in further research on development of the approach for the strategic IS change control.

The case is analyzed from the perspective of the consultants who worked on development of the strategy (in total 3 consultants were working in this project, including one of the paper author). The information used in the case is: documents provided by TLO (TLO business strategy, previous IS development plan, organizational structure), interviews with TLO management (in total 9 interviews with the heads of Department, 3 interviews with board members) and employees (in total 3 interviews with the employees) and documents created by the consultants (presentations, the description of existing situation and the IS strategy).

4   Documentation of Enterprise Architecture

4.1   Current Enterprise Architecture

The TLO is one of the leading telecommunication providers in Latvia. Besides the telecommunications services, it also provides other services (cloud computing services, video streaming etc.). The current TLO EA includes about 10 core business processes and more than 60 applications. A fragment of the high-level TLO EA logical reference model is shown in the Figure 1. The following layers are included in the reference model: 1) Users –internal and external users of applications and information; 2) Channels – what channels are used to exchange the information; 3) Operational model/core business functions–operational model, core business functions and critical processes; 4) Applications – what applications are used at TLO to support business processes; 5) Information– the TLO business information, data and the main data sources; 6) Infrastructure – what kind of IT infrastructure is used at TLO; and 7) Access points – type and location of the information and applications access points.

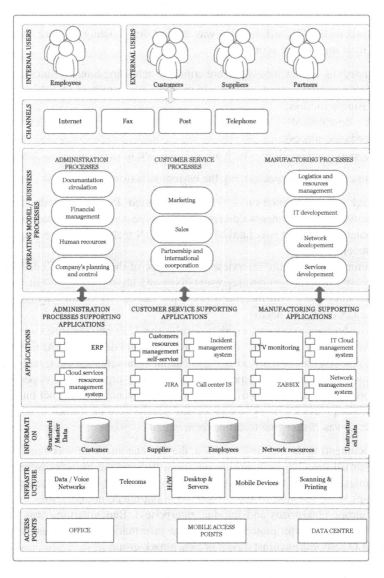

Fig. 1. A fragment of the high-level TLO logical reference model

4.2   Analysis of Current Enterprise Architecture

To identify and evaluate the current EA, firstly analysis of the existing situation was performed. The following concerns were assessed: IS, their architecture and integration level, IS support to business processes, IT infrastructure, IT organizational structure, IT governance, IT security aspects, current and planned IS/IT development projects etc. The analysis included documentation analysis (enterprises business strategy, IS documentation, agreements with suppliers and customers etc.) and interviews with TLO employees (management, process owners, IT specialists, board members etc.). Analysis of the IS portfolio also was carried out: existing IS were assessed according to their importance score [28]:

- strategic – applications which are critical to achieving future business strategy;
- high potential – applications which might be important in achieving future business success;
- key operational – applications upon which the organization currently depends for success;
- support – applications which are valuable but not critical to business success.

The main challenges characterizing the current situation were:

- Lack of documentation – TLO had limited IS technical documentation (Software requirements description, Software architecture description, User manual etc.) so it was hard to understand IS technical architecture and data model;
- Limited scope of the interviews – the scope of the project included the interviews with management representatives and board members, but there were few interviews with the end users, what causes risk of missing out some of the EA evolution needs;
- Low business processes maturity level – the TLO business processes maturity was in level 1 (according to CMMI maturity level definition: "At maturity level 1, processes are usually ad hoc and chaotic. The organization usually does not provide a stable environment. Success in these organizations depends on the competence and heroics of the people in the organization and not on the use of proven processes."). As the processes mainly were performed in ad/hoc manner, it was challenging to define them in EA.

After documenting the existing situation, the IT benchmarking was done. The TLO was asked to fill the IT benchmarking questionnaire and the answers were collected and benchmarked against the results of other companies in the same benchmark group (three groups were relevant to the project – Global telecommunications enterprises, Northern Europe enterprises and Latvian enterprises). Benchmarking was used as a measurement tool that promoted learning and information sharing and allowed to compare TLO responses against a peer or benchmark group.

As the result the existing EA was identified and evaluated, including assessment of the current IS support level to the TLO business processes. The main conclusions/identified issues were:

1. **Insufficient IS Support to the TLO Business Processes.** Several areas were identified where the IS support is not sufficient and/or does not meet the business needs (for example, the financial management, HR etc.). Overall, the TLO business processes automation level was low and extensive manual work was performed to process the same information in different sources (MS Excel files, different IS, MS Word documents etc.).
2. **Limited Options for Business Analysis due to the Lack of Integration among the Existing IS.** The current integration level was low, only 3 of more than 60 IS were partially integrated. The same data was maintained and processed in different IS, so also the data quality level was low.
3. **Business Continuity and IT Security Risk.** Several issues in IT security governance processes were identified. In recent years no internal or external IT security audits were performed. Also the related documentation did not exist (IT security policy, Business continuity plan, Disaster recovery plan etc.).
4. **Limited Options for the IS Development.** So far, the IS development was not a priority for TLO, in recent years no investments in TLO internal IS development was made, so the core business IS were physically and morally outdated and their development possibilities were limited.

Even before starting the project, TLO had started an initiative to improve the situation: the data quality audit was underway, the first default values and embedded classifiers were implemented in IS, the access control to IT resources was initiated as well as several other activities. TLO had understood that to remain competitive they need to improve effectiveness of the business processes and IT can be a mechanism that can help to do this.

4.3 IS Development Scenarios

Based on the identified IS development areas and the TLO business strategy, the long-term IS development vision was created. The long-term vision included TLO IS development for the next 6-8 years period. However, given that an IS strategy optimal live cycle is no longer than 3 years (because business processes and technologies are changing continuously), three IS development scenarios have been proposed for the next 3 years period:

A. Strengthening IS support for customer service processes;
B. Strengthening IS support for manufacturing processes and cooperation with the clients and partners;
C. Strengthening IS support for administration processes optimisation and internal communication.

All proposed scenarios are oriented towards the long-term IS development vision, though they focus on strengthening IS support for different business processes segments (for example, in Scenario A majority of the changes in IS are related to customer service improvement, while the manufacturing and administration processes are changed to a lesser degree). The consultants also gave recommendations concerning preferable scenarios to be implemented.

4.4   IS Strategy

The proposed IS development scenarios were discussed with the TLO board members and CIO and the IS development direction was selected. The development direction was based on the consolidation of the Scenarios A and B (these scenarios were selected because they directly correlated with the TLO business strategy and provided better return on investment). The selected IS development direction included strengthening IS support for the following TLO business strategy objectives:

- **Substantial Expansion of Operations in the SMEs Segment.** To help to achieve this objective, IS support to the customer service processes is to be increased, including additional IS support to customer problems, incidents and requests management processes by centralizing several existing uninte-grated systems in a unified service desk platform. The IS strategy includes also the new customer service processes requiring implementation of new applications implementation (CRM, Customer portal) to improve electronic communication with TLO customers.
- **Decrease of the operational costs** through an optimisation of resource man-agement processes and the existing IS. In the envisioned EA the number of existing IS should be significantly reduced by centralizing similar functional-ity in core IS. It is also planned to optimize the resource management proc-esses by implementing the workflows management functionality in the re-source management system.
- **Development of the cloud computing services** (Saas, ITaS etc). To help to achieve this objective, it is planned to improve configuration management for the cloud computing services and to prepare the working environment for development of future cloud computing services (e.g., Customer portal, cen-tralized monitoring and Configuration management database).

The IS strategy was created according to these directions. The IS strategy included the envisioned or the ideal EA, IS development rules and IT governance development. The TLO IS strategy defined following key activities that need to be done:

- Phasing-out of the physically and morally aged IS by transferring and cen-tralizing their functionality in the existing strategic IS and/or new IS;
- Implementation of centralized monitoring, starting with monitoring of the business critical infrastructure and gradually expanding monitoring to all other infrastructure and services;
- Expanding role and functionality of the strategic IS (e.g. ERP system);
- Implementation of new IS (CRM, Configuration management database, Cus-tomer portal etc.);
- Implementation of the integration platform and sequential IS integration, starting with the integration among the strategic IS;

- Data quality improvement by data auditing and implementation of master data management procedures (system, responsible person etc.);
- Improvement of the IT organisation and IT management processes through the development of an effective cooperation model between the IS/IT and the business.

Besides the IS strategy, the IS strategy implementation plan was also created, what includes IS development project portfolio (projects, timeline, expenses, cost-benefit analysis and risks).

The main challenges of the IS strategy development were:

1. Limited resources – the TLO resources for implementation of the IS strategy were limited, so the strategy was based on using open-source solutions, and it was clear that within three years the TLO business needs could be covered just partially;
2. Hard to prioritize the business needs – as the strategy was based mainly on the needs of TLO management and board, they all were relatively high-level and of similar important to TLO business development, so it was hard to prioritize them;
3. Uncertain business strategy implementation plan – although the TLO business development goals were set it was not clear what actions TLO plan to take for reaching the goals, so the planned IS support may be not sufficient for these actions.

5   Elaboartion of Enterprise Architecture

5.1   Ideal Enterprise Architecture

Based on the IS development direction, the envisioned or ideal EA is elaborated. A fragment of the future high-level TLO EA logical reference model is shown on Figure 2. Main changes are planned in the Applications architecture layer, what closely relates to other layers, so information, business processes and channels architecture layers also need to be changed. The main changes in other layers include:

- New communication channel – as a result of the planned implementation of Customer portal, a new communication channel between TLO and their customers will be created;
- Changes in EA business processes – level of automation of EA business processes (sales, financial management, logistics and resources management, network development, information management and others) will be increased as the result of implementing the new IS (CRM, Customer portal etc.) and significantly improving the existing IS (ERP, Call center IS etc.).
- The new structured data set (configuration management data) will be stored and maintained as the result of the Configuration management database implementation. Quality of the existing data will be increased (customer data, network resources) as the result of implementation of the integration platform.

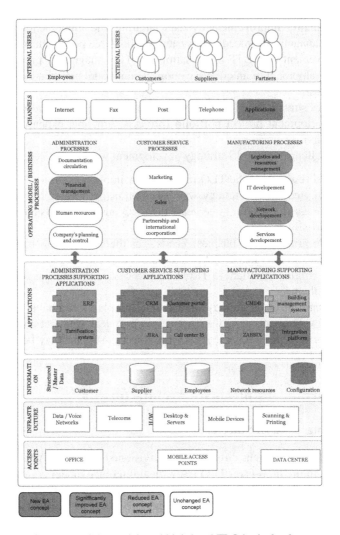

Fig. 2. A fragment of the envisioned high-level TLO logical reference model

5.2   Implementation Risks

As of now information about implementation of the TLO IS strategy is not available. However, we have identified several high - priority risks associating with realizing the IS strategy:

- Communication risk – due to the TLO existing organization culture and low internal communication, the risk exists that IS development requirements will not be specified the sufficient level of detail.
- Human resources risk – TLO may lack needed competences and human resources to implement all IS development projects.

- Cooperation risk – due to the existing sub-optimal cooperation between the business and IT departments, the risk exists the business will not contribute sufficiently to implementing the IS strategy implementation (for example, data correction, IS testing etc).
- Management risk – the IS strategy is a workable program which needs to be fully implemented to reach the benefits (business processes efficiency improvement, cost reduction etc). However, the risk exists that middle-level management will introduce add-hoc changes to the plan.

The mentioned risks mainly arise from the existing organizational culture and cooperation between the different level TLO employees. The IS strategy implementation requires strong management involvement to minimize these risks. The IS strategy implementation process and progress must be periodically reviewed by high-level management and discussed in all management levels.

6   Conclusion

In this paper, we examined typical practical challenges arising in IS strategy development and EA elaboration. These challenges were identified by investigating the enterprise architecting case at a Latvian telecommunication company . These challenges also have been observed in other similar cases not reported in the paper (the authors have participated in similar projects in more than 6 large Latvian private and public sector organizations in the last two years).

The initial results show that the enterprise IS strategy has an important role in EA architecting, both concepts are closely inter-related and partly dependent of one other, e.g. the IS strategy can be used as a tool for defining the ideal EA and it must guide the enterprise to reach the ideal EA.

The main conclusions of the study are the following:

- EA architecting should be performed by comparing and analyzing different EA layers, states, landscapes and their relations (including gap analysis between current EA state and existing reference models).
- The current and envisioned EA must be included in the IS strategy to provide enterprise with a clear and demonstrative EA development vision.
- The main objective of development of IS strategy is identify the business needs and possible IS support for reach the business strategy.
- All stakeholders (management, board, end users) should be involved in development and implementation of the IS strategy.
- As EA is changing constantly, the IS strategy must be reviewed and updated on a regular basis. It is suggested that optimal planning horizon for the IS strategy is no longer than 3 years.
- The enterprise IS strategy is an important source of information guiding the EA architecting, evolution and implementation of the changes.
- If the IS strategy is defined at a high level of abstraction, it is harder to evaluate whether the EA changes are performed according to the IS strategy;

- To implement the envisioned EA, the planned application architecture changes must be assessed in accordance with the envisioned EA and the IS strategy guidelines and rules.

Typical challenges arising in development of the IS strategy and EA architecting observed in this case and other related cases are:

- Lack of business strategy or uncertain business strategy – if enterprise's business strategy and business development plans and related actions are not clear it is hard to align IS development plans with them.
- Insufficient level of involvement of all employees and end user in defining the business needs;
- Unclear business needs – the business is not certain about needed IS support in future;
- Low business processes maturity level – if the business processes maturity level is low it is hard to evaluate existing IS support level and IS support needed in future;
- Difficult to predict and access the impact of external conditions – this challenge mainly arise in public sector organizations, because there are many decisions that are taken outside the organization and it cannot change them (for example the market liberation, changes in regulatory);
- Sub-optional cooperating between the IT and the business departments – if the cooperating between the IT and business departments is weak, both sides are not interested in IS strategy development making it difficult to analyze the existing situation (for example, anecdotally, it has been observed that the business value everything related to IT as low quality while IT claims that the business cannot specify their needs).

References

1. Erlikh, L.: Leveraging legacy system dollars for e-business. IT Professional 2(3), 17–23 (2000)
2. Hanschke, I.: Strategic IT Management. A Toolkit for Enterprise Architecture Management. Original German edition, 342p., 130. Hanser Fachbuch (2009)
3. Goknil, A., Kurtev, I., van den Berg, K., Spijkerman, W.: Change Impact Analysis for Requirements: a Metamodeling Approach. Information and Software Technology (in press, 2014)
4. Pulkkinen, M.: Systemic Management of Architectural Decisions in Enterprise Architecture Planning. Four Dimensions and Three Abstraction Levels. In: Proceedings of the 39th Hawaii International Conference on System Sciences (2006)
5. Diefenthaler, P., Bauer, B.: Gap Analysis in Enterprise Architecture Using Semantic Web Technologies. In: 15th International Conference on Enterprise Information Systems (ICEIS), Angers, France (2013)
6. Lautenbacher, F., Diefenthaler, P., Langermeier, M., Mykhashchuk, M., Bauer, B.: Planning Support for Enterprise Changes (2013)

7. Buckl, S., Schweda, C.M.: On the State-ofthe- Art in Enterprise Architecture Management Literature. Technical Report, Technische Universitat Munchen, Chair for Software Engineering of Business Information Systems (2011)
8. Winter, R., Fischer, R.: Essential layers, artefacts, and dependencies of enterprise architecture. In: 2006 10th IEEE International Enterprise Distributed Object Computing Conference Workshops (EDOCW 2006), pp. 30. IEEE Computer Society (2006)
9. Armour, F.J., Kaisler, S.H., Liu, S.Y.: A Big Picture. Look at Enterprise. In: Proceedings of the 39th Hawaii International Conference on System Sciences 8 Architectures, IT Pro, pp. 35–42. IEEE (1999)
10. Armour, F.J., Kaisler, S.H., Liu, S.Y.: Building an Enterprise Architecture Step by Step. In: IT Pro, pp. 31–39. IEEE (1999)
11. Armour, F.J., Kaisler, S.H.: Enterprise Architecture: Agile Transition and Implementation. In: IT Pro, pp. 30–37. IEEE (2001)
12. CIO Council: Practical Guide to Federal Enterprise Architecture. Chief Information Officer Council, FEAPMO Federal Enterprise Architecture Program Management Office, http://www.feapmo.gov
13. Jarvis, R.: Enterprise Architecture: Understanding the Bigger Picture - A Best Practice Guide for Decision Makers in IT, The UK National Computing Centre, Manchester, UK (2003)
14. Spewak, S.H.: Enterprise Architecture Planning: Developing a Blueprint for Data, Applications and Technology. John Wiley & Sons (1992)
15. Tang, A., Lau, M.G.: Software architecture review by association. Journal of Systems and Software 88, 87–101 (2004)
16. Wegmann, A.: On the Systemic Enterprise Architecture Methodology (SEAM). In: Camp, O., et al. (eds.) Proceedings of the International Conference on Enterprise Information Systems, Angers, France (2003)
17. Nakakawa, A., van Bommel, P., Proper, H.A.: Definition and Validation of Requirements for Collaborative Decision-Making in Enterprise Architecture Creation. Int. J. Cooperative Inf. Syst. 20(1), 83–136 (2011)
18. Gringel, P., Postina, M.: I-pattern for gap analysis. In: Engels, G., Luckey, M., Pretschner, A., Reussner, R. (eds.) Software Engineering. Lecture Notes in Informatics, pp. 281–292. Gesellschaft fur Informatik, Bonn (2010)
19. Postina, M., Sechyn, I., Steffens, U.: Gap analysis of application landscapes. In: 13th Enterprise Distributed Object Computing Conference Workshops, pp. 274–281. IEEE Computer Society (2009)
20. Earl, M.H.: Management Strategies for Information Technology. Prentice-Hall, Inc., New York (1989)
21. Sabherwal, R., Chan, Y.E.: Alignment between business and IS strategies: a study of prospectors, analyzers, and defenders. Information Systems Research 12(1), 11–33 (2011)
22. Peppard, P.: Information systems strategy as practice: Micro strategy and strategizing for IS (2003)
23. Lederer, A.L., Sethi, V.: The implementation of strategic information systems planning methodologies. MIS Quarterly 12(3), 445–461 (1998)
24. Premkumar, G., King, W.: Assessing strategic information systems planning. Long Range Planning 24(5), 41–58 (1991)
25. Flynn, D.J., Goleniewska, E.: A survey of the use of strategic information systems planning approaches in UK organizations. Journal of Strategic Information Systems 2(4), 292–319 (1993)

26. Premkumar, P., King, W.: Organizational characteristics and information systems planning: an empirical study. Information Systems Research 5(2), 75–109 (1994)
27. Bergeron, F., Buteau, C., Raymond, L.: Identification of strategic information systems opportunities: applying and comparing two methodologies. MIS Quarterly 15(1), 89–103 (1991)
28. McFarlan, F.W.: Information technology changes the way you compete. Harvard Business Review (1984)
29. Jarratt, T.A.W., Eckert, C.M., Caldwell, N.H.M., Clarkson, P.J.: Engineering change: An overview and perspective on the literature. Res. Eng. Des. 22, 103–124 (2011)
30. Ying-jie, S.: Integration IS strategy planning: Five stages framework based on the business strategy. In: International Conference on Management Science and Engineering, ICMSE 2009, pp.1224–1229, 14–16 (2009)

A Canvas for Establishing Global Software Development Collaborations

Inna Smirnova[1], Jürgen Münch[1], and Michael Stupperich[2]

[1] Department of Computer Science
University of Helsinki
Helsinki, Finland
[2] Daimler Research & Development Ulm
Daimler
Ulm, Deutschland
inna.smirnova@helsinki.fi, juergen.muench@cs.helsinki.fi,
michael.stupperich@daimler.com

Abstract. There is an increasing need and interest for organizations to collaborate with internal and external partners on a global scale for creating software-based products and services. Potential risks and different strategies need to be addressed when setting up such collaborations. Aspects such as cultural and social features, coordination, infrastructure, organizational change processes, or communication issues need to be considered. Although there are already experiences available with respect to setting up global collaborations, they mainly focus on specific areas. It is difficult for companies to quickly assess if they have considered all relevant aspects. An overall aid that guides companies in systematically setting up global collaborations is widely missing. In this paper we present a study based on the snowballing method as a systematic approach to literature review. Based on this literature review and inputs from industry we investigated what aspects and practices need to be considered when establishing global software development collaborations and how to prioritize them. Based on that we created activity roadmaps that aggregate existing experiences. Reported experiences were structured into nine main aspects each containing extracted successful practices for setting up global software development collaborations. As a result we came up with an initial version of a canvas that is proposed as guidance for companies for setting up global collaborations in the software development domain.

Keywords: Global software development, global collaborations, activity roadmaps.

1 Introduction

Today's era of globalization already affected and is still in the process of influencing many fields. Particularly software development has a great impact [8]. Nowadays the phenomenon of Global Software Development (GSD) with process' distribution all over the world is seen as a normal way of doing things [8].

G. Dregvaite and R. Damasevicius (Eds.): ICIST 2014, CCIS 465, pp. 73–93, 2014.
© Springer International Publishing Switzerland 2014

A major benefit that companies expect from global distribution and joint international collaborations is the access to low-cost resources, particularly a large remote labor pool with diverse expertise and working skills that could scale up development teams fast and might potentially lead to financial savings - *"Hourly onshore costs are typically three to four times higher than offshore rates"* [11]. Other reasons could include potential expectations on speeding up the time for product development, shortage of onsite resources, freeing up local resources for new projects, overall optimization of resources, accessing new huge markets, foreign know-how and technologies, and gaining valuable market competitiveness [12–17].

However, along with potential benefits GSD brings many new challenges, especially regarding communication, culture, coordination and project management areas [18]. For practitioners who do not yet have enough experience with setting up GSD collaborations it is necessary to be aware of the challenges and risks, different strategies and aspects along with existing practices and experiences. Such knowledge might help to reduce possible future negative effects leading to GSD projects' failures such as cost overruns, exceeding timeframes, low product quality, and overall decreased customer satisfaction [6, 8, 19]. As GSD collaborations suffer from geographical, temporal, socio-cultural distance, the organizations should adapt their current software development practices in order to benefit and gain competitive advantage in new Global Software Engineering conditions [20].

Although there are already many scientific papers and experiences available with respect to challenges, risks, mitigation advice, best actions and practices regarding establishing GSD collaborations, they are mainly focusing on specific areas such as examining trust or communication aspects [21–24]. Therefore the question how they can be used and integrated in an overall guide for setting up GSD collaborations still remains unclear. An overall holistic approach that synthesizes knowledge and guides companies in systematically setting up global collaborations for software-based products and services is widely missing [21].

To address the need for a holistic approach to setting up GSD collaborations, we performed a literature study and cooperated closely with a partner company from the industry side that operates in the automotive domain. Based on the results from the literature study and advice from the industrial partner we investigated what principal aspects and practices need to be considered when establishing global collaborations in the software development domain. Afterwards, we prioritized them and created activity roadmaps that aim at aggregating existing experiences that are relevant, credible and helpful for practitioners. Reported experiences were structured into nine main aspects. Each of them contains extracted practices for setting up GSD collaborations. Furthermore, we present the initial version of a worksheet, the so-called "Global canvas", that is proposed to be practically used as a guidance for companies intending to start global collaborations in the software development domain.

The original and new *contribution* of this study is the creation of a holistic "shopping list" of things to think of when establishing global collaborations in the software development domain. The goal is to provide a worksheet that presents scientific results to industry in an effective way and helps to identify what needs to be considered when setting up global collaborations. The aim of this study is to come up with an initial proposal for such a holistic prescriptive worksheet that is driven and validated against the needs and requirements of our case company. A mature and detailed validation of the configuration of aspects and practices is out of the scope of this study and planned as future work.

The article is structured as follows. Section 2 gives an overview of existing research with a focus on establishing global collaborations. Section 3 explains the research method that was used for collecting data. Section 4 presents the results found through literature study and industry consultation. This section explains in detail what aspects and practices were discovered with respect to establishing GSD collaborations. The proposed worksheet "Global canvas" is described in section 5. Finally, section 6 discusses the conclusions, limitations of the study and the potential for future research.

2   Related Work

There already exist many studies that analyze globally distributed software development projects, new challenges and risks compared to traditional co-located development, risk-mitigation advice, practices and experiences. Most studies focus on presenting an overview of challenges and problems which might occur as an impact of the distance that brings global orientation to software development, or examine in detail a specific aspect of GSD collaborations. In contrast, our research is aimed at a synthesis of relevant aspects with the purpose of creating a guide for companies that want to set up global collaborations and require a holistic view of the relevant aspects that need to be considered.

Nurdiani et al. performed a systematic literature review among GSD research literature that resulted in a checklist of 48 GSD challenges and 42 mitigation recommendations [6]. Another systematic literature review was done by Verner et al., who reported the risks of GSD collaboration with some mitigation recommendations structured into 12 areas starting from vendor selection and requirements engineering and finishing with coordination and control areas [7]. Šmite et al. conducted a systematic literature review of GSD experiences and came up with seven most commonly discussed practices that are aimed at overcoming GSD problems [8]. Mettovaara et al. performed interviews at Nokia and Philips and identified 10 common problems and 11 success factors based on the experiences in interorganizational collaborations in the two studied companies [25]. However, all those studies are risk- and problem-oriented in the first place. Our study takes these findings into account. However, instead of identifying relevant risks, we aim at providing a constructive guide that contains helpful practices and a sequence of activities for setting up global collaborations.

3   Context and Research Method

This study was performed in collaboration with the automotive OEM "Daimler AG" that served as case company for this study. The respective business unit of the company that was the contact point for this study is intending to set-up a long-term, multi-national distributed global collaboration for software-based products in the automotive domain.

The company identified a set of aspects (such as collaboration structure, product structure, communication, infrastructure) that were seen as highly important when setting up global collaborations. The company also provided a proposal for a sequence in which these aspects should be considered. These aspects and the information about the sequence were elicited from project leaders and reflect their experience from leading global projects in the business units "Daimler Trucks" and "Daimler Buses". The elicitation was done at Daimler via interviews and through company-internal workshops with the project leaders. The interviews and workshops were conducted by the one co-author of the paper who works at Daimler. In addition, members of the case company attended several ICGSE (International Conference on Global Software Engineering) conferences and input from these conferences implicitly influenced the selection of the aspects.

The aspects provided by the case company are used in this study as means for structuring the areas with practices for setting up global collaborations in the software development domain. This was the main rationale for selecting the aspects. We used existing systematic literature reviews (SLRs) to make small adjustments to the list of aspects provided by the case company, especially with respect to their definition and naming.

The research of this study was performed as backward snowballing [1, 2, 47]. Snowballing as a research method for data collection was chosen as an instance of a systematic approach to literature review that helps to collect all the necessary literature without performing a full systematic literature review. The chosen topic of interest was originally very broad, so that we decided not to perform a full SLR, but to choose a different systematic approach. Snowballing was found to be suitable for the exploratory research we aimed at.

Based on Webster and Watson [1] as well as Wohlin [47] the starting point for the backward snowballing research approach is the analysis of main contributions to the topic. We have decided to analyze four key SLRs related to setting up GSD collaborations as a starting point [5–8]. These SLRs aggregate already existing knowledge with respect to topics such as risks, mitigation solutions, and strategies. Therefore, they were seen as a suitable starting point. The next step in the backward snowballing method according to Webster and Watson as well as Wohlin is to "go backward" by reviewing the citations in the papers that serve as the starting point with the goal to identify topic-relevant studies that need to be considered [1, 2, 47]. We have performed a review of the bibliographic reference lists of the four SLRs and selected studies that fit to the aspects defined by the case company. This snowballing step was iteratively performed up to four times depending on the suitability of the results found.

In order to identify more topic relevant literature, we additionally reviewed scientific papers from major GSD conferences, i.e, from the International Conference on Global Software Engineering (ICGSE, 2006-2013), and from the International Conference on Software Engineering Approaches For Offshore and Outsourced Development (SEAFOOD, 2007-2010).

After the search for relevant literature, the found set of papers was examined with respect to content relevance. As a result, a collection of primary studies was defined as a literature pool for our study. The next step of the research study represented data extraction from the found literature, followed by further analysis regarding the identification of strategies and practices that need to be addressed in global software development projects. Following Whittemore and Knafl [3], the gathered strategies and practices were grouped together in an integrative way, and prioritized and described as a guidance framework that aims at supporting practitioners in setting up global software development collaborations.

As an initial validation, the results were frequently presented to the key stakeholders in the case company and reviewed. Feedback was used to revise the worksheet "Global canvas" and create the final version presented in the article.

4   Results from the Literature Study

In the following section we present the results found in the literature study. The results are structured into nine main aspects that are proposed to be addressed by the companies while setting up global collaborations in the software development domain. Each aspect contains extracted success practices and experiences.

4.1   Strategy

"Global Software Engineering becomes part of the everyday business", many software companies today recognize the need for globalization [5]. Organizations that have the intention of transferring software development work into a global context, need to understand how to start global software development, the reasons, first steps and actions for setting up global collaborations [5, 27]. Thus the first important aspect that we identified in our study is *Strategy* that is aimed to be the initial step and help software companies to answer such questions as - Why do we collaborate globally? What are the benefits that global collaborations might bring to the business? How do we do the collaborations, according to what model and where to? This step represents the whole high level framework of establishing global software development collaborations and therefore cannot be avoided by the companies engaged in performing such collaborations.

We identified five principal practices that need to be considered at the very initial stage of global collaborations.

First of all, the organization needs to see distinctly what the goals and potential benefits of collaboration are [17]. Based on the investigations of Forbath et al. [17] the main benefits and therefore goals of doing global collaboration for software-based products can be classified into three areas. The primary driver is financial savings. Development costs might lower due to access to a large labor pool in countries with lower wages or access to many resources needed for development and easily available for use at the offshore destination. Another potential could be the access to foreign know-how, expertise, new technologies that might not be obtainable onshore. Furthermore, the proximity to new offshore markets could be a driver for customization and localization of products that might lead to new customers and bigger revenues.

Next, after understanding the reasons for setting up global collaborations, the organization has to choose an appropriate collaboration model that suits a specific company context and goals. Based on the inputs from the industrial partner, we have identified and focused on three possible scenarios for launching GSD collaboration named Offshore outsourcing, Offshore insourcing and Innovative offshoring [5, 7, 19, 29]. Offshore outsourcing refers to consuming of resources and development services from an external 3rd party that is located in a different country, often representing client-subcontractor relationships [5]. Offshore insourcing means consuming of internal organizational resources that are located in a foreign country [5, 19, 29]. The company establishes, for instance, a foreign branch in a different country, in order to customize products for a dedicated market. The model of Innovative offshoring refers to consuming of innovative R&D services from the offshore partner company that is situated abroad. Those innovative services could, for instance, aim at improving the headquarter's product [5, 19, 29].

The following recommended steps that organizations should follow at the beginning of setting up global collaborations are the investigation of the foreign legal system regarding contract and IP laws; the selection of a suitable vendor with desired expertise, efficient capabilities and sufficient technological infrastructure; and the planning of financial budget for collaboration including possible risks and therefore hidden costs [7]. One of the main motivations for performing GSD collaborations by the company could be cost savings, therefore financial planning should be considered early on [7].

4.2   Collaboration Structure

In order to maximize the potential positive effects that global software development collaborations might promise and minimize possible negative risks, it is necessary to choose the right way for establishing collaborations, to determine the most advantageous form of dividing task distribution, responsibilities, peer-to-peer connections between involved sites. Our defined aspect *Collaboration structure* is dedicated to these questions of global collaborations. This aspect is aimed at determining the approach of development task allocation between locations based on collaboration goals, at creating roles and responsibilities along with the way of distributing them; at defining an organizational structure and peer-to-peer connections between sites [16, 20, 31–33, 46]. Clear understanding of work division, roles and responsibilities might help to decrease coordination and project management efforts when actual global software development takes place. Therefore it is important to address this aspect already at the planning stage of setting up global collaborations.

Regarding the aspect of *Collaboration structure* we identified two main practices which need to be considered. Those are to define the approach to distributed process breakdown and task allocation and to determine and specify the organizational structure and peer-to-peer links between sites.

Based on Šmite's case study in a Latvian software company [16, 26], Nissen's case study report from an inter-organizational cooperation in telecommunications domain [31], and the research of Faiz et al. [32] we have identified three models of process-based task distribution between sites which are suitable for collaboration scenarios described in the aspect *Strategy*. The first model was considered as a typical outsourcing model where most of the intellectual work stays onsite and only actual software development tasks are transferred offshore. In this model, requirements creation, system analysis, design are done onsite, while coding and testing phases can be performed jointly with work division, for example, by modules [16, 31–33]. The main challenges of this kind of task distribution consist of troublesome system requirements clarification, system integration and bug fixing along with coordination and control efforts. The second model is considered to be more suitable for the Offshore insourcing collaboration model where, in contrast to the first model, requirements creation, system analysis, design are performed as joint activity between collaboration partners [16, 31–33]. Such task distribution might suit product customization goals and help to create better common understanding and social ties between locations. However, this model requires good domain business knowledge from the vendor site that might be effortful to create. The last third model was considered to be used for the Innovative offshoring scenario that represents close collaboration between locations where the offshore partner performs most of the intellectual and implementation work such as R&D, requirements creation, system analysis and design, actual implementation [16, 31–33]. This model might be based on a prototyping strategy that refers to creation of innovative prototypes by the offshore site. Later the developed prototype can be used onsite as a base for building new functionality or a complete product on top.

Another practice that was aimed to be a part of the *Collaboration structure* aspect is to specify organizational structure and peer-to-peer links between collaboration sites. The main aim of the organizational structure is to clearly list roles, responsibilities and to draw communication channels between locations involved in collaboration at management, project and team levels. The examples on what roles and sites' connections the global collaboration can include were presented in the studies of Braun [34] and Faiz et al. [32]. Defined and documented organizational structure is aimed to achieve easier coordination and control, to make the information flow more transparent and traceable. It helps to make communication between parties less challenging and reach project-related common understanding faster, which eventually might reduce some efforts and investments needed for setting up distributed collaboration [24, 32–34].

4.3   Product Structure

The development process breakdown and the following task distribution, which were considered to be identified in the aspect of *Collaboration strategy*, affect the definition of the product architecture. The aspect *Product structure* addresses how the product architecture could be adapted for global software development compared to co-located development, the product ownership boundaries between locations, and how modifications to the product part at one location can affect work at other locations. Therefore it has an impact on work division between GSD teams at different locations. Clearly identified work division and product ownership boundaries between collaboration sites are expected to improve communication, reduce project coordination efforts, and help to avoid rework and duplications [7, 20, 26, 35, 46]. Thus the aspect *Product structure* is an important step for companies and needs to be already considered at the preparation and planning stages of global collaborations. It is strongly connected with the *Collaboration structure* aspect, especially with detailed definition of organizational structure, roles and responsibilities.

We have distinguished the following practices that need to be considered by the organizations. Those are to determine the product architecture, to specify product ownership between locations and to define product-based work distribution among GSD teams at different locations.

Depending on the collaboration scenarios we have identified in the aspect *Strategy*, the possible way for a *Product structure* definition might differ greatly. Referring to the Offshore outsourcing model, the strategy with one core product and full onsite ownership where the offshore partner is responsible for allocated tasks in the product development lifecycle is considered to be most suitable [36, 41, 45]. In contrast, the model of Offshore insourcing can be based on a product line architecture with variants which are built on top of a core product. The ownership of the core product can be kept onsite, while the offshore site might be responsible for the full development of one of the variants from the product line [9]. Such a variant can be customized and market-specific. In this model the offshore site has a great responsibility for the whole product variant, and thereby global collaboration might have a form of peer-to-peer partnership [26, 36]. The Innovative offshoring scenario is intended for the development of new innovative products or prototypes by the offshore site with different possibilities of product ownership boundaries depending on the initial collaboration goals and model.

Considering the approach to detailed software system architecture and following development work distribution between locations, our main suggestions are to use modular architecture and decoupling that allow having well-defined software work packages which can be distributed between different locations based on available resources and expertise. Salger [35] demonstrates an example structure of the software work package based on the experience at Capgemini sd&m. The software work package might consist of the following parts: *Software requirement specifications* describing use cases, user interface, domain objects, and specifications of functional test cases; *Design artefacts* including an external technical view on a software module and internal high level design view;

Project management artefacts containing a list of work units described in earlier parts, schedules, budget, definition of quality objectives and work acceptance criteria [35]. Such a well-defined work package structure promises to ease work transfer between locations and to achieve low dependencies between locations during actual implementation work [7, 8, 12, 14, 20, 26, 36–41]. This way it might be possible to reduce communication and coordination needs between different locations. However, system integration could become a troublesome bottleneck.

4.4   Coordination

Global software development brings geographical distance and cultural diversity into the software development process compared to co-located development. Thus globally distributed software development teams need to be effectively managed and controlled in order to complete software projects successfully, to be inside a financial and technological budget, and to use available resources and capabilities beneficially for the collaboration goals [20]. Therefore competent coordination, communication and control procedures should be attentively planned and later performed by companies on an everyday basis. Coordination can be seen as work integration in a way that each involved unit contributes to the completion of the overall task [12, 40]. Coordination procedures describe how collaboration sites communicate between each other in order to complete commonly defined tasks and to achieve collaboration goals [12, 40]. The *Coordination* aspect represents the set of activities that aim at managing dependencies within the global software development project workflow, so the work can be completed faster and more effectively. According to a study by Nguyen-Duc and Cruzes [39] such dependencies in a GSD context might include technical views such as system integration, configuration change management; temporal issues such as synchronization of schedules, deliveries between sites; software development process organization; resource distribution such as infrastructure, budget, or development tools. This aspect promises to be very important for setting up global collaborations, because coordination and project management efforts might become a cause of project hidden costs. Therefore coordination challenges need to be minimized by the organizations starting from a planning phase. For instance, differences in organizational policies, lack of common processes, variation of coding and testing standards between collaboration sites might affect coordination and project management efforts, and also might lead to insufficient end product quality and additional costs [39].

Within the aspect of *Coordination* we have specified two main practices that need to be addressed by organizations, i.e., Project management and Project control.

Project management aims at planning and organizing software development project-related activities in such a way that they lead to successful work completion. Such activities might include creating shared synchronized understanding of main milestones between collaboration sites, concrete tasks to perform, deliveries schedules, project budget constraints, peer-to-peer contact links between collaboration sites, and managing the whole project execution [39]. Project management can be seen as a mechanism that integrates software, human, and economic relations in order to use existing technology, resources, time, capabilities in the most productive and effective way [43]. Project control procedures refer to the process of monitoring work status and ensuring that the work process goes in the right direction according to the planned budget, timeframes and quality expectations [12]. Among project control procedures, a formal reporting structure concerning updates, changes and escalation path can be seen to play an important role for achieving visibility of software project status and work progress, for detecting project bottlenecks and work conflict situations and reacting to them early on [7, 10, 20, 39].

Different collaboration scenarios might have different coordination mechanisms working better in particular situations. Based on a case study by Hossain et al. in an Australian-Malaysian cooperation [44] we have identified different possible ways of performing coordination processes and discovered how they can suit different global collaboration models. For instance, the Offshore outsourcing model might require a high degree of defined standard policies, direct supervision and centralized project organization for the offshore team from the headquarter company. For the Offshore insourcing and the Innovative offshoring scenarios the software development work might be managed better with a high degree of mutual adjustment when collaboration is based on building trust and social relationships between sites, thus, many software project activities and decisions are often performed jointly [7, 9, 12, 20, 23–26, 29, 33, 35–40, 43, 44].

4.5   Development Process

As soon as the collaboration model, the process breakdown, the product structure, the task distribution, the coordination and the control mechanisms are identified, a solid foundation for defining and/or customizing a development process is laid. The aspect *Development process* aims at defining the model for software development activities between the collaboration sites. Based on experience from the authors it is recommended to mainly define the processes at the interfaces between the collaborating sites and not to aim at unification of all processes at all sites, especially when the sites belong to different organizations. Typically the specific local characteristics at each site make it hard to prescribe unique internal processes at all sites. Defining a software development process model also helps to clarify roles and responsibilities, the level of independency between sites, and the product quality expectations. Frictions such as role confusions can be avoided. Moreover, a development process can affect coordination and communication efforts, infrastructure needs, change management mechanisms and system integration efforts. In the Offshore outsourcing scenario or the Innovative offshoring scenario the collaboration sites might keep their own development processes if these processes are already established and well-working [20, 24]. However, it is essential to synchronize project milestones and schedules for important software product deliveries in order to achieve project transparency, continuous frequent integrity and early feedback on the quality of developed software [20, 24]. In the case of the Offshore insourcing scenario that has peer-to-peer close partnership orientation, it could be suitable to establish standardized guidelines for a common software development process and tools between sites. This promises to create a joint corporate level of work standards [7, 37, 43].

4.6 Communication

Communication can be seen as the exchange of information that helps to reach a common shared understanding between remote sites, including information and knowledge sharing [12, 40]. The aspect *Communication* addresses all kinds of communication activities between the different development sites. As global software development collaborations are to a large degree human-based, communication becomes crucial and needs to be considered early on, i.e., starting from the planning and negotiating phases of the collaboration till its full establishment and maintenance. Numerous studies based on industrial project investigations report the importance of communication in the GSD context and usually come to the conclusion that it is the number-one problem. Studies focusing on communication include the study by Mettovaara et al. in Nokia and Philips [25], the case study by Leszak and Meier on embedded product development in the telecommunications domain in Alcatel-Lucent between Germany and China [36], the study by Paasivaara and Lassenius based on interviews in 8 global software projects distributed across Europe, North America and Asia [24], and the study by Oshri et al. at LeCroy (Switzerland and USA), SAP (India and Germany), and Baan (India and The Netherlands) [30].

Geographical distances between teams often cause difficulties with using traditional communication paths such as face-to-face meetings and informal communication. Remote sites often need to rely on asynchronous ways of communication (tools such as E-mails, chats, blogs) or phone/video conferences that bring certain risks like misunderstandings, delays, unnecessary work, reduced trust, or absence of team spirit and partnership feeling. Those challenges might result in additional project costs, customer dissatisfaction, and barriers to maintaining long-time global collaborations. Thus companies need to consider and plan communicational strategy early on in the first stages of collaborations.

With the aspect *Communication* we have identified five practices that aim at building a successful communication strategy when establishing GSD collaborations.

Communication protocol aims at identifying who is supposed to communicate with whom within the company such as, communication channels, interface points among collaboration teams and team members, sufficient frequency of communication, information exchange paths, official corporate language [24, 42]. A detailed description of a communication protocol based on the organizational structure should be documented and distributed among team members at all collaboration sites. It is expected to create awareness of team members from whom they will get work inputs and to whom they need to distribute work output results. This way the software development project might gain more transparency and traceability [24, 42].

Team awareness channels aim at making collaboration team members become more familiar with remote colleagues and their skills, their expertise and availability, as well as their project activities and work status. It is expected that teamness and trust between remote collaboration sites help to achieve project visibility and to reduce delays for finding the right person to contact in case of some questions [38]. Team awareness can be supported, for instance, by organizational charts, project websites, or shared calendars [23, 24].

Social relationships between collaboration sites represent the result of all communication activities and efforts. Relationship building is a long process and therefore needs to be seen as a constant activity when doing global collaborations. Face-to-face meetings are a highly efficient way for building social interrelations between collaboration sites, thereby frequent visits and staff exchanges between sites are necessary. Even though face-to-face visits might cause additional investment and time, they need to be present especially in the first phases of global collaborations [7, 12, 14, 23–25, 33, 36, 40, 44].

Rich *communication tools* aim at supporting all the above-mentioned communication practices. Collaboration sites are often located at remote places, so tools often provide the only way for software development teams to get connected. Thus a variety of different communication tools such as web meetings, phones, e-mails and mailing lists, chats, file transfer tools, groupware and shared services tools should be provided by organizations [28, 37, 42].

All communication activities are expected to make global collaborations more peer-to-peer partnership-oriented. Thus it helps to build up a *common knowledge base* between collaboration sites. This promises to create the "organizational memory", shared collective understanding of the domain knowledge, technology and business needs. It accumulates the experience of a collaboration in a specific organizational context and might help collaboration sites to learn and improve their way of working together [28, 37, 42].

4.7   Social Aspects

Global distribution of software development implies that individuals are usually not only geographically dispersed but also culturally. Thus the process of socialization and cultural integration is important when setting up global collaborations. With *Social aspects* we refer to the process through which team members gain the knowledge on behavioral and communication norms, attitudes, cultural and social patterns of each other in order to work together in cooperation [30]. The process of socialization and getting to know the partners is expected to create a mutual vision on the collaboration and specific project goals, to create the understanding of remote partners' way of working and behavior, and to make global collaboration function successfully and beneficially for all the sites. *"When there is a win-win situation the motivation is usually high and the chances of success get better"* [25]. Socio-cultural distance might bring many challenges and negative effects into the collaboration process such as difficulties and inability of sites to communicate, unawareness of remote colleagues' qualification, unwillingness to exchange information, conflicts of tasks interpretation and unsuccessful end results. These challenges might have a great negative impact on the collaboration process between sites and the quality of the end product. Therefore, organizations need to consider social aspects and stimulate socio-cultural integrity between collaboration sites [7].

Within *Social aspects* we have specified two categories that need to be considered - *Trust* and *Cultural understanding*.

Trust is considered to be one of the keys for establishing effective, productive, reliable, and longitude collaborative social relationships between teams in global software development contexts [22, 23, 40]. Trust can be defined as the willingness of individuals to cooperate with others based on the belief that partners are reliable, competent and will do actions which are beneficial for the cooperation rather than for individual purposes [40]. *"Trust is a pre-requisite for globally distributed software development"* [40]. Trust promises to create the ability of remote collaboration sites to work together, and to build up the feeling of teamness. Trust stimulates the willingness of sites to communicate and work towards the completion of shared project goals - not "we and you" relations but "us" [22, 29]. Lack of trust might lead to a situation of non-cooperation, social conflicts, absence of information exchange, overall decrease in productivity and end product quality, and eventually to job dissatisfaction among employees [29]. Thus a lot of efforts are needed to be done by organizations in order to build trust between collaboration sites. Such efforts, for instance, are face-to-face visits, frequent remote communication via a rich variety of tools, staff exchanges, socio-cultural trainings, social activities. Trust needs to be built and maintained through the whole partnership history from the first collaboration stages till its end [11, 22, 25, 29, 33, 40].

Cultural understanding represents shared norms and beliefs which are historically situated and followed by people belonging to a concrete society [4]. In the context of global collaborations socio-cultural diversity among sites might be interpreted as a facilitator for promoting creativity, innovativeness, and knowledge sharing. However, at the same time cultural diversity might become a barrier for communication and effective coordination. Cultures differentiate especially with respect to the sense of time, social hierarchy, power distance, and preferable communication styles. All these distinctions affect the norms for organizational and working culture. Therefore culture-specific understanding and training should be addressed by organizations in order to create mutual awareness and avoid conflicts and misinterpretations [4, 25, 30, 40, 42].

4.8   Infrastructure

Infrastructure refers here to all tools, platforms, and other technical means that support technical, organizational, and managerial activities in the context of distributed software development, maintenance, and operation. The term infrastructure subsumes here, for instance, tool support for coordination and communication, IDEs, and quality assurance tools. Although the infrastructure already plays an important role in co-located development, the global distribution of development tasks imposes additional and new requirements that should be considered early on. It is necessary for organizations to identify infrastructure-related requirements, to analyze the existing infrastructure, and to invest into the infrastructure in order to reach the stated requirements. In addition, there is a need to analyze how the existing infrastructure at different sites can be modified so that it fits to a new distributed setting. One essential requirement for the infrastructure is the compatibility between sites. For instance, collaboration sites should have equal internet connections, bandwidths, and communication facilities. Compatibility is important, for instance, for configuration management environments, for development tools, and for coordination support. Coordination tools and communication tools promise to help mitigate communication risks that are due to temporal, geographical, and cultural distances. A rich set of groupware tools is expected to help reduce the impact of distance in global software development, to increase the frequency and ease the communication between sites, to lessen coordination efforts, and to provide equal accessibility to all project-related artefacts. A compatible infrastructure at all collaboration locations is highly important for conducting the distributed development process effectively and efficiently [7, 28].

4.9   Organizational Change Process

When organizations start setting up global software development collaborations, there is clear evidence that a sufficient amount of time is needed in order to gain desired efficiency [27]. At first, challenges such as communication, coordination, trust building, awareness of partners and integration of working procedures imply significant reductions of the overall efficiency. Reasons for the decrease in the work efficiency in the first collaboration stages are usually the time necessary for building a compatible infrastructure, establishing the necessary communication ways, providing domain, technology and cultural training, as well as building social relationships and teamness. After the first stages of a global collaboration, there is typically a period of time when partners learn to know each other and better understand the ways of working together. In this phase, the software development efficiency is usually recovering gradually. After this phase, global collaborations might exploit scaling effects with respect to efficiency that go beyond the efficiency of co-located development [9, 27, 41]. Gaining these scaling effects requires the establishment of systematic process improvement procedures.

The accumulated working history with respect to the transfer from co-located software development into a GSD working style gives a lot of insights and thus should later be examined by organizations for potential improvements [9, 26, 27]. New ideas for process changes and improvement actions should be discussed and analyzed jointly by the collaboration sites on a regular basis during the whole period of the collaboration. The improvement of the distributed collaboration can follow different process improvement approaches such as the continuous or the model-based improvement. However, there is a lack of improvement approaches and experience that are focused on global collaborations. Therefore, we recommend to deploy a problem-oriented, continuous improvement approach. The continuous process improvement aims at reaching a high level of standardization of the overall global software development process that might lead to improved end product quality and customer satisfaction [19].

5   Canvas

While setting up global software development collaborations different phases can be distinguished. Each collaboration phase can be characterized by a specific set of activities that need to be performed by the organizations. We have distinguished four main phases that organizations face when setting up global collaborations. Based on defined collaboration phases and aspects that need to be addressed by organizations, we have structured them as activity roadmaps that can be adjusted for specific organizational contexts. The initial sequence of activities was provided by the case company and refined at a joint workshop of Daimler and the University of Helsinki. The final order of activities was created mainly based on experiences reported by project leaders from the case company and results from the literature study. Some relations between activities also have an underlying inner logic. The proposed activity roadmaps are aimed to be a guidance and reminder for organizations about activities that need to be performed when setting up global collaborations and moving from a local to a globally distributed working mode. For practical industry use, we propose an initial version of a visualized structure of activity roadmaps that we named "Global canvas" (Fig.1). The proposed activity roadmaps for organizations intending to establish global software development collaborations are described as follows.

Phase 1. **Initiate:** In this phase an organization intends to transfer co-located software development into a global context as one of its business strategies. Thus the organization should investigate the potential benefits of transition into a GSD environment, what models of global collaboration exist and what model will suit the specific organizational context. Moreover, the organization makes its first decisions on the partnership type and selects collaboration partners. Thus, the proposed sequence of activities to be addressed by the organization at the initiation phase might look as follows:

a) Identify needs and goals for doing a global software development collaboration. Analyze carefully what benefits and outcomes are expected of the global collaboration.
b) Choose a global collaboration model that is suited for the specific organizational context and the business needs.
c) Investigate the foreign legal system(s) concerning IP and contract laws.
d) Choose appropriate partner(s)/vendor(s) with sufficient infrastructure, capabilities and expertise needed for the chosen collaboration model.
e) Define a budget plan for doing global software development projects. Include possible hidden costs such as communication tools or face-to-face visits.

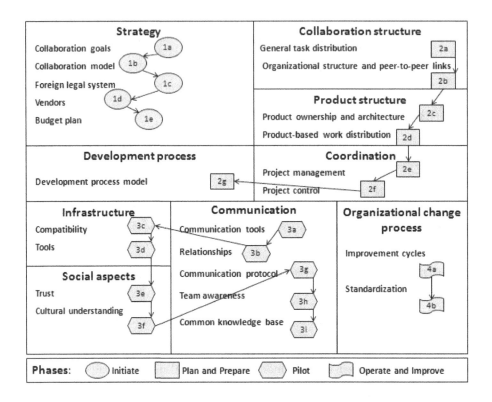

Fig. 1. Global canvas

Phase 2. **Plan and Prepare:** This phase aims at building all the conditions needed for global collaboration to start functioning. An organization defines a product structure, a work distribution, and responsibilities between collaboration sites based on available resources. The model for work coordination and the development process organization is chosen. In this phase, the organization still keeps ongoing product development mainly onsite. However, at the same time, the organization pilots first practices of setting up global software development collaboration. The potential set of activities that need to be done by companies at the preparation phase is described as follows:

a) Identify a development process breakdown and subsequent task distribution.
b) Define and document the organizational structure including specific roles, responsibilities and peer-to-peer contact channels.
c) Identify an architecture and the product ownership between sites (based on the collaboration model defined earlier and the process breakdown).
d) Define a product-based task distribution between sites based on available resources and capabilities.

e) Define the coordination mechanisms between collaboration sites. Choose an appropriate project management model that suits the agreed partnership model.

f) Specify project control procedures for monitoring work progress and detecting problems as early as possible. For instance, the data on channels for status reporting should be assigned, documented and distributed to team members.

g) Choose a model according to which the software development process will be working.

Phase 3. **Pilot:** This phase focuses on systematic testing of practices. This phase aims at detecting the problems of collaboration - if some things do not work at first, they can be changed early on. The proposed activities to be performed are described as follows:

a) Provide a rich variety of communication tools in order to stimulate communication between sites and to avoid misunderstandings.

b) Start gradual building of social relationships between sites (e.g., organize face-to-face visits, joint social activities, staff exchanges).

c) Ensure that the remote partner(s) has sufficient infrastructure needed for software development projects. Provide compatibility of internet connections, bandwidths, communication facilities (for instance, video conference rooms) between sites.

d) Introduce groupware tools that are aimed to ease the collaboration process between sites.

e) Consider socio-cultural aspects between partners. Start building trust between sites early on.

f) Ensure the teams' awareness of cultural differences and perceptions that might occur in collaboration between partners belonging to distinct societies.

g) Establish rules for a communication protocol. Identify who should communicate with whom and how often. Make team members understand that communication is an important part of everyday work.

h) Ensure team awareness channels. Team members need to be aware of remote colleagues' contact details, expertise, roles and responsibilities, work schedules. Ensure that the teams are aware of the project status.

i) Accumulate the experience based on the working history between sites, and create a collective shared knowledge base - the "organizational memory".

Phase 4. **Operate and Improve:** The overall operation of a global software development process is ongoing. Partners accumulate working history, learn, propose and handle process changes and improvements. This phase aims at a seamless operation and a continuous improvement of the collaboration. The set of activities at this stage is suggested as follows.

a) Analyze the working history, discuss potential process changes and improvements.

b) Improve the process continuously and thereby aim at achieving a high level of process standardization.

The proposed prioritization of activities in the different phases is not a strict order but meant as guidance for practical use. The order of activities can be customized based on specific organizational context and needs.

6 Conclusions

In this article we investigated and aggregated the aspects and main practices that need to be addressed by companies when establishing global software development collaborations. Furthermore, necessary activities were grouped into collaboration phases and structured in a form of activity roadmaps that can be used by industry as guidance for setting up global projects. The initial version of a "Global canvas" presents the visualization of activity roadmaps. The canvas provides a holistic view on setting up global collaborations, aggregates all the main necessary aspects and presents the activities as feasible roadmaps.

However, the sequence of activities proposed in our canvas is not mandatory and based on assumptions, literature findings, and industry inputs. The presented aspects are derived from the case company and might differ in other contexts. Therefore, the general applicability is limited and more experience is needed to better understand context-specific customization needs. As global software development is gaining a growing interest and many companies in the domain search for new business opportunities in a transition from co-located development into the global environment, a practice-oriented worksheet that guides decision making such as the canvas promises high potential. Besides using the canvas for guidance, it could also be used for other purposes. Another use case could be, for instance, using the canvas as an assessment scheme. We are planning to further evolve the canvas based on findings from applications in industry. In addition, we are planning to systematically analyze the dependencies between different practices and strategies as well as the suitability of the canvas for other purposes than guidance.

References

1. Webster, J., Watson, R.T.: Analyzing the past to prepare for the future: Writing a literature review. MIS Quarterly 26(2) (2002)
2. Betz, S., Fricker, S., Moss, A., Afzal, W., Svahnberg, M., Wohlin, C., Gorschek, T.: An Evolutionary Perspective on Socio-Technical Congruence: The Rubber Band Effect. In: Replication in Empirical Software Engineering Research (RESER) Workshop, pp. 15–24 (2013)
3. Whittemore, R., Knafl, K.: The integrative review: updated methodology. Journal of Advanced Nursing 52(5), 546–553 (2005)
4. Huang, H., Trauth, E.M.: Cultural Influences on Temporal Separation and Coordination in Globally Distributed Software Development. In: ICI (2008)

5. Šmite, D., Wohlin, C., Galvina, Z., Prikladnicki, R.: An empirically based terminology and taxonomy for global software engineering. In: Empirical Software Engineering, pp. 1–49 (2012)
6. Nurdiani, I., Jabangwe, R., Šmite, D., Damian, D.: Risk identification and risk mitigation instruments for global software development: Systematic review and survey results. In: Global Software Engineering Workshop (ICGSEW), pp. 36–41 (2011)
7. Verner, J.M., Brereton, O.P., Kitchenham, B.A., Turner, M., Niazi, M.: Risks and risk mitigation in global software development: A tertiary study. Information and Software Technology 56, 54–78 (in press, 2014)
8. Šmite, D., Wohlin, C., Gorschek, T., Feldt, R.: Empirical evidence in global software engineering: a systematic review. Empirical Software Engineering 15(1), 91–118 (2010)
9. Bhadauria, A., Bhattacharjee, S., Anandkumar, C.B., Puthiyonnan, S.: Sustaining High Performance in an Offshore Team in Globally Distributed Development: A Success Story. In: Global Software Engineering (ICGSE), pp. 120–123 (2013)
10. Bhadade, D.: A Guide to Escalation in Project Management (February 27, 2013) (unpublished)
11. Rottman, J.W.: Successfully outsourcing embedded software development. Computer 39(1), 55–61 (2006)
12. Agerfalk, P.J., Fitzgerald, B., Holmstrm, H., Lings, B., Lundell, B., Conchuir, E.O.: A framework for considering opportunities and threats in distributed software development. In: International Workshop on Distributed Software Development, pp. 47–61 (2005)
13. Kobitzsch, W., Rombach, D., Feldmann, R.L.: Outsourcing in India. IEEE Software 18(2), 78–86 (2001)
14. Lings, B., Lundell, B., Agerfalk, P.J., Fitzgerald, B.: A reference model for successful Distributed Development of Software Systems. In: Global Software Engineering, ICGSE 2007, pp. 130–139 (2007)
15. Šmite, D., Wohlin, C., Aurum, A., Jabangwe, R., Numminen, E.: Offshore insourcing in software development: Structuring the decision-making process. Journal of Systems and Software 86, 1054–1067 (2013)
16. Šmite, D.: Global software development projects in one of the biggest companies in Latvia: is geographical distribution a problem? Software Process: Improvement and Practice 11(1), 61–76 (2006)
17. Forbath, T., Brooks, P., Dass, A.: Beyond cost reduction: Using collaboration to increase innovation in global software development projects. In: Global Software Engineering, ICGSE 2008, pp. 205–209 (2008)
18. Herbsleb, J.D., Paulish, D.J., Bass, M.: Global software development at siemens: experience from nine projects. In: Software Engineering, ICSE 2005, pp. 524–533 (2005)
19. Prikladnicki, R., Audy, J.L.N., Damian, D., de Oliveira, T.C.: Distributed Software Development: Practices and challenges in different business strategies of offshoring and onshoring. In: Global Software Engineering, ICGSE 2007, pp. 262–274 (2007)
20. Richardson, I., Casey, V., McCaffery, F., Burton, J., Beecham, S.: A process framework for global software engineering teams. Information and Software Technology 54(11), 1175–1191 (2012)
21. Beecham, S., OLeary, P., Richardson, I., Baker, S., Noll, J.: Who are we doing Global Software Engineering research for? In: Global Software Engineering (ICGSE), pp. 41–50 (2013)

22. Piri, A., Niinimäki, T., Lassenius, C.: Fear and distrust in global software engineering projects. Journal of Software: Evolution and Process 24(2), 185–205 (2012)
23. Pyysiäinen, J.: Building trust in global inter-organizational software development projects: problems and practices. In: International Workshop on Global Software Development, pp. 69–74 (2003)
24. Paasivaara, M., Lassenius, C.: Collaboration practices in global interorganizational software development projects. Software Process: Improvement and Practice 8(4), 183–199 (2003)
25. Mettovaara, V., Siponen, M.T., Lehto, J.A.: Collaboration in Software Development: Lesson Learned from Two Large Multinational Organizations. In: PACIS (2006)
26. Šmite, D.: A case study: coordination practices in global software development. In: Product Focused Software Process Improvement, pp. 234–244 (2005)
27. Šmite, D., Wohlin, C.: Lessons learned from transferring software products to India. Journal of Software: Evolution and Process 24(6), 605–623 (2012)
28. Thissen, M.R., Page, J.M., Bharathi, M.C., Austin, T.L.: Communication tools for distributed software development teams. In: Proceedings of the 2007 ACM SIG-MIS CPR Conference on Computer Personnel Research: The Global Information Technology Workforce, pp. 28–35 (2007)
29. Moe, N.B., Šmite, D.: Understanding a lack of trust in Global Software Teams: a multiple case study. Software Process: Improvement and Practice 13(3), 217–231 (2008)
30. Oshri, I., Kotlarsky, J., Willcocks, L.P.: Global software development: Exploring socialization and face-to-face meetings in distributed strategic projects. The Journal of Strategic Information Systems 16(1), 25–49 (2007)
31. Nissen, H.W.: Designing the inter-organizational software engineering cooperation: an experience report, pp. 24-27 (2004)
32. Faiz, M.F., Qadri, U., Ayyubi, S.R.: Offshore software development models. In: Information and Emerging Technologies, ICIET 2007, pp. 1–6 (2007)
33. Cusick, J., Prasad, A.: A practical management and engineering approach to offshore collaboration. IEEE Software 23(5), 20–29 (2006)
34. Braun, A.: A framework to enable offshore outsourcing. In: Global Software Engineering, ICGSE, pp. 125–129 (2007)
35. Salger, F.: On the use of handover checkpoints to manage the global software development process. In: Meersman, R., Herrero, P., Dillon, T. (eds.) OTM 2009 Workshops. LNCS, vol. 5872, pp. 267–276. Springer, Heidelberg (2009)
36. Leszak, M., Meier, M.: Successful Global Development of a Large-scale Embedded Telecommunications Product. In: Global Software Engineering, ICGSE 2007, pp. 23–32 (2007)
37. Silva, F.Q., Prikladnicki, R., Frana, A.C.C., Monteiro, C.V., Costa, C., Rocha, R.: An evidence-based model of distributed software development project management: results from a systematic mapping study. Journal of Software: Evolution and Process 24(6), 625–642 (2012)
38. Chang, K.T., Ehrlich, K.: Out of sight but not out of mind?: Informal networks, communication and media use in global software teams. In: Proceedings of the, Conference of the Center for Advanced Studies on Collaborative Research, pp. 86–97 (2007)
39. Nguyen-Duc, A., Cruzes, D.S.: Coordination of Software Development Teams across Organizational Boundary–An Exploratory Study. In: Global Software Engineering (ICGSE), pp. 216–225 (2013)

40. Hofner, G., Mani, V.S.: TAPER: A generic framework for establishing an offshore development center. In: Global Software Engineering, ICGSE 2007, pp. 162–172 (2007)
41. Mockus, A., Weiss, D.M.: Globalization by chunking: a quantitative approach. IEEE Software 18(2), 30–37 (2001)
42. Deshpande, S., Richardson, I.: Management at the Outsourcing Destination-Global Software Development in India. In: Global Software Engineering, ICGSE 2009, pp. 217–225 (2009)
43. Casey, V.: Virtual software team project management. Journal of the Brazilian Computer Society 16(2), 83–96 (2010)
44. Hossain, E., Babar, M.A., Verner, J.: How Can Agile Practices Minimize Global Software Development Co-ordination Risks? In: Software Process Improvement, pp. 81–92 (2009)
45. Hyysalo, J., Parviainen, P., Tihinen, M.: Collaborative embedded systems development: survey of state of the practice. In: 13th Annual IEEE International Symposium and Workshop on Engineering of Computer Based Systems, pp. 1–9 (2006)
46. Lamersdorf, A., Münch, J., Rombach, D.: Towards a Multi-criteria Development Distribution Model: An Analysis of Existing Task Distribution Approaches. In Global Software Engineering (ICGSE), pp. 109–118 (2008)
47. Wohlin, C.: Guidelines for Snowballing in Systematic Literature Studies and a Replication in Software Engineering. In: 18th International Conference on Evaluation and Assessment in Software Engineering, EASE 2014, pp. 321–330 (2014)

Timed Automata with Action Durations – From Theory to Implementation

Souad Guellati, Ilham Kitouni, Riadh Matmat, and Djamel-Eddine Saidouni

MISC Laboratory, Constantine 2 University, 25000, Algeria
{guellati,kitouni,matmat,saidouni}@misc-umc.org

Abstract. Symbolic model checking is a technique for verifying finite-state concurrent systems that has been extended to handle real-time systems. Timed automata are widely used to model such systems behavior. In this paper we are concerned by durational actions timed automata (daTA) which is a timed automata handling action durations and true concurrency. Our aim is to compute efficiently the state space of (daTA) in order to verify quantitative timing requirements and preserve the true concurrency property.

We present a novel approach to compute quantitative information about the system and exploring the state space of daTA based on maximality semantics.

We have designed a new zone graph under the maximality semantics, named Maximality-based Zone Graph (MZG), for describing symbolic execution of daTA. In the implemented tool TaMaZG, daTA description is compiled into a MZG and represented symbolically using the Difference Bounded Matrices data structure (DBM).

Keywords: Real-time systems, maximality semantics, (durational actions) timed automata, zone graph, DBM.

1 Introduction

Timed automata (TA) was proposed to specify quantitative requirements expressed by timed constraints [3], they are an extension of finite state automata with a finite number (but arbitrary) clocks in continuous time. TA are very suitable for modeling and verifying real-time systems, indeed they ensure a good balance between expressiveness and tractability and they are supported by many verification tools in spite of this, the model suffers from many problems, principally state space explosion which impeding the scalability.

Its decidability has been proved using the so-called region graph construction. Region graph provides timed abstraction for the behavior of timed automata, but it is not used for implementing practical tools because of the complexity of size and algorithms. A zone graph was proposed as an alternative efficient implementation of timed automata based on an adapted data structures like Difference Bound Matrices (DBM) [16]. Most real-time model checking tools like UPPAAL [21] and Kronos [26] apply zones, which are much more practical and efficient symbolic states.

G. Dregvaite and R. Damasevicius (Eds.): ICIST 2014, CCIS 465, pp. 94–109, 2014.
© Springer International Publishing Switzerland 2014

Timed automata assume a "global clock" semantics, i.e., all clocks advance simultaneously and at the same rate (and there is a common initial instant). All possible executions of TA are then represented by a transition system where, from any given state, the system may evolve in two possible ways: either it executes an action or it delays with a given amount of time the potential execution. In order to model urgency, invariants constrain how long the automaton can delay in a given location, at which point it is expected that some action (i.e., the one the modeler has intended as urgent) can be executed.

It's well known that timed automata model is developed under the hypothesis that transitions represent atomic action executions (actions are instantaneous and indivisible). Modeling non atomic actions requires two sequential transitions; the first one models the action start and the second, the action end. The duration (of action) is captured by the elapsed time in the intermediate state.

In the practice of the timed automata model, splitting non-atomic actions into start and end actions aggravates the problem of state space explosion [4]. Another direct consequence of the interleaving semantics is the interleaved interpretation of concurrency, this is justified by the assumption that all actions are atomic, this means that two actions cannot occur simultaneously.

It's obvious that in real world systems, actions are not instantaneous and have durations. This realistic characteristic is important in many cases.

Instead of the interleaving semantics, maximality semantics [25] has been proved necessary and sufficient for carrying both the refinement process and action durations. Accordingly, models based on maximality semantics present concurrent actions differently from choice [12], because of non atomicity of actions. These models advocate modeling durational actions without splitting them.

The durational actions timed automata (daTA) [24] [20] [5] are a form of timed automata that admit a more natural representation of action durations and advocates carrying true concurrency. It's based on maximality semantics [25]. daTA model has been defined and a nice characterization of the model was presented in [20]. More recently, daTA is defined as a semantic support of temporally timed Petri nets [5]. The daTA model advocates capturing durations of actions and true concurrency, which are realistic assumptions for specifying in natural way systems.

To model duration of actions, every edge of the automaton is annotated by constraints on clocks which implicitly enclose them, of course those that are already started. A single clock is reset on every edge. When clock is reset it corresponds to the beginning of event. The termination of action will be captured by information on locations of the automaton, precisely on the destination location of transition, a set of temporal formulas identify actions in execution at state. In fact, the duration of an action is either in the constraint of the following edge, if there is dependence between the following actions, otherwise it is in the next locations and that means: action is not over yet. This elegant way to capture the durations is the effect of the maximality semantics.

Another important aspect of real time systems is the urgency i.e., actions whose execution cannot be delayed beyond a certain time bound, in daTA model urgency is represented by deadlines as proposed in [9] [18] [8]. This representation of urgent actions is more natural and has the advantage of avoiding the most common form of time locks [11].

In daTA deadlines replace invariants as time progress conditions (TPC). Deadlines are clock constraints associated directly with edges in the automaton, which express the set of states where the corresponding action is expected to be executed without delay. Thus, in daTA, every state either allows time to pass or allows actions to be executed (i.e., daTA are time-reactive).

Unfortunately, there are a few tools supporting models which use deadlines as urgency representation. The exception is given by the IF tool [13] and MoDeST specifications [7].

[19] was a tentative to use UPPAAL tool for verifying daTA by a translation of daTA structure to safety timed automata (TA à la UPPAAL). The main idea consists in translating deadlines in a form of invariants and preserving actions durations at all levels of analysis.

In the same order of idea; in [18] networks of timed automata with deadlines (TAD) are translated to UPPAAL modeling language. The implementation of this translation algorithm was described; this allows UPPAAL to aid the design and analysis of TAD models.

Our Contribution. In order to preserve all achievements of the maximality semantics namely duration of actions and true concurrency, we will use the daTA information when creating the zone graph. We think it'll allow us to keep the maximality semantics even on the symbolic representation of executions of daTA. The fundamental interest of this new approach is to propose a structure based on zone (i.e implementable) for model checking and all other validation needs of concurrent real-time systems (possibly distributed).

We propose an extension of zone graph definition based on the maximality semantics called Maximality-bases Zone Graph (MZG). We present an algorithm and a set of operations to generate MZG graph.

A tool implementing the proposed algorithm has been done. Furthermore, we illustrate the results on a simple example of automatic teller machine (ATM) system.

Paper Outlines. Section 2 recalls some basic definitions about durational actions timed automata model. Section 3 proposes the definition of Maximality-based Zone Graph (MZG). Section 4 describes the Difference Bound Matrices (DBM) data structure for representing the clock zone. Section 5 presents the construction algorithm of MZG and in Section 6 the implemented tool is described. Section 7 concludes the paper and gives some perspectives.

2   Durational Actions Timed Automata

The durational actions timed automata (daTA) model is a form of timed automata that admit a more natural representation of action duration and urgent actions. daTA model was proposed and used for interpreting specifications written in D-LOTOS [24] and durational timed Petri nets (DTPN) real-time specification models [5]. Several characteristics and good properties of daTA model are established in [20] such as determinization and expressiveness.

Indeed, this model extends the timed automata model by the maximality semantics [25]. Another interesting particularity of the daTA model is the fact that only a single clock is reset on transitions. The reset clock models the beginning of action. The action terminates when the associated clock attains the action duration.

From operational point of view, each action has its own (associated) clock which is reset at the start of the action. This clock will be used in the construction of the timing constraints as guards of the transitions.

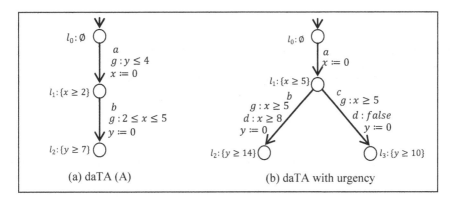

(a) daTA (A)   (b) daTA with urgency

Fig. 1. Two simple examples of daTA

An example of a daTA A is shown in Fig. 1 (a). The automaton consists of three localities l_0, l_1, l_2 and two clocks x, y. A transition form l_0 to l_1 represents the *start of action* a (indicating the beginning of its execution), the transition from l_1 to l_2 is labeled by b.

Assuming a time granularity of seconds, the automaton A starts in locality l_0. As soon as the value of y is less than or equal to 4, the automaton can make an a transition to l_1 and reset the clock x to 0. On the locality l_1 the temporal formula $\{x \geq 2\}$ represents information about the duration of the action a (it is important to differentiate it from invariant in timed automata). When x is at most 2 and is at least 5, transition to l_2 can be started (b executed) and y is reset. In the same logic the temporal formula $\{y \geq 7\}$ represents duration of the action b.

Another important aspect raised by the durational actions timed automata model (daTA) is the urgency. daTA admits a more natural representation of urgent actions, namely: deadlines, which are clock constraints associated directly with edges in the automaton (for illustration see Fig.1 (b)).

We also assume that the condition $d \Rightarrow g$ guarantees that if time cannot progress at some state, then at least one action is enabled from this state [9].

Formalization

In the following we consider $\mathbb{R}^+$ a set of nonnegative real numbers. Clocks are real variables take values from $\mathbb{R}^+$. Let X be a set of clocks, a clock valuation over X is a function that assigns a nonnegative real number to every clock. V_X is the set of total valuation functions from X to $\mathbb{R}^+$. A valuation is noted $v \in V_X$, and for $d \in \mathbb{R}^+$,

$v + d$ maps every clock x to $v(x) + d$. For $\lambda \subseteq X$, the valuation $v[\lambda := 0]$ is defined by: $(v[\lambda := 0])(x) = 0$ if $x \in \lambda, v(x)$ otherwise.

The set $C(X)$ of clock constraints C is defined by the grammar:
$C ::= true \mid false \mid x{\sim}c \mid C \wedge C$, where $x \in X$, $c \in \mathbb{N}$ and ${\sim}\in \{<,>,\leq,\geq\}$. We write $v \vDash C$ when the valuation v satisfies a clock constraint C over X iff C evaluates to true according to the values given by v.

We also use a subset of constraints where only the atomic form of clocks comparison is allowed. This set is defined by $C_d(X)$ by the grammar: $C ::= x \geq c$, where $x \in X$ and $c \in \mathbb{N}$. This subset represents condition duration over Act.

Definition 1 (daTA). A daTA A is a tuple (L, l_0, Act, M, X, E) where: L is a finite set of locations. $l_0 \in L$ is an initial location. Act represents a set of actions (finite). X is a finite set of clocks. $E \subseteq L \times C(X) \times C(X) \times Act \times X \times L$ is a finite set of edges. An edge $e = (l, g, d, a, x, l') \in E$ represents an edge from location l to l' that launch the execution of action a whenever guard g becomes true. In addition, deadline d imposes an urgency condition: the transition cannot be delayed whenever d is satisfied, x is a clock to be reset at this transition.

$M: L \to 2^{C_d(X)}$ is a maximality function which decorates each location by a set of timed formulas named actions durations. These formulas indicate the status of action execution at the corresponding state. $M(l_0) = \emptyset$ means that no action is yet started.

We define Clock Label Occurrence $CLO: C(X) \to 2^X$, as a function which gives clock names occurred in a given timed formulas, recursively by:

$$
\begin{cases}
CLO(true) = CLO(false) = \emptyset \\
CLO(\{x{\sim}c\}) = \{x\} \\
CLO(F_1 \wedge F_2 \wedge \ldots \wedge F_n) = \displaystyle\bigcup_{i=1..n} CLO(F_i)
\end{cases}
$$

Such as $F_i \in C(X), x \in X, {\sim}\in \{<,>,\leq,\geq\}$ and $c \in \mathbb{N}$.

Definition 2 (Semantics of daTA). The semantics of a daTA $A = (L, l_0, Act, M, X, E)$ is a Timed Transition System $TTS_A = (Q, q_0, \to)$, where: $Q = \{(l, v) \mid l \in L \text{ and } v \in V_X\}$. $q_0 = (l_0, v_0)$ such that $\forall x \in X, v_0(x) = 0$. $\to \subseteq Q \times (Act \cup \mathbb{R}^+) \times Q$ consist of the discrete and continuous transitions:

— The discrete transition is defined for all $e \in E$ by R1 $\quad \dfrac{(l,g,d,a,x,l') \in E \quad v \vDash g}{(l,v) \xrightarrow{a} (l',v[x := 0])}$

— The continuous transition is defined for all $d \in \mathbb{R}^+$ by

R2 $\dfrac{d \in \mathbb{R}^+ \quad \forall d' < d, v + d' \vDash TPC(l)}{(l,v) \xrightarrow{d} (l,v+d)}$,where $TPC(l) = \neg\bigvee(d \mid \exists\, e \in E: e = (l,g,d,a,x,l'))$

is the time progress condition in l [9] [18].

Rule R1 states that an edge $l \xrightarrow{g,d,a,x} l'$ defines a discrete transition from current location l whenever the guard holds in current valuation v and clock x is reset to 0. According to R2, time can progress in l only when $TPC(l)$ is true, that is as long as no deadline of an edge leaving l becomes true.

Product of Durational Actions Timed Automata

We proceed to definition of product construction for durational actions timed automata (daTA), so that a complex system can be defined as a product of component systems.

Definition 3 (Product of daTA). Let $A_1 = (L_1, l_1^0, Act_1, M_1, X_1, E_1)$ and $A_2 = (L_2, l_2^0, Act_2, M_2, X_2, E_2)$ be two daTA. Let Act_3 be a set of synchronization actions where $Act_3 \subseteq Act_1 \cap Act_2$. Assume that the clock sets X_1 and X_2 are disjoint except for clock associated to the synchronization actions. Then, the product, denoted $A_1 \| A_2$, is the daTA $(L_1 \times L_2, (l_1^0, l_2^0), Act_1 \cup Act_2, X_1 \cup X_2, M, E)$, where $M(l_1, l_2) = M_1(l_1) \cup M_2(l_2)$ and the transitions are defined by:

1. For $a \in Act_3$, for every $(l_1, a, g_1, d_1, x, l_1')$ in E_1 and $(l_2, a, g_2, d_2, x, l_2')$ in E_2, E has $((l_1, l_2), a, g_1 \wedge g_2, d_1 \wedge d_2, x, (l_1', l_2'))$.
2. For $a \in Act_1 \backslash Act_3$, for every (l, a, g, d, x, l') in E_1 and every t in L_2, E has $((l, t), a, g, d, x, (l', t))$.
3. For $a \in Act_2 \backslash Act_3$, for every (l, a, g, d, x, l') in E_2 and every t in L_1, E has $((t, l), a, g, d, x, (t, l'))$.

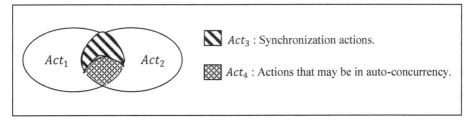

Act_3 : Synchronization actions.

Act_4 : Actions that may be in auto-concurrency.

Fig. 2. Partitioning the set of actions

Thus, locations of the product are pairs of component-locations and its duration conditions set is composed by the duration conditions sets (of the component locations). The transitions are obtained by synchronizing transitions with identical labels.

All actions a in $Act_1 \cap Act_2$ and not concerned by the synchronization (in Act_3) represent actions that can be in auto-concurrency. This set is denoted Act_4. This means that actions having the same names can be executed simultaneously see Fig.2.

An example of the product construction is illustrated in Fig. 3.

3   Zone Graph under the Maximality Semantics

It's well known that when exploring the semantics of timed automata the problem was the infinity of transition system. There exists an exact finite state abstraction based on convex polyhedra called zones [1] (a zone can be represented by a conjunction of clock constraints in $C(X)$).

When considering durational actions timed automata model we investigate maximality-based semantics and the particular considerations of urgency.

In the follow we recall zone definitions and notations; we explore the extensions induced by maximality.

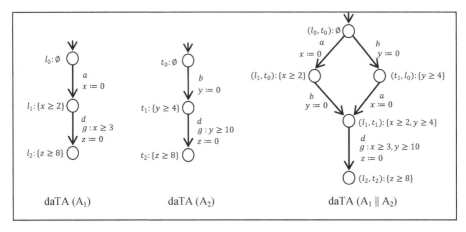

Fig. 3. Product construction of daTA

3.1   Clock Zones

Clock zone is a set of clock interpretations described by conjunction of constraints each of which puts a lower or upper bound on a clock or on difference of two clocks [1]. The set of clock zones are defined by the grammar $Z ::= x \prec c \mid c \prec x \mid x - y \prec c \mid Z \wedge Z$, where $\prec$ is in $\{<, \leq\}$.

Three operations on zones are important for the reachability analysis,

- Intersection: For two clock zones Z_1 and Z_2, the intersection of the two zones is a zone, denoted $Z_1 \wedge Z_2$.
- Future: for a clock zone Z, $Z \Uparrow$ denote the set of clock interpretations $v + d$ for $v \in Z$ and $d \in \mathbb{R}^+$. Thus $Z \Uparrow$ denotes the set of clock interpretations obtained by letting time elapse from some clock interpretation in Z.
- Reset: for a subset λ of clocks and a clock zone Z, $Z[\lambda := 0]$ is the set of clock interpretations $v[\lambda := 0]$ for $v \in Z$.
NB: The set of clock zones is closed under these operations.

3.2   Calculating Successor of Maximality Clock Zone

We build a transition system whose states are zones; a zone is a pair (l, Z) for a location l and a clock zone Z. Consider a zone (l, Z) and a transition $e = (l, g, d, a, x, l') \in E$ of a daTA A. Let $succ(Z, e)$ be the set of clock interpretations v' such that, for some $v \in Z$ the state (l', v') can be reached from the state (l, v) by letting time elapse and launching the transition e. That is, the set $(l', succ(Z, e))$ describes the successor of the zone (l, Z) under the transition e.

The clock zone $succ(Z, e)$ is obtained after the following steps:

4. Intersect Z with the time progress condition (TPC) of l to find the set of possible clock assignments for the current state.
5. Let time elapse in location l using the future operator, $\Uparrow$.
6. Take the intersection with the time progress condition of location l again to find the set of clock assignments that still satisfy the time progress condition.
7. Take the intersection with the guard g of the transition e to find the clock assignments that are permitted by the transition.
8. Set the clock x (that is reset by the transition) to 0.

The first and third steps ensure that intersection with the time progress condition is satisfied during elapse of time (since the time progress condition is convex, it suffices to ensure that the start and the final states satisfy the time progress condition) [1].

The resulting function which combines all of the above phases into one formula, we obtain: $succ(Z, e) = \left(\left(Z \wedge TPC(l) \right) \Uparrow \wedge\, TPC(l) \wedge g \right)[x := 0]$.

The set $succ(Z, e)$ is also a clock zone because of closure of clock zones under different used operations.

Definition 4 (Symbolic Semantics of daTA). Let $Z_0 = TPC(l_0) \wedge \bigwedge_{x \in X} x = 0$ be the initial clock zone. The symbolic semantics of a daTA (L, l_0, Act, M, X, E) is defined as a transition system $(S, s_0, \Rightarrow)$ called the maximality-based symbolic graph, where: $S \subseteq L \times C(X)$ is a set of symbolic states. $s_0 = (l_0, Z_0)$ is the initial state. $\Rightarrow$ is a transition relation defined by the following rule:

For all $e = (l, g, d, a, x, l') \in E$

$$(l, Z) \xrightarrow{CLO(g), a, x} \left(l', \left(\left(\left(Z \wedge TPC(l) \right) \Uparrow \wedge\, TPC(l) \wedge g \right)[x := 0] \right) \right)$$

3.3   Maximality-Based Zone Graph

A Maximality-based Zone Graph (MZG) of daTA named maximal reachability graph is a zone graph extended by maximality information which conserves true concurrency property at all levels of analysis.

On Transition: in addition to action label, transition is labeled by a set of clock labels occurred in the guard formula. Those clock names capture the signature of actions which depends the current one.

On States: information about actions potentially on execution is captured by the set of clock names coming from duration conditions. The function ψ operates on duration conditions of each locality to give the set of maximal events which materialize the true concurrency.

It is important to note that, transitions starting from the initial location l_0(initial transitions) are particular case. The initial transitions can indeed be guarded by formulas, using clocks names that are not yet attributed. These guards allow either delaying action or limiting its offer time. In accordance with the principle that the guard is formed by temporal formulas containing clocks which correspond to actions whose depends the current one, it's obvious that the set of event names that label initial transition in the zone graph remains empty without lost of generality.

For example, consider a daTA and the corresponding MZG shown in Fig. 4.

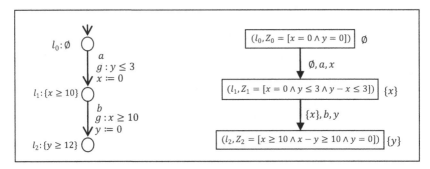

Fig. 4. A daTA and its Maximality-based Zone Graph

Definition 5 (Maximality-based Zone Graph). For a daTA $A = (L, l_0, Act, M, X, E)$, a Maximality-based Zone Graph of A, $MZG(A) = (LZ, LZ_0, T, \psi)$ is a transition system where: $LZ = \{(l, Z) | l \in L \text{ and } Z \subseteq C(X)\}$. $LZ_0 = (l_0, Z_0)$ is the initial state, such that $\forall x \in X, Z_0(x) = 0$. $T \subseteq LZ \times (2^X \times Act \times X) \times LZ$ is a transition relation defined for all $e \in E$ by: $(l, Z) \xrightarrow{CLO(g), a, x} (l', succ(Z, e))$.

$\psi: LZ \to 2^X$ is a function which associates to each state a finite set of clocks representing maximal event names present in this state. It's defined as: $\psi(l, Z) = \{x \mid x \geq c \in M(l)\}$.

4   Generating Maximality-Based Zone Graph

In this section we propose an algorithm which constructs the Maximality-based Zone Graph for durational actions timed automata. It is based on the successor function and maximality semantics to create novel zones by using daTA structure.

4.1   The Construction Algorithm

The following algorithm describes how to construct a Maximality-base Zone Graph $MZG(A)$ from a durational actions timed automata A. Clock zones are represented by Difference Bound Matrices (DBM) and the set $succ(Z, e)$ is computed by the three operations on DBM described above rather than by operations directly on clock zones. The initial state is given by (l_0, Z_0). However the unbounded clock values may render an infinite Maximality-based Zone Graph and thus might the construction algorithm not terminate (the symbolic state space is infinite). The solution problem is to introduce a *K-approximation* version of the infinite symbolic semantics. The idea is to utilize the maximum constant appearing in clock constraints in the daTA, to render a finite symbolic semantics (see [23] for more details).

Algorithm : Construction of Maximality-based Zone Graph
Input: Durational actions timed automata $A = (L, l_0, Act, M, X, E)$
Output: Maximality-based Zone Graph $MZG(A) = (LZ, \ LZ_0, T, \psi)$

Variables

$l \in L$ locality of daTA ; Z, Z', Z'': zones;
$EXL: 2^X \times Act \times X;\ Leb \in EXL$ /* EXL extended labels set */
T:set of tuples $LZ \times EXL \times LZ;$ /*transition relation of MZG(A) */
P, LZ: set of pairs $L \times Z;$ /* states of MZG(A)*/

Begin

1:    $P, LZ := \{(l_0, Z_0)\}; T := \emptyset; EXL := \emptyset; \psi((l_0, Z_0)) = \emptyset$ /* $\forall x \in X, Z_0(x) = 0$ */

2:    **While** $P \neq \emptyset$ **do**

3:       Choose and remove (l, Z) from P;

4:       **For** all transition $e = (l, g, d, a, x, l') \in E$ s.t $Z \wedge g \neq \emptyset$ /*this ensures Z' is not empty*/ **do**

5:          $Z' := Approx_k(Succ\ (Z, e));\ Leb := (CLO(g), a, x); EXL := EXL \cup \{Leb\};$

6:          $\psi(l', Z') = \{x \mid x \geq c \in M(l')\};$

7:          **If** $\exists (l', Z'') \in LZ$ such as $Z' \subseteq Z''$ **ten**

8:             $T := T \cup \{(l, Z) \xrightarrow{Leb} (l', Z')\};$

9:          **Else** $T := T \cup \{(l, Z) \xrightarrow{Leb} (l', Z')\}; LZ := LZ \cup \{(l', Z')\}; P := P \cup \{(l', Z')\};$

         End if. End for. End while

End

Application to the example in Fig. 4:

Initialization: $LZ := \{(l_0, Z_0)\};\ P := \{(l_0, Z_0)\};\ T := \emptyset;\ EXL := \emptyset;\ \psi((l_0, Z_0)) = \emptyset;$

Step 3: $(l, Z) := (l_0, Z_0);\ P := P\backslash\{(l_0, Z_0)\};$

Step 5: $Z' := Z_1;\ Leb := (\emptyset, a, x);\ EXL := \{(\emptyset, a, x)\};$

Step 6: $(l_1, Z_1) = \{x\}$;

Step 9: $T := \{(l_0, Z_0) \xrightarrow{\emptyset, a, x} (l_1, Z_1)\};\ LZ := \{(l_0, Z_0), (l_1, Z_1)\};\ P := \{ (l_1, Z_1)\};$ and so on.

4.2   The Implementation: The DBM Data Structure

A clock zone can be represented efficiently by matrices. The most common data structure used for representing a state space of timed automata is the Difference Bound Matrices (DBM) [16]. The DBM structure allows easier representation and lower complexity algorithms. A detailed presentation of DBM can be found in [6] [14].

Definition 6 (Difference Bounded Matrix). A Difference Bounded Matrix over n clocks *in* X is an $(n + 1)$ square matrix of pairs $(c, \prec)$ with $\prec \in \{<, \leq\}$ and $c \in \mathbb{Z} \cup \{\infty\}$. Where ∞ is a special value denoting that no bound is present.

The semantics of a DBM $D = (c_{i,j}, \prec_{i,j})_{0 \leq i, j \leq n}$ over a set of clocks $\{x_1, x_2, ..., x_n\}$, is the zone defined by the constraint $\bigwedge_{0 \leq i, j \leq n} x_i - x_j \prec c_{i,j}$.

A special clock called x_0 is introduced, its value is always 0. This leads to more uniform notations for clock constraints. With the help of x_0, we only need one form of clock constraints. Each element in such a matrix represents a bound on the difference between two clocks and $D_{i,j}$ denotes the (i, j)th element of zone D.

For a zone D, the DBM representation is computed first by numbering all clocks in $\{X \cup x_0\}$ to assign one row and one column in the matrix to each of them. The row is used for storing lower bounds on the difference between the clock and all other clocks while the column is used for upper bounds. The elements in the matrix are then computed in three steps.

1. For each constraint $x_i - x_j \prec c$ of D, let $D_{ij} = (c, \prec)$.
2. For each clock difference $x_i - x_j$ that is unbounded in D, let $D_{ij} = (\infty, <)$.
3. Finally add the implicit constraints that all clocks are positive, i.e. $x_0 - x_i \leq 0$, and that the difference between a clock and itself is always 0, i.e. $x_i - x_i \leq 0$.

As example, consider the zone $D = x \geq 3 \wedge y < 5 \wedge x - y < 2$. To construct the matrix representing D, we number the clocks in the order x_0, x, y. The resulting matrix is shown below:

	x_0	x	y
x_0	$(0, \leq)$	$(-3, \leq)$	$(\infty, <)$
x	$(\infty, <)$	$(0, \leq)$	$(2, <)$
y	$(5, <)$	$(\infty, <)$	$(0, \leq)$

An efficient use of DBMs requires two operations on bounds:

- Comparison, it's defined by $(c, \prec) < \infty, (c_1, \prec_1) < (c_2, \prec_2)$ if $c_1 < c_2$ and $(c, <) < (c, \leq)$.
- Addition, defined by $c + \infty = \infty, (c_1, \leq) + (c_2, \leq) = (c_1 + c_2, \leq)$ and $(c_1, <) + (c_2, \prec) = (c_1 + c_2, <)$.

Though a set of clocks valuations may be expressed by different conjunctions of constraints, there exists a unique form, called canonical form, which allows comparing zones together. A canonical form of a zone D is the representation with tightest bounds on all clock differences. Its computation is based on the shortest path Floyd-Warshall's algorithm [17].

Basic Operations on DBM [14]

For computing the successor of zone $succ(Z, e)$, we show how to achieve required operations handling zones, namely Conjunction of two zones, the future of zones ($Z \Uparrow$) and the reset operation ($Z[\lambda := 0]$) from the representation of a zone Z [1]. These operations correspond to those defined on clock zones in section 3.1.

Let D, D^1, D^2 be a representations of zones

Intersection noted $D = D^1 \wedge D^2$.

For $D_{i,j}^1 = (c_1, \prec_1)$ and $D_{i,j}^2 = (c_2, \prec_2)$, $D_{i,j} = (min(c_1, c_2), \prec)$, where $\prec$ is as follows : If $c_1 < c_2$, then $\prec = \prec_1$. If $c_2 < c_1$, then $\prec = \prec_2$. If $c_1 = c_2$, and $\prec_1 = \prec_2$, then $\prec = \prec_1$. If $c_1 = c_2$, and $\prec_1 \neq \prec_2$, then $\prec = <$.

The inclusion between two zones D_1, D_2 is a particular from of the intersection defined as $D_1 \subseteq D_2$ iff $D_1 \wedge D_2 = D_1$.

Clock reset $D = D^1[\lambda := 0]$ where $\lambda \subseteq X$ as follows: If $x_i, x_j \in \lambda$ then $D_{i,j} = (0, \leq)$. If $x_i \in \lambda, x_j \notin \lambda$ then $D_{i,j} = D_{0,j}^1$. If $x_j \in \lambda, x_i \notin \lambda$ then $D_{i,j} = D_{i,0}^1$. If $x_i, x_j \notin \lambda$, then $D_{i,j} = D_{i,j}^1$.

Elapsing of time $D = D^1 \Uparrow$ (future) is defined as follows: $D_{i,0} = (\infty, <)$ for any $i \neq 0$. $D_{i,j} = D_{i,j}^1$ if $i = 0$ or $j \neq 0$.

In each case the resulting matrix may fail to be in canonical form. Thus, as a final step we must compute its canonical form. All three of the operations can be implemented efficiently.

4.3   Complexity

Each operation in the construction algorithm can be computed using the DBM data structure. The complexity of each step of the algorithm is, as for classical timed automata, polynomial in the number of clocks. Nevertheless the cost of labeling zones using the ψ function will take just one time step.

Theorem 1: The zone-based construction algorithm has a polynomial time complexity related in the number of clocks, size of state space and the number of transitions of the daTA under analysis.

4.4   Correctness and Termination

We point out that the construction algorithm terminates because there are finitely many k-bounded zones. This for the fact that a finite k-approximations of zones can be explored for each state of the automaton.

As proved in [10], the class of timed automata for which the construction algorithm is safely used is those named diagonal-free timed automata. Diagonal-free timed automata are timed automata with restricted form of clock constraints in which difference between clocks are not allowed to appear in the guards.

Since, durational actions timed automata are subclass of diagonal-free timed automata model, so the following nice theorem holds:

Theorem 2: The construction algorithm is correct for durational actions timed automata (where the constant used for the approximation parameter is the maximum constant used in one of the clock constraints of the automaton).

4.5   Discussion (Maximality-Based Semantics and Model Checking)

Real-time model checking [14] has been mostly studied and developed in the framework of timed automata. Timed Computation Tree Logic (TCTL) [2] is adopted to describe properties of real-time systems. It's a real-time extension of the branching temporal logic CTL with clocks. The properties of reactive systems are usually divided into safety and liveness properties. Safety properties express requirements of the form "*bad things will not happen*". Liveness properties express requirements of the form "*good things will happen*".

The interest of daTA for model checking derives from the fact that the model specifies in addition of real-time constraints and deadlines, the state of execution of actions. Furthermore, semantics of daTA model captures duration of actions and their eventual concurrent execution. This will enlarge the range of properties to be verified like,

— *Actions incompatibility* meaning that actions will never be able to be executed concurrently.
— *Auto-concurrency level* checking a state in which n actions of name a are in execution simultaneously.
— *Specifying the concurrency degree* in the respect of the same idea.

Effectively, the information concerning current and concurrent executions, which are captured by timed formulas, initially on states of daTA, will be found in the localities of Maximality-based Zone Graph, what enlarges the range of properties that we are able to verify.

5   The Tool: TaMaZG

We have implemented the algorithm to compute all the reachable zones based on the maximality semantics. The tool implemented (TaMaZG) integrates a software for daTA edition and analysis.

The TaMaZG tool generates the Maximality-based Zone Graph of durational actions timed automata. It consists of two main parts: a graphical user interface and a MZG generator engine.

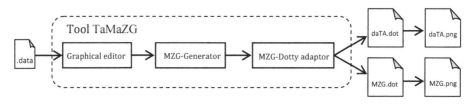

Fig. 5. Overview of TaMaZG

TaMaZG has a graphical editor to draw and edit daTA structure Fig. 6 (a). The MZG-generator generates a Maximality-based Zone Graph, and MZG-Dotty adaptor Fig. 7 produces a dot file type. Its functional view is sketched in Fig. 5.

The user interfaces and all of parts of TaMaZG are implemented in Java programming language and executed on the user's workstation.

Example (Automatic Teller Machine)
To illustrate our approach we propose the well-known example: the automatic teller machine (ATM) system. This machine allows withdrawing money from account. Its behavior is as follow: Customer has to insert card in machine. After he has to type a code, if code is correct the machine delivers money and card. If the code is wrong, the machine can keep card or reject it.

Fig. 6 (a) and Fig. 6 (b) respectively present a daTA structure of ATM system with the graph editor of the tool TaMaZG and the dotty graph editor. The resulted MZG obtained automatically is depicted by Fig. 7.

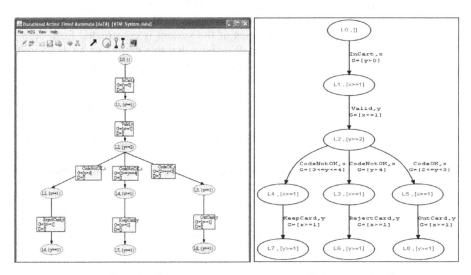

(a) TaMaZG graph editor   (b) Dotty graph editor

Fig. 6. daTA structure of ATM system

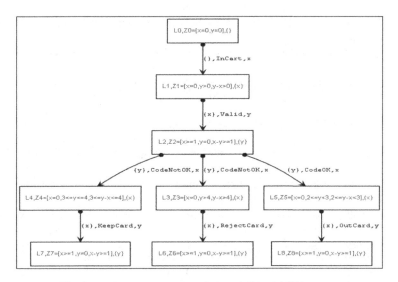

Fig. 7. MZG graph corresponding to daTA of ATM system

6   Conclusion

In this paper we have proposed a zone graph under true concurrency semantics. This model is named Maximality-based Zone Graph (MZG). Furthermore, we have developed a tool for computing quantitative properties of real-time systems. A formal zones graph based on maximality semantics of the system is constructed from durational actions timed automata description. We show that this graph can be generated using a classical DBM structure extended by functions to preserve true concurrency and action durations at all levels of analysis.

Because our proposals are based on symbolic reachability definition, they can be applied to model checking realistic systems. The approach is illustrated by means of simple example.

In its current version our proposal is able to handle timed maximality bisimulation of behaviors and formal test of concurrent real-time systems. However since the used abstraction is an over-approximation, the model based verification (model checking) can delivers spurious counterexample. Then the initial abstraction must be refined so that the spurious counterexample is eliminated.

This task is not simple; it's named the abstraction refinement possibly guided by counterexample [15] [22]. In [15] it's done automatically over a subclass of timed automata. We intend to complete this work in this direction.

References

1. Alur, R.: Timed Automata. Theoretical Computer Science 126, 183–235 (1999)
2. Alur, R., Courcoubetis, C., Dill, D.: Model-Checking in Dense Real- Time. Information and Computation 104(1), 2–34 (1993)
3. Alur, R., Dill, D.: A theory of timed automata. Theoretical Computer Science, 183–235 (1994)
4. Barbuti, R., De Francesco, N., Tesei, L.: Timed Automata with non-instantaneous Actions. Fundamenta Informaticae-Concurrency Specification and Programming 47(3-4), 189–200 (2001)
5. Belala, N., Saidouni, D.E., Boukharrou, R., Chaouche, A.C., Seraoui, A., Chachoua, A.: Time Petri Nets with Action Duration: A True Concurrency Real-Time Model. International Journal of Embedded and Real-Time Communication Systems (IJERTCS) 4(2), 62–83 (2013)
6. Bengtsson, J.: Clocks, DBMs ans States in Timed Systems. Ph.D. thesis, Department of Information Technology, Uppsala University, Uppsala, Sweden (2002)
7. Bohnenkamp, H., D'Argenio, P.R., Hermanns, H., Katoen, J.P.: MODEST: A compositional modeling formalism for hard and softly timed systems. IEEE Transactions on Software Engineering 32(10), 812–830 (2006)
8. Bornot, S., Sifakis, J.: On the composition of hybrid systems. In: Henzinger, T.A., Sastry, S.S. (eds.) HSCC 1998. LNCS, vol. 1386, pp. 49–63. Springer, Heidelberg (1998)
9. Bornot, S., Sifakis, J., Tripakis, S.: Modeling Urgency in Timed Systems. In: de Roever, W.-P., Langmaack, H., Pnueli, A. (eds.) COMPOS 1997. LNCS, vol. 1536, pp. 103–129. Springer, Heidelberg (1998)
10. Bouyer, P.: Untameable timed automata! In: Alt, H., Habib, M. (eds.) STACS 2003. LNCS, vol. 2607, pp. 620–631. Springer, Heidelberg (2003)

11. Bowman, H.: Time and action lock freedom properties for timed automata. In: Proceedings of FORTE 2001, pp. 119–134 (2001)
12. Bowman, H., Gomez, R.: Concurrency Theory, Calculi and Automata for Modelling Untimed and Timed Concurrent Systems. Springer (2006) ISBN-10: 1-85233-895-4 ISBN-13: 978-1-85233-895-4
13. Bozga, M., Graf, S., Ober, I., Ober, I., Sifakis, J.: The IF toolset. In: Bernardo, M., Corradini, F. (eds.) SFM-RT 2004. LNCS, vol. 3185, pp. 237–267. Springer, Heidelberg (2004)
14. Clarke, E.M., Grumberg, O., Peled, D.: Model Checking. MIT Press (2000)
15. Dierks, H., Kupferschmid, S., Larsen, K.G.: Automatic abstraction refinement for timed automata. In: Raskin, J.-F., Thiagarajan, P.S. (eds.) FORMATS 2007. LNCS, vol. 4763, pp. 114–129. Springer, Heidelberg (2007)
16. Dill, D.L.: Timing assumptions and verification of finite-state concurrent systems. In: Sifakis, J. (ed.) CAV 1989. LNCS, vol. 407, pp. 197–212. Springer, Heidelberg (1990)
17. Floyd, R.W.: Algorithm 97: Shortest path. Communications of the ACM 5(6), 345 (1962)
18. Gomez, R.: Model-checking timed automata with deadlines with Uppaal. Formal Aspects of Computing 25(2), 289–318 (2013)
19. Guellati, S., Kitouni, I., Saidouni, D.E.: Verification of durational actions timed automata using UPPAAL. International Journal of Computer Applications 56(11), 33–41 (2012)
20. Kitouni, I., Hachichi, H., Bouaroudj, K., Saidouni, D.E.: Durational Actions Timed Automata: Determinization and Expressiveness. International Journal of Applied Information Systems (IJAIS) 4(2), 1–11 (2012)
21. Larsen, K.G., Pettersson, P., Yi, W.: UPPAAL in a nutshell. International Journal on Software Tools for Technology Transfer 1(1-2), 134–152 (1997)
22. Nagaoka, T., Okano, K., Kusumoto, S.: An abstraction refinement technique for timed automata based on counterexample-guided abstraction refinement loop. IEICE Transactions on Information and Systems E93-D5(5), 994–1005, 5 (2010)
23. Pettersson, P.: Modelling and Verification of Real-Time Systems Using Timed Automata. Theory and Practice. PhD thesis, Uppsala University (1999)
24. Saidouni, D.E., Belala, N.: Actions duration in timed models. In: Proceedings of International Arab Conference on Information Technology (ACIT 2006), Yarmouk University, Irbid, Jordan (2006)
25. Saidouni, D.E., Belala, N., Bouneb, M.: Aggregation of transitions in marking graph generation based on maximality semantics for petri nets. In: Proceeding of the Second international conference on Verification and Evaluation of Computer and Communication Systems (VECoS 2008), pp. 6–16 (2008)
26. Yovine, S.: Kronos: A verification tool for real-time systems. International Journal on Software Tools for Technology Transfer 1(1-2), 123–133 (1997)

New Test Patterns to Check the Hierarchical Structure of Wordnets

Ahti Lohk[1], Alexander Norta[1], Heili Orav[2], and Leo Võhandu[1]

[1] Tallinn University of Technology, Akadeemia tee 15a, 12618 Tallinn, Estonia
[2] University of Tartu, J. Liivi 2, 50409, Tartu, Estonia
{ahti.lohk,alexander.norta,leo.vohandu}@ttu.ee,
heili.orav@ut.ee

Abstract. The goal of this paper is to introduce test patterns for checking inconsistencies in the hierarchical structure of wordnets. Every test pattern (displayed as a substructure) points out the cases of multiple inheritance and two of them are studied in depth by expert linguists, or lexicographers. Furthermore, this research associates test patterns with the inconsistencies they help to detect in wordnets, and presents instances of the test patterns. All examples use the Estonian Wordnet (Versions 66 or 67), some results we are shown for the Princeton WordNet (Version 3.1).

Keywords: wordnet, hierarchical structure, evaluation, test patterns, multiple inheritance.

1   Introduction

Many tasks of natural language processing, such as machine translation, information retrieval and word sense disambiguation use wordnets as a lexical resource. Therefore, wordnets are attractive due to their hierarchical structure of lexical concepts. Unfortunately, there are no good methods to study the condition of its hierarchical structure. Richens [1] and Liu [2] describe two different types of rings in the substructure of the wordnet hierarchy that point to inconsistencies like a wrongly inherited domain category or ignoring the principle of economy. A common denominator of these two type of rings is that they consist of multiple inheritance cases.

With respect to the state of the art, research has been conducted for individually testing the hierarchy substructures of wordnets. For example, David Levary gives an overview of the loops and self-references in the hierarchical structure of wordnets [3]. Liu [2] and Richens [1] show all rings of asymmetric and symmetric nature in a ring topology that is based on the same structure. In Smrž [4], the author presents 27 tests for quality control in wordnet development. Only some of those tests are for checking errors in the hierarchical structure, like "cycles", "dangling uplinks", "structural difference from the Princeton WordNet and other wordnets", or "multi-parent relations". However, there are no test pattern systems that would help to investigate a hierarchical structure in a general way, specially in the case of multiple inheritance.

G. Dregvaite and R. Damasevicius (Eds.): ICIST 2014, CCIS 465, pp. 110–120, 2014.
© Springer International Publishing Switzerland 2014

This paper fills the gap in the state-of-the-art by asking the main research question of how test patterns help to check and evaluate the multiple inheritance in the hierarchical structure of wordnets. In order to answer the question, we present different test patterns as different views on the substructures of the wordnet hierarchy in the cases of multiple inheritance. The need to check the hierarchical structure emerges because of wordnet extensions with new concepts and semantic relations that either happen manually [5], semi-automatically [6, 7], or fully automatically [8, 9]. Thus, every pattern reveals different inconsistencies in the hierarchical structure. The majority of inconsistency cases are caused by redundant, missing or wrong semantic relations between synsets. The utility of the patterns lies in supporting expert linguists who check substructures after the extensions in any human language wordnet.

We structure the paper as follows: Section 2 gives additional background for understanding the main body of the paper. Next, Section 3 shows test patterns for checking the wordnets. Section 4 discusses the inconsistency taxonomy related to these test patterns. Section 5 evaluates the test patterns providing a numerical overview and finally, Section 6 concludes the paper and presents future work.

2 Features of Wordnet-Like Dictionaries

Wordnets share properties for the concepts of polysemy that are a part of the definitions of the test patterns. On the other hand, regular polysemy is only a part of one test pattern definition, namely of the pattern *dense component*. In the remainder, Section 2.1 gives general structural features for wordnet and Section 2.2 polysemy versus regular polysemy.

2.1 Wordnet-Like Dictionaries

The fundamental approach for designing WordNet-like dictionaries came from the Princeton WordNet [10]. Each wordnet shares certain structural features. First, synonym sets (synsets) group many synonyms that share the same meaning and are referred to as concepts. Semantic relations connect synsets to each other, e.g. by hypernymy, meronymy for creating a hierarchical structure, and caused by, near synonym that do not create a hierarchical structure. In this article, we consider only hypernymy-hyponymy relations as the objects of analysis. Furthermore, there is no extension limitation for approaching different semantic relations that shape the hierarchical structure.

For details about Estonian Wordnet, we refer the reader to [5]. Furthermore, Princeton WordNet has 117,773 synsets and 88,721 hypernym-hyponym relations. In Estonian Wordnet Version 66, these values are 58,566 and 51,497 respectively, while for Versions 67, the values are 60,434 and 52,678, respectively. Princeton WordNet has hypernym-hyponym relations only in the cases of nouns and verbs; in the Estonian Wordnet in the case of nouns, verbs and adjectives.

2.2   Regular Polysemy vs the Regularity of Multiple Inheritance

According to Ravin and Leacock [11], polysemy is the multiplicity of meanings of words. The best-known definition of regular (also systematic or logic) polysemy is given by Apresjan [12]. According to Langemets [13], regular polysemy is a status where at least two words have at least two meanings with a similar relation between those meanings. For example, if the word school has the meaning institution and building, then the same is true about a hospital. The latter is also an institution as well as a building. According to Freihat et al. [14], institution building is an example of a polysemic pattern.

Multiple inheritance in wordnet hierarchies is the case where one synset has at least two parents, i.e., the synset inherits properties from many concepts. The regularity of multiple inheritance is comparable to regular polysemy in that instead of words, there are synsets and instead of a polysemic pattern, there exists a pattern of many parents. It is important to mention that if synsets are singletons, then there is no difference between the meanings of regular polysemy and the regularity of multiple inheritance.

Next, the set of test patterns for checking wordnet hierarchy-inconsistency is given.

3   Test Patterns

For every form of inconsistency, we will give a specific test pattern that is applicable to every language wordnet. Every pattern addresses a specific substructure of the hierarchical structure in wordnets and has the property of multiple inheritance, i.e. polysemy. For the sake of test pattern set's completeness, the patterns presented in Section 3.1 are inspired by Liu and Richens [2, 1] while the remainder are entirely original work.

3.1   Rings

This pattern is a substructure where one superordinate has a subordinate via two branches, e.g. in Figure 1 and 2, U_1 has the subordinate L_1. We distinguish two types of rings. In the case of a symmetric ring topology (SRT) the lengths of all chains in the branches are equal, i.e. $m = n$ in Figure 1. In an asymmetric ring topology (ART) the lengths are different, i.e. $m \neq n$ in Figure 2. Note that while Figures 1 and 2 only show two branches, this pattern extends to more branches.

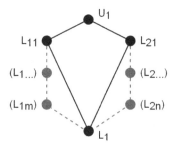

Fig. 1. Pattern of a symmetric ring topology

When a synset has information about a domain category, then both types of rings allow to detect a certain inconsistency automatically, e.g. in a situation where L_{1m} and L_{2n} are from different domain categories. Research in [2] confirms that one synset as a concept cannot inherit properties from different domain categories.

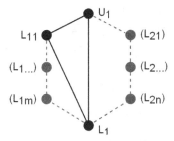

Fig. 2. Pattern of an asymmetric ring topology

The asymmetric ring topology with one redundant branch as in the center of Figure 2 indicates that the branch connecting U_1 to L_1 is not allowed because this connections already transitively exists via L_{11} [10].

3.2   Closed Subset (CS)

A modified equivalence-class-finding algorithm [15] yields the following pattern. As Figure 3 shows, and based on the sequence of hypernym relations, our algorithm separates all coherent bipartite graphs. The inconsistency occurs when the location information about the root synset equals the upper level of a bipartite graph, e.g. U_1 in Figure 3. This information indicates that the upper base involves concepts that should be on different levels. Thus, a root synset may either be added to a higher level, or connected to pre-existing higher-level concepts.

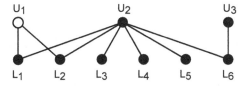

Fig. 3. Pattern of a closed set

3.3   Dense Component (DC)

A dense component is a substructure of the hierarchical structure of wordnets that has at least two synsets with at least two identical parents. Every such kind of substructure presents the case of regular polysemy, i.e., systematic polysemy. Therefore, in the evaluation process, expert linguists/lexicographers have to check if regular polysemy is justified or not. The lower level synsets in Figure 4, L_1 and L_3, have at least two identical parents, U_2 and U_3. Additionally, dense components may have synsets in common that have at least two parents in the upper level's set of nodes. For example in Figure 4, L_1 and L_3 have in common not only the synset L_2 but also the nodes U_1 to U_4 from the upper level. Separating this information keeps the polysemic context clear while every dense component is presented with related synsets to simplify the work of expert linguists/lexicographers.

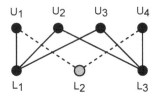

Fig. 4. Pattern of a dense component

3.4 Heart-Shaped Substructure (HSS)

In the case of a heart-shaped substructure, two upper level synsets have one common subordinate directly in common. For example in Figure 5, U_1 and U_2 have one common L_1 and simultaneously the upper level synsets also have L_3 partially transitively in common via L_2. Linguists from Princeton University have found that this pattern is helpful for detecting wrong semantic relations, mostly role and type relations. Unfortunately, a complete analysis has not been done for the Estonian Wordnet yet, but Figure 11 shows an example.

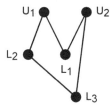

Fig. 5. Pattern of a heart-shaped substructure

3.5 Substructures through a Synset Member or a Part of a Compound Word (COM)

The Estonian Wordnet consists of many cases where an upper level synset's lexical unit relates to the main word in a compound word which is a member of the subordinates set, e.g. U_2 to L_1 to L_5 in Figure 6. Additionally, an upper level synset's lexical unit may also relate to subordinates that have the same lexical unit, e.g. L_1 to L_5. Furthermore, this pattern must simultaneously have at least one additional superordinate, e.g. U_1 from among L_1 to L_5 in Figure 6.

To evaluate this kind of pattern, expert linguists/lexicographers must ask: if U_1 is connected to L_1, why it is not connected to L_2, L_3, L_4 or L_5? This question helps to make a decision regarding inconsistencies that this pattern may have. In case of the Estonian Wordnet, we found that sometimes this pattern points to a situation where a subordinate should have additional synsets with different meanings, e.g. L_1.

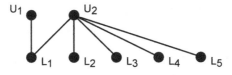

Fig. 6. Pattern of COM

In the next section, we will introduce the inconsistencies that relate to respective test patterns.

4   Inconsistencies of Substructures

The purpose of our test patterns is to check after presenting a pattern if an instance of that wordnet's substructure contained inconsistencies. Thus, in Section 4.1, we will list these inconsistencies and in Section 4.2, we will give examples.

4.1   Inconsistency Taxonomy

Any correction a linguist/lexicographer carries out affects a substructure by either deleting, inserting, merging or modifying a synset.

1. **Regularity of Polysemy** – in accordance with Section 2.2, linguists have to check if the regularity of multiple inheritance is justified or not. Linguists also check which synsets have to be connected to a pattern of parents.
2. **Ignoring the Principle of Economy (Redundant Semantic Relation)** – for building a wordnet as a lexical inheritance system, we consider the following: every synset in a wordnet hierarchy has to be connected to the nearest concept. Here we focus on cases where one synset (S1) is connected to specific parents (S2) and at the same time to parents that are ancestors (S3) to both synsets (S1 and S2).
3. **Inappropriate Semantic Relationship** – it implies that the semantic relationship's type must change. Atserias et al. [16] point to a situation that occurs in PrincetonWordNet "the IS-A link is used to code other types of relations (e.g. similar or place)". The same problem holds for a role and type relation that wordnets have not defined yet [17].
4. **Wrongly Inherited Domain Category** – if one synset inherits many different concepts from different domain categories, at least one of them represents an exception to the linguistic theory [2] that a concept has to inherit properties only from the super-concept of the same domain category. The gloss of the synset indicates which of the categories is most appropriate [10].
5. **Root synset on the wrong level** – this is a sub-problem of the unique-beginners problem that Smrž [4] defines and means that dangling uplinks occurred.

The assignment options of inconsistencies to test patterns are given in Table 1 comprises. The sequence numbers in the first column correspond to the inconsistency enumeration above while the test pattern abbreviations are given in the first row.

Table 1. The kinds of inconsistencies the test patterns help to detect

		ART	SRT	CS	DC	HSS	COM
1	Regularity of multiple inheritance				x+		
2	Ignoring the principle of economy	x+			x		
3	Inappropriate semantic relation	x	x	x	x	x+	x+
4	Wrongly inherited domain category	x+	x+	x	x	x	x
5	Root synset on the wrong level			x+			

The symbol "+" added to the table cells in addition to *x* denotes that a respective test pattern is particularly suitable for detecting a specific inconsistency type. Note that column ART has two "+" assignments as Figure 2 shows two different examples, namely with and without a redundant link.

4.2   Some Examples

In this subsection, we will present the examples that cover the test patterns that are given in Section 3. Figure 7 represents the case of an asymmetric ring topology with an empty branch. Here the *human* is connected to *bootlegger* directly (dotted line) and indirectly.

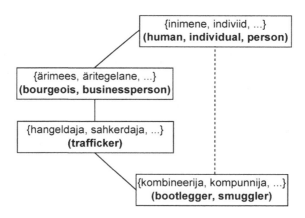

Fig. 7. Instance of an asymmetric ring topology

According to the understanding that a wordnet is a lexical inheritance system, only the nearest concepts in the hierarchy have to be connected. Therefore, in Figure 7, the dotted line as a connection between the specific *bootlegger* and the too general *human* is redundant.

Figure 8 depicts a closed subset. Two general concepts are related to specific ones. The concept with a colored background indicates to the root synset or unique-beginner case or concept without any parents. In order to solve this situation, this kind of dangling uplink needs to be connected to a more general concept.

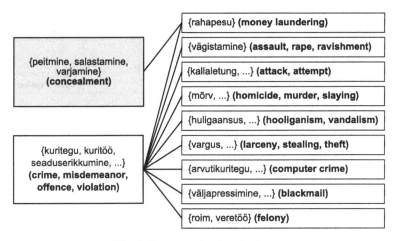

Fig. 8. Instance of a closed subset

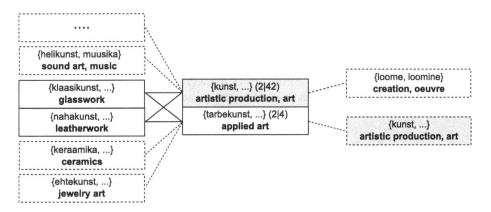

Fig. 9. Instance of a dense component

Figure 9 presents an example of a dense component where the dashed lines present background information and the colored background points to the same concept. This kind of additional information is for the linguist who does not need to check the wordnet management system for the background of every instance of a dense component.

As the co-hypernyms are concepts of a different level, due to *artistic production* involving also *applied art*, it means „kunst" must be the parent of „tarbekunst" and the links between „kunst" and „klaasikunst" and also „kunst" and „nahakunst" are redundant. In Figure 10, the key synset is „madu" (*serpent*) that is included in three compound words as „boamadu" (*boa*), „lõgismadu" (*Crotalus*) and „mürkmadu" (*Vipera aspis*). „Boamadu" (*boa*), in turn, simultaneously has the superconcept of „sall" (*scarf*).

Finally, Figure 11 shows an instance of a heart-shaped substructure. The question arises why "homöopaatia" (*homeopathy*) is not a subcase of "loodusravi" (*naturopathy*). Secondly, are "mudaravi" (*mud cure*) and "homöopaatia" (*homeopathy*) subcases of "alternatiivmeditsiin" (*alternative medicine*) or of "ravimeetod" (*method of*

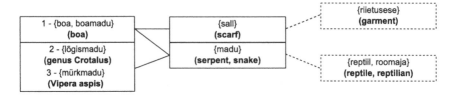

Fig. 10. A substructure via a synset member or a part of a compound word

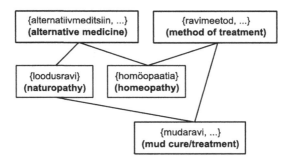

Fig. 11. Instance of a heart-shaped substructure

treatment)? On the basis of the definitions of these concepts, lexicographers decided that both are subcases of the method of treatment and that *alternative medicine* is connected to them via a *holonymy* relation.

5   Evaluation

We focused on two test patterns, namely the dense component (DC) and asymmetric ring topology with index zero (ART$_0$), i.e. with a redundant link as depicted in Figure 2. Since the test patterns overlap, correcting the instance of the dense components test pattern also affects other test pattern instances, as shown in Table 2. The test pattern system of the Estonian Wordnet Version 66 indicated that the number of multiple inheritance cases reduced from 1,677 to 1,164 in comparison to the Estonian Wordnet Version 67.

Table 2. The number of occurrences of test patterns

		EstWN (v66)	EstWN (v67)	PrWN (v3.1)
1	ART$_0$	119	79	41
2	ARTx	821	611	1,181
3	SRT	567	270	531
4	CS	21	11	9
5	DC	121	24	107
6	HSS	450	167	149
7	COM	932	406	366

In the process of using all test patterns to check the wordnets the lexicographer has to use the following typical actions:

- add a new synset
- merge synsets
- remove a synset
- add or remove lexical units from a synset
- change a semantic relation
- add or remove a semantic relation

These actions usually take place through the wordnet management system and will be repeated after every extensive change in the hierarchical structure of wordnet.

6   Conclusion

In this paper, we proposed the use of test patterns for detecting inconsistencies in the substructures of wordnet hierarchies. After specifying how these patterns relate to the types of inconsistencies, examples of real cases demonstrated test pattern applications. In the evaluation, we showed that test pattern application yields many reductions in inconsistencies in the substructures of wordnet hierarchies. Consequently, linguists and lexicographers have a set of heuristics available for locating inconsistencies faster.

Different test patterns, covering often same hierarchical structures (but in different perspective) help to check wordnet hierarchy in the multiple inheritance cases. It turns out, those different perspectives point to different type of inconsistencies intended to evaluate for lexicographer. Lexicographer evaluates the instances of test patterns and if it is needed, corrects the wordnet hierarchical substructure, which the test patterns are pointing. The test pattern system introduced here helps to detect at least five different kinds of inconsistencies: *regularity of multiple inheritance, ignoring the principle of economy, inappropriate semantic relation, wrongly inherited domain category, root synset on the wrong level.* In order to solve these problems, the lexicographer has to typically add, remove, or change the semantic relations or synsets.

After the first correction of wordnet hierarchical structure through test patterns, the same process may repeat.

As future work, we plan to investigate wordnets further to come closer to pattern-set completeness. Additionally, the currently conceptually specified patterns must be formalized. That way it would be possible to meaningfully automate the detection of patterns in wordnet substructures, which would also include a recommendation system for inconsistency detection.

References

1. Richens, T.: Anomalies in the WordNet verb hierarchy. In: Proceedings of the 22nd International Conference on Computational Linguistics, Manchster, UK, vol. 1, pp. 729–736 (2008)
2. Liu, Y., Yu, J., Wen, Z., Yu, S.: Two kinds of hypernymy faults in WordNet: the cases of ring and isolator. In: Proceedings of the Second Global WordNet Conference, Brno, CzechRepublic, pp. 347–351 (2004)

3. Levary, D., Eckmann, J.-P., Moses, E., Tlusty, T.: Loops and Self-Reference in the Construction of Dictionaries. Phys. Rev. X. 2(3), 031018-1–031018-10 (2012)
4. Smrž, P.: Quality Control and Checking for Wordnet Development: A Case Study of BalkaNet. Romanian Journal of Information Science and Technology 7, 1–9 (2004)
5. Orav, H., Kerner, K., Parm, S.: Snapshot of Estonian Wordnet. Keel ja Kirjandus, Estonia, pp. 96–106 (2011)
6. Navigli, R.: Semi-Automatic Extension of Large-Scale Linguistic Knowledge Bases. In: FLAIRS Conference, Florida, USA, pp. 548–553 (2005)
7. Beneventano, D., Bergamaschi, S., Sorrentino, S.: Extending WordNet with compound-nouns for semi-automatic annotation in data integration systems. In: International Conference on Natural Language Processing and Knowledge Engineering, pp. 1–8. IEEE, Dalian (2009)
8. Sagot, B., Fišer, D.: Extending wordnets by learning from multiple resources. In: LTC 2011: 5th Language and Technology Conference, Poznan, Poland, pp. 526–530 (2011)
9. Mihàltz, M., Sass, B., Indig, B.: What Do We Drink? Automatically Extending Hungarian WordNet With Selectional Preference Relations. In: Joint Symposium on Semantic Processing, pp. 105–109 (2013)
10. Fellbaum, C., WordNet, D.: An Electronic Lexical Database. The MIT Press, Cambridge (1998)
11. Ravin, Y., Leacock, C.: Polysemy: Theoretical and computational approaches. MIT Press (2000)
12. Apresjan, J.D.: Regularpolysemy. Linguistics 12(142), 5–32 (1974)
13. Langemets, M.: Nimisõna süstemaatiline polüseemia eesti keeles ja selle esitus eesti keelevaras. Eesti Keele Sihtasutus. Tallinn, Estonia (2010)
14. Freihat, A.A., Giunchiglia, F., Dutta, B.: Approaching Regular Polysemy in WordNet. In: The Fifth International Conference on Information, Process, and Knowledge Management, Nice, France, pp. 63–69 (2013)
15. Knuth, D.E.: The Art of Computer Programming, vol. 1. Addison-Wesley (2012)
16. Atserias, J., Climent, S., Moré, J., Rigau, G.: A proposal for a Shallow Ontologization of WordNet. In: Proceedings of the 21st Annual Meeting of the Sociedad Española para el Procesamiento del Lenguaje Natural, Granada, Spain, vol. 5, pp. 161–167 (2005)
17. Lohk, A., Võhandu, L.: Independent Interactive Testing of Interactive Relational Systems. In: Man-Machine Interactions, vol. 3, pp. 63–70. Springer International Publishing (2014)

Enhancing Spatial Datacube Exploitation: A Spatio-semantic Similarity Perspective

Saida Aissi[1], Mohamed Salah Gouider[1], Tarek Sboui[2], and Lamjed Bensaid[1]

[1] SOIE Laboratory, High Institute of Management, Tunisia
{saida.aissi,ms.gouider,lamjed.bensaid}@isg.rnu.tn
[2] ESSPCR (UR 11ES15) & CONTOS,
Faculty of Sciences, Department of Geology, Tunisia
Tarek.sboui@ulaval.ca

Abstract. Due to the enormous amount of data stored in spatial multidimensional databases (also called spatial datacubes) and the complexity of multidimensional structures, extracting interesting information by exploiting spatial data cubes becomes more and more difficult. Users might overlook what part of the cube contains the relevant information and what the next query should be. This could affect their exploitation of spatial datacubes.

In order to help users to better exploit their spatial datacubes, we propose to use a collaborative filtering recommendation approach. The approach is based on computing the similarity between the user's behaviors in term of their spatial MDX queries launched on the system.

This paper introduces a new similarity measure for comparing spatial MDX queries. The proposed measure could directly support the development of spatial personalization and recommendation approaches. The presented measure takes into account both the semantic similarity as well as the basic components of spatial similarity assessment models: the topology, the direction and the distance.

Keywords: Spatial datacube, semantic similarity, spatial similarity, recommendation, personalization.

1 Introduction

Spatial datacubes store generally important volume of historical information and multidimensional structures become increasingly complex to be explored easily. Extracting relevant information becomes costly and hard, and decision makers using SOLAP (Spatial online analytical processing) tools may get frustrated.

On the other hand, personalization and recommendation systems play a major role in reducing the effort of decision-makers to find the most relevant information. Personalization is a research topic that has been the subject of many works in the fields of Information Retrieval (Adomavicius and Tuzhilin, 2005) and Web Usage Mining (Srivastava et al, 2000). Personalization consists in adapting the system to the preferences, needs and goals of user analysis. In recent years, several studies have been

G. Dregvaite and R. Damasevicius (Eds.): ICIST 2014, CCIS 465, pp. 121–133, 2014.
© Springer International Publishing Switzerland 2014

conducted for personalizing OLAP systems (Garrigos et al., 2009; Glorio et al., 2012; Golfarelli et al., 2009; Biondi et al., 2011; Giacometti et al., 2009; Khemiri et al., 2012) and GIS (Aoidh et al., 2009; Bellatore et al., 2010; Wilson et al., 2010).

The notion of similarity has been considered as an important component for the development of personalization and recommendation systems (Wilson et al., 2010; Bellatore et al., 2010; Giacometti et al., 2009, 2011). Similarity measures are used to identify the degree of similarity between two entities. Collaborative filtering recommendation approaches are based on comparing the similarity of the recommended items (Giacometti et al., 2011). In the content- based filtering approaches, establishing similarity between user's profiles is an important step in the recommendation process. In GIS, similarity measures between trajectories, roads, map's layers or spatial objects is widely used to establish recommendation systems. For example, In OLAP systems, (Giacometti et al., 2009) establish similarity between user's sessions for the personalization of OLAP systems. (Yang et al., 2010) propose a similarity measure based on the spatial proximity and the semantic similarity for the personalization of spatial services. The similarity between the objects is well developed in the spatial similarity assessment models (Rodríguez et al., 2004; Holt et al., 1997; 1999; Goyal et al., 2000; Lee et al., 2006). Although SOLAP users have specific preferences, needs and goals, SOLAP personalization and recommendation is a search field not well developed. The only work proposing personalization of SOLAP systems is presented by (Glorio et al., 2010, 2012). It presents an adaptation of the datacube schema by integrating the required spatiality at the conceptual level.

To better support this process, we propose to assist the user during the datacube exploitation by recommending a relevant anticipated query adapted to his needs and preferences basing on a collaborative filtering approach. Collaborative filtering explores techniques for matching similarity between user's interests and making recommendations on this basis (Beel et al., 2013). The idea in this paper is to detect the similarity between the spatial datacube users through their lunched MDX queries and to exploit it to recommend to the current user a relevant MDX query.

To the best of our knowledge, there is no proposed similarity measure between spatial MDX queries and no developed recommendation approaches in the field of Spatial OLAP systems.

In this paper, we aim to present a key tool for the development of personalization and recommendation approaches in spatial datacubes by allowing implicit similarity assessment between user's preferences and needs through their posed MDX queries on SOLAP systems. SOLAP users interrogate spatial data cubes using MDX queries and handle both thematic and spatial data having specific characteristics such as topology and direction (Lee et al, 2006., Bruns and Egenhofer, 1996). Thus, in this paper we propose a spatio-semantic similarity measure between spatial MDX queries. The similarity measure takes into account the spatial similarity between spatial MDX queries as well as the semantic similarity. We (i) formalize an MDX query as a set of references (ii) propose a semantic similarity measure between MDX queries using a knowledge representation model (iii) develop a spatial similarity measure between

MDX queries composed of a topological similarity/distance, a metric similarity/distance and a directional similarity/distance (iv) implement the CoSIM system for MDX query similarity assessment and validate the proposal using the human evaluation technique.

The proposed similarity measure allows implicit detection of SOLAP user's preferences and needs according to the data stored in the spatial cube and supports the development of spatial personalization and recommendation approaches.

2   Basic Formal Definitions

In order to introduce and itemize the spatio-semantic similarity measure, we give, in this section the formal definitions of the basic concepts used in our proposal.

Cube, Schema and Dimensions
An N-dimensional Cube C is denoted $C = (D_1, D_2,..., D_n, F)$ where:

For each $i \in [1,n]$, D_i is a dimension table of schema Sch $(Di)=\{A_i^0,...,A_i^j\}$. For each dimension $i \in [1,n]$, A_i^j describes an attribute of the dimension D_i . A_i^0 represents the primary key of D_i. F is a fact table of the N-dimensional cube C.

We present in Figure 1 a multidimensional schema allowing the analysis of the crop (production). The constellation schema diagram is presented using the formalism of (Malinowski et al., 2004). It allows the analysis of the weight and the amount of the production according to the dimensions *zone*, *time* and *product*. It allows to answer queries such as: "what is the total production of biological products in 2014 produced in Norths regions?", "what is the total production of high quality products in the suds regions in 2014"?

Query References
Given a cube *C* and an MDX query *qc* over *C*. We define the set of the references corresponding to an MDX query as follows: $Rqc=\{R_1,...,R_n, M_1,...,M_N\}$ where:

$\{R_1,...,R_n\}$: is the set of dimension members *Di* adduced in the MDX query. It represents the set of members of the dimension *Di* that is adduced from the SELECT and WHERE clause.

$\{M_1,...,M_N\}$: is the set of measures used in the MDX query.

Example: Given the following MDX queries:
q1: SELECT {[Product]. [All Products]. [nonbiological]} ON COLUMNS, FROM [Production] WHERE {[Measures]. [Weight]} AND {[Region]. [All R gion]. [Region1]. [Zone1]

The references of the query q1 are Rq1= {nonbiological, Zone 1, weight}q2: SELECT {[Product]. [All Products]. [biological]} ON COLUMNS,

FROM [Production] WHERE {[Measures]. [amount]} AND {[Region]. [All Region]. [Region1]. [Zone 2].[Zone 3]}

The references of the query q2 are Rq2: {biological, Zone 2, Zone 3, amount).

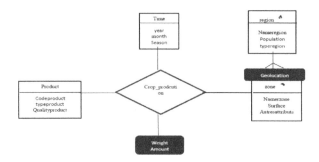

Fig. 1. A constellation schema for the analysis of the crop production

3   Semantic Similarity Measure for Comparing MDX Queries

To compute the semantic distance between two spatial MDX queries, we propose to compute the semantic distance between the different references of each query. Several similarity measures between concepts are proposed in the literature. The similarity measures are based on knowledge representation model offered by ontologies and semantic networks (Rezgui et al., 2013).The concepts is our proposal are representd by the query references.To compute the semantic distance between references of each query we use an edge counting method by applying the Rada distance (Rada et al., 1989) using an application ontology representing the differents concepts of the multi-dimensional database model (dimensions, measures and attributes).The Rada distance computes the minimum number of edges which separate the query references in the ontology. We opted for the Rada distance because it is simple, accurate and efficient (Rada et al, 1989).

Definition: Given $q1, q2$: Two spatial MDX queries, where :

$R_1 = \{R_1^1, R_1^2 \ldots R_1^i, R_1^n, M_1^1 \ldots M_1^p, \ldots M^m_1\}$: the set of references of the query q1; $1 \leq i \leq n$ and $1 \leq p \leq m$

$R_2 = \{R_2^1, R_2^2, R_2^j \ldots R_2^n, M_2^1, M_2^k, \ldots M_2^h\}$: the set of references of the query q2; $1 \leq j \leq n$ and $1 \leq k \leq h.i,j,p,k,m,n,h$ *are positive integers*

Let $A = (dr_{ij})_{1 \leq i \leq n, \ 1 \leq j \leq n}$: Denote the matrix of the semantic distances between the references R_1^i $(1 \leq i \leq n)$ of the query $q1$ and the references $R_2^j (1 \leq j \leq n)$ of the query q2; $1 \leq i \leq n$ and $1 \leq j \leq n$; dr_{ij}: The distance between the reference R_1^i of the query $q1$ and the reference R_2^j of the query q2 using the Rada distance basing on the knowledge representation model offered by the application ontology.

Let $B = (dm_{pk})_{1 \leq p \leq m, \ 1 \leq k \leq h}$: Denote the matrix of the semantic distances between the references M_1^P $(1 \leq p \leq m)$ of the query q1 and the references M_2^k $(1 \leq k \leq h)$ of the query q2 (in term of measure); $1 \leq p \leq m$ and $1 \leq k \leq h$; dm_{pk} : The distance between the reference M_1^P of the query $q1$ and the reference M_2^k of the query q2 using the Rada distance basing on the knowledgerepresentation model offered by the application ontology.

The semantic distance between the query *q1* and the query *q2* denoted *Dsem* *(q1, q2)* is obtained as follows:

$$Dsem\ (q1, q2) = \sum_{i=1}^{n}\sum_{j=1}^{n} drij + \sum_{p=1}^{m}\sum_{k=1}^{h} dmpk \ ; \ 1 \leq i, j \leq n, \ 1 \leq p \leq m \text{ and } 1 \leq k \leq h \qquad (1)$$

The semantic similarity measure is derived from the semantic distance as follows:

$$Sim_{sem}(q1, q2) = 1 \ / \ (1 + Dsem\ (q1, q2)) \qquad (2)$$

4   A Spatial Similarity Measure for Comparing Spatial MDX Queries

Spatial similarity assessment is hard to address because of the complexity of spatial properties and relations. Since it is believed that spatial relations, mainly topology, direction and distance, capture the essence of spatial similarity assessment (Li et al., 2006; Bruns and Egenhofer, 1996). Thus, in order to measure the spatial distance between two spatial queries, we can measure the topological distance, the metric distance and the directional distance between the spatial objects adduced in each query.

4.1   Distance between Spatial MDX Queries in Term of the Spatial Direction

To compute the distance between two spatial MDX queries in term of the orientation, we propose to measure the distance between the orientations of the spatial objects adduced in the queries. In the literature, nine types of directions are used namely: {north, northwest, west, southwest, south, southeast, east, northeast, and equality}. The cost of converting a direction into a close direction is equal to 2 (Li et al., 2006). The following diagram shows the conceptual neighborhood and the cost of moving from one direction to another.

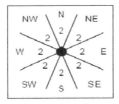

Fig. 2. Graph of spatial directions and the costs of transformation (Li et al, 2006)

Definition: Given two spatial MDX queries q1 and q2,

$OB_{q1} = (ob_1^1, ob_1^2, ..., ob_1^i)$ where $ob_1^1, ob_1^2, ..., ob_1^i$: the spatial references adduced in the spatial query q1

$OB_{q2}=(ob_2^1, ob_2^2, ..., ob_2^j)$ where $ob_2^1, ob_2^2, ..., ob_2^j$: the spatial references adduced in the spatial query q2

Let B=aij: Denote the matrix used to measure the distance in term of the direction between the spatial objects of the query q1 and the spatial objects of the query q2, *$1 \leq i \leq n, 1 \leq j \leq m$ and aij:* the direction distance between the object i in the query q1 and the object j of the query q2 ; *aij= MCT* (ob_1^i, ob_2^j): presents the minimum cost of transformation of the orientation of an object *i* in the spatial query q1 to the orientation of an object *j* in the spatial query *q2*.

The distance in term of the direction between the query q1 and the query q2 denoted $D_{dir}(q1, q2)$ is computed as follows:

$$D_{dir}(q1, q2) = \sum_{i=1}^{n}\sum_{j=1}^{m}a_{ij} \; ; \; 1 \leq i \leq n \text{ and } 1 \leq j \leq m \tag{3}$$

Example: *Given the following queries q1 and q2*

q1: SELECT {[Product]. [All Products]. [nonbiological]} ON COLUMNS,
    FROM [Production]WHERE {[Measures]. [Weight]} AND {[Region]. [All Region]. [Region1]. [Zone1]
        The spatial references of the query q1 are OBq1= {Zone 1}

q2: SELECT {[Product]. [All Products]. [biological]} ON COLUMNS,
    FROM [Production] WHERE {[Measures]. [Weight]} AND {[[Region]. [All Region]. [Region1]. [Zone 2].[Zone 3]}
        The spatial references of the query q2 are OBq2: {Zone 2, Zone 3}

For example, we have the zone 1 exists in the north, the zone 2 in the northwest and the zone 3 in the South. Computing the directional distance between the query q1 and the query q2 refers to computing the directional distance between the couple of spatial references of each query.
    Ddir (q1, q2)= Ddir (zone1,zone2)+ Ddir (zone1, zone3)= Ddir (north, northwest)+ Ddir (north, south)=2+6=8.

4.2   Distance between Spatial MDX Queries in Term of the Metric Distance

To compute the metric distance between a pair of queries, we propose to measure the metric distance between spatial objects adduced by each query. For this purpose, we propose to use the traditional model composed by four possible situations for the distances (equal, near, medium and far). The cost of transition from one situation to another is equal to 1. Figure 3 shows the various possible situations and the cost of transition from one situation to another (Li et al, 2006).

Definition: Given two MDX queries *q1 and q2*

$OB_{q1} = (ob_1^1, ob_1^2, ..., ob_1^i)$ where $ob_1^1, ob_1^2, ..., ob_1^i$: the spatial objects adduced in the query *q1*;

$OB_{q2} = (ob_2^1, ob_2^2, ..., ob_2^j)$ where $ob_2^1, ob_2^2, ..., ob_2^j$: the spatial objects adduced in the query

Let B=aij: Denote the matrix used to measure the metric distance between the spatial objects of the query q1 and the spatial objects of the query *q2, 1≤i≤n, 1≤j≤m and aij:* the metric distance between the object i in the query q1 and the object j of the query q2.

The metric distance between the query *q1* and the query *q2* denoted D_{met} (*q1*, *q2*) is computed as follows:

$$D_{met}(q1, q2) = \sum_{i=1}^{n} \sum_{j=1}^{m} a_{ij} \quad ; 1 \leq i \leq n \text{ and } 1 \leq j \leq m \qquad (4)$$

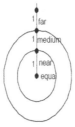

Fig. 3. The metric distance network (Li et al, 2006)

Example: *Given the previous queries q1 and q2 (Section 4). The spatial references of the query q1 are OBq1= {Zone 1}. The spatial references of the query q2 are OBq2: {Zone 2, Zone 3}.If we have the distance between zone 1 and zone 2 is far and the distance between zone 1 and zone 3 is near. Computing the metric distance between the query q1 and the query q2 refers to computing the metric distance between the couple of spatial references of each query.*

Dmet (q1, q2)= Dm (zone1,zone2)+ Dm (zone1, zone3)= 3+1=4.

4.3   Topological Distance between Spatial MDX Queries

Computing the topological similarity between two queries depends on computing the topological distance between the pairs of spatial reference of each query. To compute the topological distance between spatial references, we propose to use the conceptual neighborhood graph proposed by (Bruns and Egenhofer,1996).

As an extension to the conceptual neighborhood (Bruns and Egenhofer,1996), (Li et al., 2006) propose in the TDD model for spatial similarity assessment to decompose the conceptual neighborhood graph into three groups of topological relationships.

As such, the distance between two arcs in the same group (intra-group) is 2. However, the distance between two arcs belonging to two different groups is equal to 3. Except for the distance between the two nodes (meet and overlap) where the transformation cost is equal to 1. Figure 4 presents the conceptual neighborhood network and the cost of transformation of the topological relationships as presented in the TDD model (Li et al., 2006).

Definition: Given two MDX queries $q1$ and q.

$OB_{SS1} = (ob_1^1, ob_1^2, ..., ob_1^i)$ where $ob_1^1, ob_1^2, ..., ob_1^i$: the spatial objects adduced in the query q,

$OB_{SS2} = (ob_2^1, ob_2^2, ..., ob_2^j)$ where $ob_2^1, ob_2^2, ..., ob_2^j$: the spatial objects adduced in the query $q2$

Let A=aij: Denote the matrix used to measure the topological distance between the spatial objects of the query q1 and the spatial objects of the query q2, $1 \leq i \leq n$, $1 \leq j \leq m$ and *aij:* the topological distance between the object i in the query q1 and the object j of the query q2.

The topological distance between the query $q1$ and the query $q2$ denoted D_{topo} $(q1, q2)$ is computed as follows:

$$D_{topo}(q1, q2) = \sum_{i=1}^{n} \sum_{j=1}^{m} a_{ij} \; ; \; 1 \leq i \leq n \text{ and } 1 \leq j \leq m \tag{5}$$

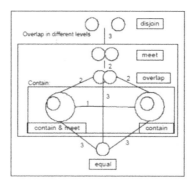

Fig. 4. Conceptual neighborhood network and topological relationships (Li et al, 2006)

Example: *Given two queries q1 and q2 (Section 4). The spatial references of the query q1 are OBq1 = {Zone 1}. The spatial references of the query q2 are OBq2: {Zone 2, Zone 3}. For example, we have zone 1 and zone 2 are disjoin and zone 1 contains Zone 3. The topological distance between q1 and q2 is computed as follows: Dtopo (q1, q2)= Dtopo (disjoin, contain)= 7.*

4.4   The Spatial Distance between MDX Queries

The spatial distance between queries varies proportionally to the topological distance, the orientation distance and the metric distance (Li et al, 2006., Bruns and Egenhofer,1996). Computing the spatial distance between two queries is derived from the topological, directional and metric distance between couple of references of each query. The spatial distance between two query is computed as follows:

Definition:
Given q1, q2: two MDX queries. The spatial distance between q1 and q2 is computed as follows:

$$D_{Spatial}(q1, q2) = D_{topo}(q1, q2) + D_{dir}(q1, q2) + D_{met}(q1, q2) \tag{6}$$

Where:
$D_{topo}(q1, q2)$*:the topological distance between q1 and q2.*
$D_{dir}(q1, q2)$**:** *the distance in term of orientation between q1 and q2.*
$D_{met}(q1, q2)$: *the metric distance between q1 and q2.*

4.5   A Spatial Similarity Measure between MDX Queries

The similarity is inversely proportional to the distance, the higher is the distance, the lower is the similarity and vice versa. Thus, we define the spatial similarity based on the spatial distance between queries as follows:

Given two spatial MDX queries q1 and q2. The spatial similarity between q1 and q2 denoted $Sim_{spatial}(q1, q2)$ is computed as follows:*q2*

$$Sim_{spatial}(q1, q2) = 1/ (1 + D_{spatial}(q1, q2)) \tag{7}$$

5   A Spatio-semantic Similarity Measure between MDX Queries

The spatio-semantic distance between two queries represents the degree of spatial similarity and semantic relatedness between them. In assessing similarity between spatial MDX queries we take into account both the spatial and semantic apect .Thus, The spatio-semantic distance between two queries is derived from the spatial and semantic distance as follows:

Definition: Given q1 and q2 two MDX queries, $D_{Sem}(q1, q2)$ and $D_{Spatial}(q1, q2)$ denote respectively the semantic distance and the spatial distance between the queries q1 and q2. The spatio-semantic distance and similarity between q1 and q2, denoted resepectively $D_{SPS}(q1, q2)$ *and* $S_{SPS}(q1, q2)$,are computed as follows :

$$D_{SPS}(q1, q2) = (D_{Sem}(q1, q2) + D_{Spatial}(q1, q2))/2 \tag{8}$$

$$S_{SPS}(q1, q2) = 1 / (1 + D_{SPS}(q1, q2)) \tag{9}$$

6   Performance Evaluations

In the experimental evaluation, we developed the CoSIM (Compute SIMilarity) system using Java language. CoSIM system implements our proposal of the spatio-semantic similarity measure. It identifies the references of a given MDX query and computes the semantic measure/distance, the spatial distance/measure and the spatio-semantic similarity measure/distance between two MDX queries according to the crop production spatial datacube (Figure 1). An example of a spatio-semantic similarity measure/distance computed between two MDX queries using CoSIM is presented in figure 5.

In order to evaluate the performance of our proposed similarity measure, we used the method of the human evaluation based on the Spearman's correlation coefficient (Spearman, 1904). The Spearman's correlation coefficient is widely used to assess the degree of the closeness of the rankings of a set of data. The value of the Spearman's correlation coefficient ranges from 1 to -1. A value of 1 indicates exactly identical rankings, a value of -1 indicates opposite rankings and a value of 0 indicates that there is no correlation between the rankings. The other values of the coefficient indicate the existence of intermediate levels of correlation.

In the evaluation process, we proposed 30 pairs of spatial MDX queries that have different degrees of spatio-semantic relatedness as assigned by the proposed similarity measure and we asked 15 human subjects to assign the degrees of similarity between the different pairs. We chose 10 pairs having a high degree of relatedness according to our similarity measure, 10 pairs having a weak degree of similarity and 10 pairs having an intermediate degree of similarity. The MDX queries are generated using an MDX queries generator that we developed in Java. The MDX queries are generated from the crop production database (Figure 1) that we developped using the database management system MySQL.

In order to evaluate the semantic similarity between the MDX queries, we define an ontology regrouping the different concepts of the multidimensional schema (attributes, dimensions, measures and instances). These concepts could be invoked in the MDX query launched by the user. For experimental purpose, we developed an application ontology related to the production schema presented in section 2. The ontology regroups and presents the different concepts included in the multidimensional schema for crop production. Figure 5 presents the developed ontology.

The experimental evaluation gave us a Spearman's correlation coefficient equal to 0,82. The obtained value of the Spearman's correlation presents a high degree of positive correlation between the similarity values, accorded to the evaluated queries, using the human evaluation and the similarity values obtained through our proposal. The obtained correlation coefficient proves the efficiency of the proposed measure.

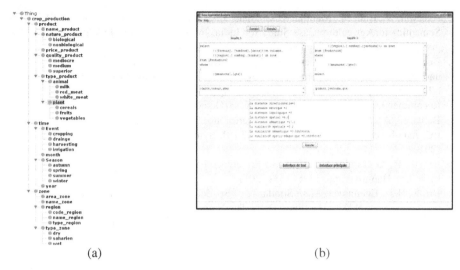

(a)   (b)

Fig. 5. (a) An agricultural crop production ontology and (b) CoSIM system

7   Conclusion

The research presented in this paper focuses on the role of the spatial and the semantic similarity in the development of SOLAP recommendation techniques. The contribution of the paper can be summarized as follows. First, It proposes a user centric spatio-semantic similarity measure between spatial MDX queries in the context of SOLAP manipulations. The spatial similarity measure integrates both the semantic aspect as well as the spatial aspect of the similarity. The spatial similarity addresses the basic spatial similarity component defined in the literature: (1) the spatial proximity (2) the distance in term of the orientation between the spatial objects and (3) the directional distance between the spatial MDX queries. To the best of our knowledge, our proposal is the first work proposing a similarity measure between spatial MDX queries for spatial personalization. Second, experimental evaluations are presented and validate the efficiency of our work. This proposal offers several research perspectives. First, we plan to integrate other comparison factors in our similarity measure as the spatial distribution and the comparison between the geometric attributes of the spatial objects. Second, the presented similarity measure will be used for the development of a collaborative filtering approach for the recommendation of spatial personalized MDX queries.

References

1. Adomavicius, G., Tuzhilin, A.: Toward the next generation of recommender systems: A survey of the state-of-the-art and possible extensions. IEEE Trans. Knowl. Data Eng. 17(6), 734–749 (2005)
2. Aoidh, E.M., McArdle, E., Petit, M., Ray, C., Bertolotto, M., Claramunt, C., Wilson, D.C.: Personalization in adaptive and interactive GIS. Annals of GIS 15(1), 23–33 (2009)

3. Agarwal, N., Rao, M., Mantha, S., Gokhale, J.A.: Annotation of Geospatial Data Based on Semantics forAgriculture:Case Study for India. In: 3rd International Conference onComputer Research and Development (ICCRD), pp. 139–142 (2011)

4. Beel, J., Langer, S., Genzmehr, M., Gipp, B.: Research Paper Recommender System Evaluation: A Quantitative Literature Survey. In: Proceedings of the Workshop on Reproducibility and Replication in Recommender Systems Evaluation (RepSys) at the ACM Recommender System Conference (RecSys) (October 2013)

5. Bellatore, A., McArdle, G., Kelly, C., Bertolotto, M.: RecoMap: An interactive and adaptive map-based recommender. In: SAC 2010: Symposium on Applied Computing. ACM (2010)

6. Biondi, P., Golfarelli, M., Rizzi, S.: Preference-based datacube analysis with MYOLAP. In: ICDE, Hannover, pp. 1328–1331 (2011)

7. Bruns, H.T., Egenhover, M.J.: Similarity of Spatial Scenes. In: Seventh International Symposium on Spatial Data Handling, Delft, The Netherlands, pp. 4A.31–4A.42 (1996)

8. Jerbi, H., Pujolle, G., Ravat, F., Teste, O.: Recommandation de requêtes dans les bases de données multidimensionnelles annotées. Ingénierie des Systèmes d'Information 16(1), 113–138 (2011)

9. Garrigós, I., Pardillo, J., Mazón, J.-N., Trujillo, J.: A Conceptual Modeling Approach for OLAP Personalization. In: Laender, A.H.F., Castano, S., Dayal, U., Casati, F., de Oliveira, J.P.M. (eds.) ER 2009. LNCS, vol. 5829, pp. 401–414. Springer, Heidelberg (2009)

10. Giacometti, A., Marcel, P., Negre, E.: Recommending Multidimensional Queries. In: Pedersen, T.B., Mohania, M.K., Tjoa, A.M. (eds.) DaWaK 2009. LNCS, vol. 5691, pp. 453–466. Springer, Heidelberg (2009)

11. Giacometti, A., Marcel, P., Negre, E., Soulet, A.: Query Recommendations for OLAP Discovery-Driven Analysis. In: IJDWM, pp. 1–25 (2011)

12. Glorio, O., Mazón, J., Garrigós, I., Trujillo, J.: Using web-based personalization on spatial data warehouses. In: EDBT/ICDT Workshop, Lausanne (2010)

13. Glorio, O., Mazón, J., Garrigós, I., Trujillo, J.: A personalization process for spatial data warehouse development. Decision Support Systems 52, 884–898 (2012)

14. Golfarelli, M., Rizzi, S.: Expressing OLAP Preferences. In: SSDBM, Louisiana, pp. 83–91 (2009)

15. Holt, A.: Spatial Similarity and Gis: The Grouping of Spatial Kinds. In: The 11th Annual Colloquium of the Spatial Information Research Centre (1999)

16. Holt, A., Benwell, G.L.: Using Spatial Similarity for Exploratory Spatial Data Analysis: Some Directions. In: Proceedings of the 2rd International Conference on GeoComputation, University of Otago, New Zealand (1997)

17. Khemiri, R., Bentayeb, F.: Interactive Query Recommendation Assistant. In: DEXA Workshops (2012)

18. Li, B., Fonseca, F.T.: TDD - A Comprehensive Model for Qualitative Spatial SimilarityAssessment. Spatial Cognition and Computation 6, 31–62 (2006)

19. Rada, A., Mili, A.H., Bicknell, E., Bletterner, C.: Development and application of a metric on semantic nets. IEEE Transactions on Systems, Man and Cybernetics 19(1), 17–30 (1989)

20. Rezgui, K., Mhiri, H., Ghédira, K.: Theoretical Formulas of Semantic Measure: A Survey. Journal OfEnerging Technologie. In: Web Intelligence 5(4) (November 2013)

21. Rodríguez, A., Egenhofer, M.: Determining Semantic Similarity among Entity Classes from Different Ontologies. IEEE Transactions on Knowledge and Data Engineering 15, 442–456 (2003)

22. Spearman, C.: The proof and measurement of association between two things. The American Journal of Psychology 15(1), 72–101 (1904)
23. Srivastava, J., Cooley, R., Deshpande, M., Tan, P.-N.: Web usage mining: Discoveryand applications of usage patterns from web data. SIGKDD Explorations 1(2), 12–23 (2000)
24. Wilson, D.C., Bertolotto, M., Weakliam, J.: Personalizing map content to improve task completion efficiency. International Journal of Geographical Information Science 24(5), 741–760 (2010)

A Semi-supervised Learning Framework
for Decision Modeling of Software Project Management

Ali Tizkar Sadabadi[*]

Department of Software Engineering, Advanced Informatics School,
Universiti Teknologi Malaysia, Kuala Lumpur, 54100, Malaysia
al_tz2@yahoo.com

Abstract. Managing the decisions in organizations raises substantial challenges in regards of the associated processes. In software project management decision making has the critical role in this scenario since it defines the manager's responsibilities and stems from the various sources linked to the process. The decision making constructs the essential foundation and thereby it needs a reliable framework for modeling of the decision structure. In this paper a conceptual multi-method simulation based framework will be introduced in a modality to cover multiple levels of the decision structure over software project management process. The framework is base on a model in which is inspired by a semi-supervised learning technique known as partially observable Markov decision process (POMDP). The methods used are integrated towards a multi-method simulation model whereas each of these methods exclusively realizes distinct aspect of software project management. The framework evolves the manner of decision making by a paradigm which establishes the foundation for a tactical level understanding and decision support for practitioners. At the results section an optimal decision policy for the framework will be presented.

Keywords: *Index Terms*—software project management, decision modeling, semi-supervised learning, multi-method simulation technique, partially observable Markov decision process, discrete event simulation, system dynamics.

1   Introduction

Software project management (SPM) is basically defined by the ability of decision making. It is the responsibility of managers to design this process and optimize it to minimize costs and maximize production. Decision makings are based on resources and constraints which are planned for the target project and the plan could change hardly in line with new requirements during project progress. But what could be done accordingly to confront changes which are contingent in every project, is to define an optimal plan with effective decisions.

Decision making is a cognitive process resulting in the selection of a course of action among several alternative scenarios. This process finally leads the decision maker to take an action or make a choice [3]. Thereby it is an ability based on experience

---

[*] Corresponding author.

G. Dregvaite and R. Damasevicius (Eds.): ICIST 2014, CCIS 465, pp. 134–149, 2014.
© Springer International Publishing Switzerland 2014

and knowledge that enables a leader of a process to succeed. The nature of software projects on the other side add other complexity in which development process has intangibility that makes it difficult for managers to design a suitable strategy for decision making.

SPM requires special mindset to make practitioners be able to conduct management process in an effective and efficient manner. These mindsets are from any point of view considered as a high level experience and management capabilities, since it originates from a complex process and organizational understanding [4]. Therefore Management of this knowledge requires special strategies for an effective knowledge management.

It is evident that an effective approach for modeling the decision making process and redefining the decision structure over SPM is necessary. This model should be able to deal with high level of intangibility and continuous change requests within the software project.

In this paper a framework which constructs the basis for modeling of decision making process over SPM will be introduced. This framework incorporates knowledge management discipline and simulation methods as well as the methodology that is supported by SPM discipline. In the framework new concepts will be introduced and the possibility of distinct levels of view over SPM would be realized.

2   Related Literature

DSS (Decision support systems) are generally implemented as expert systems to SPM process. The frameworks have been introduced in the literature of Software Project Management Decision Support (SPMDS). With study in the respective literature, it is stated the improvement of decision making by implementation of expert systems in SPM as follow. Cho [5] developed An exploratory project expert system to overcome the uncertainties of the project management and the surrounding environment. Then he stated that, it is worth trying to develop an estimation technique to learn from the past experience. Sadabadi [6] mentioned the possibility of developing a certain framework with implementation of simulation technique and expert systems to realize a game-based environment for software development process. Donzelli [7] presented a hybrid process modeling technique whereas to provide both qualitative and quantitative suggestions for SPM. His technique bridges the gap between the manager and the modeler by reusing the knowledge available in the organization. Neap and Celik [8] present COMVOB, a knowledge based system for determination of marginal value of building project management. They stated that the dicision made by managers are traditionally during thee stages of buiding projects while value of their decision and their effects are important for successful projects. Olteanu [9] develops a decision support system tailored for Romanian biodesiel industry that system optimizes the main activities of the biodiesel value chain and supports the decision making process at management level. In addition the DSS enables the user to perform sensitivity analysis based on varying various input parameters. Janczura and Golinska [10] privided a computer application based on expert systems that helps software developer to choose appropriate model with the possublity of learning from this application along with participation in development process. Plaza and Turetken [11] aimed to improve the body of knowledge on estimating project durations. Projects that are impacted by learning and knowledge transfers in the early phases prove to be very difficult to control with linear control methods. As stated by Antony and Santhanam [12] with supporting decision-making ability, the use of knowledge-base systems could implicitly improve the learning process as a stimulus. Olteanu [9] addresses the necessity of implementation of DSS in project management to identify all opportunities for improvement of decision value and lowering the production cost. Janczura and Golinska [10] defines the DSS implementation as an appropriate criteria for choosing a model for software development life cycle. At the end the author mentions that selecting an appropriate software development life cycle model is a complex and a challenging task, which requires not only broad theoretical knowledge, but also consultation with experienced expert managers. Therefore, the computer application presented should be perceived as the first step towards building a system that could be applied in practice. Besir and Birant [13] stated the DSS use in SPM could avoid the possible erroneous results and help the companies to perform the managing and planning functions easier. As Yang and Wang [14] acclaimed, Project management is an experience-driven and knowledge-centralized activity. Therefore, project managers require some assistance to reduce the uncertainty at the early stage of constructing project plans. Authors applied cased–based reasoning technique for formulating the project requirements.

Other scholars have implemented simulation technique as a method for modeling software engineering process. That is significant to mention there are two types of efforts in the literature focused on SPM modeling. Bolin et al [15], Fang and Marle [1], Huang, Lin and Hsu [16], Navarro [17] and Mittermeir et al [18] named software development process learning improvement (SDPLI) but implicitly they have tried to digest topics of SPM. Also Bollin, Hochmuller and Mittermeir [19], Gao and Xie [20], Salas, Wildman and Piccolo [21], Nembhard, YIP and Shtub [22] and Rodríguez et al [23] that explicitly addressed and focused on SPM experience acquisition solution. As noticed in the literature of SDPLI, approaches for improvement of learning scheme for software development process mainly paid attention to provide a set of facilities from models to applications to support learning process of SPM.

The summary of existing works with implementation of simulation and DSS in regards to SPM knowledge acquisition is shown in table 1. Thereby the legends on table 1 are described as follow:

Based on the level of understanding over SPM process as E-D: explicit direct view, O: operational, M: managerial, T: tactical, S: strategic and the concepts that are in this paper introduced based on decision support paradigm as DS: decision support, In-P: in-process decision support, Off-P: off-process decision support, N: not considered, Y: considered, P: partially considered. A brief explanation for the levels of view, according to Targowski [24] categorization of organizational and managerial understanding (tacit knowledge) basic, whole, global and universal mind. In this paper they are specified as (1) operational, (2) managerial, (3) tactical and (4) strategic levels. Accordingly in this paper two terms are specified as: The "in-process decision support" which resolves short-term and real-time decision issues and is assumed on the tactical level over SPM process. The "off-process decision support" resolves long-term and past decision issues and is assumed on managerial level over SPM process. Also in the discipline coverage column in table 1, SPMDS stands for software project management decision support and SPMLI for software project management learning improvement.

Table 1. Characteristics of existing works with implementation of simulation and DSS in SDPEI

Name	Reference	Discipline Coverage	Explicit E-D	Tacit O	M	T	S	DS In-P	Off-P
AMEISE	Bollin et al., 2011	SPMDS	Y	Y	Y	N	Y	Y	N
PMA	Dufner et al., 1999	SPMDS	Y	N	Y	N	N	N	Y
DSS for SR ESS	Rus and Collofello, 1999	SPMDS	P	Y	Y	N	Y	Y	Y
DSS for SPM	Donzelli, 2006	SPMDS	N	N	P	N	N	N	Y
SRNMDSPRM	Fang and Marle 2012	SPMDS	Y	Y	P	N	N	N	Y
EPECCS	Cho 2006	SPMDS	N	Y	P	N	N	N	P
AKBS	Antony and Santhanam, 2007	SPMDS	P	N	P	N	N	N	P
SimSE	Navarro, 2006	SPMLI	Y	Y	N	N	P	N	N
SESAM	Drappa and Ludewig,	SPMLI	Y	Y	N	N	P	N	N
OSS	Sharp and Hall, 2000	SPMLI	Y	P	N	N	N	N	N
PMT	Davidovitch et al.,	SPMLI	Y	Y	N	N	N	N	N

3   Framework Formation

3.1   Simulation Model

Simulation model is accountable to provide a basis for animation of SPM process. This operability is conducted through the implementation of multi-method simulation technique. The simulation techniques which are applied to this framework are discrete event simulation (DES), system dynamics (SD) and partially observable Markov decision process (POMDP). Therefore these methods will be used to model exhaustive simulation logic and engine.

Discrete Event System Specification (DEVS) [25] atomic formalism allows to develop a DES based system. An atomic DEVS model is defined as a 7-tuple: $M = < X, Y, S, ta, \delta ext, \delta int, \lambda >$.

Accordingly simulation model specification according to atomic DEVS would be:
Set of input events $X = \{useraction\}$
Set of output events
$Y = \{message, endofphase, startsimulation, endsimulation\}$
Set of sequential states

$$S = \left\{ (d, a) \mid d \in \left\{ \begin{array}{l} start, phase1, phase2, \\ phase3, phase4, end \end{array} \right\}, \\ a \in ((0, lenghtofphase] \cap T\infty) \right\}$$

Where phase1,…, phase4 are software development life cycle phases considered, $T\infty = [0,\infty]$,

$$\text{lenghtofphase} = \begin{Bmatrix} \text{lenghtofphase1, lenghtofphase2,} \\ \text{lenghtofphase3, lenghtofphase4} \end{Bmatrix}$$

is the elapsed time during the phase. This variable is dependent on predetermined value of scheduled time for the phase (based on input variables before the start of simulation) and decisions the performer of simulation will make during progress of the phase. In this simulation it is supposed that "lenghtofphase" never will be zero. For a, the reason we accounted zero for the range (in $T\infty$ range) is just because of {start, end } states that their lifespan are considered$\approx \varepsilon$.

c= the time value of loading simulation, d= the time value of ending simulation and showing results as stated: $c = d = \varepsilon$.

Initial state $S_0 = \{\text{start}, c\}$

Time advance function ta(s) = a for all s $\in$ S

External transition function

$\delta\text{ext} = \{((\text{phase1}, T\infty), (\text{phase2}, T\infty), (\text{phase3}, T\infty), (\text{phase4}, T\infty), (\text{end}, d))\}$

Internal transition function

$$\delta\text{int} = \left\{ \left(\begin{matrix} (\text{start}, c), (\text{phase1}, \text{lenghtofphase1}), (\text{phase2}, \text{lenghtofphase2}), \\ (\text{phase3}, \text{lenghtofphase3}), (\text{phase4}, \text{lenghtofphase4}), (\text{end}, d) \end{matrix} \right) \right\}$$

Output function

$\lambda = \{(\text{startsimulation}, \text{message}, \text{endofphase}, \text{endsimulation})\}$

SD is an approach to understanding the behavior of complex systems over time. It deals with internal feedback loops and time delays that affect the behavior of the entire system [26]. There mainly two topics in SD: (a) Causal loop diagrams, is a simple map of a system with all its constituent components and their interactions. By capturing interactions and consequently the feedback loops, a causal loop diagram reveals the structure of a system. By understanding the structure of a system, it becomes possible to ascertain system's behavior over a certain time period. (b) Stock and flow diagrams, to perform a more detailed quantitative analysis, a causal loop diagram is transformed to a stock and flow diagram. The graphical presentation of the SD model designed for this study is illustrated in fig 1. This design is developed based on Vensim version 6 application.

A POMDP models an agent decision process in a Markov Decision Process, but the agent cannot directly observe the underlying state. Instead, it must maintain a probability distribution over the set of possible states, based on a set of observations and observation probabilities, and the underlying Markov Decision Process [27]. An exact solution to a POMDP yields the optimal action for each possible belief over the world states. The optimal action maximizes the expected reward of the agent over a possibly infinite horizon. Briefly a POMDP consists of 6 elements plus the belief state condition; set of states, actions, observations, state conditional transition probability function, conditional observation probability function and reward function. The specification of POMDO model for this study would be described in section 4.

Simulation Methods and Their Correspondence to the Level of Views. Each method projects specific level of perspective over simulation process. They operate at different level of abstraction and comprises of distinct elements. DES is the basis for constructing the simulation operability which is the SPM process. SD which entails the highest level of simulation abstraction that provides strategic view from the system behavior. Yet the multi-method simulation approach is not coherent and there is a gap between these two levels. POMDP fills out this gap and provides tactical view level of process. This level is as much significant as, on one side to coordinate the two different techniques of DES and DS and on the other side to adapt the continuous technique, of SD with the discrete one, of DES. The simulation methods and their correspondence to level of operation from each distinct perspective are illustrated in fig 2.

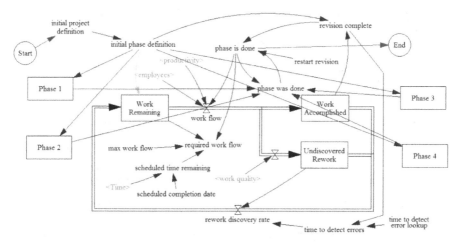

Fig. 1. SD model designed for the framework

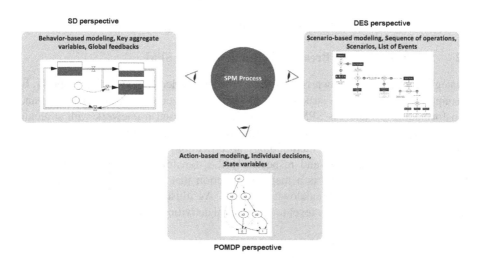

Fig. 2. Process perspectives of each simulation method

Simulation Engine. Simulation engine is formed by interrelated operability of DES and SD. The simulation engine is responsible to provide the basis for dynamism of simulation events. DES is adequately rich to develop simulation system, but on the other hand the lack of high-level abstract view of simulated environment makes it insufficient to bring in the critical characteristics of SPM. For this reason SD complements the operability of DES that allows the simulation system to be a strategic planning-decision-making platform for SPM process. Fig 3 illustrates the elements of multi-method simulation engine.

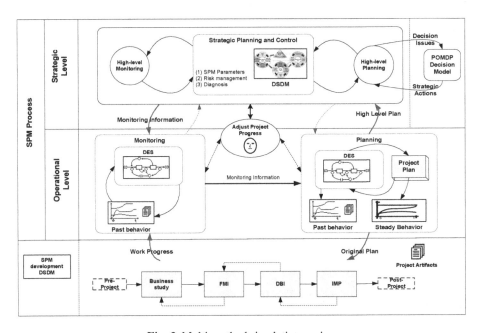

Fig. 3. Multi-method simulation engine

3.2   Strategic Decision Breakdown Framework for SPM

Strategic decision breakdown is an approach to model decision structure properly. In this approach the decision structure would be categorized by domain, objective and transformation. To address SPM decisions in the proposed framework with strategic perspective, type of decisions will be identified. These types are stereotypes of SPM activities according to SPM methodology specification. With identification of decision stenotypes, objectives and respectively the transformation function would be determined. Transformation is a mapping function that links a decision frame into related operational work breakdown structure. As illustrated in fig 4, the decision design process from strategic level to operational activities is depicted.

4   Implementation

4.1   Generating Policy

For the proposed framework given the follow definition for POMDP model as S is the set of states, A is the set of actions and O is the set of observations:

S1= phaseproceeding, S2= phasedone
A1= noact, A2= hire, A3= fire, A4= planreview, A5= buytool   , A6= determineiteration
O1= slowphaseprogress, O2= lowquality,
O3= behindschedule, O4= lowbudget

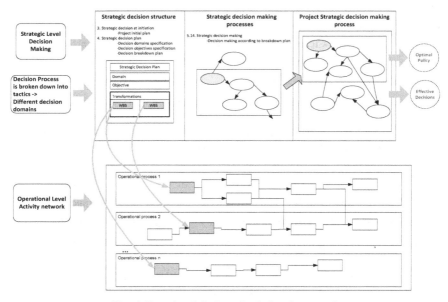

Fig. 4. Functional design of solution framework

The set of actions, observations and transition functions are elicited according to [1] risk prioritization, for the considerable actions and related observations. The action set labeled as "action stereotypes" helps to categorize the decision domains and to model the decision process effectively. Definition of transition functions are based on (1) and (2) respectively for actions and observations:

$$P(\text{action}) = \frac{\text{observ} + 0.5 \times \text{semiobserv}}{\text{total observations}} \tag{1}$$

$$P(\text{observ}) = \frac{\text{risks} + 0.5 \times \text{semirisks}}{\text{totalriks}} \tag{2}$$

P(action) is probability function of action over states, "observ" is the number of related observations, "semiobserv" is the number of semi-related observation, P(observ) is the probability function of observation over states and risks are related risks to the observations, "semiriks" is semi-related risks. Table 2 shows the project risk list.

Table 2. Project risk list [1]

Risk ID	Risk name	Nature
R01	Low budget	Cost and time
R02	Infractions against law	Contract
R03	Low communication and advertising for the show	User/ customer
R04	Unsuitable cast	Organization
R05	Unsuitable ticket price-setting	Strategy
R06	Unsuitable rehearsal management	Controlling
R07	Cancellation or delay of the first performance	Cost and time
R08	Poor reputation	User/customer
R09	Lack of production teams organization	Organization
R10	Low team communication	Organization
R11	Bad scenic, lightning and sound design	Technical performance
R12	Bad costume design	Technical performance
R13	Low complicity between cast members	Technical performance
R14	Too ambitious artistic demands compared to project means	Requirements
R15	Few spectators/lukewarm reception of the show	User/ customer
R16	Technical problems during a performance	Technical performance
R17	Low cast motivation	Organization
R18	Unsuitable for family audiences	Strategy
R19	Low creative team leadership	Controlling
R20	Low creative team reactivity	Controlling

Algorithm used to find the optimal policy is SARSOP [2] as described in fig 5. We have a set of states, but we could never be certain where we are. A way to model this situation is to use probabilities distribution over the belief states. For better management of SPM process phases, the phase is divided into two states, "phaseproceeding" state which implies the process of the phase and "phasedone" which implies the phase is done. In a real SPM process each phase could be different dependant of manager's strategy but for formulating the process the same situation is considered for all phases of SPM. Therefore, the probability distribution over the two states is, $\Pr(s = \text{phaseproceeding}) = 0.50$, $\Pr(s = \text{phasedone}) = 0.50$ where s= state at time t. In this model there are advantages which would reduce the complexity of the algorithm of finding an optimal policy; 1-we know the initial belief point and 2-we know the initial action 3-belief state transition is one-way which only transition is from "phaseproceeding" to "phasedone". These three conditions of the model reduce the complexity of an exponential algorithm. There are 6 actions and 4 observations, according to (3):

$$\text{Number of policies} = (\text{number of actions})^{(\text{number of observations})} \quad (3)$$

$$=6^4=1296$$

Algorithm SARSOP

---

1. Initialize the Γ set of α-vectors, representing the lower bound $\underline{V}$ on the optimal value function V^*. Initialize the upper bound $\overline{V}$ on V^*.
2. Insert the initial belief point b_0 as the root of the tree $T_{\mathcal{R}}$.

3. repeat
4. SAMPLE($T_{\mathcal{R}}, \Gamma$).

5. Choose a subset of nodes from $T_{\mathcal{R}}$. For each chosen node b, BACKUP($T_{\mathcal{R}}, \Gamma, b$).

6. PRUNE($T_{\mathcal{R}}, \Gamma$).

7. until termination conditions are satisfied.
8. return Γ.

Fig. 5. SARSOP algorithm [2]

It is a considerable large number to find an optimal policy from 1296 existent policies.

$$E^\pi(b_0) = \sum_{t=0}^{\infty} \gamma^t E[r(s_t, a_t)|b_0, \pi] \qquad (4)$$

Where in (4), π is the policy, $0<\gamma<1$ is discount factor, r is reward function, b0 is initial belief state and Eπ is expected value for policy π.

Then the optimal policy would be (5):

$$\pi^* = \underset{\pi}{\text{argmax}} \, (E^\pi(b_0)) \qquad (5)$$

Determining the Optimal Policy. The optimal policy for the simulation framework is described in table 3. The transition of belief state with Piecewise linear and convex strategy, is converted into partitions, the belief space (state=phasedone).

Table 3 shows an optimal policy for this framework since there are only two states, belief state can be represented with a single value. In doing so it is not much more than a table lookup and using of Bayes Rule.

Generally finding an optimal policy over the POMDP is a very complex calculation form the complexity of algorithm chosen over an infinite number of horizons for the purpose. One of major issues in computing the optimal policy over belief states is the continuity. In finding POMDP optimal policy, it is more effective to divide the continuous belief space into several partitions and then to assign one action for each of the partitions. The set of partitions is resulted from the calculation of policy from infinite horizons and see the intersection for each of action-observation set of lines resulted from the value function called Piecewise linear and convex (PWLC). Fig 6 shows the visual PWLC presentation of computed optimal policy over the belief state partitions for the framework. The Y axis accounts for value of action and the x axis accounts for belief space probability distribution. Briefly, this figure illustrates the action segmentation for the considered belief space whereas in this case is the project progress. Simply PWLC visualizes the segmentation of belief space; each line is the value function of actions that are defined in specification of the model. The value function is a computed by SARSOP algorithm which is presented in section 4 (fig 5). Each intersection point of these lines on x axis, determines the respective partition point.

Table 3. Optimal policy over continuous belief

Partition No	Pr(state=phasedone)	Action
1	0.0000 to 0.3607	A2
2	0.3607 to 0.4537	A5
3	0.4941 to 0.6523	A3
4	0.6523 to 0.7566	A6
5	0.7566 to 0.7882	A1
6	0.5037 to 1.0000	A4

Policy Graph of POMDP. Policy graph is another form of a policy presentation for acting in a POMDP. A finite state controller, which each node of the graph is an associated action, and the edge out of the node going to other node is each observation that is possible. For this framework, a "policy graph" is shown in fig 7. Since the actual graph is very complicated, for simplification, maximum branches starting from a node to show is implemented. Fig 7 illustrates the same policy with 1 maximum branch starting from a node. This graph on the other hand provides a vision and clear visual for the analyzer to have a better insight on actions, observations and their impact on decision process. Also policy graph reveals the central tendency of decision; nevertheless this strategy makes the complexity of POMDP mitigated. The legends of symbols used in fig 7 are, A as action, O as observation and Y as state. For all symbols array number, the value in parentheses starts from zero and the value beside O is the probability of observation and Y is the belief point value.

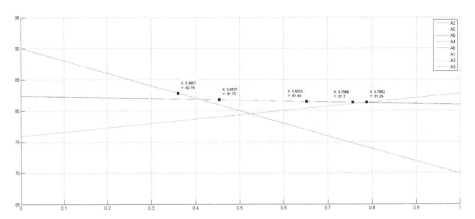

Fig. 6. PWLC Visualization of optimal policy

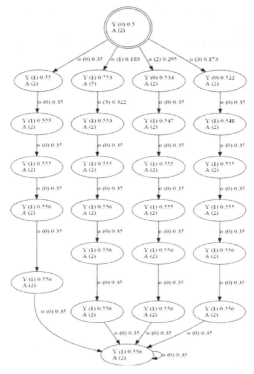

Fig. 7. A policy graph with maximum of 1 branch out for optimal policy

5   Discussion

Policy based decision paradigm is part of a comprehensive decision support framework to open new horizons over SPM decision modeling. This feature is employed by the specified policy of POMDP to model the decision process and evaluate decision values. The framework helps practitioner to adjust their short-term perspectives over SPM process and see their actual decision feedback with regards to project constraints. The significance of decision modeling and an evaluation course for SPM decision process that roots from the complexity of this practice, inculcates that constructing a decision modeling framework is complicated. Nevertheless, the proposed framework intends to form a different decision paradigm system from synthesis of decision support and decision management systems. Decision management systems automate operational decisions (so called they take actions); they mitigate the burden of decision making but restrict the freedom of users [28]. On the other hand decision support systems only provide recommendations for users and don't interfere in the process of decision making. This paradigm reduces the efficacy of the system in multi-level processes and in fact doesn't reduce the effort needed for decision making. By combination of these two systems, it is possible to develop a multi-level decision modeling framework to support both paradigms. Although as the optimal policy demonstrated the feasibility of such a framework for automating the decision making, but it should not be taken as a replacement for the domain expert. Therefore the decision model is not intended to make decisions. The existence and cooperation of the domain expert is necessary for ultimate assessment of the framework performance (according to the decision model) and determination of actual course of action. SPM and related knowledge areas in regards to decision modeling and new decision paradigm are illustrated in fig 8. In fig 8, the knowledge of SPM is categorized with planning and decision making domains for the purpose.

The goals of this study can be discussed from two aspects: (1) From a practical aspect, we try to find a solution to improve decision making process, that it has likely better effect. (2) From a scientific aspect, we presented a model which maps actual decision process to an optimal policy. This paper demonstrated the possibility of this model. Also based on the pragmatic approach of this study in which employs constructive methodology, the practical aspect is highly considered. Therefore, the impact of the conceptual framework in any case, whether an operational solution is developed or not, shall identify potentially interesting and practically significant tendencies towards future studies.

6   Future Work

By integration of expert systems into the framework, the idea of reaching for having common features of decision support systems and decision management systems entirely will be accomplished. The goal is to develop a framework that involves in planning and decision making stages of SPM. The role of an expert system in the framework would be to specify structure for long-term perspective adjustment and help practitioners to acquire knowledge from past decisions.

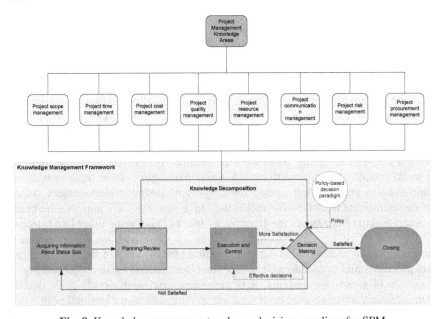

Fig. 8. Knowledge management and new decision paradigm for SPM

With minor alteration to the POMDP model, this framework could be generalized for a greater purpose of project management. As detailed in section 4, the specific process of software development has been chosen for action-decision analysis. With a model builder embedment for POMDP policy generation, multi-process analysis of decision modeling for other branches of management is feasible.

The presented framework based on the pragmatic approach of the research would be transformed into an operational solution. The performance of the solution would be evaluated according to the acquired knowledge of SPM in two domains of planning and decision making. The optimal policy which is a decision model is the basis for in-process decision support for the proposed solution.

7   Conclusion

The presented framework provides different views over SPM training and knowledge management, which were hardly considered in the existing approaches. These views are ranged from strategic, tactical, managerial and operational dimensions of SPM experiential knowledge.

The intention of implementing POMDP into the framework is to deal with complex aspect of SPM decision making process in which specifies tactics and principles to evaluate decision values. SD with underlying basis of simulation supported by DES, provides a comprehensive simulation engine that on one hand makes the possibility of developing an operational framework upon the conceptual architecture and on the other hand transforms the simulation framework into a strategic planning-training platform. The framework brings on a delicate feature for SPM practitioner which is called in-process decision support. With this feature it is possible to assess the decision issues and deal with them according to the designated strategy in a real time fashion.

Acknowledgements. Special thanks to Advanced Informatics School, UTM for cooperation and providing resources.

References

1. Fang, C., Marle, F.: A simulation-based risk network model for decision support in project risk management. Decision Support Systems 52, 635–644 (2012)
2. Kurniawati, H., Hsu, D., Lee, W.S.: SARSOP: Efficient Point-Based POMDP Planning by Approximating Optimally Reachable Belief Spaces. In: Robotics: Science and Systems, pp. 65–72 (Year)
3. Reason, J.: Human error. Cambridge university press (1990)
4. Rodríguez, D., Satpathy, M., Pfahl, D.: Effective Software Project Management Education through Simulation Models: An Externally Replicated Experiment. In: Bomarius, F., Iida, H. (eds.) PROFES 2004. LNCS, vol. 3009, pp. 287–301. Springer, Heidelberg (2004)
5. Cho, S.: An exploratory project expert system for eliciting correlation coefficient and sequential updating of duration estimation. Expert Systems with Applications 30, 553–560 (2006)

6. Tizkar, A.S.: A decision support system for game-based simulative environment of software development project management. International Journal of Machine Learning and Computing 2, 173–177 (2012b)

7. Donzelli, P.: A Decision Support System for Software Project Management. IEEE Software 23, 67–75 (2006)

8. Neap, H.S., Celik, T.: A knowledge-based system for determination of marginal value of building projects. Expert Systems with Applications 21, 119–129 (2001)

9. Olteanu, A.P.: A Decision Support System (DSS) for Project Management in the Biodiesel Industry. Informatica Economică 15, 189–202 (2011)

10. Janczura, G.H., Golinska, I.: Decision support system for choosing model for a software development life cycle. Operations Research and Decisions 1, 61–77 (2010)

11. Plaza, M., Turetken, O.: A model-based DSS for integrating the impact of learning in project control. Decision Support Systems 47, 488–499 (2009)

12. Antony, S., Santhanam, R.: Could the use of a knowledge-based system lead to implicit learning? Decision Support Systems 43, 141–151 (2007)

13. Besir, S., Birant, K.U.: A Case for Decision Support Systems on Project Management. In: ICT Innovations, Web Proceedings, pp. 71-76. (Year)

14. Yang, H.L., Wang, C.S.: Recommender system for software project planning one application of revised CBR algorithm. Expert Systems with Applications 36, 8938–8945 (2009)

15. Bollin, A., Hochmüller, E., Mittermeir, R., Samuelis, L.: Experiences with Integrating Simulation into a Software Engineering Curriculum. In: 25th IEEE Conference on Software Engineering Education and Training, pp. 62–71. (Year)

16. Huang, S.T., Lin, W.H., Hsu, M.C.: Embracing Business Context in Pedagogical Simulation Games-A Case with Process Disciplined Project Management. In: CSEETW 2008 Proceedings of the 2008 21st IEEE-CS Conference on Software Engineering Education and Training Workshop, pp. 9–12 (2008)

17. Navarro, E.O.: SimSE: A Software Engineering Simulation Environment for Software Process Education. Donald Bren School of Information and Computer Sciences, vol. Doctoral, pp. 298. University of California, Irvine (2006)

18. Mittermeir, R.T., Hochmüller, E., Bollin, A., Jäger, S., Nusser, M.: AMEISE - A Media Education Initiative for Software Engineering: Concepts, the Environment, and initial Experiences In: Proceedings International Workshop ICL - Interactive Computer Aided Learning (Year)

19. Bollin, A., Hochmuller, E., Mittermeir, R.T.: Teaching Software Project Management using Simulations. In: 24th IEEE-CS Conference on Software Engineering Education and Training (CSEE&T), pp. 81–90 (Year)

20. Gao, Z., Xie, C.: The Study of Content Simulation Using in the Software Project Management Teaching. In: Second International Workshop on Education Technology and Computer Science, pp. 576–578 (2010)

21. Salas, R., Wildman, J.L., Piccolo, R.F.: Using Simulation-Based Training to Enhance Management Education. Academy of Management Learning & Education 8, 559–573 (2009)

22. Nembhard, D., Yip, K., Shtub, A.: Comparing Competitive and Cooperative Strategies for Learning Project Management. Journal of Engineering Education 181–192 (2009)

23. Rodríguez, D., Sicilia, M.A., Gallego, J.J.C., Pfahl, D.: e-Learning in Project Management Using Simulation Models: A Case Study Based on the Replication of an Experiment. IEEE Transactions on Education 49, 451–463 (2006)

24. Targowski, A.: From Data to Wisdom in the Global and Civilizational Context the Cognitive Perspective. In: Quintela Varajão, J.E., Cruz-Cunha, M.M., Putnik, G.D., Trigo, A. (eds.) CENTERIS 2010, Part I. Communications in Computer and Information Science, vol. 109, pp. 21–30. Springer, Heidelberg (2010)
25. Zeigler, B., Kim, T.G., Praehofer, H.: Theory of Modeling and Simulation,Second Edition:Integrating Discrete Event and Continuous Complex Dynamic Systems. Academic Press (2000)
26. Sterman, J.D.: System Dynamics Modeling. California Management Review 43, 8–25 (2001)
27. Kaelbling, L.P., Littman, M.L., Cassandra, A.R.: Planning and acting in partially observable stochastic domains. Artificial Intelligence 101, 99–134 (1998)
28. Taylor, J., Raden, N.: Smart Enough Systems: How to Deliver Competitive Advantage by Automating Hidden Decisions. Pearson Education, Upper Saddle River (2007)

Methods for Smart Home Environment's Intellectualization: The Comparative Analysis

Raimundas Jasinevicius, Vaidas Jukavicius, Agnius Liutkevicius,
Vytautas Pertauskas, Agne Taraseviciene, and Arunas Vrubliauskas

Kaunas University of Technology, Real Time Computer Systems Centre, Kaunas, Lithuania
{raimundas.jasinevicius,vaidas.jukavicius,agnius.liutkevicius,
vytautas.petrauskas,agne.paulauskaite-taraseviciene,
arunas.vrubliauskas}@ktu.lt

Abstract. The difference between smart home (or smart agent) and intellectualized smart home (or intellectual smart agent) is delivered, and the framework for their modelling is described. Question of a sophisticated adequacy evaluation is raised to compare the reality and its model. The proposed approach was used to evaluate four different decision making technologies implemented in the models of the intellectualized smart home environment, and the comparison of those experimental technologies prepared by expert is presented.

Keywords: intellectualized home environment, multi-agent system, systems training, retraining, self-training, modeling adequacy, decision making technologies.

1 Preliminaries

First of all here we deliver our own point of view regarding the difference between the smart and intellectualized home environment [1]. In general, the intellectualized smart home environment is a software/hardware entity which interacts in a prescribed way with the environment's user and as such, - inherits a functional organization, based on a deterministic or stochastic (fuzzy) description of its external activity and internal operations as well. If the environment's behavior does not require from a user any programming activity, we have a smart or intelligent environment.

In case when the home environment's external interaction with the user and its in- ternal operations are based on a crisp algorithmic logic, we have smart home envi- ronment (SHE).

When the SHE's external interaction with the user and its internal operations are based on fuzzy algorithmic logic, we have the intellectualized smart home environment (I_SHE).

The level of smart home environment's intellectics depends on two types of characteristics: 1) the type of possible agent actions to be performed in the environment, and 2) the type of interactions between those agents performing and supplying certain services to the user of the environment. Four types of smart home environment obtained from possible combinations of those two features are presented in Table 1.

G. Dregvaite and R. Damasevicius (Eds.): ICIST 2014, CCIS 465, pp. 150–159, 2014.
© Springer International Publishing Switzerland 2014

Table 1. Types of smart or/and intellectualized home environments

Type of interaction (type of service) / Type of agent	SMART	INTELLIGENT
SA - SMART AGENT	SS_HE	SI_HE
IA – INTELLIGENT AGENT	IS_HE	II_HE

The process of development and intellectualization of such a smart home system must include the modelling environment adequate to the complexity of the reality. Main questions to be analyzed and answered in the model are shown in the Fig. 1.

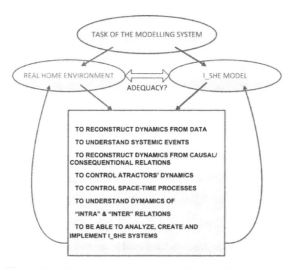

Fig. 1. Questions to be solved during the modelling process

Must be emphasized that in general the system's development as well as systems modelling deals with not only crisp but rather the fuzzy information, concerning users' requirements and the systemic intelligent inference along the whole value chain: smart home environment's user - systems developer. Dynamically interacting processes of system's actions and services predetermine a modular structure of the whole system.

2   Modelling

The modelling system must play a significant role not only in the simulation itself, but in the process of system's implementation according to the user's needs and industrial requirements for a concrete application area. General idea of the universality of the modelling system under consideration can be seen and elaborated by the simulation environment proposed, implemented and used in the framework of the BIATech project (see Fig.2). Here a simplified modelling block, called BIAsim is presented as a significant part of the whole smart home environment's modelling and development system.

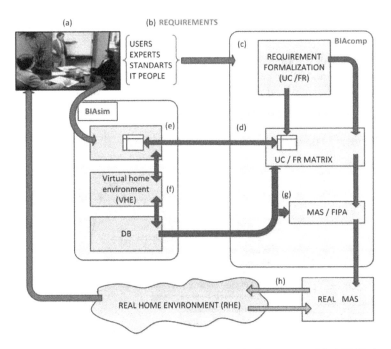

Fig. 2. Simulation environment implemented and used in the framework of the BIATech project

A role of the BIAsim can be clearly seen after the generalized analysis of the whole I_SHE development process' sketch. Usually the team (a), consisting of users, professional experts and IT people accumulate, discuss and prepare a set of requirements (b) to be formalized (c) and presented in the form of a special type of user cases (UC) and systems functional requirements (FR) matrix (d). At the same time an analogous FRxUC matrix must be created, which serves as an information necessary to produce a virtual home environment (f) where the user and IT people are able to model, visualize and simulate in 3D-coordinate system all effects and consequences of requirements' changes. The "on a shelf ready" approach based software and hardware artefacts' prototypes for the smart home environment's intellectualization are selected from the data base (DB) and are transferred to the virtual multi agent system (MAS) (g) to be implemented in the real MAS (h) serving for the direct intellectualized smart home environment's control [2].

3   Adequacy

One of the very important problems to be solved in BIAsim implementation is a problem of the real home environment (RHE) and the virtual one (VHE) adequacy evaluation.

In order to answer the question: how to evaluate system's model's adequacy to the reality (when the reality's role plays the smart home environment to be intellectualized during the modelling and development processes), everybody looks for an opportunity to compare model's data with the corresponding data produced by the reality under investigation. In any case such a comparison covers input (I), output (O) as well as internal state (S) variables wherever they occur: in the entity Ω, or in its smaller elements. In Figure 3 the corresponding differences ε (ε_I, ε_S and ε_O) between the reality and its model are determined.

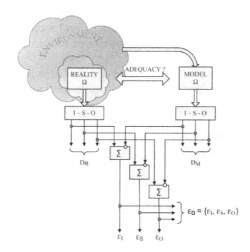

Fig. 3. Evaluation of adequacy of the model and the reality based on data differences

Nowadays, neither ICT people nor scientists, experts or decision makers from different applied fields use so-called raw data. And in general, the object of computerized system analysis, decision making processes and information processing (especially when the problem deals with artificially intellectualized environment) shifts from raw data towards more sophisticated computerized evaluation processes according to the following scheme:

Data → Information → Knowledge → Wisdom.

As a matter of fact, each step in this transformation scheme is performed on the basis of certain operations. For example, the transformation of raw data into information includes the procedure of data mapping on some context (CR – in case of a reality, and CM – in case of a model), as it is shown in Figure 4. Here DR and DM stand for data obtained from the reality and from the model correspondingly.

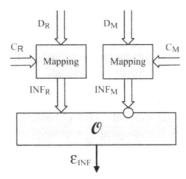

Fig. 4. Raw data transformation into information by mapping on a context

More sophisticated operations are involved in the process when information is to be transformed into knowledge. Such a mapping is usually based on a test feedback paradigm: information used in a closed feedback control loop to reach a certain goal becomes the knowledge which guarantees positive or negative result with some degree of uncertainty [3].

The last step in this scheme (transformation of knowledge into wisdom) is still under discussion and thorough investigation, and we do not know any suitable formalized procedures except for knowledge implementation and summarizing of obtained results.

So, more reliable and more understandable evaluation of smart home environment model's adequacy to the reality can be obtained on the level of knowledge as it is schematically shown in Figure 5.

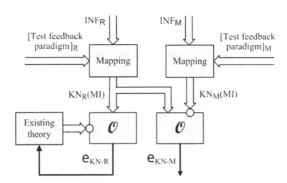

Fig. 5. Adequacy of model and reality evaluation based on knowledge differences

In this case, adequacy is evaluated qualitatively and/or quantitatively by a certain measure ε_{KN} based on a causal/consequential analysis of functional organization of both the reality and the model under investigation.

It must be emphasized that the reasoning on the knowledge level (on the level of meta information MI) enables us to compare existing theories with the results KN-R received from the investigation of a reality and even to correct the existing theories, if necessary.

4   Experimental Simulation

A simplified version of BIAsim was successfully and efficiently used on the initial stages of a real project dedicated to the research and industrial implementation of the smart home environment's intellectualization BIATech ("Research on Smart Home Environment and Development of Intelligent Technologies (BIATech)" [project VP1-3.1-ŠMM-10-V-02-020]).

Assume that the light sources should be controlled according to user preferences in a simple environment which is depicted in Fig. 6a). The two existing light sources can be controlled differently. The first light source on the left is a halogen lamp and can be controlled by an actuator which has 100 positions (0 – the light source is off, 100 – the light source lights at maximum intensity). The second light source on the right is a fluorescent lamp and can be controlled by an actuator only by switching the lamp on or off. Two illumination sensors are placed on each table below the light sources.

Only three features describing the situation are taken into consideration: the illumination of each light source, each user's location sensor's measures and additional feature, indicating the presence of each user in the room. Only one user is interacting in this environment, and his preferences are: 1) all light sources should be turned off when he is in the middle of the room, 2) halogen lamp intensity should be adjusted by selecting thirtieth actuator position when he is near the table on the left, 3) fluorescent lamp should be switched on when he is near the table on the right. The testing results are obtained by using BIAsim simulation tool. They are depicted in Fig. 6b).

As it was mentioned earlier, situations are described by several properties: the user presence, which in this case is chosen to be 1 when the user is in the room, X and Y coordinates and light illumination measures L1 and L2 of the halogen and fluorescent lamps illumination sensors'. The feature, denoting the user presence could also have other values, indicating when the user is or is not in the room. The modelled situations simply denote when the light intensity of the halogen lamp should be increased, decreased or left unchanged according to certain features' values obtained when the user had made corresponding actions.

The questions under consideration were two.

The first one - how the reality (a real home environment - RHE) is able to react to the actions and stimulus received from the intellectualized MAS elements. Practically acceptable results were received concerning the speed and accuracy of all intellectualized services. An example of a significant part of the virtual 3D testing environment of the RHE and the 2D map of equipment for the light intensity control and user's movements is shown on the Fig. 6 a) and b).

The second question under investigation was connected with the decision making technologies (DM_technologies) to be recommended for use in the MAS agents. Four different algorithms for the implementation of the RHE intellectualization paradigm were tested on the virtual environment (VHE) of the BIAsim: 1) the neural network based intellectics (NN_technology), 2) fuzzy logic based intellectics (FL_technology), 3) linear programming procedures based intellectics (LP technology), and 4) an intellectics based on Bayes decision making procedures (BA_technology).

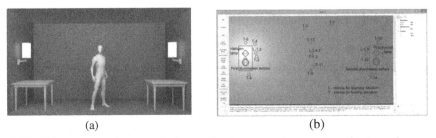

(a)   (b)

Fig. 6. The light sources to be controlled according to user preferences in a simple environment (a), and testing results obtained by BIAsim simulation tool (b)

Sketches of functional organization of the VHEs controlled by MAS built according to those four technologies are delivered in Fig.7 a) - d) correspondingly. Detailed descriptions of those decision making algorithms are delivered in [4, 5].

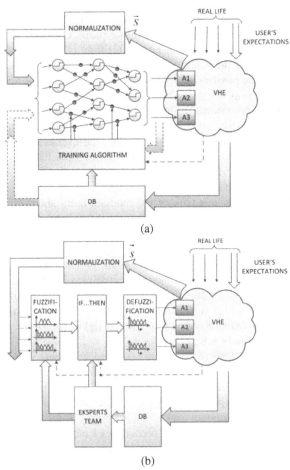

Fig. 7. Model of I-SHE built according to the NN_technology-a), FL_technology-b) LP_technology-c) BA_technology-d)

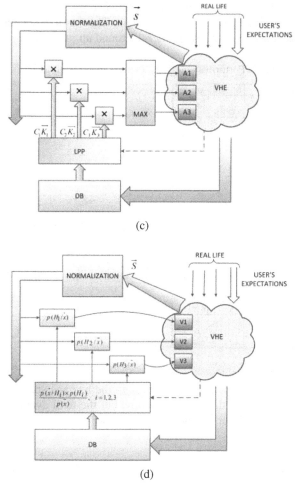

(c)

(d)

Fig. 7. (*continued*)

It is worth to mention the fact that in the sketches S stands for sensors' signals pro- duced by the VHE and describing its situation, and A - for the actions proposed by the decision making algorithm and performed in the VHE to achieve and satisfy user's wishes and expectations in the current situation.

All four DM technologies were tested and compared on the VHE using the BIAsim according to the speed and data amount used for the action performance when: 1) the training process takes place; 2) decision is made for action; 3) the retraining process takes place in two different regimes – when user's wishes change momentarily and when those changes are accumulated gradually; 4) when the intellectualized smart environment is under permanent observation starting "from zero information" (the self- training regime) and obtains possibility to react adequately to the implicit user's wishes. The received simulation results were evaluated by eight independent decision making experts according to the 10 degree system. Their average evaluations are presented in the Table 2: a) - before and b) after the round up procedure.

Table 2. Performance evaluation in both cases: a) and b)

(a)

Training process		NN	FL	LP	BA
	Speed	5,88	8	7,13	8,88
	Space	6,25	6,75	6,88	7,63
	Σ	6,06	7,38	7	8,25
Decission making					
	Speed	9	8,75	7,88	8,63
	Space	8,38	8,25	7,75	8,5
	Σ	8,69	8,5	7,81	8,56
Retraining process (momentary wish)					
	Speed	4,88	9,13	7,38	8,25
	Space	6,25	6,63	6	7,5
	Σ	5,56	7,88	6,69	7,88
(weighted average wish)					
	Speed	8	5,25	6,13	9
	Space	6,5	5,5	5,5	8,25
	Σ	7,25	5,38	5,81	8,63
Self training process					
	Speed	5,38	8,13	6,88	8,63
	Space	6,5	7,5	6,75	8
	Σ	5,94	7,81	6,81	8,31
Σ (speed)		6,63	7,85	7,08	8,68
ΣΣ		6,7	7,39	6,83	8,33

(b)

No.	Feature / characteristics		Evaluation			
			Type of DM- technology			
			NN	FL	LP	BA
1	Training process					
		Speed	6	8	7	9
		Space	6	7	7	8
		Σ	6	7	7	8
2	Decission making					
		Speed	9	9	8	9
		Space	8	8	8	9
		Σ	9	9	8	9
3	Retraining process					
3.1	(momentary wish)					
		Speed	5	9	7	8
		Space	6	7	6	8
		Σ	6	8	7	8
3.2	(weighted average wish)					
		Speed	8	5	6	9
		Space	7	6	6	8
		Σ	7	5	6	9
4	Self training process					
		Speed	5	8	7	9
		Space	7	8	7	8
		Σ	6	8	7	8
	Σ (speed)		7	8	7	9
	ΣΣΣ		7	7	7	8

The Table 2 b) clearly shows that according to the average speed performance the preference must be given to the BA technology, but the total average summary confirms the opinion that all four technologies are approximately equal for the purpose under investigation.

5   Summary

There is an increasing trend towards modelling smart as well as intellectualized home environment under multi-agent systems control. This paper presents our point of view concerning the difference between smart home/agent and intellectualized smart home/agent. More sophisticated evaluation of adequacy of the reality and its model is delivered. Four different intellectual decision making technologies are implemented on the modelling framework, and their results are evaluated by expert team. Concluding reasoning and experimental simulation results permit us to consider the general approach as positively highly promising.

References

1. Nakashima, H., Aghajan, H., Augusto, J.C.: Handbook of Ambient Intelligence and Smart Environments, p. 1293. Springer (2010)
2. Park, S., Sugumaran, V.: Designing multi-agent systems: a framework and application. Expert Systems with Applications: An International Journal 28, 259–271 (2005)

3. Jasinevicius, R., Petrauskas, V.: On Fundamentals of Global Systems Control Science(GSCS). In: ISCS 2013: Interdisciplinary Symposium on Complex Systems, Emergence, Complexity and Computation, vol. 8, pp. 77–87 (2014)
4. Guarracino, M.R., Jasinevicius, R., Krusinskiene, R., Petrauskas, V.: Fuzzy hyperinference-based pattern recognition. In: Borgelt, C., Gil, M.Á., Sousa, J.M.C., Verleysen, M. (eds.) Towards Advanced Data Analysis. STUDFUZZ, vol. 285, pp. 223–240. Springer, Heidelberg (2013)
5. Konar, A.: Computational Intelligence Principles, Techniques and Application, p. 708. Springer, Heidelberg (2005)

Fuzzy Rule Base Generation Using Discretization of Membership Functions and Neural Network

Henrikas Pranevicius, Tadas Kraujalis, Germanas Budnikas,
and Vytautas Pilkauskas

Department of Applied Informatics, Kaunas University of Technology,
Studentu 56-301, LT-51424 Kaunas, Lithuania
henrikas.pranevicius@ktu.lt

Abstract. Paper presents a technique for fuzzy rule extraction. It applies a division of a feature space into fuzzy grids and a selection of discrete values as inputs for neural network. A neural network generates fuzzy rules that are simplified using a decision table analysis tool Prologa. The tool detects and fixes cases of redundancy and ambivalence in a fuzzy rule base. A case study contains an illustration of the proposed technique and a comparison of the results to other sources. A comparative analysis of a productivity of traffic light controllers developed using an expert rule base and a rule base formed using our technique is given. Iris classification problem is considered too. Comparison results prove better accuracy of the technique suggested.

Keywords: neural network, fuzzy grid, automatic fuzzy rule generation, discretization value.

1 Introduction

Fuzzy Logic has been successfully applied to the solution of problem in control and classification areas [1]. Fuzzy logic allows incorporating the knowledge of human experts into expert systems. These systems consist of two main components: knowledge base and fuzzy inference. The composing entire rule base of a fuzzy rule base system by an expert is one of the most important and time consuming task and sometimes the performance of the designed fuzzy system is far from the optimum. Generally, this task can be done using two different approaches. One approach is by extracting the necessary rules directly from human experts, the other by automatically generating a set of fuzzy rules from a set of training data. With an increasing number of inputs and fuzzy sets, the number of rules is increasing exponentially, thus it takes the expert a lot of time to modify and tune fuzzy rules for good system performance. For this reason, the method that automatically generates fuzzy rule base using neural network from a set of example data is proposed.

Various approaches have been proposed for the automatic generation of fuzzy rule base from numerical data. Some of proposed rule extraction techniques were successfully applied to medicine [2], fault detection [3] [4], credit card screening [5].

G. Dregvaite and R. Damasevicius (Eds.): ICIST 2014, CCIS 465, pp. 160–171, 2014.
© Springer International Publishing Switzerland 2014

Several researchers have applied artificial neural network (ANN) for generation fuzzy rules from a training data. Huang and Xing [6] present an approach that represents continuous-valued input parameters using linguistic terms. In the first step, the continuous-valued input parameters are converted into binary input parameters. The sets are represented in a binary form as follows— if there are three sets (*small, medium, large*) the set *small* will be represented as [1 0 0], the set *large* as [0 0 1]. A number of neurons in the output layer of neural network is equal to the number of classes of a classification problem. Input data vector is assigned to the class, neuron of which is most dominant in the output of neural network. The constructed neural network is trained using back-propagation algorithm; during the training process, the binary vector is presented to the NN input layer. Finally, the fuzzy rules are extracted by equation $\sum_{i=1}^{n} \sum_{j=1}^{m} w_{ij} \times x_{ij} - B > 0$, (where n – number of inputs, m – number of sets, w_{ij} – weight, x_{ij} – input value, B - threshold value) and the most dominant values are selected. In the pruning process, an input parameter affects the activation of an output neuron that depends only on the maximum weight of the parameters and not on the minimum weight, hence, the accuracy of the inference system decreases. To overcome this disadvantage, more efficient, simpler technique has been presented in [7]. The absolute difference between the maximum and minimum weights is calculated for each input parameter. Finally, the algorithm prunes each input parameter so long as the neuron remains activated.

Ishibuchi and Nii [8] proposed fuzzy arithmetic based approach for extracting fuzzy rules from ANN. The n-dimensional linguistic vector Ap=(x_1 small, x_2 medium ...) is presented to the trained three-layer feed-forward ANN, the output value of the ANN shows to which class the input pattern belongs. Finally, the consequent class and the grade of certainty are determined by an inequality relation between fuzzy outputs.

Özbakır et al. [9] proposed a method for knowledge extraction by combining advantages of artificial neural networks and swarm intelligence. The proposed approach makes use of particle swarm optimization algorithm to transform the behaviors of trained ANNs into accurate and comprehensible classification rules. Particle swarm optimization with time varying inertia weight and acceleration coefficients is designed to explore the best attribute-value combination via optimizing ANN output function. Later a novel approach for fuzzy rule extraction from neural networks was proposed [10].

The construction of the rule base can be viewed as partitioning the multidimensional feature (input) space. The partitioned two-dimensional input space is depicted in Fig. 1. Feature space is partitioned into a set of separate regions (or units), which form a fuzzy grid. Single fuzzy if-then rule is generated for each fuzzy grid unit. A fuzzy rule generation technique from training data using a fuzzy grid was presented by [11]. Obviously, the technique performance depends on the amount of training data. Generating a rule base from a small number of training data it is likely that the training data will not cover all fuzzy grid units and many regions remain undefined. This may lead to a poor classification performance. In order to overcome this problem, Ishibuchi and Yamamoto [12] suggest a fuzzy discretization approach. An advantage of fuzzy discretization is the overlap between neighboring fuzzy sets while, there is no overlap in the method presented in [11]. This means that in the case of fuzzy discretization, more rules can be generated from a small number of training patterns and more training patterns are involved in the generation of each fuzzy rule. Unfortunately, the training data still do not cover all regions using this rule generation technique. This is actual when the number of attributes is large and each attribute is divided into a large number of fuzzy sets. The fuzzy rules extracted by Ishibuchi and Yamamoto [12] method are able to classify more accurately a pattern than this is done by using Wang et al. [11] technique. If training data would cover all fuzzy grid units, the rules derived from such a feature space could classify data with the higher accuracy. However, an expert usually provides only a small amount of training data. This causes a small coverage of fuzzy grid by training data. In order to cover all fuzzy grid units with the small amount of the training data we propose applying a neural network that forecasts a class label to be assigned to a corresponding fuzzy grid unit.

The approach suggested in the paper generates a fuzzy rule for every fuzzy grid unit using artificial neural network while inputs to ANN are discretized values of membership functions. A number of the generated fuzzy rules increases along with the increasing number of fuzzy sets and increasing number of inputs. Their simplification is topical for an expert to be employed to check the generated rule base as well as for the further use. One of the ways used in the approach proposed is to remove redundant antecedent parts from the rules. The simplification of the fuzzy rule base is performed using a decision table analysis tool Prologa [13]. The tool also is employed for verification of redundancy and ambivalence cases (the tool suits well for verification of formal specifications too [14]). The technique for automated fuzzy rule generation using neural network was applied to solution of Iris classification problem and to traffic signal control.

This paper is organized as follows: section 2 presents the fuzzy rule extraction technique; section 3 gives a brief description of a simplification mechanism and definition of verified properties; a case study where applications of the proposed technique to the Iris classification problem and Traffic lights control problem are explored in section 4. A comparison of the results obtained with respect to other sources is presented there too. Conclusions summarize the paper in section 5.

2   Fuzzy Rule Extraction Technique

In a fuzzy approach, the most important part of a classification system is a fuzzy rule base consisting of a set of fuzzy *if-then* rules. The fuzzy rules consist of the conclusions from one or more conditions connected by *and, or* logical junctions. In this approach, fuzzy *if-then* rules of the following type are used:

$$R_i : \text{if } input_1 \text{ is } A_{p1} \text{ and } ... \text{ and } input_n \text{ is } A_{pn} \text{ then } Class \text{ } C_p$$

where R_i is the i-th rule label, A_{pi} is antecedent fuzzy set on the unit interval [0,1], C_p is the consequent class.

A proposed technique consists of the following steps: (1) definition of membership functions for each input; (2) constructing and training neural network; (3) division of feature space into fuzzy grid units; (4) selection of discrete values as inputs for ANN and (5) extract fuzzy rules using neural network.

Steps 1 and *2* are performed with respect to a classic procedure of membership function definition and constructing and training a neural network (e.g. [15]).

Step 3: Dividing feature space into fuzzy grid units. Each input *input$_i$* is partitioned into N_i linguistic values (e.g. *small, medium, large*). This causes a division of a feature space into units – *fuzzy grid units*. A number of linguistic variables depends on a problem under consideration. An expert selects its quantity. However, this number is independent with respect to a number of data in a training set of neural network. Assume that inputs *input$_1$*

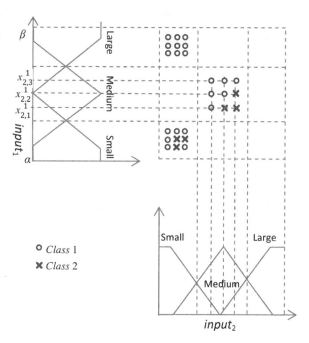

○ *Class* 1

✗ *Class* 2

Fig. 1. Fuzzy grid

and *input$_2$* are partitioned by three linguistic values. Then a feature space is divided into 9 two-dimensional fuzzy grid units, as shown in Fig.1.

Step 4: Selection of discrete values as inputs for ANN. The selection of discrete values consists of two stages. During the first one, a numerical attribute domain is partitioned into intervals. We assume that the domain of a numerical attribute ranges from α to β, and $\{x_1, x_2, ..., x_d\}$ denotes d cut points. The cut points are used in determining the intervals as defined in the following equations:

$$[\alpha; x_1)[x_1; x_2) ... [x_{d-1}; x_d)[x_d; \beta],$$

where $x_1: \mu_1(x_1) = \mu_2(x_1)$ and $x_i: \mu_{i-1}(x_i) = \mu_i(x_i), i = \overline{2, d}$, and μ_i is i-th membership function.

During the second stage, the determined intervals are used to obtain discrete values. The last will be used to train a neural network. A quantitative interval can be discretized by using an *equal width discretization* method [16]. According to the method, we choose a number of sub-intervals equal to k. Experiments with changing a value of k have showed such a dependency. If k was set less than 4, average classification accuracy was 20 % less than at $k = 4$. While if k was greater than 4, average classification accuracy was almost the same as at $k = 4$ along with exponentially increasing time of calculations. Further, in the paper we use k value equal to 4.

The i-th interval of the j-th input is divided into the k equal sub-intervals between v_{min} and v_{max} values, where v_{min} is a start of the interval, v_{max} is an end of the interval.

The sub-intervals have widths $w = (v_{max} - v_{min}) / k$, and the cut points:

$$x_{i,1}^{j} = v_{min} + w,$$

$$x_{i,2}^{j} = v_{min} + 2w, \qquad i = \overline{1,m} \ (m - \text{the number of membership functions})$$

$$x_{i,3}^{j} = v_{min} + 3w,$$

from the set $X_i^j = \left\{ x_{i,1}^j, x_{i,2}^j, x_{i,3}^j \right\}$ correspond to the selected discrete to be used as inputs to a neural network.

Step 5: Generation of fuzzy rule using neural network. Once the network is trained (Step 2) and discrete values are selected (Step 4), a fuzzy rule base can be generated. Its consequent part is obtained by presenting a Cartesian product $X_1^j \times \cdots \times X_m^j$ as an antecedent part of the rule to the trained neural network, where m is the number of membership functions, j – number of input. The number of patterns, required to generate one fuzzy rule, is r^n, where r is a cardinality of the set X_i^j ($r = 3$ w.r.t. Step 4).

A fuzzy rule represents a relation between input data and output in a fuzzy grid unit. The fuzzy grid unit may contain several outputs corresponding to different classes. In order to define a dominating class, counters for each class occurrence in the grid unit are used. A class with the highest value of a counter corresponds to the dominating one. The procedure of rule generation algorithm is outlined in Fig. 2.

Let us consider an example of fuzzy rule extraction. An abstract fuzzy system is described by two inputs and one output. Assume, each input is described by 3 fuzzy sets — *small, medium, large* and the output has two possible classes ($class_1$ or $class_2$).

A finite set of possible inputs is obtained after a discretization of membership functions. For example, discretized values of the membership function *"medium"* of $input_1$ are $X_2^1 = \left\{ x_{2,1}^1, x_{2,2}^1, x_{2,3}^1 \right\}$ the values of membership function *"medium"* of $input_2$ are $X_2^2 = \left\{ x_{2,1}^2, x_{2,2}^2, x_{2,3}^2 \right\}$. After discretization, a Cartesian product $X_2^1 \times X_2^2$ is presented to the trained neural network. When all possible combinations are explored (9 variants in our case) the consequent part of the rule is taken as a class label with the highest number of instances being assigned as the class of the fuzzy rule. E.g., if antecedent part of the rule is "If $input_1$ is *Medium* and $input_2$ is *Medium*" then the neural network assigns input patterns to $class_1$ six times and to $class_2$ three times (see Fig.1). Thus, the dominating class is $class_1$ and the consequent part of the rule contains an assignment to $class_1$.

3   Simplification and Verification of the Generated Rule Base

Our proposed technique enables a generation of fuzzy rule base covering all possible input alternatives, and the question about a consistency of the generated output is very important. Preece and Shinghal [17] identify four general cases of anomalies in rule bases. They are redundancy, ambivalence, deficiency and circularity. Due to a specific nature of rules in our fuzzy rule base, i.e.

- all possible input alternatives are covered by the rules, thus deficiency anomaly is not possible;
- generated rules do not make inference chain between themselves, thus circularity anomaly is not the case,

verification of the generated rule base became a checking of redundancy and ambivalence. Along with the verification task, another important problem is reconstruction and simplification of the generated rule base in order to reduce the number of rules in a rule base, since in real applications, a generated rule base consists of hundreds of rules. These two issues can be solved using a computerized tool – Prologa [13]. Prologa is an interactive design tool for a computer-supported construction and manipulation of decision tables. It offers additional features assisting reconstruction, simplification and verification of decision tables.

The decision table DT is a function from the Cartesian product of the condition states (SB) to the Cartesian product of the action values (VB), by which every condition combination is mapped onto action configuration:

$$DT: SB_1 \times SB_2 \times \ldots \times SB_m \rightarrow VB_1 \times VB_2 \times \ldots \times VB_n.$$

As it is stated in [18] "a decision table is equivalent to a set of production rules," which are the output of rule generation machine. Redundancy and ambivalence issues in the generated rule base might have the following cases (see summarizing Fig.2).

The reconstruction and simplification of decision tables that represent fuzzy rules is performed with respect to [18]. As Prologa tool uses decision table representation, each rule is represented in a form of a decision table column. Upper part of the table contains condition subjects and values; lower part of the table contains action subjects and values. Since the rules conclude assignments of a certain class, they do not form an inference chain between themselves. Thus, entire rule base corresponds to single decision table. Decision table columns with the same action combinations (i.e. assignment to the same class) are contracted. This results in a possible reduction of a number of condition value combinations due to elimination of redundant condition parts. For example, decision table columns that represent rules r_1: if a is *High* and b is *High* then *Class*$_1$; r_2: if a is *High* $\wedge$ b is *Low* then *Class*$_1$ are contracted to single column representing the rule r: if a is *High* then *Class*$_1$. Another possibility to reduce a number of rules is a changing a condition order. The condition order, at which the minimum number of contracted columns is found, is selected. Next section contains an illustration of the proposed technique.

4   Case Study

Accomplished case study consists of application of the proposed technique of automated generation of fuzzy rule base to a solution of Iris classification problem [19] and traffic signal control in Kaunas city [20]. The goal of experiments was evaluation of effectiveness of our technique with respect to [6, 12, 21, 22] as well as to illustrate an applicability of the technique proposed to well-known classification tasks and to actual problems in traffic management.

In production rule	In decision table
\multicolumn{2}{c}{Redundancy}	
Subsumed rule	Subsumed column pair
A rule R is redundant if another rule R' subsumes it, i.e.: $\exists \delta: R \rightarrow R'\delta$, where δ is some substitution.	A DT contains a subsumed column pair, if and only if it includes a pair of columns $(SB_j;\ VB_j)$, $(SB_k;\ VB_k)$ $(1 \leq j, k \leq t)$, $j \neq k$ for which: $SB_j \subseteq SB_k$ ir $VB_j \supseteq VB_k$.
Duplicated rules	Duplicate column pair
Rule is redundant if and only if $\exists \delta: (R \rightarrow R'\delta) \wedge (R' \rightarrow R\delta)$.	A DT contains a duplicate column pair if it includes a pair of columns SL_j, SL_k $(1 \leq j, k \leq t)$, $j \neq k$ for which: $SL_j = SL_k$.
\multicolumn{2}{c}{Ambivalence}	
Ambivalent rule pair	Subsumed column pair
A pair of rules R and R' are ambivalent if the *antece*dent of R' subsumes the antecedent of R, and their *conseq*uents infer a semantic constraint C: $\exists \delta((antec(R) \rightarrow antec(R')\delta) \wedge (\{conseq(R), conseq(R')\delta\} \in C))$ where δ is some substitution.	An ambivalent column pair occurs when two columns of a DT have incompatible action values specified – which specify execution of different actions or violate a semantic constraint, for overlapping set of input cases. A DT contains an ambivalent column pair $(SB_j; VB_j)$, $(SB_k; VB_k)$ $(1 \leq j, k \leq t)$, $j \neq k$ if $SB_j \cap SB_k \neq \varnothing$ and $VB_j \cap VB_k = \varnothing$.

Fig. 2. Redundancy and ambivalence issues in production rules and decision tables. Source: [17, 18].

4.1   Application to Iris Classification Problem

The Iris classification problem is a standard benchmark problem for evaluating different classification methods. It contains 150 patterns, which fall into three different classes containing an equal number of patterns (50 in each): Iris - *Setosa*, Iris - *Versicolor*, Iris - *Virginica*. The classification problem consists of finding the correct Iris class on the four input attributes — sepal length, sepal width, petal length and petal width. The Iris flower data set [19] was used for the experiments.

The three–layer feed forward neural network was trained with 15 patterns (five samples from each of the classes: *Setosa*, *Versicolor* and *Virginica*). The training patterns were obtained via a random process from the original Iris data set [19]. The neural network generates a fuzzy rule base. A fuzzy inference engine was develop to test rule base performance with new (unseen) patterns. After few experiments (up to 10), the average accuracy of the generated rule base was evaluated.

As our example contains 4 attributes: *sepal length* and *width*, *petal length* and *width*, and each attribute has 3 fuzzy sets — *small*, *medium* and *large*, $3^4 = 81$ rules had been generated. The last were imported to Prologa tool to perform simplification and verification activities. These tasks permitted to reduce a number of rules up to 8 times by removing redundant antecedent parts of the rules. The analyzed and simplified rule base is depicted in Fig.3.

1. petal_length	small		medium				large			
2. sepal_length	·		small		medium or large	small or medium		large		
3. petal_width	·	small or medium	large		·	·		small		medium or large
4. sepal_width	·	·	small	medium	large	·		·	small	medium or large	·
1. setosa	x		·	·	·			·	·	·	·
2. versicolor	·	x	·	x	·	x		·	·	x	·
3. virginica	·	·	x	·	x	·	x	x	·	x
	1	2	3	4	5	6	7	8	9	10

Fig. 3. Simplified rule base of Iris classification problem

We compared the results of the proposed approach application to Iris classification problem with the results reported in [12]. As it can be seen from Table 1, the accuracy of the proposed technique increases with the increasing number of fuzzy sets.

Table 1. Comparison of experimental results for the Iris data set

Number of fuzzy sets for each input	Average accuracy of proposed technique	Accuracy of [12] technique
3	94.6	94
4	95.8	89
5	96.3	89

In Table 2 we present a comparison of the proposed method to other techniques. The experimental results showed that the accuracy of the proposed approach varied from 98% to 99.3% and the average accuracy was 98.9%.

Table 2. Technique classification accuracy compared to other sources

Proposed technique	[6]	[12]	[21]	[22]
98- 99.3 (*)	86-96	96.7- 98	95.4-96	99.3

* The number of fuzzy sets was between 6 and 12.

4.2 Application to Traffic Lights Control

Another case study considers application of the proposed technique to traffic lights control in Kaunas city order to reduce traffic jams. A schematic view of the considered junction is presented in paper [23]. There are many intelligent approaches used to manage the flows of traffic in response of real time traffic situation at junctions [23], such as fuzzy logic, fuzzy-neural network, evolutionary algorithms, reinforcement learning.

In this case study, we compare performances of traffic lights controllers (TLCs) developed by using automatically generated rule base, which was produced using the proposed technique and rule base created by an expert [1].

The criterion used for the evaluation is the average stopped delay [25], i.e. the delay that occurs when a vehicle is fully immobilized. The better control strategy is the one that provides the lowest average delays.

In order to create the traffic lights controller, 15 training patterns were provided by a domain expert as training data. A neural network with 3 input neurons and two output neurons was used. The three-dimensional vectors were presented to the trained neural network. In order to define which control action to undertake – "extend current green" or "terminate current green", a dominating class is defined using class counters. A total of 48 rules were obtained after rule generation. The rules were imported to Prologa tool to perform simplification and analysis tasks. Six rules were left after the simplification (see Fig.4) and were used creating a traffic lights controller. Here in the table *Terminate* action value "–" corresponds to "extend current green" and permits checking an ambivalence property.

The fuzzy logic controller described in [1] determines whether to stay in the current green phase or switch to the next phase after a time of a green light. A green time of 10 seconds is given for the first time. If the TLC concludes to switch to the next phase, then the current green light will be terminated. Otherwise, the current phase will be extended for the time interval of 6 seconds and so forth until the maximum green time is reached (40 seconds). Extension time and its number is selected with respect to an intensity of transport flows in the junction. The same schema was used in the controller designed by our technique. Input parameters for the TLC are: Average number of vehicles in the lanes of current green phase; Arrival rate of current green phase; Average number of vehicles in the lanes of the next green phase.

The number of vehicles of current green phase and the number of vehicles in next green phase are divided into four fuzzy sets: *short*, *medium*, *long* and *very long*. Arrival rate has three fuzzy sets: *low*, *medium* and *high*.

The controller control action is obtained as follow. The input data (most often crisp values) are fed to the fuzzification part of the TLC. Then fuzzified input data are entered into the fuzzy inference system where the most appropriate rules are selected from the fuzzy rule base. To obtain a decision from this fuzzy output, the fuzzy set is defuzzified. There are several defuzzification methods [15] and the mean of maximum method is used in the proposed approach.

1. Queue1		Short				Medium		Long or Very long
2. Queue2		Short	Medium or Long or Very long	Short or Medium or Long	Very long			·
3. Arrival rate	Small	Medium or High	·	·	·			·
1. Terminate	x	–	x	–	x			–

Fig. 4. Simplified rule base for Traffic Lights Controller problem

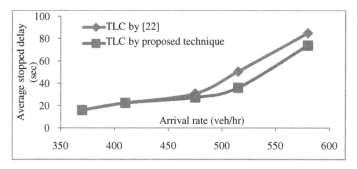

Fig. 5. Comparison of the approach proposed and [1] at the same traffic volumes

During the simulation, arrival rate of vehicles in the lane varied between 0,08 and 0,19 vehicles per second (288-680 veh/hr). Comparisons were made by considering two cases of traffic volumes: equal and different at the approaches of junctions.

Results of TLCs developed by our and [1] techniques are almost identical at low and medium vehicle arrival rates (Fig.5). During higher traffic volume, both controllers are able to control the traffic flows quite well. However applying the TLC designed by our technique average stopped delay is lower than [1] technique at the equal traffic volumes. Table 3 represents the average stopped delays when traffic volumes at each approach are different. The first row of the table shows the lanes of the analyzed intersection. The arrival rate in the lane is shown in the second row of the table. The rest rows of the table show the results of the case study.

The TLC by [1] control method has similar delays at low and medium traffic volumes, while the TLC by proposed in the paper technique seems to be effective at high volumes of traffic flows. The overall average stopped delay value at the different arrival rates was 15.64% lower if used proposed technique for TLC control as compared to [1] technique. While at the same arrival rates in each lane, the TLC designed using suggested approach produced 14.22% lower average stopped delays w.r.t. to TLC designed using [1].

Table 3. Average stopped delays at different traffic volumes

Lane	Arrival rate (veh/hr)	Average stopped delay (sec)	
		Proposed technique	**[1]**
1,2,3	470		
4,5	360	17.99	19.08
6,7	288		
1,2,3	470		
4,5	470	20.95	19.75
6,7	288		
1,2,3	600		
4,5	470	28.51	31.69
6,7	360		
1,2,3	680		
4,5	510	44.23	51.34
6,7	360		
1,2,3	680		
4,5	600	70.39	93.89
6,7	470		

5   Conclusions

An approach for fuzzy rule extraction using discretization of membership functions and neural network was presented in this paper. Its accuracy was compared during case studies. An effectiveness of the technique proposed is compared with the results of [6, 12, 21, 22] by analyzing the Iris classification problem. A comparison showed the main advantage of the suggested technique—the accuracy increases with the increasing number of fuzzy sets.

Another case study considered a problem of traffic lights control. Fuzzy logic controllers were designed using rule base developed by an expert and the proposed techniques. Control effectiveness of traffic junctions was measured in terms of average stopped delays at the same and different vehicle arrival rates. Results demonstrated the better productivity with respect to [1] of the approach proposed by the average 14.9 %.

Acknowledgements. The work described in this paper has been carried out within the framework the Operational Programme for the Development of Human Resources 2007-2013 of Lithuania „Strengthening of capacities of researchers and scientists" project VP1-3.1-ŠMM-08-K-01-018 „Research and development of Internet technologies and their infrastructure for smart environments of things and services" (2012- 2015), funded by the European Social Fund (ESF).

References

1. Zhang, L., Honglong, L., Prevedouros, P.D.: Signal Control for Oversaturated Intersections Using Fuzzy Logic. In: TRB 2005 Annual Meeting, Hawaii, pp. 24–32 (2005)
2. Cui, Y., Dong, M.: Extracting Fuzzy Rules from Hierarchical Heterogeneous Neural Networks for Cardiovascular Diseases Diagnosis. In: Motoda, H., Wu, Z., Cao, L., Zaiane, O., Yao, M., Wang, W. (eds.) ADMA 2013, Part II. LNCS, vol. 8347, pp. 243–249. Springer, Heidelberg (2013)
3. Siah, Y.K., Wong, S.Y., Tiong, S.K.: Compressing and improving fuzzy rules using genetic algorithm and its application to fault detection. In: IEEE 18th Conference on Emerging Technologies & Factory Automation (ETFA), pp. 234–242 (2013)
4. Deepika, B., Bansal, R.K., Gupta, H.O.: Function analysis based rule extraction from artificial neural networks for transformer incipient fault diagnosis. Int. J. Electrical Power & Energy Systems 43(1), 1196–1203 (2012)
5. Rudy, S., Baesens, B., Mues, C.: Rule extraction from minimal neural networks for credit card screening. Int. J. Neural Systems 21(04), 265–276 (2011)
6. Huang, S.H., Xing, H.: Extract intelligible and concise fuzzy rules from neural networks. Fuzzy Sets and Systems 132(2), 233–243 (2002)
7. Muslimi, B., Capretz, M.A.M., Samarab, J.: An Efficient Technique for Extracting Fuzzy Rules from Neural Networks. Int. J. Computer Systems Science and Engineering, 930–936 (2006)
8. Ishibuchi, H., Nii, M.: Generating fuzzy if–then rules from trained neural networks: Linguistic analysis of neural networks. In: IEEE International Conference on Neural Networks, vol. 2, pp. 1133–1138 (1996)

9. Özbakır, L., Delice, Y.: Exploring comprehensible classification rules from trained neural networks integrated with a time–varying binary particle swarm optimizer. Engineering Applications of Artificial Intelligence 24(3), 491–500 (2011)
10. Sinem, K., Özbakır, L., Baykasoğlu, A.: Fuzzy DIFACONN–miner: A novel approach for fuzzy rule extraction from neural networks. Expert Systems with Applications 40(3), 938–946 (2013)
11. Wang, L.X., Mendel, J.M.: Generating fuzzy rules by learning from examples. IEEE Transactions on Systems, Man, and Cybernetics Part B: Cybernetics 22(6), 1414–1427 (1992)
12. Ishibuchi, H., Yamamoto, T.: Performance Evaluation of Fuzzy Partitions with Different Fuzzification Grades. In: Proc. of IEEE International Conference on Fuzzy Systems, pp. 1198–1203 (2002)
13. Vanthienen, J.: Prologa v.5 User's manual, Katholieke Universiteit Leuven (2000)
14. Pranevicius, H., Budnikas, G.: Creation of ESTELLE/Ag Specifications Using Knowledge Bases. Informatica 14(1), 63–74 (2003)
15. Rajasekaran, S., Vijayalakshmi Pai, G.A.: Neural Networks. Fuzzy Logic and Genetic Algorithms: Synthesis and Applications (2004)
16. Dougherty, J., Kohavi, R., Sahami, M.: Supervised and unsupervised discretization of continuous features. In: Proc. of the 12th International Conference on Machine Learning, pp. 194–202 (1995)
17. Preece, A., Shinghal, R.: Foundation and application of knowledge base verification. Int. J. Intelligent Systems 9(8), 683–702 (1994)
18. Vanthienen, J., Mues, C., Aerts, A.: An illustration of verification and validation in the modelling phase of KBS development. Data & Knowledge Engineering 27, 337–352 (1998)
19. Fisher, R.: The Use of Multiple Measurements in Taxonomic Problem. Ann. Eugenics 7(II), 179–188 (1936)
20. Pranevicius, H., Kraujalis, T.: Fuzzy traffic control for three–sided intersection. In: Proc. of International 12th Conference Transport Means, pp. 52–55 (2008)
21. Gadaras, I., Mikhailov, L., Lekkas, S.: Generation of Fuzzy Classification Rules Directly from Overlapping Input Partitioning. In: Fuzzy Systems Conference, pp. 1–6 (2007)
22. Matthews, C., Jagielska, I.: Fuzzy rule extraction from a trained multi–layered neural network. In: Proc. of IEEE International Conference on Neural Networks, pp. 744–748 (1995)
23. Pranevicius, H., Kraujalis, T.: Knowledge based traffic signal control model for signalized intersection. Transport 27(3), 263–267 (2012)
24. Liu, Z.: A Survey of Intelligence Methods in Urban Traffic Signal Control. Int. J. Computer Science and Network Security 7(7), 105–112 (2007)
25. Darma, Y.K., Mohamad, M.R., Abdullah, S.J.: Control delay variability at signalized intersection based on HCM method. In: 6th Conference of the Eastern–Asia–Society–for–Transportation–Studies, vol. 5, pp. 945–958 (2005)

Directed Acyclic Graph Extraction from Event Logs

Olegas Vasilecas, Titas Savickas, and Evaldas Lebedys

Information Systems Research Laborary, Vilnius Gediminas Technical University,
Saulėtekio al. 11, LT-10223
{Olegas.Vasilecas,Titas.Savickas,Evaldas.Lebedys}@vgtu.lt

Abstract. The usage of probabilistic models in business process mining enables analysis of business processes in a more efficient manner. Although, the Bayesian belief network is one of the most common probabilistic models, possibilities to use it in business process mining are still not widely researched. Existing process mining approaches are incapable to extract directed acyclic graphs for representing Bayesian networks. This paper presents an approach for extraction of directed acyclic graph from event logs. The results obtained during the experiment show that the proposed approach is feasible and may be applied in practice.

Keywords: Process mining, direct acyclic graph, event log, Bayesian belief network.

1 Introduction

Business processes are the most important aspect of every business as they define an activity or a set of activities that must be accomplished to achieve the organizational goals. Modelling and analysis of the processes is critical in identifying existing processes and understanding the contributions of new processes to the system [1].

Process mining techniques are used to discover and analyze business processes in an automated way. Using all kinds of recorded process data, process mining techniques attempt to automatically discover the structure and properties of the business process that can be visualized in business process models.

Existing process mining solutions extract information from event logs and, for each business intelligence question, they require to iterate through the log each time. Also, the existing methods often extract models that do not semantically conform to existing processes as they allow transitions between activities that do not exist in the existing BP.

To attempt to solve these problems, probabilistic models could be used. Although, the Bayesian belief network is one of the most common probabilistic models, possibilities to use it in business process mining are still not widely researched.

Existing business process mining algorithms cannot extract process models suitable for Bayesian belief networks (BBN), because BBN requires a DAG. The goal of this paper is to present an approach on how to acquire a DAG from an event log suitable for the generation of BBN.

G. Dregvaite and R. Damasevicius (Eds.): ICIST 2014, CCIS 465, pp. 172–181, 2014.

The paper is structured as follows: Section 2 provides a high-level view of the pro-posed approach. Section 3 formulates a background for the approach by presenting the view of the event logs. Then, Section 4 describes problems with existing process mining algorithms for DAG extraction and presents directed acyclic graph extraction algorithm of our proposed approach. Section 5 presents experimental results of an exemplary case and section 6 provides overview of related literature. The paper con-cludes with conclusions and future work.

2   Proposed Approach

The goal of our ongoing research is generation of BBN from event logs extracted from an information system. Since BBN is based on DAG, the focus of this paper is extraction of a DAG from event logs. For this purpose we propose an approach which attempts to extract a graph from event logs but avoids loops while extracting it. The algorithm is presented in Figure 1.

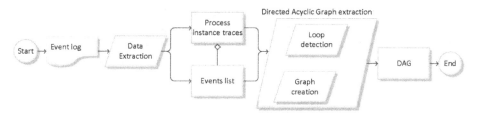

Fig. 1. Algorithm for event log transformation into belief network

The proposed approach starts with an event log (for details, see Section 3) extracted from existing information systems. The steps of the algorithm are:

1. Data is extracted from an event log – process instance traces reflecting each indi-vidual process execution are extracted into a set for loop detection and all individ-ual events (which are associated to some trace) are extracted into additional set for graph creation.
2. The graph nodes are created/modified/updated while enumerating the event set.
3. Upon possible loop detection, the loop source is identified and if the loop exists in the traces it is saved for last step, otherwise the graph is modified to reflect control flow but avoid the loop.
4. When the event set is enumerated, additional dummy activities are created reflect-ing loops in the process.

The output of the algorithm is a DAG reflecting a one-way flow through the activi-ties represented in the event log.

3   Event Logs

Process mining focuses on extraction of knowledge from event logs commonly available in today's information systems. One of the purposes of business process mining is to discover business process models or to check conformance of/enhance existing models [2]. The process mining starts from the events stored in information systems (i.e. transaction logs, audit trails, etc.).

For this paper, we adapt the van Dogen definition of event logs [3]. We introduce two additional elements – M and δ. The definition is as follows:

Definition 1. *An event log over a set of activities A and time domain TD is defined as* $L_{A,TD} = (E, C, M, \alpha, \gamma, \beta, \succ)$, *Where:*

- *E is a finite set of events,*
- *C is a finite set of cases (process instances),*
- *M is a finite set of attributes,*
- $\delta: M \to E$ *is a function assigning each data attribute to an event,*
- $\alpha: E \to A$ *is a function assigning each event to an activity,*
- $\gamma: E \to TD$ *is a function assigning each event to a timestamp,*
- $\beta: E \to C$ *is a surjective function assigning each event to a case,*
- $\succ \subseteq E \times E$ *is the succession relation, which imposes a total ordering on the events in E*

The trace in the definition above reflects each business process case. In our context, we call it a trace, since it is a trace of execution history of a business case.

Table 1. Event log example

Trace ID	Event	Timestamp	Organization Resource	Data
1	*Incoming claim*	2014.01.05 8:05	*{actor A}*	*{claimant }*
1	*Register claim*	2014.01.05 8:30	*{actor A}*	*{claim size}*
1	*End*	2014.01.05 13:57	*{actor A}*	*{rejected}*
2	*Incoming claim*	2014.01.07 13:07	*{actor B}*	*{claimant}*
2	*Register claim*	2014.01.07 13:13	*{actor B}*	*{claim size}*
2	*Initiate payment*	2014.01.10 11:15	*{actor B}*	*{payment size}*
2	*End*	2014.01.10 11:17	*{actor B}*	*{complete}*

There are many difficulties in extraction of the process models – the events are intertwined, the logs might contain noise or they could lack data [4].

Event logs used in process mining are more formal. At the moment, there are 2 types of event logs in use for process mining purposes. They are MXML [5] and XES[6]. Both of these formats are based on XML markup language and are used for storing information about the execution of the business processes – metadata, business process instance (case) information and events captured in the information system about the execution of the business processes. Since the XES format is a newer version and is an upgrade of the MXML, we use the XES for the purposes of this paper. An example fragment of event log in XES format looks like this:

```
<trace>
    <string key="concept:name" value="0" />
    <string key="description" value="Example process instance" />
    <event>
        <string key="org:resource" value="employee age 30-39" />
        <date key="time:timestamp" value="1970-01-01T01:00:00.000+01:00" />
        <string key="lifecycle:transition" value="complete" />
        <string key="concept:name" value="activity completed" />
    </event>
```

4   Directed Acyclic Graph Extraction

Existing business process mining approaches are not suitable for DAG extraction. This is because they allow edges in the graph that would form a loop (for example see experimental results in Section 5). The loops in those graphs appear because:

- The business process contains a loop and it is extracted as such from the event log;
- The business process contains parallel activities which are extracted as sequences from the event log. This extraction renders the model semantically incorrect and modeled activities become causally dependent, while in reality they are independent.

For example, there may be traces "ABCD", "ACBD" and "ABBCD". The first two traces do not have any repeated activities and have no loops, but standard process mining tools would extract it in a way to allow a loop (fig. 2a). The correct way would be to model them as independent activities (fig. 2b). For the third trace, the process allows the loop and it would look like shown in figure 2c. As it can be seen, there are two problems to be solved for DAG extraction – avoidance of loops not appearing in the event logs and restructuration of loops into single blocks to hide them.

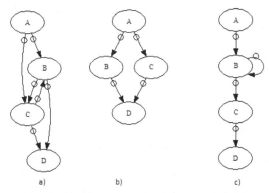

Fig. 2. Incorrect (a) and correct (b) graphs for traces "ABCD" and "ACBD"; graph of trace "ABBCD" (c)

We define directed acyclic graph as follows:

Definition 2. *Directed acyclic graph over event log L is defined as* $T_L = (N, D, \propto)$, *where:*

- *N is a set of nodes,*
- $\propto: N \rightarrow E$ *is a function mapping nodes to events,*
- $D = \{N \times N: n_i, n_j \in N, N \in c, c \in C \; n_i \succ n_j \& n_i \nprec n_j\}$ *is a set of edges connecting nodes, whose representative events follow each other but do not form a loop and exist in the same trace;*

A process instance loop in our context is defined as a set of events that are ordered in sequence, but the first and last events in the set appears in the log more than once and they belong to the same trace:

Definition 3. *A process instance loop in an event log L is a set of events* $P=\{p_0, p_1, ..., p_{i-1}, p_i\}$ *where:*

- *P is a finite set of events,*
- $\forall p \in P: p \in E$ *all events in the set belong to the event log,*
- $\forall p_k, p_j \in P : p_k \succ p_j$, *where* $k > j, k > 0, j > 0, k < i, j < i$, *all events inside the loop are ordered,*
- $p_0 \succ p_i \& p_i \succ p_0$, *first and last elements follow each other in the trace*
- $\forall p \in P, E \rightarrow c \in C$, *all events in a loop belong to the same trace*

An incorrect model level loop in our context is defined as a set of nodes that are ordered in a sequence and its first and last elements and their corresponding events never form a loop in any trace in an event log.

As we can see, the objective of DAG generation is to transform an event log into a graph, where events follow each other in a way that would not form a loop. The loops existing in the event log must still be reflected in the graph to represent the semantics of the process flow.

To solve this task, our approach is to iterate through the set of events and build the graph. While iterating the events and creating the graph, we must check if it would create a loop. To check if adding a node or creating an edge would create a loop, we go through the tree from bottom to top from the point where the edge/node would be added and check if we find a node with the same name. If we find one, then the arc/node would create a loop.

If it does create a loop and there exists corresponding loop in event logs, it must be saved for additional processing. If a loop does not exist in the event log, there needs to be an additional step removing the loop but still reflecting the data and ordering as it is presented in the event log. For this purpose, we save the loop for later processing.

For the problem of an incorrect model level loop, we find nearest common previous event for the child and parent nodes and make the nodes independent of each other, since we are sure that they never form a loop and are independent of each other (since their execution order is independent).

Finally, after the creation of the directed acyclic graph, we enumerate loops existing in the event logs but not yet reflected in the graph that were saved in previous steps. For each loop, we create dummy graph nodes and place them directly after the last event in the loop and before the next event, since the execution of the loop depends on the activity before the control flow activating the loop.

The algorithm used in our approach to form a directed acyclic graph is shown in pseudo code below:

```
For each trace in traces
  For each event in trace
    If Graph.NodeCount = 0
      CreateRootNode(event.previous)
    Else if not Graph.HasNode(event.previous)
      Graph.AppendNode(event.previous)
    If Graph.CreatesLoop(event,event.previous)
      If ExistsLoopInTrac-
es(event.name,Parent(event).name)
        SaveLoop(event,Parent(event),Next(event))
      Node x =
Graph.NearestCommonParentNode(event,Parent(event))
      Graph.AppendChild(x,event)
    Else
      Graph.AppendChild(event,Parent(event))
For each loop in SavedLoops
  Graph.AppendDummyNode(loop)
```

The result of the algorithm is a DAG which reflects the control flow of the process but avoids any possible loops.

5   Experimental Results

In order to test the proposed approach, a custom tool was made for XES event log processing and DAG extraction.

For comparison with other approaches, we used alpha algorithm [7], Heuristics-Miner [8] and manual event log review to see if the extracted graph reflects the process control flow.

For experimental test data, two event logs were selected – a synthetic log composed of 3437 traces consisting of up to 11 events and BPI 2012 challenge real-life log taken from financial institute, containing 262200 events in 13087 traces.

The experiments tested two parameters – performance and correctness. Performance was tested by extracting the process model 5 times and making the average of the amount of time it takes to visualize the model. Correctness in our case is how well the proposed approach reflects the control flow of the process model. The performance results are presented in table 2.

Table 2. Performance comparison of proposed approach and existing approaches

Approach	Presented approach	Alpha algorithm	HeuristicsMiner
Synthetic log	4.15s	3.27s	1.63s
Real-Life log	40.63s	10.27s	5.67s

The performance of the proposed approach appears to linearly depend on the amount of events in the event log. It is because the custom tool does not keep history – every time it checks for loop in the traces, it does so by iterating through all the event traces. The performance might be improved by optimizing the loop detection algorithm and implementing caching of already found event transitions. At the moment the algorithm's performance is comparable with the other approaches only when the event log does not contain a lot of events. In case of many events in the log, the execution of the approach is slow.

To present the structural testing, we present some fragments of extracted processes. In case of the synthetic logs, by manually reviewing the event log, it was noticed that the log does not contain any loops allowing for "*check on advice complete -> advice claimant ->initiate payment*", but the alpha algorithm extracted the process that allows for the loop to exist (figure 4). That is because the algorithm does not differentiate between model level loop and process instance level loop. Our proposed approach successfully avoided creating the loop (figure 3).

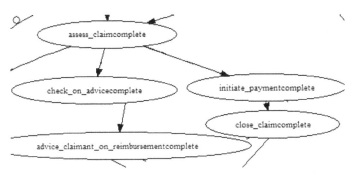

Fig. 3. Fragment of the extracted DAG by the proposed approach

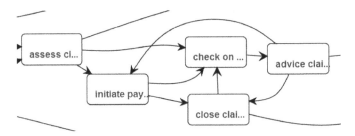

Fig. 4. Fragment of the extracted graph by alpha algorithm

For the second log, there were some loops that were avoided by the presented approach, but the log contained some loops in the process model too. One of the loops in the event log was "*w_afhandelen_leadsstart->w_afhandelen_leadcomplete*". For this loop, the approach created dummy node "*d*" which has an edge out of the last event of the loop and edges to the nodes that correspond to the next events in the event log. The fragment of the extracted graph is shown in figure 5.

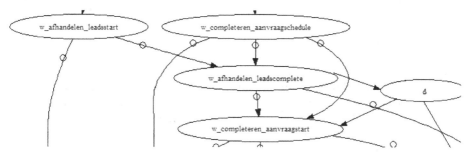

Fig. 5. Fragment of the extracted graph showing dummy node

6   Related Work

The paper proposes custom graph extraction algorithm with a purpose of loop removal to get a DAG for Bayesian belief network. There are quite a few process discovery algorithms [9] that are based on petri net (graph) extraction from event logs. Existing algorithms, i.e. HeuristicsMiner [8], Fuzzy miner [7] or Genetic Miner [4], extract graphs with loops or with loops that do not actually exist in the process rendering them unusable for generation of Bayesian belief networks. There's been research on generic DAG extraction from sequential data, i.e. [10], but the generic methods do not take into account the semantics of business processes, where loops are important and have to be presented in the graph in some way.

Process mining has seen quite a few applications in business process analysis. It has been used for time prediction – in [11] authors use regression equations based on event logs to prepare model for prediction on when the process instance (case) will be finished; in [12] authors generate transition system from an even log which is used for time prediction of a case. Authors of [13] propose to simulate discovered models for use in decision support.

Bayesian networks is not a new research area, but its application in process mining has not been widely researched. In [16], authors extract Bayesian network from an event log. The authors do not take into account the possible extracted structure, but rather attempt to extract it by analyzing dependency between events in the log. In our approach, we use custom network structure extraction approach to model dependency.

7   Conclusions and Future Work

This paper tackles the problem of Directed Acyclic Graph (DAG) extraction from an event log to be used for Bayesian belief networks generation. The main problem of the existing approaches that makes them not suitable for this task is their inability to avoid loops in the extracted graph.

The presented approach is suitable for DAG extraction, because it checks if the extracted graph conforms to the ordering of event in an event log and transforms loops into dummy nodes representing loops.

The experimental results show that the algorithm is able to work with both simple (synthetic) and complicated (real-life) logs, although it needs optimization, since it scales linearly with the amount of events in the event logs.

Extracted DAGs allow creation of Bayesian belief networks which simplify the task of business intelligence extraction and future work includes combination of DAG extraction and event log transformation into Bayesian Belief network for complicated probabilistic analysis of the event logs. The Bayesian Belief networks could be used for business knowledge extraction and simulation of business processes based on real data.

References

1. Aytulun, S.K., Guneri, A.F.: Business process modelling with stochastic networks. Int. J. Prod. Res. 46, 2743–2764 (2008)
2. Rozinat, A., Mans, R.S., Song, M., van der Aalst, W.M.P.: Discovering simulation models. Inf. Syst. 34, 305–327 (2009)
3. van Dongen, B.F., Crooy, R.A., van der Aalst, W.M.P.: Cycle time prediction: When will this case finally be finished? In: Meersman, R., Tari, Z. (eds.) OTM 2008, Part I. LNCS, vol. 5331, pp. 319–336. Springer, Heidelberg (2008)
4. van der Aalst, W.M.P., de Medeiros, A.K.A., Weijters, A.J.M.M.: Genetic process mining. In: Ciardo, G., Darondeau, P. (eds.) ICATPN 2005. LNCS, vol. 3536, pp. 48–69. Springer, Heidelberg (2005)
5. Van Dongen, B.F., van der Aalst, W.M.P.: A Meta Model for Process Mining Data. EMOI-INTEROP 160, 30 (2005)
6. Verbeek, H.M.W., Buijs, J.C.A.M., van Dongen, B.F., van der Aalst, W.M.P.: XES, xE-Same, and proM 6. In: Soffer, P., Proper, E. (eds.) CAiSE Forum 2010. LNBIP, vol. 72, pp. 60–75. Springer, Heidelberg (2011)
7. Van der Aalst, W.M.P., Rubin, V., Verbeek, H.M.W., van Dongen, B.F., Kindler, E., Günther, C.W.: Process mining: a two-step approach to balance between underfitting and overfitting. Softw. Syst. Model. 9, 87–111 (2010)
8. Weijters, A.J.M.M., Van Der Aalst, W.M.P., Medeiros, A.K.A.: De: Process Mining with the HeuristicsMiner Algorithm. Cirp Ann. Technol. 166, 1–34 (2006)
9. van Dongen, B.F., Alves de Medeiros, A.K., Wen, L.: Process mining: Overview and outlook of petri net discovery algorithms. In: Jensen, K., van der Aalst, W.M.P. (eds.) ToPNoC II. LNCS, vol. 5460, pp. 225–242. Springer, Heidelberg (2009)

10. Mannila, H., Meek, C.: Global partial orders from sequential data. In: Proceedings of the sixth ACM SIGKDD International Conference on Knowledge Discovery and Data Mining, pp. 161–168 (2000)
11. van Dongen, B.F., Crooy, R.A., van der Aalst, W.M.P.: Cycle time prediction: When will this case finally be finished? In: Meersman, R., Tari, Z. (eds.) OTM 2008, Part I. LNCS, vol. 5331, pp. 319–336. Springer, Heidelberg (2008)
12. Van der Aalst, W.M.P., Schonenberg, M.H., Song, M.: Time prediction based on process mining. Inf. Syst. 36, 450–475 (2011)
13. Liu, Y., Zhang, H., Li, C., Jiao, R.J.: Workflow simulation for operational decision support using event graph through process mining. Decis. Support Syst. 52, 685–697 (2012)
14. Rozinat, A., Van Der Aalst, W.M.P.: Decision Mining in Business Processes
15. De Leoni, M., van der Aalst, W.M.P.: Data-aware process mining: discovering decisions in processes using alignments. In: Proceedings of the 28th Annual ACM Symposium on Applied Computing, pp. 1454–1461 (2013)
16. Sutrisnowati, R.A., Bae, H., Park, J., Ha, B.-H.: Learning Bayesian Network from Event Logs Using Mutual Information Test. In: 2013 IEEE 6th Int. Conf. Serv. Comput. Appl., pp. 356–360 (2013)

Comparison of Genetic Programming, Grammatical Evolution and Gene Expression Programming Techniques

Evaldas Guogis and Alfonsas Misevičius

Kaunas University of Technology, Department of Multimedia Engineering,
Studentų st. 50–400/416a, LT–51368 Kaunas, Lithuania
`evaldas.guogis@singleton-labs.lt`,
`alfonsas.misevicius@ktu.lt`

Abstract. The purpose of this paper is to compare the efficiency of three different evolutionary programming techniques – Genetic Programming, Grammatical Evolution and Gene Expression Programming. These algorithms were applied to different type test problems with the same set of parameters. The results of the experiments and some insights on similar experiments of the other authors are provided.

Keywords: genetic programming, grammatical evolution, gene expression programming, symbolic regression problem, multiplexer problem, artificial ant problem.

1   Introduction

Genetic programming is an evolutionary algorithm with the goal to evolve computer programs to solve user-defined tasks. This field enjoys growing popularity, modifications of existing techniques are proposed or new techniques are created. In this paper, we analyse one such technique – gene expression programming (GEP), proposed by Ferreira [3]. Information about the performance of this technique is contradicting. While Ferreira reported few orders of magnitude better performance compared to genetic programming, Oltean and Grossan [4] observed generally poor GEP performance on the so-called symbolic regression problems. Results published by different authors are often hard to compare because, for the same test problems, different parameter sets are used. We decided to address this issue and to compare performance of three different genetic programming techniques – "classical" tree-based Genetic Programming (later in the article it will be called Genetic Programming, or GP), Grammatical Evolution (GE), and GEP. Three different problem types were used in the experiments – symbolic regression, multiplexer and artificial ant.

The paper is organized as follows. Genetic programming techniques are introduced in Section 2. The test problems that were used to compare these techniques are

G. Dregvaite and R. Damasevicius (Eds.): ICIST 2014, CCIS 465, pp. 182–193, 2014.

discussed in Section 3. Further, the results of the experiments are presented and, finally, brief concluding remarks are given.

2   Background Information

To evolve program to solve a given task by the means of genetic programming, the following steps must be performed [1, 8]. First, a set of *terminals* (program's external inputs, zero arity[1] functions and constants, for example, $T = \{X, 1.0\}$) and a set of *functions* (functions with arity of one or higher, for example, $F = \{+, -, *, /\}$) that are sufficient to solve given problem must be composed. In this article, these sets of terminals and functions will be called *GPTerminals* and *GPFunctions*, to avoid the confusion with terminals in Backus Naur Form grammar (see Section 2.2). The next step is to create a fitness function that evaluates how good a given solution as a single figure of merit is. Then, initial generation consisting of available GPTerminals and GPFunctions is generated, fitness of each individual is evaluated, and a new set of individuals (called generation) is produced by applying genetic operations with specified probabilities on best-fit individuals. This step is repeated until an acceptable solution has been found or a maximum allowed number of generations has been reached.

The following sections provide a brief introduction to GP, GE and GEP and highlight the main differences between these techniques.

2.1   Genetic Programming

The tree-based Genetic Programming was introduced by Koza [1]. Individuals are seen as parse trees (Fig. 1). The tree leaves represent GPTerminals, whereas the internal nodes represent GPFunctions.

While such tree representation is convenient to use in some programming languages (such as LISP) it might not always be the case and efficiency may be lost. In addition, some genetic operations may be harder to use or implement. For example, for the tree representation, different mutation operations must be used for the leaves and internal nodes.

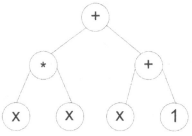

Fig. 1. GP individual expressed as a parse tree. This parse tree can be decoded to $X*X+X+1$

---

[1]   Arity – the number of arguments a function takes.

2.2   Grammatical Evolution

GE was introduced by O'Niel and Rayan [2]. This technique uses Backus Naur Form[2] grammar. BNF grammar can be expressed as $G = \{N, T, P, S\}$, where N denotes a set of non-terminals, T is a set of terminals[3], P denotes a set of production rules of mapping of the elements of N to the elements of T, and S is a start symbol (S must belong to N). For example:

$$N = \{expr, op, var\}$$

$$T = \{+,-,*,/, X, 1.0\}$$

Production rules P:

```
<expr> ::= <expr> <op> <expr>      (a0)
         | (<expr> <op> <expr>)    (a1)
         | <var>                   (a2)
<op> ::= +                         (b0)
       | -                         (b1)
       | *                         (b2)
       | /                         (b3)
<var> ::= X                        (c0)
        | 1.0                      (c1)
```

$$S = expr$$

GE individual is represented as a binary string of variable length. Consecutive groups of 8 bits (*codons*) are converted to the corresponding integers and are used to select a production rule from BNF grammar using the following mapping function:

$$Rule = (Codon\_value)\mathrm{mod}(Number\_of\_rules)$$

Consider the BNF grammar from the example above and GE individual in Figure 2. The start symbol is <expr>. From production rules, one can see that, for <expr>, three different rules – (a0), (a1) or (a2) – can be applied. To make a choice, the first codon value (72) is taken and used in the mapping function. Then, $72 \bmod 3 = 0$ means that the first rule (a0) has to be used. Thus, <expr> is replaced with <expr><op><expr>.

Now, the left-most not terminal symbol is <expr>. The second codon value is 18. If the mapping function is applied ($18 \bmod 3 = 0$), the rule (a0) has to be used again. The expression becomes: <expr><op><expr><op><expr>.

In the next step ($128 \bmod 3 = 2$), the rule (a2) is applied, which produces the following result: <var><op><expr><op><expr>.

---

[2]   Backus Naur Form is a notation to describe the syntax of a given language in the form of production rules.

[3]   It should be noted that GE terminal set consists of GPTerminals and GPFunctions.

The mapping continues until there are no non-terminal symbols left in the expression. The final result is X * X + (X + 1).

If there are extra codons left after mapping, they are ignored. If the end of the individual is reached before finishing the mapping, a wrapping operator is invoked – codons are read from the start of individual once again. If wrapping operator is invoked certain number of times, the mapping process is stopped and an individual gets the lowest possible fitness score.

| 72 | 18 | 128 | 212 | 86 | 11 | 158 | 120 | 35 | 98 | 8 | 113 | 75 |

Fig. 2. An example of GE individual (codons expressed as integers)

Compared to other techniques, GE has few major advantages. The use of BNF grammar allows easy transformation of programs into any programming language that can be expressed by BNF grammar. In addition, domain knowledge can be incorporated into the grammar and no other parts of the system need to be modified. The representation of individuals in the form of binary strings is very flexible and convenient to use. Genetic operators are easy to apply. Wrapping is an effective way to reduce the number of unfit individuals.

2.3   Gene Expression Programming

GEP individuals are composed of one or more genes. Each gene is a fixed length string and consists of two different parts, called domains. *Head domain* contains function and terminal symbols, *tail domain* contains only terminal symbols (it acts as a buffer of the terminal symbols). The head length (h) can be chosen, the tail length (t) is calculated by the formula: $t = h(n-1)+1$, where n is the highest function arity.

Consider a gene in Figure 3. For the function set $F = \{+,-,*,/\}$, $n = 2$. If the head length $h = 5$, then the tail length $t = 6$, consequently the total length of the gene is $5+6 = 11$. This gene can be expressed as a tree (equivalent to the tree shown in Figure 1) or decoded to the expression: X * X + X + 1. First seven symbols of this gene are used, others are simply ignored.

head					tail					
0	**1**	**2**	**3**	**4**	**5**	6	7	8	9	0
+	*****	**+**	**X**	**X**	**X**	**1**	1	**X**	1	1

Fig. 3. GEP gene example

The main advantage of the GEP technique is that it always produces syntactically correct individuals. Genetic operators are easy to implement, but must be applied on the head and on the tail separately, which makes it slightly inconvenient.

More details of the GEP algorithm and its' strengths and weaknesses can be found in [3] and [4] respectively.

3   Test Problems

Three problem types used in the experiments are described in this section: symbolic regression, multiplexer, and artificial ant. This is a popular collection of the test problems widely used in the field of genetic programming.

Two different test variants for each problem type were used.

3.1   Symbolic Regression Problem

The objective of this problem is to find a function in symbolic form whose output matches a given set of inputs and outputs. One of the most common symbolic regression test problems is quartic polynomial function $x^4 + x^3 + x^2 + x$ examined in [1,2,3,4]. GEP performance results on this problem were inconclusive. Ferreira[3] found that GEP greatly surpasses GP, while Oltean and Grosan [4] found the opposite. Note that Ferreira used a smaller functions set (sin, cos, exp, log were not allowed). In addition, data points were from a different interval. To our opinion, this is the main reason of the difference in performance. Therefore, we have examined both test instances. They are denoted as follows:

P1 – the functions set used by Koza[1] and randomly generated data set.
P2 – the functions set and predefined data set (Table 2) used by Ferreira [3].

Table 1. General parameters for symbolic regression problems **P1** and **P2**

	P1	**P2**
GPTerminals:	x (the independent variable)	x (the independent variable)
GPFunctions:	+, -, *, /, sin, cos, exp, log	+, -, *, /
Fitness cases:	The given sample of 20 data points in the interval (-1, +1)	The given sample of 10 data points in the interval (0, 20)
Raw Fitness:	The sum of the error over the 20 fitness cases	The sum of the error over the 10 fitness cases
Success predicate:	$\|f(x_i) - y_i\| \leq 0.01$ for all 20 data points	$\|f(x_i) - y_i\| \leq 0.01$ for all 10 data points

100 sets of data points in the interval (-1, +1) were generated (1 set for each run) for the problem **P1**. The same predefined data set (Table 2) was used in all 100 runs.

Table 2. Data set for the symbolic regression problem **P2**

x	2.81	6	7.043	8	10	11.38	12	14	15	20
$f(x)$	95.2425	1554	2866.55	4680	11110	18386	22620	41370	54240	168420

3.2   Multiplexer Problem

The goal of Boolean multiplexer problem is to discover a composition of Boolean functions that can return correct value of a Boolean function after seeing a certain number of examples.

An N-multiplexer has N inputs and one output. Inputs consist of k address bits a_i ($i = 1, ..., k$) and 2^k data bits d_j ($j = 1, ..., 2^k$). The total number of multiplexer inputs is: $N = k + 2^k$.

The Boolean N-multiplexer has inputs: $a_0, a_1, ..., a_{k-1}, d_0, d_1, ..., d_{2k-1}$. The output of the Boolean multiplexer function is a value of one of the data bits. Which data bit to select is determined by the values of the address bits. For example, in Figure 4, 6-multiplexer is shown. If address bits $a_0 a_1$ are 01, the Boolean 6-multiplexer output will be the data bit d_2 ($d_2 = 0$).

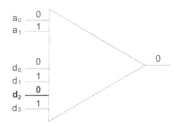

Fig. 4. Example of 6-multiplexer with the input values 010101 and the output value 0

The examined multiplexers are as follows: **P3** (3-multiplexer) and **P4** (6-multiplexer).

Table 3. General parameters for the multiplexer problems **P3** and **P4**

	P3	P4
GPTerminals:	a_0, d_0, d_1	$a_0, a_1, d_0, d_1, d_2, d_3$
GPFunctions:	AND, OR, NOT	AND, OR, NOT, IF
Fitness cases:	$2^3 = 8$ (all possible input combinations)	$2^6 = 64$ (all possible input combinations)
Raw Fitness:	Number of the correct outputs for fitness cases	Number of the correct outputs for fitness cases
Standardized Fitness:	8 minus raw fitness	64 minus raw fitness
Success predicate:	Correct output for all fitness cases	Correct output for all fitness cases

3.3   Artificial Ant Problem

The purpose of this problem is to control an artificial ant, attempting to find all food lying on the grid. Food items form a twisting trail. The ant is facing east and the start is in the upper left corner of the trail in the square marked X (Fig. 5). The ant can perform one of the following operations: move forward one square in the direction it is currently facing, turn left or turn right (all consumes one step) or sense food ahead (free). When the ant moves into square, it eats the food if there is any. The ant can also use a binary sensing operator "food ahead". This sensing operator enables to look into the square the ant is currently facing and executes one of its arguments depending upon whether the square ahead contains food or is empty. An ant control program is repeated until a limit of steps is reached or all food items are eaten.

Two instances of the artificial ant problem were used:
P5 –Santa Fe Trail (as described by Koza [1]);
P6 – Trail from Dynamic Ant Trail problem (proposed by Fagan et al. [7]).

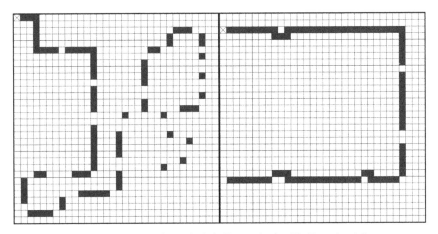

Fig. 5. Santa Fe Trail on the left, Dynamic Ant Trail on the right

The identical parameters were used for both problems (see the table below). Steps limit in Santa Fe Trail was increased from 600 (used by Koza) to 650, as suggested by Georgiou and Teahan [8]. 500 steps limit was used in Dynamic Tail.

Table 4. General parameters for both artificial ant problems

GPTerminals:	LEFT, RIGHT, MOVE
GPFunctions:	IF_FOOD_AHEAD
Fitness cases:	One fitness case
Raw Fitness:	Number of the food items found
Standardized Fitness:	Total number of the food items minus raw fitness
Success predicate:	All food items found

4   Computational Experiments

4.1   Experimental Setup

The extensive computational experiments have been carried out using x86 series computer with an Intel 2.8 GHz four core processor, with 4GB RAM and 32-bit MS Windows operating system. Java library EpochX [9] was used to solve GP and GE problems. EpochX library extension developed by the authors of this paper was used for GEP problems.

4.2   General Experiment Settings

For each problem, 100 independent runs were performed, 50 generations in each run. Population size $M = 100$ was used for problems **P2** and **P3**, $M = 500$ for the rest of the problems. Tournament selection (tournament size − 7) was used in all the experiments while comparing all techniques. One-point crossover was used with a probability of $p_{cr} = 0.9$.

BNF grammars used in the experiments can be seen in Table 5. It should be noted that the grammar used for artificial ant problem is different from the grammar used by O'Niel and Rayan [2]. As Robilliard et al. [5] noticed, the grammar used by O'Niel and Rayan does not allow multiple <op> inside THEN and ELSE blocks of the function IF-FOOD-AHEAD (thus reducing a search space and giving GE unfair advantage).

Table 5. BNF grammars for all examined problems

P1. Symbolic regression	**P2**. Symbolic regression

<pre>S ::= <expr>
<expr> ::= <expr> <op> <expr>
        | (<expr> <op> <expr>)
        | <pre_op>(<expr>)
        | <var>
<op> ::= + | - | * | /
<pre-op> ::= Sin | Cos | Exp | Log
<var> ::= X | 1.0</pre>
	<pre>S ::= <expr>
	<expr> ::= <expr> <op> <expr>
	        | (<expr> <op> <expr>)
	        | <var>
	<op> ::= + | - | * | /
	<var> ::= X | 1.0</pre>

P3. 3-multiplexer	**P4**. 6-multiplexer

<pre>S ::= <expr>
<expr>::= <expr> <op> <expr>
       | (<expr> <op> <expr>)
       | <pre-op>
       | <var>
<op> ::= AND | OR
<pre-op> ::= NOT (<expr>)
<var>::= A0 | D0 | D1</pre>
	<pre>S ::= <expr>
	<expr> ::= <expr> <op> <expr>
	        | (<expr> <op> <expr>)
	        | <pre-op>
	        | <var>
	<op> ::= AND | OR
	<pre-op> ::= NOT (<expr>)
	          | IF ((<expr>) (
	<expr>) ELSE (<expr>))
	<var> ::= A0 | A1 | D0 | D1 | D2 | D3</pre>

P5, P6. Artifitial ant problem	

<pre>S ::= <expr>
<expr> ::= <line> | <expr> <line>)
<line> ::= IF-FOOD-AHEAD THEN (<expr>) ELSE (<expr>)
         | op
<op> ::= move | left | right</pre>	

4.3   Results

The results of the experiments are presented in this section. The success rate over the number of generations for each tested problem can be seen in figures below.

GP found more solutions for the problem **P1** at the early generations but later got overtaken by both GE and GEP which almost tied at the end (Fig 6.).

GP found more solutions for the problem **P2** at early generations again. All algorithms performed well and found correct solution in more than 90% of runs (Fig 7.).

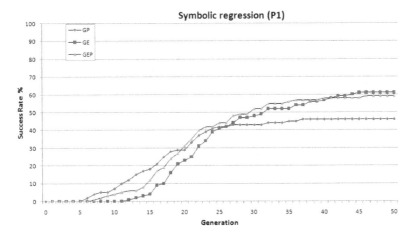

Fig. 6. Success rate on the symbolic regression problem **P1** (population size $M = 500$)

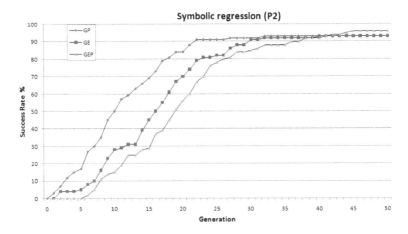

Fig. 7. Success rate on the symbolic regression problem **P2** (population size $M = 100$)

Very similar trend can be seen for the 3-multiplexer problem. GP finds more solutions early and finishes just below 90% success rate threshold. GE and GEP show approximately equally good results again (Fig. 8).

The different behaviour has been observed on the 6-multiplexer problem (Fig. 9). This time, GE performed best with 61% success rate, GEP performed worst with 43% success rate, and GP was almost exactly in the middle with 51% success rate.

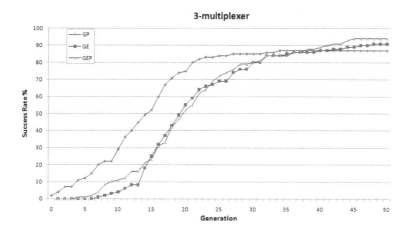

Fig. 8. Success rate on the 3-multiplexer problem (population size $M = 100$)

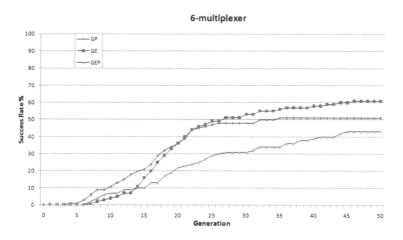

Fig. 9. Success rate on the 6-multiplexer problem (population size $M = 500$)

The Santa Fe Trail problem turned out to be the hardest problem. As can be seen in Fig. 10, only a few solutions were found with GP and GE, and GEP found no solutions at all.

The experiments were repeated with the obviously less complicated trail taken from Dynamic Ant benchmark. This time, GP showed the best performance, but, overall, the efficiency remained poor for all the algorithms.

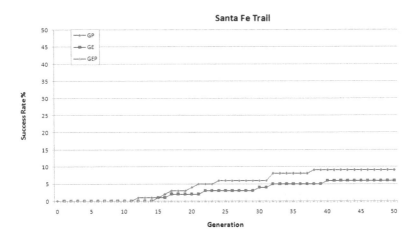

Fig. 10. Success rate on the Santa Fe Trail problem (population size $M = 500$)

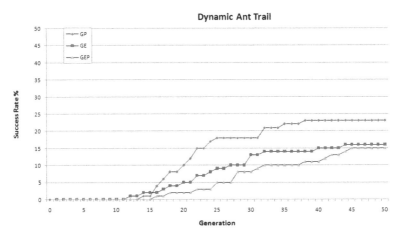

Fig. 11. Success rate on the Dynamic Trail problem (population size $M = 500$)

5   Concluding Remarks

We have examined the GEP technique on the symbolic regression and multiplexer test problems. Additionally, we have analysed the GEP performance on the artificial ant test problems and this is, to our knowledge, the first attempt of testing of the efficiency of the GEP technique on these problems. For the sake of the fair examination, we have studied also the GP and GE techniques on the above mentioned test problems. The same set of controlling parameters was applied in all cases.

Overall, the results were not conclusive. As a whole, GE performance was best, but difference was not drastic. We strongly suspect that these differences could be most likely reduced even more by fine-tuning of the algorithm parameters (like the maximum tree depth on GP or the head size on GEP), using other selection procedures or different tournament schemes.

By analysing the results got by the other authors [3,4], we offer some insights.

In the experiments, we used tournament size 7 selection. When we changed tournament to binary, we noticed the success rate drop for both symbolic regression problems and 6-multiplexer problem. In Oltean and Grosan [4] experiments, binary tournament was applied. This might be one of the reasons why GE and GEP performance is quite poor in [4]. A huge performance difference between GP and GEP reported by Ferreira [3] can be explained by the fact that the comparison was not fair enough. A different set of functions, which reduces a search space, was used for the symbolic regression problem in [3]. Also, a fitness function designed to decode addresses one by one was used for 11-multiplexer problem in [3]. More sophisticated fitness function could better explain the difference in GP and GEP performance.

References

1. Koza, J.R.: Genetic Programming: On the Programming of Computers by Means of Natural Selection. MIT Press, Cambridge (1992)
2. O'Neill, M., Ryan, C.: Grammatical Evolution: Evolutionary Automatic Programming in a Arbitrary Language. Genetic programming, vol. 4. Kluwer Academic Publishers, Norwel (2003)
3. Ferreira, C.: Gene Expression Programming: A New Adaptive Algorithm for Solving Problems. Complex Systems 13, 87–129 (2001)
4. Oltean, M., Grosan, C.: A Comparison of Several Linear Genetic Programming Techniques. Complex Systems 14 (2003)
5. Robilliard, D., Mahler, S., Verhaghe, D., Fonlupt, C.: Santa Fe Trail Hazards. In: Talbi, E.-G., Liardet, P., Collet, P., Lutton, E., Schoenauer, M. (eds.) EA 2005. LNCS, vol. 3871, pp. 1–12. Springer, Heidelberg (2006)
6. Georgiou, L., Teahan, W.J.: Grammatical Evolution and the Santa Fe Trail Problem. In: Filipe, J., Kacprzyk, J. (eds.) IJCCI (ICEC), pp. 10–19. SciTePress (2010)
7. Fagan, D., Nicolau, M., Hemberg, E., O'Neill, M., Brabazon, A.: Dynamic Ant: Introducing a new benchmark for Genetic Programming in Dynamic Environments. University College Dublin, Ireland, Technical Report UCD-CSI-2011-04 (2011)
8. Poli, R., Langdon, W. B., McPhee, N. F.: A field guide to genetic programming (2008), Published via http://lulu.com and freely available at http://www.gp-field-guide.org.uk (with contributions by Koza, J. R.)
9. Otero, F.E.B., Castle, T., Johnson, C.G.: EpochX: Genetic Programming in Java with Statistics and Event Monitoring. In: Proceedings of the 2012 Genetic and Evolutionary Conference Companion (GECCO 2012), Philadelphia. ACM Press (2012)

GoalDAG – ArchiMate Integration

Cahit Gungor[1,2] and Halit Oguztuzun[2]

[1] Central Bank of Republic of Turkey, Ankara, Turkey
cahit.gungor@tcmb.gov.tr
[2] Middle East Technical University, Computer Engineering Department, Ankara, Turkey
oguztuzun@ceng.metu.edu.tr

Abstract. Organizational alignment is an important issue in various interest areas such as Strategy, Business Process Management, Requirements Engineering, and Enterprise Architecture. From IT perspective the most holistic approach on alignment and control is Enterprise Architecture. Enterprise Architecture's eminent standard framework is TOGAF with companion architecture modeling language ArchiMate. Although ArchiMate proposes Motivation Extension to facilitate strategic alignment, this extension does not offer any facility to verify and/or validate the architecture model. Moreover, the Motivation Extension proposes its model elements to be linked to the core elements only through the *stakeholder* element. This paper proposes an ArchiMate Profile for *GoalDAG*. GoalDAG is a simple goal model that can be linked to the different model elements seamlessly and enables to validate the existing model. To represent GoalDAG integration with Enterprise Architecture, ArchiMate - GoalDAG profile is developed and exemplified through TOGAF's ArchiSurance fictitious case study.

Keywords: Strategic Alignment, Enterprise Architecture, TOGAF, ArchiMate, Goal Modeling.

1 Introduction

One of the main concerns in Business Management and IT Management is business – IT alignment. In fact, the business-IT alignment is a function of strategic alignment of the organization. According to findings in the literature, CIO and CEO main concerns are mainly alignment or related to alignment to some extent [1–3]. From our point of view, Organizational Strategy, Enterprise Architecture, Requirements Engineering, and Business Process Management are varied view points for the same problem handling the issues of alignment in an organization.

A holistic approach, covering and integrating different focus areas –Organizational Strategy, Requirements Engineering, Enterprise Architecture, Business Process Management- and abstract levels of the organization from top to bottom, is missing. Authors proposed a generic goal model -*GoalDAG*- that covers abstract levels and the tools used in those abstract levels.

G. Dregvaite and R. Damasevicius (Eds.): ICIST 2014, CCIS 465, pp. 194–210, 2014.
© Springer International Publishing Switzerland 2014

Fig. 1. Research Areas in Relation to Alignment

- High Level
    - o Strategy Map, Balanced Scorecard, VMOST, Strategy Theme Based Analysis, EA Strategy Layer
- Middle Level
    - o Business Processes, EA Business Architecture
- Low Level
    - o IT implementation, EA Information Architecture

GoalDAG, a generic goal-graph based framework, is implemented to engage different interest areas, with different concerns of the high - middle - low levels of the organization. Those different interest areas use different approaches, and different tools for their own needs. The proposed capacity of covering all levels and tools of that abstraction level is highly ambitious. However the GoalDAG is basically a simple graph, the simplicity enables it to connect to an existing structure easily. Even more, the hierarchically the GoalDAG connected to a structure within an abstraction level of the organization, can be connected to a lower level structure seamlessly. In this study, GoalDAG integration with Enterprise Architecture through ArchiMate Modelling Language Extension is presented and illustrated using the ArchiSurance case study [4]. The aim is to lay the foundation of validation of ArchiMate Motivation Extension through GoalDAG.

This paper is further structured as follows. 2Section 2 provides an overview of the goal and goal hierarchy concepts specific to this study and discusses the rationale behind this research. Section 3 briefly describes Enterprise Architecture, TOGAF and ArchiMate with emphasis on ArchiMate Motivation Extension and Language Extension Mechanism of ArchiMate. The concepts of GoalDAG and its model are introduced in Section 4. Section 5 describes how ArchiMate Motivation Extension is extended to be linked with GoalDAG. Case study of ArchiSurance and results are presented in Section 6. Finally, Section 7 presents our conclusions and points to future work.

2   Rationale behind GoalDAG

Goal has different meanings, connotations, and nuances in different contexts (Defense, Psychology, Biology, Business, Software, e.g.). In this study, *Goal* word is used with the broadest possible meaning. The definition for *Goal* covers different terminology such as *mission*, *objective*, and *outcome*. *Goal* is any measurable specific result that is to be achieved. *GoalDAG* is the hierarchical organization of goals defined in this broad context. The detailed definitions of *Goal* and *GoalDAG* are presented in Section 5.

Following this simple foundation, evidently there are quite a few frameworks and methodologies to model goals. Thagard coherence model [5], GSN (Goal Structuring Notation) [6], GQM (Goal Question Metric) [7], KAOS [8], and TROPOS[9] are eminent examples of goal models.

In those models, goals and their relations are defined very clearly. Additionally, users are able to add information into the model to define goal relations distinctively. In Fig. 2, a goal model for requirements engineering is presented [10]. This model is selected since the representation is very similar to GoalDAG model presented in this study with its weighted graph structure.

Literature consists of complex, rich in meaning goal models[11]. So, what GoalDAG proposes, what is the contribution of GoalDAG? All goal models are built with expert knowledge; however, there are limited validation studies of those models. A goal model is built on expert knowledge and heuristics, still the model is a representation built on assumptions about the system. It resembles to human practical reasoning based on beliefs [12], obviously, it can be argued that an organization is more deterministic than a human being.

There are two types of validation methods to validate a goal model. First one is analyzing the correlation between two variables, which are measurements   related to the goals [13]. Second one is the animation of the system [14–16].

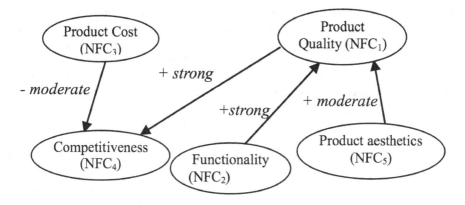

Fig. 2. An example of a goal model with weights

Correlation analysis does not take into account the whole goal hierarchy. So, assume you have two goals which are contributors of the same parent goal. They may both have positive correlation with their parent goal. What if they are in conflict with each other? Correlation analysis is a good start for initial goal hierarchy structuring, unfortunately, it fails to analyze whole goal hierarchy [17].

Validation through animation (or simulation) is well-suited solution for requirements engineering for IT systems. If the system behavior is known, which is generally true for technical systems, validation can be done through animation very effectively. Though, the strategic – tactical - operational level activities level cannot be validated through animation, since the system behavior cannot be described precisely as in a technical module. Consequently, animation cannot be applied to higher level activities of an organization.

GoalDAG model and its accompanying methodology proposes that the goal hierarchy can be validated as a whole and can also be applied to higher level goals other than technical ones. The whole structure can be covered through a simple, generic GoalDAG structure of weighted directed graph. *and/or, composition* relations can be expressed with a single attribute of goal relation, namely, contribution weight. The resulting structure becomes analogous of SEM (Structural Equation Model) [18]. SEM can be analyzed statistically to validate the goal hierarchy as a whole.

3   Enterprise Architecture

In the context of high level understanding and controlling the organization from strategic level to technical level, Enterprise Architecture (EA) comes forward as the main concept with respect to IT. TOGAF 9 defines EA as a formal description of enterprise, which is a detailed plan at component level to guide its implementation. The plan consists of structure of components, their interrelationships, and the principles and guidelines governing their design and evolution over time [19]. This definition is constructed over IEEE's definition of Architectural Description of Software Intensive

Systems which was "fundamental organization of a system embodied in its components, their relationships to each other, and to the environment, and the principles
guiding its design and evolution" [20]. But a more distinctive definition is offered by
Gartner by defining EA as the process of translating business vision and strategy into
effective enterprise change by creating, communicating and improving the key requirements, principles and models that describe the enterprise's future state and enable
its evolution. The scope of the enterprise architecture includes people, processes,
information and technology of the enterprise, and their relationships to one another
and to the external environment. Enterprise architects compose holistic solutions that
address the business challenges of the enterprise and support the governance needed
to implement them [21]. Gartner's definition is much more distinctive since it puts
more emphasis on business vision and strategy. The previous definitions given by
TOGAF and IEEE are more IT centric, so they fail to address the main concern of
guidance by business and strategy, although it is one of the top concerns of IT executives [22–25]. Business vision is originated from organizational strategy. Business
Architecture (BA) is built upon the business vision through elements of Business
Processes (BP). The other point at this stage is that BP should be layered to enable
different stakeholders to advance their interest and their expertise aspects. There are
many studies focusing on the rest of the structure which are mainly implementations
of business processes by information systems[26–34]. In other words, the concern
hierarchy, from top to bottom, should be as follows; strategic decision as top , business vision, BP hierarchy as middle and conveying those key elements through the
technical architecture as bottom. The main concern of business owners and strategic
bodies is to align IT with enterprise goals. EA's central focus is BA, BA's functional
elements are BPs, and IT's target is to implement those BPs.   Diffusion of goals from

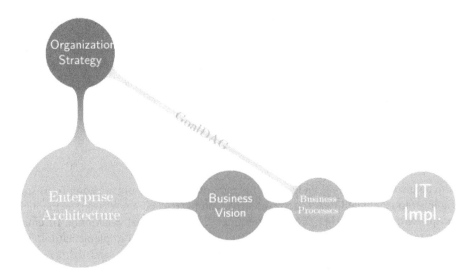

Fig. 3. Organizational Strategy Operation

strategic level to technical detail is described by GoalDAG in a quantitative way guided with professional expertise to model initial GoalDAG modeling. Fig. 3 illustrates, overall strategic operations followed in an IT intensive organization. The GoalDAG links the strategy with BPs.

3.1 Overview of ArchiMate® Architecture Modelling Language

ArchiMate®, an Open Group Standard, is an open and independent modelling language for enterprise architecture that is supported by many tool vendors and consulting firms. ArchiMate® provides instruments to enable enterprise architects to describe, analyze and visualize the relationships among business domains unambiguously [35]. There was no goal relation to the model elements in the first version of ArchiMate®, which was added in the second version. Fig. 4 presents Motivation Extension of ArchiMate®.

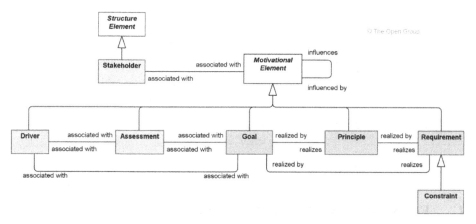

Fig. 4. ArchiMate Motivation Extension Metamodel (Property of The Open Group)

The relationship between a motivational element and architecture element is defined through stakeholder element of the model. Generally, each stakeholder defines their requirements, especially constraints to the implementations, from their specific points of view. When these requirements are evaluated in isolation from each other, some strategic concerns may be lost or the resulting implementation may conflict with the organization's strategy. Therefore, goals should diffuse to all main model elements independent of the stakeholder. Moreover, strategic goals and decisions are high level guidelines which cover all tactical and operational aspects of the implementations and actions on the system.

3.2 Overview of ArchiMate® Architecture Modelling Language

ArchiMate® consortium states that ArchiMate® contains only the concepts and relationships that are necessary for general architecture modeling [36]. The intention to keep ArchiMate® as generic as possible to cover most modelling needs, results in limited capability of expressiveness for special needs. To overcome such limitations, ArchiMate® offers Language Extension Mechanism, called "*Profiling*", to facilitate specialized or domain-specific purposes.

In profiling specialization mechanism, a *profile* is a data structure, defined separately from the ArchiMate® language, but can be dynamically coupled with concepts or relationships [36]. Profiles can be considered in two types. One is *Pre-defined profiles* which are embedded into tools that support ArchiMate® but in the meantime, enabling their specialized capability features defined as attributes and relationships. The other type of profile is *User-defined profiles*, in which user can define their own profiles according to their needs. The Fig. 5 shows examples for specialization of ArchiMate®.

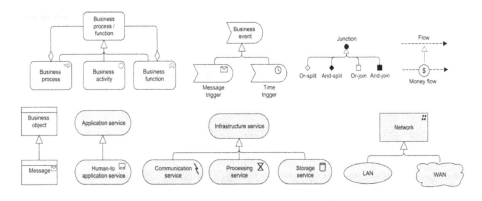

Fig. 5.   Examples of Specialized Concepts and Relationships (Property of the Open Group)

4   Formal Representation of GoalDAG

This study models goal-hierarchy as a directed acyclic graph (DAG) with weighted edges, and relation functions. The weights of the edges are called contribution weights. DAG is a graph which has no loops, no multiple arcs, and no directed cycles [37].

Ordinary DAG has at least one node with in-degree zero. In the DAG used in this study, called GoalDAG, nodes represent goals and edges represent the relation between two calls, defining direction and contribution weight. GoalDAG is an inverted DAG, where the direction of the edges is from dependent to the dependee objective. Each node is representative of a metric. The relations between metrics are depicted as edges, from dependent to dependee.

The formal definition is as follows:

$$GoalDAG = < V, E >$$

where

V is the set of nodes in G and E is the set of edge.

Measurement; is a function *m* that evaluates the value, of the node representing a metric at any given time *t*, as a real number.

$$m(i,t); i \in V, t \in Date$$

Relation Function; is a function that represents how two objectives are correlated with each other, as a real number

$$rf(i,j); i,j \in V$$

Contribution Weight; is a value that represents the degree of contribution of a goal to the parent goal, with respect to other goals which are also contributing to the same parent objective.

$$cw(i,j); i,j \in V$$

$$0 \leq cw(i,j) \leq 1$$

$$\forall i \in V : \sum_{j \in edge(i,j)} cw(i,j) \leq 1$$

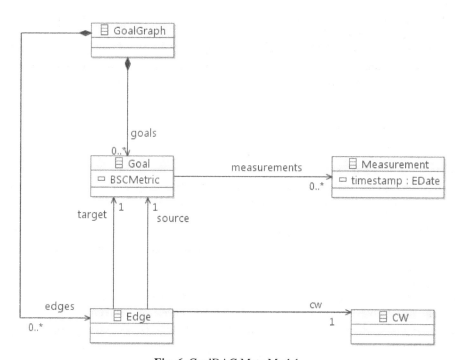

Fig. 6. GoalDAG Meta Model

Since *rf* is a function, it can represent a wide range of correlations between two goals. In this context, it is generally used to represent a linear relation of two metrics, however, the relation function can be adopted according to the best curve fitting mathematical function, such as polynomial, exponential and especially natural logarithmic.

GoalDAG meta-model is presented in Fig. 6. In this figure, the *GoalGraph* is the container element that keeps all elements related to GoalDAG. *Goal* element corresponds to a node in GoalDAG. *Edge* element is the link between two *Goals*, one of which is the *source*, the other is *target*, and with an attribute keeping *cw*. *cw* is the contribution weight that shows the degree of the relation between source and target goals. Every goal is related with a set of *Measurements*, which are keeping the measurements that is an instance of *Goal Metric*.

The meta-model for GoalDAG is developed with Eclipse EMF. When this meta-model is used with Eclipse GEF, graphical editor for GoalDAG will be finalized as an Eclipse plug-in.

5   GoalDAG Profile for ArchiMate®

A mapping from GoalDAG to architecture definition language is a first step to integrate enterprise architecture to goal hierarchy definition. This section first describes the preliminary mapping of GoalDAG model elements to the ArchiMate® model elements.

Upon initial mapping, the specialized versions of ArchiMate® model elements that represent corresponding GoalDAG elements are introduced.

To define the GoalDAG - ArchiMate® mapping, ArchiMate® concepts, especially Motivation Extension, are investigated. According to the mapping, if it is possible to keep the concept as it is, the ArchiMate® concept is directly used; otherwise specialized versions are introduced.

5.1   Concept Mapping

The concepts from GoalDAG meta model, presented in Section 4, is mapped to ArchiMate® Motivation Extension in Table 1..

In Motivation Extension, a *stakeholder* represents a person or a group of persons, or an organization that influences, guides, or constrains the enterprise. The motivation landscape relates to the architecture through *stakeholder*. In addition to the *stakeholder* relation, core elements can be related to the requirement model element of Motivation Extension through *Realization Relation*, although *stakeholder* is depicted to be the only structure that relates goal element to the core architecture through *association* relation. For instance, in an organization there are many business services which have different stakeholders involved. Even though, all stakeholders have their own concerns and goals, the main goal of the business service undertaken might be different. The goal of the business service can be linked to GoalDAG element with *association* relation.

Table 1. Concept Mapping from GoalDAG to ArchiMate

GoalDAG Concept	ArchiMate Concept
GoalGraph	Motivation Extension and related ArchiMate Elements
Goal	Goal - Driver - Principle - Requirement
Edge	Influence Relation Aggregation Relation between Goals Association Relation between Driver Goal Realization Relation between Requirement and Principle
Measurement	Assessment
Contribution Weight	influences attribute of the relations
-	Stakeholder

In fact, the *association* relation is defined as to be linking any pair of elements in the ArchiMate model. This, generic feature of the *association* relation facilitates linking GoalDAG Goal element with the rest of the architecture with additional attributes, namely, *direction* and *contribution weight*. *Stakeholder* element does not have corresponding model element in GoalDAG, since GoalDAG is only related to the goals and their hierarchical order. All subclasses of Motivational Elements, except *Assessment,* are mapped to the *Goal* element of GoalDAG. One can argue that the generalization of all *Driver, Goal, Principle, Requirement* elements into one *Goal of GoalDAG* may result in loss of information. In fact, GoalDAG is not a replacement of ArchiMate Motivation Extension, and all those elements stay same with enriching information. Moreover, as a rule of thumb, only the measurable elements with influence on higher goals should be used in relation with GoalDAG.

Any Motivational Element relation that is related to Edge of GoalDAG should be related to an *assessment*, which corresponds to the *Measurement of GoalDAG*. The relation should define *influences* attribute that corresponds to the *Contribution Weight of GoalDAG*.

6   Case Study: ArchiSurance

The Open Group introduced ArchiSurance as an example to illustrate the use of the ArchiMate modeling language in the context of the TOGAF framework [4]. ArchiSurance involves an insurance company concerned with insurance which constructed from the merger of three previously independent companies.

In our study most important part of the ArchiSurance is architecture vision, consisting of business goals. The elements related to business goals are also important to the case study. Architecture elements that are in relation with business goals can belong to different architectures, namely, the business, application, data, and technology architecture.

As we focused on the Architecture Vision phase for exploration of the motivational elements, the initial output is the first artifact to be worked on. Fig. 7 depicts, Stakeholder Viewpoint to identify the main stakeholders in the architecture engagement and their concerns.

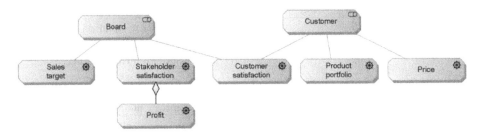

Fig. 7. Fragment of Stakeholder View

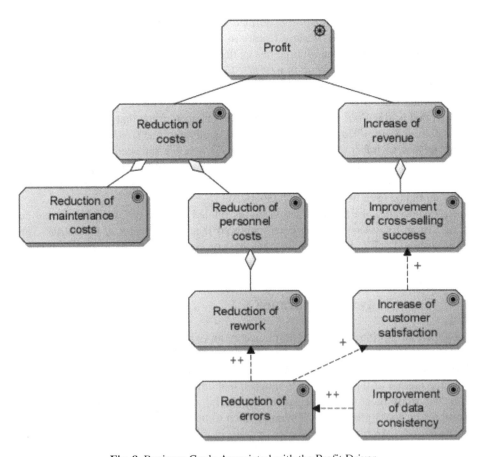

Fig. 8. Business Goals Associated with the Profit Driver

Once the high level motivational elements are defined, *Profit Driver* is investigated in detail to represent goals, which is shown on Fig. 8.

After Profit Driver goals are defined, Principles View is created in Fig. 9. Following this view, Goal Refinement view, represented more concrete low level goals with emphasis on relation types in Fig. 10.

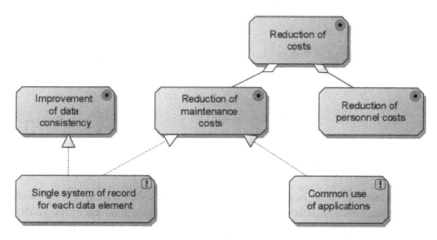

Fig. 9. Principles View Extended

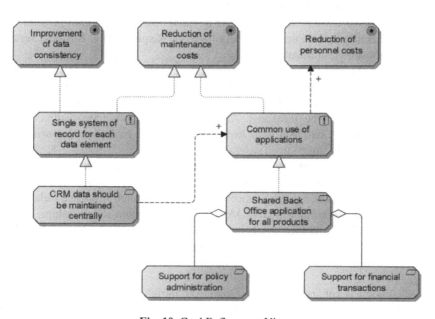

Fig. 10. Goal Refinement View

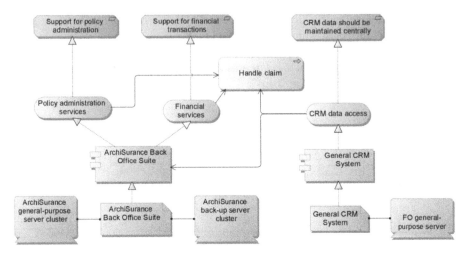

Fig. 11. Requirements Realization View

Goal Refinement view is followed by Requirements Realization View, shown in Fig. 11. Requirements Realization View guides the implementations of the goals. We represent a consolidated total view of motivational elements of ArchiMate model for ArchiSurance in Fig. 12.

The Open Group approach to define Architecture Vision starts with the definition of the stakeholders and their drivers. After defining the first level drivers, the goals related to the drivers, are defined. Goals are detailed hierarchically until principles are identified. Identified principles guide definitions of Requirements. Business services are built on those Requirements.

The GoalDAG and ArchiMate Motivation Extension are examined in two areas, namely, Technical and Methodological. Technically, GoalDAG keeps the basic structure of advised approach but differs in two aspects: Assessments and Relations. Any GoalDAG goal should be measured. All GoalDAG relations have a direction and weight. To integrate GoalDAG with ArchiMate, not only goals, but also drivers and principles are actually linked to an *assessment*.

Even though interrelations between the Goals of ArchiMate model, have direction, Driver - Goal relations have no direction, which are undirected association. Fortunately, ArchiMate allows Goals to be connected to Drivers through Influence Relation, so, in order to match ArchiMate to GoalDAG; those Association Relationships between Drivers and Goals are replaced with Influence Relationship. Relations in ArchiMate are enriched with *influences* attribute, which corresponds to the *contribution weight* of GoalDAG to keep GoalDAG model consistent. The corresponding GoalDAG graph is in Fig. 13.

Methodological enhancement that GoalDAG introduces to ArchiMate approach can be simply called *detailed hierarchical goals for validation*. Meanwhile, Archi-Mate Motivation Extension, depicted to branch the hierarchy to guide Business Service definitions. The Business Service definitions constitute the requirement specification as shown in Fig. 11. GoalDAG methodology proposes goal hierarchy to be deepened to a level that is covering Business Processes. Although, Business Process are very important component for GoalDAG in organization alignment, ArchiSurance case study do not include example Business Processes. Thus, we cannot show any branching through the business process in corresponding GoalDAG instance.

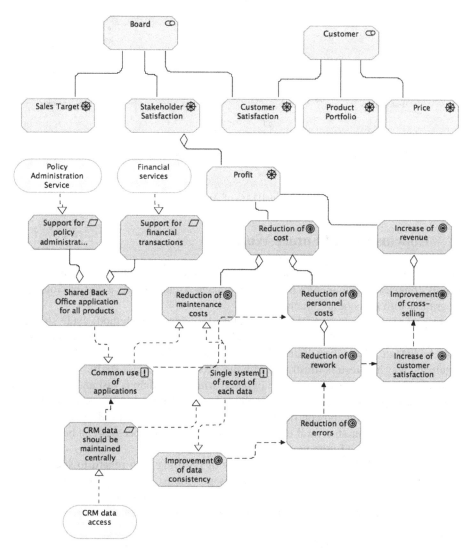

Fig. 12. Total view of ArchiMate Model related to Motivational Elements

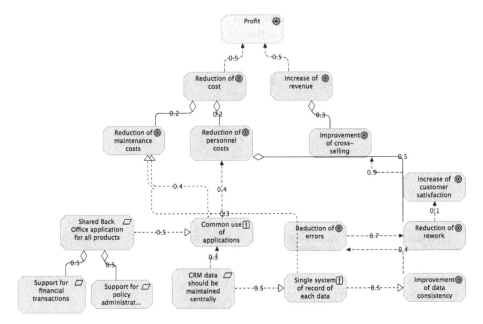

Fig. 13. GoalDAG of ArchiSurance

7   Conclusion and Future Work

This study illustrates GoalDAG integration with Enterprise Architecture, on TOGAF with its companion architecture modeling language ArchiMate, as a part of GoalDAG integration with tools of alignment.

TOGAF methodology's ADM (Architecture Development Method) cycle strategic phase covers the on Architecture Vision phase using ArchiMate Motivation Extension. ArchiMate Motivation Extension is mapped to GoalDAG model elements in a systematic way and results illustrated with the ArchiSurance case study.

GoalDAG concept mapping and integration with ArchiMate is fast and easy thanks to the generic nature of ArchiMate. GoalDAG specific model attributes, namely, direction of contribution and contribution weight, are embedded into Motivation Extension. Moreover, other structural elements such as business processes can be linked to the goal hierarchy as a future work.

Although ArchiMate allows a prolific way of profiling with regard to specific extensions, validation of the extended model is not robust. A well-formed GoalDAG model is highly related to the expertise and craft of the strategic analyst. Firstly, a robust and user friendly model validating facility is the target of the successor of this study.

Secondly, however, ArchiSurance is a well-known and widely used case study; it is still a fictitious scenario. A real-world case study, covering strategic decision making process and Architecture Vision phase, is the best way to assess the validity of the GoalDAG integration with ArchiMate. Obviously, an ADM cycle, in any ordinary organization, is highly complicated and takes a long period to implement. Even more, organizations generally shift from ArchiMate to sophisticated Enterprise Architecture tools, after getting accustomed to the TOGAF and architectural approaches, according to our field search. Given those complexities, authors plan to exemplify the ADM cycle in a subdivision of an organization.

To sum up, fundamental ArchiMate Profile for GoalDAG is constructed and exemplified with ArchiSurance case study. A full-fletched real world case study will be able to show the validity, usefulness, and value of the GoalDAG-ArchiMate integration.

References

1. Nash, H.: Harvey Nash 2013 CIO Survey (2013)
2. Economist, T.: The Strategic CIO (2013)
3. CIO: 2013 State of the CIO (2013)
4. Jonkers, H., Band, I., Quartel, D.: ArchiSurance Case Study. The Open Group (2012)
5. Thagard, P., Millgram, E.: Inference to the Best Plan: A Coherence Theory of Decision. Goal-driven Learning, pp. 439–454. MIT Press (1995)
6. Limited, O.C. (York): GSN COMMUNITY STANDARD VERSION 1 (2011), http://www.goalstructuringnotation.info/documents/GSN_Standard.pdf
7. van Solingen, R., Basili, V.R., Caldiera, G., Rombach, H.D.: The Goal Question Metric Approach. Encyclopedia of Software Engineering (2002)
8. Dardenne, A., Lamsweerde, A., van Fickas, S.: Goal-directed requirements acquisition. Science of Computer Programming 20, 3–50 (1993)
9. Bresciani, P., Perini, A., Giorgini, P., Giunchiglia, F., Mylopoulos, J.: Tropos: An Agent-Oriented Software Development Methodology. Autonomous Agents and Multi-Agent Systems 8, 203–236 (2004)
10. Bendjenna, H., Charrel, P.J., Zarour, N.E.: Identifying and Modeling Non-Functional Concerns Relationships. Journal of Software Engineering and Applications 3, 820–826 (2010)
11. van Lamsweerde, A.: Goal-oriented requirements engineering: a guided tour. In: Proceedings of the 5th IEEE International Symposium on Requirements Engineering, pp. 249–262. IEEE Computer Society (2001)
12. Bratman, M.E., Israel, D.J., Pollack, M.E.: Plans and resource-bounded practical reasoning. Computational Intelligence 4, 349–355 (1988)
13. MacGregor, J.M.: Apparatus and method for strategy map validation and visualization. US Patent 7,730,023 (2010)
14. Sutcliffe, A.: Scenario-based requirements analysis. Requirements Engineering 3, 48–65 (1998)
15. Heymans, P., Dubois, E.: Scenario-Based Techniques for Supporting the Elaboration and the Validation of Formal Requirements. Requirements Engineering 3, 202–218 (1998)
16. Mashkoor, A., Matoussi, A.: Towards validation of requirements models. In: Frappier, M., Glässer, U., Khurshid, S., Laleau, R., Reeves, S. (eds.) ABZ 2010. LNCS, vol. 5977, p. 404. Springer, Heidelberg (2010)
17. Kavakli, E., Loucopoulos, P.: Information Modeling Methods and Methodologies. Advanced Topics in Database Research, pp. 102–124. Idea Group Publishing (2005)

18. Simon, H.A.: Causal ordering and identifiability. Models of Discovery, pp. 53–80. Springer Netherlands (1977)
19. Group, T.O.: The Open Group Architecture Framework (TOGAF). The Open Group (2011)
20. IEEE: IEEE 1471-2000 IEEE Recommended Practice for Architectural Description of Software- Intensive Systems – Description. IEEE (2000)
21. Gartner, I.: IT Glossary: Enterprise Architecture (2012),
    http://www.gartner.com/technology/it-glossary/
    enterprise-architecture.jsp
22. Luftman, J., Maclean, E.: Key issues for IT executives. MIS Quarterly Executive 4, 89–104 (2005)
23. Reich, B.H., Nelson, K.M.: In their own words: CIO visions about the future of in-house IT organizations. SIGMIS Database 34, 28–44 (2003)
24. Tallon, P.P., Kraemer, K.L., Gurbaxani, V.: Executives' Perceptions of the Business Value of Information Technology: A Process-Oriented Approach. Journal of Management Information Systems 16, 145–173 (2000)
25. Watson, R.T., Kelly, G.G., Galliers, R.D., Brancheau, J.C.: Key Issues in Information Systems Management: An International Perspective. Journal of Management Information Systems 13, 91–115 (1997)
26. Neubauer, T.: An empirical study about the status of business process management. Business Process Management Journal 15, 166–183 (2009)
27. Dumas, M., van der Aalst, W.M.P., ter Hofstede, A.H.M.: Process-Aware Information Systems. John Wiley and Sons, Inc. (2005)
28. Jeston, J., Nelis, J.: Business Process Management. Routledge (2013)
29. Rigby, D., Bilodeau, B.: Management Tools and Trends. Bain and Company Inc. (2013)
30. Ko, R.K.L., Lee, S.S.G., Lee, E.W.: Business process management (BPM) standards: a survey. Business Process Management Journal 15, 744–791 (1997)
31. Kettinger, W.J., Teng, J.T.C., Guha, S.: Business Process Change: A Study of Methodologies, Techniques, and Tools. MIS Quarterly 21, 55–80 (1997)
32. Zairi, M., Sinclair, D.: Business process re-engineering and process management: A survey of current practice and future trends in integrated management. Business Process Management Journal 1, 8–30 (1995)
33. Grover, V., Jeong, S.R., Kettinger, W.J., Teng, J.T.C.: The Implementation of Business Process Reengineering. Journal of Management Information Systems 12, 109–144 (1995)
34. van der Aalst, W.M.P., ter Hofstede, A.H.M., Weske, M.: Business Process Management: A Survey. In: van der Aalst, W.M.P., ter Hofstede, A.H.M., Weske, M. (eds.) BPM 2003. LNCS, vol. 2678, pp. 1–12. Springer, Heidelberg (2003)
35. Group, T.O.: Business Layer Metamodel (2009),
    http://www.opengroup.org/archimate/doc/ts_archimate/
36. Group, T.O.: Archimate Language Extension Mechanism (2013)
37. Robinson, R.W.: Counting unlabeled acyclic digraphs. In: Little, C.C. (ed.) Combinatorial Mathematics V, pp. 28–43. Springer, Heidelberg (1977)

FMEBP: A Formal Modeling Environment of Business Process

Imed Eddine Chama, Nabil Belala, and Djamel-Eddine Saidouni

MISC Laboratory, University Constantine 2, 25000, Algeria
{i.chama,belala,saidouni}@misc-umc.org

Abstract. This paper proposes a formal environment, named FMEBP, for modeling business processes. This environment is based on a transformation approach that translates Web services, described in BPEL language, to abstract specifications, written in a high-level real-time language called D-LOTOS. The interest of D-LOTOS language is provided from the fact that it is based on true-concurrency semantics and supports both timing constraints and actions durations. For assessing the proposed environment we study a specification of a Web services application.

Keywords: Web services, BPEL, specification, D-LOTOS, timed constraints, business processes.

1   Introduction

Formalization, analysis and verification of Web services composition benefit from a considerable attention in the research community. This is due to the lack of formal semantics of Web services composition languages that are essentially syntactic and ignore the specification stage. In the literature, different approaches and methods have been proposed to formalize these languages and standards that are used to specify business process behavior based on Web services [4]. We quote in this matter the approaches that are proposed to formalize and verify Web Services Business Process Execution Language (abbreviated to BPEL) which is one of the highly used languages for model the composition of Web services and that has become the standard specification language for business process compositions and interactions.

Major part of the proposed works is grounded on BPEL untimed behavior. In [12], [16], authors are interested in mapping from BPEL to Petri Nets. A verification method based on a WSDL/BPEL to LOTOS NT transformation was proposed in [15]. In [7], [5] two-way mapping between BPEL and LOTOS was proposed. However these works have two major drawbacks. First, they provide only a partial coverage of BPEL language. On the other hand, they do not take into account the timed aspects (both timing constraints and durations of activities) induced by the interactions of BPEL Web services. This is due to the use of untimed formal models in which time is abstracted. Unfortunately, the lack of temporal aspects formalization reduces the accuracy of the obtained formal BPEL model and does not allow the analysis of quantitative properties.

G. Dregvaite and R. Damasevicius (Eds.): ICIST 2014, CCIS 465, pp. 211–223, 2014.

In the literature, only few approaches have been developed to formalize the timed aspects induced by the interaction of Web services. In [6] the authors applied their approach to FIACRE specifications to model timed aspects of BPEL by covering both the relative and the absolute time of BPEL. Nevertheless, the properties are specified logically in LTL and MITL which makes it difficult to handle. In [13] a transformation from BPEL to dtLTS (discrete-time Labeled Transition Systems) has been done in order to capture the timed behavior of BPEL. However this approach only considers a discrete notion of time and ignores a dense model of time.

In this paper, we are interested in formal modeling and analysis of the Web services composition. We present a formal environment, named FMEBP, for formalizing and verifying Web services described in BPEL. This platform is based on a transformation approach that translates the timed behavior of a BPEL process into a D-LOTOS specification. In this work, we have not only to verify the qualitative requirements, such as liveness, safety and deadlock freeness in the composition execution, but also to analyze the quantitative properties, i.e., the timed properties of BPEL Web services compositions. This verification is done via the check of behavioral properties related to the composition scenario, expressed using temporal logic. To do this the obtained D-LOTOS specification is transformed into DATA model [2]. The user can then use UPPAAL [11] to simulate the running process and model-check various properties he need.

The rest of this paper is organized as follows: in Section 2, we briefly introduce the real-time model D-LOTOS and BPEL. In Section 3, we focus on the transformation of the BPEL code to D-LOTOS specifications using the FMEBP. In order to illustrate the application of the proposed environment, we describe the *PurchaseTripOrder* Web service case-study in Section 4. Finally, Section 5 concludes the paper and gives some perspectives provided by our approach.

2   Preliminaries

2.1   D-LOTOS

D-LOTOS language [14] is a high-level specification model for modeling real-time systems. It extends Basic LOTOS language [3], [8] with timing and urgency constraints, in addition to a function "τ" giving to each action a duration.
The grammar of D-LOTOS is defined as follows:

$E ::=$ **Behaviors**
   $stop \mid exit\{d\} \mid \Delta^d E \mid X[L] \mid g@t[SP]; E \mid i@t\{d\}; E \mid E[]E \mid E/[L]/E \mid$
   $hide\ L\ in\ E \mid E \gg E \mid E\ |[L>|\ E \mid E\ [> E$

This syntax concerns the syntax of behavior expression E. The informal semantics of syntactic items is the following:
Let a be an action (observable or internal), E a behavior expression and $d \in D$ a value in a countable time domain (for example, D is $\mathbf{Q}^+$). Intuitively, $a\{d\}$ means that the action a must start its execution in the temporal domain $[0,d]$. $\Delta^d E$ means that no

evolution of E is allowed before a time delay equal to d. In $g@t[SP];E$ (resp. $i@t\{d\};E$), t stores the time passed since the enabling of the action g (respectively i) and which will be substituted by zero when this action finishes its execution.

The other operators are those of process algebras as nondeterministic choice ($E[]E$), parallel composition ($E/[L]/E$), interiorization (*hide L in E*), sequential composition ($E \gg E$), and preemption ($E[>E$). In the expression ($E|[L>|F$) the process E evolves independently of F. Two cases may occur: In the first case, E terminates its execution, and then the system terminates. In the second case, E synchronizes with F on an action in L, in this case E is preempted and F takes the control. Note that processes that are synchronized with F are not preempted.

2.2   The BPEL Web Services Composition Language

Web Services Business Process Execution Language [9] (BPEL for short) is an XML based language for specifying business process behavior based on interactions between a group of Web services partners. This interaction occurs through *<partnerLinks>*. In BPEL, we have two parts of modeling.

The first is the abstract part. It is written in a WSDL document that describes the various Web services, their data types, port types and the messages exchanged between different partners without specifying any internal behavior. Specifically, in BPEL each *<partnerLinks>* may contain two roles (*<myRole>* and *<partnerRole>*) typed by *<portType>*. In each *<portType>*, we can declare several operations that are used to receive (input) or to send (output) *<messages>*. The second is the dynamic part which is described by two categories of activities:

- *Basic activities*: are those which do not contain any other activity like *<Receive>*, *<Reply>*, *<Invoke>*, etc.
- *Structured activities*: are obtained by composing other primitive and/or structured activities recursively. They are used to define the order in which their enclosed activities are executed. For example, sequential and parallel processing may be modeled respectively by *<Sequence>* and *<Flow>*. Finally, the *<Scope>* activity which allows the decomposition of the BPEL process into sub-processes.

A scope can be associated with a set of:

(a) *Event handlers*: which can be run concurrently and invoked when the corresponding event occurs (inbound messages events: *<onEvent>*, or alarm events: *<onAlarm>*);
(b) *Fault handlers*: to handle error messages when a fault occurred;
(c) *Compensation handler*: to compensate the scopes which are completed successfully in case where exceptions occur or a partner requests a backtrack;
(d) *Termination handler*: that controls the forced termination of a scope.

3   Formal Modeling Environment of Business Process (FMEBP)

3.1   The FMEBP Functionality

FMEBP is a formal environment that automates the transformation process of BPEL descriptions to D-LOTOS specifications. This platform is implemented with Java as a plugin to Eclipse development environment. Its functional view is sketched in Fig. 1. The input is a BPEL executable file [9], that is, an XML document which specifies the behavior of business process, while the output is a D-LOTOS process that formalizing the input BPEL file. The user only needs to give a BPEL file as input, and then the plugin will automatically transform it into D-LOTOS process. The obtained D-LOTOS process can be directly and automatically transformed into other low-level timed structures (such as Durational Action Timed Automata (DATA) [2]), that can supply formal verification methods like model checking or bisimulation. The user can then use UPPAAL [11] to simulate the running process and check properties assessing the well system behavior.

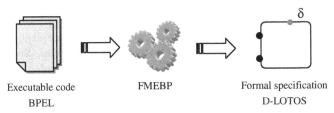

Executable code   FMEBP   Formal specification
      BPEL   D-LOTOS

Fig. 1. Functionality of FMEBP

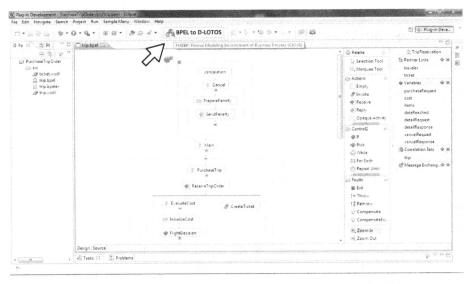

Fig. 2. The Formal Modeling Environment of Business Process (FMEBP)

Once the BPEL process is fully translated to a D-LOTOS specification using FMEBP, the generated D-LOTOS specification is translated to a low-level real-time structure, named Durational Action Timed Automata (DATA for short) [2] . Hence, the UPPAAL tool [11] may be used for simulating the running of the process, as well as checking both qualitative and quantitative properties stated in temporal logic like TCTL [1]. These properties concern: safety (something bad never occurs), liveness (something good eventually occurs) and deadlock freeness.

By taking into account the duration of the actions, we can easily verify the behavior properties besides the time performance as well.

3.2   Translating in FMEBP

BPEL services and D-LOTOS processes correspond to each other. A formal modeling of BPEL services is based on the observation that a BPEL definition is interpreted as a formal D-LOTOS specification.

In BPEL we have two parts for modeling: the abstract part and the dynamic part. In this paper we are interested in formal modeling the second part which is the BPEL executable processes that specify the behavior of business processes (various activities of BPEL description) in full detail. In our presentation, we refer to Table 1 where we show sample code of both languages. The correspondence is the mapping from BPEL Structured Behaviors model to D-LOTOS model.

Mapping for the Basic Activities

This part introduces the representation of basic BPEL activities in the specification language D-LOTOS. Basic activities are those which do not contain any other activity (for example, *<invoke>*, *<receive>*, and *<reply>* activity). In our approach, each BPEL simple activity is represented by a specific D-LOTOS process.

Consider the mapping illustrated in Fig. 3 where *act* denotes a basic BPEL activity, and *g* and *d* represent respectively guard and duration. "*act{g}*" means that the action *act* has to begin its execution within *g* time units, and "*act[τ(act)]*" means that the necessary time for the complete execution of the action *act* is $d=\tau(act)$.

```
process BPELBasicActivity [act[τ(act)],…] :=
               act{g}; exit
Endproc
```

Fig. 3. Mapping for a BPEL basic activity

Mapping for the Structured Activities

Structured activities are obtained by composing other primitive and/or structured activities recursively. They are used to define the order in which their enclosed activities are executed. In Table 1, we define D-LOTOS processes that represent structured BPEL activities.

First of all, the *<Sequence>* and the *<flow>* activities in BPEL are formalized by the D-LOTOS sequential composition construct "≫" and the two parallel composition operators "|[…]| or ‖" respectively. Intuitively, the D-LOTOS recursive process calls correspond either to the *<while>* activity enabling repeated execution as long as its boolean condition evaluates to *"true"* at the beginning of each iteration, or to the *<repeatUntil>* activity that is used to express repetitive execution. In contrast to the *<while>* activity, the encapsulated activities of the *<repeatUntil>* activity are executed at least once as its boolean condition is evaluated at the end of each iteration. Note that the provided condition in both of them (a boolean expression) is not represented in our formalization. Thus, we use directly the non-deterministic choices between a recursive call (recursive behavior) and the *exit* action (ending behavior).

The branching conditions in the *<if>* activity, might comprises boolean expressions that are not represented in our formalization. Again, we use directly the non-deterministic choices "[]" (possibly multiple) to choose a possible activity which may be executed.

Table 1. Transformation rules of BPEL structured activities into D-LOTOS model

BPEL	D-LOTOS
Sequence	**process** sequence[$\cup_{i=1}^{n}\ G_i[d_i]$] := activity1[…] $\gg$ activity2[…] $\gg$ … $\gg$ activityN-1[…] $\gg$ activityN[…] **Endproc**
If	**process** if[$\cup_{i=1}^{n}\ G_i[d_i]$] := condition$_1$; activity$_1$[…] [] … [] condition$_2$; activity$_2$[…] [] exit **Endproc**
While	**process** while[$\cup_{i=1}^{n}\ G_i[d_i]$] := (activity[…] $\gg$ while[…]) [] exit **Endproc**
RepeatUntil	**process** repeatUntil[$\cup_{i=1}^{n}\ G_i[d_i]$] := activity[…] $\gg$ (repeatUntil[…] [] exit) **Endproc**
Flow + Links	**process** flow[$\cup_{i=1}^{n}\ G_i[d_i]$]:= activity$_1$[…] |[*link$_i$*]| activity$_2$[…] |[*link$_i$*]| … |[*link$_i$*]| activity$_n$[…] **Endproc**
FaultHandlers	**process** faultHandlers[…]:= catch$_1$[*faultName$_1$*, …] [] … [] catch$_n$[*faultName$_n$*, …] [] catchAll[*faults*, …] **Endproc**

Modeling of BPEL Timed Aspects

The behavior of a BPEL Web service comprises not only the concurrency, synchronization and communication between its various activities, but also the delay of response of the service. These aspects can be modeled using D-LOTOS model.

In BPEL, there are two expressions to manage the time. The *<for>* expression which specifies a duration for a certain period of time (takes into account a relative time) and the *<until>* expression that specifies a delay until a certain deadline is reached (takes into account an absolute time). These expressions are used either in the *<wait>* activity, or in the *<onAlarm>* element of a *<pick>* or an <eventHandlers>.

The formal modeling of the relative time of BPEL (the *<for>* expression) is straightforward in D-LOTOS. This could be considered as synchronization on a timer gate which its delay is the indicated duration ($\Delta^{duration\text{-}expr}$). Regarding the absolute time of BPEL (the *<until>* expression), it could be treated by bounding the temporal domain between the starting date of the BPEL process and the indicated deadline.

In order to formalize the reception time of a request i.e. of the *<receive>* activity and the *<onMessage>* events of both the *<eventHandlers>* and the *<pick>* activity, we should annotate the BPEL code before transforming it to D-LOTOS specification by time constraints [10]. This can allow specifying bounds of the activity duration and guarantees that any action will take place at the right moment of time. In this formalism, we assume that the execution time of each BPEL activity and the response time of a synchronous invoke of a Web service (request-response invocation) are bounded.

Moreover, the fact that some BPEL activities may take certain period of time to terminate their executions is treated in FMEBP by using D-LOTOS actions with durations "a[τ(a)]" and clock guards "a{g}". The τ(a) function gives the execution time of this action and the g guard guarantees that this action will take place at the right moment of time.

4   Case Study

In order to show how a BPEL code is translated into a D-LOTOS specification using FMEBP, we give the *PurchaseTripOrder* example "Fig. 4" which is a BPEL Web service issued from electronic commerce. It describes a service that processes an on-line purchase of a trip. We will transform this latter into D-LOTOS and we show how the relative and the absolute times are treated in our approach as well as how we formalize the interactions between a customer and the *PurchaseTripOrder* service. Because of the relative complexity of this Web service, we do not detail its textual BPEL and WSDL descriptions, but we present its workflow graphically using the BPEL graphical representation.

In the following, we explain how to generate D-LOTOS specification from the *PurchaseTripOrder* BPEL process given in Fig. 4. The system is composed of one customer and one *PurchaseTripOrder* service; this is because of the *createInstance* value which is declared "yes".

— The behavior of a customer is as follows:

- The customer sends a *purchaseTrip* request.
- After the reservation of the flight, the hotel and the car, the customer receives an invoice.
- Then, the customer can request for the trip detail as well as cancel the trip, until a fixed deadline.

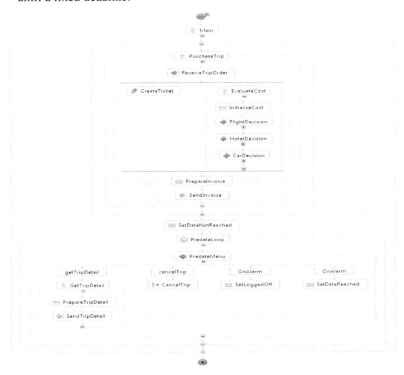

Fig. 4. Timed *PurchaseTripOrder* example

— The behavior of the *PurchaseTripOrder* BPEL Web service is as follows:

- When the *PurchaseTripOrder* Web service receives a *purchaseTrip* request, it creates a new instance to handle the requests of the customer. This is due to the "*createInstance = yes*" attribute.
- Then, the service asks the customer for the allocation of flight, hotel and car in order to calculate the cost, then it send the invoice to the customer.
- Finally, the service enables the customer to do some operation as long as the specified deadline has not been reached. Note that each access is available during a certain period of time *d*.

In FMEBP, each BPEL activity, either primitive or structured, is represented by a specific D-LOTOS process. Consider the mapping illustrated in Fig. 5 where *receive_ReceiveTripOrder[...]* is a D-LOTOS process that models the receive activity named *ReceiveTripOrder*. *purchaseRequest* denotes a communication point (gate) in which the BPEL Web service receives the *purchaseTrip* requests from customers. *g* and *d* represent respectively guard and duration. "*purchaseRequest{g}*" means that the action *purchaseRequest* has to begin its execution within *g* time units, and "*purchaseRequest[d]*" means that the necessary time to complete the execution of the *purchaseRequest* action is *d*.

```
<sequence name="Main">
  <scope name="TripPurchase">
    <sequence name="PurchaseTrip">
      <receive name="ReceiveTripOrder"
               createInstance="yes"
               operation="purchaseTrip"
               partnerLink="traveler"
               … />
      <flow>   …   </flow>
      <assign name="PrepareInvoice" … >
               …   </assign>

      <reply name="SendInvoice"
             operation="purchaseTrip"
             partnerLink="traveler" … >
               …   </reply>
    </sequence>
  </scope>

  <assign name="PrepareInvoice" … >
             …   </assign>
  <while name="PredateLoop">
  </while>
</sequence>
```

```
process sequence_Main[…]  :=
       scope_TripPurchase[…]
    >> assign_PrepareInvoice[…]
    >> while_PredateLoop[…]
Where

  process scope_TripPurchase[…]:=
         sequence_PurchaseTrip[…]
  where

    process sequence_PurchaseTrip[…]:=
           receive_ReceiveTripOrder[…]
        >> flow_PurchaseTrip[…]
        >> assign_PrepareInvoice[…]
        >> reply_SendInvoice[…]
    where
      process receive_ReceiveTripOrder
                  [purchaseRequest[d]]:=
               purchaseRequest{g}; exit
      Endproc
        …
    Endproc

  Endproc
Endproc
```

Fig. 5. D-LOTOS process corresponding to the *Main* sequence activity

Upon receiving a purchase order from a customer, the service initiates simultaneously two paths: a sequence activity, named *EvaluateCost*, which are used

```
<flow>

  <invoke name="CreateTicket"
          operation="createTicket"
          partnerLink="ticket" … >
          …
  </invoke>

  <sequence name="EvaluateCost">
    <assign name="InitializeCost" … >
          …   </assign>

    <if name="FlightDecision">
      <condition>...</condition>
      <scope name="FlightReservation">

        <compensationHandler>
          <assign
          name="ReimburseHotel" … >
          …   </assign>
        </compensationHandler>

        <assign name="ChargeHotel"… >
          …   </assign>
      </scope>
    </if>

    <if name="HotelDecision"> … </if>
    <if name="CarDecision"> … </if>

  </sequence>

</flow>
```

```
process flow[…]  :=
       invoke_CreateTicket[…]
       |||
       sequence_EvaluateCost[…]
where
  process invoke_CreateTicket[…]  :=
         ticketRequest{g}; exit
  Endproc
  process sequence_EvaluateCost[…]  :=
         assign_InitializeCost[…]
      >> if_FlightDecision[…]
      >> if_HotelDecision[…]
      >> if_CarDecision[…]
  where
    process if_FlightDecision[…]  :=
           ( condition1{g};
             scope_FlightReservation[…] )
           [] exit
    where
      process scope_FlightReservation[…]:=
             (
             (assign_ChargeHotel[…] >>
             enableComp_fr;exit)

             ) |[enableComp_fr, undoPurchase_fr]|
               compensationHandler_FR[…]
           where
             process compensationHandler_FR[…]:=
                    enableComp_fr; undoPurchase_fr;
                    assign_ReimburseHotel[…]
             Endproc
      Endproc
    Endproc
      …
  Endproc
Endproc
```

Fig. 6. D-LOTOS process corresponding to *flow* activity of the *PurchaseTripOrder* process

to evaluate the cost, and an invoke activity, named *CreateTicket*, to create a ticket for the customer. Once the two concurrent paths are completed, the service sends an invoice to the customer. The formalization of such activities is given in Fig. 6 where we show how the *EvaluateCost* activity is formalized as a sequential composition of four D-LOTOS processes: *assign_InitializeCost[...]*, *if_FlightDecision[...]*, *if_HotelDecision[...]* and *if_CarDecision[...]*.

To formalize the *FlightReservation* scope activity "Fig. 6" we have to formalize its behavior and the behavior of its compensation handler. The *scope_FlightReservation[...]* D-LOTOS process given in Fig. 6 is the result of these behaviors. In the case where no fault occurs during the execution of the *FlightReservation* scope, this scope completes if all its enclosed activities complete. In this case, the corresponding D-LOTOS process enables synchronization on the *enableComp* port to indicate the successfully completion of this scope in order to make available its compensation handler for invocation. Moreover, the *compensationHandler_fr[...]* compensation handler process "Fig. 6" can only be executed when the enclosing scope completes successfully (the synchronization with the *enableComp* port is enabled) and is triggered by the *compensate_TripPurchase[...]* compensation process using the *undoPurchase* port "Fig. 8". If these two conditions are fulfilled, the compensation handler is executed. Any other attempt to compensate this scope will be ignored.

```
<while name="PredateLoop">                     ...   Alarm[…]   |[pause]|    ...
  <condition> … </condition>
  <pick name="PredateMenu">                process while_PredateLoop[…]  :=
    <onMessage operation="getTripDetail"
(1)            partnerLink="traveler" … >  ( pick_PredateMenu[…] >>
      <sequence name=" GetTripDetail">           while_PredateLoop [...] )
        …                                  [] exit
      </sequence>
    </onMessage>                           where
                                             process pick_PredateMenu[…]:=
    <onMessage operation="cancelTrip"
(2)            partnerLink="traveler" … >  (1)  getTripDetail{g};
      <throw                                    sequence_GetTripDetail[…]
         faultName="tns:cancelation"            []
         name="CancelTrip"/>               (2)  cancelTrip{g};throw_CancelTrip[…]
    </onMessage>                                []
                                           (3)  delay(d)assign_SetLoggedOff[…]
    <onAlarm>                                   []
(3)    <for>'PT2M'</for>                   (4)  Pause;assign_SetDateReached[…]
       <assign name="SetLoggedOff">
        …                                    where
       </assign>                               process sequence_BalanceSeq[…]  :=
    </onAlarm>                                    assign_PrepareTripDetail[…]
                                                  >> reply_SendTripDetail[…]
    <onAlarm>                                Endproc
(4)    <until>'2002-12-24T18:00+01:00'
       </until>                               process throw_CancelTrip[…]  :=
       <assign name="SetDateReached">            cancelation{g};exit
        …                                     Endproc
       </assign>                              …
    </onAlarm>                              Endproc
  </pick>
</while>                                   Endproc
```

Fig. 7. The *PredateLoop* while activity and their corresponding D-LOTOS process

The *PredateMenu* pick activity “Fig. 7” is itself decomposed of *getTripDetail*, *cancelTrip*, *loggedOff* and *dateReached* branches which are specified respectively: the consultation of the trip details, the annulation of the trip, the closing the current session and the ending the service. The *getTripDetail* branch is a sequence of two activities (*prepareTripDetail* and *SendTripDetail*), while the *cancelTrid* branch is a throw activity. If the customer does not select any one of the desired operations within 5 minutes the *loggedOff* branch is triggered and the assign activity (*SetLoggedOff*) is executed. Finally the *dateReached* branch is used to specify a delay in which the service is only offered until the specified deadline is passed or reached. If the deadline is reached, the assign activity (*SetDateReached*) will be executed and the Web service will proceed by replying a negative response to the customer.

When the *cancelation* fault occurs during the execution of the BPEL process, i.e., the *throw_CancelTrip[...]* process enables synchronization on the *cancelation* port “Fig. 7”, the execution of the main process will be stopped and the *faultHandlers[...]* process will catch this fault and executes the *catch[...]* process “Fig. 8”. Note that the strong termination forced by an enclosing scope is respected in our approach.

```
<process>
   <faultHandlers>

      <catch
        faultName="tns:cancelation">

        <sequence name="Cancel">

          <compensateScope
              name="UndoPurchase"
              target="TripPurchase"/>

          <assign
              name="PreparePenalty"
              validate="no">
               ...  </assign>

          <reply name="SendPenalty"
               operation="cancelTrip"
               partnerLink="traveler"
                ... />
        </sequence>
      </catch>

   </faultHandlers>

   <sequence name="Main">
      ...
   </sequence>

</process>
```

```
hide enableComp, executeComp, faultName in

process purchaseTripOrder[...] :=
     sequence_Main[...]   |[cancelation>|
     faultHandlers[...]

where
   //  sequence_Main[...] (Fig. 5)

   process faultHandlers[...]:=
        catch[cancelation]
   Where
     Process catch[cancelation[d]] :=
       cancelation{g};sequence_Cancel[...]
     Where
       Process sequence_Cancel[...] :=
           compensate_TripPurchase[...] >>
           assign_PreparePenalty[...] >>
           reply_SendPenalty[...]
       Where
         Process compensate_TripPurchase[...]
             undoPurchase;exit
             [ ] empty[...]
         Endproc
         ...
       Endproc
     Endproc

   Endproc
Endproc
```

Fig. 8. Formalizing *PurchaseTripOrder* BPEL process by D-LOTOS

5   Conclusion and Future Work

In this paper, we have presented a formal modeling environment of business process, named FMEBP. It is a formal environment that automates the transformation process of BPEL code to D-LOTOS language. By using FMEBP, we transform BPEL activities into D-LOTOS processes. This transformation allows us to verify not only the reliability and correctness of service composition but also the timed properties of BPEL.

The use of D-LOTOS formal language has several advantages. First of all, its structure is very close to the programming structures of a Web service process and enables to model directly and easily a Web service (which is a process). In addition, the obtained D-LOTOS process can be directly and automatically transformed into other low-level timed structures (such as Durational Action Timed Automata [2] (DATA)), that can supply formal verification methods like model checking or bisimulation.

The proposed formal environment is based on the formalization of both behavioral and timed aspects of BPEL descriptions. Therefore, our transformation approach allows us to model and verify a richer set of properties compared to the other approaches that exist in the literature.

As perspective, we look for proposing another formal environment based on the translation of BPEL directly into real-time low-level model such as DATA models [2], without using an intermediate specification language. This can optimize the obtained low-level structure and accelerate the formal verification of the Web services composition.

References

1. Alur, R., Courcoubetis, C., Dill, D.L.: Model-checking in dense real-time. Information and Computation 140(1), 2–34 (1993)
2. Belala, N., Saïdouni, D.E.: Actions Duration in Timed Models. In: Proceeding of International Arab Conference on Information Technology (ACIT 2006), Yarmouk University, Irbid (2006)
3. Bolognesi, T., Brinksma, E.: Introduction to the ISO specification language LOTOS. In: Computer Networks and ISDN Systems, pp. 14:25–14:59 (1987)
4. Breugel, F.V.: Koshkina, M.: Models and verification of BPEL (2006), http://www.cse.yorku.ca/~ranck/research/drafts/tutorial.pdf
5. Chirichiello, A., Salaün, G.: Encoding abstract descriptions into executable web services: Towards a formal development. In: Proc. of the 3rd IEEE/WIC/ACM Intl. Conf. on Web Intelligence (WI 2005), pp. 457–463 (2005)
6. Fares, E., Bodeveix, J.P., Filali, M.: Verification of Timed BPEL 2.0 Models. Enterprise, Business-Process and Information Systems Modeling 81, 261–275 (2011)
7. Ferrara, A.: Web services: a process algebra approach. In: Proceedings of the 2nd International Conference on Service Oriented Computing (ICSOC 2004), New York City, NY, USA, pp. 242–251 (2004)

8. ISO/IEC. LOTOS: A Formal Description Technique Based on the Temporal Ordering of Observational Behaviour. In: International Standard 8807. International Organisation of Standardization — Information Processing Systems — Open Systems Interconnection. Genève (1988)

9. Jordan, D., et al.: Web Services Business Process Execution Language (WSBPEL), OASIS Standard (2007), http://docs.oasis-open.org/wsbpel/2.0/OS/wsbpel-v2.0-OS.html

10. Kazhamiakin, R., Pandya, P., Pistore, M.: Representation, verification, and computation of timed properties in Web Service Compositions. In: Proceedings of the IEEE International Conference on Web Services, pp. 497–504. IEEE Computer Society, Washington, DC (2006)

11. Larsen, K.G., Pettersson, P., Yi, W.: UPPAAL in a nutshell. IJSTTT 1, 134–152 (1997)

12. Lohmann, N.: A feature-complete Petri net semantics for WS-BPEL 2.0. In: Hee, K.V., Reisig, W., Wolf, K. (eds.) Proceedings of the Workshop on Formal Approaches to Business Processes and Web Services (FABPWS 2007), University of Podlasie, pp. 21–35 (June 2007)

13. Mateescu, R., Rampacek, S.: Formal Modeling and Discrete-Time Analysis of BPEL Web Services. International Journal of Simulation and Process Modeling (2008)

14. Saïdouni, D.E., Courtiat, J.P.: Prise en compte des durées d'action dans les algèbres de processus par l'utilisation de la sémantique de maximalité. In: Ingénierie des Protocoles (CFIP 2003), France, Paris, pp. 51–66 (2003)

15. Thivolle, D.: Langages modernes pour la modélisation et la vérification des systèmes asynchrones. PhD thesis. Grenoble: Grenoble University (laboratory of computing) (2011)

16. van der Aalst, W.M.P., Mooij, A.J., Stahl, C., Wolf, K.: Service interaction: Patterns, formalization, and analysis. In: Bernardo, M., Padovani, L., Zavattaro, G. (eds.) SFM 2009. LNCS, vol. 5569, pp. 42–88. Springer, Heidelberg (2009)

Object-Oriented Development of Adaptive Workflows for Customer Flow Management Processes

Vladimirs Rusakovs and Jānis Grabis

Institute of Information Technology, Riga Technical University
Kalku 1, LV-1658, Latvia
{vladimirs.rusakovs,grabis}@rtu.lv

Abstract. Customer Flow Management (CFM) systems are used to manage queues and support customer service business processes at various companies. The customer experience could be improved and waiting time reduced, if the service provisioning adapts to the context. To solve this problem, an approach for design and implementation of CFM systems on the basis of adaptive workflows is proposed. The adaptive workflows are modeled using BPMN and implemented using the object-oriented approach. To support model-driven implementation of adaptive workflows, the BPMN meta-model is extended to represent adaptive features and to support reuse of workflow activities across multiple alternative implementations of workflow execution variants. To illustrate the approach, a prototype of the dynamic luggage registration and online ticket re-registration in case of flight cancellation CFM system is developed.

Keywords: adaptive workflows, customer flow management.

1 Introduction

Queues are reality of daily life, for instance, in the shopping centers, governmental institutions, entertainment events, airports, and other queuing areas. The studies show that the queues can cause loss of person's control, boredom feeling as well as physical discomfort [1]. The queues point to the fact that waiting and service time is not managed effectively and underlying business process can be improved.

Workflow management (WfM) systems are used to manage the business processes [2,3,4] This kind of systems has become one of the most successful ways of process coordinating and automating [5]. As time goes by, programming and software development becomes more agile and dynamic. In past, development of the system began with in detail design and planning of all functions. Nowadays, developers should take into consideration the fact that system will change and evolve during the utilization period to adapt to changes in the organization, business processes and business environment. Traditional WfM systems were not intended for such scenario, that's why adaptive workflows have been receiving much attention in recent years [7,8,9].

The interest about implementing flexibility into business processes has increased for the last decade because of the fact that in a dynamic business environment organization's economic success depends on ability to rapidly react on changes in the mar-

G. Dregvaite and R. Damasevicius (Eds.): ICIST 2014, CCIS 465, pp. 224–235, 2014.
© Springer International Publishing Switzerland 2014

ket. The changes are usually caused by product or service customization, production process optimization, customer service enhancement or amendments of law [10]. One of the key benefits of using adaptive workflows is possibility to modify running processes on the fly, to manage process exceptions without or with minimal person interaction, to adapt to context and to work with external systems and sensors, to run diagnostics [11]. The adaptive workflow is a logical extension of traditional workflows and the new generation of business process execution.

Nowadays, many information systems, which fit different organization functional needs, are available. That includes operational systems, database management systems and specific enterprise applications. Customer flow management (CFM) systems, which aimed at organizing customer service processes and ensuring that the service level is maintained regardless of the customer flow intensity, can be perceived as specialized WfM systems. However, there can be many more things that can be done to free additional time for the customer until his/her turn comes [30]. A conceptual method for designing CFM systems was developed in [12] although implementation issues were not further elaborated.

In this paper, possibilities to use adaptive workflows to enrich the functionality of CFM system are investigated. The aim of this research is to develop solutions for CFM system design and implementation, which use an adaptive workflow object-oriented approach, to enhance CFM process adaptability, workflow execution variants flexibility and implementation reusability.

The rest of this paper is structured as follows. Section 2 presents results of related work analysis and theoretical justification of the adaptive workflow development and usage in CFM system optimization. Section 3 presents main concepts of the proposed object-oriented adaptive workflow development approach. In Section 4, we introduce our prototype of airline CFM system for dynamic luggage registration and online ticket re-registration in case of flight cancellation. This paper concludes with future research directions and evaluation of the approach in Section 5.

2   Related Work

During the related works investigation, the key focus fields were business processes management (BPM), WfM and BPM systems, including investigation of the basics of operations, aims and tasks of adaptive workflows, development history and implementation approaches, CFM disadvantages and development possibilities.

Waiting time is essential and can dramatically influence the level of the customer's satisfaction [13]. Studies show that queues can cause the loss of control and overestimation of waiting time. Boredom and physical discomfort are also identified [1]. The fact that customers have to waste their precious time to get desired or needed services can negatively influence the evaluation of service provider [14, 15].

In recent years there is increase in interest for implementing flexibility into business processes because traditional WfM systems were not intended to be more agile and dynamic during a utilization period of a system. In a dynamic business environment organization's economic success is dependent on ability to rapidly and flexibly react on changes in the market. As a result, workflow should be easily and rapidly modifiable both in the development and maintenance phases [4]. Adaptive workflow effectively reacts to system, environment, or context changes [16].

What is an adaptive workflow? Taking into consideration that workflow is computerized consequent execution of business process tasks, it can be stated that adaptive workflow is execution of an adaptive process. Adaptive process is process that is not fully standardized and can adapt to environment, e.g. consultancy or business startup process, engineering problem solving process, audit, evaluation of sophisticated insurance cases, complex medical cases etc [16]. Many researchers [11, 17, 18, 19, 20]) have defined adaptive workflow as a mechanism, that can implement strategies, that allow to avoid exceptions, discover and process them in different application levels. The ability to change process behavior during the run time is critical factor for adaptive workflows. [21] considers adaptive workflows as a vast and important research field. They are confident that these systems improve service quality and are focused on users.

There are many approaches to implement adaptive workflow. These are single model and open point approaches [6, 8, 22, 23], event-based processing [19, 24] and agent and web-service based approach [17, 20] and also adaptation using business process variants [4, 25, 26, 27]. Recently the new approach was proposed – execution model approach, which uses object-oriented paradigm in business process development [28]. There is not a standard way for technical implementation of Adaptive workflows. Also designing the adaptive workflows using one of the most popular modeling standards – BPMN, it is hard to visualize business process variants in a model and to define inheritance between main elements – tasks. These problems results in three tasks of this paper – understand how to implement the adaptive workflow; choose the most appropriate implementation approach that allows enhancing CFM system functionality; make sure, that nowadays adaptive WfM systems are available.

Nowadays, usual CFM systems are used in many spheres most commonly for queue organization [29]. Developers of MobiQ prototype and researchers [30] state, that two disadvantages are identified in CFM systems. Firstly, customers have to go to organization office to reserve a place in the queue for service. Secondly, after the ticket is received, customer have to wait for his turn inside the organization premises, as systems does not update information on remaining waiting time remotely and online. In other words, customer could use waiting time for his personal needs – for instance rest in the nearby park, or travelling time to the nearest service point. CFM systems do not provide dynamic processing depending on the current exception situation. These problems allow defining this paper's aim and 4th task – design and implement the adaptive workflow to optimize functionality of a CFM system.

3   Adaptive Workflow Development

The CFM system is built on the basis of the underlying workflow. It is assumed that there is a general workflow defining the main high level activities. There are also several alternative ways these activities can be performed. Appropriate combinations of these alternative activities form workflow execution variants. In order to provide for workflow adaptability, appropriate process variant is selected for the execution depending on the current context. The object-oriented approach is used to design and implement the adaptive workflow in order to reduce development effort associated with implementation of the multiple workflow variants.

3.1   Workflow Design

The adaptive workflow underlying the CFM system is developed as an object-oriented workflow (OOWF). The first step is to identify main activities of OOWF and alternatives of performing these tasks. In the terms of notation used by [25], the general process is expressed as

$$BP = (N, E, G, C),$$

where N is the set of tasks in the process, E is the set of events, G is the set of gateways and $C: N \times E \times G$ is the set of connectors.

The general process is enriched by specifying alternatives for execution of each task:

$$BP^* = (N, E, G, C, \alpha),$$

where $\alpha: N \to A$ associates alternatives with tasks and A is the set of alternatives.

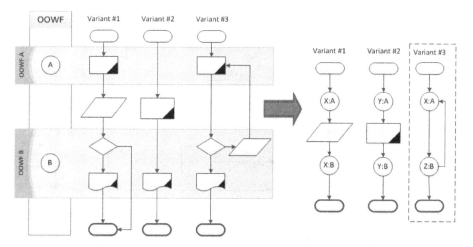

Fig. 1. Reusability and flexibility using OOWF tasks

The general process and variants elaborated by specifying alternatives of the tasks are illustrated in Fig. 1. The tasks of general OOWF are circles - A, B, and the alternatives are X:A, Y:A, X:B, Y:B, Z:B (shaded lanes show association among the general tasks and their execution alternatives). The workflow variants also contain tasks and activities, which are not present on the general process. Each alternative task has its own specific implementation, e.g. specific user interface.

3.2   BPMN Extension

The workflows can be modeled using BPMN. However, in order to represent workflow execution variants and to support their object-oriented implementation, the standard BPMN meta-model is extended. The meta-model extension is developed for the `Activity` flow element (Fig. 2). `Class of Task` is introduced to represent the task object-oriented implementation. This element captures general aspects of the task while the `Task Alternatives` element represents variant specific implementation of the task. The specific implementation inherits general features of the tasks thus allowing for reduction of the development effort. `Switching Rules` class defines adaptive behavior of the workflow and is used to select appropriate workflow execution variant according to the current context represented by the `Context Data` element. In order to represent human interaction with the CFM system, the `GUI` class implementing user interface for each task is also introduced.

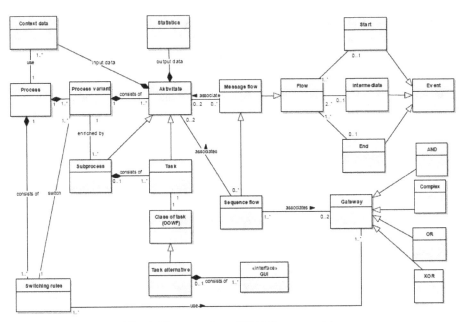

Fig. 2. The extension of BPMN meta-model

These extensions are intended for supporting object-oriented implementation of the adaptive workflow while the standard BPMN focuses on analysis and design issues. That allows for model-driven implementation of adaptive workflows in a spirit of executable modeling as proposed by [28]. The Object-Oriented programming (OOP) approach differs from procedural and modular paradigms in a fact that objects can interact with each other using interfaces. The fundamental concepts in OOP include: object, classes of objects, methods, messages, abstraction, encapsulation, object inheritance and polymorphism. OOWF derives it features and concepts from OOP. The OOP and OOWF comparison of main concepts is represented in Table 1.

OOWF structure is made of attributes which are used to store data of incoming or outgoing messages. Methods describe behavior of an OOWF. When a message from the context data is received, the state of the workflow can be changed. The main objective of the OOWF is to achieve adaptive process management. As a result business process becomes more flexible and agile. Moreover, the adaptive workflows provide a mechanism of an exception handling, dynamic adjustment of business process based on contextual data, and effective implementation of evolutionary changes.

Table 1. OOP and OOWF main features and concepts

Basic concepts	OOP	OOWF
Object	Is an instance of a class.	Is the implementation of the task, where task executor, task functionality and adaptation mechanisms are known.
Class	Represents a set of objects with similar structure and behavior.	An abstract business task, which describes tasks with similar structure and behavior.
Message	The instrument of object communication – call to object's method	Input and output data of a workflow.
Method	Defines an algorithm, which is executed by an object as a reaction to message. Method is a piece of code that is connected to class or object.	Specific functionality which can change the workflow instance task behavior, state and identity. Usually is an implementation of a subprocess.
Abstraction	It is a simplified description of something that highlights its most important characteristics and aims and at the same time ignores unimportant details. Distinguishes the most essential characteristics of the object so that the object can be uniquely identified and clarifies its conceptual boundaries.	The workflow is divided in 3 levels – abstract, definition and instance levels. The first level also indicative of the fact that workflows inherent characteristic of abstraction. If an implementation of a workflow is not known over OOWF class, then it can be empty and implemented in the inherited classes.
Encapsulation	Describes the ability of an object to hide its data and methods from outside.	The access control of workflow development and implementation. Only the process manager can create, modify, and delete process elements.
Inheritance	Subclass inherits the superclass structure and behavior. Used to promote the use of existing code with little or no modifications.	Specific business task can inherit the structure and behavior from another abstract business task. Inheritance enhances reusability and flexibility of workflow development and maintenance process.
Polymorphism	OOP polymorphisms principle is usually used for functions and operations, when multiple functions with the same name execute different actions.	It is possible to implement polymorphism in OOWF by using input data and branching mechanism.

3.3   Workflow Implementation

The adaptive workflow is implemented as an expanded business process explicitly showing all alternative tasks and execution paths:

$$BP^E = (N', E', G', C', \Phi, R),$$

where function $\Phi = (\phi_1, \phi_2, \phi_3, \phi_4)$ defines transformation from BP^* to BP^E, for example, $\phi_1 \colon N \cup A \to N'$ defines transformation of initial nodes and their execution alternatives into the set of tasks in the expanded model. Process variants, switching rules and context data are used to design the expanded model and implement the adaptive process in adaptive WfM systems (Fig. 3). The context data are input of business process that affects behavior of the workflow. The switching rules and process variants are used to adapt business process. The statistical data are an output of the executed adaptive workflow. These data can be used to monitor and compare with targeted customer service requirements.

Implementation of the expanded business process implies merging all process variants into a single model (Fig. 3). The adaptive behavior is represented using the context-dependent gateway, where decisions concerning execution of the appropriate process variant are made. The context data trigger the switching rules, and the CFM processes execution is adjusted accordingly. The tasks in the process variants are implemented as objects of the `Task Alternative` class and inherit characteristics of the general task. The process variants can packaged as templates for further reuse in other workflows. The exception handling for the adaptive workflow is provided.

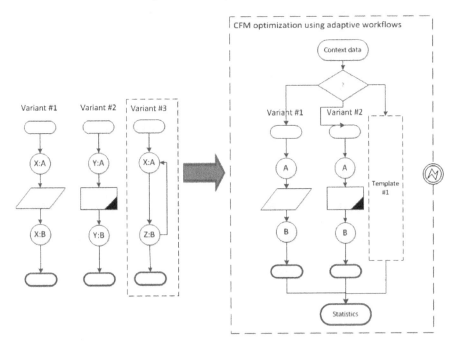

Fig. 3. Implementation of an adaptive workflow using OOWF

4   Implementation Example

In this section, to illustrate the proposed development approach, we discuss ideas and techniques for the prototype's case applied to the passenger airlines and the CFM in airports. This does not narrow at all the application spectrum and generalization of the solution and it is meant to assist flow of ideas.

Nowadays, airlines provide many more services than just ticket sales and registration via mobile devices and web sites. A passenger can be served from the moment he decided to buy a ticket till the end of round trip flight collecting feedback and statistics from whole process. Moreover, adaptive workflows integration with CFM system could improve, firstly, luggage registration process using sensor's data and, secondly, ticket registration with car rent and hotel reservation processes case of flight cancelation to make it possible offering online re-registration.

BPMN model is shown in Figure 4. The first process variant is for management of flight cancelation. The other process variants provide sensor data processing at a luggage registration checkpoint and sending messages to passengers with information about current state at checkpoint and proposed instructions. The message depends on the amount of passengers in queue, who has not registered their luggage yet. For example, there are three options available: if queue length is less than 5 people, then message is sent to inform about possibility to arrive later; if queue length is less than 20 people and greater than 5 people, then message is sent to inform about necessity to arrive immediately; if queue length is greater than 20 people, then message is sent to inform about only one possible variant - use the "VIP" registration.

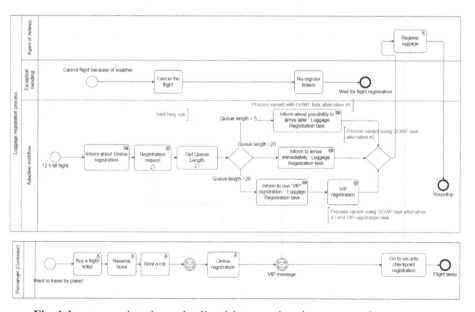

Fig. 4. Luggage registration and online ticket re-registration processes improvement

The prototype has been implemented using a commercial WfM system (Microsoft SharePoint Server 2010) and a 3-d party extension (Nintex Workflow for SharePoint) to create the adaptive workflow for optimization of CFM system business processes.

As a result two main OOWF tasks "Registration task" and "Sensor", four of first level inherited OOWF tasks "Luggage Registration task" and "Ticket Registration task", "Queue sensor" and "Weather sensor" were created. Also there were implemented three alternative tasks of "Luggage Registration task": "Inform about possibility to arrive later", "Inform to arrive immediately" and "Inform to use "VIP" registration" Only one adaptive workflow to manage the whole business process is needed, and it consists of four process variants (Appendix A).

5   Evaluation and Conclusions

In this paper we have concentrated on design and implementation solutions of CFM systems to reach development reusability and flexibility including exception handling. We have shown that the dynamic flow management problem has many facets and is therefore a worthwhile area of study. We have proposed the BPMN meta-model extension. We demonstrated its suitability for the specification of adaptive workflows to optimize CFM system in our prototype called AdaptFly. Its main purpose is optimization of luggage registration and re-registration processes. The presented prototype serves as a proof of concept that the approach is feasible and efficient. The chosen platform has a few of unresolved technical errors, but nevertheless it has many advantages, such as features to provide workflow objects inheritance, intuitional and robust capabilities of GUI elements to create, store and manage adaptive workflows and rich monitoring tools.

This approach provides three main advantages. First of all, analysis of business process can be realized with UML. Business logic of process is distributed into classes as it happens in real life and then is visualized using BPMN modeling language, which is preferable in Non-IT world. Secondly, in the future OOWF tasks can be used in other business processes or easily improved by adding new task alternatives. So, complex business requirements can be realized using OOP best practices. Last but not least, one of main disadvantages of rules based approach is reduced. Usually there are some external rules that manage process behavior. The process and rules are hard related. There is no problem to realize evolutionary changes in such scenario, but there is no fast answer on question: "What would happen with business processes and rules if reengineering process of organization has been started?" It means that all related rules with old processes are no longer valid and must be reconfigured or redeveloped. In turn, process variants with OOWF tasks could be just regrouped or enriched by new task alternatives.

Future steps include enhancing the alert mechanisms using Short Message Service (SMS) and social networks in order to be able to give fast possibilities of interaction with customers. Moreover the prototype is ready to use external sensors. Also Gartner analysts [31] pay attention to the cloud technologies that enables organizations to use such technology as a service, reducing the investment needed and the time of implementation lifecycle. It means that the next step is to upgrade the prototype providing cloud solutions.

References

1. Nie, W.: Waiting: integrating social and psychological perspectives in operations management. Omega 28(6), 611–629 (2000)
2. Chang, J.F.: Business Process Management Systems, Strategy and Implementation. Auerbach Publications (2005)
3. Georgakopoulos, D., Hornick, M., Sheth, A.: An overview of workflow management: From process modeling to workflow automation infrastructure. Distributed and Parallel Databases 3(2), 119–153 (1995)
4. Kumar, A., Yao, W.: Design and management of flexible process variants using templates and rules. Computers in Industry 63(2), 112–130 (2012)
5. van der Aalst, W.M.P., ter Hofstede, A.H.M., Weske, M.: Business process management: A survey. In: van der Aalst, W.M.P., ter Hofstede, A.H.M., Weske, M. (eds.) BPM 2003. LNCS, vol. 2678, pp. 1–12. Springer, Heidelberg (2003)
6. Han, Y., Sheth, A., Bussler, C.: A taxonomy of Adaptive Workflow Management. Paper Presented at the Proceeding SAC, Proceedings of the, ACM Symposium on Applied Computing, New York, NY, USA (2000)
7. Lu, R., Sadiq, S., Governatori, G.: On managing business processes variants. Data & Knowledge Engineering 68(7), 642–664 (2009)
8. Reichert, M., Dadam, P.: ADEPT flex—supporting dynamic changes of workflowswithout losing control. Journal of Intelligent Information Systems 10, 93–129 (1998)
9. Richardson, C., Miers, D.: BPM Suites The Forrester Wave™ Q1, 23 (2013)
10. Weber, B., Reichert, M., Rinderle-Ma, S.: Change patterns and change support features – Enhancing flexibility in process-aware information systems. Data & Knowledge Engineering 66(3), 438–466 (2008)
11. Günther, C.W., Reichert, M., Van Der Aalst, W.M.P.: Supporting flexible processes with Adaptive Workflow and Case Handling. Paper Presented at the Proceedings of the 17th IEEE International Workshop on Enabling Technologies: Infrastructure for Collaborative Enterprises, WETICE 2008, Rome, Italy (2008)
12. Grabis, J.: Using Process Variants in Design of Flow Management Systems. In: Kobyliński, A., Sobczak, A. (eds.) BIR 2013. LNBIP, vol. 158, pp. 34–47. Springer, Heidelberg (2013)
13. Reijers, A., van der Aalst, W.M.P.: The effectiveness of workflow management systems: Predictions and lessons learned. International Journal of Information Management 25(5), 458–472 (2005)
14. Daskin, M.S.: Service Science: Service Operations for Managers and Engineers (2010)
15. Evenson, R.: Customer Service Management Training 101: Quick and Easy Techniques That Get Great Results (2011)
16. Kraft, F.M.: What is an Adaptive Process?, BPMN Forum (2014)

17. Buhler, P.A., Vidal, J.M., Verhagen, H.: Adaptive Workflow = Web Services + Agents. Paper Presented at th. In: Proceedings of the International Conference on Web Services (2003)
18. Kammer, P.J., Bolcer, G.A., Taylor, R.N., Hitomi, A.S., Bergman, M.: Techniques for supporting dynamic and adaptive workflow. Computer Supported Cooperative Work: CSCW: An International Journal 9(3), 269–292 (2000)
19. Müller, R., Greiner, U., Rahm, E.: AGENTWORK: A workflow system supporting rule-based workflow adaptation. Data and Knowledge Engineering 51(2), 223–256 (2004)
20. Xu, H., Tang, B., Gui, Y.: An adaptive workflow engine based on web services and agents. Journal of Information and Computational Science 7(4), 941–950 (2010)
21. Smanchat, S., Ling, S., Indrawan, M.: A survey on context-aware workflow adaptations. Paper presented at the MoMM 2008 Proceedings of the 6th International Conference on Advances in Mobile Computing and Multimedia, New York, NY, USA (2008)
22. Adams, M., Ter Hofstede, A.H.M., Edmond, D., Van Der Aalst, W.M.P.: Worklets: A service-oriented implementation of dynamic flexibility in workflows. In: Meersman, R., Tari, Z. (eds.) OTM 2006. LNCS, vol. 4275, pp. 291–308. Springer, Heidelberg (2006)
23. Cardoso, J., Sheth, A. (2005). Adaptation and Workflow Management Systems. Paper Presented at the Proceedings of the IADIS International Conference on WWW/Internet, Lisbon, Portugal (October 2005)
24. Aoumeur, N., Saake, G., Rautenstrauch, C.: An adaptive ECA-centric architecture for agile service-based business processes with compliant aspectual.NET environment. In: Proceedings of the 10th International Conference on Information Integration and Web-based Applications and Services, pp. 240–247 (2008)
25. Dijkman, R., Dumas, M., van Dongen, B., Käärik, R., Mendling, J.: Similarity of business process models: Metrics and evaluation. Information Systems 36(2), 498–516 (2011)
26. Hallerbach, A., Bauer, T., Reichert, M.: Configuration and Management of Process Variants. In: International Handbooks on Information Systems: Handbook on Business Process Management (1), pp. 237–255 (2010)
27. Li, C., Reichert, M., Wombacher, A.: Mining business process variants: Challenges, scenarios, algorithms. Data & Knowledge Engineering 70(5), 409–434 (2011)
28. Mellor, S.J.: Executable Modeling for Agile Development RTU, Riga (2013)
29. Q-MATIC AB, An introduction to Customer Flow Management (2009)
30. Paschou, M., Sakkopoulos, E., Sourla, E., Tsakalidis, A.: MobiQ: Mobile based processes for efficient customer flow management. In: Bider, I., Halpin, T., Krogstie, J., Nurcan, S., Proper, E., Schmidt, R., Soffer, P., Wrycza, S. (eds.) EMMSAD 2012 and BPMDS 2012. LNBIP, vol. 113, pp. 211–225. Springer, Heidelberg (2012)
31. Dixon, J., Jones, T.: Hype Cycle for Business Process Management, Gartner Research (2011)

Appendix A. Adaptive Workflow Using SharePoint 2010

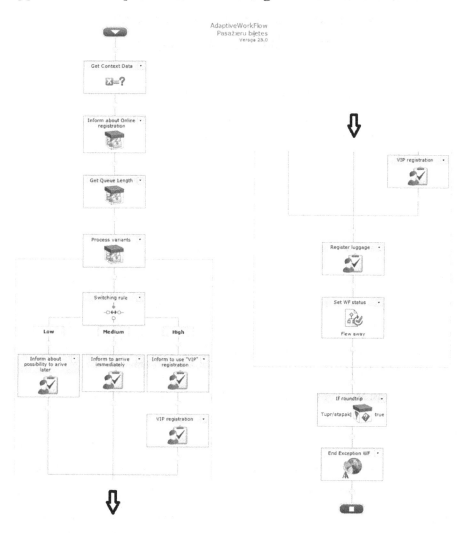

Formalization of Mobile UML Statechart Diagrams Using the π-calculus: An Approach for Modeling and Analysis

Aissam Belghiat[1,2], Allaoua Chaoui[2], Mourad Maouche[3], and Mokhtar Beldjehem[4]

[1] Département d'informatique, Université 20 Août 1955-Skikda, Algérie
[2] MISC Laboratory, Department of Computer Science, University of Constantine 2, Algeria
[3] Department of Software Engineering, Philadelphia University, Amman, Jordan
[4] University of Ottawa, Canada
belghiatissam@gmail.com, a_chaoui2001@yahoo.fr,
mmaouche@hotmail.com, mbeldjeh@uOttawa.ca

Abstract. Mobile UML (M-UML) has been proposed as an extension of UML to model mobile agent-based software systems. As UML, M-UML suffers from lack of semantics due to its semi-formal structure. Formal methods have been used largely in order to deal with such problems. π-calculus is one of these formal methods that deal with mobile computation. In this paper, we propose a formalization of M-UML statechart diagrams using π-calculus in order to provide a formal semantics for such diagrams. The generated π-calculus specifications are then used to analyze and check systems using π-calculus analytical tools (e.g. MWB tool). We illustrate our approach by an example.

Keywords: Mobile UML (M-UML), π-calculus, formalization, MDA.

1 Introduction

UML (Unified Modeling Language) is a language to visualize, specify, build and document all the aspects and artifacts of a software system [1]. It has been extended in [2] to model mobile agent-based software systems by covering the mobility aspects which represent the novel concept inherent to such systems. UML has no formal semantics and hence, it is often needed to tackle incompleteness and ambiguity of their diagrams by means of formalization. This later uses Object Constraint Language (OCL) (which is normally comes with and used for describing rules that apply to UML) or any other formal language. Analogously, M-UML suffers from the same problems and in the case of mobile statechart diagrams, OCL is not the most appropriate formal language, as it does not provide appropriate constructs to represent behavior and mobility aspects modeled in these diagrams correctly. In addition, OCL has ambiguous nature which will not help in reasoning and formal proofs [3]. On the other hand, using π-calculus to formalize M-UML diagrams can help in providing precise semantics to M-UML statechart diagrams. Thus, we propose in this paper an integrated approach *M-UML statechart diagram/π-calculus specification* for modeling and analysis of

G. Dregvaite and R. Damasevicius (Eds.): ICIST 2014, CCIS 465, pp. 236–247, 2014.
© Springer International Publishing Switzerland 2014

mobile agent-based software systems by mapping mobile statechart diagrams to π-calculus specifications. The generated π-calculus specification will be considered as a formal semantic used in analysis; such as early detection of errors (deadlock, livelock,...), check if certain properties are satisfied, or check the equivalence between different diagrams by using π-calculus analytical tools like the Mobility Workbench (MWB) [9][10].

The rest of the paper is organized as follows. In Section 2, we present some related works. In Section 3, we recall some concepts of M-UML. In Section 4, we present the π-calculus computation model. In Section 5, our approach is presented. In Section 6, we illustrate our approach through an example. Section 7 concludes the paper and gives some perspectives of the work.

2   Related Works

There is a large body of work in the literature which attempt to formalize the semantics of UML statechart diagrams and it is impossible to review all of them. Thus, we consider the most related ones to our contribution. The authors in [19] provided a categorization and comparison of 26 approaches of state machines semantics formalization. In [16], a formal semantics of statechart diagrams is given by a temporal logic-based formalization. In [11] and [17], CSP is used to define a formal semantics of statechart diagrams. Other formalizations of statechart diagrams using PROMELA [13], Esterel [14], and Petri nets [18] formalisms are developed.

Other works can be considered since they seem very close to our work in using π-calculus to formalize UML diagrams. In fact, the authors in [15] have proposed a formalization of statechart diagrams in the π-calculus by a bottom-up approach. In [5] and [6], the π-calculus is used to formalize UML activity diagrams. In [7] an automatic translation of UML specifications made up of sequence and state diagrams into π-calculus processes is provided.

The semantics of UML statechart diagrams with mobility was handled in [20] and [8]. Actually, the authors in [20] have proposed an approach for transforming mobile UML statecharts diagrams to nested nets using meta-modeling and graph grammars for modeling and analysis purposes. In [8], a formalization of mobile state machines using the TLA logic is presented and used to define the notions of refinements.

With regard to all these previous studies, we notice the following concerns:

- Although there exists already a formal semantics of M-UML statechart diagrams in [20], the target semantic domain chosen is very limited in semantics and in tools.
- The work presented in [15] was done without considering mobility, besides the fictive strategy adopted in formalization which often consider that it exist fictive (non-identified) processes which accomplish some tasks behind the door. By examination of this approach, we quickly detect that it is impossible to analyze and verify a pi-calculus specification generated by this formalization using specialized tools (e.g. MWB [9][10]). This is what discourages us to pick this formalization and extend it to M-UML statecharts.

- The informal definition of the semantic mapping in large of all previous works, especially in [15], [20], which make them insufficient to full define the translation.
- The authors in [8] propose a formalization of mobile UML state machines by means of MTLA which is an extension of Lamport's Temporal Logic of Actions (TLA) with spatial modalities. The approach can be classified in the ones using statechart diagrams for refinement purposes besides the poverty of the target model (MTLA formalism) in theory and tools.

In contrast to all these works, our contribution provides multiple benefits over them:

- We use in our work the pi-calculus as the target semantic domain; this will facilitate describing these diagrams and capturing the mobility feature. In addition, the pi-calculus provides a rich theory and tools for concurrent systems and mobile communication. This makes it more appropriate for analyzing and verifying mobile systems modeled as M-UML statechart diagrams than other formalisms including nested nests (in [20]) which focus only on dynamic behavior.
- Our study provides a full formal definition of the semantic mapping between M-UML statechart diagrams and the pi-calculus. In contrast to [15], [20] and [8], our approach allows making easy the automation of the translation and its scalability.
- We present a complete and a persistent approach at least for analyzing and verifying the mobility feature captured in these diagrams. This will allow to import the generated pi-calculus specifications into the specialized tools (e.g. MWB [9][10]) and proceed to analysis.

3   M-UML Statechart Diagrams (MSDs)

M-UML Statechart Diagrams (MSDs) [2] have been introduced to model the behavior of a mobile agent/object by exposing their different states. We present bellow (Fig. 1) structural elements of MSDs, and we focus on the new elements introduced by M-UML to deal with mobility in statechart diagrams.

An object is at the beginning in the initial state, and after that it can be found in other states at a given time. A state with a box (M) is a mobile state; it is a state reachable by the object out of its base platform. A transition is a link that comes from a source state and reaches a target state. A mobile transition is a transition with a box (M) between two states reachable by the agent/object in two different platforms; it has several forms as illustrated in Fig. 1. All states reached by an object either at its base or away will be depicted with a dashed box (M). A remote transition which carries a box (R) is a state reached by a mobile agent while interacting with another agent remotely. A transition with <<agentreturn>> stereotype represents the return of the mobile agent to its original platform by reaching a state in it. If the object finishes the execution, it will attain the final state.

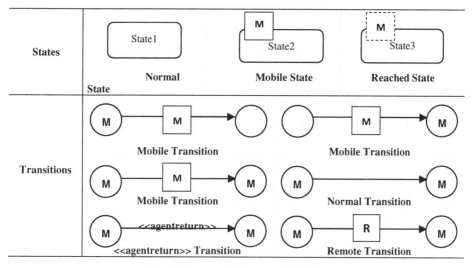

States	State1	State2	State3
	Normal State	**Mobile State**	**Reached State**

Fig. 1. Structural elements of MSDs

4 π-calculus

The π-calculus [4] is a process algebra which has been introduced as a rigorous sematic model for mobile systems. It is developed to cover the limitation of others calculus in terms of expression power by authorizing the passage of "channels" between processes. It can be used for the representation, the analysis, the verification and simulation of mobile systems. The π-calculus uses two concepts to model mobile systems: a process that is an active communicating entity in the system, and a name that is anything else, e.g. a communication link, variable, data, etc. The abstract syntax for the π-calculus is given by:

$$
\begin{aligned}
\mathbf{P} ::= \quad & \mathbf{0} & & \text{Nil; empty process} \\
\mid \quad & \mathbf{x\,(y)\,.\,P} & & \text{Input prefix; receive y along x} \\
\mid \quad & \mathbf{x\,<y>\,.\,P} & & \text{Output prefix; send y along x} \\
\mid \quad & \mathbf{\tau\,.\,P} & & \text{Silent prefix; an internal action} \\
\mid \quad & \mathbf{P\mid P} & & \text{Parallel composition} \\
\mid \quad & \mathbf{P+P} & & \text{non-deterministic choice} \\
\mid \quad & \mathbf{(v\,x)\,P} & & \text{Restriction of name x to process P} \\
\mid \quad & \mathbf{!\,P} & & \text{Replication of process P} \\
\mid \quad & \mathbf{[x=y]\,P} & & \text{Match; if x = y then P} \\
\mid \quad & \mathbf{[x\neq y]\,P} & & \text{Mismatch; if x = }y\text{ then P} \\
\mid \quad & \mathbf{A(y_1, \ldots , y_n)} & & \text{Process Identifier}
\end{aligned}
$$

And, we define the following shortcuts:

$$\sum_{i\in I} P_i \stackrel{def}{=} P_1 + \ldots + P_n \text{ (summation of all processes)}, \quad \prod_{i\in I} P_i \stackrel{def}{=} P_1 \mid \ldots \mid P_n$$

(composition of all processes), and $\quad \overrightarrow{x_1} \stackrel{def}{=} x_1, x_2, \ldots, x_n \quad$ (series of channels)

5   The Proposed Approach

In this section, inspired by [5], [6] and [12], we define a textual abstract syntax as a formal definition of an M-UML statechart diagram. Then, we start our formalization by formally define the mapping toward the π-calculus.

5.1   Formal Definition of MSDs

— Definition 1: (MSDs Definition)

Mobile statchart diagrams (MSD) are defined as:

- S = NS U MS U RS is the set of states where:

> NS is the set of normal states
> MS is the set of mobile states
> RS is the set of reached states

- K = {NT, MT, RT, AT} is the set of transitions kinds where:

> NT represents normal transitions
> MT represents mobile transitions
> RT represents remote transitions
> AT represents *agentreturn* transitions

- $E = \{E_1, E_2, ..., E_n\}$ is the set of events.

- $C = \{C_1, C_2, ..., C_m\}$ is the set of conditions.

- $A = \{A_1, A_2, ..., A_k\}$ is the set of actions.

- $T = KxSxExCxAxS$ is the set of all transitions.

A mobile statechart diagram is a 9-tuple:

$$MSD = (MSDname, S, T, \delta_K, \delta_{src}, \delta_{trg}, \delta_E, \delta_C, \delta_A) \text{ where:}$$

- MSDname   is the name of the mobile statechart diagram.

- $\delta_K : T \longrightarrow K$ returns the kind of a transition.

- $\delta_{src} : T \longrightarrow S$ returns the source of a transition.

- $\delta_{trg} : T \longrightarrow S$ returns the target of a transition.

- $\delta_E : T \longrightarrow E$ returns the event of a transition.

- $\delta_C : T \longrightarrow E$ returns the condition of a transition.

- $\delta_A : T \longrightarrow S$ returns the action of a transition.

— Definition 2: (Mapping Function)

We define a function Ψ for representing each mobile statechart diagram as process expressions in the π-calculus. The function Ψ is defined as follows:

$$\Psi(.) : MSD \longrightarrow \text{Pi-calculus}$$

- MSD is the set of all mobile statechart diagrams.
- Pi-calculus is the set of pi-calculus process expressions.

This function defines for each mobile statechart diagram M ∈ MSD, its corresponding pi-calculus specification Ψ(M) ∈ Pi-calculus.

— Definition 3: (Process Expression Function)

We define the following bijective sub-functions:

$$\Psi_{e \in ELM} : ELM^{MSD} \longrightarrow \sum_{\{PI,N\}}^{\pi}$$

- ELM^{MSD} represents a set of elements of MSD.
- $\sum_{\{PI,N\}}^{\pi}$ is the set of process identifiers "PI" and channels "N".

This function translates each element of the mobile statechart diagram into a pi-calculus process identifier or a channel.

— Definition 4: (Equivalence Class)

We define an equivalence relation R on the set of states S as:

$$R = \{<S_1, S_2> \mid S_1, S_2 \in S \text{ are two states which run on the same platform}\}$$

Then, this equivalence relation defines a partition of the set S where:

$$[s]_R = \{x \in S \mid (s, x) \in R\}$$

The quotient set (equivalence classes set) is defined as:

$$S_{/R} = \{[s]_R \mid s \in S\}$$

The quotient set represents the set of platforms of the mobile statechart diagram.

— Definition 5: (Platforms Distinction)

We define a surjective function which returns for each diagram its platforms.

$$\delta_P : S \longrightarrow S_{/R}$$

Which localizes for each state its platform of execution such that:

$$\forall s \in S, \exists p \in S_{/R}, \text{ where } \delta_P(s) = p.$$

5.2   Formalization of MSDs

The technique adopted to formalize mobile UML statechart diagrams is to define the appropriate π-calculus representation of the reached state (current state) of the object in terms of a process identifier. This later interacts with other processes such as the platforms scheduler, the conditions evaluation process, the events wrapper, and the actions handler to dynamically progress toward other states processes regarding the communication results.

— Rule 1: (the platforms scheduler)

Let P1, P2, ... $\in$ $S_{/R}$, $\Psi_p(P1) = p_1$, $\Psi_p(P2) = p_2$, ... , the platforms scheduler is the process that deals with the platform where the mobile agent/object is currently executed on. The behavior of the platforms scheduler is given by the process:

$$PS(migrate, p_1) \overset{def}{=} \overline{p_1}.PS(migrate, p_1) + migrate(newp).PS(migrate, newp)$$

In the platforms scheduler process, "p_i" is used to model a particular platform "i" in the system and this channel will be changed dynamically when we switch to another platform. This channel is used to model the interaction between the states and the platform where they have performed on. "migrate" is a channel for requesting a migration from a platform to another. PS continues to interact with states by the output action "$\overline{p_i}$" recursively. The need for the migration is modeled by an input on the migration channel that represents the next new platform. The modeling of the mobility feature is guaranteed by the interaction between the platform process and states processes. The formalization is built upon this process; it is the manager of the movements of an object from a state to another in different platforms.

— Rule 2: (Events wrapper)

Let T1, ... , Tn $\in$ T, $\delta_E(T1) = E_1$, ... , $\delta_E(Tn) = E_n$ $\Psi_E(T1) = e_1$, ... , $\Psi_E(Tn) = e_n$, rtc is a channel to represent the run-to-completion of events. An event is something occurring in a system that triggers a potential change. We model the semantics of the occurred events by the behavior of the process ER(rtc, e_1,... ,e_n) as follows:

$$ER(rtc, e_1,...,e_n) \overset{def}{=} \tau.!\overline{e_1}.\overline{rtc}.....\tau.!\overline{e_n}.\overline{rtc}.ER(rtc, e_1,...,e_n)$$

We model the occurrence of something as an internal action "τ" that is produced in the events process "ER". After that, the channel corresponding to the event is sent. We use the replication operator "!" to indicate that the event process makes multiple copies of an event, since the same event can triggers several transitions. The sequential outputs of events in the events process ensures that one event will be performed at a time and the output action "$\overline{rtc}$" guarantees the run-to-completion of events such that the environment will dispatch an event only if the previous was finished.

— Rule 3: (conditions evaluation)

Let T1, ... , Tn $\in$ T, $\delta_C(T1) = C_1$, ... , $\delta_C(Tn) = C_n$, $\Psi_C(T1) = c_1$, ... , $\Psi_C(Tn) = c_n$. *true* and *false* are two channels to represent the current evaluation of a condition (true or false), the semantics of conditions evaluation are modeled by the process CE(true,false,c_1, ... ,c_n) as follows:

$$CE(true,false,c_1, ... ,c_n) \overset{def}{=} \prod_{i=1}^{n} c_i(g).(\overline{g}<true> + \overline{g}<false>).CE(true,false,c_1, ... ,c_n)$$

A guard condition is a logical expression that must be true to take the transition. The process receives a request for the evaluation of a condition by the input action "$c_i(g)$". It then uses the received channel to return the Boolean value by outputting the channel "true" or "false" according to the evaluation. The parallel choice used in the conditions process will guarantee that all the conditions evaluations are performing in parallel, and the invoked one will be executed.

— Rule 4: (actions handler)

Let $T1, \ldots, Tn \in T$, $\delta_A(T1) = A_1, \ldots, \delta_A(Tn) = A_n$, $\Psi_A(T1) = a_1, \ldots, \Psi_A(Tn) = a_n$, We model the semantics of the actions by the behavior of the parameterized process $AH(a_1, \ldots, a_n)$ as follows:

$$AH(a_1, \ldots, a_n) \overset{def}{=} \sum_{i=1}^{n} a_i.\tau.AH(a_1, \ldots, a_n)$$

On receiving the input action "a_i", the actions handler process executes the action (modeled as an internal action "τ") and recursively iterates to perform other actions. The non-deterministic choice is used to treat the adequate action.

— Rule 5: (state + simple transition)

Let $S1 \in S$, $S2 \in S$, $T1 \in T$, $\delta_P(S1) = P1$, $\delta_P(S2) = P1$, $\delta_{Src}(T1) = S1$, $\delta_{Trg}(T1) = S2$, $\delta_K(T1) = NT$, $\delta_E(T1) = E_1$, $\delta_C(T1) = C_1$, $\delta_A(T1) = A_1$, $\Psi_P(P1) = p_1$, $\Psi_E(E1) = e_1$, $\Psi_C(E1) = c_1$, $\Psi_A(A1) = a_1$, and $\Psi_S(S1) = S1(p_1, e_1, c_1, a_1)$. We model the semantics of a state with a transition which has an event, a condition and an action by the behavior of the parameterized process $S1(p_1, e_1, c_1, a_1)$ as follows:

$$S1(p_1, e_1, c_1, a_1) \overset{def}{=} p_1.S1(p_1, e_1, c_1, a_1) + e_1.(v\ g)\overline{c_1}<g>.g(y).$$

$$([y=true]\ \overline{a_1}.S2(p_1) + [y=false]\ S1(p_1, e_1, c_1, a_1))$$

A state is localized in a platform and waits to be reached. This is modeled as an input action "p_1", and in this case the process modeling the state continues to communicate with the platforms scheduler (see Rule 1) until an event occurs i.e. receipt of the adequate channel "e_1" from the events wrapper (see Rule 2).

A condition is represented as a channel "c_1" which will be used to evaluate the guard condition. Actually, after an event occurs, the process modeling the state creates a new channel "$v\ g$" and uses the output action "$\overline{c_1}<g>$" and the input action "$g(y)$" to retrieve the current evaluation of the condition by communicating with the process of conditions evaluation (see Rule 3). The matching construct "[y=true]" indicates that the condition is verified. The matching construct "[y=false]" indicates that the condition is not verified, i.e. the transition can't be realized.

An action is represented as an output action "$\overline{a_1}$". After the occurrence of an event and the evaluation of the condition, the action is executed by communicating with the actions handler process (see Rule 4) and consequently there is a change to the state S2 if the condition is verified. Otherwise, the transition can't be taken, the action is not executed and the object continues as itself.

— Rule 6: (state +remote transition)

Let $S1 \in S$, $S2 \in S$, $T1 \in T$, $\delta_P(S1) = P1$, $\delta_P(S2) = P1$, $\delta_{Src}(T1) = S1$, $\delta_{Trg}(T1) = S2$, $\delta_K(T1) = RT$, $\delta_E(T1) = \varepsilon$, $\delta_C(T1) = \varepsilon$, $\delta_A(T1) = A_1$, $\Psi_P(P1) = p_1$, $\Psi_A(A1) = a_1$, "remote" is a channel for remote interaction and $\Psi_S(S1) = S1(p_1, \text{remote}, a_1)$. We model the semantics of a state with a remote transition by the behavior of the parameterized process $S1(p_1, \text{remote}, a_1)$ as follows:

$$S1(p_1, \text{remote}, a_1) \overset{def}{=} p_1.S1(p_1, \text{remote}, a_1) + \tau.((v\ r_1)\ \overline{\text{remote}}< r_1> \mid r_1(a_1)).\overline{a_1}.S2(p_1)$$

The interaction between a local agent with a remote agent is modeled by sending an output action using the channel of remote interaction "remote" and in parallel waits to receipt the result. These input and output action will retrieve the remote action channel which will be used to execute the corresponding action by communicating with the actions handler process (see Rule 4).

— Rule 7: (state + mobile transition)

Let $S1 \in S$, $S2 \in MS$, $T1 \in T$, $\delta_P(S1) = P1$, $\delta_P(S2) = P2$, $\delta_{Src}(T1) = S1$, $\delta_{Trg}(T1) = S2$, $\delta_K(T1) = MT$, $\delta_E(T1) = \varepsilon$, $\delta_C(T1) = \varepsilon$, $\delta_A(T1) = \varepsilon$, "migrate" is the channel used to request a migration, and $\Psi_S(S1) = S1(p_1, \text{migrate})$. We model the semantics of a state with a mobile transition by the behavior of the parameterized process $S1(p_1, \text{migrate})$:

$$S1(p_1, \text{migrate}) \overset{def}{=} p_1.S1(p_1, \text{migrate}) + \tau.(v\ p_2)\overline{\text{migrate}}< p_2>.S2(p_2)$$

A process modeling a state is in contact with the process modeling the platforms and their location in a particular platform is specified using the channel "p_1". The process S1 modeling the state S1 interacts with the platforms scheduler process PS by sending and receiving the "p_1" channel in a recursive way. When an agent/object moves from the state S1 on platform P1 to another state S2 on the platform P2, a new channel p_2 is created and sent towards the scheduler PS using the "migrate" channel to indicate the movement and the process modeling the state S1 behaves like the process modeling the mobile state S2. The channel "p_2" will become the new parameter of the process PS (see Rule 1). All types of mobile transitions will be modeled in our proposition in the same manner.

— Rule 8: (state + <<agentreturn>> transition)

Let $Sn \in S$, $S1 \in NS$, $T1 \in T$, $\delta_P(Sn) = Pm$, $\delta_P(S1) = P1$, $\delta_{Src}(T1) = Sm$, $\delta_{Trg}(T1) = S1$, $\delta_K(T1) = AT$, $\delta_E(T1) = E_1$, $\delta_C(T1) = C_1$, $\delta_A(T1) = A_1$, $\Psi_P(Pm) = p_m$, $\Psi_P(P1) = p_1$, and $\Psi_S(Sn) = Sn(p_m, \text{migrate})$. We model the semantics of a state with a <<agentreturn>> transition by the behavior of the process $Sn(p_m, \text{migrate})$ as follows:

$$Sn(p_m, \text{migrate}) \overset{def}{=} p_m.Sn(p_m, \text{migrate}) + \tau.(v\ p_1)\ \overline{\text{migrate}}< p_1>.S1(p_1)$$

A <<agentreturn>> transition is similar to a mobile transition. It only differs by the fact that the mobile agent/object makes a return to the original/base platform i.e. the platform from which it is dispatched at the first time. We describe this using the first interacting channel "p_1".

— Rule 9: (MSDs)

Let $MSD = (MSDname, S, T, \delta_K, \delta_{src}, \delta_{trg}, \delta_E, \delta_C, \delta_A)$ a mobile statechart diagram and $\Psi(MSD) = MSDname$, The behavior of this mobile statechart diagram is defined in the π-calculus by the process expression:

$$\text{MSDname} \overset{def}{=} (v \overrightarrow{msd}) (S1 \mid PS \mid EW \mid AH \mid CE)$$

Here, we have to assemble as a process the whole system formed by a restricted composition of five processes and which evolved dynamically by message passing between themselves. $\overrightarrow{msd}$ are different channels used.

6   Example

Let us apply our approach on the mobile statechart diagram illustrated in (Fig. 2) and borrowed from [2]. It models a mobile voting system (MVS), where a mobile agent VC (vote collector) gets a list of voters from a stationary agent VM (vote manager) and visits the VO's (voters) stations which already have the list of candidates to collect the results of the votes and returns them to the VM that mandated the VC in action. The example in (Fig. 2) shows a simple state behavior of the mobile agent VC. Firstly, the VC is in the state ReadyToMove (RTM) at its base platform (P1) while it gets an event StartVotingProcess to move by a mobile transition to the state Voting-ManagerReached (VMR) in another platform (P2). At VMR, the mobile agent performs an action GetVotersList to get the list of voters and moves by a transition to the state WaitForList (WFL) and waiting for the list. At WFL, when the mobile agent receives an event VotersList, it executes the LogList action while interacting remotely with the Logger and moves to the state ReadyToCollectVotes (RCV). After that, the mobile agent performs the action GetVote and moves to the state WaitingForVote (WFV) in the first VO platform (P3). Finally the mobile agent performs a <<agentreturn>> transition to return to its base platform.

The execution semantics of the mobile voting system (MVS) modeled as a mobile statechart diagram is given by the following π-calculus specification:

RTM $(p_1, migrate, vmstartvotingprocess) \overset{def}{=} p_1.RTM (p_1, migrate, vmstartvotingprocess) + vmstartvotingprocess.(v p_2)\overline{migrate}< p_2>.VMR(p_2, migrate, vmgetvoterslist)$

VMR$(p_2, migrate, vmgetvoterslist) \overset{def}{=} p_2.VMR(p_2, migrate, vmgetvoterslist) + \tau.\overline{vmstartvotingprocess}. WFL(p_2, vmvoterslist, loggerloglist)$

WFL$(p_2, vmvoterslist, loggerloglist) \overset{def}{=} p_2.WFL(p_2, vmvoterslist, loggerloglist) + vmvoterslist.\overline{loggerloglist}. RCV(p_2, migrate, vogetvote)$

RCV$(p_2, migrate, vogetvote) \overset{def}{=} p_2.RCV(p_2, migrate, vogetvote) + \tau.\overline{vogetvote}.(v p_3)\overline{migrate}<p_3>.WFV(p_3, migrate)$

WFV$(p_3, migrate) \overset{def}{=} p_3.WFV(p_3, migrate) + \tau.(v p_1)\overline{migrate}<p_1>.WFV(p_3, migrate)$

PS$(migrate, p_1) \overset{def}{=} p_1.P(migrate, talk) + migrate(newp). PS(migrate, newp)$

ER$(rtc, vmstartvotingprocess, vmvoterslist) \overset{def}{=} \tau.!\overline{vmstartvotingprocess}.\overline{rtc}.\tau.!\overline{vmvoterslist}.\overline{rtc}.ER(rtc, vmstartvotingprocess, vmvoterslist)$

$$AH(\text{vmgetvoterslist, loggerloglist}) \overset{def}{=} \text{vmgetvoterslist}.\tau.\ AH(\text{vmgetvoterslist, loggerloglist}) + \text{loggerloglist}.\tau.AH(\text{vmgetvoterslist, loggerloglist})$$

$$MVS \overset{def}{=} (v \text{ migrate,vmstartvotingprocess,vmgetvoterslist, vmvoterlist, loggerloglist,} \\ \text{vogetvote, } p_1, \text{rtc}) (RTM \mid ER \mid AH \mid PS)$$

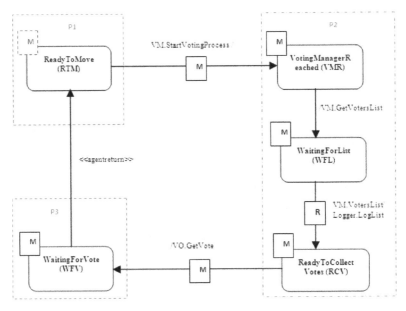

Fig. 2. The mobile statechart diagram of the VC

7   Conclusion

Mobile UML (M-UML) is an extension of UML to model mobile agent-based software systems. As UML, Mobile UML is a semi-formal language and consequently lacks for a precise semantics and formalization. In this paper, we have proposed an approach to formalize UML mobile statechart diagrams using π-calculus. It consists of defining a set of rules mapping the elements of mobile statechart diagrams to theirs corresponding pi-calculus expressions. We have focused on the main elements which affect the mobile behavior of object/agent in these diagrams. In a future work, we plan to extend our approach to take into account all notational elements of UML mobile statechart diagrams, and consequently more mobile agent-based software system will be covered. We plan also to develop a full integrated environment for the automatic generation and analysis of pi-calculus specifications and formalize more M-UML diagrams such as mobile sequence diagrams and mobile activity diagrams since they represent different aspects of a mobile system.

References

1. OMG:OMG Unified Modeling Language, Superstructure, v2.3 (May 2010), http://www.omg.org/
2. Saleh, K., El-Morr, C.: M-UML: an extension to UML for the modeling of mobile agent-based software systems. Journal of Information and Software Technology 46, 219–227 (2004)
3. Evans, A., France, R.B., Lano, K.: The UML as a formal modeling notation. In: Bézivin, J., Muller, P.-A. (eds.) UML 1998. LNCS, vol. 1618, pp. 336–348. Springer, Heidelberg (1999)
4. Milner, R.: Communicating and Mobile Systems: The π-calculus. Cambridge University Press (1999)
5. Lam, V.S.W.: On π-calculus semantics as a formal basis for UML activity diagrams. International Journal of Software Engineering and Knowledge Engineering 18(4), 541–567 (2008)
6. Yang, D., Zhang, S.S.: Using π-calculus to formalize UML activity diagrams. In: 10th Int. Conf. and Workshop on the Engineering of Computer-based Systems, pp. 47–54. IEEE Computer Society (2004)
7. Pokozy, K., Priami, C.: Toward Extracting π- calculus from UML Sequence and State Diagrams. Electronic Notes in Theoretical Computer Science 101, 51–72 (2004)
8. Knapp, A., Merz, S., Wirsing, M.: Refining Mobile UML State Machines. In: Rattray, C., Maharaj, S., Shankland, C. (eds.) AMAST 2004. LNCS, vol. 3116, pp. 274–288. Springer, Heidelberg (2004)
9. Victor, B.: A Verification Tool for the Polyadic π-Calculus. Department of Computer Systems, Uppsala University, Licentiate thesis (1994)
10. Victor, B., Moller, F.: The Mobility Workbench -A Tool for the π-calculus. In: Dill, D. (ed.) CAV 1994. LNCS, vol. 818, pp. 428–440. Springer, Heidelberg (1994)
11. Ng, M., Butler, M.: Towards formalizing UML state diagrams in CSP. In: SEFM 2003 (2003)
12. Posse, E.: Mapping UML-RT state machines to kiltera. Technical Report 2010-569, School of Comp., Queen's Univ (2010)
13. Lilius, J., PaltorI, I.P.: The Semantics of UML State Machines. TUCS Technical Report No. 273. Turku Centre for Computer Science (1999)
14. Seshia, S.A., Shyamasundar, R.K., Bhattacharjee, A.K., Dhodapkar, S.D.: A Translation of Statecharts to Esterel. In: Wing, J.M., Woodcock, J., Davies, J. (eds.) FM 1999. LNCS, vol. 1709, pp. 983–1007. Springer, Heidelberg (1999)
15. Lam, V.S.W., Padget, J.: Formalization of UML Statechart Diagrams in the π-Calculus. In: Proceedings of Software Engineering Conference, Australian. IEEE (2001)
16. Rossi, C., Enciso, M., de Guzmàn, I.P.: Formalization of UML statemachines using temporal logic. SoftwSyst Model 3, 31–54 (2004)
17. Yeung, W., Leung, K., Wang, J., Dong, W.: Improvements towards formalizing UML state diagrams in CSP. In: APSEC 2005 (2005)
18. Saldhana, A., Shatz, J.: UML diagrams to object Petri net models: An approach for modeling and analysis. In: Proceedings of the International Conference of Software and Knowledge Engineering, SEKE 2000, pp. 103–110 (2000)
19. Crane, M., Dingel, J.: On the semantics of UML state machines: Categorization and comparison. Technical Report, 2005-501, School of Comp., Queen's Univ, 55 p. (2005)
20. Bahri, M.R., Hettab, A., Chaoui, A., Kerkouche, E.: Transforming Mobile UML Statecharts Models to Nested Nets Models using Graph Grammars: An Approach for Modeling and Analysis of Mobile Agent-Based Software Systems. In: SEEFM 2009, pp. 33–39. IEEE Computer Society, Washington (2009)

Detecting Missing Requirements in Conceptual Models

Zheying Zhang, Peter Thanisch, Jyrki Nummenmaa, and Jing Ma

School of Information Sciences, University of Tampere, Tampere, Finland
{Zheying.Zhang,Peter.Thanisch,Jyrki.Nummenmaa,Jing.Ma}@uta.fi

Abstract. Completeness of requirements has persisted as a challenge in software development projects. Particularly, in an iterative and incremental development process, only a small portion of requirements are specified before iterations start. Initial versions of the models may be developed in parallel whilst requirements elicitation is still ongoing. In this paper, we propose a metamodel approach for automating the detection of incompleteness in requirements during the conceptual modeling process. Our approach utilizes the metamodel information to allow the modeler to record explicitly each of the model's "known-unknowns", i.e. items of information which are needed to make the model complete, yet which cannot be inferred from the available requirements.

Keywords: Known, unknown, requirements, metamodel.

1 Introduction

Completeness of requirements has persisted as a challenge and motivation over the last 30 years for research in requirements engineering [1, 2]. Much research effort has been put on developing requirements methodologies to improve the completeness, consistency, and accuracy of requirements. It has resulted in standards [3], syntax models [4, 5, 6], language [7], etc. for requirements specification. Incompleteness however still remains a common phenomenon.

Incompleteness problems persist because they are just too difficult to predict all of the details required by a project. Particularly, in an iterative and incremental software development process, only a small portion of requirements are specified before iterations start. The missing information required is rarely written down in a form where it is immediately useable by the project. The delay between the point in time at which the developer realizes that an item of information is needed and the point in time at which the requirements analyst is able to elicit the required information straddle successive time-boxed increments of the development process.

Detecting missing requirements forms an important issue throughout a software development life cycle. A variety of techniques and tools [1, 8, 9, 10, 11] have been proposed and developed to validate requirements and to detect missing information in a requirements document. During a modeling process, it is common to uncover uncertainties over the content of the model [9]. The uncertainties identified by the modeler can imply the missing information about requirements, and remind the development team to elicit the omissions in requirements.

G. Dregvaite and R. Damasevicius (Eds.): ICIST 2014, CCIS 465, pp. 248–259, 2014.
© Springer International Publishing Switzerland 2014

In this paper, we aim at clarifying the known and unknown state of requirements, and propose a metamodel approach to detecting the unknown requirements. Taking entity-relationship (ER) diagrams [12, 13] as an example, we have implemented a metamodel database for storing ER diagrams. The database allows the conceptual modeler to state explicitly that an item of information concerning the detail of the model is, at present, unknown. Using this information structure, we are able to generate a comprehensive list of questions for which the requirements analyst must obtain answers in order to make the requirements complete with respect to the conceptual model.

The rest of this paper is organized as follows. Section 2 introduces different states of knowledge from a requirements analyst point of view and discusses the possible state change. Section 3 presents our approach to detecting missing requirements by using a metamodel specification. The approach is further demonstrated in Section 4, which explains how we store known unknown information in the metamodel database and subsequently use it in order to generate a list of questions that help to discover missing requirements. Our approach and the implementation is further discussed in Section 5, as well as the future work and concluding remarks.

2   Knowns and Unknowns

Importance of dealing with the "knowns" and "unknowns" has been discussed and debated in science and technology communities over the past two decades. The terms refer not only to the presence and absence of knowledge possessed by people, but also to their awareness of what they do not know and to their unawareness of what they do actually know. In the context of software development, a tacit knowledge framework [11, 16] has been proposed to distinguish between the known and unknown requirements using the properties of expressible, articulated, accessible, and relevant. In this section, we further clarify the different states of knowledge possessed by a requirements analyst and discuss how the unknown detected by a conceptual modeler triggers the state change of knowledge possessed by the analyst.

2.1   Knowns and Unknowns in Requirements

Known and unknown form two statuses of knowledge perceived and processed by individuals. The status varies when the knowledge possessor changes. That is to say, the stakeholders possess a body of knowledge about a proposed system which is not necessarily possessed by the analyst at the beginning of the project. Requirements analysis is the process of transforming that knowledge into a coherent set of requirements and communicating that knowledge to the project team [1, 17]. Along with improved understanding of the universe of discourse, the known and the unknown is continuously shaped, and maintains a dynamic relationship. This entails that we must clarify both the *point of view* and the *point in time* when discussing the status of knowledge.

We look retrospectively at a completed project and adapt the requirements taxonomy [11, 16] to distinguish between four states of knowledge at any given point in time in a project, and they are known-known (KK), known-unknown (KU), unknown-known (UK), unknown-unknown (UU).

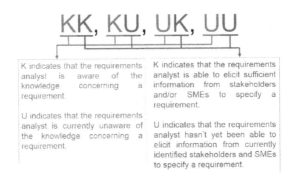

Fig. 1. States of requirements analyst's knowledge concerning requirements at any given time

The four states of knowledge is laid out in Fig. 1. The left-hand K or U indicates the requirements analyst's awareness of the knowledge concerning a requirement. The right-hand K or U indicates whether or not the needed knowledge is possessed by stakeholders and/or SMEs at a given point in time. If yes, the knowledge is a KK or a UK, depending on how the analyst is aware of the knowledge; otherwise, it is a KU or a UU.

KKs refer to requirements which an analyst is able to elicit from the stakeholders and SMEs. A KK is explicit and clear at that time, and the project team proceeds with the subsequent development activities.

KUs refer to the knowledge which the requirements analyst is aware of, but (s)he has not yet been able to elicit from the stakeholders. That is to say, the analyst may encounter difficulties in acquiring the required knowledge [11]. The simplest form of a KU can be a missing business rule [18, 19], which likely exists only in the heads of individuals [1]. As long as the source is unreachable or unidentified, the knowledge is not elicited, and remains unknown to a requirements analyst.

UKs refer to the knowledge that the stakeholders and/or SMEs possess, but of which the requirements analyst is unaware at the time. That is to say, a stakeholder or an SME can provide the knowledge, but has not been asked for the knowledge by the requirements analyst. The knowledge is not transferred to the analyst. Such knowledge is tacit, i.e. embedded in individual experience. Once its value is recognized by the analyst, requirements can be elicited, and UKs evolve into KKs.

UUs refer to the knowledge which the analyst is unaware of, and is not possessed by the currently identified stakeholders and SMEs. As the software system becomes increasingly complex and faces constant changes, it is impossible to predict and specify the large body of knowledge about the system and complex environment where the system operates [2, 20]. There might be unexpected changes, e.g. in the regulatory framework, occurring during the project life cycle. It would be unreasonable to expect that the UU could have been foreseen by the analyst or the stakeholders. A UU is unknowable [14], unpredictable, and emerges during the project life cycle.

It is important to mention that the left-hand U indicates the analyst's unawareness of the knowledge concerning requirements at a given point in time. A UU or a UK can only be brought into consciousness when problems occur and make analysts realize the value of the serendipitous knowledge, and ascribed in retrospect.

2.2   Techniques for Detecting Unknown Requirements

As the project progresses, the knowledge concerning a requirement can transfer from one state to another. On the way of transferring from unknown requirements to known ones, it is important to make analysts become aware of the unknown but relevant knowledge, especially when it is absent, as it forms a pre-condition to activate requirements elicitation for missing and vague information.

Various techniques can help to detect missing and vague requirements. They include requirements review, checklist, planning testing cases, preparing for user manual, model-checking, prototypes, etc [1, 6, 15]. In addition, a lot of research addresses the problems of missing requirements, and presents a variety of approach for discovery of omissions in requirements. For example, Lee and Rine [8] presented an integrated framework to construct proxy viewpoints model from legacy status requirements; Salay et al. [9] presented partial models to manage uncertainty uncovered over the content and structure of requirements models; Yang et al. [10] proposed a machine learning approach for identifying uncertain cues in requirements documents; and Sutcliffe and Sawyer [11] review a number of elicitation techniques and tools that support discovering unknowns in requirements. Specifically, model checking is a powerful technique for checking and reasoning about the syntactical and semantic completeness and consistency of a software specification [6]. Although various model checking techniques and tools are developed to analyze the completeness and consistency of models, they mostly put the focus on requirements models, and rarely elaborate on the linkage between requirements and software design models. There is no systematic approach for eliciting and updating unknowns in the conceptual modeling process.

Detecting unknowns is threaded throughout the project life cycle backwards and forwards. In particular, in an iterative and incremental development process, requirements are no way complete before the design and implementation starts in iterations. Problems and questions regarding the incompleteness and vagueness of knowledge arise. If developers cannot get the required information, they have to make their own interpretations, which are not always correct and explicitly specified, and may lead to substantial effort on detecting and fixing the improper interpretations.

2.3   Detecting and Eliciting Missing Requirements Based on a Modeler's Unknown

Models are commonly used to describe different views or perspectives of the software system for implementation. It is not always the case that a modeler is provided with a complete and consistent description of the world-to-be-modeled, and (s)he may face problems of what and how to model [21]. As shown in Fig. 2, the grids represent the knowledge developers possess at a given point in time. The left grid represents the knowledge concerning requirements, and the right one represents the knowledge concerning design. The UKs and UUs are in grey, as they can only be ascribed in retrospect. The identified KKs and KUs are in black.

When an unknown issue concerning a model is identified, we call it a modeler's KU, as the model is always directed by a known specification, e.g. a metamodel, with which a modeler is acquainted. Generally speaking, a modeler's KU implies the missing information which (s)he cannot retrieve from the existing documents. Requests for missing information can be forwarded to the requirements analyst, and they reveal what the analyst was either unaware of (i.e. a UK or a UU in the left grid) or did not know even though (s)he was aware of the missing (i.e. a KU in the left grid). The tracing paths are shown in thick arrows connecting the two grids.

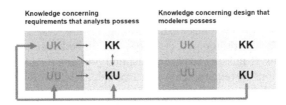

Fig. 2. A modeler's unknown triggers the state change of knowledge possessed by the analyst

When a modeler consults the analyst and SMEs about his KUs, the knowledge of which the analyst used to be unaware becomes explicit, and its state starts changing too. Arrows inside the left grid show possible transitions between the knowledge states. Such transitions can be complicated and in particular, it may alternate between different states several times before finally reaching a KK state. Basically, the transition from a KU to a KK implies a successful requirements elicitation process, and the reverse one indicates the probability of identifying new unknowns from existing known ones. The other transitions imply the awareness process of the required knowledge as being known or unknown by the analyst.

It is worth mentioning that such a process fits in different software development process models. As long as there is a modeling activity, the modeler's unknowns can be collected as requests for elicitation requirements at the time.

3   Metamodel and Unknown Requirements

Whereas the process of detecting UKs and UUs at the requirements stage is often counted as a matter of luck [11], detecting KUs in the modeling phase is a relatively tractable problem where the model is described in a modeling formalism which has an associated metamodel. Essentially, the metamodel comprises a collection of constructs and rules for what constitutes a valid concrete model in the modeling language. [22, 23]. Constructs are normalized elements in a particular model instance, and rules specify the way of integrating construct instances into a model.

When a modeler construct a model on the basis of available requirements, if the model conforms to the metamodel, there are no KUs; otherwise, if insufficient information has been provided about the constructs in the model, each such omission constitutes a modeler's KU. The above observation forms the basis of how we can enumerate, automatically, the set of all KUs associated with the model constructed on the basis of available requirements. We now describe in detail one particular modeling formalism, i.e. the Entity-Relationship (ER) model, in order to illustrate these concepts.

3.1   An Entity Relationship Metamodel

We adapt a metamodel for the enhanced entity relationship model, based on Fidalgo et al. [13]; see the upper division in Fig. 3. We follow Fidalgo's terminology by referring to entities in the metamodel as meta-entities. Distinct meta-entities are constructs to represent the entities, relationships and attributes in an ER model. The attributes of a meta-entity are referred as meta-attributes, and examples include "Participation", "Is_Weak", etc. which are presented in ovals in the metamodel diagram.

An ER model is shown in the lower division in Fig. 3. It is an excerpt derived from the scenario of a conceptual view of the database in an organization [21]. In the excerpt, there are three entities, i.e. Employee, Department and Dependent, and two relationships, i.e. Employment and Dependency.

3.2   KUs in an ER Model and the Match in the Metamodel

When constructing an ER model, the modeler, working from the requirements, has considerable latitude in the design of the model's structure. As shown in Fig. 3, having creatively defined the meta-entity instances, e.g. Employee, Department and Employment, however, the modeler is highly constrained by the business rules with regard to the integration of instances. For example, Employment is a relationship connecting an Employee with a Department. When defining the relationship's cardinality, the modeler may be unclear as to whether the requirement is for a model which allows the possibility that an employee can work in more than one department. In other words, is there an unstated requirement that the proposed system must be capable of modelling such relationships? If such a rule is not available in documents, the modeler detects one unknown issue about the cardinality of the relationship_link connecting the Employment relationship and the Department entity, which is marked as "1 or more?" in Fig. 3. As the modeler is aware of the unknown, we call it a modeler's KU. In order to clarify the value to the cardinality, (s)he shall contact the analyst or other stakeholders to obtain a precise or complete statement of the requirements (see thick arrows in Fig. 2).

The definition of instances in a model depends largely on the requirements and the modeler's design, whereas the integration structure and the constraints is sometimes determined by business rules [18, 21, 24], which encompass statements of goals, policies, or constraints with respect to states and processes in an organizations [1]. These statements are subsumed as part of notation schemes in conceptual modeling [24]. When business rules are not explicitly specified in requirements, the underlying rationale for a modeler to construct a conceptual model might be insufficient. One consequence of this is that a delay in discovering relevant rules will tend to delay completion of the model's construction.

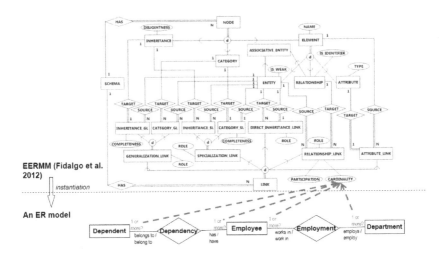

Fig. 3. Relations between the modeler's KUs and the metamodel

Thanisch et al. [21] identified twelve categories of incompleteness that a conceptual modeler may encounter in the process of constructing an ER model, as summarized in the left column of Table 1. The incompleteness encompasses unknown attributes of entities (e.g. Categories 1-4) and relationships (e.g. Categories 5-11), and an unknown concerning whether an attribute belongs to an entity or a relationship (Category 12).

Table 1. KUS identified in an ER model and their associated meta-entities or –attributes

	Category of KUs in an ER model [21]	Related meta- entities/attributes in the metamodel [13]
1	One entity or two?	*Entity*
2	Weakness of an entity	*Entity.is_weak*
3	Attribute value multiplicity	*Attribute.type*
4	Attribute status: identifier or a part of a composite identifier	*Attribute.type*
5	Degree of a relationship	*"N"* in the *Target* relationship connecting *Relationship* and *Relationship_Link*
6	Connectivity of a relationship	*Relationship_link.cardinality*
7	Optionality of the occurrence of an entity in a relationship	*Relationship_link.participation*
8	Generalization: subtypes overlapping or disjoint	*Inheritance.disjointness*
9	Multiple relationships: inclusive or exclusive OR	-
10	Aggregation hierarchy redundancy	*Category*
11	Relationship redundancy	*Relationship*
12	Attribute of a relationship or an entity	*Source* relationship between *Attribute_link* and *Element*

In the following sections, we describe our implementation of the metamodel database, and how we have extended it to allow the modeler to state that an item of information pertaining to the concrete model is currently unknown. Once a concrete model has been loaded into our metamodel database, our software identifies the constructs and the attributes that are subsumed by the metamodel and are related to the incompleteness, as shown in the left column of Table 1. Such a match is also exemplified in Fig. 3, and the examples illustrate omissions in the cardinality of relationship links (Category 6 in Table 1).

4 A Tool to Detect the Incompleteness of ER Model

It is straightforward to implement the metamodel as an ordinary relational database. We have implemented such a metamodel database which can store all of the details of any ER model in such a way that the database design for the model can be generated from the content of the metamodel database. As explained below, we have designed our metamodel database so that it explicitly stores information about a modeler's KUs.

4.1 The Metamodel Database Design

We have incorporated into our implementation of the metamodel database the capability of explicitly stating whether a value corresponding to a meta-attribute is known or unknown. There is a table for each of the meta-entities in the metamodel. Each of the meta-attributes associated with a meta-entity is implemented as a field in the table. This is particularly important in the present context because this is where we are able to store the information about a KU. For example, in our metamodel database, there is a table for the "Entity" meta-entity, which we have named "tblEntity". Once we have loaded the example ER model from the lower division of Fig. 3 into our metamodel database, we can query tblEntity, as illustrated in Fig. 4.

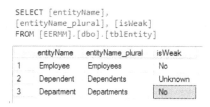

Fig. 4. An example query of the tblEntity table

As shown in Fig. 4, we have included Fidalgo et al.'s "is_Weak" meta-attribute as an attribute in our table. However, instead of restricting the values to "Yes" and "No", we allow the modeler to assign a third value, "Unknown". A rule of ER modeling is that an entity name is unique. Hence entityName is the primary key for the table.

Note that we require the modeler to provide both a singular and a plural form of the entity name. This is to facilitate the automatic generation of natural language questions from the content of the metamodel database.

4.2 The Application

As well as the database tables, we have implemented three sets of stored procedures which facilitate interaction with our metamodel database whilst shielding the details of the metamodel from the users. The first set of procedures allow the conceptual modeler to insert the description of a concrete ER model (with KU, of course) into our database. The second set of stored procedures generate data definition language statements to create the concrete database design for the target database, using the information stored in our metamodel database. These stored procedures take into account the KUs, producing a "worst-case" design. The third set of procedures is most relevant to the present paper. This set comprises one procedure for each of the categories of KU. Each procedure automatically generates a set of natural language questions which attempt to elicit the information required to eliminate incomplete information concerning requirements and business rules. The procedure does this by extracting each of the records in the unique table associated with this particular KU which as the value "Unknown" in the field corresponding to the meta-attribute. When the procedure finds such a record, it prints out a natural language question which solicits the information needed to translate this KU into a KK.

In Table 2, we give the T-SQL code which is executed to generate questions relating to cardinality KUs (i.e. Category 6 in Table 1). The code needs to identify every relationship link record which (a) is associated with a binary relationship and (b) has the value 'Unknown' in the cardinality field of the record. This set of records is obtained by joining the Relationship table with the RelationshipLink table on relationship_ID.

Table 2. T-SQL code to generate questions for each cardinality KU

```
BEGIN
  DECLARE @relationship_ID INT
  DECLARE @entityName_1 SYSNAME, @entityName_2 SYSNAME
  DECLARE @link_1 INT, @link_2 INT
  DECLARE @role_1_plrl SYSNAME;
  DECLARE db_cursor CURSOR FOR
  SELECT DISTINCT L.relationship_ID,
               L.relationshipLink_ID,
               L.[entityName], L.role_plrl
    FROM (   SELECT * FROM tblRelationship
             WHERE [degree] = 'binary'
           ) AS R INNER JOIN
         (   SELECT * FROM tblRelationshipLink
             WHERE [cardinality] = 'Unknown'
         ) AS L ON R.relationship_ID = L.relationship_ID;

  OPEN db_cursor
  FETCH NEXT FROM db_cursor INTO
               @relationship_ID, @link_1,
               @entityName_1 , @role_1_plrl
  WHILE @@FETCH_STATUS = 0
  BEGIN
    SELECT @link_2 = relationshipLink_ID,
           @entityName_2 = [entityName]
    FROM [dbo].[tblRelationshipLink]
    WHERE relationship_ID = @relationship_ID
    AND   relationshipLink_ID <> @link_1;

    PRINT 'Can '
        + fn_addIndefiniteArticle(@entityName_1)
        + ' ' + @role_1_plrl + ' more than one '
        + @entityName_2 + '?';
    FETCH NEXT FROM db_cursor INTO
               @relationship_ID, @link_1,
               @entityName_1 , @role_1_plrl
  END
  CLOSE db_cursor
  DEALLOCATE db_cursor
END
```

With the ER model in Fig. 3, our metamodel information system recognizes that the modeler has not provided any information about (a) whether participation in the relationships is mandatory or optional and (b) the maximum cardinality of the set of relationship instances in which a given entity instance can participate. When the code in Table 2 is executed, it automatically generates a set of questions to elicit more information about the generality of the requirements and/or the business rules of the organization, as shown in Fig. 5.

```
Can an Employee work in more than one Department?
Can a Department employ more than one Employee?
Can an Employee have more than one Dependent?
Can a Dependent belong to more than one Employee?
```

Fig. 5. Generated questions of cardinality Unknowns

Answers to these questions must be obtained before a complete ER model can be constructed. Meanwhile, however, a database design can be generated which is based on the "worst case" that the requirements are for the most general database design. In the above example, this worst case corresponds to a "yes" answer to each of the questions above. This would mean extra tables are needed to model many-to-many relationships between the entity classes, making updates slower and maintenance more complex. If, subsequently, it is discovered that some of answers to the above set of questions is "no" then it may be possible to refactor the database in order to simplify the design.

5   Discussion

Requirements constrain the design solution and the exact balance of satisfying these requirements cannot be known in advance of producing a design [18]. The main aim of our approach has been to detect and report missing constraints through a) the metamodel of conceptual models and b) the linking between the metamodel specification and requirements. Information specified in a metamodel forms a basic schema to represent a software system under development, and serves as a reliable and effective checklist for detecting omissions. The automated detection and report process guarantees that requirements of which analysts or modelers may not be aware will always be made explicitly, which helps the development team to detect and manage missing requirements when planning subsequent development activities.

As a proof of concept we used the ER model to illustrate our approach, implemented it in the relational database environment, and demonstrated how omissions in an ER model are detected and reported. The generated questions enumerate various requests for missing requirements. As an ER model's main constructs are entities and relationships that can exist among them, the detected unknowns are mainly about entities' attributes and their relationships. Requirements regarding action assertions, mathematical calculations, inference rules, etc. [1, 19] are associated with events, guards, conditions, etc. which are specified and reflected in different modeling techniques. Similarly, our approach works as long as the linking between requirements and the metamodel specification is understood and explicitly specified.

In our current implementation, besides setting up the metamodel database environment, we have developed procedures to insert an ER model, to report requests for missing requirements, and to create concrete database design to the target database. All these can also be implemented in a metaCASE tool or a modeling tool which includes a metamodeling language to specify methods. Comparing with the metamodel database, a metaCASE tool facilitates the syntactic and semantic specification of a methods and provides flexibility of method specification. Implementing our approach in a metaCASE tool and analyzing how it supports the detection of missing requirements in a specific application domain forms the next step of our research on this issue.

Concerning the implementation of reporting function in our metamodel database, we have developed procedures to detect KUs that are illustrated in Table 1, with an exception of Category 9 (i.e. Multiple relationships: inclusive or exclusive OR), which is about the constraint on multiple relationships, and is related to the semantic meaning of the model. Such specification is not in the current metamodel, and hard to define a meta-entity or attribute that matches it. The lack of detecting unknowns in the semantic meaning of a model forms a limitation of our approach. In addition, it is easy to see that the detected unknowns are from the instances that have been created and specified in an ER model. If there is any important instance missing from the model, omission regarding the instance's attributes or constraints cannot be detected.

Clearly, these limitations are derived from the nature of the metamodel. As metamodels can express the logical syntactical structures of models only, the semantic completeness and semantic constraints of a model cannot be specified in the current metamodel specification. In order to deal with the unknowns associated with the semantics of a model, formal methods with rigorous semantic basis can be applied combined with the modeling technique. Besides, domain ontology provides a thesaurus of concepts and the inference rules. The inference rules can be used to detect semantic inconsistency. Detecting the semantic incompleteness and inconsistency in a model forms one important direction of our future work.

In summary, our main contribution is twofold. First, we clarified four states of knowledge from the requirements analyst point of view at any given time in a software development project, as well as the possible paths of the state transition triggered in other development activities. Second, we demonstrated and discussed how the transition is triggered by using our metamodel approach in the modeling process. On the basis of our implementation, we shall further study how our approach can be combined with the different model checking techniques to support the missing requirements detection process in a more effective and flexible way.

References

1. Wiegers, K.E.: Software Requirements, 2nd edn. Microsoft Press (2003)
2. Jarke, M., Loucopoulos, P., Lyytinen, K., Mylopoulos, J., Robinson, W.: The brave new world of design requirements. Information Systems 36(7) (2011)
3. IEEE: In: IEEE Recommended Practice for Software Requirements Specifications. Technical report, IEEE Std 830-1998
4. Mavin, A., Wilkinson, P., Harwood, A., Novak, M.: EARS(Easy Approach to Requirements Syntax). In: Proceedings of the 17th IEEE International Requirements Engineering Conference. IEEE computer society (2009)

5. Guo, J., Wang, Y., Zhang, Z., Nummenmaa, J., Niu, N.: Model-driven approach to developing domain functional requirements in software product lines. IET Software 6(4), 391–401 (2012)
6. Lamsweerde, A.V.: Requirements Engineering: From System Goals to UML Models to Software Specifications. Wiley (2009)
7. Gilb, T.: Quantifying the Qualitative: How to Avoid Vague Requirements by Clear Specification Language. Requirenautics Quarterly 12, 9–13 (1997)
8. Lee, S., Rine, D.: Missing Requirements and Relationship Discovery through Proxy Viewpoints Model. In: Proceeding of the 19th Annual ACM Symposium on Applied Computing, pp. 1513–1518 (2004)
9. Salay, R., Chechik, M., Horko, J.: Managing Requirements Uncertainty with Partial Models. In: The 20th IEEE International Conf. on Requirements Engineering, pp. 1–10 (2012)
10. Yang, H., Roeck, A.D., Gervasi, V., Willis, A., Nuseibeh, B.: Speculative requirements: Automatic detection of uncertainty in natural language requirements. In: the 20th IEEE International Conference on Requirements Engineering, pp. 11–20 (2012)
11. Alistair, S., Sawyer, P.: Requirements elicitation: Towards the unknown unknowns. In: The 20th IEEE International Conference on Requirements Engineering, pp. 92–104 (2013)
12. Chen, P. P.: The Entity-Relationship Model - Toward a Unified View of Data. ACM Trans. Database Syst., 9–36 (1976)
13. Do Nascimento Fidalgo, R., De Souza, E.M., España, S., De Castro, J.B., Pastor, O.: EERMM: A Metamodel for the Enhanced Entity-Relationship Model. In: Atzeni, P., Cheung, D., Ram, S. (eds.) ER 2012 Main Conference 2012. LNCS, vol. 7532, pp. 515–524. Springer, Heidelberg (2012)
14. Gomory, R.: The Known, the Unknown and the Unknowable. Scientific American, p. 120 (June 1995)
15. Kontoya, G.: SommervilleI.: Requirements Engineering: Processes and Techniques. Wiley (1998)
16. Gacitua, R., Ma, L., Nuseibeh, B., Piwek, P., Roeck, A.N., De Rouncefield, M., Sawyer, P., Willis, A., Yang, H.: Making Tacit Requirements Explicit. In: Proc. 2nd International Workshop on Managing Requirements Knowledge (MARK 2009), Atlanta, pp. 85–88 (2009)
17. Pohl, K.: The Three Dimensions of Requirements Engineering. In: Rolland, C., Cauvet, C., Bodart, F. (eds.) CAiSE 1993. LNCS, vol. 685, pp. 275–292. Springer, Heidelberg (1993)
18. Wan-Kadir, W.M.N., Loucopoulos, P.: Relating evolving business rules to software design. Journal of Systems Architecture 50(7), 367–382 (2004)
19. Loucopoulos, P., Wan, K., Wan, M.N.: BROOD: business rules-driven object oriented design. Journal of Database Management 19(1), 41–73 (2008)
20. Cheng, B.H.C., Atlee, J.M.: Research Directions in Requirements Engineering. In: Future of Software Engineering (FOSE 2007). IEEE (2007)
21. Thanisch, P., Niemi, T., Nummenmaa, J., Zhang, Z., Niinimäki, M., Saariluoma, P.: Incompleteness in Conceptual Data Modelling. In: Skersys, T., Butleris, R., Butkiene, R. (eds.) ICIST 2013. CCIS, vol. 403, pp. 159–172. Springer, Heidelberg (2013)
22. Zhang, Z., Lyytinen, K.: A Framework for Component Reuse in a Metamodelling based Software Development. Requirements Engineering Journal 6(2), 116–131 (2001)
23. Gonzalez-Perez, C., Henderson-Sellers, B.: Metamodelling for Software Engineering. John Wiley & Sons, Ltd. (2008)
24. Gottesdiener, E.: Discovering an Organization's Knowledge: Facilitating Business Rules Workshops. In: Proceedings of Annual Meeting of the International Association of Facilitators, Williamsburg, Virginia (1999)

Model-Driven Approach and Implementation of Partial Model-to-Model Transformations in a CASE Tool

Tomas Skersys[1,2], Saulius Pavalkis[1], and Ingrida Lagzdinyte-Budnike[1]

[1] Center of Information Systems Design Technologies, Kaunas University of Technology
[2] Department of Information Systems, Kaunas University of Technology
Studentu str. 50, Kaunas, Lithuania
{tomas.skersys,saulius.pavalkis,ingrida.lagzdinyte}@ktu.lt

Abstract. One of the main features of Model Driven Architecture is a model-to-model (M2M) transformations, which improve the overall model-driven systems development process by speeding up the development process itself and also enabling the reusability of the existing models within a single or even multiple projects. However, CASE tool-supported M2M transformations quite often lack so needed flexibility and customization options. The main goal of this paper is to present a practical model-driven approach to improve the usability of partial model-to-model transformations in a CASE tool environment. The approach is currently implemented in the CASE tool MagicDraw; however, it can be adopted by any other CASE tool that meets certain capability requirements.

Keywords: model-to-model transformation, drag-and-drop actions, MDA, UML profile, DSL, CASE tool.

1 Introduction

Since the advent of Model Driven Architecture (MDA) [1] in 2003, its impact on the overall process of model-driven systems development becomes more and more evident. Additional boost to it was given by the introduction of UML 2.0, which brought into play the powerful model extension mechanism. Today, every advanced CASE tool utilizes at least few features of MDA, such as platform-independent and platform-specific modeling, model integration, model-to-model (M2M) transformations featuring model reusability and traceability [2]. When talking about M2M transformations [3], one should mention that the usability of this feature quite often lacks so needed flexibility and customization options – in many cases, this is due to the fact that the feature itself is implemented as a hard-coded solution, rather than a model-based one. Moreover, number of such M2M transformations in a CASE tool might also be quite limited and not always satisfy the needs of a user.

Our current practical experience with various CASE tools, as well as the feedback from our professional partners also indicates that a certain subtype, i.e. user-interacted *partial* M2M transformations are in particular demand by many, especially when it comes to agile, highly iterative model-driven development. By the term *partial M2M transformation* we assume the case where not the whole model, but only a user-defined

G. Dregvaite and R. Damasevicius (Eds.): ICIST 2014, CCIS 465, pp. 260–271, 2014.
© Springer International Publishing Switzerland 2014

part (fragment) of the model (i.e. a set of selected source model concepts) is being transformed into a fragment on another model (i.e. a set of target model concepts). In general, a CASE tool user prefers to have a certain degree of "freedom of choice" when it comes to selecting a process of work, ability to create few models at a time while reusing each other's concepts, modifying these models on demand, etc. This is where the advantage of *partial M2M transformations* over traditional *complete M2M transformations* is the most obvious.

As a rule, any kind of M2M transformation in a CASE tool is either a hard-coded one or implemented using a dedicated transformation language (ATL [4] and QVT [5] are arguably the most widely-used ones). In both these cases, the possibility for a user to somehow modify the predefined transformations or even add new ones is highly limited. In this paper, we present a practical model-driven approach to improve the usability of partial M2M transformations in a CASE tool environment. This approach provides a capability not only to customize the existing M2M transformations but also to develop new ones in a model-driven way.

Currently, one can find a great number of research papers, project reports and all kinds of discussions related to various aspects of M2M transformations. However, none of the analyzed sources delivers a practical, well-defined solution for model-driven management of user-interacted partial M2M transformations in the environment of an actual CASE tool. Due to this fact and also taking into account the paper size limitations, we will omit the related work discussion as such and concentrate more on other high priority aspects of our research. Further, the paper is structured as follows: in Section 2, we present basic requirements for a CASE tool to support the proposed approach; in Section 3, the approach itself is presented and discussed in more details; in Section 4, some illustrative examples of the core component of the approach (i.e. drag-and-drop action specifications) are presented; conclusions are drawn in Section 5.

2   Requirements for a CASE Tool to Support the Approach

The proposed M2M transformation approach is highly dependent on certain features of a CASE tool; therefore, we will define basic set of requirements for a CASE tool, which should be met in order to use the approach:

- *Support of UML extension mechanism* to introduce language extensions, custom DSLs or even other modelling languages (e.g. BPMN, SoaML). Today, the majority of state-of-the-art CASE tools (e.g. Visual Paradigm, ArgoUML, MagicDraw, Modelio, ObjectIF, Papyrus) support this kind of extensibility through UML profiling [6, 7]. This capability can also be achieved by providing the ability to develop custom metamodels from scratch (e.g. Rational Software Architect); however, such approach is more time- and effort-consuming as a rule. Our approach is based on UML profiling.
- *Extensibility of CASE tool functionality.* In this regard, UML CASE tools can be divided into functionally extensible and non-extensible ones. This capability of functional extensibility is inherent to open source solutions or/and the ones supporting plug-in-based implementation architectures with stable public API. Our approach is based on (but the conceptual part is not bound to) the latter.

- *DSL engine and its extensibility.* If a CASE tool has an implemented UML extension mechanism, then it certainly has some DSL engine as well. The critical question is, if that engine is extensible and how this is achieved. If the previous two requirements are satisfied by quite many CASE tools, the third one limits this number to quite few. Today, only several reviewed CASE tools support model-based DSL customization. Here, the strongest are MagicDraw by No Magic Inc. [8] and Enterprise Architect by Sparx Systems [9]. However, to our knowledge, only MagicDraw has extended its DSL engine to allow the customization of so called D&D handlers that play a crucial part in our approach [10].

Provided all the above mentioned capability requirements are met, each CASE tool still has its own ways of implementing things. Further on, we will use a CASE tool MagicDraw to present basic aspects of the approach.

3   The Approach of Partial Model-to-Model Transformations

3.1   Illustrative Example

Before we go into conceptual and technological details of the approach itself, let us start with two simple examples that will illustrate the usability of the approach in actual modeling activities, and its capability of enabling one to create new and configure the existing M2M transformations in a model-driven way.

For the first example, let us assume a business analyst has a BPMN business process model (BPM) designed for some business domain. Now, it is up to another member of the project team, namely, a system analyst to develop a user functional requirements model based on the business knowledge provided by the designed BPM (and some other sources of knowledge, which we will omit for simplicity reasons). Our system analyst starts doing it by designing a UML use case diagram (UCD). This is not nearly a straight forward process; therefore, the analyst would normally start designing this diagram from the scratch just by looking at some process diagrams of the BPM. But instead of creating new UML concepts and putting them into UCD, the analyst starts selecting certain concepts from the BPM itself and then dragging and dropping them right into the worksheet of UCD; at the same time, CASE tool reacts to each analyst's drag-and-drop action by creating sets of new interrelated UML use case model (UCM) concepts and automatically deploying them into the diagram. An illustrative example of one of such drag-and-drop actions is presented in Figure 1: a selected task from BPMN business process model (Tag 1) is being transformed into a set of interrelated concepts (*Actor-Association-UseCase*) of UML UCM, which are then automatically deployed into a use case diagram (Tag 2).

For the second example, let us assume our system analyst is not really happy with the limited set of predefined partial M2M transformations that he has at his disposal. While working with UML use case models, he wants to have the same drag-and-drop-invoked transformation not only for BPMN *Task* concepts (as shown in Figure 1) but for *SubProcess* concepts as well. To make this happen, he simply opens up the BPMN_BPM-to-UML_UCM transformation model, finds the transformation specification dedicated to BPMN *Task*, and uses it as a pattern to develop a new transformation dedicated to BPMN *SubProcess*. With a bit of practical experience, it all took him less than five minutes to have a new partial M2M transformation ready for use.

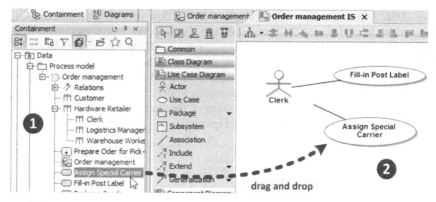

Fig. 1. Illustrative example of a partial M2M transformation using D&D action

The two above mentioned examples illustrate main "selling" features of the proposed approach, which will be described in more details further below.

3.2   Basic Principles of the Approach

Figure 2 describes the basic concepts of structural composition of the approach.

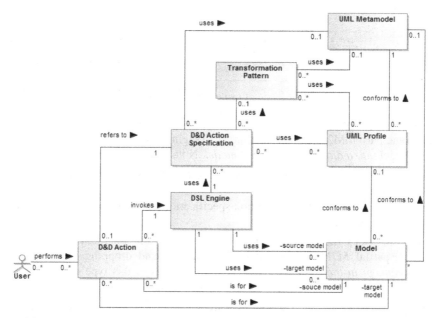

Fig. 2. Basic structural composition of the approach in a CASE tool environment

After a user of a CASE tool performs a predefined D&D action (*D&D Action*) on a particular concept from a source model (*Model*), it acts as a trigger to invoke a DSL engine (*DSL Engine*), which uses certain D&D action specification (*D&D Action Specification*) to perform M2M transformation. Each D&D action specification uses model concept types from either UML metamodel (*UML Metamodel*) or/and one or more UML profiles (*UML Profile*), which are used in that particular M2M transformation. D&D action specification may also be related to a transformation pattern (*Transformation Patter*) in case of more complex M2M transformations.

Further, two basic scenarios of application of the implemented M2M transformation approach are presented (Figure 3 and Figure 4).

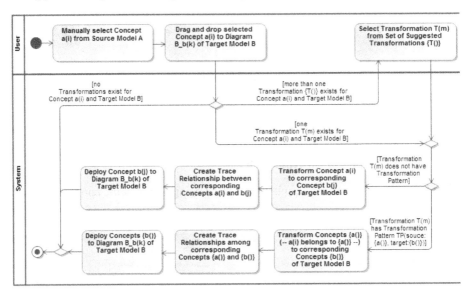

Fig. 3. The 1st scenario of *using* partial M2M transformation

Figure 3 describes the first scenario of a user-system interaction when a user initiates some partial M2M transformation by dragging and dropping a concept from a source model *into a diagram of a target model*. Note that the scenario has two cases:

- The 1st case is when a transformation specification is supplemented with a transformation pattern;
- The 2nd case is when a transformation specification does not have a supplementary transformation pattern.

Figure 4 describes the second scenario of a user-system interaction when a user initiates a partial M2M transformation by dragging and dropping a concept *onto another concept in the same diagram*. Transformations of this type do not use supplementary transformation patterns. Note that this scenario also has two cases:

- The 1st case is when dragging and dropping a concept onto another concept assigns the first concept as a new *value* to a predefined *property* of the latter concept;
- The 2nd case is when dragging and dropping a concept onto another concept creates a new *relationship* between these concepts.

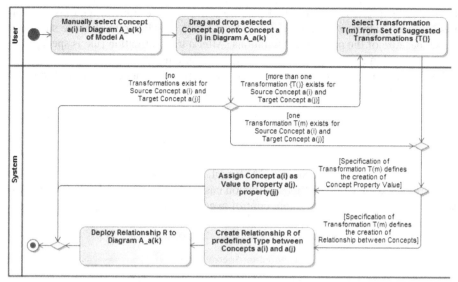

Fig. 4. The 2nd scenario of *using* partial M2M transformation

However, in order to actually start running the application scenarios (Figure 3 and Figure 4), one needs to develop a set of partial M2M transformation specifications first (unless they are already provided by someone else). The distinctive feature of our approach is that this stage is done in a model-driven way. Basic steps of the scenario for the development of partial M2M transformations are shown in Figure 5.

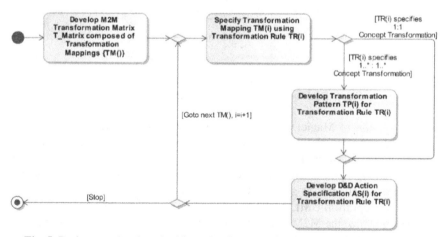

Fig. 5. Basic scenario of mode-driven *development* of partial M2M transformations

The scenario starts from two conceptual level steps: first, the development of a transformation matrix that specifies transformation mappings among corresponding concept types of source and target models, and second, the specification of each transformation mapping using transformation rules. These two steps are not mandatory; however, they help to specify the transformations in a formalized manner and keep them organized. For this conceptual part we use a specific transformation specification approach, which was presented in [11]; we will not elaborate on these steps any further because of the paper size limitations. After a transformation rule is specified, it can be realized in a model-driven way using our implementation.

The main composing elements of M2M transformation model itself are presented in the next subsections of Section 3.

3.3   Drag-and-Drop Action Metamodel

Drag-and-drop (D&D) actions are one of the core elements of the proposed partial M2M transformation approach. In a CASE tool, D&D capability may be implemented as a hard-coded (which is the most common case) or a model-based solution. Model-based solution provides much more control over the customization options and extensibility of D&D actions.

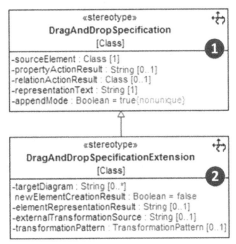

Fig. 6. D&D action metamodel for M2M transformations

Current version of MagicDraw already uses some extension to UML metamodel (Tag 1 in Figure 6), which allows one to specify properties of D&D actions responsible for dragging and dropping one model concept onto another within the same diagram and creating relationships between these concepts or assigning some property values to a target concept as a result. Other D&D action behavior (e.g. dragging and dropping a concept from UML model into a diagram) is still hard-coded.

In order to realize the M2M transformation approach, the existing D&D action metamodel was extended with additional specialization metaclass (Tag 2 in Figure 6).

Description of the properties of D&D action metaclasses is presented in Table 1.

Table 1. Description of properties of D&D action metaclasses

Metaclass property	Description
sourceElement	The mandatory property defining a type of a source model concept that will be dragged onto some target model concept or a target diagram. The property can specify a class, a metaclass, or a stereotype.
representationText	The property defines a short description of a D&D action.
relationActionResult	When the property is not empty, the result of the D&D action is a new *relationship* between two concepts. The property *relationActionResult* defines a *type* of a relationship that will be created.
propertyActionResult	When the property is not empty, the result of the D&D action is a new *value* assigned to a property of a concept after another concept was dragged and dropped onto the first concept. The property defines *property* of a target concept, to which the dragged and dropped source concept (*SouceElement*) will be set as a *value*.
appendMode	The property is of Boolean type and complements *propertyActionResult*. If the value is set to "true", then each time the specified D&D action is performed, new value is stacked to the already existing values of the specified property of a target concept; if the value is set to "false", then the new value will be set over the old one.
targetDiagram	Defines a type of a target diagram, on which the D&D action will be performed.
newElementCreationResult	The property is of Boolean type. If the value is set to "true", then a new concept will be created in a target model after the source concept (*sourceElement*) is dragged and dropped into a diagram of the target model (*targetDiagram*); if "false", then the new element will not be created.
elementRepresentationResult	The property complements *newElementCreationResult*. It specifies the graphical representation of the newly created (or just represented) concept in a target diagram (*targetDiagram*).
externalTransformationSource	Defines a class from the custom M2M transformation plugin, which implements custom M2M transformation rules of more complex transformation cases.
transformationPattern	Defines a class, whose structure specifies a transformation mapping between concepts of a source and a target models. When specified, this transformation pattern supplements D&D action specification.

An example of instantiated D&D action metaclasses is presented in Figure 7. Note that a non-mandatory *TransformationPattern* property binds this D&D action specification with the supplementary transformation pattern (Figure 8); in other words, a complete M2M transformation model may or may not have a supplementary transformation pattern (see Section 3.4 for more information).

Lastly, in order to actually start using newly developed M2M transformation, its D&D action specification needs to be assigned to a specific stereotyped *customization* class, which binds the main target concept with one or more D&D action specifications (Figure 7). If customization class for the main transformation target concept does not yet exist, it also has to be created before assigning any D&D action specification to it.

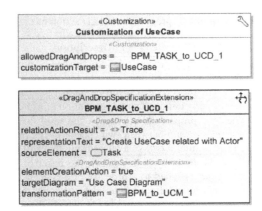

Fig. 7. Example of D&D action specification and customization classes

3.4   Transformation Pattern Specification

In our approach, one-to-one concept transformation within a single or two different models can be realized using the extended D&D action definition alone (see the illustrative examples in Section 4). However, for many-to-many concept transformations, D&D action definition is not enough – additional specification of concept types' mappings is required. We call this specification a *Transformation Pattern*.

When used together, D&D action definition and transformation pattern compose a complete partial M2M transformation model, which provides the following possibilities to the transformation:

- Any concept type or its property can be mapped to any other concept type or its property.
- One can specify mappings within a single model or between different models expressed in the same or even different modeling languages (e.g. UML and BPMN, BPMN and SoaML).
- Many-to-many mapping can be specified.

A transformation pattern is identified by a custom stereotype <<*TransformationPattern*>>, which is derived from the UML metaclass *Class* (Figure8).

The pattern itself is realized as a structured class that has its internal structure, called *Structure Compartment*. The structure compartment of a transformation pattern holds two parts: *Source* and *Target*. In the source part, there is one or more inner parts deployed – these represent concept types and/or properties of concept types of a source model.   In the target part, there is also one or more inner parts deployed – these represent concept types and/or properties of concept types of a target model. In each part, inner parts are interconnected using connectors – these interconnected inner parts define certain common patterns of the particular type of model. In its turn, mappings between source and target models are also defined using connectors (pay attention, however, the semantics of using connectors in the first and second cases differs).

An example of a transformation pattern is presented in Figure 8. The pattern specifies: a source part describing BPMN Process Model pattern composed of a *Task* that is deployed in a *Lane*, and a *Resource* assigned to a *Lane*; a target part describing UML

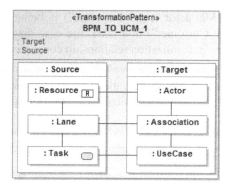

Fig. 8. Transformation pattern example

Use Case Model pattern composed of an *Actor* associated with a *UseCase*; mapping between certain inner parts of the source and target parts.

Note that in general the validity of a model is ensured by a CASE tool's model validation engine (provided, the CASE tool supports certain metamodel). In other words, if a CASE tool supports a certain level of enforcement of model correctness, an incorrect model cannot be created or at least syntactical errors are highlighted for correction. On the other hand, at this stage of development, our M2M transformation approach does not restrict a user from developing incorrect *transformation patterns*; in its turn, this should lead to incorrect target model fragments after certain transformation is performed. However, on the execution of such transformation, a MagicDraw user will get a warning message that the action could not be executed as it leads to the creation of an incorrect model (such message is generated if the creation of a model fails).

4   Illustrative Examples of D&D Action Specifications

In this section, we will present four D&D action specification examples illustrating four basic cases that were introduced in Section 3.2. Short description of the presented cases (Table 2) is as follows:

- The first case: a *BPMN data object* (e.g. "Order") is being dragged from BPMN process model and dropped into a UML class diagram. The result of the transformation is a new UML class ("Oder") deployed in the diagram.
- The second case: a BPMN task (e.g. "Assign Special Carrier") is being dragged from BPMN process model and dropped into a UML use case diagram. The result of the transformation is three new concepts deployed in the diagram: actor ("Clerk"), use case ("Assign Special Carrier") and association connecting the actor to the use case. Transformation pattern is also used in this transformation specification. This case is described in more details throughout the whole paper.
- The third case: a SoaML interface class (e.g. "Receiver") is being dragged and dropped onto a consumer or provider class (e.g. "Consumer") in a SoaML diagram. The result of the transformation is a new value ("Receiver") set to a predefined property ("Type") of the consumer or provider class ("Consumer").

- The fourth case: a UML actor (e.g. "Customer") is being dragged onto another UML actor (e.g. "VIP Customer") in a UML use case diagram. The result of the transformation is a new generalization relationship connecting the two actors.

In Table 2, some cells are marked as *"no value"*, which means that the corresponding properties of certain D&D action specifications have no values. A property with no value means that it is not relevant to a particular D&D action specification.

Table 2. Examples of D&D action specifications

Metaclass property	Case			
	1st	2nd	3rd	4th
<<Customization>> stereotype				
customizationTarget	Class	Use Case	SoaML Consumer, SoaML Provider	Actor
<<DragAndDropSpecification>> stereotype				
sourceElement	DataObject	Task	Interface	Actor
representationText	Create Class	Create Actor related with Use Case	Set Type	Create Generalization relationship
relationActionResult	Trace	Trace	*not filled-in*	Generalization
propertyActionResult	*no value*	*no value*	Type	*no value*
appendMode	*no value*	*no value*	False	*no value*
<< DragAndDropSpecificationExtention>> stereotype				
targetDiagram	Class diagram	Use Case diagram	*no value*	*no value*
newElementCreationResult	True	True	False	False
elementRepresentationResult	*no value*	*no value*	*no value*	*no value*
externalTransformationSource	*no value*	*no value*	*no value*	*no value*
transformationPattern	*no value*	BPM_TO_UCM_1	*no value*	*no value*

5   Conclusions

In this paper, we presented the approach and implementation of user-interacted partial model-to-model (M2M) transformations. One of the key features of this approach is the model-driven development and customization of M2M transformations, which greatly increases the flexibility and usability of this capability when used in a CASE tool environment. Our current implementation works as an extension to the CASE tool MagicDraw; however, the conceptual part of the approach could be reused in other advanced CASE tools that meet the defined requirements.

One more distinctive feature of the proposed approach is that it can be applied to any graphical modeling language that is based on UML metamodel. Within the IDAPI project (see Acknowledgements), the approach is currently being experimented with four modeling languages: UML, BPMN, SoaML and SBVR. CASE tool MagicDraw supports UML profiles for BPMN [12] and SoaML [13]; also, UML profile for SBVR [14] was introduced by the authors of this paper.

The plans of the nearest future involve further improvements of the D&D Action metamodel and DSL engine itself to bring even more usability features to user-interacted partial M2M transformations.

Acknowledgements. The work described in this paper has been carried out within the framework of the Operational Program for the Development of Human Resources 2007-2013 of Lithuania „Strengthening of Capacities of Researchers and Scientists" project VP1-3.1-ŠMM-08-K-01-018 „Research and Development of Internet Technologies and their Infrastructure for Smart Environments of Things and Services (IDAPI)" (2012-2015), funded by the European Social Fund (ESF).

References

[1] Object Management Group: Model-Driven Architecture – MDA Guide. OMG spec. v. 1.0.1 (2003), http://www.omg.org/cgi-bin/doc?omg/03-06-01

[2] Pavalkis, S., Nemuraitė, N., Butkienė, R.: Derived Properties: A User Friendly Approach to Improving Model Traceability. Information Technology and Control 42(1) (2013)

[3] Biehl, M.: Literature Study on Model Transformations. Embedded Control Systems. Royal Institute of Technology, Stockholm, Sweden (2010)

[4] The Eclipse Foundation: ATL – a model transformation technology (2014), http://www.eclipse.org/atl/

[5] Object Management Group: Meta Object Facility (MOF) 2.0 Query/View/Transformation, v1.1, OMG. www.omg.org/spec/QVT/1.1/ (2011)

[6] Object Management Group: Unified Modeling Language. OMG spec. v. 2.4.1 (2011), http://www.omg.org/spec/UML/2.4.1/

[7] Fuentes-Fernández, L., Vallecillo-Moreno, A.: An Introduction to UML Profiles. UPGRADE, European Journal for the Informatics Professional 5(2), 5–13 (2004)

[8] No Magic, Inc.: MagicDraw – Architecture Made Simple (2014), http://www.nomagic.com

[9] Sparx Systems: Enterprise Architect – UML Modeling and Lifecycle Tool Suite (2014), http://www.sparxsystems.com.au

[10] No Magic, Inc.: UML Profiling and DSL. User Guide, v 17.0.5 (2011)

[11] Skersys, T., Danenas, P., Butleris, R.: Approach for Semi-automatic Extraction of Business Vocabularies and Rules from Use Case Diagrams. In: Fitch, J. (ed.) EUROSAM 1984 and ISSAC 1984. LNCS, vol. 174, pp. 182–196. Springer, Heidelberg (1984)

[12] Object Management Group: UML Profile for BPMN Processes. OMG spec. v. 1.0 beta (2010), http://www.omg.org/cgi-bin/doc?ab/10-06-01

[13] Object Management Group: Service oriented architecture Modeling Language (SoaML). OMG spec. v. 1.0.1 (2012), http://www.omg.org/spec/SoaML/

[14] Skersys, T., Pavalkis, S., Nemuraite, L.: Implementing Semantically Rich Business Vocabularies in CASE tools. In: 4th Symposium on Computer Languages, Implementations and Tools (SCLIT2014) at 12th International Conference of Numerical Analysis and Applied Mathematics (ICNAAM 2014). AIP proceedings (2014) (to be published)

Impact of Cloud Computing Technology on E-Government

Omar Ali, Jeffrey Soar, and Jianming Yong

University of Southern Queensland, Australia
{Omar.Ali,Jeffery.Soar,Jianming.Yong}@usq.edu.au

Abstract. Electronic business uses ICT to support its activities. This has positively impacted business performance. Recognizing the successful implementation of e-business, governments have decided to use ICT in public services in order to improve the performance of government organizations in providing best possible information and services to citizens, businesses and other public departments. Computing technologies have grown by leaps and bounds, and governments of all nations plan to make optimum use of such advanced technologies across public service organizations. However, due to financial crises, governments have resorted to cost-cutting, which in turn has resulted in a cap on their ICT budget. As a large-scale facility, e-government requires large monetary investment from the government. Some new inventions in the field of computing technologies have made cost reduction possible, while also increasing the efficiency and flexibility of government sectors. One such invention is cloud computing, which provides information and computing services as utilities. Cloud-based e-government provides the best possible services to its citizens and businesses at an affordable cost. This is because governments do not need to purchase and install ICT equipment on their premises. In this paper we analyse cloud computing and its applications in the context of e-government.

Keywords: E-Government, E-Business, Cloud Computing, Service-Oriented Cloud.

1   Introduction

The concept of e-government was inspired by e-business and e-commerce in the late 1990s [1]. The use of information and communication technology (ICT) in business was tremendously enhancing business performance. Successful implementation of e-commerce and e-business led governments worldwide to introduce ICT in the public sector, too. Their main aim was to provide information and services to citizens, businesses and other public departments using the Internet and the World Wide Web (www). Slowly, the plan came to fruition, thanks to the already existing concepts of e-commerce and e-business. Today almost all countries in the world are efficiently and effectively using the e-government concept.

Advances in computing technology have resulted in evolutionary changes in e-business and e-commerce, such as the introduction of Service-Oriented Architecture (SOA). The emergence of SOA has led to the outsourcing of business establishment and functioning to online services [2]. According to [3], "Cloud computing is the realization

G. Dregvaite and R. Damasevicius (Eds.): ICIST 2014, CCIS 465, pp. 272–290, 2014.

of SOA". The use of 'cloud computing in e-business' poses a significant question: Would the use of cloud computing services be possible in the e-government domain?

In e-government, public sector organizations provide information and services to citizens and businesses with the help of modern ICT. This results in better performance of these organizations by increasing their effectiveness and efficiency, and facilitates interaction between citizens and government. The concern here is that if governments invest huge amounts of money in creating an e-government system, the system should be reliable, easy to maintain, cost efficient and satisfactory [4]. However, e-government faces several challenges, primarily budget shrinking for ICT, increasing public demand for information and services and continuous advances in technology. In order to overcome these challenges, governments should be willing to adopt innovative ideas for e-government such as advanced computing technologies. The current economic crisis has forced governments to cut down on costs, and therefore, cap their ICT budget. In such a situation, the traditional e-government model has become difficult to operate.

2   Cloud Computing Background

Cloud computing is a result of significant innovations in virtualization, utility computing, elasticity, distributed computing, grid computing, storage, content outsourcing, security and Web 2.0, networking, the World Wide Web and software services [5][6]. Since the concept is described in different ways by various authors, no single agreed-upon definition of cloud computing exists. However, one well-known definition is as follows: "Clouds, or clusters of distributed computers, provide on-demand resources and services over a network, usually the Internet, with the scale and reliability of a data centre" [7]. Another definition is provided by the [8], "A paradigm in which information is permanently stored in servers on the Internet and cached temporarily on clients that include desktops, entertainment centres, computers, notebooks, wall computers and handhelds". The U.S. National Institute of Standards and Technology (NIST) includes some other important aspects of cloud computing in its definition: "A model for enabling ubiquitous, convenient, on-demand network access to a shared pool of services (e.g., networks, servers, storage, applications and services) that can be rapidly provisioned and released with minimal management effort or service provider interaction" [9]. This definition promotes the availability of cloud computing and describes its five essential characteristics in addition to its three delivery models and four deployment models [9].

2.1   Cloud Computing Characteristics

The five characteristics of cloud computing mentioned in the NIST definition are as follows:

- **On-Demand Self-Service**: With the help of the cloud service provider, consumers can avail themselves of the cloud service, that is, computing capabilities, network storage and application, 24/7 without the need for any human interaction.
- **Broad Network Access**: The availability of cloud computing services on the Internet makes it easily accessible through standard mechanisms by both thick and thin clients (e.g., laptops, mobile phones, or Personal Digital Assistants 'PDAs').

- **Resource Pooling**: Cloud computing uses a multi-tenant model to assign and re-assign physical and virtual resources to consumers according to their demands [10].
- **Rapid Elasticity**: Cloud computing can scale resources both up and down as required. The cloud appears to be infinite to consumers, who can purchase as much or as little computing power as they need.
- **Measured Service**: One of the essential characteristics of cloud computing is measured service, whereby the usage of services and resources is constantly monitored, controlled and reported for fair pay-as-you-go model implementation.

2.2   Cloud Service/Delivery Models

Cloud services can be categorised on the basis of the following three service/delivery models: See Figure (1).

- **Software as a Service (SaaS):** The SaaS service model enables consumers to use the service provider's applications running on a cloud infrastructure. Consumers can access the applications using various client devices through a thin client interface such as a Web browser (e.g., Web-based email). However, they do not have the access to manage or control the underlying cloud infrastructure, that is, network, servers, operating systems, storage or even individual application capabilities. Though consumers do have access to limited user-specific application configuration settings [10][11].
- **Platform as a Service (PaaS):** The PaaS service model enables the consumer to deploy consumer-created or -acquired applications onto the cloud infrastructure with the help of programming languages and tools the provider supports. Once again, as in the SaaS model, the consumer does not manage or control the underlying cloud infrastructure, but can control the deployed applications and possibly the application-hosting environment configurations [11].
- **Infrastructure as a Service (IaaS):** The IaaS service model provides the consumers with processing, storage, network and other fundamental computing resources. The consumer can deploy and run arbitrary software, including operating systems and applications. Like in the other two models, the consumer cannot manage or control the underlying cloud infrastructure but has control over operating systems, storage and deployed applications and possibly has limited control over select networking components, such as host firewalls [10].

Fig. 1. Cloud architecture [4]

Depending on the different stages of workflow or different phases of business processes of an e-government system, government decision-making bodies and the Chief Information Officer (CIO) can select from these three service models to satisfy demands from different government departments and various requirements of citizens. Table (1) depicts a comparative study of the three service/delivery models of government cloud.

Table 1. Comparison of service models

Model	Characteristics	Target Business
SaaS	Focus on using application	Government online services (e.g., portal), productivity tools (e.g., online office), collaboration (e.g., e-meeting), EaaS, DaaS.
PaaS	Focus on developing and sunning applications	Development, debugging and deployment of the government application, security services, database management.
IaaS	Control over operating systems, applications and data	Business of the network administrators and IT department of the organization.

2.3   Cloud Deployment Models

More recently, the cloud community has categorised four cloud deployment models; [10][11][12][13][14], as follows:

- **Private Cloud:** In this model, the cloud infrastructure is deployed solely for a single organization. The organization may itself manage the infrastructure or outsource it to a third party, and the cloud infrastructure may exist in the organization's premises or be based off-premise [12].
- **Community Cloud:** This model deploys the cloud infrastructure to several organizations at the same time and supports a specific community that shares similar concerns (e.g., mission, security requirements, policy and compliance considerations). The cloud infrastructure may be managed by the organizations or by a third party and may exist in the organisations' premise or be based off-premise [12].
- **Public Cloud:** This model enables the cloud infrastructure to be made available to the general public or to a large industry group. The infrastructure is owned by an organization that provides cloud services [12].
- **Hybrid Cloud:** In this model, the cloud infrastructure is composed of two or more clouds (private, community or public) that remain unique entities, but are bound together by standardized or proprietary technology that enables data and application portability (e.g., cloud bursting for load-balancing between clouds) [11].

Government decision-making bodies and the CIO can choose from these four deployment models according to the control capacity over government cloud, data sensitivity, users, business requirements and budget. Table (2) depicts a comparative study of the four deployment models of government cloud.

Table 2. Comparison of deployment models

Model	Security	Cost	Target Department
Public	Low	Low	Departments directly providing public services
Private	High	High	Departments storing sensitive data and calling for high security
Hybrid	Depends	Depends	Large government organizations
Community	Medium	Medium	Departments sharing same concerns and calling for collaboration

2.4   Cloud Computing Benefits

The potential benefits of cloud computing are numerous. The sharing of ICT capabilities in the cloud helps individuals, businesses and government agencies use their resources more efficiently and effectively (US Committee on Science, Technology and Space). Individuals use cloud computing for email, content and information sharing; file storage and payment services; among other services. Businesses and government agencies use it for basic office tools, project management, collaboration and design of custom applications. In addition, government agencies also are helped by cloud computing to improve the quality of the services they provide to citizens through e-government solutions (EU Directorate General for Public Policies, Cloud Computing). Cloud computing is indeed better than the traditional widely used computing model in use today, in which organizations have to purchase all the equipment and software and then operate them by themselves [7]. In contrast, cloud computing is a usage-based model, wherein the user pays only for the resources used. Moreover, installation and configuration of expensive machines and applications on one's own premises is not required, and this results in reduced capital expenses. Another key benefit of cloud computing is scalability. Cloud-based storage services can easily manage the huge amounts of data, which are difficult to manage using the traditional databases. Cloud computing also offers flexibility and freedom; that is, it allows customers hassle-free service provider portability so that they can enjoy more up-to-date solutions.

2.5   Growth of Cloud Computing

The global IT expenditure reached $3.4 trillion in 2008, although that year the aggregate spending was expected to decline for the first time since 2001. The decline would continue up to 2010 [15]. Indeed, across the private sector, IT spending has been constantly decreasing. This is the result of inter-related impacts of economic recession and the credit crisis, which has led to significant decline in capital budgeting and credit availability for large IT projects. The only developing areas of IT in the wake of the crisis are outsourced IT and IT-enabled services [16]. As these new areas enter the marketplace, many of them have associated themselves with the cloud system. Thus, the expenditure involved in these services is likely to reduce over the next few years, and competition seems imminent between larger, traditional models and these upstart firms [17].

According to IDC estimates, approximately 10 per cent of the nearly $64 billion spent on business applications worldwide in 2008 was on cloud computing applications delivered remotely [18]. Analysts like Gartner correctly projected a growth rate of 20 per cent or more for cloud computing over the years to come [19]. The global market for cloud computing services reached $42 billion in 2012, a growth rate of 30 per cent [20]. It reached the $150 billion annual mark in 2013 [21].

3   E-Government and Its Benefits

As mentioned above, e-government uses ICT to provide public services to citizens, businesses and other public service departments. The ultimate goal of any government is to improve the efficiency and effectiveness of its organizations, so that they can provide the best possible services to its stakeholders, that is, citizens, businesses and other public service departments [22]. In the 1990s, governments came under increasing pressure to achieve these two objectives. Hence, they resorted to the e-government concept. Today almost every country in the world is making optimum use of modern computing technologies in order to provide proper services to its citizens and businesses, and also to interact with other governments.

Any technology needs constant advancement for better progress, and so does e-government. Innovation is the key here. E-government should adapt to latest developments in ICT to keep itself up to date. Cutting-edge ICT facilitates an effective and efficient e-government system. The traditional e-government model is also effective; however, its effectiveness can be further enhanced by introducing innovative computing technologies like cloud computing into its system.

4   Cloud Values in E-Government

The e-government service platform uses the cloud computing environment to its advantage in order to create the corresponding values for government, public, environment.

4.1   Values For Government

The government shifts the e-government system to the cloud computing environment to create the following values:

4.1.1   Benefitting the Public

E-government tends to bring service to the core of its function to bring about a change. Cloud computing can systematise the IT resource service, thus standardising resource deployment. Thus, it makes possible measuring and tracing back of IT resources [23], which in turn provides services to the public via a network. Moreover, this facility can be used as per public demand and usage and can be paid for in accordance with the application usage. Thus it provides the public with an innovation service model of IT resources. In addition, the government can enhance computing and storage capacity of the system, thereby providing the public with more diversified value-added services via cloud computing [57][58].

4.1.2   Promoting Cooperation With Enterprises

If the government uses cloud computing, it can provide not only the traditional support of policy and environment to local high-tech development zones and software parks, but also a variety of IT support, thus attracting more business and a higher inflow of funds. Cloud computing service platforms would create more opportunities for the government to cooperate with enterprises; thus the government can use enterprise background strength to support local development and to easily manage the procurement and outsourcing tasks [57][58].

4.1.3   Promoting Public Construction

The current requirements for power system capacity are increasing gradually in the power construction, especially in the construction of smart grids. The existing power system capacity is unable to bear the load. Toward this end, countries resorted to the idea of a power system based on cloud computing. Cloud computing has powerful processing capabilities and high-level system integration to support the construction of smart grids. In addition, it can make full use of the existing hardware resources of the power system and reduce investment in new hardware [59].

4.1.4   Increasing the Utilization Rate of Resources

It is difficult to anticipate the number of system resources required. This results in uneven distribution of data centre resources. However, the virtualization technology of cloud computing can virtualize servers, storage devices and other physical hardware, thus building the e-government system on the logic hardware. In this way, a single physical device can be shared by different services across various government agencies. It also avoids poor resource utilization by allowing isolated management of the physical device [59].

4.1.5   Improving Administrative Efficiency

Cloud computing can save the deployment time required to create new applications, and is conducive to data sharing and cooperation, thereby improving administrative efficiency [60][61].

- *Rapid provision*
  At present, in the e-government system, the process of creation of new applications and updates is tedious and time consuming. It has to pass through a lengthy route of budget provision approval, fully funding and finally the actual implementation. However, in a cloud computing environment, systems can dynamically adjust resources according to the needs of the new application. This implies that in the case of unused resources, the system will immediately make itself available to new applications, thus saving deployment time.

- *Sharing and cooperation*
  The present e-government network data is in a state of 'distributed storage, distributed access [24]. The data centre resembles several isolated islands of information, lacking the support of data sharing or a collaboration platform. However, the network distributed computing feature of cloud computing can integrate data from storage devices of various government agencies into a data resource pool. This will help data sharing and accelerate search speed. It will also prove beneficial for establishing platforms for different government agencies, making cooperation with each other from different places possible.

4.1.6   Reducing the Budget

The e-government system using a cloud computing environment can reduce the cost associated with hardware, software, human resource and electricity, thereby reducing the overall system budget [62][63].

- *Hardware*
  Cloud computing facilitates the sharing of physical devices and the dynamic allocation of system resources, thus reducing hardware requirements and depreciation costs of the data centre.

- *Software*
  Currently, the system software license can be bought for a one-time payment. In a cloud computing environment, the government will be able to use the mode of software as services and platform as services paying as per the usage, thus reducing cost.

- *Human resources*
  Cloud computing can upgrade systems and configure settings, thereby reducing human dependence. This will reduce the overall cost incurred by the human resources departments.
- *Electricity*
  Cloud computing can increase the utilization rate of resources, and can help in energy optimization, thus reducing the electricity cost of data centres.

4.1.7   Increasing Robustness

The e-government system making use of cloud computing has improved its accuracy, compatibility, security and disaster recovery capability [62][65][66] [67][68].

- *Accuracy*
  At present, upgrading and maintaining e-government systems involves several repetitive steps by people. This leads to tiredness, which in turn causes operational errors. However, cloud computing can decrease the dependence on humans, thus avoiding human error.
- *Compatibility*
  Currently, there is lack of integration in the e-government system; hence, the compatibility and stability of the system suffer. Cloud computing can prove conducive to the e-government system by providing government officials with a unified work environment, which will significantly improve compatibility and stability.
- *Disaster recovery*
  The current e-government backup system and disaster recovery capabilities are unable to meet the demand for IT development. Cloud computing can provide systems with virtually unlimited storage capacity and a more comprehensive backup mechanism. Moreover, systems in a cloud computing environment can back up each other between the backup centres in different places.

4.2   Values For Society

The e-government service platform based on cloud computing creates the following values for the society [65][69][70][71]:

4.2.1   Reducing the Initial Capital Investment

Commercial activities and IT are closely linked. This is because performing numerous business operations simultaneously increasingly needs IT support. Thus, entrepreneurs have to invest heavily to acquire such support. In this respect, the cloud computing services platform can provide enterprises with IT resource services, including computing, storage, software, to name just a few. With the help of cloud computing, entrepreneurs can transform the capital input of information construction into actual operating expenses. Moreover, the cloud computing environment also reduces the demand for technical staff, thereby reducing labour cost.

4.2.2   Promoting the Transformation of Industry

Many software parks and high-tech zones have been set up by the government to promote the local software outsourcing industry. This development is promoting the industrial structure and transforming manufacturing into a service outsourcing industry, thereby upgrading the local industry. Here, the cloud computing service platform can provide developers with a development platform based on the needs, and which is conducive to collaborative development; thus it can shorten the software development cycle. In addition, the platform can also provide a test environment based on practical needs and thus improve the overall quality of software.

4.2.3   Scientific Study Supply

IT has carved a niche in the education and academic field as well, especially by providing high-performance computing resources for scientific research.

At present, IT equipment is managed by the respective project teams and owned by the respective departments of educational institutions. This does not allow resources to be shared among departments, causing resource waste. However, such institutions can procure more powerful computing resources via the cloud computing services platform. In addition, the virtualization characteristic of cloud computing can solve the problem of ownership of equipment by virtualising the physical device.

4.3   Values for Environment

The demand for global energy at present has increased enormously, and as a result, the climate and environment are gradually deteriorating. This means that protecting the environment has become important in order to save humankind. Cloud computing can greatly increase the judicious utilization rate of resources, reduce energy consumption and thus help the global economy to stride forward to a greener future [72][73].

5   Challenges in Cloud and E-Government

When the storage and processing of sensitive data are in the hands of a third party, trust becomes a major concern for e-government stakeholders. Several factors come into play to build that trust, namely, truth, reliability, faith, confidence and strength. If you believe in others' capabilities and skills, you can reasonably rely on them and leave your valuable assets to their care [25]. Trust plays an important role in the success of an e-government system. Hence, it is important that people have trust in the e-government system. Cloud computing comes with its own challenges that can directly affect the e-government system. Some of the problems are as follows:

5.1   Privacy

In a cloud computing environment, data are not stored and processed locally at the enterprise premises. Rather, third parties do that at their own sites through remote machines installed at various locations. In such a situation, it is natural for individuals to be concerned about the privacy of their personal data and information because it is the right of every individual to secure their private and sensitive information [26][74].

5.2   Lack of User Control

Lack of user control and ownership affect trust. The lesser control over our assets, the lesser the trust in the system [25]. In a cloud-based e-government system, data are stored at third-party data centres, and thus we have less control over our own data, while the cloud computing providers have complete access to it. Therefore, it becomes important for intellectual property and personal information to be protected [27][28][74][75].

5.3   System Failure

Sudden failure of the system also affects users' trust in cloud computing. Some public services must be available to citizens 24/7. However, at times these services fail to deliver in a cloud computing environment. Any loss of data or any kind of security breach cannot be compensated for by the cloud service providers as the data is irreplaceable [29].

5.4   Security

Some of the other security concerns involved with cloud computing are the "confidentiality, availability and integrity of data or information" [30]. Security helps establish users' trust in cloud computing [29]. In the e-government context, cloud computing must be secure.

5.5   On-Demand Self-Service

On-demand self-service is one of the most important characteristics of cloud computing. It is achieved through virtual environment or management interface accessible to all cloud service users. The cloud service provider is responsible for maintaining the security of the management interface from unauthorized access because the management functionality can be accessible only to a few authorized administrators. Access authorization is given to authentic users through claim-based access control, federated identity approaches and security assertion mark-up language [32][33].

5.6   Data Leakage

Data leakage also affects the trust of citizens and public sector organizations in cloud based e-government systems. Since the e-government system contains sensitive data and information about users and businesses, security of the data is important. Data leakage can discourage governments from using cloud-based e-government systems [31].

6   Cloud in Government

Public demand for services guides the development of e-government. The focus of e-government has changed from office automation and administration supervision to public services. This transformation reflects the change in government functionality. Governments around the world hope to obtain the trust and support from their people. Therefore, globally e-government systems oriented towards public services are being established, thus enhancing the national competitive strength.

Cloud computing is an innovative mode not only of computation but also of resource utilization [23][34]. It can provide users with IT resources in the form of service via network. Therefore, the government can provide its citizens with more varied service contents via cloud computing. This becomes consistent with the e-government's aim of bringing service into its core domain. Besides, as a kind of green technology, cloud computing can considerably increase the utilization rate of resources at data centres and can reduce energy consumption. For these reasons, cloud computing is the best environment to establish e-government. On the other hand, it has not gained much popularity yet. If governments around the world promote its development, the scale of cloud computing can be expanded rapidly, thus popularizing the concept. Therefore, use of cloud computing services by governments will tremendously stimulate the development of this concept. In short, cloud computing and e-government can complement each other.

Cloud application scenarios in e-government could help to foster the benefits described of cloud computing in e-government. These application scenarios would depend on a specific business case but might include using the cloud for hosting of all main data used in operations by local government. The cloud could be also be used to host or provide application software; there are cloud providers in several industries who provide both application software access and data hosting per day or per transaction fee [76].

Although the mode and degree of promoting cloud computing at present is diverse across governmental systems, establishing an e-government service platform based on cloud computing has become the main trend. The following provides the current status of cloud computing service promoted by governments across the globe.

6.1   The USA

The U.S. government is the most focused in establishing e-government based on cloud computing. The government hopes to centre all national e-government systems on the cloud computing environment, utilizing it to the fullest.

- *Data.gov*
  In May 2009, the U.S. government released its Data.gov website as a data inquiry service platform based on cloud computing [35][36]. The government believes the public could understand the government's data through this platform and thus the transparency of the government could be enhanced.

- *Apps.gov*
  In September 2009, the U.S. government released the Apps.gov website. This is the federal government portal based on cloud computing [36][37], and aims to promote cloud computing in all government departments. With the help of this portal, the government hopes to reduce the system budget, improve system security and performance, and provide the public with IT service via cloud computing.

6.2   China

Many local governments in China have taken the assistance of companies possessing rich experience in cloud computing to establish cloud computing service platforms in order to provide IT support for local enterprises, thereby stimulating economic growth and promoting industrial growth.

- *Dongying Cloud Computing Centre*
  In September 2009, the Dongying municipal government, with the aid of IBM, established its cloud computing centre in the Yellow River Delta [23]. From this centre, the government provides IT support to enterprises via cloud computing. This move has resulted in the local oil industry chain development and competitiveness of small and medium software enterprises. It has also helped promote the economic development of the Yellow River Delta region.

- *Wuxi Cloud Computing Centre*
  In March 2008, the Wuxi municipal government established a cloud computing centre with the aid of IBM [36]. The government hoped to provide cloud computing service support to the local software outsourcing industry, to accelerate the development of the software industry, thereby gradually transforming the traditional manufacturing industries into a service-led economy.

6.3   New Zealand

The Ministry of Commerce of New Zealand made an announcement in June 2009 declaring that it would be consolidating IT procurement for all its government agencies. The aim was to form 'centres of expertise' focused on rationalizing IT acquisition and investigating the significant roles of cloud computing and SaaS in the future [38].

6.4   Australia

Forbes Insights, in association with KPMG International, conducted a study among 429 government executives in 10 countries including Australia on the initiative taken by and the progress made by governments in adopting cloud computing. The result of the study indicated that the rate of cloud adoption is scaling new heights in Australia. It also indicated that adoption in the government sector is slower than in the private sector, perhaps due to perceived risks [39]. The Australian government remains cautious about the challenges of cloud computing due to the inherent security, privacy and trust issues [40][41]. However, in order to overcome these challenges, the Australian government issued a policy in April 2011 [41], devising cloud computing strategies, issues and benefits for government and guidance information. Despite the existence of this policy, use of cloud computing in the government sector remains lower than in the private sector [42].

6.5   The United Kingdom (UK)

The UK government has strategically prioritised the creation of 'G-cloud', a government-wide cloud computing network [43]. In June 2009, the joint report of the Department for Business Innovation and Skills and the Department for Culture, Media and Sport [44], entitled 'Digital Britain Report', asked the UK government to lead a wide-ranging digital strategy for the country. Prime Minister Gordon Brown made the following announcement related to the report: "Digital Britain is about giving the country the tools to succeed and lead the way in the economy of the future" [44]. The prime aim of the Digital Britain strategy is to improve IT-enabled government service and allow for more services to be provided online. To support this action, the UK's IT procurement efforts will focus on enabling the government to become a leading force in the use of cloud computing. The report states:

"The Government's impact on the digital economy goes way beyond its role as policy maker. In delivering public services, as a large customer of ICT products and services and as the owner of data systems, the public sector has enormous influence on the market. In many areas, such as education, health and defence, Government can use its position as the leading procurer of services, to drive up standards – in some cases to set standards – and to provide an investment framework for research and development" [44].

7   Cloud Migration Strategy

One observer has correctly admonished IT executives, noting that when it comes to shifting to cloud computing, "Standing pat means being left behind" [23][45]. Linda Cureton, NASA's CIO, stated the matter thus:

"I'd like to say it a little more bluntly. If CIOs don't get ready, manage fears and manage their risk, they will get run over by this disruptive technology. Your organization is doing it anyway – without you! So do something! You don't have to move your entire enterprise into the cloud, just take the first step and look at some appropriate data sets. This does not have to be an all or none decision" [46].

One should bear in mind that 'cloud computing is a tool, not a strategy' [47]. IT leaders working for the government should be well advised to take a programmed assessment of how cloud computing can fit into their overall IT strategy, in support of the mission and overall strategy of their agency. This involves a six-step process, as follow.

7.1   Learning

In order for the cloud migration strategy to begin, learning the basics of cloud computing is very important – through attending seminars, networking, talking with vendors and reading. As cloud computing is a new paradigm in computing technology, technology transfer must happen– the 'techies' in and outside of government will have to take that extra step to educate and inform the 'non-techie' policy makers (Agency executives, staffers and lawmakers) about the merits and value of cloud computing. Sufficient funding will be required for research to establish how cloud computing is working – or not – in various fields and at all levels of government. This will help ground the policy and practices of governmental use of cloud computing.

7.2   Organizational Assessment

In the second step, IT managers must assess their present IT needs, structure and capacity utilization. In a cloud computing environment, resources can be added or subtracted based on needs and demands; thus it is critical for IT managers to honestly assess their IT baseline. In terms of data centre utilization, it will be important to categorise resources based on their needs, that is, whether they are required all the time and are necessary for day-to-day operations in order to establish a baseline for internally hosted operations. Only then can decisions be made as to whether to continue to host 'excess' capacity in the data centre or to contract for cloud services as needed to scale up in order to meet seasonal, cyclical or event-based demand for greater amounts of computing resources.

7.3   Cloud Pilot

The third step is the selection of one area – or one specific project – by the IT managers to 'cloud pilot' and assess their ability to manage and bring such a project to fruition. As with any new technology, cloud computing is undergoing a great deal of experimentation. Internet users are experimenting with cloud applications in their daily lives – from Twitter to Gmail to using photo-sharing sites. In the same way, organizations are also conducting cloud computing experiments – efforts that are distanced from their core IT operations and often at the periphery of (or trying to connect to) the organization.

Many times, even in the public sector, such experiments may be considered 'rogue' operations conducted by individuals and units to test the utility of the technology. These are important efforts, and they should be supported – and reported within and outside the organization – so that others in the IT sector and in the wider community can learn about the successes and downsides of operating in the clouds. Thus, sharing both 'best practices' and 'lessons learned' in cloud computing is vital. Indeed, such demonstration - or 'science' projects - in large and small organizations will, predictably, drives the eventual acceptance and adoption of cloud computing [48].

7.4   Cloud-Readiness Assessment

After the internal assessment and external outreach stemming from the pilot effort, IT managers should conduct an overall IT cloud-readiness assessment to determine if their organization has data and applications that could readily move to a cloud environment, and if a public/private/hybrid cloud would be suitable or usable for these purposes and they need to rank potential projects. As this assessment progresses, IT decision makers must focus on establishing rules as to which data and applications can –or cannot – be housed in any form of cloud environment. In doing so, they will discover a definite field of 'cloud-eligible' and 'cloud-ineligible' data and applications.

7.5   Cloud Rollout Strategy

At this stage, it is important to roll out the cloud computing strategy – gaining buy-in from both organizational leadership and IT staffers, and communicating with both internal and external stakeholders about the goals, progress and costs/benefits of each cloud project. Now the cloud transitions from a test effort to a more mainstream system in the way the agency manages its data, operations and people. It becomes part of 'normal' organizational operations, just as other old tech innovations (From telephony to fax to the Internet to email to social media) have become IT tools, used in support of the agency's IT strategy, and more importantly, its overall strategy.

7.6   Continuous Cloud Improvement

In the final stage, the process takes the final shape–'continuous cloud improvement'– where the agency/organization/unit moves the appropriate data and applications to the cloud and back from the cloud to internally hosted operations, if necessary, after thoroughly and continuously assessing the appropriate use of cloud technologies for that particular agency. The shift to more cloud-based applications will help government agencies acquire new capabilities to communicate and collaborate. However, it will also necessitate some quick policy decision-making and the implementation of operational rules. For instance, decisions need to be made as to who can access what files and the type of access one will have (e.g., read-only, editing access) [49].

8   Conclusion

Since the 1990s, e-government has become attractive government systems worldwide. Today almost every country in the world has developed and implemented its own e-government system in some form or another in order to improve the performance of its public sector organizations. The main aim is to provide the best public services to citizens and businesses in an efficient and effective manner. Effectiveness and efficiency can be increased further if governments make good use of new and modern computing technologies like SOA. Cloud computing is the realization of SOA, which is a direct outcome of research in virtualization, utility computing, distributed computing, grid computing, content outsourcing and Web 2.0. Cloud-based e-government systems perform better than the traditional e-government systems. Cloud-based e-government provides several benefits over the traditional system. Since information and applications are hosted online in cloud computing, they are available and accessible from anywhere and at any time. In light of the current economic situation in which governments around the world are under pressure to cut their expenditure, they are putting a cap on the ICT budget as well. In such a situation, cloud-based e-government is a good option since in such a system, governments do not need to purchase ICT equipment. Rather they lease ICT resources and services according to their need. In short, capital costs are replaced by operational costs for the resources used by government organizations. Trust and security also play an important role in the success of e-government. One of the important stakeholders of e-government are the citizens, therefore, they should trust the e-government system. In cloud computing, data is stored and processed at third-party premises; and this means that citizens and businesses are concerned about the confidentiality and security of their sensitive data and information. Similarly data leakage can also affect the trust of citizens and businesses because in some cases the data loss can be irreplaceable. Nevertheless, the cloud-based e-government system is providing more benefits than loss in the form of efficiency, scalability, flexibility and cost effectiveness as compared to traditional e-government.

References

1. Alshomrani, S.: A comparative study on United Nations E-Government indicators. Journal of Emerging Trends in Computing and Information Sciences 3(3), 411–420 (2012)
2. Apps.gov, http://apps.gov (accessed December 23, 2013)
3. Barwick, H.: Cloud computing adoption increases in Australia, IDC (2013), http://www.cio.com.au/article/520964/cloud_computing_adoption_increases_australia_idc_/ (accessed August 24, 2013)
4. Beizer, D.: Cloud computing comes into focuses, Government Computer News (2008), http://gcn.com/articles/2008/06/11/cloudcomputing-comes-into-focus.aspx (accessed December 17, 2013)

5. Catteddu, D., Hogben, G.: Cloud computing: Benefits, risks and recommendations for information security. In: European Network and Information Security Agency (ENISA) (2009)
6. CCIA, 'Public Policy for the Cloud: How Policy makers Can Enable Cloud Computing', Computer and Communications Industry Association (2011), http://www.ccianet.org/CCIA/files/ccLibraryFiles/Filename/000000000528/CCIA%20%20Public%20Policy%20for%20the%20Cloud.pdf (accessed October 17, 2013)
7. Chen, G.: IBM cloud computing and government cloud computing platforms. Programmer (11), 1–10 (2008)
8. Copeland, M.V.: The client-server model: Not dead yet. Fortune (2009), http://money.cnn.com/2009/02/16/technology/copeland_oracle.fortune/index.htm (accessed September 28, 2013)
9. CSA 2009, 'Security Guidance for Critical Areas of Focus in Cloud Computing', Cloud Security Alliance
10. CSA 2010, 'Top Threats to Cloud Computing', Cloud Security Alliance
11. Cureton, L.: Cloud computing in the federal government: On a cloudy day how it will astound you. Goddard CIO Blog (2009), http://blogs.nasa.gov/cm/blog/Goddard-CIOBlog.blog/posts/post_1237089048316.html (accessed November 02, 2013)
12. Data.gov, http://www.data.gov (accessed December 23, 2013)
13. Davis, J.: Gartner and Forrester now forecast, decline in IT spending, Channel Insider (2009), http://www.channelinsider.com/c/a/News/GartneranForrester-Now-Forecast-2009Decline-in-IT-Spending-204121/ (accessed October 2013)
14. Davis, J.: Gartner: Outsourced IT services prices could fall 20%, Channel Insider (2009), http://www.channelinsider.com/c/a/News/GartnerOutsourced-ITServices-Prices-Could-Fall-20-145259/ (accessed November 02, 2013)
15. Department of Finance and Deregulation, 'Cloud Computing Strategic Direction Paper, pp. 1–45 (2011)
16. DFDAG, Cloud Computing Strategic Direction Paper, Department of Finance and Deregulations Australian Government (2011)
17. Dustin Amrhein, P.A., de Andrade, A., Armstrong, E.A.B., Bartlett, J., Bruklis, R., Cameron, K.: Cloud computing use cases. White Paper. Version 3.0 ed., pp. 1–7 (2010)
18. EU Directorate General for Public Policies, Cloud Computing, http://ec.europa.eu/information_society/activities/cloudcomputing/docs/cc_study_parliament.pdf (accessed October 16, 2013)
19. Ferguson, S.: Gartner says IT spending will decline 4 percent in 2009. e-Week (2009), http://www.eweek.com/index2.php?option=content&task=view&id=52598&pop=1&hide_ads=1&page=0&hide_js=1 (accessed December 17, 2013)
20. Forbes, Australia, Italy and Denmark Lead Government Cloud Adoption (2012), http://www.forbes.com/sites/hugomoreno/2012/03/20/governments-tip-toe-toward-the-cloud/ (accessed August 25, 2013)
21. Gansen, Z., Chunming, R., Jin, L., Feng, Z., Yong, T.: Trusted data sharing over untrusted cloud storage providers. In: IEEE Second International Conference on Cloud Computing Technology and Science, p. 97 (2010)
22. Glick, B.: Digital Britain commits government to cloud computing. Computing (2009), http://www.computing.co.uk/computing/news/2244229/digital-Britaincommits (accessed October 27, 2013)

23. Golden. B.:The case against cloud computing, part one, CIO (2009),
    http://www.cio.com/article/477473/The_Case_Against_Cloud_Com
    puting_Part_One (accessed October 09, 2013)
24. Grance, T.: 2010,The NIST Cloud Definition Framework. NIST
25. Gronlund, A., Horan, T.A.: Introducing e-government: History, definitions, and issues.
    Communications of the Association for Information Systems 15(1), 713–729 (2004)
26. Grossman, R.L.: The case for cloud computing, pp. 23–27. IEEE Computer Society (2009)
27. GUK, Department for Business Innovation and Skills and Department for Culture, Media
    and Sport, Government of the United Kingdom, Digital Britain: The Final Report (2009),
    http://www.culture.gov.uk/images/publications/digitalbritain
    -finalreportjun09 (accessed October 27, 2013)
28. GUK, Department for Business Innovation & Skills and Department for Culture, Media
    and Sport, Government of the United Kingdom, Press Release: Building Britain's Digital
    Future (2009), http://www.culture.gov.uk/reference_library/
    media_releases/6220.aspx (accessed October 27, 2013)
29. Hall, J.A., Liedtka, S.L.: The sarbanes-oxley act: Implications for large-scale IT
    outsourcing. Communications of the ACM 50(3), 95–100 (2007)
30. Hamm, S.: How cloud computing will change business. Business Week (2009),
    http://www.businessweek.com/print/magazine/content/09_24/b41
    35042942270.htm (accessed August 11, 2013)
31. Hashizume, K., Rosado, D.G., Fernández-Medina, E., Eduardo, B., Fernandez, E.B.: An
    analysis of security issues for cloud computing. Journal of Internet Services and
    Applications, 1–13 (2013)
32. Higginbotham, S.: Cloud computing is a tool, not a strategy. GigaOm (2009),
    http://gigaom.com/2009/02/19/cloudcomputing-is-a-tool-not-a-
    strategy/ (accessed August 21, 2013)
33. Hoover, J.N.: Chief of the year, InformationWeek (2009),
    http://www.informationweek.com/news/government/leadership/sh
    owArticle.jhtml?articleID=222002611&pgno=1&queryText=&isPrev
    = (accessed November 19, 2013)
34. IDC 2008. Cloud Computing Entering Period of Accelerating Adoption and Poised to
    Capture IT Spending Growth over the Next Five Years,
    http://www.idc.com/getdoc.jsp?containerId=prUS21480708 (accessed
    October 15, 2013)
35. IDC 2009, Enterprise panel, http://www.slideshare.net/JorFigOr/cloud-
    computing-2010-an-idcupdate (accessed July 11, 2013)
36. IEEE Computer Society: Definition of Cloud Computing
37. IT Industry Innovation Council 2011, Cloud Computing- Opportunities and Challenges,
    pp. 1–31
38. Karunanithi, D., Kiruthika, B.: Efficient framework for ensuring the effectiveness of
    information security in cloud computing. In: International Conference on Signal, Image
    Processing and Applications With workshop of ICEEA, pp. 1–10 (2011)
39. Khaled, M.K., Qutaibah, M.: Establishing trust in cloud computing, cloud computing. IT
    Professional 12(5), 20–27 (2010)
40. King, J.: 5 key questions about cloud storage, Computerworld (2009),
    http://www.computerworld.com/s/article/340471/Cloud_StorageI
    lluminated (accessed September 26, 2013)

41. Lv, Y.: 'Research on Construction of E-government Information Resources Sharing System Based on Cloud Computing. Information Studies: Theory and Application (4), 1–39 (2010)

42. Macias, F., Thomas, G.: Cloud computing advantages in public sector, pp. 1–7. Cisco Press (2011)

43. Mell, P., Grance, T.: Draft NIST working definition of cloud computing, vol. 15, pp. 1–7 (2009)

44. NIST 2009, Cloud computing, Computer Security Resource Centre, `http://csrc.nist.gov/groups/SNS/cloudcomputing/` (accessed August 27, 2013)

45. Nezhad, H.M., Stephenson, B., Singhal, S.: Outsourcing business to cloud computing services: Opportunities and challenges. IEEE Internet Computing, Special Issues on Cloud Computing, pp. 1–10 (2009)

46. O'Gara, M.: Washington itching to take the lead on cloud computing. SOA (2009), `http://govit.sys-con.com/node/1055764` (accessed December 23, 2013)

47. Pallis, G.: Cloud computing: The new frontier of Internet computing, pp. 1–8. IEEE Computer Society (2010)

48. Pearson, S.: Taking account of privacy when designing cloud computing services. In: ICSE Workshop on Software Engineering Challenges of Cloud Computing, p. 44 (2009)

49. Regulation of Investigatory Powers Act (RIPA), Part II, s 28, UK (2000)

50. Strecker, T.P.: Govt IT procurement in for shake- up. The Dominion Post (2009), `http://www.stuff.co.nz/technology/2521317/Govt-IT-procurement-in-forshake-up` (accessed November 12, 2013)

51. Tripathi, A., Parihar, B.: E-governance challenges and cloud benefits. In: IEEE International Conference on Computer Science and Automating Engineering (CSAE), pp. 1–10 (2011)

52. US Committee on Science, Technology and Space, Potentials of Cloud Computing, `http://democrats.science.house.gov/pressrelease/subcommittee-examines-potential-cloud-computing` (accessed November 23, 2013)

53. VijayKumar, N.: Role of ICT in e-governance: Impact of cloud computing in driving new initiatives. SET-Labs Briefings 9(2), 43–55 (2011)

54. Vouk, M.A.: Cloud computing issues, research and implementations. Journal of Computing and Information Technology, 235–246 (2008)

55. Wang, L.: Scientific cloud computing: Early definition and experience. In: IEEE International Conference on High Performance Computing and Communications, pp. 1–10 (2008)

56. Zhu, J.: Smarter cloud computing, pp. 1–8. Publishing House of Electronics Industry China (2010)

57. Cellary, W., Strykowski, S.: E-government based on cloud computing and service-oriented architecture. ACM International Conference Proceedings Series, pp. 5–10 (2009)

58. Sharma, R., Sharma, A., Singh, R.R.: E-governance and cloud computing: Technology oriented government policies. International Journal of Research in IT and Management 2(2), 1–8 (2012)

59. Aveek, M.A., Rahman, M.S.: Implementing E- Governance in Bangladesh Using Cloud Computing Technology, BRAC University, Dhaka, Bangladesh (2011)

60. Goel, S., Manuja, M., Dwivedi, R., Sherry, A.M.: Challenges of technology infrastructure availability in e- governance program implementations: A cloud based solution. Journal of Computer Engineering 5(2), 13–17 (2012)

61. Tewari, N., Sharma, M.K.: Cloud based working concept for e-governance citizen charter. International Journal of Advanced Research in Computer Science and Software Engineering 3(6), 1–12 (2013)
62. Grossman, R.L., Gu, Y.: On the varieties of clouds for data intensive computing. Data Engineering 44 (2009)
63. Marston, S., Li, Z., Bandyopadhyay, S., Zhang, J., Ghalsasi, A.: Cloud computing - The business perspective. Decision Support Systems 51(1), 176–189 (2011)
64. West, F.: Ten Reasons Why Cloud Computing is the Wave of the Future for the Recruitment Sector (2011), http://www.westtek.co.uk/Users/frmBlogDetail.aspx?id=2 (accessed January 1, 2014)
65. Leavitt, N.: Is Cloud Computing Really Ready for Prime Time? Computer 42(1), 15–20 (2009)
66. Staten, J.: USA.gov Achieves Cloud Bursting Efficiency Using Terre mark's Enterprise Cloud (Case study) (2013), http://www.terremark.com/uploadedFiles/Industry_Solutions/Federal_Government/Case%20Study%20USA.gov%20Achieves%20Cloud%20Bursting%20Efficiency%20Using%20Terremark%27s%20Enterprise%20Cloud.pdf (accessed January 27, 2014)
67. Singh, S.: Promoting e-governance through right to information: A case-study of india. International Journal of Scientific and Engineering Research 1(2), 1–10 (2010)
68. Rajkumar, B., James, B., Andrzej, M.G.: Cloud Computing: Principles and Paradigms, Hoboken, New Jersey (2011)
69. Melvin, B., Greer, J.: Software as a Service Inflection Point: Using Cloud Computing to Achieve Business Agility. iUniverse Star (2009)
70. Rastogi, A.: A model based approach to implement cloud computing in e-governance. International Journal of Computer Applications 9(7), 5–18 (2010)
71. Al-Khouri, A.M.: PKI in government identity management systems. International Journal of Network Security and Its Applications 3(3), 69–96 (2011)
72. Veljanovska, K., Zdravevska, V.: E-government based on cloud computing. Journal of Emerging Trends in Computing and Information Sciences 4(4), 377–381 (2013)
73. Sasikala, P.: Cloud computing and e-governance: advances, opportunities and challenge. International Journal of Cloud Applications and Computing 2(4), 1–21 (2012)
74. Pearson, S., Benameur, A.: Privacy, security and trust issues arising from cloud computing. In: The 2nd IEEE International Conference on Cloud Computing Technology and Science, pp. 693–702. IEEE Press (2010)
75. Karunanithi, D., Kiruthika, B.: Efficient framework for ensuring the effectiveness of information security in cloud computing. In: International Conference on Signal, Image Processing and Applications, pp. 1–10 (2011)
76. MSDN, 'Chapter 26: Designing Hosted and Cloud Services', Microsoft Application Architecture Guide, 2nd Edition Microsoft (2014), http://msdn.microsoft.com/en-us/library/ee658110.aspx (accessed June 13 2014)

Generative Learning Object (GLO) Specialization: Teacher's and Learner's View

Vytautas Štuikys, Kristina Bespalova, and Renata Burbaitė

Kaunas University of Technology, Studentų 50, 51368 Kaunas, Lithuania
{vytautas.stuikys,kristina.bespalova,renata.burbaite}@ktu.edu

Abstract. The paper introduces the stage-based specialization of the initial reusable GLOs treated as meta-programs. The aim is to support pre-programmed user-guided adaptation of the Computer Science (CS) teaching content within the educational robot environment. Specialization of GLOs by staging enables to flexibly (automatically) prepare the content at a higher level for the different contexts of use. We describe the approach along with the case study from the user's perspective taking into account the specializer tool we have developed. The contribution of the paper is the staged specialization for the pre-programmed adaptation of the learning content.

Keywords: Meta-program-based GLO, LO adaptation through specialization, GLO specialization through staging, robot-based CS teaching.

1   Introduction and Related Work

Learning Object (LO) research is a wide topic. The term defines the course-independent learning content aiming at supporting interoperability and reusability in the domain. Among multiple ideas and approaches the generative learning objects (GLOs) proposed by Boyle *et al.* [22], [17] play a significant role. GLOs are defined as *"an articulated and executable learning design that produces a class of learning objects"*[4]. GLOs being reusable and executable items (programs and meta-programs in our case [27]) may offer also new opportunities to create individual and highly adaptable learning content. The adaptability problem of LOs is broadly discussed in the literature. In e-learning, *adaptation* is thought of as the customization of the system "to the cognitive characteristics of the students and implies the study and conjunction of *technical and pedagogical aspects*" [10]. The paper [15] defines adaptation as "the adjustments in an educational environment aiming to (1) *accommodate learners' needs*, goals, abilities, and knowledge, (2) *provide appropriate interaction*, and (3) *personalize the content*". Some LO design aspects can be found in [8].

The aim of this paper is to discuss the meta-program-based GLO specialization which (if designed correctly, e.g. if criteria for adaptation are pedagogically sound) enables *the pre-programmed adaptation* of learning content. As we do not consider adaptation itself in detail here, we are able to formulate the task as *GLO specialization for adaptation*. As GLO is an executable specification (i.e. meta-program), below we introduce the main concepts of two research streams: (1) *meta-programming* and (2) *program specialization* as follows. Meta-programming [28] is a generative technology that allows achieving the

G. Dregvaite and R. Damasevicius (Eds.): ICIST 2014, CCIS 465, pp. 291–301, 2014.
© Springer International Publishing Switzerland 2014

aims of automation. It deals with how to perform manipulating programs as data. The result of the manipulation is the lower-level program. At the core of this manipulation is *parameterization*. There are many different views to understand, or to deal with this approach. Examples are generative programming [6], aspect-oriented programming, etc. (reader can learn more from [28]).

Program specialization or partial evaluation (a.k.a. refactoring [26], especially in SWE) is the technique that makes it possible to automatically transform a program into a specialized version, according to the context of use [12], [2]. Initially partial evaluation has been used to compiler generators design [13] and later as a source-to-source transformation technique whose aim was to improve program performance [14]. Now, however, there are much more applications including program obfuscation [16], model transformation [23], security improving [9] and many more [3], [2].

Program specialization also relates to *stage programming* and *meta-programming*, especially in logic programming research [24], [25]. Shortly it can be summarized as *multi-stage* programming, i.e. the development of programs in several different stages. Taha was the first to provide a formal description for a multi-stage programming language [29]. Staging is a program transformation that involves reorganizing the program execution into stages. He treats the use of the formal language MetaML to develop meta-programs as multi-stage programming. The concept relates to the fundamental principle of information hiding through the introduction of a set of abstraction levels (stages) aiming at gaining a great deal of flexibility in managing the program construction process. In fact, a *program specializer* performs the specialization process in two stages. The first is *early computations* (when some program variables are evaluated at the compile time). The second is *late computations* (when the remaining variables are evaluated at the run time).

The contribution of the paper is the *pedagogically sound* stage-based specialization of the initial highly reusable GLOs (in fact meta-programs) to support pre-programmed user-guided adaptation of the CS teaching content within the educational robot environment. By 'pedagogically sound' we mean the fact that stages are defined through functions of Bloom's taxonomy levels [7] for topic cognition. The paper's structure is as follows. Section 2 presents the GLO specialization task, section 3 – a basic idea of the approach. Section 4 provides a case study with experiments to specialization domain–specific GLO to teach CS within the educational LEGO NXT [1] robot environment. Section 5 evaluates and concludes the main result.

2   GLO Specialization Task

Here we need first to look at the *program specialization task*. Futumura [30], for example, formulates this task as a transformation process π as follows:

$$\pi(c_1', c_2', ..., c_m', r_1', r_2', ..., r_n') = \alpha(\pi, c_1', c_2', ..., c_m')(r_1', r_2', ..., r_n') \qquad (1)$$

The left side of Eq. (1) presents the state of a program to be evaluated before specialization. Here the values $(c_1', c_2', ..., c_m', r_1', r_2', ..., r_n')$ of variables $(c_1, c_2, ..., c_m, r_1, r_2, ..., r_n)$ of the program are split into two subsets: the *constants* as *compile time values* (denoted by c' with the adequate index) and *variables* as *run time values* (denoted by r' with the adequate index). The right side of the equation specifies the state of the program after specialization using the "specialization algorithm α, which evaluates $(c_1', c_2', ..., c_m')$ in the first stage and then evaluates $(r_1', r_2', ..., r_n')$ in the second stage, though the stages are not defined explicitly. The *higher-level program* that implements the "specialization algorithm" is called *specializer*. In fact, the specializer is a meta-program because it *generates* through the process π the other, i.e. a specialized program.

Now we are able to formulate the meta-program (i.e. GLO) specialization problem similarly. Let be given a set of parameters $P = \{(p_1, ..., p_m), (p_{m+1}, ..., p_n)\}$ of a GLO, where the space P is decomposed into two subsets under the following *constraint: dependent parameters* (if any, see Section 4) *have to appear in the same subset*. Similarly to (1), we formulate the problem as *the two-stage specialization* task as follows:

$$\pi(p_1, ..., p_m, p_{m+1}, ..., p_n) = \alpha(\pi, p_1, ..., p_m)(p_{m+1}, ..., p_n) \qquad (2)$$

Here, parameters $(p_1, ..., p_m)$ are evaluated in *stage 2*, thus being treated as *constants*, while the remaining parameters $(p_{m+1}, ..., p_n)$ at this stage are treated as *variables*. Stage 2 is treated as the *highest*. To be evaluated in stage 2, parameters $(p_1, ..., p_m)$ have to be *active* (meaning their usual role in the meta-program), while the remaining parameters have to be *passive* (meaning not being evaluated). Note that programming languages (e.g. C++, PHP) have a very simple mechanism to change the *state* of a variable, when it is processed or evaluated, from the *active state* to the *passive state*. For example, the record '\p' denotes that the parameter p is passive in some context.

It is the role of a specializer (formally denoted as α), among others, to *pre-program* the change of states so that parameters $(p_{m+1}, ..., p_n)$ would be passive at *stage 2* (which describes evaluation of $(p_1, ..., p_m)$ only) and they would *be active* at *stage 1* (which describes evaluation of $(p_{m+1}, ..., p_n)$). By *stage 1* in (2) we mean a sub-process of π. Stage 1 is treated as *the lowest*.

The equation (2) can be generalized by introducing the concept of multi-stage (e.g. k-stage) specialization. Indeed, we can "think" in terms of recursion, i.e. to apply "specialization" by partitioning the remaining parameters $(p_{m+1}, ..., p_n)$ in two subsets (under the stated constraints) again and again until some of *remaining parameters* will be evaluated $(k-1)$ times. Therefore, we can write:

$$\pi(p_1, ..., p_m, p_{m+1}, ..., p_n) = \alpha(\pi, p_1, ..., p_m)(p_{m+1}, ..., p_n) \; \alpha(\pi, p_{m+1}, ..., p_i)(p_{i+1}, ..., p_n) \cdots$$
$$\cdots \alpha(\pi, p_{i+1}, ..., p_j)(p_{j+1} ..., p_n) \cdots \qquad (3)$$

For increasing readability and stage visibility, we use a column-based representation of staging in Eq. (4), where the top of the right side equation represent the highest k-stage, the next represents $(k-1)$-stage and so on till 1-stage.

$$\pi(p_1, ..., p_m, p_{m+1}, ..., p_n) = \alpha(\pi, p_1, ..., p_m)(p_{m+1}, ..., p_n)$$
$$\alpha(\pi, p_{m+1}, .., p_i)(p_{i+1}, .., p_n) \cdots$$
$$\alpha(\pi, p_{i+1}, ..., p_j)(p_{j+1} ..., p_n) \cdots \qquad (4)$$

Eqs. (2-4), in fact, describe the specialization not a meta-program itself but its model expressed as a parameter set. With respect to specialization through staging, however, the parameters of different type should be evaluated differently. For example, pedagogical context should be evaluated first, the student's context next, and then the content [8]. Thus the staging should be managed adequately. For this purpose, we use the priority weights assigned to each parameter. We express the weights through fuzzy variables with values taken from the set {*HP, IP, LP*} (*HP-* high priority; *IP* – intermediate priority, *LP-* low priority). Semantically, those variables define the *specialization context* to specialize the GLO by staging without redundancy (see also sub-section 3.1 and Section 4).

3   Basic Idea of the Approach

We describe the approach from the user's perspective using the specializer (MP-ReTool – "meta-program refactoring tool") we have developed [11]. The tool transforms a heterogeneous meta-program (HMP) coded in PHP into the equivalent multi-stage representation through specialization or refactoring [26]. We are able to use the tool for GLOs because they, in fact, are HMPs. We use GLOs to automatically generate LOs to teach CS (programming). The tool accepts the initial GLO specification along with the consistent GLO parameter model as input data. The basic assumption to correctly interpret the approach is that the initial GLO should be designed *for reuse*. The latter means that the GLO implements the *enhanced learning variability* [27]. The latter includes *pedagogical, social, content,* and *specific technological variability*. Therefore, the concrete context of the GLO use requires its specialization before being adapted and used.

The tool implements the user-tool communication model to solve the specialization problem. There are two modes of using the tool. In mode 1, the user (typically teacher) indicates (through the communication model) on how GLO parameters are to be allocated to stages. In mode 2, the tool works fully automatically. In this case, however, parameters are to be supplied *with non-redundant weights* (for details see sub-section 3.1 and Table 1) introduced by the GLO designer (teacher) when the specification is coded. We explain the approach schematically in Fig. 1. Here, GLO$_R$ should be read as "designed for reuse" and GLO$_S$ - as "specialized for adaptation". The adequate GLO models are expressed through the set of parameters {P} and outlined graphically in Fig. 1(a). Here, T(S) should be read as "transformation through specialization"; PM – consistent parameter model described as a specific textual data structure; k – number of stages; {P}$_R$ – GLO model before specialization and {P}$_S$ – GLO model after specialization in terms of parameter space.

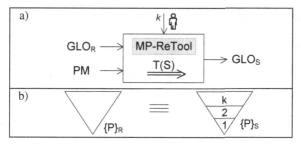

Fig. 1. Specialization phase: a) tool's level, b) GLO models before and after transformation (see right side) represented as equivalent parameter spaces

In Fig. 2, we present the simplified real task to explain the approach in some more details. The task is the straight line movement of the educational NXT robot to model (teach) linear algorithms in RobotC (it treats as a target (teaching) language in terms of HMP). Three parameters (pairs of motors, movement time and speed) along with their values characterize the initial GLO specification of the task (see Fig. 2 (a) and (b) on left side). The right side of Fig. 2 illustrates the state of the task after specialization (i.e. after the use of the tool, when the number of stages is equal to 2). This state is visible through the use of the other tool (PHP compiler), which interprets GLOs when the use of the specialized GLO takes place. Here the parameter p_1 (motors pairs) is at the stage 2 (it is visible for the user), while the remaining parameters p_2 and p_3 are at stage 1 (they are invisible at stage 2).

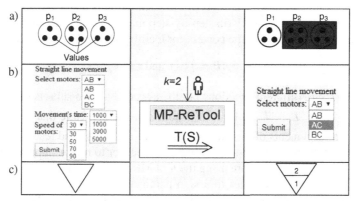

Fig. 2. a) Abstract Interfaces of GLO_R and GLO_S models; b) user's view of the GLO_R and GLO_S interfaces; c) abstract view of specialization

We only revealed one aspect of our approach, i.e. the essence of the *specialization task* (without the context of use). The other aspect is the consequent of the specialization process itself. In fact, the k-stage GLO is a generator of the other GLO, i.e. $(k-1)$-stage GLO and so on. In this context, the PHP processor is the generator that accepts the k-stage GLO as input and produces a $(k-1)$-stage GLO as output.

We can summarize the task as follows: GLO or meta-program k-stage specialization is the partitioning of the whole parameter space into k subsets first without intersecting using some prescribed rules, and then, the assigning subsets to stages with respect to prescribed constraints.

3.1 Pedagogical Aspects of GLO Specialization

In our approach, we aim at performing specialization so that automatic adaptation of the content to the user's context would be possible. There are two kinds of users (due to GLO reusability): teachers and learners. Therefore, GLO should be specialized for adaptation for both categories of actors.

Having a pedagogically sound specialization of a GLO, teacher should first make adaptation to his context and later to allow the learners to make adaptation by themselves to their context. The teacher's context has to be separated from the learner's context (such as profile, etc.), when the adaptation takes place. The content adaptation to the learner's context, on the other hand, should be the self-guided process. Such an adaptation is a cognitive process, or more precisely, the early stage of the knowledge gaining in the learning process.

In general, Bloom's taxonomy levels [7] predefine the cognitive process. We present the levels as (L_1: Remember; L_2: Understand; L_3: Apply; L_4: Analyse; L_5: Evaluate; L_6: Create). Now we are able to connect Bloom's taxonomy levels with the needed number of stages from the pedagogical perspective. As it was stated in Section 2, fuzzy variables {HP, IP, LP}, being the parameter weights, serve for managing stage selection. Indeed, the value HP is relevant to teacher's context parameters; therefore, HP can be treated as a constant because the teacher knows the teaching context. As we want to make content adaptation to the learner's context as flexible as possible, we need to accept that the values IP and LP are not constants but functions of Bloom's taxonomy levels. The basis of the assumption is that a learner should have the possibility to move gradually (in step-by-step manner) from the lowest level to the highest, when self-selecting of the content for learning takes place. Thus, we write:

$$HP = constant;\ IP = f(\lambda)\ \text{and}\ LP = f^*(\lambda), \tag{5}$$

Where f, f^* are different functions but their arguments are subsets defined on the same set $\lambda \subset \{L_1,...,L_6\}$; L_i - a level of Bloom's taxonomy; Note that what levels we need to treat as arguments of the functions depend on the task and teacher's intention. It is the reason why we left the possibility for the teacher to reason about actual values of IP and LP (see Table 1) before using the tool MP-ReTool. The more precise definition of IP and LP values enables to assign parameters to stages easily and calculate the needed number of stages automatically (e.g. for our task k=5, see Table 2).

The latter enables us to reason about the theoretically possible number of stages form the pedagogical perspective. If we assume that all teacher context parameters (labelled as HP) are placed at stage k and the content parameters at stage 1, then $k_{max}(p)$ might be equal to 6 + number of teacher-related stages (in (6) $k_{max}(p)$ - theoretically possible number of stages defined from pedagogical perspective). In practice, however, there is no need to consider all levels L_i as separate units.

Now we are able to combine technological (t) and pedagogical (p) aspects in calculating the upper bound of stages $k_m(p,t)$ to make specialization correctly as follows:

$$k_m(p,t) = \min\{k_{max}(t), k_{max}(p)\}. \tag{6}$$

Here, $k_{max}(t)$ is the upper bound of stages from the pure technological viewpoint, i.e. the number of independent parameter groups (e.g. $k_{max}(t) = 11$ in our case study, see Fig. 3); further, for simplicity reasons, we accept that the number of teacher-related stages is equal to 1 in our case study.

4   Case Study and Experiments

The aim is to demonstrate the specialization process of the real learning task using NXT robot environment [1] and the GLO approach. We have selected the "Ornament drawing by robot" task. The learning objective was to teach loops and nested loops written in RobotC [18]. The GLO specification, as teaching content for reuse, has been written manually in advance. PHP has been used as a meta-language and RobotC as a target language. Using the tool MP-ReTool, we were able to extract the dependency (interaction) models from the given specification (see Fig. 3 and Table 1). Legend below Table 1 explains the meaning of all parameters and their values.

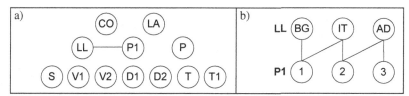

Fig. 3. Model of GLO "Ornament drawing by robot": a) parameter model; b) value interaction model of parameters LL and P1

In Fig. 3, we present the model of the task as a parameter dependency graph (a) and value interaction for parameters LL and P1 (b). The value interaction model (values within circles; lines – the constraint *requires in terms of feature modelling* [5]) predefines parameter dependency and should be read as: "It is required to draw the only one ornament with the robot's help for the beginner (BG), while for the advanced learner (AD) it is required 2 or 3 ornaments". To understand the task, learners should have previous knowledge on robots architecture and functionality. For example, learners know that there are 3 motors (A, B, C) used in pairs (AB, AC, BC), there are two kinds of velocity (drawing and idle move).

In Table 1 (see graphs on right), we present the task models in more details. There are two variants (a) and (b) of the GLO model. They differ by the assigned weights introduced by the teacher. Weights are functions of Bloom's taxonomy levels. They describe the semantics for adaptation. The made assignment enables the tool to calculate the number of needed stages. Note that for this task $k_{max}(p) = 6 + 1 = 7$; $k_{max}(t) = 11$ (the number of independent parameter groups) and $k_m(p,t) = \min\{11, 7\} = 7$. Thus, the identified numbers of stages (4 and 5) are valid for both models (a) and (b).

Table 1. Characteristics of the initial GLO (Ornament drawing by Robot)

Characteristics of GLO	Name of parameters (in bold) and their Values (in brackets), for abbreviations and meaning, see legend below
Context-based parameters	**CO** (LN); **LA** (CT; PS); **LL** (BG; IT; AD)
Content-based parameters	**S** (AB; AC; BC); **V1** (10; 30; 50); **V2** (10; 30; 50); **T** (1000; 3000; 5000); **P** (4; 5; 7); **D1** (10; 30); **D2** (10; 30); **T1** (200; 500); **P1** (1, 2; 3)

Parameters' interaction model (Line means interaction/dependency) Bloom's Taxonomy Levels (BTLs)

L1: *Remember*
L2: *Understand*
L3: *Apply*
L4: *Analyse*
L5: *Evaluate*
L6: *Create*

HP– Highest Priority
IP – Intermediate Priority as a function of BTLs
LP – Lowest Priority

Legend. **CO** – curriculum objective (LN – loops and nested loops), **LA** – learning activity (Case study (given by *Teacher*)- CT; Practise (done by *Learner*) – PS); **S** – selected motor (AB, BC, AC), **V1**, **V2**– *drawing velocity* of motors (pen on the paper), **T** – robot's drawing time, **P** – number of ornament's parts, **D1**, **D2** – *moving velocity* of motors (pen over paper), **T1** – robot's moving time, **P1** – number of ornaments. **LL** – learner's previous knowledge level (Beginner-BG; Intermediate – IT; Advanced – AD).

For example, for the model (a), 5 stages are needed (see Table 2). For the model (b), 4 stages are needed (stage 4 contains CP and LA; stage 3 contains S, V1, V2, D1 and D2; stage 2 contains T and T1; stage 1 contains LL – P1 and P). Note that the variants (a) and (b) provide slightly different possibilities for adaptation (knowledge levels to be gained already at the adaptation phase). Note that this is the "surface knowledge" in terms of "surface learning and deep learning" [20], [21]. Here, surface learning is defined as "*accepting new facts and ideas uncritically and attempting to store them as isolated, unconnected, items*". Indeed the user sees data in stages as isolated items. However, the more stages we have the more steps the adaptation includes. But the needed number stages should be linked with the task semantics. The latter dictates the teacher's intention.

Table 2 summarizes the specialized task for adaptation (model (a), see Table 1) given from the users' viewpoint, where the teacher's and learner's specializations are separated. The criteria for the learner specialization are levels of Bloom's taxonomy.

In Fig. 4, we present the results of solving the Ornament drawing task: the generated instance according to the given parameter values (a) and the Robot's view to run the task (b).

Table 2. Characteristics of GLO (Ornament drawing by Robot) obtained by using MP-ReTool

Specialization for teacher		
Teacher's context parameters	CO; LA	stage 5
Specialization for learner		
Level: Category of Bloom's Taxonomy -BT	BT Description using the verb-subsets from [19]	Visible parameters at current stage and already evaluated parameters at previous stages (blacken) as they are seen in the specialized specification	Stages for adaptation by learners
L1: Remember	recognize, recall	S*	stage 4
L2: Understand	interpret, exemplify, classify, summarize, infer, compare, explain	S; V1; V2; D1; D2	stage 3
L3: Apply	execute, implement	S; V1; V2; D1; D2; T; T1	stage 2
L4: Analyse	differentiate, organize, attribute		stage 1
L5: Evaluate	check, critique	S; V1; V2; D1; D2; T; T1; P; P1-LL	
L6: Create	generate, plan, produce		

*) Learner should have previous knowledge about LEGO NXT Robot;

```
task main(){
//Preparation for drawing
    motor[motorB] = 50;
    wait1Msec(100);
    motor[motorB] = 0;
//Drawing
    for (int j=0; j<7; j++){
        motor[motorC] = 30;
        motor[motorA] = 30;
        wait1Msec(1000);
        motor[motorC] = -30;
        motor[motorA] = 0;
        wait1Msec(1000);
    }
//Drawing of ornament is finished
    motor[motorB] = -50;
    wait1Msec(100);
    motor[motorB] = 0;
}
                                      a)
```

b)

Fig. 4. The derived instance in RobotC (a); b) the Ornament drawing task by NXT Robot

5   Evaluation and Conclusion

We have described the specialization task and approach to transform the reusable GLO (which, in fact, is a meta-program) into its multi-stage format. The aim of this transformation is to make possible the pre-programmed user-guided adaptation of GLOs when used. We have developed the tool to specialize (automatically) the real GLOs used for generating teaching topics in CS within the robot-based environment.

As our application is highly heterogeneous and includes such sub-domains as teaching content (curricular), pedagogy, programming languages, educational robotics, we are able to reflect the essential variability aspects explicitly through parameters in the developed specifications. We treat these aspects as learning variability. To make the learning variability easy manageable, we have enriched it with parameter priorities using fuzzy variables (*HP*, *IP* and *LP*). For the pedagogical evaluation, we express the variables through cognitive levels of Bloom's taxonomy. The use of fuzzy variables enables to resolve two problems: 1) to assign parameters to stages easily and calculate the needed number of stages automatically; 2) to specify adaptation as a gradually augmenting process in 'surface' knowledge gaining.

Because of the necessity of managing changeability and adaptation of the teaching content to the context of use, we have found the stage-based specialization of the GLO (this is the main contribution of the paper) as a relevant and beneficial technology. The practical needs have come from our extensive experiments in using NXT and other educational robots in the real setting (school) to teach CS topics. From the teacher's perspective, GLO specialization first to prepare the content flexibly and opens the way for the learner-guided automatic adaptation of GLOs. From the learner's perspective, the teacher's initiated adaptation then makes the learner's self-adaptation process possible and enables to generate LO to drive the learning process according to the learner's contexts and needs.

References

[1] Castledine, A., Chalmers, C.: LEGO Robotics: An authentic problem-solving tool? Design & Technology Education 16(3), 19–27 (2011)

[2] Le Meur, A.F., Lawall, J.L., Consel, C.: Towards bridging the gap between programming languages and partial evaluation. ACM SIGPLAN Notices 37(3), 9–18 (2002)

[3] ACM SIGPLAN, Workshop on Partial Evaluation and Program Manipulation (PEPM 2013), http://www.program-transformation.org/PEPM13

[4] CETL reusable learning objects. What are GLOs?, http://www.rlo-cetl.ac.uk/whatwedo/glos/whatareglos.php

[5] Czarnecki, K., Helsen, S., Eisenecker, U.: Staged configuration through specialization and multilevel configuration of feature models. Software Process: Improvement and Practice 10(2), 143–169 (2005)

[6] Czarnecki, K., Eisenecker, U.: Generative Programming: Methods, Tools and Applications. Addison-Wesley, Boston (2000)

[7] Anderson, L., Krathwohl, D.A.: Taxonomy for Learning, Teaching and Assessing: A Revision of Bloom's Taxonomy of Educational Objectives. Longman, New York (2001)

[8] Ilomäki, L., Jaakkola, T., Lakkala, M., Nirhamo, L., Nurmi, S., Paavola, S., Rahikainen, M., Lehtinen, E.: Principles, models and examples for designing learning objects (LOs). Pedagogical guidelines in CELEBRATE. A Working Paper for the European Commission, CELEBRATE Project, IST-2001–35188 (2003)

[9] Murakami, M.: An application of partial evaluation of communicating processes to system security. International Journal in Foundations of Computer Science & Technology (IJFCST) 2(4) (2012)

[10] Ruiz, M.D.P.P., Díaz, M.J.F., Soler, F.O., Pérez, J.R.P.: Adaptation in current e-learning systems. Computer Standards & Interfaces 30(1), 62–70 (2008)

[11] MP-ReTool tools, http://proin.ktu.lt/metaprogram/MP-ReTool/

[12] Jones, N.D., Gomard, C.K., Sestoft, P.: Partial evaluation and automatic program generation. Peter Sestoft (1993)

[13] Jones, N.D., Sestoft, P., Søndergaard, H.: An experiment in partial evaluation: the generation of a compiler generator. In: Jouannaud, J.-P. (ed.) RTA 1985. LNCS, vol. 202, pp. 124–140. Springer, Heidelberg (1985)

[14] Jones, N.D.: An introduction to partial evaluation. ACM Computing Surveys (CSUR) 28(3), 480–503 (1996)

[15] Bednarik, R., Moreno, A., Myller, N., Sutinen, E.: Smart program visualization technologies: Planning a next step. In: Fifth IEEE International Conference on Advanced Learning Technologies, ICALT 2005, pp. 717–721. IEEE (2005)

[16] Giacobazzi, R., Jones, N.D., Mastroeni, I.: Obfuscation by partial evaluation of distorted interpreters. In: Proceedings of the ACM SIGPLAN 2012 Workshop on Partial Evaluation and Program Manipulation, pp. 63–72. ACM (2012)

[17] Morales, R., Leeder, D., Boyle, T.: A case in the design of generative learning objects (GLOs): applied statistical methods. In: World Conference on Educational Multimedia, Hypermedia and Telecommunications, pp. 2091–2097 (2005)

[18] RobotC – Improved movement. Robotics Academy, p.19,
    https://www.doc.ic.ac.uk/~ajd/Robotics/RoboticsResources/RO
    BOTC%20-%20Improved%20Movement.pdf

[19] Martin, S., Vallance, M., van Schaik, P., Wiz, C.: Learning spaces, tasks and metrics for effective communication in Second Life within the context of programming LEGO NXT Mindstorms™ robots: towards a framework for design and implementation. Journal of Virtual Worlds Research 3(1) (2010)

[20] Shuhidan, S., Hamilton, M., D'Souza, D.: A Taxonomic Study of Novice Programming Summative Assessment. In: Proc. 11th Australasian Computing Education Conference (ACE 2009), Wellington, New Zealand, pp. 147–156 (2009)

[21] Bhattacharyya, T., Prasath, R., Bhattacharya, B.: Qualitative Learning Outcome through Computer Assisted Instructions. In: Mining Intelligence and Knowledge Exploration, pp. 567–578 (2013)

[22] Boyle, T., Leeder, D., Chase, H.: To boldly GLO – towards the next generation of learning objects. In: World Conference on eLearning in Corporate, Government, Healthcare and Higher Education, pp. 28–33 (2004)

[23] Mens, T., Czarnecki, K., Van Gorp, P.: A Taxonomy of Model Transformations. Electronic Notes in Theoretical Computer Science 152, 125–142 (2006)

[24] Sheard, T.: Accomplishments and research challenges in meta-programming. In: Taha, W. (ed.) SAIG 2001. LNCS, vol. 2196, pp. 2–44. Springer, Heidelberg (2001)

[25] Tourwé, T., Mens, T.: Identifying refactoring opportunities using logic meta-programming. In: Proceedings of Seventh European Conference on Software Maintenance and Reengineering, pp. 91–100. IEEE (2003)

[26] Štuikys, V., Bespalova, K., Burbaitė, R.: Refactoring of Heterogeneous Meta-Program into k-stage Meta-Program. Information Technology And Control 43(1), 14–27 (2014)

[27] Štuikys, V., Burbaitė, R., Damaševičius, R.: Teaching of Computer Science Topics Using Meta-Programming-Based GLOs and LEGO Robots. Informatics in Education-An International Journal 12(1), 125–142 (2013)

[28] Štuikys, V., Damaševičius, R.: Meta-Programming and Model-Driven Meta-Program Development: Principles, Processes and Techniques. Springer (2013)

[29] Taha, W.: A gentle introduction to multi-stage programming. In: Lengauer, C., Batory, D., Blum, A., Odersky, M. (eds.) Domain-Specific Program Generation. LNCS, vol. 3016, pp. 30–50. Springer, Heidelberg (2004)

[30] Futamura, Y.: Partial evaluation of computation process–an approach to a compiler-compiler. Higher-Order and Symbolic Computation 12(4), 381–391 (1999)

Efficiency Analysis of Object Position and Orientation Detection Algorithms

Tomas Uktveris

Multimedia Engineering Department, Kaunas University of Technology,
Studentu St. 50, Kaunas, Lithuania
tomas.uktveris@gmail.com

Abstract. This work presents a performance evaluation of the state-of-the-art computer vision algorithms for object detection and pose estimation. Depth information from Kinect sensor is used in this work for the estimation task. It is shown, that Kinect depth sensor is more superior for orientation estimation than a regular stereo camera setup. Accuracy and performance of a point cloud alignment ICP method is analyzed and tested. Furthermore, multiple object detectors accuracy and runtime performance is evaluated. Simple but effective techniques are provided for the comparison. Conducted experiments show a maximum object detection accuracy of 90% and speed of 15 fps for standard size VGA images, while ICP alignment performance of 2 fps is achieved. Additional optimizations would be necessary to attain better real-time object detection and pose extraction performance.

Keywords: pose estimation, performance, point cloud, iterative closest point.

1 Introduction

Accurate detection of objects and their poses from images or video data is a well-known task in computer vision. This problem as been analyzed for almost half of a century and is receiving great interest from many researchers till now. Required for many applications, the ability to detect and estimate the position and orientation of an object in different environments is highly desirable. While detection serves as an initial tool for object localization and identification in the camera frame, pose extraction - as a refinement step, gives the accurate orientation of the object in 3D space. Such knowledge obtained allows for robots or other tools to grasp and manipulate objects more precisely.

Recent advances in the field show promising results but still no perfect method exists for the given issue. The problem also arises when choosing which algorithms to apply in robotics or other field for the task. Detection accuracy, estimation accuracy and run-time speed are crucial parameters for many applications, especially in real-time ones. While many algorithms exist and can be chosen from, a combined comparison of the state-of-the-art solutions is still lacking. This work fills in the existing gap by analyzing well-known algorithms and their performance using a single evaluation methodology.

G. Dregvaite and R. Damasevicius (Eds.): ICIST 2014, CCIS 465, pp. 302–311, 2014.

2   Related Work

Over the years many object detection and pose extraction algorithms were proposed with different performance and accuracy characteristics. This section gives an overview of different algorithms used in current applications to fully understand the available solutions for the analyzed problem. As by [1] object detection methods can be classified into three main groups: pattern based, model based and feature based methods. These groups will be discussed more thoroughly further.

Pattern based methods such as the ones using fiducial markers or different color patterns attached to objects were proposed in [2] and [3] works. While this method is very accurate (due to easy to detect high-contrast markers), the requirement for direct manipulation with the object cannot be accomplished always. Moreover, this method suffers greatly from pattern occlusions by environment clutter. Multiple patterns need to be attached to the object from different sides to remedy the problem.

A more robust and less susceptible are the model based methods. In this type of algorithms the model database is known or is built a priori before detection. Such technique incorporating a prebuilt 3D CAD models were used in [4, 5]. Using the technique, model edges and corners need to be matched against extracted image edges and corners. Depending on primitive types matched (segment to segment or corner to corner) - the accuracy decreases at the expense of gained processing performance. In other model based techniques as proposed in [6], the pose was computed using iterative optimization techniques. Optimization allowed to refine the detected object pose by minimizing the orientation error. While edge based model methods are resilient to illumination changes and give an accurate pose estimate, the increased processing requirements also negatively affect processing time. Another disadvantage is the requirement to have an accurate 3D CAD model built before detection. A much more robust approach would be to learn the model dynamically before detection.

The largest feature based algorithm category contains methods that extract different interest data - color, corner or gradient information from image or video RGB frames and can use that data for object detection. First well known subcategory of such algorithms are solutions directly manipulating color information. More frequently HSV or YUV color spaces are used for object detection because of better resilience to illumination changes. Object detection by color range or by building object color histograms was proposed in [7, 8, 9]. The mentioned papers implemented simple object detection by evaluating image histograms and by doing adaptive color comparisons. Dynamically changing thresholds were used to increase adaptability to illumination changes. Additionally, Kalman filtering was integrated to improve the tracking accuracy between successive video frames. While color based detection is fast and easy to compute, the method is still highly not invariant to illumination changes, fails to discern between same objects or same color background and can be used only for tracking dominant color objects without any texture.

Other type of algorithms in the feature category is feature detectors such as SIFT, FAST, ORB, SURF, BRISK, HARRIS, SHI-TOMASI and others. Feature detectors are capable of extracting stable interest points from an image and with accompanying descriptor match them between different images. Many detectors rely on image gradient information, are invariant to translation, rotation and scale changes. SIFT feature detector for object detection was used in [10] with SVM orientation classifier.

A database of 8 image views around the target object was used. Though, average orientation detection accuracy of 90% was achieved, the method was limited to planar surface objects and one orientation axis was fixed. Similar results were received in [11] using a SURF detector. While feature detectors are a promising technique for planar object detection and image panorama stitching, it still needs highly textured surfaces (gradients) for best repeatability, matching performance and cannot be efficiently used for complex shape texture-less object detection alone.

Another object detection approach is based on image templates and ML (machine learning). Algorithms such as Haar [12] and HOG [13] were successfully used for face, human, car detection and can be trained using positive and negative image examples for any type of object detection. Haar method uses Ada boosting technique to create a strong classifier out of a cascade of weak binary classifiers. Classifiers are trained from Haar type features extracted from images. The HOG algorithm uses an SVM classifier trained using of a fixed size image window containing a grid of gradient edge histograms. The downside of the ML template based approach is the need for thousands of positive and negative images to obtain an accurate classifier.

Effective solution has been presented in [14] by fusing multiple modalities - image gradients and depth gradients acquired using Microsoft Kinect sensor. The introduced LINE-MOD algorithm was specially designed for any kind of object detection. As presented in the original paper, it allows training a database from thousands of object templates for object detection. Templates can also provide approximate initial orientation for further pose refinement. Another combined template and tracking solution - the TLD algorithm, was created by Zdanek Kalal and implemented by Georg Nebehay as OpenTLD [15]. The improvement over all other methods for TLD is the dynamic just-in-time learning and error correction.

A definitive state-of-the-art algorithm for point-model registration and alignment is the ICP (Iterative Closest Point) that was used by numerous works such as [16, 17] for different view Kinect depth registration and 3D model scanning-acquisition.

Given the initial method overview, further presented work in this paper was based on the Haar, HOG, LINE-MOD, TLD and ICP algorithm performance and accuracy evaluation.

3   Evaluation Methods

Evaluation methods presented in this section were used to assess efficiency of selected algorithms. The assessment procedure was divided into two separate tests – object detection and object orientation estimation. Each part with its own evaluation technique will be presented in further subsections. Since accurate stereo depth data was required for each step an additional depth camera data accuracy evaluation phase was conducted before all tests.

3.1   Object Detection

In order to evaluate object detection accuracy a database of objects was assembled. To create as much variety as possible – textured, non-textured and different shape objects were chosen for training and testing. The training and testing procedure is given in a diagram Fig. 1. Training flow is marked using solid line arrows and testing using dotted. The training samples were generated by recording a video of the object from different views and orientations and then manually selecting a bounding box around the object in every frame. Selected image samples were used to train each detector algorithm.

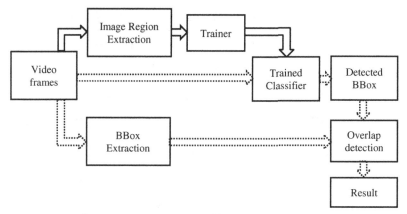

Fig. 1. Object detection training and testing procedure

Testing procedure was accomplished in a similar way – another video was recorded and ground truth bounding boxes were extracted manually. The same video frames were given to the classifier for object detection. Computed bounding boxes and ground truth boxes were tested for correctness using an overlap ratio as given by (1) equation.

$$\omega(B_1, B_2) = \frac{B_1 \cap B_2}{B_1 \cup B_2} > T \qquad (1)$$

where T – threshold for correct matches (usually 0.5), B_n – area of computed bounding boxes ($n = 1..2$).

3.2   Object Pose Estimation

The pose estimation evaluation procedure as defined in Fig. 2 was used to assess the ICP algorithm performance. To correctly evaluate object pose estimation a 3D point cloud reference model for each tested object was built in the training phase (solid arrows). This was accomplished by using a similar fiducial marker technique as described in [17] and implemented via ARToolkit+ library. In the testing phase (dotted arrows) a video was recorded with Kinect camera in various orientations of the object placed in the center of the fiducial marker plane. A point cloud of each video frame was extracted and target object point cloud separated from the scene using plane detection and Euclidean clustering methods available in the PointCloud library. For each frame the built 3D reference model was aligned with the current frame's object point cloud using the ICP algorithm. In testing phase the fiducial marker plane served only as a reference for the ground truth model pose. After the ICP alignment, the aligned and ground truth object poses were compared using techniques described further.

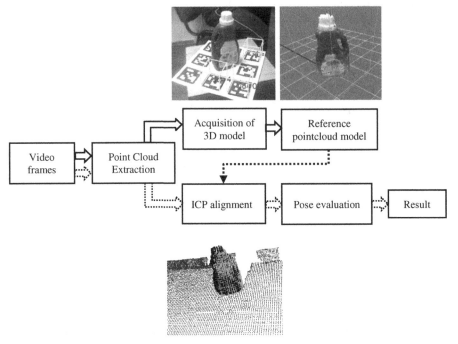

Fig. 2. Model creation and alignment testing procedure

Given a known model pose matrix $M_1=[R_1|t_1]$ and aligned model pose matrix $M_2=[R_2|t_2]$, (where R_i – is a 3x3 rotation matrix and t_i – is a 3x1 translation vector) we wish to know the alignment correctness. Extracting Euler angles (pitch, yaw, roll) from the rotation matrices R_1 and R_2 and comparing them element-wise will give ambiguous results as there are many ways to compose the same rotation matrix with different Euler angles [18]. Spherical coordinate approach was used in this work instead. Each rotation matrix is uniquely identified by a pair of rotation angles (φ, θ) on a unit sphere as shown in Fig. 3. So the final full transformation evaluation was done by transforming a unit vector $p = \{1,0,0\}$ by each of the R_1 and R_2 matrices, converting the resulting p_1 and p_2 points to spherical coordinates by equations (2), (3) and taking the angle difference (4). Pose translation parts were compared by taking the difference of the two t_1 and t_2 vectors.

$$\varphi(p) = \arctan\left(\frac{p_y}{p_x}\right) \tag{2}$$

$$\theta(p) = \arccos(p_z) \tag{3}$$

$$\delta(p_1, p_2) = \{\varphi_{p1} - \varphi_{p2}, \theta_{p1} - \theta_{p2}\} \tag{4}$$

Additionally deviation from identity matrix evaluation metric (as defined in [19]) and given by (5) was used to verify the correctness of the rotation comparison.

$$\phi(R_1, R_2) = \left\|I - R_1 R_2^T\right\|_F, \quad \phi \in [0, 2\sqrt{2}] \tag{5}$$

where I – the identity matrix and $\|\cdot\|_F$ is the Frobenius norm of a matrix.

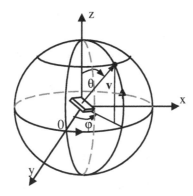

Fig. 3. Every point on a unit sphere has unique (φ, θ) spherical coordinates

4   Depth Accuracy Evaluation Results

Since the selection of a stereo system had an influence on the LINE-MOD and ICP algorithm accuracy, an initial depth accuracy experiment was conducted before any other tests. A stereo camera system consisting of two identical Prestigio PWC 2 webcams and a Microsoft Kinect sensor was compared. OpenCV library functions were used to calibrate the stereo system and SGBM disparity calculation algorithm was used to compute dense disparity map and depth map for the webcam system. For each test a large flat surface was placed in front of the depth camera at a known distance and average depth was computed from the depth image by selecting a stable region on the flat surface area. The test results are presented in Fig. 4. From acquired data it is clear that Kinect depth image information is more accurate and the error is increasing more slowly with distance. Both curves are second order polynomial functions.

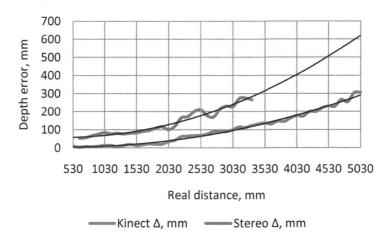

Fig. 4. Stereo webcam system and Kinect depth image error comparison

5   Object Detection Results

By the previously defined object detection evaluation methods an object database of 8 different objects were assembled for testing. The used test set is shown in Fig. 5.

Fig. 5. Objects used for training and frames from training sequence

A 1 minute video at 640x480 resolution and 30 fps of color and depth data was recorded using Kinect for each object for training. A total of 1800 color and depth images of each object encompassing bounding boxes were extracted from video frames manually. A limited amount of images were used for automated training due to high memory requirements of the training process. 1300 positive images and 3200 negative images were used for HOG training. Default OpenCV training settings and a window size of 96x96 pixels were selected. Haar method was trained with 500 positive and 1500 negative samples at a window size of 24x24 pixels, for 15 stages, minimal hit rate – 0.999, false alarm rate – 0.5 and max weak classifiers – 20.

Testing was accomplished automatically by comparing the bounding boxes for overlap in 8 different videos of approximate 1 minute in length as described in the previous section. All experiments were executed on Intel Core 2 Duo P8400 2xCore 2.26GHz CPU with 4GB of RAM. The accuracy and run-time performance test results are given in Fig. 6.

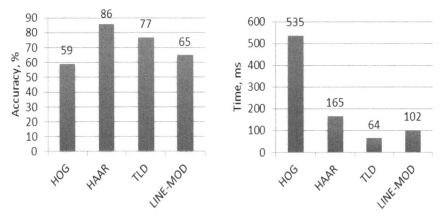

Fig. 6. Object detection method accuracy and run-time performance

Test results show that detectors are capable of achieving 60-90% detection accuracy. Haar and TLD results compared to the presented in the original papers are close (91% and 81% respectively). Using depth and color data yields more feature points. Still LINE-MOD accuracy is less than the expected 95% as presented in original paper. The least accurate HOG method also showed the worst detection run-time performance, while TLD was the fastest method compared. A maximum of 15fps speed has been achieved using TLD for 640x480 image frame processing.

6   Orientation Estimation Results

By the previously defined object pose evaluation methods the same 8 objects were tested. A voxel size of 1 cm was used to filter the test point clouds. ICP algorithm was run for a maximum of 100 iterations, using 1e-3 pose convergence epsilon and correspondence threshold set to 4 cm for all tests. Test results of all tests are given in the Table 1 further. The accuracy of the Φ metric was computed using (6) equation.

$$Acc(\phi) = \left(1 - \frac{\phi}{2\sqrt{2}}\right) \cdot 100\% \tag{6}$$

Table 1. ICP orientation estimation results

Test name	Position (abs. mean error, mm)			Rotation (abs. mean error, deg)		Φ metric		Time, ms
	X	**Y**	**Z**	**Φ**	**θ**	**Error**	**Acc. %**	
Book	37.50	31.58	54.38	5.02	7.28	0.30	89.44	621.15
Bottle	23.82	49.82	43.75	12.96	28.00	0.75	73.32	496.66
Box	31.78	18.07	52.33	6.36	5.02	0.24	91.48	456.01
Car	23.77	16.94	11.05	15.87	31.12	0.95	66.35	374.93
Cup	7.24	6.50	2.20	17.96	78.11	1.82	35.52	238.21
Sheep	30.55	23.20	41.71	25.65	39.28	1.22	56.87	340.56
Shoe	18.30	22.90	7.04	11.48	17.76	0.60	78.88	404.70
Teddy	36.22	26.34	65.76	38.67	29.76	1.25	55.89	613.95
Mean	**26.15**	**24.42**	**34.78**	**16.75**	**29.54**	**0.89**	**68.47**	**443.27**

Test results show that the depth alignment with the ICP method gives an average of 3.4 cm translation error and nearly 30 degrees average rotation error. The ICP matching is a costly operation and its performance is far from real-time with an average 640x480 frame processing time of 443.27 ms (or approximate - 2 fps). It can be seen that simpler shape objects (as a book) show better matching accuracy with respect to more complex ones (sheep, teddy). Highly symmetrical objects (cup) show poor orientation estimation results due to difficulty to discern between similar looking poses.

7   Conclusion

This work presented a simple approach for object detection and pose estimation efficiency calculation. The four selected and analyzed state-of-the-art object detection methods showed a maximum of 15fps speed when performing standard VGA 640x480 resolution image processing and detection accuracy up to 90% with the lower bound not less than 60%.

The object pose estimation ICP algorithm showed mean absolute translation error of 3.4 cm and mean rotation error of 30 degrees when aligning Kinect extracted pointcloud data. While the algorithm runs approximately at 2 fps on laptop computer, plenty of optimization or data simplification possibilities exist for future work.

By combining object detector and ICP information it is possible to exclude a significant amount of point cloud points by analyzing only the object region of interest. A possible combination of an object tracker and a detector would allow to increase the overall accuracy even more at the price of lower run-time performance.

Many applications such as robots do not require or cannot process large amounts of data, so reducing the image frame size to 320x240 could also reduce the point cloud size 4 times giving a significant performance boost. Keeping the same or achieving better estimation results would be a challenge for future work also.

References

1. Giesbrecht, J.: Development of a Vision-Based Robotic Follower Vehicle. Technical report (2009)
2. Xiaogang, G., Changhong, W., Zhenshen, Q.: Object Tracking for Autonomous Mobile Robot based on Feedback of Monocular-vision. In: Industrial Electronics and Applications, ICIEA 2007, pp. 467–470 (2007)
3. Ukida, H., Kawanami, M., Terama, Y.: 3D Object Tracking by Pan-Tilt Moving Cameras and Robot Using Sparse Template Matching and Particle Filter. In: SICE Annual Conference (SICE), pp. 2004–2009 (2011)
4. Drummond, T., Cipolla, R.: Real-Time Visual Tracking of Complex Structures. IEEE Transactions on Pattern Analysis and Machine Intelligence 24, 932–946 (2002)
5. Lepetit, V., Fua, P.: Monocular Model-based 3D Tracking of Rigid Objects, Found. Trends. Found. Trends. In: Comput. Graph. Vis. 1(1), 1–89 (2005)
6. Lowe, D.G.: Fitting Parameterized Three-Dimensional Models to Images. In: Transactions on Pattern Analysis and Machine Intelligence (1991)
7. Rui, L., Zhijiang, D., Fujun, H., Minxiu, K., Lining, S.: Tracking a Moving Object with Mobile Robot Based on Vision. In: I21E International Joint Conference on Neural Networks (2008)
8. Gönne, C., Rous, M., Kraiss, K.F.: Real-Time Adaptive Colour Segmentation for the RoboCup Middle Size League (2005)
9. Browning, B., Veloso, M.: Real-Time, Adaptive Color-based Robot Vision (2005)
10. Lin, C., Setiawan, E.: Object Orientation Recognition Based on SI6 and SVM by Using Stereo Camera. In: International Conference on Robotics and Biomimetics (2009)

11. Thachasongtham, D., Yoshida, T., de Sorbier, F., Saito, H.: 3D Object Pose Estimation Using Viewpoint Generative Learning. In: Kämäräinen, J.-K., Koskela, M. (eds.) SCIA 2013. LNCS, vol. 7944, pp. 512–521. Springer, Heidelberg (2013)
12. Viola, P., Jones, M.: Rapid Object Detection Using a Boosted Cascade of Simple Features. In: Computer Vision and Pattern Recognition, vol.1, pp.I-511–I-518 (2001)
13. Dalal, N., Triggs, B.: Histograms of Oriented Gradients for Human Detection. In: Computer Vision and Pattern Recognition, vol. 1, pp. 886–893 (2005)
14. Hinterstoisser, S., Holzer, S., Cagniart, C., Ilic, S., Konolige, K., Navab, N., Lepetit, V.: Multimodal templates for real-time detection of texture-less objects in heavily cluttered scenes. In: IEEE International Conference on Computer Vision (ICCV), pp. 858–865 (2011)
15. Nebehay, G.: Robust Object Tracking Based on Tracking-Learning-Detection, Faculty of Informatics, TU Vienna (2012)
16. Newcombe, R.A., Izadi, S., Hilliges, O., Molyneaux, D., Kim, D., Davison, A.J., Kohi, P., Shotton, J., Hodges, S., Fitzgibbon, A.: KinectFusion: Real-time dense surface mapping and tracking. In: 10th IEEE International Symposium on Mixed and Augmented Reality (ISMAR), pp. 127–136, 26–29 (2011)
17. Mihalyi, R.G., Pathak, K., Vaskevicius, N., Birk, A.: Uncertainty estimation of AR-marker poses for graph-SLAM optimization in 3D object model generation with RGBD data. In: IEEE/RSJ International Conference on Intelligent Robots and Systems (IROS), pp.1807–1813, 3–7 (2013)
18. Winkler, S.: Model-based pose estimation of 3-D objects from camera images using neural networks. Technical Report IB 515-96-12, Diplomarbeit, Institut für Nachrichten-und Hochfrequenztechnik, Technische Universität Wien, pp. 28–31 (1996)
19. Huynh, D.Q.: Metrics for 3D Rotations: Comparison and Analysis. J. Math. Imaging 35(2), 155–164 (2009)

An Idea to Apply Firefly Algorithm in 2D Image Key-Points Search

Marcin Woźniak and Zbigniew Marszałek

Institute of Mathematics, Silesian University of Technology,
ul. Kaszubska 23, 44-100 Gliwice, Poland
{Marcin.Wozniak,Zbigniew.Marszalek}@polsl.pl

Abstract. In this paper we discuss the idea to apply evolutionary computation method, in particular firefly algorithm, to search for key-points in 2D images. In the research, classic firefly algorithm is used to search for special areas in test images. Research results are presented and discussed to show potential efficiency of applied method.

Keywords: evolutionary computation, firefly algorithm, key-points search, 2D image classifier, 2D image processing.

1 Introduction

Evolutionary computation (EC) is one of most important fields in computer science. One may present it's applications in different sciences, projects and industry. EC represents power of computational intelligence (CI), where dedicated mechanisms solve complex problems. Among these methods one can name genetic algorithms (GA), evolutionary strategies (ES) and heuristic algorithms (HA). These methods are mapping behavior of real life to solve given task. They are efficient in positioning, simulating different objects and complex optimization. One can also find their efficiency in search for optimal solutions and easy implementation with high precision. Let us give some examples.

In [8] was presented application of ES to create learning sets for artificial intelligence (AI) control systems. LAN models positioning and optimization by the use of GA or ES is presented in [9], [29], [30] and [31]. GA are also efficient in optimization of medical diagnostic classifiers (see [20]) and positioning of ultrasound surgery (see [21]). They also play crucial role in manufacturing systems (see [14]). HA may be applied in industrial processes simulations, i.e. iron cast as shown in [15]. HA are adaptive to conditions of diverse fitness functions as presented in [18]. Efficiency of GA versus analytical approach for optimization of solar thermal electricity plants is discussed in [4]. While stability and convergence of EC is discussed in [2], [5], [10], [23] and [34]. Some hybrid EC methods are applied in model of airport gate scheduling as presented in [11]. EC are efficient in FUZZY-PID controllers positioning (see [28]), job scheduling problems (see [38]) and image processing (see [33]). As You see EC may be applied in various and complicated models which describe sophisticated co-working subsystems

G. Dregvaite and R. Damasevicius (Eds.): ICIST 2014, CCIS 465, pp. 312–323, 2014.

and complex problems. These convinced us to assess it's efficiency in 2D image processing.

In this paper we aim to show possibility of using EC, in particular firefly algorithm (FA), to search for key-points in 2D images. For the research were taken sample images from open test images databases *www.imageprocessingplace.com* and *www.ece.utk.edu/gonzalez/ipweb2e/*. In following sections we present classic attempt and FA application to search for key areas. Applied FA presents high precision, is easy to implement and solves given task very fast. This makes presented solution efficient.

2 Key-Points Search Methods

There are many aspects where EC can help to solve given problems and analyze 2D images. In [32] is discussed application of some algorithms in preprocessing human signatures for AI classifiers. In [12] EC methods are used to design shape imitation. Here we would like to discuss potential application of EC in the process of 2D image classification.

Computer image is composed of points, which have special position and properties. Among them are saturation, sharpness, brightness and more. All these features compose objects visible to our eyes and give information about objects in the picture. This information can help to identify somebody or something. Therefore position of each pixel (each one has measurable coordinates $X = (x, y) = (x_{i,1}, x_{i,2})$) and it's properties (i.e. brightness and saturation) are crucial for classification. We implemented EC method to find areas that contain many pixels of the same kind, which can be classified by AI system.

2.1 Classic Attempt

One of classic methods used for key-points recognition is SURF (Speeded-Up Robust Features) algorithm. This method gives description of the image by selecting characteristic key-points. Here is given only a short presentation, for more details please see [1], [3], [7], [13] and [22].

Our SURF combines selection of key-points with calculating 64-element vector (descriptor). In SURF is applied integrated image and filter approximation of block Hessian determinant. To detect interesting points is used particular Hessian-matrix approximation (see [1] and [3]). For point $X = (x, y)$ in the image is defined Hessian matrix $H(X, \sigma)$ in X at scale σ using formula

$$H(X, \sigma) = \begin{bmatrix} L_{xx}(X, \sigma) & L_{xy}(X, \sigma) \\ L_{xy}(X, \sigma) & L_{yy}(X, \sigma) \end{bmatrix}, \tag{1}$$

where the symbols are: $L_{xx}(X, \sigma)$ – convolution of Gaussian second order derivative $\frac{\partial^2}{\partial x^2}$. We define approximation D_{xx}, D_{yy} and D_{xy} using formula

$$det(H_{ap}) = D_{xx} D_{yy} - \left(\frac{|L_{xy}(\sigma)|_F |D_{xx}(\sigma)|_F}{|L_{xx}(\sigma)|_F |D_{xy}(\sigma)|_F} D_{xy} \right)^2. \tag{2}$$

Then, image is blurred to get DoG (Difference of Gaussian) images, which helps to find edges. To localize interesting points is used non maximum suppression in $3 \times 3 \times 3$ neighborhood. Maximum determinant of Hessian matrix is interpolated at scale σ, which helps to differ between first level and each octave. In [3] or [7] SURF descriptor is based on similar properties. First is fixed reproducible orientation based on information from circular region around pixel. Then, is constructed square region aligned to selected orientation and SURF descriptor is extracted from it. Please see [1] and [3] for more details.

2.2   Firefly Algorithm

Firefly algorithm (FA) maps behavior of flying insects that we all can see in the summer - fireflies. This method maps them while searching for best partner. In the research we have implemented this process for 2D image key-points search.

One of first versions of FA was presented in [34], [35] or [36]. Since then it was efficiently applied in many fields. In [6] chaotic FA is applied to reliability-redundancy optimization. In [16] FA is applied to minimum cross entropy threshold selection. In [19] this method is applied to solve traveling salesman problem. It is efficient in continuous optimization (see [37]) and multi-modal optimization (see [34]). FA is also efficient in image compression, please see [17]. All these convinced us to apply classic FA in the process of 2D image classification. Let us now present mathematical model of classic FA algorithm applied to search for image key-points.

The method describes behavior of fireflies in natural conditions, characterized by several biological traits:

- Specific way of flashing.
- Specific way of moving.
- Specific perception of other individuals.

These features are modeled with numerical values. In this way we translate natural characteristics of biological organisms on mathematical model used to develop specific EC method. Thus, in implementation of classic FA we assume:

- I_{pop}-light intensity factor for given species.
- γ-absorption coefficient of light in given circumstances.
- β-factor for attractiveness of firefly species.
- μ-factor for random motion of individual.

In description of FA we also use the following assumptions:

- All fireflies are unisex, therefore one individual can be attracted to any other firefly regardless of gender.
- Attractiveness is proportional to brightness. Thus, for every two fireflies less clear flashing one will move toward brighter one.
- Attractiveness is proportional to brightness and decreases with increasing distance between individuals.

- If there is no clearer and more visible firefly within the range, then each one will move randomly.
- Firefly and pixel (2D image point) are equal in FA algorithm.

Distance between any two fireflies i and j situated at points (pixels) X_i and X_j in the picture is defined as Cartesian metric

$$r_{ij}^t = \|X_i^t - X_j^t\| = \sqrt{\sum_{k=1}^{2}(x_{i,k}^t - x_{j,k}^t)^2}, \tag{3}$$

where the symbols are: X_i^t, X_j^t–pixels in the picture in t iteration, $x_{i,k}^t$, $x_{k,j}^t$–k-th components of spatial coordinates X_i^t and X_j^t that describe each firefly position (pixel in the image) measured in t iteration.

Light intensity I_{ij}^t from firefly i that is received by firefly j decreases with increasing distance r_{ij}^t between them. Natural light is absorbed by media, so attractiveness also vary according to absorption and distance between them. In the model light intensity varies according to

$$I_{ij}^t(r_{ij}^t) = I_{pop} \cdot e^{-\gamma \cdot (r_{ij}^t)^2}, \tag{4}$$

where the symbols are: $I_{ij}^t(r_{ij}^t)$–intensity of light from firefly i that is received by firefly j in t iteration, r_{ij}^t–distance between firefly i and firefly j defined in (3), γ–light absorption coefficient mapping natural conditions.

Attractiveness of firefly i to firefly j decreases with increasing distance. Attractiveness is proportional to intensity of light seen by surrounding individuals and can be defined by formula

$$\beta_{ij}^t(r_{ij}^t) = \beta_{pop} \cdot \frac{1}{1 - e^{-\gamma \cdot (r_{ij}^t)^2}}, \tag{5}$$

where the symbols are: $\beta_{ij}^t(r_{ij}^t)$–attractiveness of firefly i to firefly j in t iteration, r_{ij}^t–distance between firefly i and firefly j defined in (3), γ–light absorption coefficient mapping natural conditions.

Movement of individual is based on conditioned distance to other individuals surrounding it. Firefly will go to most attractive one, measuring intensity of flicker over the distance between them. In given model, natural identification of individuals and their attractiveness defined in (5) depends on light intensity defined in (4) and distance separating them defined in (3). In nature fireflies that are closer not only see themselves better, but also are more attractive to each other. Using these features in the model, calculations remap natural behavior of fireflies. Firefly i motions toward more attractive and brighter (clearer flashing) individual j using information about other individuals denotes formula

$$X_i^{t+1} = X_i^t + (X_j^t - X_i^t) \cdot \beta_{ij}^t(r_{ij}^t) \cdot I_{ij}^t(r_{ij}^t) + \mu \cdot e_i, \tag{6}$$

where the symbols are: X_i^t, X_j^t–points in the picture, $\beta_{ij}^t(r_{ij}^t)$–attractiveness of firefly i to firefly j defined in (5), $I_{ij}^t(r_{ij}^t)$–intensity of light from firefly i

that is received by firefly j defined in (4), r_{ij}^t–distance between fireflies i and j defined in (3), γ–light absorption coefficient mapping natural conditions, μ–coefficient mapping natural random motion of individuals in population, e_i–vector randomly changing position of firefly. Using these facts we build CI to map behavior of fireflies in the process of computer algorithm. Let us now present FA implementation and discuss some examples.

Start,
Define all coefficients: I_{pop}–light intensity, γ–light absorption,
β_{pop}–attractiveness, μ–natural random motion, number of $fireflies$ and
$generation$–number of iterations in the algorithm,
Define fitness function for the algorithm using (7),
Create at random initial population P of $fireflies$ in 2D image,
$t = 0$,
while $t \leq generation$ **do**
    Calculate distance between individuals in population P using (3),
    Calculate light intensity for individuals in population P using (4),
    Calculate attractiveness for individuals in population P using (5),
    Evaluate individuals in population P using (7),
    Create population O: move individuals towards closest, brightest and most
    attractive individual using (6),
    Evaluate individuals in population O using (7),
    Replace δ worst individuals from P with δ best individuals from O,
    The rest of individuals take at random,
    Next generation $t = t + 1$,
end
Values from population P with best fitness are solution,
Stop.

Algorithm 1: FA to classify 2D images key-points

3   Research Results

Algorithm 1 presented in section 2.2 was applied to search for 2D image key-points. Each firefly is representing single pixel (point in image). Population move from pixel to pixel and search for specific areas. In the research we have used simplified fitness function. This function reflects quality of image points as

$$\Phi((x_{i,1}, x_{i,2})) = \varphi_i = \begin{cases} 0.1 \ldots 1 \text{ for points of defined saturation} \\ 0 \qquad\qquad \text{other} \end{cases} , \qquad (7)$$

where symbol φ_i denotes brightness and sharpness of evaluated pixel. This measure reflects value in scale from 0.0 to 1.0, where colors might change from black to white. When fireflies fly in iteration, they pick pixels with best fitness within the range of their flight. Then from all individuals we take δ of them, where fitness function is highest or lowest (depending on experiment). These points (fireflies) are taken to next iteration and the rest of population is taken at random from all image points. Random points selection in each iteration helps to search entire image for the best points of interest.

Simulations were performed for 120 fireflies in 20 generations with set coefficients: $I_{pop} = 0.25$, $\beta_{pop} = 0.15$, $\gamma = 0.3$, $\mu = 0.25$, $\delta = 30\%$. As objects for examinations were taken standard test images, downloaded from open test image databases (see section 2). We have performed experiments on different types of pictures: sharp, blurred, landscapes, human postures and faces. In the research we were looking for special objects concerning brightness and saturation of pixels defined in standard way. Therefore, using FA from section 2.2 we searched for key areas. Each of resulting key-points (pixels) is marked in red. We have provided some close-ups of classified areas for better presentation. First we tried to find dark areas where $\varphi_i = 0$ or $\varphi_i = 0.1$. In second attempt we were looking for bright areas where $\varphi_i = 0.9$ or $\varphi_i = 1$.

3.1 Dark Areas in Images

Fig. 1. Dark key-areas in human posture images: on the left SURF, on the right FA

Dark objects are present in various images. They can represent objects in landscape (constructions, blocks, etc.), natural phenomena (tornadoes, shadows, etc.), human figures or human appearance (clothes, face features, hair, eyes, etc.). In Fig.1 - Fig.4 are presented research results for key-points representing dark areas. We can see that classic FA can easily find dark objects of different shapes like human hair, clothes and some appearance features. It is also efficient in finding some aspects in landscapes. In Fig.3 and Fig.4 are presented research results of searching for shades under constructions or dark parts of machinery. All these areas were found by FA using very small number of fireflies and iterations. Let us now present research results for bright objects localization.

Fig. 2. Dark key-areas in human face images: on the left SURF, on the right FA

Fig. 3. Dark key-areas in architecture images: on the left SURF, on the right FA

Fig. 4. Dark key-areas in machinery images: on the left SURF, on the right FA

3.2   Bright Areas in Images

Bright areas can represent objects in landscape (bright or lightened constructions, machinery, etc.), natural phenomena (clouds, sun, etc.), human figures or human appearance (gray hair, eyes, bright clothing, etc.). In Fig.5 - Fig.8 are presented research results for key-points representing bright areas in images. We can see that classic FA can easily find bright objects of different shapes. FA pointed human faces or bright clothes better than SURF (see Fig. 5 and Fig.6). It is also efficient in locating bright or lightened constructions like machinery or buildings present in Fig.7 and Fig.8.

Fig. 5. Bright key-areas in human posture images: on the left SURF, on the right FA

Fig. 6. Bright key-areas in human face images: on the left SURF, on the right FA

Fig. 7. Bright key-areas in architecture images: on the left SURF, on the right FA

Fig. 8. Bright key-areas in machinery images: on the left SURF, on the right FA

3.3   Conclusions

Application of classic FA allows to easily and reliably find key-areas in examined images. Algorithm efficiency is increased if we are looking for key-points with high contrast in relation to surroundings (see Fig.1 and Fig.3). If we are processing images where many points are of the same valor, classification may be more complicated. There, algorithms must find bright points among many pixels of similar kind or brightest/darkest among many bright/dark ones. If photos are taken during day, all objects of bright properties are lightened in some way (see Fig.8). Similarly for night photos objects are darker. Therefore FA calculations are slightly more complex. For example in Fig.7 we were looking for bright constructions in highly sun-lighted photos. Moreover there are some clouds on the sky. All these made classification process complicated. However similarly to dark areas search, all bright areas were found by classic FA even using even small number of fireflies and iterations.

In conclusions we see that presented FA can find whole areas (objects) of interest, covering them with found key-points. This feature makes it promising tool for AI recognition systems and image classifiers. Moreover calculations performed by FA method are simple. We just use formulas (3) – (6) to calculate position and perform move of each point in examined images.

4   Final Remarks

Application of EC methods, in particular classic FA, to search for key-points allows to easily and reliably select areas of interest. At the same time, EC methods allow to easily explore entire 2D image in search for selected objects without many complicated mathematical operations. Presented idea to apply FA is efficient.

EC methods are efficient in positioning or optimization of different systems, like queuing models (see [29], [31] or [30]). One can find other EC methods efficiently applied in the process of data acquisition (see [8]) or dynamic object positioning (see [24], [25], [26] and [27]). Research presented in this paper show that EC methods, in particular FA, are also excellent to perform process of 2D image classification for AI systems. Therefore similar experiments may be performed using other EC methods, their modifications and other input objects.

References

1. Abeles, P.: Speeding Up SURF. In: Bebis, G., Boyle, R., Parvin, B., Koracin, D., Li, B., Porikli, F., Zordan, V., Klosowski, J., Coquillart, S., Luo, X., Chen, M., Gotz, D. (eds.) ISVC 2013, Part II. LNCS, vol. 8034, pp. 454–464. Springer, Heidelberg (2013)
2. Baonabeau, E., Dorigo, M., Theraulaz, G.: Swarm Intelligence: From Natural to Artificial Systems. Oxford University Press (1999)
3. Bay, H., Ess, A., Tuytelaars, T., Van Gool, L.: SURF: Speeded Up Robust Features. Computer Vision and Image Understanding 110(3), 346–359 (2008)
4. Cabello, J.M., Cejudo, J.M., Luque, M., Ruiz, F., Deb, K., Tewari, R.: Optimization of the Sizing of a Solar Thermal Electricity Plant: Mathematical Programming Versus Genetic Algorithms. In: IEEE Congress on Evolutionary Computation (CEC 2009), pp. 1193–1200. IEEE (2009)
5. Clerc, M., Kennedy, J.: The Particle Swarm-Explosion, Stability and Convergence in a Multidimensional Complex Space. IEEE Transactions on Evolutionary Computation 6(1), 58–73 (2002)
6. dos Santos Coelho, L., de Andrade Bernert, D.L., Mariani, V.C.: A chaotic firefly algorithm applied to reliability-redundancy optimization. In: IEEE Congress on Evolutionary Computation (CEC 2011), pp. 517–521. IEEE (2011)
7. Decker, P., Paulus, D.: Model Based Pose Estimation Using SURF. In: Koch, R., Huang, F. (eds.) ACCV 2010 Workshops, Part II. LNCS, vol. 6469, pp. 11–20. Springer, Heidelberg (2011)
8. Gabryel, M., Woźniak, M., Nowicki, R.K.: Creating learning sets for control systems using an evolutionary method. In: Rutkowski, L., Korytkowski, M., Scherer, R., Tadeusiewicz, R., Zadeh, L.A., Zurada, J.M. (eds.) EC 2012 and SIDE 2012. LNCS, vol. 7269, pp. 206–213. Springer, Heidelberg (2012)

9. Gabryel, M., Nowicki, R.K., Woźniak, M., Kempa, W.M.: Genetic cost optimization of the GI/M/1/N finite-buffer queue with a single vacation policy. In: Rutkowski, L., Korytkowski, M., Scherer, R., Tadeusiewicz, R., Zadeh, L.A., Zurada, J.M. (eds.) ICAISC 2013, Part II. LNCS, vol. 7895, pp. 12–23. Springer, Heidelberg (2013)
10. Gazi, V., Passino, K.M.: Swarm stability and optimization. Springer, Heidelberg (2011)
11. Gómez de Silva Garza, A., Torres Campos Licastro, P.A., Ogando Justo, R.M.: A Hybrid Knowledge-Based And Evolutionary Process Model Of Airport Gate Scheduling. International Journal of Uncertainty, Fuzziness and Knowledge-Based System 12(2), 43–62 (2004)
12. Gómez de Silva Garza, A., Zamora Lores, A.: Evaluating an evolutionary method of design style imitation. Journal Artificial Intelligence for Engineering Design, Analysis and Manufacturing 25(1), 1–13 (2011)
13. Gossow, D., Decker, P., Paulus, D.: An Evaluation of Open Source SURF Implementations. In: Ruiz-del-Solar, J. (ed.) RoboCup 2010. LNCS, vol. 6556, pp. 169–179. Springer, Heidelberg (2010)
14. Guan, Z., Wang, C., Huang, J., Wan, L., Shao, X.: Optimization of Manufacturing Systems using Genetic Search and Muti-Resolution Simulation. In: IEEE International Conference on Control and Automation (ICCA 2010), pp. 1473–1480. IEEE (2010)
15. Hetmaniok, E., Słota, D., Zielonka, A.: Experimental verification of immune recruitment mechanism and clonal selection algorithm applied for solving the inverse problems of pure metal solidification. International Journal of Pure and Applied Mathematics 85(1), 171–178 (2013)
16. Horng, M.H., Liou, R.J.: Multilevel minimum cross entropy threshold selection based on the firefly algorithm. Expert Systems with Applications 38, 14805–14811 (2011)
17. Horng, M.H.: Vector quantization using the firefly algorithm for image compression. Expert Systems with Applications 39, 1078–1091 (2012)
18. Hu, M., Wu, T., Weir, J.D.: An Adaptive Particle Swarm Optimization With Multiple Adaptive Methods. IEEE Transactions on Evolutionary Computation 17(5), 705–720 (2013)
19. Jati, G.K., Suyanto: Evolutionary discrete firefly algorithm for travelling salesman problem. In: Bouchachia, A. (ed.) ICAIS 2011. LNCS (LNAI), vol. 6943, pp. 393–403. Springer, Heidelberg (2011)
20. Kupinski, M.A., Anastasioy, M.A.: Multiobjective Genetic Optimization of Diagnostic Classifiers with Implications for Generating Receiver Operating Characteristic Curves. IEEE Transactions on Medical Imaging 18(8), 675–685 (1999)
21. Lu, M., Wan, M., Xu, F., Wang, X., Zhong, H.: Focused Beam Control for Ultrasound Surgery with Spherical-Section Phased Array: Sound Field Calculation and Genetic Optimization Algorithm. IEEE Transactions on Ultrasonics, Ferroelectrics and Frequency Control 52(8), 1270–1290 (2005)
22. Mehrotra, H., Majhi, B., Gupta, P.: Annular Iris Recognition Using SURF. In: Chaudhury, S., Mitra, S., Murthy, C.A., Sastry, P.S., Pal, S.K. (eds.) PReMI 2009. LNCS, vol. 5909, pp. 464–469. Springer, Heidelberg (2009)
23. Nandy, S., Sarkar, P.P., Das, A.: Analysis of nature-inspired firefly algorithm based back-propagation neural network training. International Journal of Computer Applications 43(22), 8–16 (2012)
24. Nowak, A., Woźniak, M.: Algorithm for optimization of the active module by the use of genetic algorithm. Acta Mechanica Slovaca 3C, 307–316 (2008)

25. Nowak, A., Woźniak, M.: Multiresolution derives analysis of module mechatronical systems. Journal Mechanika 6(74), 45–51 (2008)
26. Nowak, A., Woźniak, M.: Analysis of the active module mechatronical systems. In: International Conference Mechanika 2008, pp. 371–376. Kaunas University of Technology Press (2008)
27. Nowak, A., Woźniak, M.: Optimization of the active vibroisolation system for operator's cabin with the hydropneumatical element. Transactions of the Universities of Košice 3, 113–116 (2009)
28. Rubaai, A., Castro-Sitiriche, M.J., Ofoli, A.R.: DSP-Based Laboratory Implementation of Hybrid Fuzzy-PID Controller Using Genetic Optimization for High-Performance Motor Drives. IEEE Transactions on Industry Applications 44(6), 1977–1986 (2008)
29. Woźniak, M.: On applying cuckoo search algorithm to positioning GI/M/1/N finite-buffer queue with a single vacation policy. In: Mexican International Conference on Artificial Intelligence (MICAI 2013), pp. 59–64. IEEE (2013)
30. Woźniak, M., Kempa, W.M., Gabryel, M., Nowicki, R.K.: A finite-buffer queue with single vacation policy - analytical study with evolutionary positioning. International Journal of Applied Mathematics and Computer Science 24(4) (in-press, 2014)
31. Woźniak, M., Kempa, W.M., Gabryel, M., Nowicki, R.K., Shao, Z.: On Applying Evolutionary Computation Methods to Optimization of Vacation Cycle Costs in Finite-buffer Queue. In: Rutkowski, L., Korytkowski, M., Scherer, R., Tadeusiewicz, R., Zadeh, L.A., Zurada, J.M. (eds.) ICAISC 2014, Part I. LNCS (LNAI), vol. 8467, pp. 480–491. Springer, Heidelberg (2014)
32. Woźniak, M., Połap, D., Marszałek, M.: On handwriting preprocessing for 2D object recognition systems. In: Proceedings of International Conference on Advances in Information Processing and Communication Technology (IPCT 2014). The IRED Digital Seek Library, pp. 46–53 (2014)
33. Woźniak, M., Połap, D.: Basic concept of Cuckoo Search Algorithm for 2D images processing with some research results. In: Proceedings of the 11th International Conference on Signal Processing and Multimedia Applications (SIGMAP 2014). SciTePress - INSTICC (accepted, in press, 2014)
34. Yang, X.-S., Deb, S.: Eagle strategy using Lévy walks and firefly algorithm for stochastic optimization. In: González, J.R., Pelta, D.A., Cruz, C., Terrazas, G., Krasnogor, N. (eds.) NICSO 2010. SCI, vol. 284, pp. 101–111. Springer, Heidelberg (2010)
35. Yang, X.S.: Engineering Optimization: An Introduction with Metaheuristic Applications. John Wiley & Sons, USA (2010)
36. Yang, X.-S.: Firefly algorithms for multimodal optimization. In: Watanabe, O., Zeugmann, T. (eds.) SAGA 2009. LNCS, vol. 5792, pp. 169–178. Springer, Heidelberg (2009)
37. Yang, X.S., Cui, Z.H., Xiao, R.B., Gandomi, A.H., Karamanoglu, M.: Swarm Intelligence and Bio-inspired Computation: Theory and Applications. Elsevier, Waltham (2013)
38. Yousif, A., Abdullah, A.H., Nor, S.M., Abdelaziz, A.A.: Scheduling jobs on grid computing using firefly algorithm. Journal of Theoretical and Applied Information Technology 33(2), 155–164 (2011)

Integrating Linked Data in Mobile Augmented Reality Applications

Silviu Vert and Radu Vasiu

Politehnica University of Timisoara, Timisoara, Romania
{silviu.vert,radu.vasiu}@cm.upt.ro

Abstract. Mobile devices are currently the most popular way of delivering ubiquitous augmented reality experiences. Traditionally, content sources for mobile augmented reality applications can be seen as isolated silos of information, being designed specifically for the intended purpose of the application. Recently, due to the raising in popularity and usage of the Semantic Web technologies and the Linked Data, some efforts have been made to overcome current augmented reality content sources limitations by integrating Linked Data principles and taking advantage of the significant increase in size and quality of the Linked Open Data cloud. This paper presents a literature review of the previous efforts in this respect, while highlighting in detail the limitations of current approaches, the advantages of integrating Linked Data principles in mobile augmented reality applications and up-to-date challenges in regarding this still novel approach. The authors conclude by suggesting some future research directions in this area.

Keywords: Mobile Augmented Reality, Linked Open Data, Semantic Web.

1   Introduction

Mobile augmented reality has seen significant growth in the past few years, due to the proliferation of smart mobile devices. Mobile augmented reality applications have been proved to work successfully in domains ranging from education to gaming and tourism [1]. The most popular mobile augmented reality applications are those that allow the user to explore his surroundings, most of these applications being what we call augmented reality browsers. However, the browsing experience is a quite plain one, as the user can see Points of Interest around him, access them for some more information and click a link that sends them in another application (usually the mobile browser) for full description.

In parallel, the Web of Documents, that seem to be the working base for augmented reality now, has evolved into a Web of Data, due to the adoption of a set of principles and technologies belonging to the Semantic Web [2]. Although the full vision of the Semantic Web hasn't emerged yet, a more practical part of it, named Linked Data [3], has grown in popularity and adoption. Linked Data works on standards of the Semantic Web (a representation standard, RDF [4], and a query mechanism, SPARQL [5]) and is focused on uniquely identifying things in the world, making

G. Dregvaite and R. Damasevicius (Eds.): ICIST 2014, CCIS 465, pp. 324–333, 2014.

their description accessible on the Web and interlinking them to provide more context and information. The Linked Open Data cloud of linked datasets has emerged as a proof of the adoption of such principles.

In this paper, we argue that current augmented reality applications are limited in their content workflow and that Linked (Open) Data can bring some clear advantages in this respect. We review some projects in this area and we present some concerns and discussion points on integrating Linked Data in augmented reality. In the final part we suggest some directions for future research in this field.

2   Related Work

Some of the early efforts in integrating Semantic Web in mobile applications are mSpace Mobile and DBpedia Mobile, although these applications do not leverage augmented reality technologies. mSpace Mobile is an exploring application that keeps track of location and context, while integrating various resources from the Web in a Semantic Web style [6]. The prototype was tested in London, making use of such sources as Open Guide to London, IMDb, BBC and others.

DBpedia Mobile is a client application that makes use of DBpedia content (an effort to extract Linked Data from Wikipedia) to offer a map-based interface for exploring the surroundings of a user [7]. The user can follow links to other related content and can contribute to the Linked Data content by publishing photos or reviews of nearby points of interest.

Augmented reality-based mobile applications that integrate Linked Data principles have started to emerge more clearly in 2010.

In [8], the authors describe an envisioned future of mobile augmented reality and discuss the current limitations in the landscape of mobile augmented reality applications that hinder this desirable future. Linked Data principles, with a focus on the Linked Open Data cloud, are proposed as an appropriate mechanism to override these limitations. Some concerns regarding the implementation of Linked Data, such as the perceived complexity of RDF and SPARQL technologies, along with trust issues, are presented.

A significant exploitation of sources from the Linked Open Data cloud, together with more specialized knowledge sources from the cultural heritage domain, is done in [9]. The application enables the user to search and browse cultural heritage information in Amsterdam with a location-aware mobile device which displays an "enriched local map" of Points of Interest. The authors present a detailed approach for integrating the various Linked Data sources, while highlighting some common challenges, such as harvesting, merging and aligning the information. It is concluded that Linked Open Data sources deliver limited information if processed in isolation, but integrating them, together with some other more specialized repositories, can yield a very informative location-based service.

In 2011, the authors highlight in a position paper [10] the personalization aspect of Point of Interest recommendations that can be achieved through the use of Linked Data principles in a heritage-based augmented reality application. The authors argue that Points of Interest described as Linked Data can benefit from enhanced associated metadata, through the processing of resources that are linked to the Point of Interest, thus enabling recommender systems to personalize and contextualize better. Also, Linked Data-based Points of Interest enable a browsing-like experience for the user, helping him to easily find more information.

The SmartReality project, a nationally funded project in Austria, started at the end of 2010 with the purpose of investigating the combination of augmented reality with Semantic technologies and Web services for a smarter information delivery [11]. The authors propose a general workflow for the envisioned SmartReality platform. According to this workflow, the platform is responsible for filtering, ranking and formatting Semantic Web retrieved content, based on the TOIs (Things of Interest) recognized by the augmented reality mobile client. The TOI is a modified version of the more common POI (Point of Interest) and features only a name, an identifier (unique URI) and a category (also a unique URI). The project aims to reuse current standards for augmented reality and the other technologies involved.

A demonstration of the SmartReality concept is showcased in [12], where an augmented reality client enhances common posters found on the streets with music-related content (e.g. information about the artist, booking a ticket at the concert). An annotation tool is implemented for the poster, to help content creators to link posters or parts of the posters with Semantic-based content or services. A more detailed workflow of the SmartReality platform is presented, along with tools and processes used for retrieving and processing the information. The proof of concept is limited to augmenting street posters with content from just one Linked Data source (play.fm).

In [13], the researchers take a novel approach by arguing for and implementing a model that replicates, aggregates and consolidates Linked Data graphs directly on the mobile device, thus eliminating the need for a separate processing server and an always-on Internet connection. The sensor-based augmented reality mobile application is deployed in a mountain area and uses data sources such as LinkedGeoData, DBpedia and Geonames for exploring the surroundings. The approach is currently limited to a reduced number of possible replicated RDF triples and to a sensor-based tracking, which is sufficient only in some scenarios.

ARCAMA-3D is an augmented reality location-based mobile application that facilitates surroundings discovery by overlaying 3D models of buildings on the real world as seen by the urban user [14]. The 3D models are interconnected with the Linked Open Data cloud, thus extending the information offered to the user but also extending the Linked Open Data cloud itself. The authors propose an ontology called arcama-owl to describe, in space and time, the OiIs (Objects of Interest). In a follow-up to the project [15], a web application is implemented that allows for uploading 3D models and linking them to the Linked Open Data cloud. Also, a mediator ontology is employed for linking information such as the roles of buildings with similar information from DBpedia.

Some projects highlight that further research should focus more on the semantics of the Linked Data, i.e., the augmented reality application should also be able to suggest touristic paths, not only to allow browsing links from the Points of Interest.

Previous projects show successful attempts at integrating Linked Data principles in mobile augmented reality applications, while highlighting common challenges in pursuing this approach. Further research should focus on overcoming such challenges on a wider scale (significant number of Linked Open Data sources integrated) and in more general use cases.

3   Mobile Augmented Reality and Linked Data Integration

3.1   Limitations of Current Content Sources for Augmented Reality Applications

Current efforts in mobile augmented reality applications are targeted towards better image and location recognition and improvements in rendering 3D graphics [1]. Content has always been obtained from fairly simple databases which act as isolated silos of information. This is typically found in augmented reality-based touristic guides, where a user, to find more information about a Point of Interest, has to click a link that opens another application (usually the mobile browser). The content is usually handpicked and very specific for the kind of application that it is made for and cannot be reused.

Popular augmented reality browsers on the marketplace are Wikitude, Junaio and Layar (although the latter one has recently focused on print augmented reality). These browsers issue queries to an augmented reality server, which in turn query a server that stores Points of Interest using a radius filter [16]. Due to this simple form of storing content, more complex functionalities of the augmented reality application are hard to develop (e.g. reasoning). The user can simply see the Points of Interest around him and select one to see some more details (he cannot ask, filter etc.).

Due to the heterogeneous landscape of standards (or lack of) for augmented reality applications [17], integrations and reusability are massively hindered.

3.2   Advantages of Linked Data Integration

Linked Data principles are well-suited for organizing content for mobile augmented reality applications. In [3], the authors present four characteristics of the Web of Data: data is separated from format and presentation; data is self-describing (vocabularies that describe the data can be found via URI dereferencing); data uses a standardized access mechanism (HTTP) and a standardized data model (RDF); and it is open (new data sources are constantly added and can be dynamically integrated).

In his popular W3C design note on Linked Data [18], Tim Berners-Lee issues four simple rules for publishing data: use URIs as names for things; use HTTP URIs so people can look up the names; provide useful information using the standards (RDF, SPARQL) when people look up a URI; include links to other URIs, to enable discovery of more things.

These simple yet effective rules have enabled the constant growth of the so-called Linked Open Data cloud: a significant number of datasets, published by various organizations or individuals, in various domains, with an open license, linked between them. The Linked Open Data cloud has evolved from 12 datasets in May 2007 to 295 datasets in September 2011 [19]. Some datasets have become hubs in the Linked Open Data cloud because they store information for very common concepts (e.g. DBpedia) or location-based information (e.g. Geonames).

The authors identify in [8] three ways through which Linked Data in general and the Linked Open Data cloud in particular can enhance augmented reality: through dynamic selection and integration of data sources, through enabling the utilization of a wide range of contextual data and by offering the user a Web-like browsing experience in augmented reality applications.

Previous projects have successfully demonstrated the integration of various datasets from the Linked Open Data cloud in an augmented reality application [9, 13, 14]. This integration is possible due to common encoding and standards (RDF, RDFS, OWL and SPARQL).

Moreover, easy discovery of new datasets to be integrated is enabled through various means, such as semantic search engines (e.g. Sindice), follow-your-nose principle and consulting catalogs for dataset metadata (e.g. CKAN) [20].

Previous projects have also demonstrated the possibility for the user to find additional information by following the links that are attached to the Points of Interest. Due to the way that Linked Data is working, the augmented reality application is able to show bits of additional data inside the view of the application, without requiring the user to leave the application and to open a new application (usually the mobile browser).

The following scenario reveals the advantages of integrating Linked Open Data in mobile augmented reality applications for the end user:

Maria is for the first time in Palermo, Italy, and she is interested in local cultural touristic attractions. Luckily, her augmented reality-enabled glasses can help her to explore the surroundings in every way she desires. She starts her journey in front of the cathedral. While admiring the outstanding building, she scrolls through the history of the cathedral as documented on Wikipedia. She would like to visit it, but unfortunately it is closed. She easily checks the timetable, as it was published on the open data portal of the City Hall, and finds out that she can visit it the next day in the morning. Maria is curios which other buildings nearby have so many architectural styles as the cathedral (norman, gothic, baroque and neoclassical). The augmented reality application suggests some nearby buildings that fit the criteria. Maria chooses one of them and the application highlights on her surroundings the shortest route to get there, using information from OpenStreetMap. As she walks towards this destination, she is able to see photos of how the streets of Palermo looked like in the past, superimposed on the actual view of the city.

Not only augmented reality applications benefit from the Linked Open Data cloud, but the vice versa is also true. There is an increasing amount of content created for augmented reality applications. If this content is linked into the Linked Open Data cloud, then the Linked Open Data cloud grows in size and diversity and this benefits Linked Data application developers.

3.3   Some Concerns and Discussion Points

While applying Linked Data principles to augmented reality can yield great benefits, there are some issues that need to be taken into consideration.

One of the biggest advantages of the Linked Open Data cloud, its significant size, might easily become a disadvantage, if content is used in a mobile application without specific filtering. This is because a query in the Linked Open Data cloud might yield a great number of Points of Interest around the user, which would overwhelm an experience typically provided on a small screen device. Filtering which takes into account the context (e.g. what the user is doing, what preferences he has set in his social network) is certainly necessary.

A lot of issues regard the inherent nature of Linked Open Data. Datasets are heterogeneous in terms of vocabularies used and have overlapping information. Common Linked Data publishing workflows include vocabulary mapping, interlinking datasets and cleansing data for an integrated dataset to be obtained. Entity resolution issues (deciding if two entities from different datasets are referring to the same thing or not) are worsened by ambiguity, which can be of two types: name ambiguities (due to typos, different languages and homonyms used) and structural ambiguities (inconsistent relationships to other entities). These can be resolved using ontology matching techniques [21]. Content itself can differ between datasets that have overlapping information, and integrating them involves taking a decision whether to use one source or the other.

Not only integrating various datasets can raise issues, but also the datasets in isolation, because "authors that work with user generated Linked Open Data have to deal with duplication, misclassification, mismatching and data enrichment issues" [22].

In [9], the researchers report on having to deal with multiple Semantic Web challenges while integrating sources from the Linked Open Data cloud for the cultural heritage augmented reality browser: different schemas, different labeling conventions, different geodata, errors in geodata and conflicts in typing. For the schema matching, the authors had to create around 200 mapping rules by hand. The paper reports that it typically found discrepancies of 20m, in some cases even hundreds of meters, in coordinates of the same location, as reported by various sources in the Linked Open Data cloud. Inaccuracy of the geodata required a range of at least 35 meters in order to find all possible candidates for a Point of Interest. These results indicate that a more sophisticated algorithm for integration of spatial information is required.

In [13], the researchers also report on differences in content retrieved from similar-domain Linked Open Data sources, which required aggregation and consolidation of the data.

Other Semantic Web specific issues are trust, provenance, quality, relevance, privacy and licensing. For dealing with the provenance aspect, developers can use the PROV ontology proposed by the W3C [23].

Another significant discussion point is the architectural pattern for integrating Linked Data in the augmented reality application. Three architectural patterns are

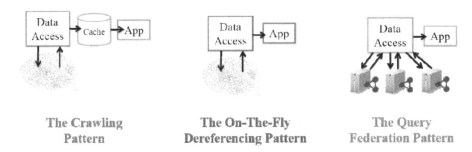

The Crawling
Pattern

The On-The-Fly
Dereferencing Pattern

The Query
Federation Pattern

Fig. 1. Linked Data architectural patterns [25]

presented in [24]: the Crawling Pattern (sources are crawled and cached in a single datastore), the On-The-Fly Dereferencing Pattern (URIs are dereferenced on the spot) and the Query Federation Pattern (a query is issued to a fixed known set of sources). The architectural patterns are depicted in Figure 2.

In augmented reality situations, where registration with the real world needs to happen in real-time, the first pattern should be the preferred one, although it has the disadvantage that the information is not always up-to-date. Depending on the use case, this might be a problem or not. In [9], the authors report on retrieving the RDF statements on-the-spot, although in some cases it takes even 50 seconds. They believe this might not be a problem if the content is preloaded as the application tries to guess in advance which Points of Interest the user is approaching.

4   Future Research Directions

Given the high potential of integrating Linked Data in mobile augmented reality scenarios, we envision some trends in this direction:

— **Towards Linked Open Repositories for augmented reality content.** We should be able to publish augmented reality content that we create to open repositories. At the same time, we should be able to easily access content that someone else created, from such open repositories, so we don't have to recreate it [26]. Such repositories would best work using Linked Data principles and technologies, because they offer the framework for heterogeneous content to be queried, processed and published using the same standards.
— **Smarter integration of geodata.** We imagine an effort towards integrating geodata at a large scale, with algorithms for schema alignment and entity reconciliation that have good performance and precision. Integration should work flawlessly, not only with very simple geographic objects, like coordinates for a point, but also with more complex geometries (such as lines and polygons). The framework that enables this integration should support dynamically adding or removing of datasets, as well as ranking the datasets, based on data quality and relevance for the task that the user has at hand.

- **Towards a generic augmented reality-based linked data browser.** There are several Linked Data browsers developed as research projects, such as Tabulator, Disco and OpenLink [27]. We envision an augmented reality-based Linked Data browser which people would use to browse content, described using Linked Data principles, that is geo-tagged around them. This would benefit the Linked Data domain, as it will allow users to browse an otherwise unfamiliar machine-readable content in a more natural and engaging way.
- **Towards more personalization and contextualization.** Linked Data has the potential of offering a huge amount of information. Even when using closed data-bases for content delivery, the number of Points of Interest returned to the user can be overwhelming. Semantic Web and Linked Data principles can enable reasoning over the data, such that results of users' queries can be more relevant. Results can be also personalized, for example by leveraging the FOAF profile of the user.

5   Conclusions

Current approaches in content delivery for mobile augmented reality applications have some limitations due to content being stored in isolated silos of information. Linked Data principles and technologies can aid in this respect, but researchers need to address some concerns that are related either to the inherent nature of Linked (Open) Data or directly to the integration of Linked Data in augmented reality applications.

We have presented in this paper the current limitations of mobile augmented reality applications regarding the content used, along with the Linked Data principles, mainly openness and standardization, that can help overcome the current issues. We highlighted some discussion points regarding the interconnection of these two fields and we pointed out to some concerns, like trust, quality and integration, which should be addressed in this endeavor. We have reviewed several projects that seem to confirm these concerns.

We suggest some future research directions in this area, namely linked open repositories for augmented reality content, smarter integration of geodata, a generic augmented reality-based linked data browser and more effort towards personalization and contextualization. These directions should highlight even more the potential of integrating Linked Data in augmented reality applications.

Acknowledgement. This work was partially supported by the strategic grant POSDRU/159/1.5/S/137070 (2014) of the Ministry of National Education, Romania, co-financed by the European Social Fund – Investing in People, within the Sectoral Operational Programme Human Resources Development 2007-2013.

References

1. Huang, Z., Hui, P., Peylo, C., Chatzopoulos, D.: Mobile Augmented Reality Survey: A Bottom-up Approach. arXiv preprint arXiv:1309.4413 (2013)
2. Shadbolt, N., Hall, W., Berners-Lee, T.: The semantic web revisited. IEEE Intelligent Systems 21, 96–101 (2006)
3. Bizer, C., Heath, T., Berners-Lee, T.: Linked Data - The Story So Far. International Journal on Semantic Web and Information Systems 5, 1–22 (2009)
4. W3C RDF Working Group: RDF 1.1 Primer,
   http://www.w3.org/TR/2014/NOTE-rdf11-primer-20140225/
5. W3C SPARQL Working Group: SPARQL 1.1 Overview,
   http://www.w3.org/TR/2013/REC-sparql11-overview-20130321/
6. Wilson, M.L., Russell, A., Smith, D.A., Owens, A., et al.: mspace mobile: A mobile application for the semantic web (2005)
7. Becker, C., Bizer, C.: Exploring the geospatial semantic web with dbpedia mobile. Web Semantics: Science, Services and Agents on the World Wide Web 7, 278–286 (2009)
8. Reynolds, V., Hausenblas, M., Polleres, A., Hauswirth, M., Hegde, V.: Exploiting linked open data for mobile augmented reality. W3C Workshop: Augmented Reality on the Web. p. 12 (June 2010)
9. van Aart, C., Wielinga, B., van Hage, W.R.: Mobile cultural heritage guide: Location-aware semantic search. In: Cimiano, P., Pinto, H.S. (eds.) EKAW 2010. LNCS, vol. 6317, pp. 257–271. Springer, Heidelberg (2010)
10. Hegde, V., Reynolds, V., Parreira, J.X., Hauswirth, M.: Utililising Linked Data for Personalized Recommendation of POI's. Presented at the International AR Standards Meeting, Barcelona, Spain (2011)
11. Nixon, L., Grubert, J., Reitmayr, G.: SmartReality: Augmented Reality + Services + Semantics. Presented at the International AR Standards Meeting, Barcelona, Spain (2011)
12. Nixon, L.J., Grubert, J., Reitmayr, G., Scicluna, J.: SmartReality: Integrating the Web into Augmented Reality. In: I-SEMANTICS (Posters & Demos), pp. 48–54 (2012)
13. Zander, S., Chiu, C., Sageder, G.: A computational model for the integration of linked data in mobile augmented reality applications. In: Proceedings of the 8th International Conference on Semantic Systems, pp. 133–140. ACM (2012)
14. Aydin, B., Gensel, J., Genoud, P., Calabretto, S., Tellez, B.: Extending Augmented Reality Mobile Application with Structured Knowledge from the LOD Cloud. In: 3rd International Workshop on Information Management for Mobile Applications. Citeseer (2013)
15. Aydin, B., Gensel, J., Genoud, P., Calabretto, S., Tellez, B.: An architecture for surroundings discovery by linking 3D models and LOD cloud. In: Proceedings of the Second ACM SIGSPATIAL International Workshop on Mobile Geographic Information Systems, pp. 9–16. ACM (2013)
16. Butchart, B.: Augmented reality for smartphones (2011)
17. Perey, C., Engelke, T., Reed, C.: Current Status of Standards for Augmented Reality. In: Alem, L., Huang, W. (eds.) Recent Trends of Mobile Collaborative Augmented Reality Systems, pp. 21–38. Springer, New York (2011)
18. Berners-Lee, T.: Linked Data - Design Issues,
    http://www.w3.org/DesignIssues/LinkedData.html
19. Cyganiak, R., Jentzsch, A.: Linking open data cloud diagram. LOD Community (2011),
    http://lod-cloud.net/
20. Hausenblas, M.: Exploiting Linked Data to Build Web Applications. IEEE Internet Computing 13, 68–73 (2009)

21. Shvaiko, P., Euzenat, J.: Ontology matching: state of the art and future challenges. IEEE Transactions on Knowledge and Data Engineering 25, 158–176 (2013)
22. Emaldi, M., Pena, O., Lazaro, J., Vanhecke, S., Mannens, E., Lopez-de-Ipina, D., et al.: To Trust, or not to Trust: Highlighting the Need for Data Provenance in Mobile Apps for Smart Cities. In: Proceedings of the 3rd International Workshop on Information Management for Mobile Applications, pp. 68–71. Riva del Garda, Italy (2013)
23. De Nies, T., Coppens, S., Verborgh, R., Vander Sande, M., Mannens, E., Van de Walle, R., Michaelides, D., Moreau, L.: Easy Access to Provenance: an Essential Step Towards Trust on the Web. In: 2013 IEEE 37th Annual Computer Software and Applications Conference Workshops (COMPSACW), pp. 218–223. IEEE (2013)
24. Heath, T., Bizer, C.: Linked Data: Evolving the Web into a Global Data Space. Synthesis Lectures on the Semantic Web: Theory and Technology 1, 1–136 (2011)
25. EUCLID project: Module 5 - Building Linked Data Applications (2013), http://www.slideshare.net/EUCLIDproject/building-linked-data-applications-27768679
26. Craig, A.B.: Understanding Augmented Reality: Concepts and Applications. Elsevier Science (2013)
27. Bizer, C., Heath, T., Idehen, K., Berners-Lee, T.: Linked data on the web (LDOW2008). In: Proceedings of the 17th International Conference on World Wide Web, pp. 1265–1266. ACM (2008)

Relevant Aspects for the Integration of Linked Data in Mobile Augmented Reality Applications for Tourism

Silviu Vert and Radu Vasiu

Politehnica University of Timisoara, Timisoara, Romania
{silviu.vert,radu.vasiu}@cm.upt.ro

Abstract. Mobile augmented reality applications have seen tremendous growth in recent years and tourism is one of the fields in which this set of technologies has been proved to be a natural fit. Augmented reality has the potential of enhancing the surroundings of the tourist in a meaningful way. In order to provide personalized and rich content for the augmented reality application, researchers have explored the use of Semantic Web and especially Linked Data principles and technologies. In this paper we review existing projects at the intersection of these technologies and current aspects, not necessarily specific, but highly relevant to the integration of Linked Open Data in mobile augmented reality applications for tourism. In this respect, we discuss approaches in the area of geodata integration, quality of the open data, provenance information and trust. We conclude with recommendations regarding future research in this area.

Keywords: Linked Open Data, Mobile Augmented Reality, Tourism, Ontology Matching, Geographic Information Systems.

1   Introduction

Mobile augmented reality has emerged as the most popular and convenient form of augmented reality, mainly due to the proliferation of mobile devices and ubiquitous computing. Several fields of use have proven to be proper for deployment of mobile augmented reality technologies. We argue for the natural fit of mobile augmented reality applications in the field of tourism and we present some research and commercial projects in this area. Next, we address the issue of content sources for mobile augmented reality applications. The usual approach of developers and content publishers in this respect is to use isolated databases for content, which limits the information depth of surroundings exploration for tourists. We identify the benefits of exploiting Linked Data principles and technologies for enriching content in mobile augmented reality applications for tourists and explore some projects that tackle this approach.

Several aspects have been identified in the literature as being relevant to Linked Data integration. We place this aspects in the context of mobile augmented reality applications for tourism and present current efforts in research in these areas. The most important aspect is geodata integration i.e. ontology matching and entity disambiguation

G. Dregvaite and R. Damasevicius (Eds.): ICIST 2014, CCIS 465, pp. 334–345, 2014.
© Springer International Publishing Switzerland 2014

during integration of several heterogeneous and overlapping datasets from the Linked Open Data cloud, with the purpose of providing a consolidated, enriched and more relevant unique dataset for tourism purposes. Other discussed aspects are the assessment of the quality of the data, usage of provenance information and inference of trust. We conclude by suggesting some further research issues in the reviewed domain.

2   Related Work and Arguments for Linked Data Integration

2.1   Mobile Augmented Reality Applications for Tourism

Mobile augmented reality has seen tremendous growth in the recent years. The set of technologies commonly called mobile augmented reality is deployed successfully in a number of fields, such as tourism and navigation, entertainment and advertisement, training and education, assembly and maintenance and so on [1].

Due to its inherent strong alignment with the real world [2], mobile augmented reality is well suited for enabling location-aware applications and services. Also, mobile augmented reality applications provide the ground for innovative services within the ecosystems of smart cities [3].

Mobile augmented reality is a natural fit for tourism applications and services, being regarded as having a significant impact in this area [4], due to its ability of enhancing the surroundings of the tourist [5]. A recent online survey [6] showed that location based services, augmented reality browsers and tourism and travel applications are the most used types of augmented reality applications, after games and entertainment applications based on these technologies.

Additional benefits of augmented reality in urban heritage tourism are presented in [7].

One of the first experiments in exploring the surrounding urban landscape with a mobile augmented reality system was the Touring Machine [8], followed by the MARS system [9].

Researchers propose in [10] a system called Wikireality which consumes text information and images from Wikipedia and overlays them on nearby Points of Interest. A more complex project is pursued in [11], where the authors describe a large-scale mobile augmented reality system that overlays 3D footprints of buildings and their name on top of urban buildings.

Several similar applications have also been developed in the commercial area. An overview [12] of mobile augmented reality applications for tourism classifies them as augmented reality browsers (such as Layar, Junaio and Wikitude), dedicated augmented reality applications (such as Acrossair, Augmented Reality UK and WhereMark) and augmented reality view-enabled applications (such as mTrip, TripWolf and Yelp).

A popular category is composed of mobile augmented reality applications that display historic images on top of the current landscape. Well known projects are PhillyHistory in Philadelphia [13], StreetMuseum in London [14] and "Paris, then and now" [15].

Cultural tourism is a subdomain that is also proper for deployment of augmented reality technologies. One of the first projects in this area is PRISMA [5], an interactive visualization system that is a combination of tourist binoculars and augmented reality. In [16], the authors describe a tracking framework that uses different tracking flows for more efficient identification of targets, to be used in augmented reality cultural heritage tours. The LIMES project is a recent augmented reality platform developed to raise awareness and present in an innovative way the ancient Roman Frontier called the Roman Limes [17]. The Points of Interest are added using the backend of the platform and are made available to users through popular augmented reality browsers.

2.2   Content-Related Limitations of Mobile Augmented Reality Applications

The plethora of research projects and commercial applications leveraging augmented reality technologies in the mobile tourism field has shown the benefits of implementing this set of technologies, but has also highlighted some challenges that need to be further tackled.

Content is one of them and is "a critical aspect for acceptance" [18], revealed a usability evaluation of the MobiAR project. The study pointed out that, when selecting a Point of Interest, people would like to be shown how to get there (route navigation) and would like to see additional information (like parking and opening hours).

This type of functionality is limited by the nature of content sources that augmented reality applications for tourism (and not only) usually use today, and for which projects like MobiAR [19] and LIMES [17] are representative: isolated silos of information, typically relational database management systems, which store only a few attributes about the Points of Interest. To provide the users with more information, the Points of Interest reference a link that typically opens another application on the mobile device (e.g. the mobile browser). Thus, the immersive experience in the augmented reality application is discontinued.

Moreover, popular augmented reality browsers (Junaio, Wikitude) consume Point of Interest information using different standards [20], which highlights the "lack of interoperability across mobile platforms" is this respect [21].

More flexible strategies are required for managing data sources and for making them consumable by different applications [1].

2.3   Linked Data in Mobile Augmented Reality Applications for Tourism

There is a trend to develop augmented reality applications that integrate heterogeneous sources of content, which have various degrees of data quality (ranging from user-generated data to open government data). [22]

This type of openness and integration can be achieved by leveraging Linked Data [23] principles and technologies. These can help by dynamically selecting and integrating data from various sources, thus providing enriched content, by means of enabling the exploitation of more contextual information, not only location, and by creating a Web-like browsing experience for the augmented reality application user [24].

The authors describe in [25] a framework in which an augmented reality application for urban navigation features content that is organized according to Semantic Web principles. Reasoning with OWL takes place to help the user navigate in the urban space.

mSpace Mobile [26] and DBpedia Mobile [27] are some early non-augmented reality-enabled applications that allow the user to discover Points of Interest that are retrieved and integrated from Semantic Web sources. In [24] the researchers propose a vision for integrating Linked Open Data content in mobile augmented reality applications, which might help these applications to overcome some of their limitations.

In [28] a mobile augmented reality application is proposed which facilitates surroundings discovery in an urban setting by overlaying 3D models of buildings on the real world. The 3D models are connected in the Linked Open Data cloud. The authors describe in [29] a framework and an implementation, the WantEat application, which provides an augmented reality browsing experience for accessing ontological described knowledge mainly in the field of gastronomic tourism.

Several augmented reality projects have been developed also in the field of cultural tourism with the help of Linked Data principles.

In Amsterdam, the researchers developed an application [30] to allow users to search and browse cultural heritage information that is retrieved and integrated from the Linked Open Data cloud and from specialized knowledge sources in the cultural heritage domain of the city.

In [31], the authors implement an augmented reality application for exploring cultural heritage sites such as popular cemeteries. They use content sources from scraped websites and DBpedia.

Integrating Linked Open Data in location-based mobile applications for touristic purposes (albeit not augmented reality enabled) is pursued also in [32] and [33]. The latter describes Telemaco, a client-server system in which the server integrates various Linked Open Data sources of content and information from social networks to offer personalized recommendations to users.

3   Relevant Aspects for Linked Data Integration

The most important type of data to be integrated in mobile augmented reality tourism applications is geodata, which is currently the backbone of the Linked Open Data

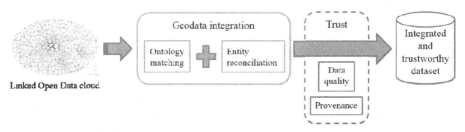

Fig. 1. Highlighting of relevant aspects for Linked Data integration in mobile augmented reality applications for tourism

cloud [34]. Also, due to the nature of open data in general, of considerable importance is the quality of the data, along with provenance, both of which trigger trust. These key concepts are depicted in Figure 1.

3.1   Integrating Geodata

Geographic information is at the center of the biggest category of information on the Web nowadays. A popular quote says that "80% of all information is geographically referenced". Due to their inherent nature, augmented reality applications treat geographic information aspects as first class citizens of the Web.

There is a trend to integrate more and more the fields of Geographic Information Systems and Augmented Reality, as this helps to reduce the gap between the real world and the virtual world by means of projecting the virtual world in space and time [35].

There are many popular sources of geographic information in the Linked Open Data cloud, such as Geonames, DBpedia and LinkedGeoData. A developer of mobile augmented reality applications, wishing to integrate several of these resources so they can complement each other, is facing a challenge due to the sources using different vocabularies to describe the data and due to duplicate records that appear after the data integration.

The first issue, of aligning different vocabularies, is known in literature as ontology matching and applies to all fields, not only to geographic information [36].

In [37], the authors enumerate 15 translation/mapping patterns that are useful in aligning ontologies. Some tools can assist in semi-automatically matching ontologies, such as the COMA++ tool [38]. Integrating multiple distributed ontologies is likely to yield inconsistencies. One example of a tool that can aid with this type of issues is RaDON [39].

The second issue is called in literature entity reconciliation and aims to identify and merge data that refers to the same real world feature.

The problem of integrating several location-based services has been studied in the literature before the proliferation of the Linked Open Data. Researchers present in [40] and [41] uncertainty issues in fusing information from various location-based services and categorize integration issues as: geographic integration (differences in geographic representation – points/line/polyline/volume – and in the reported position), place name integration (differences in spelling of location names) and semantic integration (differences in describing the data/metadata).

The author proposes in [42] a supervised machine learning approach for duplicate detection and data consolidation over gazetteer records. Features that help link the records between them are categorized by: place name similarity, geospatial footprint similarity, place type similarity, semantic relationships similarity and temporal footprint similarity.

The expansion of the Linked Open Data cloud led to early work on aligning geographic datasets, such as on interconnecting LinkedGeoData and Geonames based on type information, spatial distance and name similarity, which allow single access to an integrated dataset and validating the information, one against the other [43].

A more complex solution for aligning geographic datasets is proposed in [44–46]. It is based on constructing restriction classes using owl:sameAs links. It is well suited also for enhancing a poorly described ontology with the help of a richly described one.

In [47], the researchers publish two geospatial datasets, GADM (Global Administrative Areas) and NUTS (Nomenclature of territorial units for statistics), using a proposed NeoGeo vocabulary and integrate them with other datasets from the Linked Open Data cloud. They describe an algorithm for finding equivalent geometric shapes across multiple datasets.

The creation of such vocabularies as NeoGeo was determined by the lack of a standardized RDF vocabulary for managing geographic information in the Linked Data space. In the meantime, a W3C working group standardized GeoSPARQL, which is comprised of a small ontology for representing features and geometries and SPARQL query predicates and functions [48].

However, the implementation of GeoSPARQL in current triple stores is still in its infancy. A recent benchmark [49] on geospatial capabilities of current triple stores reveals the need for huge optimization in several aspects, such as performance of spatial indexing, query optimization and GeoSPARQL compliance.

A survey of the current geodata providers in the Linked Open Data cloud and their data modelling approach is presented in [50]. Furthermore, the authors propose an alignment process using the GeOnto vocabulary, focusing on interlinking French geodata with the Linked Open Data cloud.

The researchers describe in [51] the process of integrating several Linked Open Data and non-Linked Open Data sources, with the potential of using the integrated dataset in an augmented reality touristic application.

Further research is needed to improve precision and performance for successful integration of geographic datasets on a large scale. In the case of a mobile augmented reality tourism application, the data needs to be integrated and cached in a datastore. The time cost for integrating the data in real-time would be too high for augmented reality applications, which require registration with the real world with almost no delays for a proper experience. Even with this approach, the development of such an application is still hindered by the poor implementation of the GeoSPARQL standard in current triple stores.

3.2   Data Quality

Exploitation of Linked Data sources should take into account the quality of data. This is even more important in such areas as mobile augmented reality applications for tourism, as the tourist relies on the data for real-time exploration of the surrounding environment.

Linked Data assumes an open-world philosophy according to which anyone can say anything about anything [52]. This leads to issues such as inconsistencies in data provided for the same entity by different sources, concerns of timeliness, completeness and accuracy, just to name a few. A comprehensive list of quality criteria for

Linked Data sources, grouped by content, representation, usage and system, is proposed in [53].

Corroborated with limitations induced by the shallow expressivity of the published knowledge and the heterogeneity of the describing schemas, Linked Data runs the risk to become "merely more data" [54], in the absence of efforts to overcome these challenges.

Various approaches have been identified to tackle these issues. For example, in [55, 56], the authors describe a framework to identify data quality problems, such as missing literal values, false literal values and functional dependency violations, using generic SPARQL queries. Also, researchers have proposed vocabularies for data quality management, such as in [57].

Attempts to quantify the data quality of user-generated content have been pursued in the literature. Of interest to mobile tourism applications is, for example, the comparison between proprietary geodata and Volunteered Geographic Information (a term coined by [58]), such as OpenStreetMap (with its Linked Data equivalent LinkedGeoData). Several papers [59, 60] have reported on the high reliability of Volunteered Geographical Information in urban centers, a finding that is confirmed by the fact that the quality of data increases with the number of contributors [61].

Data quality cannot be always assessed in absolute terms. A pragmatic approach is to evaluate the data quality based on the *fitness for use* principle, which takes into account the specific task that is to be achieved [62]. This principle should be further investigated for mobile augmented reality applications for tourism.

3.3   Provenance and Trust

Along with general data quality factors, provenance is one of the main triggers for trust in Web content [63]. Although some tools for tracking provenance are hardwired in Linked Data (such as dereferenceable HTTP URIs), the ever increasing integration of various heterogeneous datasets makes it harder to keep track of detailed provenance metadata. This is the case also for mobile augmented reality applications in the field of tourism.

Usually, provenance refers to keeping track of the workflow that led to the creation of the data. In today's Web of Data, it is important to also keep track of data access information, meaning metadata about the providers of the data and the way they deliver it [64].

The Open Provenance Model [65], a vocabulary that describes provenance using the terms "artifact", "process" and "agent", is used in applications such as El Viajero, a platform for managing Linked Data in the travelling domain, which integrates several heterogeneous datasets [66].

The W3C Provenance Working Group recently proposed the PROV standard for dealing with provenance information. In [67], the authors discuss the PROV standard and propose an implementation of Tim Berners-Lee's "Oh, yeah?" button [68]. Also, the application of the PROV standard in modelling uncertain provenance is discussed in [69].

4   Conclusion

Mobile augmented reality is a promising set of technologies for the tourism field and the exploitation of Linked Data in resulting applications can yield concrete benefits. We explored several aspects relevant to this exploitation, namely integration of geodata, data quality, provenance and trust.

Further research should focus on a large scale integration approach for geodata, keeping precision and performance of ontology matching and entity disambiguation algorithms relevant for a tourist's experience. The quantity of content is ever increasing in the Linked Open Data cloud and care must be taken not to overload the augmented experience with information. The quality of the data in the Linked Open Data cloud is still a debatable issue. Thus, the integration approach should be able to prioritize between content sources based on assessed quality. The same judgment applies to provenance information, all together influencing the trust in the data. Successfully tackling this issues should lead to a fulfilling augmented reality experience for the tourists.

Acknowledgement. This work was partially supported by the strategic grant POSDRU/159/1.5/S/137070 (2014) of the Ministry of National Education, Romania, co-financed by the European Social Fund – Investing in People, within the Sectoral Operational Programme Human Resources Development 2007-2013.

References

1. Huang, Z., Hui, P., Peylo, C., Chatzopoulos, D.: Mobile Augmented Reality Survey: A Bottom-up Approach. arXiv preprint arXiv:1309.4413 (2013)
2. Azuma, R.T.: A survey of augmented reality. Presence 6, 355–385 (1997)
3. Komninos, N., Schaffers, H., Pallot, M.: Developing a policy roadmap for smart cities and the future internet. In: eChallenges e-2011 Conference Proceedings, IIMC International Information Management Corporation. IMC International Information Management Corporation (2011)
4. Gretzel, U., Law, R., Fuchs, M.: Information and Communication Technologies in Tourism 2010: Proceedings of the International Conference, Lugano, Switzerland, February 10-12. Springer (2010)
5. Fritz, F., Susperregui, A., Linaza, M.: Enhancing cultural tourism experiences with augmented reality technologies. In: The 6th International Symposium on Virtual Reality, Archaeology and Cultural Heritage VAST, pp. 1–6 (2005)
6. Tutunea, M.F.: Augmented Reality - State of Knowledge, Use and Experimentation. USV Annals of Economics & Public Administration. 13 (2013)
7. Jung, T., Han, D.-I.: Augmented Reality (AR) in Urban Heritage Tourism. e-Review of Tourism Research (2014)
8. Feiner, S., MacIntyre, B., Höllerer, T., Webster, A.: A touring machine: Prototyping 3D mobile augmented reality systems for exploring the urban environment. Personal Technologies 1, 208–217 (1997)

9. Höllerer, T., Feiner, S., Terauchi, T., Rashid, G., Hallaway, D.: Exploring MARS: developing indoor and outdoor user interfaces to a mobile augmented reality system. Computers & Graphics 23, 779–785 (1999)

10. Gray, D., Kozintsev, I., Wu, Y., Haussecker, H.: WikiReality: augmenting reality with community driven websites. In: IEEE International Conference on Multimedia and Expo, ICME 2009, pp. 1290–1293. IEEE (2009)

11. Takacs, G., El Choubassi, M., Wu, Y., Kozintsev, I.: 3D mobile augmented reality in urban scenes. In: 2011 IEEE International Conference on Multimedia and Expo (ICME), pp. 1–4. IEEE (2011)

12. Yovcheva, Z., Buhalis, D., Gatzidis, C.: Overview of Smartphone Augmented Reality Applications for Tourism. E-review of Tourism Research 10 (2012)

13. Boyer, D., Marcus, J.: Implementing mobile augmented reality applications for cultural institutions. Museums and the Web, Philadelphia, USA (2011)

14. Streetmuseum: Q&A with Museum of London, http://blog.variousbits.net/2010/06/01/streetmuseum-qa-with-vicky-lee-museum-of-london/

15. Hutchings, E.: Time Travel Through Paris With Augmented Reality App, http://www.psfk.com/2013/07/paris-travel-augmented-reality-app.html

16. Seo, B.-K., Kim, K., Park, J., Park, J.-I.: A tracking framework for augmented reality tours on cultural heritage sites. In: Proceedings of the 9th ACM SIGGRAPH Conference on Virtual-Reality Continuum and its Applications in Industry, pp. 169–174. ACM (2010)

17. Dorrzapf, L., Kratz, N., Schrenk, M.: LIMES App - Mobile applications as an opportunity for cultural tourism along the Roman Limes in Europe. Presented at the International Conference on Cultural Heritage and New Technologies, Vienna (2012)

18. Linaza, M.T., Marimón, D., Carrasco, P., Álvarez, R., Montesa, J., Aguilar, S.R., Diez, G.: Evaluation of mobile augmented reality applications for tourism destinations. In: Information and Communication Technologies in Tourism 2012, pp. 260–271. Springer (2012)

19. Marimon, D., Sarasua, C., Carrasco, P., Álvarez, R., Montesa, J., Adamek, T., Romero, I., Ortega, M., Gascó, P.: MobiAR: Tourist Experiences through Mobile Augmented Reality. In: Telefonica Research and Development, Barcelona, Spain (2010)

20. Butchart, B.: Augmented reality for smartphones (2011)

21. Kounavis, C.D., Kasimati, A.E., Zamani, E.D.: Enhancing the Tourism Experience through Mobile Augmented Reality: Challenges and Prospects. International Journal of Engineering Business Management 4 (2012)

22. Emmanouilidis, C., Koutsiamanis, R.-A., Tasidou, A.: Mobile guides: Taxonomy of architectures, context awareness, technologies and applications. Journal of Network and Computer Applications 36, 103–125 (2013)

23. Bizer, C., Heath, T., Berners-Lee, T.: Linked Data - The Story So Far. International Journal on Semantic Web and Information Systems 5, 1–22 (2009)

24. Reynolds, V., Hausenblas, M., Polleres, A., Hauswirth, M., Hegde, V.: Exploiting linked open data for mobile augmented reality. In: W3C Workshop: Augmented Reality on the Web, p. 12 (June 2010)

25. Schmalstieg, D., Reitmayr, G.: The World as a User Interface: Augmented Reality for Ubiquitous Computing. Presented at the Central European Multimedia and Virtual Reality Conference (2005)

26. Wilson, M.L., Russell, A., Smith, D.A., Owens, A., et al.: mspace mobile: A mobile application for the semantic web (2005)

27. Becker, C., Bizer, C.: Exploring the geospatial semantic web with dbpedia mobile. Web Semantics: Science, Services and Agents on the World Wide Web 7, 278–286 (2009)
28. Aydin, B., Gensel, J., Genoud, P., Calabretto, S., Tellez, B.: Extending Augmented Reality Mobile Application with Structured Knowledge from the LOD Cloud. In: 3rd International Workshop on Information Management for Mobile Applications. Citeseer (2013)
29. Grillo, P., Likavec, S., Lombardi, I.: Using mobile phone cameras to interact with ontological data. In: Moreno-Díaz, R., Pichler, F., Quesada-Arencibia, A. (eds.) EUROCAST 2011, Part II. LNCS, vol. 6928, pp. 568–576. Springer, Heidelberg (2012)
30. van Aart, C., Wielinga, B., van Hage, W.R.: Mobile cultural heritage guide: Location-aware semantic search. In: Cimiano, P., Pinto, H.S. (eds.) EKAW 2010. LNCS, vol. 6317, pp. 257–271. Springer, Heidelberg (2010)
31. Matuszka, T., Kiss, A.: Alive Cemeteries with Augmented Reality and Semantic Web Technologies. International Journal of Computer, Information Science and Engineering 8, 32–36 (2014)
32. Fouad, R.A., Badr, N., Talha, H., Hashem, M.: On Location-Centric Semantic Information Retrieval in Ubiquitous Computing Environments. International Journal of Electrical & Computer Sciences 10 (2010)
33. Martín-Serrano, D., Hervás, R., Bravo, J.: Telemaco: Context-aware System for Tourism Guiding based on Web 3.0 Technology. In: 1st Workshop on Contextual Computing and Ambient Intelligence in Tourism, Riviera Maya, Mexico (2011)
34. Cyganiak, R., Jentzsch, A.: Linking open data cloud diagram. LOD Community (2011), http://lod-cloud.net/
35. Hugues, O., Cieutat, J.-M., Guitton, P.: Gis and augmented reality: State of the art and issues. In: Handbook of Augmented Reality, pp. 721–740. Springer (2011)
36. Shvaiko, P., Euzenat, J.: Ontology matching: state of the art and future challenges. IEEE Transactions on Knowledge and Data Engineering 25, 158–176 (2013)
37. Rivero, C.R., Schultz, A., Bizer, C., Ruiz, D.: Benchmarking the Performance of Linked Data Translation Systems. LDOW (2012)
38. Massmann, S., Raunich, S., Aumüller, D., Arnold, P., Rahm, E.: Evolution of the coma match system. Ontology Matching 49 (2011)
39. Ji, Q., Haase, P., Qi, G., Hitzler, P., Stadtmüller, S.: RaDON — repair and diagnosis in ontology networks. In: Aroyo, L., Traverso, P., Ciravegna, F., Cimiano, P., Heath, T., Hyvönen, E., Mizoguchi, R., Oren, E., Sabou, M., Simperl, E. (eds.) ESWC 2009. LNCS, vol. 5554, pp. 863–867. Springer, Heidelberg (2009)
40. Karam, R., Favetta, F., Laurini, R., Chamoun, R.K.: Uncertain geoinformation representation and reasoning: A use case in lbs integration. In: 2010 Workshop on Database and Expert Systems Applications (DEXA), pp. 313–317. IEEE (2010)
41. Karam, R., Favetta, F., Kilany, R., Laurini, R.: Integration of similar location based services proposed by several providers. In: Zavoral, F., Yaghob, J., Pichappan, P., El-Qawasmeh, E. (eds.) NDT 2010. CCIS, vol. 88, pp. 136–144. Springer, Heidelberg (2010)
42. Martins, B.: A supervised machine learning approach for duplicate detection over gazetteer records. In: Claramunt, C., Levashkin, S., Bertolotto, M. (eds.) GeoS 2011. LNCS, vol. 6631, pp. 34–51. Springer, Heidelberg (2011)
43. Hahmann, S., Burghardt, D.: Connecting linkedgeodata and geonames in the spatial semantic web. In: 6th International GIScience Conference (2010)
44. Parundekar, R., Knoblock, C.A., Ambite, J.L.: Linking and building ontologies of linked data. In: Patel-Schneider, P.F., Pan, Y., Hitzler, P., Mika, P., Zhang, L., Pan, J.Z., Horrocks, I., Glimm, B. (eds.) ISWC 2010, Part I. LNCS, vol. 6496, pp. 598–614. Springer, Heidelberg (2010)

45. Parundekar, R., Knoblock, C.A., Ambite, J.L.: Aligning ontologies of geospatial linked data. Workshop On Linked Spatiotemporal Data. In: Conjunction with the 6th International Conference on Geographic Information Science (GIScience 2010), Zurich, September 14 (2010) (forthcoming)

46. Parundekar, R., Ambite, J.L., Knoblock, C.A.: Aligning unions of concepts in ontologies of geospatial linked data. In: Proceedings of the Terra Cognita 2011 Workshop in Conjunction with the 10th International Semantic Web Conference. Bonn, Germany (2011)

47. Salas, J., Harth, A.: Finding spatial equivalences accross multiple RDF datasets. In: Proceedings of the Terra Cognita Workshop on Foundations, Technologies and Applications of the Geospatial Web, pp. 114–126 (2011)

48. Battle, R., Kolas, D.: GeoSPARQL: Enabling a Geospatial Semantic Web. Semantic Web Journal 3, 355–370 (2011)

49. GeoKnow Consortium: Deliverable 2.1.1 - Market and research overview (2013), http://svn.aksw.org/projects/GeoKnow/Public/D2.1.1_Market_an d_Research_Overview.pdf

50. Atemezing, G.A., Troncy, R.: Comparing vocabularies for representing geographical features and their geometry. In: Terra Cognita 2012 Workshop, p. 3 (2012)

51. Matuszka, T., Kiss, A.: Geodint: Towards Semantic Web-Based Geographic Data Integration. In: Nguyen, N.T., Attachoo, B., Trawiński, B., Somboonviwat, K. (eds.) ACIIDS 2014, Part I. LNCS, vol. 8397, pp. 191–200. Springer, Heidelberg (2014)

52. Resource Description Framework (RDF): Concepts and Abstract Data Model, http://www.w3.org/TR/2002/WD-rdf-concepts-20020829/#xtocid48014

53. Flemming, A., Hartig, O.: Quality Criteria for Linked Data sources, http://sourceforge.net/apps/mediawiki/trdf/index.php?title=Q uality_Criteria_for_Linked_Data_sources

54. Jain, P., Hitzler, P., Yeh, P.Z., Verma, K., Sheth, A.P.: Linked Data Is Merely More Data. In: AAAI Spring Symposium: Linked Data Meets Artificial Intelligence (2010)

55. Fürber, C., Hepp, M.: Using SPARQL and SPIN for data quality management on the semantic web. In: Abramowicz, W., Tolksdorf, R. (eds.) BIS 2010. LNBIP, vol. 47, pp. 35–46. Springer, Heidelberg (2010)

56. Fürber, C., Hepp, M.: Using semantic web resources for data quality management. In: Cimiano, P., Pinto, H.S. (eds.) EKAW 2010. LNCS, vol. 6317, pp. 211–225. Springer, Heidelberg (2010)

57. Fürber, C., Hepp, M.: Towards a vocabulary for data quality management in semantic web architectures. In: Proceedings of the 1st International Workshop on Linked Web Data Management, pp. 1–8. ACM (2011)

58. Goodchild, M.F.: Citizens as sensors: the world of volunteered geography. GeoJournal 69, 211–221 (2007)

59. Zielstra, D., Zipf, A.: A comparative study of proprietary geodata and volunteered geographic information for Germany. In: 13th AGILE International Conference on Geographic Information Science (2010)

60. Haklay, M.: How good is volunteered geographical information? A comparative study of OpenStreetMap and Ordnance Survey datasets. Environment and Planning B: Planning and Design 37, 682–703 (2010)

61. Haklay, M.(M.), Basiouka, S., Antoniou, V., Ather, A.: How Many Volunteers Does it Take to Map an Area Well? The Validity of Linus' Law to Volunteered Geographic Information. The Cartographic Journal 47, 315–322 (2010)

62. Celino, I., Contessa, S., Corubolo, M., Dell'Aglio, D., Della Valle, E., Fumeo, S., Krüger, T.: Linking smart cities datasets with human computation – the case of urbanMatch. In: Cudré-Mauroux, P., et al. (eds.) ISWC 2012, Part II. LNCS, vol. 7650, pp. 34–49. Springer, Heidelberg (2012)

63. Gil, Y., Artz, D.: Towards content trust of web resources. Web Semantics: Science, Services and Agents on the World Wide Web 5, 227–239 (2007)

64. Hartig, O.: Provenance Information in the Web of Data. In: LDOW (2009)

65. Moreau, L., Clifford, B., Freire, J., Futrelle, J., Gil, Y., Groth, P., Kwasnikowska, N., Miles, S., Missier, P., Myers, J., et al.: The open provenance model core specification (v1. 1). Future Generation Computer Systems 27, 743–756 (2011)

66. Garijo, D., Villazón-Terrazas, B., Corcho, O.: A provenance-aware linked data application for trip management and organization. In: Proceedings of the 7th International Conference on Semantic Systems, pp. 224–226. ACM (2011)

67. De Nies, T., Coppens, S., Verborgh, R., Vander Sande, M., Mannens, E., Van de Walle, R., Michaelides, D., Moreau, L.: Easy Access to Provenance: an Essential Step Towards Trust on the Web. In: 2013 IEEE 37th Annual Computer Software and Applications Conference Workshops (COMPSACW), pp. 218–223. IEEE (2013)

68. Berners-Lee, T.: Consistent User Interface, Section - The "Oh yeah?" button, http://www.w3.org/DesignIssues/UI.html

69. De Nies, T., Coppens, S., Mannens, E., Van de Walle, R.: Modeling uncertain provenance and provenance of uncertainty in W3C PROV. In:Proceedings of the 22nd international con-ference on World Wide Web Companion, pp. 167–168. International World Wide Web Conferences Steering Committee (2013)

Educational Robots for Internet-of-Things Supported Collaborative Learning

Ignas Plauska[1] and Robertas Damaševičius[2]

[1] Centre of Real Time Computer Systems
[2] Software Engineering Department,
Kaunas University of Technology,
Studentų 50, Kaunas, Lithuania
{ignas.plauska,robertas.damasevicius}@ktu.lt

Abstract. We present a vision of using educational robots as smart mobile components ("things") of Internet-of-Things. Such robots, beside their primary mission to facilitate learning, are able to communicate; have computing capabilities; as well as have sensors and actuators to sense and change their physical context. The robot serves both as the educational service that allows to visualize knowledge through explicit actions and behaviour as well as the enabler of learning and providing student engagement through immersion and instant feedback. The vision is based on the principles of contextualization, physicality and immersion. The pedagogical background is the proposed Internet-of-Things Supported Collaborative Learning (IoTSCL) paradigm based on constructivism, which provides a highly motivating learning environment in university, promoting collaboration among students, and achieving the creation of new knowledge in a reflexive process directed by the teacher. We demonstrate the implementation of the paradigm in the project-based setting at the university course and evaluate it using the Four-Phased Model of Interest Development.

Keywords: Internet-Of-Things, educational robotics, collaborative project-based learning.

1 Introduction

Recent achievements in educational technologies,such as educational robotics, augmented reality or semantic web, open new opportunities for increasing attractiveness of technological specialties and stimulating engagement of students in the learning process. However, new technologies require additional efforts (both methodological and technological) to integrate and construct teaching and learning environments to enhance delivery of subject material [1]. In this paper we analyse the potential of the Internet-of-Things (IoT) [2] technologies for supporting education. IoT is a vision of a world penetrated by embedded smart devices, which have identities, sensing and actuation capabilities, are connected via Internet, can communicate with each other and with humans, and can provide some useful services (definition based on [3]).

Currently IoT is emerging as one of the major trends shaping the development of technologies in the ICT sector [4]. IoT has connections with Ambient Intelligence [5],

G. Dregvaite and R. Damasevicius (Eds.): ICIST 2014, CCIS 465, pp. 346–358, 2014.
© Springer International Publishing Switzerland 2014

which refers to digital environments that are sensitive and responsive to the presence of people; Augmented Reality [6], where physical users and virtual reality are merged together, Semantic Web [7], which enables human knowledge to be machine-readable, Ubiquitous Computing [8], which allows Web services to serve anything, forming a bridge between virtual world and real world; Cloud Robotics [9], where cloud computing is used to augment the capabilities of robots by off-loading computation and providing services on demand; Wireless Sensor Networks [10], which connect spatially distributed autonomous sensors to monitor physical or environmental conditions and to cooperatively send their data through the network, Web mashups [11], where users can create applications mixing real-world devices, such as home appliances, with virtual services on the Web; and Web-Squared [12], which is an extension of Web 2.0 [13] aimed at integrating web and sensing technologies.

The theoretical background for the application of IoT for education is Norman's foundational theory of action [14], which states seven stages of activity from its conception to formation: 1) establish a goal, 2) form an intention, 3) specify an action sequence, 4) execute an action, 5) perceive the system state, 6) interpret the state, and 7) evaluate the system state with respect to the goals and intentions. Another theoretical concept is immersive learning, whichsimilarly to IoT is based around networking and could be combined with IoT in an educational setting [15].

Conceptually, IoT is similar to Object-Oriented Programming (OOP): the "things" have a state and represent real-world entities, which can be accessed only via interfaces ("services"). Currently, OOP dominates the field of software programming. However, students often face difficulties when trying to assimilate the concepts of OOP. Several approaches tried to assist student understanding of programming concepts by moving towards visualization of learning content, tools and materials, which includes, e.g., programming environments in which the structure of program code is visualized [16], or using highly abstract visual programming languages (VPLs), which use visual elements rather than machine instructions [17]. VPLs are more attractive to non-professional or novice programmers because ofsimpler description of domain [18], and immediate visual feedback [19] instead of textual languages.

On the other hand, there is a strong trend towards increasing the role of robotics in the education [1, 20, 21]. Robotics is a complex domain that includes both hardware and software parts and requires deep knowledge of embedded systems, real-time systems, artificial intelligence, mechanics, kinematics, navigation, sensors, communication and control protocols and robot programming languages.

The novelty of this paper is an approach that combines robotics, IoT and Computer Supported Collaborative Learning (CSCL) for project-based learning based on a vision of robots as *mobile smart learning objects*.The aim of the paper is to discuss the proposed concept of IoT Supported Collaborative Learning (IoTSCL) and describe its application in the university course using educational robots.

The structure of the remaining parts of the paper is as follows. Section 2 discusses the role and model of using IoT for educational purposes. Section 3 proposes the concept of IoTSCL and discusses its advantages for education. Section 4 presents a case study application of the proposed ideas in the university course. Section 5 evaluates and discusses results and Section 6 presents conclusions.

2   Role and Model of Internet of Things for Education

IoT is based on the concept of "smart objects", or "things". Miorandi et al. [4] define smart objects as entities that are *physical*; can communicate (accept incoming messages and reply to them); have a unique identifier and are associated to at least one name and one address; have some computing capabilities; and have means to sense physical phenomena (sensors) or to trigger actions having an effect on the physical reality (actuators). These properties allow smart objects to be *context-aware*, i.e., smart object can analyse the data received from its sensors and can use recognition algorithms to detect activities and events [22], as well as to be *social*, i.e., share their data, learn about each other and perform intelligent behaviours based upon each other's states [23], and provide services to both humans and robots in real-world environments [24].

Structurally, IoT consists of three major layers of abstraction:

1) *Hardware* (sensors, actuators and communication devices), which is built upon the existing global Internet communication infrastructure that links physical and virtual services [25]. Sensors allow users to get information about their environment, enable new forms of user interaction, and connect the real world with information.

2) *Middleware* (computing tools), which is used for data capture, aggregation and analysis. Secondary information inferred from sensor data also can be used for synchronizing learning activities with the physical environment and user feedback about their interaction with objects [26].

3) *Presentation* (or web service) *layer*, which allows Things to participate in business processes and provide capabilities to query things and change their state as well as support visibility (therefore, abstract concepts to be learned can be made visible and hence more understandable).

The main challenge in developing educational IoT systems is integration of functionalities and/or resources provided by smart things into educational services [27]. This requires the definition of the educational IoT architectures and models for seamlessly integrating and composing the resources/services of smart objects into educational services for learners.

For educational purposes, the IoT Reference Model [3] can be adopted. The IoT Reference Model identifies the generic IoT scenario in which a User (a human person or a software agent) needs to interact with a Physical Entity (a discrete, identifiable part of the physical world). A Physical Entity can be represented in the electronic world by a uniquely identifiable Digital Entity such as avatars, or even a social network account. Smart Object is the extension of a Physical Entity with its associated Digital Proxy. For Smart Object to be represented in both physical and digital world, it has embedded or attached Devices such as Sensors or Actuators that allow for interacting with or gaining information about the Physical Entity. Users can interact with Smart Objects through the use of Resources which provide services to Users.

In the next Section, we discuss how IoT can be used to support collaborative learning using mobile physical robots as Smart Objects as defined by the IoT Reference Model.

3   The Concept of IoT Supported Collaborative Learning

Computer supported collaborative learning (CSCL) refers to a technological environment in which students interact actively, share experiences and build knowledge [28].
Face-to-face CSCL provides a highly motivating learning environment, changing the
classroom dynamics and promoting collaboration among students for achieving good
results [29]. The inclusion of educational robotics to CSCL as Mobile Robotic Supported Collaborative Learning (MRSCL) [30] has added a new dimension to this
learning environment. While maintaining the face-to-face interactions, collaboration,
and the underlying technological assistance, Educational Robotics provides a way to
embrace real-world capabilities [30]. This real environment (as opposed to virtual
learning environments common in e-learning [31]) provides students with a common
resolution space where mobility enables world exploration and immersion. On the
other hand, the robot, empowered with mobility and autonomous navigation, becomes
a new actor capable of interacting with both, the physical world and a group of students. Moreover, MCSCL introduces a space that favours constructivism to achieve
creation of new knowledge in a reflexive process directed by the teacher
[32].Conceptually, the role of robots in the educational IoT-based environment is
threefold:

1) **Robot as a mobile smart "thing"**. Knowledge is created, enhanced, and rebuilt
through interaction between smart objects. Learning materials and processes can be
self-organized and adapted according to students' real-time interest and psychological
statuses [33]. Things are implemented as Mobile Robots, which can move and interact
with their environments [34].

2) **Robot as a Service (RaaS)** [35] enables an agent to enlist a robotic entity to
perform actions. The robot becomes a service end point for a user to command.

3) **Robot as Learning Object (RaLO),** which extends the notion of an LO beyond
the virtual domain (learning content) to a physical domain (robot hardware and physical processes that are demonstrated by the hardware) [36, 37].

Connecting learning services and materials to physical objects enriched with sensors is a next step in the evolution of Learning Objects and e-learning environments.
As noted by Specht [38],"*the connection between digital and physical objects builds a
new landscape for learning of the future.*" The vision of robot as "smart thing" allows
to extend the MRSCL into the IoT domain as the IoT Supported Collaborative Learning (IoTSCL). The main contribution of IoT for education is as follows:

1) Providing a technological background for *contextualised* learning by embedding
technology (gadgets, devices, sensors, etc.) in the natural environment in which learning takes place. It enriches the learning experience by contextualising learning activities and synchronizing learning content with the learner's context and reflection [38].
Contextualization is an essential step towards personalization of delivery of learning
services, i.e., IoT comes forward as a technological platform for such personalization.

2) Achieving immersion of learners, where the learner rather than interacting with
the outside learning environment, actually is inside of the learning environment, with
smart physical mobile robotic learning objects surrounding him. A core component of

the efficient learning is the instant feedback in these rich and interactive environments. In a real-time environment each action of the robot programmer and user may trigger instant feedback and subsequent reflective thought processes [38]. Such learning through immersion can contribute to the construction of new knowledge which is based on the pre-existing knowledge of students.

3) Increasing student engagement by using *physical* rather than virtual things. This engagement plays a fundamental role in skill development, because behaviour of the physical thing provides immediate feedback that helps the student to gain knowledge and correct the errors[39],and has positive influence on algorithmic thinking [40].

4   Case Study

The use of educational robotics and IoT technologies combined with project-based collaborative learning was explored during the laboratory works of "Robot Programming Technologies", a course delivered at Faculty of Informatics, Kaunas University of Technology (Lithuania)to the 4th year bachelor students [41]. The course was attended by 34 students in 2012 and by 22 students in 2013. The course aims to teach students of the basic principles of robot control and robot programming. The main concepts to learn are state (property of the robot), action/reaction (change of the state of the robot due to external or internal factors), behaviour (specific sequence of actions aimed to achieve a pre-set objective), decision (ability to undertake a specific sequence of actions from a set of alternatives), autonomity (ability to function independently), communication (ability to send/receive messages from external devices).

This case study describes the development of one project in the group project-based educational setting.Following the Norman's foundational theory of action [14], the goal of the project has been formulated as the development of the mobile webcam for home security applications and its evaluation. The functions of the robot to be implemented is home patrolling (free roaming with obstacle avoidance as well line following in room environment), image capturing and sending to the server computer, as well as fire detection and user warning using the temperature sensor.

The robot has been assembled using .NET Gadgeteer components and programmed using object-oriented language C#. For data transmission wireless internet is used. Robot control commands are sent to robot using UDP and images from robot camera

Fig. 1. Implementation of robot

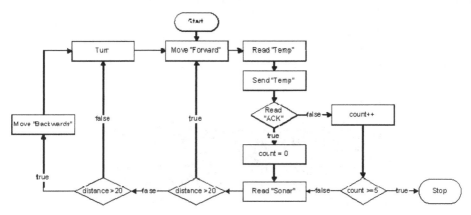

Fig. 2. Flowchart of the robot algorithm

are sent using TCP (TCP ensures faster data transmission). The hardware implementation of the robot can be seen in Fig. 1, while a fragment of the behaviour algorithm is shown in Fig. 2. The fragment demonstrates obstacle avoidance of the robot.

The line following algorithm modelled using Microsoft Visual Programming Language, a part of the Microsoft Robotics Developer Studio, is presented in Fig. 3. Using a high-level visual language rather than code-level textual programming language such as C# for description of algorithms is positively rated by students as it allows to deal with complexity of robotics and IoT domains more effectively [41].

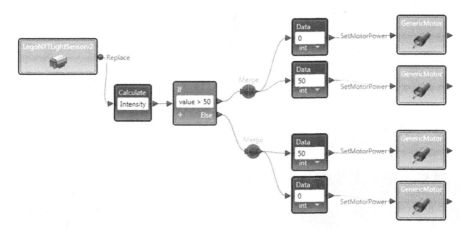

Fig. 3. Line following algorithm in Microsoft Visual Programming Language

The constructed robot is also able to measure temperature of its environment (see Fig. 4), to send values to the server for storage and further analysis (if needed), and to send SMS to the user, if the temperature value exceeds a predefined value. This service allows to demonstrate the communication capabilities of the robot as a mobile sensor platform in the context of Internet-of-Things.

Fig. 4. Example of temperature measurement results

In the research part of the project, the student group was asked to experiment-tally evaluate different strategies for turning a robot, i.e., to change the direction of its movement using different values of motor power applied to its wheels, in terms of their speed and accuracy. Three variants of turning a robot were devised (see Fig. 5).

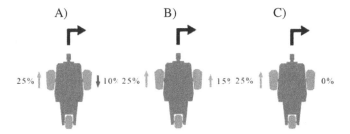

Fig. 5. Motor power and wheel turning direction in different robot turning scenario

The experiments were performed using two different line following algorithms: One Bounce and One Inside [42], and two different types of route for robot driving. One route (see Fig. 6, a) is aimed to evaluate the ability of the robot to complete rounded turns while frequently changing the direction of movement. Another route (Fig. 6, b) is made of 10 sharp angles which test the ability of the robot to complete sharp turns. The results of robot time trial are presented in Table 1.

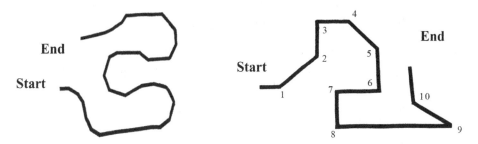

Fig. 6. Routes: a) with rounded turn angles, b) with 10 sharp turns

Table 1. Experimental results of robot driving

Route	Algorithm	Turning variant	Time (min:s.ms)	Accuracy evaluation
1	One Bounce	A	2:52.8	Completed
1	One Bounce	B	1:30.8	Completed
1	One Bounce	C	-	Failed
1	One Inside	A	2:16.7	Completed
1	One Inside	B	1:27.5	Completed
1	One Inside	C	1:09.9	Completed
2	One Bounce	A	1:35.7	Completed 8/10 turns
2	One Bounce	B	0:35.5	Completed 7/10 turns
2	One Bounce	C	0:24.7	Completed 7/10 turns
2	One Inside	A	1:26.1	Completed 10/10 turns
2	One Inside	B	0:16.3	Completed 3/10 turns
2	One Inside	C	0:21.1	Completed 6/10 turns

Project Findings. The project results were discussed during student self-evaluation sessions with a teacher as well as presented during course workshop for all course students. The students noted that the most important factor determining the accuracy of robot movement is noise in sensor data. While in theory all analysed line following algorithms should allow the robot to complete the intended route, random factors such as dust or unevenness of ground caused errors in sensor interpretation of line colour beneath the robot, which caused change or movement direction and, eventually, missing of the route. Also the students have noted that the sharpness of angles of the route could cause problems for the robot. When comparing different line following algorithms, One Bounce algorithm proved to be more reliable, but also slower and visually observed robot movement was more similar to stepping. One Inside algorithm allowed the robot to complete the route faster but sometimes also caused the robot to miss the line, especially when driving at sharp angles.

5   Evaluation and Discussion

To measure students' satisfaction we took a survey of 22 students after the lab exercise. The majority of students was satisfied with the class and expressed positive opinion. Fig. 7 shows the survey results.The students were asked three questions:

1) First question *"What is your opinion of the course?"* surveyed the emotional disposition of students towards the course.

2)   Second question *"What advantages does this course have?"* surveyed the cognitive disposition of students towards the course.

3) Third question *"Would you prefer to have more practical exercises with mobile robots in the next semester?"* surveyed their disposition to reengage.

The questionnaire allows to measure emotional/cognitive interest vs. short-time/long-time engagement.

The students' satisfaction was evaluated using the Four-Phase Model of Interest Development proposed by Hidi and Renninger [43] which introduces four types of interest as follows:

1) *Triggered Situational Interest:* short-term changes in affective (i.e. emotional) and cognitive processing sparked by content (e.g. information, tasking).

2) *Maintained Situational Interest:* a psychological state that involves focused attention and persistence over an extended period of time for content/tasks that an individual considers meaningful or relevant.

3) *Emerging Individual Interest:* the beginning of enduring predisposition for an individual to seek repeated engagement with particular content or tasks over time.

4) *Well-Developed Individual Interest:* an enduring predisposition to reengage with particular content or tasks over time characterized by positive feelings, more stored knowledge and more stored value for the content.

The answers of students are interpreted using the matrix presented in Table 2 and summarized in Fig. 7 (in percents). When analysing we assume that long-term interest subsumes short-term interest and cognitive interest subsumes emotional interest.

Table 2. Interpretation of Four-Phase Model of Interest Development [43]

Four-Phase Model of Interest Development	**Short-term engagement → Long-term engagement**	
Emotional interest ↓ **Cognitive interest**	Triggered Situational Interest	Maintained Situational Interest
	Emerging Individual Interest	Well-Developed Individual Interest

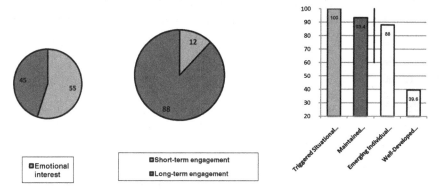

Fig. 7. Results of survey and their interpretation using four-phase interest model

6   Conclusions

This paper has studied and analysed the basic components of the Internet of Things (IoT) Supported Collaborative Learning (IoTSCL) environment defining and implementing the robot as a mobile physical smart learning object and service. Such smart learning objects and services can create contextualized learning ecosystems that enhance both learning outcomes and motivational states of students interacting with them. The paper has discussed the experience of using a mobile robot development project in the context of IoT for joining hardware and software subjects in the learning process. A case study presented an example implementation of a mobile home webcam project in which students interacted with a robot as a contextualized learning object and service within the context of IoT. The experience has been done in the 4th course of software engineering studies with the aim to motivate students. Students acquired problem-oriented skills (knowledge and competences) in software and hardware. The course experience demonstrated that mobile robots can be used as physical smart learning objects. The evaluation of the course using Four Phase model of Interest Development [43] demonstrated that a majority of students have developed long-term cognitive interest into the subject of study. The use of mobile robots as physical learning objects allowed to enrich the learning experience by providing instant feedback and subsequent reflection, and achieving full immersion of learners into the learning environment with smart physical learning objects surrounding them.

Future work will focus on the development of a learning environment that supports visual modelling language for mobile robotics as well as elements of IoT (sensors, actuators and communications). The environment will be used in the context of group-based collaborative project learning and its pedagogical efficiency will be evaluated using student and expert surveys.

Acknowledgement. The work described in this paper has been carried out within the framework of the Operational Program for the Development of Human Resources 2007-2013 of Lithuania „Strengthening of Capacities of Researchers and Scientists"

project VP1-3.1-ŠMM-08-K-01-018 „Research and Development of Internet Technologies and their Infrastructure for Smart Environments of Things and Services" (2012-2015), funded by the European Social Fund (ESF).

References

1. Lye, N.C., Wong, K.W., Chiou, A.: Framework for educational robotics: a multiphase approach to enhance user learning in a competitive arena. Interactive Learning Environments (ILE) 21(2), 142–155 (2013)
2. Future Generation Computer Systems: Internet of Things (IoT): A Vision, Architectural Elements, and Future Directions. Elsevier, The Netherlands (2013)
3. Serbanati, A., Medaglia, C.M., Ceipidor, U.B.: Building Blocks of the Internet of Things: State of the Art and Beyond. In: Turcu, C. (ed.) Deploying RFID - Challenges, Solutions, and Open Issues. InTech (2011)
4. Miorandi, D., Sicari, S., De Pellegrini, F., Chlamtac, I.: Internet of things: Vision, applications and research challenges. Ad Hoc Networks (ADHOC) 10(7), 1497–1516 (2012)
5. van Kranenburg, R.: The Internet of Things. A critique of ambient technology and the all-seeing network of RFID. Network Notebooks 02. Institute of Network Cultures, Amsterdam (2008)
6. Gimenez, R., Pous, M.: Augmented reality as an enabling factor for the Internet of Things. In: W3C Workshop: Augmented Reality on the Web, Barcelona, Spain (2010)
7. Ruta, M., Scioscia, F., Di Sciascio, E.: Enabling the Semantic Web of Things: framework and architecture. Proc. of 6th IEEE International Conference on Semantic Computing (ICSC 2012), pp. 345–347 (2012)
8. Greenfield, A.: Everyware: The dawning age of ubiquitous computing. New Riders (2007)
9. Hu, G., Tay, W.P., Wen, Y.: Cloud robotics: architecture, challenges and applications. IEEE Network 26(3), 21–28 (2012)
10. Dargie, W., Poellabauer, C.: Fundamentals of wireless sensor networks: theory and practice. John Wiley and Sons (2010)
11. Zang, N., Rosson, M.B., Nasser, V.: Mashups: who? what? why? In: Proc. of CHI 2008 Extended Abstracts on Human Factors in Computing Systems. ACM, Florence (2008)
12. Calma, G., Palazzi, C.E., Bujari, A.: Web squared: paradigms and opportunities. In: Proc. of the 5th Int. ICST Conference on Simulation Tools and Techniques (SIMUTOOLS 2012), Brussels, Belgium, pp. 256–261 (2012)
13. Anderson, P.: Web 2.0 and Beyond: Principles and Technologies. Chapman & Hall/CRC (2012)
14. Norman, D.: Cognitive engineering. In: Norman, D., Draper, S.W. (eds.) User Centered Systems Design, pp. 31–62. LEA, Hillsdale (1986)
15. Callaghan, V.: Buzz-Boarding; Practical Support For Teaching Computing, Based On The Internet-Of-Things. Presentation at 1st Annual Conference on the Aiming for Excellence in STEM Learning and Teaching. Imperial College (2012)
16. Henriksen, P., Kölling, M.: Greenfoot: combining object visualisation with interaction. In: Companion to the 19th Annual ACM SIGPLAN Conference on Object-Oriented Programming Systems, Languages, and Applications (OOPSLA 2004), pp. 73–82. ACM, New York (2004)
17. Bentrad, S., Meslati, D.: Visual Programming and Program Visualization – Towards an Ideal Visual Software Engineering System. IJIT- ACEEE International Journal on Information Technology 1(3), 56–62 (2011)

18. Clarisse, O., Chang, S.-K.: VICON: A Visual Icon Manager. In: Visual Languages, pp. 151–190. Plenum Press, New York (1986)
19. Burnett, M.: Visual Programming. In: J. Webster (ed.), Encyclopedia of Electrical and Electronics Engineering. John Wiley & Sons (1999)
20. de Cristóforis, P., Pedre, S., Nitsche, M., Fischer, T., Pessacg, F., Di Pietro, C.: A Behavior-Based Approach for Educational Robotics Activities. IEEE Trans. Education (TE) 56(1), 61–66 (2013)
21. Barreto, F., Benitti, V.: Exploring the educational potential of robotics in schools: A systematic review. Computers & Education (CE) 58(3), 978–988 (2012)
22. Kortuem, G., Kawsar, F., Sundramoorthy, V., Fitton, D.: Smart Objects as Building Blocks for the Internet of Things. IEEE Internet Computing 14(1), 44–51 (2010)
23. Faludi, R.: Socialable Objects. MSc thesis, New York University (2007)
24. Möller, A., Roalter, L., Kranz, M.: Cognitive Objects for Human-Computer Interaction and Human-Robot Interaction. In: 6th ACM/IEEE Int. Conference on Human-Robot Interaction (HRI 2011), Lausanne, Switzerland, pp. 207–208 (2011)
25. EU FP7 Project CASAGRAS: CASAGRAS Final Report: RFID and the Inclusive Model for the Internet of Things (2009)
26. European Technology Platform on Smart Systems Integration: Internet ofthings in 2020, Report of Beyond RFID - the Internet of Things, Joint EU-EPoSS workshop, Brussels, Belgium (2008)
27. Guinard, D., Trifa, V., Karnouskos, S., Spiess, P., Savio, D.: Interacting with the SOA-based Internet of Things: discovery, query, selection, and on-demand provisioning of Web services. IEEE Trans. Serv. Comput. 3(3), 223–235 (2010)
28. Roschelle, J., Teasley, S.: The construction of shared knowledge in collaborative problem solving. In: O'Malley, C.E. (ed.) Computer Supported Collaborative Learning, pp. 69–97. Springer, Heidelberg (1995)
29. Cortez, C., Nussbaum, M., Santelices, R., Rodriguez, P., Zurita, G.: Teaching science with mobile computer supported collaborative learning (MCSCL). In: 2nd IEEE Int. Workshop on Wireless and Mobile Technologies in Education (WMTE 2004), pp. 67–74. IEEE CS Press (2004)
30. Mitnik, R., Nussbaum, M., Soto, A.: Mobile Robotic Supported Collaborative Learning (MRSCL). In: Lemaître, C., Reyes, C.A., González, J.A. (eds.) IBERAMIA 2004. LNCS (LNAI), vol. 3315, pp. 912–921. Springer, Heidelberg (2004)
31. Piccoli, G., Ahmad, R., Ives, B.: Web-Based virtual learning environments: a research framework and a preliminary assessment of effectiveness in basic IT skills training. MIS. Q. 25(4), 401–426 (2001)
32. Zurita, G., Nussbaum, M.: A constructivist mobile learning environment supported by a wireless handheld network. Journal of Computer Assisted Learning 20(4), 235–243 (2004)
33. Zhuge, H.: Semantic linking through spaces for cyber-physical-socio intelligence: A methodology. Artif. Intell. 175(5-6), 988–1019 (2011)
34. Turcu, C., Turcu, C., Gaitan, V.: Merging the Internet of Things and Robotics. In: Recent Researches in C ircuits and Systems, pp. 499–504. WSEAS (2012)
35. Chen, Y., Hu, H.: Internet of intelligent things and robot as a service. Simulation Modelling Practice and Theory (2012)
36. Burbaite, R., Stuikys, V., Damasevicius, R.: Educational Robots as Collaborative Learning Objects for Teaching Computer Science. In: Proc. of IEEE Int. Conference on System Science and Engineering (ICSSE 2013), Budapest, Hungary, pp. 211–216 (2013)

37. Burbaite, R., Damasevicius, R., Stuikys, V.: Using Robots as Learning Objects for Teaching Computer Science. In: Proc. of 10th IFIP World Conference on Computers in Education (WCCE 2013), Torun, Poland, vol. 1, pp. 101–111 (2013)

38. Specht, M.: Learning in a technology enhanced world - context in ubiquitous learning support. In: OCE in the Netherlands (2009)

39. Pásztor, A., Pap-Szigeti, R., Lakatos Török, E.: Effects of Using Model Robots in the Education of Programming. Informatics in Education 9(1), 133–140 (2010)

40. Liu, A.S., Schunn, C.D., Flot, J., Shoop, R.: The role of physicality in rich programming environments. Computer Science Education 23(4), 315–331 (2013)

41. Plauska, I., Lukas, R., Damasevicius, R.: Reflections on using robots and visual programming environments for project-based teaching. Electronics and Electrical Engineering 20(1), 71–74 (2014)

42. Gray, J.A.: Toeing the Line: Experiments with Line-following Algorithms (2003), http://www.fll-freak.com/misc/01-jgray_report.pdf (retrieved)

43. Hidi, S., Renninger, K.A.: The Four-Phase Model of Interest Development. Educational Psychologist 41(2), 111–127 (2006)

Towards Empirical Modelling of Knowledge Transfer in Teaching/Learning Process

Robertas Damaševičius

Software Engineering Department
Kaunas University of Technology
Studentų 50, Kaunas, Lithuania
`robertas.damasevicius@ktu.lt`

Abstract. Educational systems are complex adaptive systems with basic properties of openness, nonlinearity, feedback and adaptivity. Modelling and assessment of a teaching/learning process is a difficult task that involves many factors at multiple dimensions (pedagogical, technological, organizational, social, etc.). Common methods used for evaluation of teaching/learning effectiveness such as surveys, questionnaires and tests are subjective and lack of statistical control and standards for comparison. In this paper, we propose an empirical knowledge transfer model for closed teacher-learner systems and its extension for open teacher-learner systems. The model is based on the theory of communication in noisy channels with additive white Gaussian noise. We describe the pedagogical interpretation of the model's parameters and describe its application in modelling the transfer of knowledge in the teaching/learning process.

Keywords: knowledge transfer modelling, information theory, noisy channel, teaching, learning, education.

1 Introduction

A complex system is defined as a system comprising of a large number of interacting agents with nonlinear activity and self-organization [1]. Complex adaptive system denotes systems that have some or all of the following attributes [2]: the number of relations between the parts is non-trivial; the system has memory or includes feedback; the system can adapt itself to its environment; the relations between the system and its environment are non-linear; the system is highly sensitive to initial conditions.

Educational systems, institutions and practices exhibit many features of complex adaptive systems, being dynamical and emergent, sometimes unpredictable, and operating in changing external environments [3]. Educational systems involving teachers and learners also possess these properties: non-trivial relations between agents (teacher-student, student-student), memory of previous learning states, adaptation to new learning conditions, and influence of external learning factors, sensitivity to teacher qualifications and student initial knowledge and prejudice. For example, the teaching-learning process is an activity that occurs in a complex system consisting of a teacher and one or multiple learners using a particular curriculum and textbook [4].

G. Dregvaite and R. Damasevicius (Eds.): ICIST 2014, CCIS 465, pp. 359–372, 2014.
© Springer International Publishing Switzerland 2014

The implication of understanding education as a complex phenomenon include acknowledging complicity of learners and teachers in the education process, allowing for improvisation in communication and rethinking evaluation of learning results [5]. Interaction of agents requires some means and media of communication to ensure transmission of information between interacting agents. Self-organization requires information to be transmitted in a structured and organized way. Such organized information provided by a teacher during the teaching process becomes a part of the learner's knowledge.

There are many kinds of structural organization of information that can be used in the teaching process, e.g., textbooks, slides, handouts, notes, video tutorials, etc. In the context of e-learning [6], Learning Objects (LOs) are leading as an instructional technology of choice for delivering information [7]. LOs can be delivered over the Internet where they can be accessed and used by many learners simultaneously. Though computer networks and internet technologies are considered as a prerequisite for e-Learning [8], well-designed LOs can be used not only for different types of distance education, but also directly in the classroom environment as one of the education resources available to the teacher [9]. LOs are not equal in their ability to produce learning [10]. Some LOs can be specifically created to represent and transfer knowledge explicitly thus achieving higher knowledge transfer than others [11].

Multiple reasons affect suitability of LOs for learning: composition and structure of learning material, visual presentation, pedagogical methods used, technological appeal, etc. Objective evaluation of the pedagogical effectiveness of LOs and the results of learning process is difficult [12]. We can distinguish four types of evaluation: evaluation of a teaching material (e.g., learning object or entire course), evaluation of a teaching method, evaluation of a teacher (instructor), and evaluation of a learner. These all types of evaluation are intertwined and the results of evaluation can be interpreted differently. For example, what was the reason for student's failure: bad presentation of teaching material, unsuitable teaching method, lack of competence and qualification by an instructor, or personal reasons of a learner (lack of motivation, illness, lack of abilities, etc.).

Traditional learner assessment tools include exams, quizzes, problem-sets, papers, and projects [13]. Student usage logs provide information about when, how often and how much time students spend with a learning object. Teacher surveys allow the teaching institution to rate a learning object in terms of what teachers think it added to their class, and also collect information about how a learning object was used by the teacher [14]. Analysis of the exam and survey results can help to identify successful or unsuccessful learning objects. Interviews can be used to detail what factors contributed (or did not contribute) to success of a learning object. A typical form of the Learning Object assessment used by numerous authors is knowledge surveys presented in the form of a questionnaire [15]. The disadvantage of questionnaires and surveys is that a large number of participants are required to ensure that the results will be statistically meaningful [16]. These assessment methods have many disadvantages. Grading and surveys are subjective and depend upon many external factors. Exams are limited by time constraints, cover narrow ranges of content and cognitive levels of inquiry, are generally quite stressful, and are subject to problems of reliability. Knowledge surveys are hampered by the lack of a control and suitable standard for comparison [13]. Student evaluations of courses often have little correlation with learning process results [17].

The primary key to effective teaching and learning in higher education is knowledge transfer [18]. Primarily, this is an informal social process that can be aided by technological means by which a teacher shares his/her knowledge with the learner. The process is shaped by one basic constraint — the limited rate of flow of information into human sense channels [19]. Knowledge transfer does not mean that the knowledge has to be transmitted and reproduced in exactly the same structure or sequence. Transformations of content can be used to reduce sensing time while preserving the content of information transferred. The success of knowledge transfer is usually measured by testing memory content or the ability of the learner to execute certain tasks given by the teacher.

In this paper we claim that the knowledge transfer process in a closed system consisting of one teacher and multiple learners can be modelled empirically. We propose a knowledge transfer model based on the information-theoretic concepts of communication in a noisy channel with additive white Gaussian noise, and its extension for open teacher-learner systems with economical parameters introduced. We also present a pedagogical interpretation of the model's parameters and discuss its application for modelling transfer of knowledge.

2   Related Work

In the Kanagaretnam & Thevaranjan's model [20], the relationship between acquired knowledge K and efforts α and β is measured using a linear equation

$$K = m\alpha + \beta, \quad 0 < m < 2/3 \tag{1}$$

here m is the motivation level of the student, and α, β are components of student effort.

Acquired knowledge and effort are unobservable and cannot be measured directly; therefore, the teacher determines the grade based on learner performance measure y:

$$y = K + \varepsilon_y, \quad y \in [0,1], \quad \varepsilon_y \sim N(0,n) \tag{2}$$

here, ε_y is the noise in the true performance measure, which is assumed to be normally distributed with zero mean and finite variance n.

The disadvantage of Kanagaretnam & Thevaranjan's model is that all students are treated as equal individuals with equal perceptory and understanding abilities. Amount of transferred knowledge only depends upon student's efforts and its grading can be slightly adjusted by the teacher. There are no teacher-related parameters; therefore, it cannot be used to evaluate the characteristics of the teaching process.

Cordier et al. [21] consider entropy as a measure of the learning process, while learning is considered as complex motor behaviour. Entropy is used to measure the degree of structuring in the successive states of the subject-environment system during the learning of a complex task. The study shows that entropy decreases as learning progresses, and that the shape of the entropy curve is a function of the learner's expertise. A model of constraint relaxation is proposed to describe the learning process.

Singh *et al.* [22] propose an entropy based performance index (Sp) based on item response curves (IRCs) for monitoring the teaching-learning process. IRC is treated as an explicit function of the ability, and Sp plays a role analogous to entropy, student ability is compared to inverse temperature, and teacher's instruction is similar to an ordering (magnetic) field. The study shows that low (high) entropy implies high (low) ability, while the instruction efficiency and information on the state of knowledge of the student group are key variables in this process.

Bordogna and Albano [23] use the Ising model that describes magnetism in materials, and model a classroom as a piece of iron [23]. Individual students play the role of atoms, and their knowledge of a subject is similar to the atoms' magnetic orientations. The teacher behaves like an external magnetic field trying to align the student's knowledge into the "right" direction (understanding the curriculum). But like atoms, students can be distracted by other students, which could cause the students to become disoriented. Student ability is modelled as inverse temperature and student performance is treated as entropy. The theory correctly predicts that team-work aids learning, which is similar to the aligning force between neighbouring atoms.

Yeung [24] reformulates the Ising model for the collaborative learning induced by group interactions between students. The model considers prior knowledge of students, student-student and student-other interactions, individual student's cognitive and metacognitive abilities for learning, and educational aspects of the tutoring system (instructional appropriateness and attractiveness of content presentation, feedback, motivation).

Nitta [25] proposes a phenomenological theory of peer instruction that describes a short-time process of learning. The model considers the number of students answering correctly at multiple-choice questions before and after peer discussions.

Ogawa *et al.* [26] simulate knowledge gain of students engaged in collaborative learning. The knowledge is assumed to be a dynamic variable influenced by the cognitive impact, which depends upon the knowledge level of the student, and the influence of the teacher and other students on the student.

Patriarcheas and Xenos [27] propose using a formal language defined in mathematical terms (with an alphabet for terminals, a grammar and semantics) to describe communication between tutors and students in the context of distance education. The formal grammar-based model eases the understanding of forums used for distance learning, to improve data processing and analysis in identifying best practices and erroneous patterns of behaviour, and to improve quality of learning in distance education. The language among others includes the concepts of time, group size and volume of information transmitted during communication.

Considering the advantages and disadvantages of the discussed empirical teaching-learning process models, we propose our information theory based knowledge transfer model described in Section 3.

3   Information Theory Based Knowledge Transfer Model

First, we begin with the definition of what knowledge is. We understand knowledge as a description of all concepts and their relationships in the domain of interest. This knowledge can be represented formally as domain ontology. Ontology can be described using OWL (Web Ontology Language) language and resolved into a set of facts represented in the form of RDF (Resource Description Framework) triples. An RDF triple says that some relationship, indicated by the predicate, holds between the things denoted by subject and object of the triple. Each triple represents a fact of domain knowledge, and all triples represent entire domain knowledge specified in domain ontology. The aim of the knowledge transfer model is to model the transfer of knowledge from the teacher's ontology to the learner ontologies.

Let T be a transmitter (teacher). Let O^T be knowledge, which a teacher has in the form of ontology. Let L be a set of receivers (learners) $L = \{L_1, ..., L_n\}$. Let O_i^L be knowledge acquired during learning process by learner L_i. Let knowledge transfer be a continuous process of transferring O^T to O_i^L via a noisy communication channel:

$$O_i^L \leftarrow \varphi_i\left(O^T, t\right), \tag{3}$$

here t is time (duration of a teaching process), and φ_i is the transfer function for a learner L_i.

The effectiveness of the teacher-learner communication process can be evaluated by the similarity of their respective ontologies O^T and O^L. As ontologies in fact are sets of facts, their similarity can be measured using the Jaccard index as follows:

$$J\left(O^T, O^L\right) = \frac{\left|F^T \cap F^L\right|}{\left|F^T \cup F^L\right|}, \tag{4}$$

here F^T and F^L are the sets of facts in ontologies O^T and O^L, respectively.

Knowledge gain by the learner during knowledge transfer is a derivative of the transfer function φ_i:

$$\varphi_i' = \sum_k p_i\left(f_k^T\right), \tag{5}$$

here $f_k^T \in F^T$ is a fact, and p_i is a probability function of fact transfer without any error (i.e., distortion or loss) during knowledge transfer session.

Let F_T^L be a set of true facts that were correctly acquired by the learner L during the learning process. Let F_F^L be a set of false facts that were incorrectly acquired by the learner L during the learning process. Let F_F^T be a set of facts that were not acquired (e.g., due to noise, communication breakdown, etc.) by the learner L during the learning process. Given F_T^L, F_F^L and F_F^T, the following identities are valid:

$$F^L = F_T^L \cup F_F^L, \quad F^T = F_T^L \cup F_F^T \tag{6}$$

Given a probability of fact transfer p, the size of sets can be estimated as follows:

$$\left|F_T^L\right| = p \cdot \left|F^T\right|, \quad \left|F_F^L\right| + \left|F_F^T\right| = (1-p) \cdot \left|F^T\right|. \tag{7}$$

Assuming that probability of information loss is equal to probability of information corruption, we can write:

$$\left|F_F^L\right| = \left|F_F^T\right| = \frac{(1-p)}{2} \cdot \left|F^T\right|. \tag{8}$$

Then we can rewrite Eq. 4 as follows:

$$J\left(O^T, O^L\right) = \frac{\left|F^T \cap F^L\right|}{\left|F^T \cup F^L\right|} = \frac{\left|F_T^L\right|}{\left|F^T\right| + \left|F^L\right| - \left|F_T^L\right|} = \frac{2p}{3-p}. \tag{9}$$

The transfer of information over a noisy channel is determined by the Shannon's channel theorem [28], which establishes that for any given degree of noise contamination of a communication channel, it is possible to communicate discrete data nearly error-free up to a computable maximum communication rate R through the channel:

$$R = \frac{C}{1 - H(p)}, \tag{10}$$

here C is the channel capacity and $H(p)$ is the binary entropy function:

$$H(p) = -(p \cdot \log_2(p) + (1-p) \cdot \log_2(1-p)). \tag{11}$$

If $R > C$, information cannot be guaranteed to be transmitted reliably across a channel at rates beyond the channel capacity.

Transmitted information is also affected by noise. Here we assume that noise in the knowledge transfer medium can be modelled as additive white Gaussian noise (AWGN). AWGN is a channel model in which the only impairment to communication is a linear addition of white noise with a constant spectral density and a Gaussian distribution of amplitude. An application of the channel capacity concept to an AWGN channel is defined by the Shannon–Hartley theorem:

$$C = B \cdot \log_2(1 + SNR), \tag{12}$$

here B is the bandwidth of the channel, and SNR is the signal-to-noise ratio.

Assuming that the bandwidth of the communication channels follows the normal distribution, we can model the individual channel B_i as

$$B_i \sim N\left(B_\mu, \sigma^2\right), \; 1 \le i \le n,$$

(13)

here B_μ is mean bandwidth, σ^2 is variance, and n is the number of channels.

Given Eqs. 10, 11, 12, the probability of correct fact transfer can be calculated:

$$p_i = 1 - H^{-1}\left(1 - \frac{B_i}{R}\log_2(1 + SNR)\right),$$

(14)

here H^{-1} is the inverse of binary entropy function, which can be fitted ($R^2 = 0.999$) using the following analytically discovered function:

$$H^{-1}(x) \approx \frac{1}{2}\left(1 \pm \sqrt{1-x}\right).$$

(15)

We formulate the aim of a teaching process as to achieve maximum similarity of teacher ontology O^T and learner ontologies O_i^L subject to the existing temporal constraints (i.e., the time of teaching t is limited) and teaching media constraints (e.g., level of noise, etc.). The solution to this problem can be treated as a typical optimization problem. There can be several variants of the aim function as follows.

Function ψ_1 maximizes the average effectiveness of knowledge transfer to a group of learners:

$$\psi_1 = \max \; \frac{1}{n}\sum_{i=1}^{n} J\left(O^T, \varphi_i\left(O^T, t\right)\right),$$

(16)

here J is the Jaccard index for evaluating similarity of two sets.

Function ψ_2 maximizes knowledge transfer function for learners with poorer learning abilities:

$$\psi_2 = \max \; \min_{1 \le i \le n} \; J\left(O^T, \varphi_i\left(O^T, t\right)\right),$$

(17)

Function ψ_3 maximizes the number of learners passing the evaluation test.

$$\psi_3 = \max \; \sum_{i=1}^{n}\left[J\left(O^T, \varphi_i\left(O^T, t\right)\right) \ge \theta\right],$$

(18)

here θ is the threshold value of acquired knowledge required to pass the knowledge evaluation test, and square brackets are the Iverson bracket operator.

The knowledge transfer model is summarized as follows:

$$K\left(\psi(R), SNR, B_\mu, n, \sigma^2, \theta\right),$$ (19)

here $\psi(R)$ is a pedagogical aim function for optimization of communication rate R:

$$\psi(R) = \begin{cases} \max\limits_{R} & \dfrac{1}{n}\sum\limits_{i=1}^{n}\dfrac{2p_i}{3-p_i}, \\[2ex] \max\limits_{R} & \min\limits_{1\le i\le n}\dfrac{2p_i}{3-p_i}, \\[2ex] \max\limits_{R} & \sum\limits_{i=1}^{n}\left[\dfrac{2p_i}{3-p_i} \ge \theta\right]. \end{cases}$$ (20)

p_i is the probability of the correct fact transfer:

$$p_i = 1 - H^{-1}\left(1 - \frac{B_i}{R}\log_2(1 + SNR)\right),$$ (21)

B_i is the channel bandwidth for the individual receiver (learner):

$$B_i \sim N\left(B_\mu, \sigma^2\right),$$ (22)

SNR is the signal-to-noise ratio of the communication channels (assumed constant for all channels); σ^2 is variance, n is the number of communication channels (i.e., receivers); and θ is the threshold value of acquired knowledge required to pass the knowledge evaluation test.

4 Pedagogical Interpretation of the Model's Parameters

Knowledge transfer will always be incomplete because people always know more than they can tell. However, we can evaluate what and how much was told, and how much the learners understood from what was told using content-independent informa-tion-theoretic measures. For example, teaching efficiency can always be evaluated as the ratio of the amount of learned facts divided by the amount of transferred facts.

The knowledge transfer model defined in Section 3 has a number of parameters (channel bandwidth, communication transfer rate, noise), which so far have been defined and used only in terms of information theory. In this Section we provide the pedagogical interpretation of these concepts as follows:

1) *Channel bandwidth* can be interpreted as the perceptory ability of a learner to receive and assimilate the teaching content. There are a number of metrics for assess-

ing hearing and reading abilities of a learner. Words per minute (wpm) is a common metric for assessing reading speed and is often used in the context of skill evaluation, where it is used as a measure of reading performance [29]. Rate for a human reading text is on the order of 100 bits/sec [30]. The average adult reads text on paper at 250 to 300 wpm, and 180 wpm on a computer monitor [31]. The range that people comfortably hear and vocalize words are usually 150–160 wpm [32]. Assuming that the average word length in English is 5 letters and that each letter carries about 6 bits of information, the estimation of bandwidth as 100 bits/sec is fairly accurate.

2) *Communication rate* can be interpreted as the ability of the teacher to present information to the learner. Slide presentations are about 100 wpm, while average talking speed is about 200 wpm [33], i.e., ~ 100 bits/sec, although differences between speaking rates of males and females have been noted.

3) *Noise* can be interpreted as a set of external or internal distracters such as fatigue or mental state of the learner that hinder the ability of a learner to assimilate information. Noise can arise due to factors such as mood of a student on the exam day, clarity of the exam questions, time pressure faced by the student, classroom environment, etc. When the class size is very small, most of these factors may not even be present, as there will be a better understanding between the professor and the students. But as the class size increases many of these factors come into play and begin to cause significant difference between student knowledge and true performance on the different assignments. Normal speech is about 60 dB, and noise in actual classroom conditions can reach 40 dB, therefore a typical signal-to-noise ratio is 15 dB [34].

4) *Number of communication channels* can be interpreted as the number of students in a class, while each student represents a receiver with his/her own unique characteristics. The average number of students in a regular class is considered to be about 21-26 [35], though the number depends on the national and administrative policies, demographical situation, the age of students as well as on the subject of teaching. Reducing this number usually improves student achievement [36]. In small classes, the teacher has the ability to quickly identify the needs of the student and provide feedback, which favours the more able students. In large classes, the ability of students to obtain feedback from the teacher on whether their studying style is appropriate for the course rapidly declines with increased class sizes, while the teacher usually focus on the less able students [37]. Also large class sizes and higher student loads are correlated with less critical and analytical thinking, less clarity in class presentations, and lower ratings on the instructor's ability to stimulate student interest [38].

5) *Variance* can be interpreted as variability of student abilities. There are number of metrics to measure variability in human population. A common metric to assess intelligence is an Intelligence Quotient (IQ), a score derived from one of several different standardized tests. Human IQ scores are approximately normally distributed with the mean of 100 and standard deviation (a square root of variance) of 15 [39].

6) *Threshold level* is a minimal passing score that is required to pass a test of exam. A typical passing score is 50% of correct answers.

The parameters of the knowledge transfer model are summarized in Table 1.

Table 1. Summary of model's parameters and their pedagogical interpretation

Parameter	Typical value	Property of	Pedagogical interpretation
Channel bandwidth	100 bits/sec	Learner	Ability to receive teaching content
Communication rate	100 bits/sec	Teacher	Speed of teaching
Signal-Noise Ratio	15 dB	Environment	Affects learner's ability to focus on learning and overcome disruptions
Number of channels	25	Environment	Number of students in a classroom
Variance	15	Learner	Statistical deviation of learner abilities from the mean
Threshold	50%	Environment	Passing score of an exam or test

Graphically the knowledge transfer model is depicted in Fig. 1.

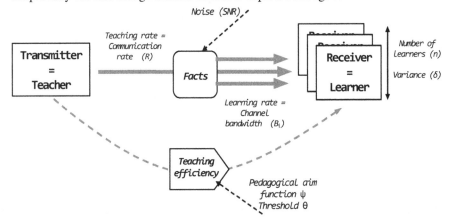

Fig. 1. Knowledge transfer model

In an ideal world, where a teacher and a teaching institution is driven only by pedagogical motives and a teacher is not limited with temporal constraints, the most favourable teaching rate could be selected so that all students including the least able ones would eventually assimilate all knowledge and would pass the knowledge tests.

In a real world, temporal, organizational and, especially, economical motives play a major role, and the teacher workload and economics of teaching must be taken into account. Therefore, we supplement the pedagogical model with economical parameters and constraints as follows:

$$\xi = \max \quad c_p \cdot \psi_3(R) - c_l n \frac{M}{R} - c_c , \tag{23}$$

here ξ is the economical aim function, c_p are financial benefits to the teaching institution associated with students, who pass the exams (such as tuition fee, government funding, etc.); c_l are the financial expenditures associated with student teaching process; M is the amount of teaching material to be communicated to students; and c_c are constant expenditures of the teaching institution not directly related to the number of students (e.g., cost of infrastructure).

Given a standard rate of communication as 100 bits/sec and the duration of typical lecture as 90 min, the total amount of information M transferred during a lecture from a teacher to a student is about 65 kB. Teaching costs and tuition fees have very wide variability depending upon national differences, standard of living, subject of teaching, etc. and must be given for a specific teaching institution in mind. Assuming that a student pays full cost of this education, and other expenditures of teaching are fully covered (e.g., by state budget), we can simplify Eq. (23) as follows:

$$\xi = \max \quad c \cdot \left(\psi_3(R) - n\frac{M}{R} \right), \tag{24}$$

here c is a cost multiplier.

5   Modelling Results

Since the teacher cannot change parameters of the communication channel (SNR, number of learners), which depend upon learning environment and personal capabilities of learners to learn (channel bandwidth, variance), the teacher can optimize learning process by selecting the rate of presentation that is optimal to his students. The pedagogical efficiency is evaluated using the percentage of students passing the knowledge test. In Table 2, we present the experimental modelling results.

Table 2. Experimental modelling results

Parameter	Value
Mean bandwidth, B_μ (bits)	100
Variance, σ^2	15
Number of learners, n	25
Signal-to-noise ratio, SNR (dB)	15
Threshold, θ	75%
Optimal communication rate, R (wpm)	269
Percentage of students passing, %	88

The results of knowledge transfer modelling are presented in Fig. 2. See that optimal communication rate of 269 wpm (corresponds to the peak of the aim function) can be established. Larger values of teaching rate lead to lower knowledge assimilation and subsequently to lower percentage of students passing, while smaller values of teaching rate increases time required to teach and subsequently increases associated teaching costs.

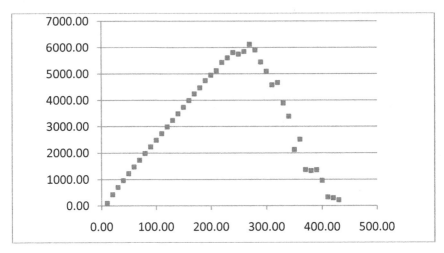

Fig. 2. Value of economical aim function vs. communication rate

6   Conclusions

In this paper we have presented an empirical model for describing knowledge transfer in a closed teacher-learner system based on a theory of communication in noisy channels with additive white Gaussian noise. We provide the pedagogical interpretation of the model's parameters and describe its application in modelling transfer of knowledge in the teaching/learning process. The modelling results show that if the teaching-learning process is bounded only by the ability of human senses to receive information, then the teachers will focus on the less able students and will adopt a slower teaching rate to maximize the number of students passing the exam. When a model is supplemented with the economical parameters and constrains, which includes financial costs associated with the teaching process, the model becomes bounded, and the optimal value of the communication rate can be calculated.

The proposed model can be used as a useful tool to evaluate the student passage rates in the context of changing parameters of the educational environment such as the number of students in a classroom, the number of teaching hours allocated for a course, or the amount of information contained in teaching materials that should be transferred to students.

Future work will focus on the extension of the knowledge transfer model with further parameters relevant to the teaching/learner process such as teaching material repeatability and memorability as well as for modelling knowledge transfer processes in group-based learning.

References

1. Rocha, L.M.: Complex Systems Modeling: Using Metaphors From Nature in Simulation and Scientific Models. In: BITS: Computer and Communications News. Computing, Information, and Communications Division. Los Alamos National Laboratory (1999)
2. Johnson, N.F.: Two's Company, Three is Complexity: A simple guide to the science of all sciences. Oneworld, Oxford (2007)
3. Morrison, K.R.B.: Complexity Theory and Education. In: APERA Conference, Hong Kong (2006)
4. Jorg, T., Davis, B., Nickmans, G.: Towards a new, complexity science of learning and education. Educational Research Review 2, 145–156 (2007)
5. Clarke, A., Collins, S.: Complexity science and student teacher supervision. Teaching and Teacher Education 23, 160–172 (2007)
6. Khan, B.H.: Managing E-Learning: Design, Delivery, Implementation and Evaluation. Information Science Pub. (2005)
7. Wiley, D.A.: Learning Object Design and Sequencing Theory. PhD Thesis, Brigham Young University (2000)
8. Piskurich, G.M.: The AMA Handbook of E-Learning: Effective Design, Implementation, and Technology Solutions. AMACOM (2003)
9. Janson, A., Janson, R.: Integrating Digital Learning Objects in the Classroom: A Need for Educational Leadership. Innovate 5(3) (2009)
10. Hannum, W.: A Pedagogy for Learning Objects: The Theoretical and Empirical Basis. In: Interactive Mobile and Computer Aided Learning Conference, Amman, Jordan (2007)
11. Štuikys, V., Damaševičius, R.: Towards Knowledge-Based Generative Learning Objects. Information Technology and Control 36(2), 202–212 (2007)
12. Haughey, M., Muirhead, B.: Evaluating learning objects for schools. E-Journal of Instructional Science and Technology 8(1) (2005)
13. Wirth, K.R., Perkins, D.: Knowledge Surveys: An Indispensable Course Design and Assessment Tool. Innovations in the Scholarship of Teaching and Learning (2005)
14. Martin, J.R.: Evaluating Faculty Based on Student Opinions. Issues in Accounting Education, 1079–1094 (November 1998)
15. Nuhfer, E.B., Knipp, D.: The knowledge survey: A tool for all reasons. To Improve the Academy 21, 59–78 (2003)
16. Schoner, V., Buzza, D., Harrigan, K., Strampel, K.: Learning objects in use: 'Lite' assessment for field studies. Journal of Online Learning and Teaching 1(1), 1–18 (2005)
17. Cohen, P.A.: Student ratings of instruction and student achievement: A meta-analysis of multisection validity studies. Review of Educational Research 51(3), 281–309 (1981)
18. Ju, T., Lin, C., Tran, H., Ju, P.: Knowledge transfer in higher education. In: Effective Teaching in Taiwan vs. Thailand, 2006 ACME Annual Meeting, Honolulu, Hawaii USA (2006)
19. Heilprin, L.B., Goodman, F.L.: Analogy Between Information Retrieval and Education. American Documentation 16, 163–169 (1965)
20. Kanagaretnam, K., Thevaranjan, A.: Grade inflation: causes and cures. Syracuse University (1999)
21. Cordier, P., France, M.M., Pailhous, J., Bolon, P.: Entropy as a global variable of the learning process. Human Movement Science 13(6) (1994)
22. Singh, V.A., Pathak, P., Pandey, P.: An entropic measure for the teaching-learning process. Physica A 388, 4453–4458 (2009)

23. Bordogna, C.M., Albano, E.V.: Theoretical Description of Teaching-Learning Processes: A Multidisciplinary Approach. Phys. Rev. Lett. 87(11), 118701 (2001)
24. Yeung, Y.: Scientific Modeling of Technology-Mediated Collaborative Learning Processes. In: Proc. of Conference on Learning by Effective Utilization of Technologies: Facilitating Intercultural Understanding, pp. 249–256. IOS Press, Amsterdam (2006)
25. Nitta, H.: Mathematical theory of peer-instruction dynamics. Physical Review Special Topics - Physics Education Research 6, 020105-1– 020105-4(2010)
26. Ogawa, K., Nakamura, Y., Yasutake, K., Yamakawa, O.: Mathematical Model For Collaborative Learning: Acquiring Hierarchic-Structured Knowledge. In: Proc. of the 21st International Conference on Computers in Education, Bali, Indonesia (2013)
27. Patriarcheas, K., Xenos, M.: Modelling of distance education forum: Formal languages as interpretation methodology of messages in asynchronous text-based discussion. Computers & Education 52(2), 438–448 (2009)
28. Shannon, C.E.: Communication in the presence of noise. Proc. of Institute of Radio Engineers 37(1), 10–21 (1949)
29. Bruggeman, H., Legge, G.E.: Psychophysics of Reading XIX. Hypertext Search and Retrieval with Low Vision. Proceedings of the IEEE 90, 94–103 (2002)
30. Reed, C.M., Durlach, N.I.: Note on Information Transfer Rates in Human Communication. Presence 7(5), 509–518 (1998)
31. Ziefle, M.: Effects of display resolution on visual performance. Human Factors 40(4), 555–568 (1998)
32. Williams, J.R.: Guidelines for the use of multimedia in instruction. In: Proc.of the 42nd Annual Meeting on Human Factors and Ergonomics Society, pp. 1447–1451 (1998)
33. Yuan, J., Liberman, M., Cieri, C.: Towards an integrated understanding of speaking rate in conversation. In: Proc. of Interspeech 2006, pp. 541–544 (2006)
34. Dillon, H., Massie, R.: The Impact of Sound-Field Amplification. Australian Journal of Education 50(1), 62–77 (2006)
35. Resnick, L.B., Zurawsky, C.: Class Size: Counting Students Can Count. Research Points 1(2) (2003)
36. Bressoux, P., Kramarz, F., Prost, C.: Teachers Training, Class Size and Students Out-comes: Learning from Administrative Forecasting Mistakes. The Economic Journal 119(536), 540–561 (2009)
37. Bandiera, O., Larcinese, V., Rasul, I.: Heterogeneous Class Size Effects: New Evidence from a Panel of University Students. The Economic Journal 120(549), 1365–1398 (2010)
38. Monks, J., Schmidt, R.: The impact of class size and number of students on outcomes in higher education. Cornell University (2010)
39. Becker, K.A.: History of the Stanford-Binet Intelligence Scales: Content and Psychometrics. Stanford-Binet Intelligence Scales, 5th Edition Assessment Service Bulletin, vol. 4. Riverside Publishing, Itasca (2003)

Testing Phylogenetic Algorithms in Linguistic Databases

Valery Solovyev, Renat Faskhutdinov, Venera Bayrasheva

Kazan Federal University, Kazan, Russia
maki.solovyev@mail.ru

Abstract. Phylogenetic algorithms are a tool that is frequently used in biology and linguistics for reconstruction of the evolution trees for species or languages. However, there is no a definitely superior algorithm: various algorithms have shown the best results in various studies. In this paper we test four most popular algorithms. We make recommendations which algorithm is better to choose in different cases. In particular, the influence of the feasibility of the lexical clock hypothesis is shown. It is shown that the results are also affected by the choice of metric, and that the results can be improved by using the λ-measure instead of the Hamming's measure. The results of the paper are obtained using both the simulation method and real data.

Keywords: phylogenetic algorithms, evolution trees, measures, linguistic databases.

1 Introduction

In a number of papers [1-3, 5, 8, 17] attempts have been made to apply approaches developed in biology for reconstructing trees of species evolution to linguistic data. These methods can be useful in solving some problems that are not solved using the traditional comparative historical method. Recently compiled large databases like The World Atlas of Language Structures [14] and "Jazyki mira" [10], which have introduced a great deal of new data for comparative research, hold the promise of producing new results in comparative linguistics. The two databases are compared in [10].

Phylogenetics and cluster analysis suggest different algorithms for constructing evolution trees and many questions are still not answered – which algorithm is better, which metrics (distance between languages) is preferable. The most popular algorithms in evolutionary biology include UPGMA (Unweighted Pair Group Method with Arithmetic mean), NJ (Neighbour Joining), MP (Maximum Parsimony), which are available in the packages PAUP* (paup.csit.fsu.edu) and Phylip (evolution.genetics.washington. edu/phylip.html).

The results described in published papers are contradictive. In research [16] the NJ and MP algorithms were compared, the UPGMA algorithm was excluded from the comparison. In [8] the evolution of Indo-European family was studied various algorithms were compared and it was ascertained that NJ provides better results than UPGMA. In fact NJ is the most frequently used algorithm. In [6] only different versions of NJ and one more phylogenetic algorithm, Greedy Minimum Evolution, were

G. Dregvaite and R. Damasevicius (Eds.): ICIST 2014, CCIS 465, pp. 373–383, 2014.

compared. According [5] "the Neighbor Joining algorithm …has emerged as the de facto standard".

However, the situation is not as simple as it seems. In [3] the evolution of Sumba languages, belonged to Austronesian family was studied. The paper also deals with comparison of different algorithms and proves that better approximation to the tree established by comparatively historical method is provided by UPGMA algorithm. It is quite natural to determine factors that cause such divergence.

It is clear why in the research [8] UPGMA algorithm gave worse results than other algorithms. One of possible factors that influence the accuracy of the results of the phylogenetic algorithm is a relative rate of language changing in the group under consideration. The principle "molecular clock" of the Pauling [18] is well-known in evolution biology. According to it mutations take place with the same rate for all the species on the segments of chromosomes with the same functions. By analogy to the "molecular clock" in linguistics there is a "lexical clock" assumption and we introduce "grammar clock" assumption, which implies the hypothesis of a constant rate of change in lexical and grammatical parts of languages correspondently. It in turn causes the same number of changes in the languages that had been existed after separation for the same period of time.

According [8]: "The UPGMA … algorithm … is designed to work well when the evolutionary processes obeys the lexical clock assumption". In [8] a lot of languages were considered, including both existing today (Latvian, Albanian, etc.) and extinct ones, disappeared at different time (Hittite, Old Church Slavonic, etc.) It is clear that languages that existed different periods of time have accumulated different amounts of changes, therefore algorithms oriented on equal number of changes cannot give good results. But if all considered languages are existing today (and the absolute majority of investigations are carried out for such sets of languages), then it has sense to test UPGMA along with the other algorithms.

Appearance of concrete examples, like in paper [3], which obviously contradict the conclusions of paper [12], demands returning to the problem of comparative evaluation of NJ and other phylogenetic algorithms.

It has been shown in [12] that NJ gives better results than UPGMA. However, the arguments mentioned in the paper are far from being exhaustive. The other reason for revaluation of conclusions [12] on the NJ advantages is that NJ was suggested in this paper for analysis of biological data. It is quite natural that the evolution of languages differs from biological evolution, and mechanical transfer of bioinformatics methods to linguistics can be sometimes improper. We need a model of language evolution trees and analysis of efficiency of the phylogenic algorithms applied to linguistic data.

The question what phylogenic algorithm gives better results has not only applied but also a theoretical value. If UPGMA shows better results it means greater advantage of lexical clock and grammar clock hypothesis and will provide better understanding the basic cognitive mechanisms of language evolution.

Another question under analysis in our paper is the choice of metrics. Languages as well as biological objects are described by a set of features. However, distance-based algorithms, such as NJ and UPGMA need to represent data as distances between classified objects. The use of Hamming metrics is standard. Its use occurring almost everywhere is explained by its simplicity being a tribute to tradition. There are many other metrics and there are no results which can prove that Hamming measure is better than other possible metrics.

Thus, there is a certain clearance for choosing an instrument at this stage of constructing phylogenic trees. In [17] λ-metrics was suggested and it was stated that it gives better results than Hamming metrics in many applications of cluster analysis, which phylogeny belongs to. The definition of λ-metrics is given in the third part of the paper; there are detailed explanations of the ideas the definition is based on and the methods of its application is illustrated by real example (from [17]). The example shows that there are situations in linguistic phylogeny when λ-metrics turns out to be better than Hamming metrics.

This paper is dedicated to problems of choosing tools and presents results of testing different algorithms and metrics on different sets of related languages.

2   Algorithms

Let us consider paper [12], which states that algorithm NJ is better than UPGMA. Careful analysis of the argumentation of the paper shows that NJ displayed better results only on the trees of certain topology (structure). In fact in [12] they tested only two very specific topologies of trees, given in Fig.1.

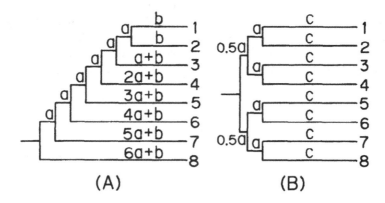

Fig. 1. Trees from paper [12], with permission

Tree (A) is extremely unbalanced. Trees of such structure are not found in language evolution. Tree (B) is balanced, but has other very specific properties: there are edges of only three different lengths, the edges close to the root being very short (a = 0.01), and the edges to the leaves being very long (c = 0.07). It results in the fact that the distances between leaves (the sum of edges lengths) are not very different: the shortest equals 2c = 0.14, the longest is 2c + 3a = 0.17, i.e. the longest distance is only 20% greater than the shortest one.

The trees of a language family level are not usually like these ones: the distances (the time from the moment of language divergence) between, for example, the

Russian and the Ukrainian languages are much shorter than between Russian and Albanian. Besides, the edge lengths in the trees of language evolution have many different values. These observations show that the results of paper [12] bear no direct relation to linguistic phylogeny. Structure of the real evolution trees of language groups is also far from "ladder" on Fig. 1 (a), the real trees are usually more "bushy".

That is why the problem of systematical comparison of algorithms UPGMA and NJ on the trees of various configurations becomes actual. Unfortunately, at the present time there is no a formal model of language evolution trees. For algorithms testing we will generate trees with random typology. Data available today allow to include in the model the estimations of relative length of edges, i.e. the period of existence of (proto-)languages from their appearance and till their decay or present time.

We shall analyze the time of independent life of all languages of a certain family based on descriptions from literature. One of the most complete descriptions has the tree of languages' evolution of Turkic family, given in [13]. Lengths of all the edges in the tree are calculated and ordered from minimum to maximum. The results are represented in Fig. 2. Here x-axis denotes number of the edge in the numeration of all edges in the order of length increase. Y-axis denotes the length of edge (period of existence of the (proto-)language).

It is easy to notice that there are several super-long edges and there is also one abnormally short edge – 30 years. The lengths of most edges – from the second to the 66th – lie on the direct line on the diagram. The lengths of these edges are from 90 to 650 years. The fact that most of edges except several ones lie on the direct line means that the length of the edges can be considered a value with uniform distribution on interval (90, 650).

Thus, the average value of the edge length (without considering the shortest and 10 longest ones) is 370 years. The declination of the edge length from the average value does not exceed 280 years that equals 0.75 of the average length. Let us

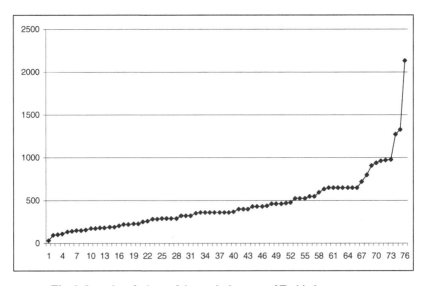

Fig. 2. Lengths of edges of the evolution tree of Turkic languages

designate this value as p (p ≤ 1). Analogous results are obtained for evolution trees of language families from completely different regions. For Mande [15] from Africa we obtained 0.81, for Maya [7] from America – 0.73. Let us take p = 0.8 in further calculations. Of course, it is not possible to calculate the values of p for all or many families, because there are no relevant data (trees with the length of edges calculated using glottochronology method) or such data are very debatable.

We made an experiment with generation of random binary trees of arbitrary topology. There are no suppositions in the first variant of algorithms that all languages can exist till nowadays. The trees were generated with a given number of leaves and the length of each edge was determined as a random number on a given interval. Then, matrixes of distances between leaves were made for every generated tree T. After that, trees T-UPGMA and T-NJ were determined by methods UPGMA and NJ.

To assess how big the difference between two trees is we used the Robinson-Foulds distance [9] between them, which stands for the number of elementary transformations needed for conversion of one tree into another.

To be more precise one can describe the whole algorithm as the following:

1. A random binary tree T with a given number of leaves r is generated, and all the edges are of equal length 1.
2. In the generated tree the length of each edge is changed by adding a random number from interval $[- p, + p]$, where p is a constant smaller 1.
3. The matrix of distances between leaves is constructed by the data.
4. Trees T-UPGMA and T-NJ are constructed by the distance matrix by methods UPGMA and NJ.
5. The Robinson-Foulds distance between the obtained trees and tree T is calculated.

Parameter p is introduced to consider the influence of historical randomness, which determine the time from the moment of a language appearance to the moment of its branching.

The trees with 24 leaves are generated for comparison with data from [8] (24 is the number of languages in [8]). We generated 500 arbitrary trees and averaged the results. As a result UPGMA constructs trees that in average differ by 12.3 from the initial one by Robinson-Foulds measure and for NJ the corresponding difference equals 11.5. As we expected the NJ result is better.

The second algorithm models the situation when all languages exist at present moment. Trees with 19 leaves are generated for comparison with data from [3] with the help of the second algorithm (19 is the number of languages in [3]). With this statement even UPGMA gives better results than NJ: average Robinson-Foulds measure 5.3 to 7.6. It exactly corresponds to data [3]: Robinson-Foulds measure between genuine tree and the trees constructed by UPGMA and NJ algorithms is 6 to 10 accordingly.

Thus, we can recommend using UPGMA algorithm while constructing phylogenic trees for the groups of existing languages.

3   Metrics

The UPGMA algorithm benefit shown on the model of trees relevant to language evolution is an advantage of lexical clock and grammar clock hypothesis. If these hypothesis are true for any language group at least approximately, one can use the algorithm of constructing ultrametrical trees (let us denote it as U-tree), described in [4]. The ultrametrical tree is a phylogenetic tree for which the hypothesis of a "molecular clock" holds true. If such a tree really exists for the data analyzed, the U-tree algorithm constructs it, otherwise it gives an approximate decision, namely the closest ultrametrical tree [4].

The UPGMA, NJ, and U-tree algorithms are clustering algorithms. They are based on the distances between the objects compared. Usually such distance-oriented methods use the simplest type of distances, namely the Hamming metrics (also known as City or Manhattan metrics). However, a number of researches of cluster analysis [17] showed that, in some cases, the best results are achieved by using another metrics.

It was established, that not only the distances but also the relations between them play an important role in many applied problems of data analysis. The fact draws more attention homogeneity than the absolute value of distances and was called the "λ-compactness hypothesis".

Let us formally determine the λ-distance (according [17]). Let the Hamming distance between all pairs of points of the set be defined, then one can draw a complete graph connecting all the points. We find the longest edge of the graph, i.e. the graph diameter (D). Let us designate the length of the connecting edge as $\alpha(i, j)$ for every pair of points i and j. We consider the value $d(i, j) = \alpha(i, j) / D$ to be a normalized distance between the points.

Among the edges adjacent to the edge (i, j) we find the shortest one, and designate its length as β. Let $r^* = \alpha / \beta$. Let us normalize r* dividing by the maximum value rmax. The value $r = r^* / rmax$ is a fixed characteristics of local density of set near the points (i, j). The value $\lambda = f(r, d)$ is called λ-distance between points i and j. Using the function $f(r, d) = r2\ d$ is the most advisable.

Let's consider the effect of λ-transformation in example on Fig. 3 (left part), where distance between points A and B, and also between points B and C equals 1; distance between points C and D equals 3; distance between points D and E, also between points E and F equals 5. As the calculations for λ-distance are fulfilled we obtain the following Fig. 3 (right part):

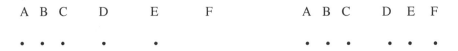

Fig. 3. Example of thew effect of λ-transformation

After λ-transformation distances between points A, B, C, and D remain the same. Distance between D and E equals 1.67, and between E and F equals 1. It is clear, that after λ-transformation points are divided into two clusters: A, B, C and D, E, F.

According to the "λ-compactness hypothesis" metrics can be spatially heterogeneous. The λ-metrics is spatially varied depending on the local density, distorting the space, like matter concentration distorts the physical space in the General Relativity by Einstein. Intuitively, λ-metrics smoothes objects density.

Thus it is necessary to test algorithms at least with two different metrics: Hamming and λ-distance. Contemporary state of science does not give an answer on the question – which problems each metrics should be used for. This is a subject for future investigations. In this paper we confine ourselves to describing a concrete example from linguistic phylogeny, which shows that λ-distance may be more effective than Hamming one.

Algorithms using λ-distance are defined as λ-UPGMA, λ-NJ and so on. MP algorithm is a symbolic one, i.e. it is not based on distances and, therefore, doesn't depend on metrics. We used algorithms from PAUP* package in the experiments described. First of all we made one experiment on the following language sample.

We used the following six pairs Americas languages from six different families (also considered in [16]):

1. Athapaskan: Slave, Navajo
2. Uto-Aztecan: Yaqui, Comanche
3. Chibchan: Ika, Rama,
4. Aymaran: Aymara, Jaqaru
5. Otomanguean: Chalcatongo Mixtec, Lealao Chinantec
6. Carib: Hixkaryana, Carib.

The choice of these languages is motivated by the following circumstances. Firstly, we use the WALS database, as the most eastablished database with the most reliable data. Secondly, while not all languages in WALS are described in enough details, there are enough data on the chosen languages. Finally, belonging of these languages to different families is beyond question among experts.

Following [16], utilize WALS descriptions, classified by the 17 best features. In Table 1 below we show how many pairs of languages had been correctly defined by the algorithms tested.

The main conclusions on the results of the experiment:

1. UPGMA algorithm has a better result than NJ on the test (in accordance with the results of the previous section).
2. Using λ-metrics we got a better result almost every time.
3. The UPGMA algorithm (with λ-metrics) turned out to be the best.
4. The results given by the MP algorithm are not good enough (it proves the conclusions of works [8, 17]).

The tree constructed by λ-UPGMA algorithm in the Newick format:

(((Aymara, Jaqaru), (Yaqui, Comanche)), ((((Hixkaryana, Carib), (Ika, Rama)), (Chalcatongo Mixtec, Lealao Chinantec)), (Slave, Navajo)))

Table 1. The results of testing different algorithms

Algorithms	The number of accurately recognized pairs of languages
UPGMA	5
λ-UPGMA	6
NJ	3
λ-NJ	3
U-tree	4
λ-U-tree	5
MP	3

The pairs of languages selected for the experiments are far removed both genetically and geographically. This reduces the influence of borrowing. Perhaps in this case one can fix approximately the same speed of structural changes and this could explain the rather good results of the UPGMA and U-tree algorithms for American languages.

Let's consider an example of λ-metrics calculation and its influence on real data clusterization. Let's examine a set of four languages Hixkaryana, Carib, Ika, Rama in the space of 17 WALS-features, selected in [16]. In several cases the features are not determined for all languages, in [16] this is denoted by the '?' symbol. We will interpret '?' as a new feature value, different from the values realized in other languages. Hamming distances are shown in Table 2.

UPGMA will start by joining the closest languages Hixkaryana and Carib in the one cluster. This gives the Table 3:

Table 2. Hamming distances between four test languages

	Hixkaryana	Carib	Ika	Rama
Hixkaryana	0	5	6	7
Carib		0	7	8
Ika			0	7
Rama				0

One can see from this table that Ika is closer to the Hixkaryana-Carib cluster than to Rama. Therefore, joining Ika with the Hixkaryana-Carib cluster will take place on the next stop.

Table 3. Hamming distances, step 1 of the UPGMA

	Hixk – Carib	Ika	Rama
Hixk – Carib	0	6,5	7,5
Ika		0	7
Rama			0

To calculate λ-metrics for the table 2 we fulfill the following steps. First of all we find the largest distance (8) and divide all the distances by this quantity, obtaining Fig. 4.

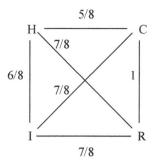

Fig. 4. Calculation λ-metrics, step 1

Then, we divide the length of each edge by the length of the shortest edge, contiguous to the one under consideration. We obtain Fig. 5.

To simplify our calculations let's skip normalization and calculation of the λ = f (r, d) function. This will not affect the final result in given case. On Fig. 5 distances are already modified due to local languages density, and this will influent clusterization result.

Again Hixkaryana and Carib are the closest, and will be joined on the first step, providing distances matrix in Table 4.

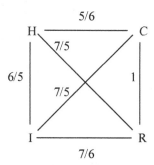

Fig. 5. Calculation λ-metrics, step 2

Table 4. λ-metrics, step 1 of the UPGMA

	Hixk – Carib	Ika	Rama
Hixk – Carib	0	13/10	15/10
Ika		0	7/6
Rama			0

But now it turns out that Ika is closer to Rama languages (7/6 < 13/10) and cluste-rization process will be accomplished in another way. Languages considered here belong to two different families: Ika, Rama to Chibchan, and Hixkaryana, Carib to Carib.

Consequently, this example demonstrates that λ-metrics can provide a more precise language classification, than the Hamming one.

4   Conclusion

The paper introduces the results of comparison of different phylogenetic algorithms. Numerical analysis of tree structure of well-described language families let us pro-pose the model of language evolution trees, which describes the distribution of edge lengths in a tree. The main phylogenic algorithms UPGMA and NJ have been com-pared on a set of trees randomly generated in accordance with this model of trees. It turned out that in the absence of dead languages UPGMA provides better result that corresponds with the results of paper [3] and supports the hypothesis of the same tempos of language changes. The advantages of UPGMA over NJ are for the first time demonstrated with the use of methods of mathematical modeling, not just on the base of examples from particular language families.

Further improvement of the phylogenic methods can be connected with the use of different metrics. It is shown, that λ-metrics, suggested in cluster analysis, gives better results than traditionally Hamming metrics, at least for one example of language tree.

Thus, currently there is no the best phylogenetic algorithm or metric. When select-ing tools for data analysis, it is not necessary to use only the most frequently used NJ algorithm and Hamming metric. Other tools may lead to better results. Testing of other algorithms, as well as testing of other metrics should be continued.

Acknowledgements. The research has been carried out with the support of Russian Foundation for Basic Research, grant № 13-06-97065.

References

1. ASJP. The Automated Similarity Judgment Program Project (2014),
   http://email.eva.mpg.de/~wichmann/ASJPHomePage.htm
2. Cysouw, M., Comrie, B.: How varied typologically are the languages of Africa? In: Botha, R., Knight, C. (eds.) The Cradle of Language, Oxford, vol. 2 (2009)

3. Donwey, S., Halmark, B., Cox, M., Norquest, P., Lansing, S.: Computational Feature-Sensitive Reconstruction of Language Relationships: Developing the ALINE Distance for Comparative Historical Linguistic Reconstruction. Journal of Quantitative Linguistics 15, 340–369 (2008)
4. Gusfield, D.: Algorithms on String, Trees, and Sequences. Cambridge University Press (1997)
5. Jäger, G.: Phylogenetic Inference from Word Lists Using Weighted Alignment with Empirically Determined Weights. Language Dynamics and Change 3, 245–291 (2013)
6. Jager, G.: Evaluating distance-based phylogenetic algorithms for automated language classification (2014), `http://www.sfs.uni-tuebingen.de/../njFastme.pdf`
7. Lachaume, R.: Tree of Maya languages (2009),
   `http://en.wikipedia.org/wiki/file:Tree_of_maya_languages.svg`
8. Nakhleh, L., Warnow, T., Ringe, D., Evans, S.N.: A Comparison of Phylogenetic Reconstruction Methods on an IE Dataset. The Transactions of the Philological Society 3(2), 171–192 (2005)
9. Pattengale, N., Gottlieb, E., Moret, B.: Efficiently Computing the Robinson-Foulds Metric. Journal of Computational Biology 14(6), 724–735 (2007)
10. Polyakov, V.N., Solovyev, V.D.: Komp'juternyemodeli i metody v tipologii i komparativistike. Kazan (2006) (in Russian)
11. Polyakov, V., Solovyev, V., Wichmann, S., Belyaev, O.: Using WALS and Jazyki Mira. Linguistic Typology 13, 135–165 (2009)
12. Saitou, N., Nei, M.: The Neighbor-joining Method: A New Method for Reconstructing Phylogenetic Trees. Mol. Biol. Evol. 4, 406–425 (1987)
13. Tenischev, E.R. (ed.): Sravnitel'no-istoricheskaja grammatika tjurkskih jazykov. Nauka, Moscow (2002) (in Russian)
14. Haspelmath, M., Dryer, M.S., Gil, D., Comrie, B. (eds.): The World Atlas of Language Structures. Oxford University Press, Oxford (2005)
15. Vydrin, V.: On the Problem of the Proto-Mande Homeland. Journal of Language Relationship 1, 107–142 (2002)
16. Wichmann, S., Saunders, A.: How to use typological database in historical linguistic research. Diachronica 24, 373–404 (2007)
17. Zagorujko, N.G.: Prikladnyemetodyanalizadannyh i znanij. IM SO RAN, Novosibirsk (1999) (in Russian)
18. Zuckerkandl, E., Pauling, L.B.: Molecular disease, evolution, and genetic heterogeneity. In: Kasha, M., Pullman, B. (eds.) Horizons in Biochemistry, pp. 189–225. Academic Press, New York (1962)

A Platform to Exploit Short-Lived Relationships among Mobile Users: A Case of Collective Immersive Learning

Jack Fernando Bravo-Torres[1], Martín López-Nores[2],
Yolanda Blanco-Fernández[2], and José Juan Pazos-Arias[2]

[1] Área de Ciencias Exactas, Universidad Politécnica Salesiana
Calle Vieja 12-30 y Elia Liut, Cuenca, Ecuador
jbravo@ups.edu.ec

[2] AtlantTIC Research Center for Information and Communication Technologies
Departamento de Enxeñaría Telemática, Universidade de Vigo
EE Telecomunicación, Campus Universitario s/n, 36310 Vigo, Spain
{mlnores,yolanda,jose}@det.uvigo.es

Abstract. Online social networks are largely failing to engage people in relevant interactions with people, contents or resources in their physical environment. We motivate the potential of automatically establishing sporadic social networks among people (acquaintances or strangers) who happen to be physically close to one another at a certain moment. We present the design of one platform intended to provide solutions from the lowest level of establishing ad-hoc connections among nearby mobile devices, up to the highest level of automatically identifying the most relevant pieces of information to deliver at any time. A number of application scenarios are presented, along with conclusions from redesigning a former system that delivered immersive learning experiences in museums according to the constructs of the sporadic social networks.

Keywords: Sporadic social networks, ad-hoc networking, mobile cloud computing, knowledge management.

1 Introduction

Research in the field of information services has made significant progress in exploiting the knowledge contained (explicitly or implicitly) on social networks like Facebook, Twitter or LinkedIn. Despite having radically different approaches and objectives, these Web 2.0 sites are always based on semi-permanent relationships among people. These relations (bidirectional, as friends, or unidirectional, as followers/followees) serve to gradually build knowledge bases in the form of graphs, with elements representing the pieces of information shared by the individuals: comments, documents, images etc. The analysis of such meshes of contents enables additional features like recommending potentially interesting contents for each individual, launching of advertising campaigns aimed at specific groups or segments of the population, identifying affinities among people or synergies between different areas of activity, etc.

G. Dregvaite and R. Damasevicius (Eds.): ICIST 2014, CCIS 465, pp. 384–395, 2014.
© Springer International Publishing Switzerland 2014

The interactions enabled by the aforementioned sites are largely confined to the virtual world of the Internet. These are not accompanied by face-to-face interactions except in cases in which people communicate to arrange physical meetings for entertainment or work. Moreover, it is noticeable that the individuals' interactions are increasingly focused on the set of people included in their social graphs, which are now accessible at any time. This causes a side effect of de-socialization, in which the individual is isolated from his/her environment and voluntarily (though perhaps not quite consciously) gets trapped in a bubble of communication with his/her contacts. This social phenomenon is being widely studied [10], but its effects in the medium-to-long term are still unknown.

This paper is about applying technology to enable new forms of social interaction outside the aforementioned bubble. We are building a platform called SPORANGIUM ("*SPORAdic social networks in the Next-Generation Information services for Users on the Move*") that aims at facilitating the creation and exploitation of sporadic (short-lived) social networks, communicating each individual with the people that surround him/her at a given moment —both acquaintances and strangers— and considering the information that may be relevant to them in different contexts and at different levels (room, building, street, city, province, etc). The goal is to allow individuals to make the most of their environment at all times. The proposal is applicable in various areas, from the formation of groups and the orchestration of activities around events or venues that attract people with potentially-related interests (e.g. museums, concert halls or campsites) to opportunities for enhanced communications and access to relevant information on the road (advanced information services to vehicular networks) or advances in the vision of the smart cities (related to the planning of personal mobility or the celebration of location-based urban games).

The paper is organized as follows. In Section 2, we present the architecture of the SPORANGIUM platform, followed by some of the functionalities we aim to support in different areas. Section 3 provides an overview of our ongoing experiments with the SPORANGIUM concepts in the context of History-related museums. Conclusions are given in Section 4.

2   The SPORANGIUM Platform

We are developing the SPORANGIUM platform as an extension of the technology that is already available to people, aiming to incorporate sporadic social networks (henceforth, SSNs) and the mechanisms that make them possible into the technological landscape of the well-known Web 2.0. Conceptually, its architecture has four levels, as shown in Fig. 1.

The sporadic social networks rely firstly on ad-hoc networks laid dynamically among the mobile devices of the people who happen to be close to one another at a given moment. With proper foundations, ad-hoc networks are arguably the most natural and efficient way to exchange information among people who are very close to each other, instead of proceeding "*the Whatsapp way*", i.e. sending data packets out to servers that may be very far away, only to have

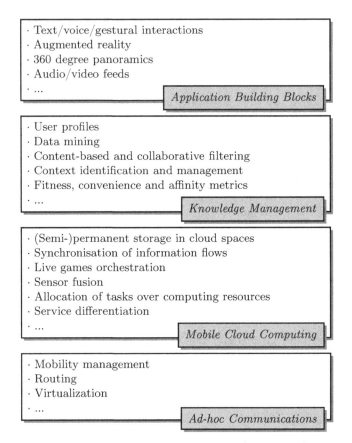

Fig. 1. The conceptual layers of the SPORANGIUM platform

the server echo the same packets downlink [19]. In this regard, SPORANGIUM provides mechanisms to establish connections proactively and transparently to the users whenever deemed appropriate by the information from higher levels of the architecture. It incorporates virtualization constructs introduced in [3] to use the ad-hoc networks as reliable channels and repositories of the information available to the members of an SSN. Virtualization provides scalable mechanisms by which the mobile devices can collaborate to support communications from, to and through them, directly or in a multihop fashion, even with the ability to differentiate a range of QoS demands.

Whenever the ad-hoc networks are not stable or reliable enough, the "*Mobile Cloud Computing*" (MCC) layer can use the infrastructure accessible through 2G/3G/4G connections or Wi-Fi access points to maintain connectivity as far as possible and to store information temporarily during periods of disconnection. Unlike the classical vision of mobile cloud computing, focused on individuals that would do practically nothing without access to the Internet (see [6]), the goal of MCC in SPORANGIUM is to enable value-added services for groups of people already in the level of ad-hoc communications, harnessing the resources available to each one of them through their mobile devices. There are plenty of things to be done without access to the Internet, which can nonetheless be exploited to offer more advanced functionalities and more abundant contents. Following this philosophy (which is explicit in the diagram of Fig. 2) the MCC layer in SPORANGIUM provides the following services, with only the last and the last-but-one depending on connectivity out of the ad-hoc networks:

- Storing information in spaces in the cloud, linked to source/target devices, creating/consuming users, location, etc.
- Accessing and serving information of high-level user profiles during the formation of ad-hoc networks.
- Synchronizing multiple flows of information coming from the connected devices.
- Supervising and enforcing interaction patterns to support live games.
- Pooling data from various sensors on multiple devices to achieve greater precision in geolocation.
- Delegating complex tasks on remote machines, to overcome the limitations of the mobile devices in terms of battery, memory and/or computing power.
- Providing access to cloud services on the Internet: maps, databases, semantic repositories, etc.

Upper in the architecture, the *"Knowledge Management"* layer is the place to put solutions from the areas of data mining, recommender systems and the Semantic Web to automatically drive the selection of pieces of information for the greatest benefit of the members of an SSN, while personalizing the contents delivered by each device either to a single person (as typically happens with mobile phones) or several people using the same device (as might be the occupants of a vehicle). In this regard, we are doing our early experiments by reusing semantic reasoning and personalisation mechanisms from previous works of our own, out of the realm of mobile devices and social networking [13].

The top level of the architecture, *"Application Building Blocks"*, conceptually contains the software components that provide value-added services to the members of an SSN, plus the interfaces that help make the most of those new features: augmented reality, 360 degree panoramic pictures, gestural interactions, etc.

2.1   SPORANGIUM Features for Venues

The use of the SPORANGIUM platform in venues has to do with the formation of groups, the orchestration of activities, the synchronization of multiple flows of information and the collective use of the devices in the hands of the different individuals. Museums, concert halls, campsites, kindergartens, stadiums, ... they are all places where many people get close together and, even though they may not know each other, it is likely that they have common interests (e.g. in History or Science, in a certain kind of music, in nature, in children stuff, in sports, etc). Hereafter, we will focus on features enabled by SSNs in museums, which put forward ideas that can be easily extrapolated to other venues.

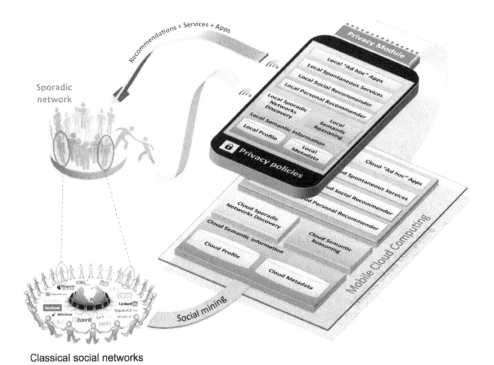

Fig. 2. The combined vision of ad-hoc networks and mobile cloud computing

People go to museums during their spare time purposefully to learn about a specific subject, which makes them propitious places to go beyond the individual use of mobile devices promoted by the many previous pieces of work that provided personalized itineraries within the buildings, continuity of experiences from one visit to another, etc [20]. With the corresponding SSN application, a museum visitor would be ready to start interacting with people out of the everyday contacts upon entering the building. To begin with, the user could browse a virtual bulletin board containing a selection of messages posted on Twitter by other current visitors with similar profiles. Short reviews and photos of areas to visit, ratings of activities and exhibitions, ... may be a very good starting point for newcomers to get to know the place and to meet new people, with no need to ever have browsed their Twitter profiles and, of course, with no need to have previously established follower-followee relationships.

The platform may also take the lead in gathering groups of visitors to engage in guided tours inside the museum, considering such parameters as language, country/province of origin, gender and age. Having identified a number of visitors for the task, their mobile devices could be used to agree on the hour, the duration and the topic of the tour in close interaction with the museum staff. Then, when the tour is running, the mobiles devices of the visitors and the guide would be contributing contents (textual comments, pictures, recorded audio, etc) to one space in the cloud, to be shared accessed by others to the criteria decided by the owner of each device: *"this comment is open for all the others to read"*, *"this picture can be only seen by the people who appear on it"*, ...

Contents coming from multiple devices in an SSN are automatically aggregated, annotated and synchronized at the MCC layer to allow accessing them in different ways. For example, they can be displayed on a virtual timeline that the user could scroll to remember what the guide had said minutes before, to compare a picture in display with another one in the preceding room, etc. They can also be displayed on a scrollable map or as augmented-reality items overlaid on the live output of a camera.

2.2   SPORANGIUM Features for the Smart City

Many institutions are promoting the concept of the smart city as a strategic move to improve the efficiency of the public services, to boost the activity of the local businesses and to improve the quality of life of the citizens. The sporadic social networks may enable new forms of communication and collaboration among acquaintances or strangers for several purposes.

To begin with, SSNs may support *time banking* initiatives as a means to forge stronger inter-community connections. Time banking is a pattern of reciprocal service exchange that uses units of time as currency: the time one spends providing these types of community services earns time that he/she can spend to receive services. This has been primarily used to provide incentives and rewards for work such as mentoring children or caring for the elderly, which a pure market system devalues. However, it also works with otherwise paid jobs like doing haircuts or gardening. Despite their growing interest in the context of global economic crisis [16], time banks usually fail to involve more than a few dozens of people, often from relatively close circles. This is where SSNs may bring benefits, inasmuch as the ability to trigger communications among strangers in close vicinity can greatly facilitate the discovery of potentially interesting offerings and people who might be interesting in what each one can contribute.

SSNs can provide means to deliver publicity of local shops and stores more effectively. For example, one user's positive valuation of a restaurant could be made visible not only to his/her contacts in some of the Web 2.0 sites, but also to other people with similar profiles in the surroundings. The valuation could become a coupon that, when redeemed by a new client, would yield free coffee/dessert to the former. Likewise, SSNs could be used to dynamically identify opportunities to trade batches of products in advantageous conditions (e.g. to offer 20% discount for one smartphone if at least 20 people come within the next 20 minutes to buy one unit each). Businesses could join the SSNs to tailor their offerings, and even collaborate to offer packs, e.g. dinner + disco tickets + private taxi for the break of dawn.

The SSNs could also become a basic element to improve the classical navigation/guidance systems based on GPS. Most of those systems work only with street names, which forces the user who receives instructions to look for signposts that may be hard to locate or even missing. One would certainly expect more useful and natural indications from the smart city, for example, to advance "*towards the red building at the bottom*" or "*to the roundabout with a Botero statue*". These indications —that should be tailored to each individual (not everyone can recognize a Botero statue)— could be derived from the activity of the citizens in Web 2.0 sites enhanced with the mechanisms of the SSNs, geolocation features, the possibility of making and sharing pictures, etc. For instance, it usually happens that one person (A) asks another (B, probably a stranger) for indications to go to a given place. Beyond a certain distance, the explanations become longer and more complicated, to the point that it is often necessary to ask a third person. The SPORANGIUM mechanisms could simplify the process by establishing a short-lived connection between the mobile phones of A and B. Thereby, A could follow the first indications given by B up to a certain point, and then send a 360° panorama to B asking where to go on... and thus proceed in three or four rounds, already in the distance.

Finally, the SSNs could provide suitable foundations for running urban games (aka location-based games) that involve groups of people —again, acquaintances or strangers— in entertainment or educational activities in the context of the smart city. Participants in flashmobs could be recruited on the fly, too. The experiences run up to now in several cities worldwide [7, 18] reveal great possibilities for community building in the exploitation of new tools for communication, interaction and personalization of contents.

3   Experiences with SSNs in Museums

During the last few years, there have been many approaches to improve the pedagogy of History through technology, with smartphones and tablets being around for some time [1], just like videogames for learning [4], location-based and virtual reality educational tools [9] and, of course, social networking on top of the traditional sites of the Web 2.0 [2, 5]. We started developing the REENACT system in late 2012 as an approach to bring augmented reality (AR) technologies into the scene as well, aiming to engage groups of people into immersive collective experiences that would make them learn about the prelude, the course and the aftermath of historical battles with the aid of tactile mobile devices, repositories of multimedia contents and remote experts. The system was originally implemented on top of the technological facility provided by the EXPERIMEDIA FP7 project, which features four functional components (see [17]):

- The *Experiment Content Component* (ECC) monitors, derives experimental data from, and manages the other components, taking control of installation, deployment at the experimentation venues, running and termination.
- The *Social Content Component* (SCC) gathers and manages data that is generated on social networking sites during the course of an experiment.
- The *AudioVisual Content Component* (AVCC) provides services related to the management and delivery of audiovisual contents, including acquisition from a media producer, adaptation and distribution to different platforms, live edition and realisation, and data and metadata synchronization.

– The *Pervasive Content Component* (PCC) provides means to track the users' locations as a means by which augmented reality content can be delivered and user-generated data can be mapped to a spatial location. It hosts an augmented reality platform and an online environment for the orchestration of distributed live games.

As shown in Fig. 3, REENACT supplemented the EXPERIMEDIA facility with one server installation and three interfaces (further details in [14]):

– The *REENACT server* centralised access to pre-recorded contents and live streaming through the AVCC, to store the records of events raised during the experiences and to control what was displayed on whichever screens. Besides, it provided a repository to store the static images and the text documents that might be used for illustration purposes at any time.
– The *reenactors' front-end* was an Android that relied on the PCC to render the AR contents on the participants' devices, and on the SCC to support messaging and rating of contents and comments. It also interacted with the AVCC to control the flows of text, images and audio entering and leaving each device.
– The *expert's front-end* was a web application providing the controls needed by the expert to deliver explanations and control the presentation of contents from a remote location, interacting internally with the AVCC and the SCC.
– Finally, the *administrator's front-end* provided the interfaces needed to supervise the operation of the rest of the elements during the REENACT experiences, including manual control over the orchestration of events and the gathering of information for later evaluation in cooperation with the ECC.

The REENACT system built on top of the EXPERIMEDIA facility was put to the test between June and August 2013, in collaboration with the Foundation

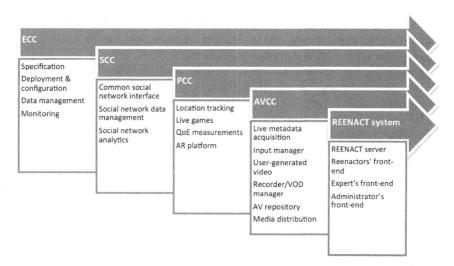

Fig. 3. Blocks and features of the EXPERIMEDIA facility and the REENACT system

of the Hellenic World, a not-for-profit cultural institution based in Athens with a unique technological infrastructure. The Foundation provided support from expert historians to develop historically rigorous scripts for the experiences and sets of questions and topics for games and debates. Besides, their virtual reality department contributed 3D models for the AR features as well as some pictures and audio/video footage to put into the content repositories. The experiments were largely successful, revealing —among other facts— that the participants in the different experimentation sessions could actually be seen as a sporadic social network of people doing something together for some time, rather than just a group of people doing something in the same room.

In parallel with the running of the experiments, we have entirely refactored the implementation of the REENACT system according to the constructs of the SPORANGIUM platform. This way, the new scheme to support the many flows of information generated during the REENACT experiences relies on two main ideas at the applications layer, namely connection sharing and parallel downloads among a mesh of cooperating peers:

- On the one hand, the mobile devices can activate any 2G/3G/4G connections whenever WiFi is not available (or performing poorly), and those connections can be shared in a MANET so that other devices can download anything from the Internet. The nodes that have permanent or transient access to the Internet advertise themselves as HTTP proxies by using the push protocol presented in [8].
- On the other hand, content downloading and sharing happens in a Torrent-like fashion, so that different nodes can get different parts (*chunks*) of the contents from the Internet and then seek for the the pieces they are missing from other nodes in the MANET. Here, we have adopted the protocol presented in [11, 15], which includes a gossip mechanism to propagate content availability information and a proximity-driven piece selection strategy.

At the transport layer, the REENACT app relies on UDP to deliver live video streams from the expert, advertisements and gossip messages; TCP is used for everything else (pictures, audio clips, comments, etc).

By replicating the sequences of events and the mobility traces recorded during the experimentation sessions of Athens and Vigo, we have confirmed that the new communications scheme beats the former one in terms of better connectivity, lower latencies (an average saving of 18% in downloading images and pieces of audio or video), lower battery consumption (3% saving despite the overhead due to virtualization, advertising and gossiping) and greater capacity to serve more participants in the experiences (nearly four times as many, from 17 to 60, thanks to reducing the burden on the content servers and the Internet connection behind the WiFi access points).

Figure 4 links the features of the system to the SPORANGIUM layers that support them. Probably, the most significant evolution lies within the disappearance of the REENACT server, due to the fact that we do no longer need a centralized point for communications. Instead, the *"Mobile Cloud Computing"* module can perfectly accommodate the server's tasks over all the devices connected to the SSN. The A/V delivered to the participants' devices are initially stored only in the expert's computer (quite a natural place for them, by the way) and they are distributed therefrom collaboratively in such a way that the computer does not need to upload the files more than once.

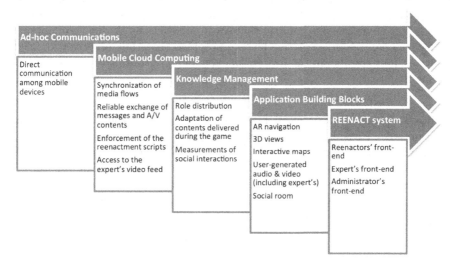

Fig. 4. REENACT features provided by the new SPORANGIUM implementation

Other specific points of research relate to the formation of groups of people who may like reenacting together —we have checked that parameters like age and gender differences do condition the way people interact—, the distribution of roles in the game, the adaptation of the contents delivered to each user according to his/her cognitive profile (borrowing ideas put forward in another EXPERIMEDIA experiment [12]) and the synchronized recording of the actions and contents generated during the reenactment, replay and debate stages. Overall, we can say that the reenactors' and the expert's perception of the REENACT experiences did not change with the refactoring of the system, whereas we have attained advantages in terms of openness, flexibility and scalability: simpler deployment, message packets flowing only inside the museum, lower bandwidth requirements, lower battery consumption, etc.

4   Conclusions

The SPORANGIUM platform aims at providing mechanisms to exploit the potential of the short-lived social networks that may be built around an individual to make the most of the people and the resources around him/her. Ad-hoc networking provides natural foundations for direct or hop-by-hop communications among people who happen to be close to each other. Mobile cloud computing concepts serve to leverage the resources contributed by multiple mobile devices, including Internet access to provide richer services than those available with ad-hoc communications only. Finally, modern knowledge management techniques are the key to bringing together the right groups of people to make the most of the resources present in their environment. There are plenty of scenarios in which SSNs ideas may enable new service opportunities, e.g. for communication, resource sharing or advertising, and our early experiments in the area of museum-like environments confirm that social interactions among acquaintances or strangers can be an attractive feature provided that they are given the right incentives, for example, in the form of unexpected entertainment or special commercial offers.

Acknowledgment. This work has been supported by the European Union 7th Framework Programme (FP7/2007-2013) under grant agreement no. 287966 (EXPERIMEDIA project), the European Regional Development Fund (ERDF) and the Galician Regional Government under agreement for funding the Atlantic Research Center for Information and Communication Technologies (AtlantTIC), and the Ministerio de Educación y Ciencia (Gobierno de España) research project TIN2013-42774-R (partly financed with FEDER funds).

References

1. Akkerman, S., Admiraal, W., Huizenga, J.: Storification in History education: A mobile game in and about medieval Amsterdam. Computers & Education 52(2), 449–459 (2009)
2. Arends, M., Weingartner, M., Froschauer, J., Goldfarb, D., Merkl, D.: Learning about Art History by exploratory search, contextual view and social tags. In: Proceedings of the 12th IEEE International Conference on Advanced Learning Technologies (ICALT), Rome, Italy (July 2012)
3. Bravo-Torres, J., López-Nores, M., Blanco-Fernández, Y.: Virtualization support for complex communications in vehicular ad hoc networks. MTA Review 23(2), 121–140 (2013)
4. Charsky, D., Ressler, W.: "games are made for fun": Lessons on the effects of concept maps in the classroom use of computer games. Computers & Education 56(3), 604–615 (2011)
5. Díaz, P., Paredes, P., Alvarado, D., Giaccardi, E.: Co-designing social games with children to support non formal learning. In: Proceedings of the 12th IEEE International Conference on Advanced Learning Technologies (ICALT), Rome, Italy (July 2012)
6. Fernando, N., Loke, S., Rahayu, W.: Mobile cloud computing: A survey. Future Generation Computer Systems 29(1), 84–106 (2013)
7. Gentes, A., Guyot-Mbodji, A., Demeure, I.: Gaming on the move: Urban experience as a new paradigm for mobile pervasive game design. Multimedia Systems 16(1), 43–55 (2010)
8. Helal, S., Desai, N., Verma, V., Lee, C.: Konark: A service discovery and delivery protocol for ad-hoc networks. In: Proceedings of 3rd IEEE Conference on Wireless Communication Networks (WCNC), New Orleans, USA (March 2003)

9. Jacobson, A., Militello, R., Baveye, P.: Development of computer-assisted virtual field trips to support multidisciplinary learning. Computers & Education 52(3), 571–580 (2009)

10. Kuss, D., Griffiths, M.: Online social networking and addiction: A review of the psychological literature. International Journal of Environmental Research and Public Health 8, 3528–3552 (2011)

11. Lee, K., Lee, S.H., Cheung, R., Lee, U., Gerla, M.: First experience with CarTorrent in a real vehicular ad hoc network testbed. In: Proceedings of Mobile Networking for Vehicular Environments, Anchorage, USA (May 2007)

12. Lykourentzou, I., Naudet, Y., Tobias, E., Antoniou, A., Lepouras, G., Vassilakis, C.: BLUE experiment: Description, problem statement and requirements. EXPERIMEDIA project deliverable D4.8.1 (2013), http://www.experimedia.eu/publications

13. López-Nores, M., Blanco-Fernández, Y., Pazos-Arias, J.: Cloud-based personalization of new advertising and e-commerce models for video consumption. Computer 56(5), 573–592 (2013)

14. López-Nores, M., Blanco-Fernández, Y., Pazos-Arias, J., Gil-Solla, A., García-Duque, J., Ramos-Cabrer, M.: REENACT experiment - experiment problem statement, requirements and PIA review. EXPERIMEDIA project deliverable D4.9.1 (2012), http://www.experimedia.eu/publications

15. Nandan, A., Das, S., Pau, G., Gerla, M., Sanadidi, M.: Cooperative downloading in vehicular ad hoc networks. In: Proceedings of 2nd International Conference on Wireless On-Demand Network Systems and Services (WONS), St. Moritz, Switzerland (January 2005)

16. Ryan-Collins, J., Stephens, L., Coote, A.: The new wealth of time: How timebanking helps people build better public services, http://www.timebankingwales.org/userfiles/NEW

17. Salama, D., Garrido Ostermann, E., Ljungstrand, P., Softic, S., Prettenhofer, S., Boniface, M., Crowle, S., Phillips, S., Halb, W., Konstanteli, K.: First blueprint architecture. EXPERIMEDIA project deliverable D2.1.3 (2012), http://www.experimedia.eu/publications

18. Sintoris, C., Yiannoutsou, N., Demetriou, S., Avouris, N.: Discovering the invisible city: Location-based games for learning in smart cities. Interaction Design and Architecture(s) Journal 16 (2013)

19. Sun, J.Z.: Mobile ad hoc networking: an essential technology for pervasive computing. In: Proceedings of International Conference on Info-tech and Info-net (ICII), Beijing, China, vol. 3 (October 2001)

20. Wang, Y., Stash, N., Sambeek, R., Schuurmans, Y., Aroyo, L., Schreiber, G., Gorgels, P.: Cultivating personalized museum tours online and on-site. Interdisciplinary Science Reviews 34(2-3), 139–153 (2009)

Sharp-Edged, De-noised, and Distinct (SDD) Marker Creation for ARToolKit

Dawar Khan, Sehat Ullah, and Ihsan Rabbi

Department of Computer Science and IT,
University of Malakand, Pakistan
{dawar,sehatullah,ihsanrabbi}@uom.edu.pk

Abstract. Fiducial markers are widely used in many Augmented Reality (AR) applications such as to manipulate AR objects, robot navigation, education and AR based games. ARToolKit is an open source, easy to configure and well-documented tracking system which is widely used for designing marker based AR applications. The quality of ARToolKit markers plays a vital role in the performance of these AR applications, but currently there is neither algorithm nor quantitative measure to guide users for designing high quality markers in order to achieve their reliable tracking. In this paper we studied the effect of edge sharpness, noise and markers distinction on markers reliability. We also developed the specialized algorithms for designing Sharp-edged, De-noised and Distinct (SDD) markers, which have low inter-marker confusion and are highly reliable.

Keywords: Fiducial markers, ARToolKit, Augmented Reality, Vision based tracking, pattern recognition.

1 Introduction

Augmented Reality (AR) is the technology in which computer generated information such as graphs, text, objects or audio are superimposed over some part of the real world environment in order to enhance the user perception of the real world environment [1]. Augmented Reality aims to mix virtual world in the real world so that the viewer perceives that virtual objects are part of the real environment [2,3]. AR has many applications including media teaching and learning [4,5], mobile robot navigation [6], and video conferencing [7]. Other application areas include medical, entertainment, military, engineering design, robotics and tele-robotics, manufacturing, maintenance and repairing [8].

Fiducial markers are images placed in a real world scene, to be detected by a video camera and identified by comparing their similarities with pre-stored templates [9]. These are used in indoor AR, hand-held objects for showing user pose to the camera, message tags to obtain some feature from marker, or general pose calculation for industrial setting [9]. Fiducial markers are used in a wide range of AR applications, including mobile robot navigation [6], 3D modeling [10], and education and learning aids [4,5]. Music AR is described in [11] as

G. Dregvaite and R. Damasevicius (Eds.): ICIST 2014, CCIS 465, pp. 396–407, 2014.
© Springer International Publishing Switzerland 2014

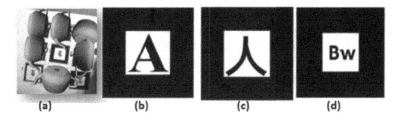

Fig. 1. Examples of ARToolKit markers (a–d), where in (a) virtual objects are overlaying the detected markers

an AR based game for children to enhance their attraction using webcam and to allow them to toggle on/off members of the musical team, or their musical instruments. ASR (Augmented Sound Reality) is another project developed in ARToolKit that mixes AR with a 3D sound environment [11]. Apart from AR applications, fiducial markers are used in other areas including robot localization, television, industrial, video conferences, and human machine interactions [12,13]. Similarly, some types of markers contain other data, such as phone number, a URL, or a GPS coordinate, and are used in mobile applications, giving URL to web browser and obtaining GPS data from a marker [14]. Marker based tracking is used in various AR applications to determine the camera pose by detecting one or more fiducial markers [15]. Pose can be determined with accuracy and low cost because fiducial markers only require a camera, which is already existent in many AR systems. Some examples of ARToolKit markers are shown in the Fig. 1(a–d); where Fig. 1(a) shows a screenshot of virtual solid teapots overlaying the detected markers. For designing various marker based applications different toolkits such as ARTag, ARToolKit and ARToolKit Plus are used. ARToolKit is open source, easy to configure, well documented and widely used in AR applications. Although ARToolKit is simple, users still have problems in designing high quality markers and achieving robust tracking. Although example patterns for fiducial markers are available, users have no clearly defined guidelines about various attributes while designing high quality markers. During markers designing noise may appear which causes inter-marker confusion and some time lead to miss detection. Similarly sharp edges that have abrupt change from black to white are highly reliable but it may be impractical to design sharp-edged markers. The most challenging task for a marker designer is to ensure that the new marker is distinct from all the existing markers in the library. So far there is no algorithm available to ensure that all the makers in the library are distinct and have no confusion in shape. Similarly there are no algorithms available for making the markers noise free and sharp edged. In this paper, we studied the effect of edge sharpness, noise, and markers distinction on the reliability of recognition. We found that sharp-edged, de-noised and distinct markers are highly reliable and have minimal inter-marker confusion. We also developed algorithms for making the markers sharp-edged and de-noised and to predict the possible inter-marker confusion in the ARToolKit markers library.

SDD markers are highly reliable and have minimal inter-marker confusion. The remaining paper is organized as follows: in section 2 related work about fiducial markers, quality of fiducial markers and existing problems are discussed. In section 3 the the effect of edge sharpness, noise and marker distinction along with the algorithms for these factors are discussed. Finally, in section 4 the conclusion of the work and some future work is described.

2   Related Work

Various studies have been conducted in the field of marker based Augmented Reality on the quality and applications of fiducial markers. This section covers the literature review on fiducial markers, and their quality. In addition, ARToolKit and some alternative marker tracking systems such as ARTag and ARToolKit Plus are discussed.

2.1   Fiducial Markers

Fiducial markers are images placed in the environment and are detectable by a video camera [6]. Marker based tracking is one of the popular methods in AR where predefined markers are placed in real scene, from which their position can be calculated [2]. ARToolKit [16] uses markers to translate and rotate virtual objects over the real world environment [17]. ARToolKit is the first marker tracking system used for marker-based AR applications while ARTag and ARToolKit Plus were later introduced [10]. ARTag is designed by the National Research Council of Canada and is also gaining popularity in the recent AR systems due to its improved performance [9,18]. ARToolKit uses square markers [19]. Markers of ARTag are also square in shape where the marker is divided into *10×10* segments [18]. The square shape is better for easy pose calculation [14]. Black and white markers are robust in various light intensity levels and are easy to print [20] whereas color markers allow a comparatively large number of distinct markers [12]. An ideal fiducial marker should contain at least four points in approximately squared fashion. However in some marker tracking systems, the shape of the marker is not necessarily square [19]. Minimal inter-marker confusion rate, low false negative rate, and immunity to various lighting conditions and partial occlusion are the key advantages of ARTag over ARToolKit and ARToolKit Plus [10]. The main problem with ARTag is computational workload which makes it incompatible with modern mobile devices [14]. Compared to ARToolKit, ARTag has two main limitations: no reduction of vertex jitter (noise at the corner) upon defocusing and longer processing time [21]. Source code unavailability is an other disadvantage of ARTag [22]. ARToolKit Plus also has the same limitation of longer execution time [17]. ARToolkit is the only toolkit which provides free source codes. Although some other toolkits are also freely available, they are not open sourced [17]. ARToolkit is widely used in AR and Human Computer Interaction (HCI) systems due to its freely available source code [9]. ARToolKit runs on a range of different operating systems, including SGI IRIX, PC Linux and PC Windows, each with a separate version of ARToolKit [16]. In addition ARToolKit has short execution time and is most suitable for real time applications [17].

2.2 Quality of Fiducial Markers

The best fiducial marker is one that can be detected with an easy and reliable fashion in all situations [14]. The selection of the best fiducial marker depends upon the application [14]. When following a proper designing method, marker can be constructed with high reliability [9]. The requirements for high quality markers are that: the marker should be distinct from the surrounding, unique in existing library of markers, passive (not coated with electronic substances), quickly detectable and effective in low light and noisy environment using a robust image processing algorithm [9]. The use of black and white markers enable easy detection in various lighting conditions [14], whereas using more colors support a greater number of unique markers [12]. The main challenge in AR applications is to achieve high speed and accuracy with low cost and minimal changes in the applications [3]. Rencheng Sun et al. have designed new kinds of markers (i.e. QMarkers), and have carried out comparison with ARToolKit in terms of the marker recognition speed and its reliable tracking [2]. Similarly in [18], new type of markers (called diagonal connected component markers) are introduced and the results are compared with ARToolKit markers in terms of detection time. Camara et al. [12] use color based markers to create up to 65000 unique markers with comparatively greater accuracy. They mentioned that their markers may be misdetected due to low quality cameras. The paper also concluded that larger quantity of distinct markers can be achieved by increasing their size [12]. However there is no experimental proof given. In [9], Fiala proposes eleven evaluation criteria for the quality of the marker system, namely: 1. the false positive rate (the rate at which absent markers are falsely reported as present), 2. the inter-marker confusion rate (the rate at which wrong id is reported), 3. the false negative rate (the rate of misdetection of a present marker), 4. the minimal marker size (the minimal size in pixel for reliable detection) 5. the vertex jitter characteristics (the noise in marker) 6. the marker library size (the number of unique markers in the library), 7. immunity to lighting conditions, 8. immunity to occlusion, 9. immunity to photometric calibration, 10. perspective support and 11. the performance speed.

2.3 Problems in Designing High Quality Markers

In ARToolKit, marker designing, registration (storing templates of markers) and their tracking are challenging tasks. During their designing, noise may be left in the marker which leads to inter-marker confusion and miss detections. Similarly for reliable recognition the edges are required to have abrupt change from black to white (sharp), but currently there is no algorithm available for edge sharpness of the markers. In addition there is neither any assistance nor algorithm available to make the markers noise free. The information inside the white region of ARToolKit markers are usually textual and create confusion [23]. One of the most challenging tasks for a marker designer is to ensure that the new marker is distinct from all the existing markers and that the it causes no inter-marker confusion in the library. Designing distinct markers is impractical to be done manually without using an automatic tool. Currently, there is no specialized algorithm that automatically checks the inter-marker confusion in markers library. Similarly, there is neither any clear guideline nor quantitative measurements available for designing high quality markers. Due to all the previously-discussed challenges, ARToolKit marker tracking has high rate of false identifications (false positive rate), high inter-marker confusion, high rate of miss detections of a present marker (false negative rate).

3   Designing Highly Reliable Markers

Marker designing has a great effect in marker recognition and reduction of the inter-marker confusion. Edge sharpness, de-noising, and ensuring the distinction among the markers in the library are the key tasks needed to reduce inter-marker confusion. These tasks are discussed in the following subsections.

3.1   Edge Sharpness

Edge sharpness means how the intensity change has occurred in the marker? Whether it is an abrupt change from black to white (sharp) or a slow and smooth change? We found that sharp edges are better for all circumstances because there is no ambiguity in such a case. Markers with sharp edges are identified accurately and inter-marker confusion can be reduced with sharp-edged markers. Example of markers having different levels of edge sharpness are shown in Fig. 2. To experimentally identify the effect of edge sharpness on marker

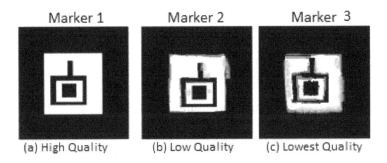

Fig. 2. Edge Sharpness: from left to right edge sharpness is decreasing so quality is decreasing

quality we used three markers, as shown in Fig. 2. We rotated and translated each of the marker in front of the camera for five minutes and stored the above three measurement (i.e. True identifications, False identification and CF value) and finally the results were compared. The CF value is the value from the range [0 1] which shows that how much the marker tracking system is sure that the marker is exactly as the identified one. In [23] the CF value has been used with the alternative name as the 'degree of similarity' of the detected marker with its pre-stored template. The lower value means higher ambiguity (i.e. low accuracy) and the higher value means lower ambiguity (i.e. high accuracy). In short for high quality the first and last parameters (i.e. true detections and CF value) are desired to have higher value and the second parameter (i.e. false detections) is required to have low value. We have identified that the sharper edges are better in detection. Marker1, Marker2 and Marker 3 as shown in the Fig. 2 are three markers such that the edge sharpness decreases in order: Marker1, Marker2 , Marker3. The results of five minutes experiments are shown in Fig. 3 such that Fig.3 (a) shows the true and false identifications per five minutes and in Fig. 3 (b) the CF values are plotted graphically after sorting in ascending. Here we found Marker 1 being sharper in edges the best one in number of true identifications as well as in CF value. Noise are small spots over the marker surface which creates difficulties in detection, because noise may become invisible in a non-optimal light intensity or with changing the orientation of the marker with respect to camera. We have developed an algorithm for noise removal and edge sharpness which is given in the coming subsection.

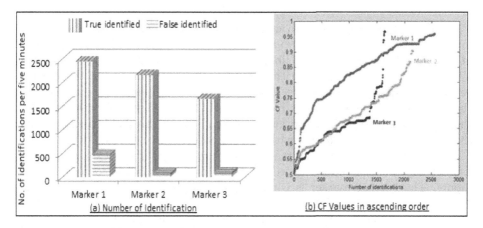

Fig. 3. Results of experiments on edge sharpness

Edge Sharpness and Noise Removal Algorithm. In this algorithm the input marker is first converted into binary. Then we use morphological operators to remove small objects from the binary image. The algorithm is given as:

$SmallObjectsRemoval(current\ marker)$
$(1)\ m := convert2black_white(current\ marker)$
$(2)\ m := RemoveArea(m,\ 30,\ 4)$
$(3)\ m := RemoveArea(\sim m,\ 30,\ 4)$
$(4)\ m := RemoveArea(m,\ 60,\ 8)$
$(5)\ current\ marker := RemoveArea(\sim m,\ 60,\ 8)$
$(6)\ return\ current\ marker$
$(7)\ end$

In the first step, the marker is converted into black and white, which makes the edges sharper as intensity changes become abrupt. In the second step, all closed regions of size $\leq$ 30 pixels 4-connected are removed. Then the negation (conversion of 0 to 1 and 1 to 0) of the marker is taken and cleaned from noise (regions of size $\leq$ 30 pixels 4-connected). Next, the regions of size $\leq$ 60 pixels 8-connected are also removed. In the $5th$ step, the marker is again negated to get its original binary values and the regions of size $\leq$ 60 pixels 8-connected are removed. The first and last steps remove small black objects from the white areas of the marker whereas the $2nd$ and $3rd$ step remove white objects from the black areas of the marker.

3.2   Marker Distinction

The most challenging task for a marker designer is to ensure that the current marker is distinct from all existing markers in the library. If there exist two or more similar markers in the library, they will cause inter-marker confusion. We have implemented an algorithm that checks the similarity of the *current marker* with all existing markers. A degree of similarity below the recommended threshold of T = 0.46 produces a *no confusion* message. On the other hand if the degree of similarity is greater than or equal to the threshold, the algorithm shows the most similar marker with the computed degree of similarity.

The algorithm takes the current marker cm, the library of existing makers $Library(n)$, and the recommended threshold for inter-marker confusion T as inputs. The current marker is compared with all markers of the library and the most similar marker, if exists, is displayed. In the first step variables key, $SimilarMarker$ and $MAXCR$ (maximum correlation) are initialized to *black and white of the current marker*, $NULL$ and *zero* respectively. In the second step, the key is checked with each marker in the library using the $DoS()$ algorithm, which will be discussed later. Here $Library(i)$ represents the ith marker of the library and CR is the computed degree of similarity. In this step the most similar marker with the key (current marker) is found. In the 3rd step, if $MAXCR$ is greater than or equal to the recommended threshold, the similar marker is shown with the value of the degree of similarity. The algorithm is given below:

PredictConfusion(cm, Library(n), T)
(1) *Initialization* :
    (i) *key* := *im2bw(cm)*
    (ii) *MAXCR* := 0
    (iii) *SimilarMarker* := *NULL*
(2)*For i* = 1 *to n*
    CR := *DoS(key, Library(i))*
        if(CR > MAXCR)
            MAXCR := *CR*
        end if
        if(CR ≥ threshold)
            SimilarMarker := *Library(i)*
        end if
    end for loop
(3) *if(MAXCR ≥ threshold)*
    (i) *Showmarker(SimilarMarker)*
    (ii) *Print"Degreeofsimilarity* = ". *MAXCR*
    end if
(4) *End*

Fig. 4. A screenshot of the checking inter-marker confusion

The screenshot in Fig. 4 is showing the result of inter-marker confusion check between two markers.The algorithm for checking the inter-marker confusion is based on the image correlation which checks the degree of similarity between the two markers and is given below:

$$DoS(key,\ marker)$$
$$(1)\ Initialization:$$
$$(i)\ W := marker$$
$$(ii)\ X := imrotate(marker,\ 90)$$
$$(iii)\ Y := imrotate(marker,\ 180)$$
$$(iv)\ Z := imrotate(marker,\ 270)$$
$$(2)\ corr = maxcorr2(key,\ W,\ X,\ Y,\ Z)$$
$$(3)\ return\ corr$$
$$(4)\ End$$

Firstly, the *marker* (an existing marker of the library) is rotated in four ori-

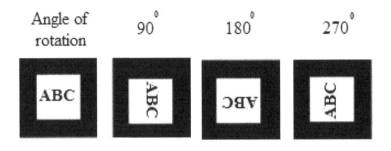

Fig. 5. Four orientations of an existing marker for checking its similarity with current marker

entations (see Fig. 5). These orientations are stored in variables W, X, Y and Z. Image correlation is then used to find out the degree of similarity of the *key* (current marker) with each orientation of the existing marker and the maximum similarity is returned.

Experimental Evaluation of the Algorithm. The experiments were to examine the meaningful relationship between the numerical value for *degree of similarity* that our algorithm provides and the marker matching algorithm in the ARToolKit. In other words, we aim to prove their semantic similarity. For this purpose we designed ten markers and stored them as a testing set. We designed a key marker to be moved in front of camera for detection in ARToolKit. The ARToolKit markers library contained five markers: first is the key marker, second is a marker from the testing set and three other markers (to enlarge the library size to an average case). We rotated the key marker in front of the camera for ten minutes and counted the number of detections as the key marker (true detections), as testing marker (confusion caused by testing marker) and the total number of detections. The testing marker was replaced by another marker from testing set and the same experiment was performed. Similarly the same experiment was repeated for the remaining markers of the testing set. For each experiment we calculate the percentage of inter-marker confusion (key marker is falsely detected as the testing marker) using equation 1, where '$\sum i(t_0)$' shows the sum of identifications as the testing marker and '$\sum i(T)$' shows the total numbers of identifications.

$$\% \text{ inter-marker confusion} = \frac{\sum i(t_0)}{\sum i(T)} * 100 \tag{1}$$

Table 1. Results of experiments on the inter-marker confusion

Serial no.	similarity between key and testing marker by $DoS()$ algorithm	% inter-marker confusion (caused by testing marker, using ARToolKit)
1	0.1535	8.49%
2	0.2263	9.53%
3	0.3197	12.17%
4	0.4202	12.35%
5	0.4318	16.02%
6	0.4516	20.38%
7	0.5462	30.43%
8	0.6523	30.67%
9	0.7140	31.89%
10	1.0	41.15%

We also checked the degree of similarity of the key marker with each marker of the testing set using $DoS()$ algorithm. The degree of similarity equal to 1 means that the key marker and the testing marker were exactly the same. The results are shown in table 1, which show that the degree of similarity that the our algorithm provides has a direct relation with inter-marker confusion in ARToolKit and hence we can use it for the prevention of inter-marker confusion in ARToolKit.

4   Conclusion and Future Work

We have studied the effect of noise and edge sharpness on the marker recognition and developed an algorithm for designing sharp-edged and de-noised markers. We have also developed an algorithm for checking the similarity a *key marker* with a number of markers to ensure marker distinction and predict a possible inter-marker confusion. Using the two algorithms the possible inter-marker confusion can be reduced and a robust recognition can be achieved. For future we are working to implement these algorithms in a GUI based application which will be used as an ARToolKit markers designing tool.

References

1. Patkar, R.S., Singh, S.P., Birje, S.V.: Marker Based Augmented Reality Using Android OS. International Journal of Advanced Research in Computer Science and Software Engineering (IJARCSSE) 3(5), 64–69 (2013)
2. Sun, R., Sui, Y., Li, R., Shao, F.: The Design of a New Marker in Augmented Reality. In: Proc. Int. Conf. on Economics and Finance Reasearch, Singapore, vol. 4, pp. 129–132. IACSIT Press, Singapore (2011)
3. Rabbi, I., Ullah, S.: A Survey on Augmented Reality Challenges and Tracking. Acta Graphica 24(1-2), 29–46 (2013)
4. Thiengtham, N., Sriboonruang, Y.: Improve Template Matching in Mobile Augmented Reality for Thai Alphabet Learning. International Journal of Smart Home 6(3), 25–32 (2012)
5. Shetty, C.G., Ujawal, U.J., Joseph, J., Chidananda, K.: Interactive Digital Learning System (IDLS). International Journal of Advanced Research in Computer Science and Software Engineering (IJARCSSE) 2(10), 479–494 (2012)
6. Luke, R., Bradshow, K.: Fiducial Marker Navigation for Mobile Robots. In: Honours Project, RHods University Garahamstown, South Africa, pp. 129–132 (2012)
7. Kato, H., Billinghurst, M.: Marker Tracking and HMD Calibration for a Video-based Augmented Reality Conferencing System. In: Proc. 2nd IEEE and ACM International Workshop on Augmented Reality (IWAR 1999), San Francisco, USA, pp. 85–94 (1999)
8. Vallino, J.R., Brown, C.M.: Interactive Augmented Reality. Ph. D. Thesis, Rochester (1998)
9. Fiala, M.: Designing highly reliable fiducial markers. IEEE Transactions on Pattern analysis and machine intelligence 32(07), 1317–1324 (2010)
10. Fiala, M.: Comparing ARTag and ARToolkit Plus Fiducial Marker Systems. In: HAVE 2005: IEEE International Workshop on Haptic Audio Visual Envirements and Applications, Ottawa, Ontario, Canada, pp. 148–153 (2005)
11. Kumar, M., SahityaPriyadharshini, K.: A Survey of ARToolkitBased Augmented Reality Applications. Journal of Computer Applications 5(3), 261–264 (2012) ISSN: 0974-1925
12. Da Camara Neto, V.F., De Mesquita, D.B., Garcia, R.F., Campos, M.M.: On the design and evaluation of a precise, robust and scalable fiducial marker framework. International Journal of Pattern Recognition and Artificial Intelligence 26(02), 386–390 (2012)
13. Radkowski, R., Oliver, J.: A Hybrid Tracking Solution to Enhance Natural Interaction in Marker-based Augmented Reality Applications. In: ACHI 2013: Proc. The 6th Int. Conf. on Advances in Computer-Human Interactions, pp. 444–453 (2013)
14. Siltanen, S.: Theory and applications of Marker based Augmented Reality. V. Science, VTT Technical Research Centre of Finland, P.O Box 1000 (Vuorimiehentie 5, Espoo), FI-02044 VTT, Finland (2012)
15. Russel, M.F., Julier, S.J., Steed, A.J.: A Method for Predicting Marker Tracking Error. In: Sixth IEEE and ACM International Symposium on Mixed and Augmented Reality, ISMAR 2007, pp. 157–160 (2007)
16. Kato, H., Billinghurst, M., Poupyrev, I.: ARToolKit version 2.33, http://www.tinmith.net/lca2004/ARToolkit/ARToolKit2.33doc.pdf (accessed August 17, 2013)
17. Vriends, T., Coroporaal, H.: Evaluation of High Level Synthesis for the implementation of Marker Detection on FPGA. Master Thesis Embedded systems, Eindhoven University of Technology (2011)

18. Wu, H., Shao, F., Sun, R.: Research of quickly identifying markers. In: Proc. IEEE Int. Conf. on Augmented Reality, Advanced Management Science (ICAMS), Chengdu, pp. 671–675 (2010)
19. Owen, C. B., Fan, X., Middlin, P.: What is the best fiducial?. In: The First IEEE International Workshop In Augmented Reality Toolkit, Media and Entertainment Technologies Lab, Media Interface and Network Design Lab, Michigan State University, 3115 Engineering Building, East Lansing, MI (2002)
20. Atcheson, B., Heide, F., Heidrich, W.: CALTag: High Precision Fiducial Markers for Camera Calibration. In: Koch, R., Kolb, A., Rezk-Salama, C. (eds.) Vission, Modeling and Visualization (2010)
21. Fiala, M.: ARTag, a Fiducial Marker System Using Digital Techniques. In: Proceeding of Computer Vission and Patteren Recognition, pp. 590–596 (2005)
22. Fernandez, V., Orduna, J.M., Morillo, P.: Performance characterization of mobile phones in Augmented Reality marker tracking. In: Proc. of the 12th Int. Conf. on Computational and Mathematical Methods in Science and Engineering, CMMSE, Spain (2012)
23. Badeche, M., Benmohammed, M.: Classification of the Latin alphabet as Pattern on ARToolkit Markers for Augmented Reality Applications. World Academy of science, Engineering and Technology 6(9), 386–390 (2012)

Shell Failure Simulation Using Master-Slave and Penalty Methods

Dalia Čalnerytė and Rimantas Barauskas

Kaunas University of Technology, Faculty of Informatics, Kaunas, Lithuania
dalia.calneryte@ktu.edu, rimantas.barauskas@ktu.lt

Abstract. Failure simulation for the flat structure assembled of the degenerated shell elements and referred as unidirectional composite is considered in this paper. Master-Slave and penalty methods are implemented in order to describe connections between elements. The results are compared for 2D simulation by both methods if structure is loaded in longitudinal and transverse directions.

Keywords: Degenerated shell element, failure criteria, Master-Slave method, penalty method.

1 Introduction

Finite element method has been used for linear elasticity problems since the origins of the finite element analysis. Nowadays it is also applied for non-linear elasticity problems and failure simulation.

The principal problems of nonlinear shell analysis are damage simulation and delamination. A zero-thickness rigid bar connecting master and slave nodes which belong to different layers of the shell is used in [7] to simulate delamination. Similar approach is used to simulate damage evolution in this article.

The general theory of element failure criteria is described in [10]. Failure criteria used for fiber reinforced unidirectional composites are summarized in [5]. Failure criteria varies from simple forms such as maximum stress (element fails if stress in the principal material direction reaches critical value), maximum strain (element fails if strain reaches critical value) to more complex criteria such as Tsai-Wu or Hashin-Rotem. Same criteria can be used to simulate failure of the layer and delamination between layers. One of the most popular criteria used in simulation is the Hashin criteria used in this paper. This criteria is used in [9] to predict damage evolution properties and failure strengths of composite laminates. The same criteria is also used in [11] to predict layer failure with additional component for delamination of the layers.

Two methods used for connecting shell elements are compared in this work. Flat structure is divided to degenerated shell elements. Each element has 4 individual nodes. The elements are connected by fictitious bar elements. In this work, we use two different methods to constrain connections between elements. Master/Slave and penalty methods are implemented and results for longitudinal and transverse loads are compared. The orthotropic material corresponding unidirectional fiber reinforced

G. Dregvaite and R. Damasevicius (Eds.): ICIST 2014, CCIS 465, pp. 408–418, 2014.

composite in mezzo scale is used in simulation. Total Lagrangian formulation is employed in dynamic analysis where all variables are referred to the initial configuration of the finite element model.

2   Explicit Solution

The global system of discretized equations of motion at the nth time step is given by [9]:

$$\mathbf{M}\ddot{\mathbf{u}}_n + \mathbf{C}\dot{\mathbf{u}}_n + \mathbf{K} \cdot \mathbf{u}_n = \mathbf{R}_n \tag{1}$$

Where $\mathbf{M}$ is the mass matrix, the damping matrix $\mathbf{C} = \alpha\mathbf{M}$, α – damping constant, $\mathbf{K}$ is the tangential stiffness matrix, $\mathbf{u}_n$ is the displacement vector at the moment after n time steps, $\mathbf{R}_n$ is a vector of the external forces. In the nonlinear explicit analysis component $\mathbf{K} \cdot \mathbf{u}_n$ is replaced with a vector of the internal forces $\mathbf{F}_n$ in order to simplify calculations [8]:

$$\mathbf{F}_n = \int_{V_0} (\mathbf{B}_L^T)_n \hat{\mathbf{S}}_n dV \tag{2}$$

Where $\mathbf{B}_L$ is a matrix such that $\boldsymbol{\varepsilon} = \mathbf{B}_L\mathbf{u}$ and $\boldsymbol{\varepsilon}$ is Green – Lagrange strain, $\hat{\mathbf{S}}$ is a vector corresponding the 2nd Piola–Kirchhoff stress. This follows from the total Lagrangian formulation that relates the 2nd Piola–Kirchhoff stress to the Green–Lagrange strain and where all variables of the element are referred to the initial configuration [1].

Displacements at the $(n+1)\Delta t$ moment are explicitly computed using formula

$$\mathbf{u}_{n+1} = \Delta t^2 \mathbf{M}^{-1}(\mathbf{R}_n - \mathbf{F}_n - \mathbf{C}(\mathbf{u}_n - \mathbf{u}_{n-1})/\Delta t) + 2\mathbf{u}_n - \mathbf{u}_{n-1} \tag{3}$$

3   Degenerated Shell Element (Reissner-Mindlin Assumptions)

Degenerated shell element also called basic shell model was developed from solid model in order to represent in-plane and bending behavior and corresponds to the plate element of the Reissner-Mindlin mathematical model [3, 4]. Basic shell element is developed with the plane stress assumption $\sigma_{33} = 0$ which is a contradiction to a consequence of the Reissner-Mindlin kinematic assumption that the strain component $e_{33} = 0$. These assumptions are substantiated by considering kinematical assumptions with additional thickness variable at each node for the higher order elements [4].

Any shell element is defined by material properties, nodal point coordinates, shell mid-surface normal and shell thickness at each mid-surface node. For convenience this relation can be written in respect to midsurface coordinates and a vector connecting upper and lower points:

$$\begin{Bmatrix} x \\ y \\ z \end{Bmatrix} = \sum N_k(\xi,\eta) \cdot \left(\begin{Bmatrix} \tilde{x}_k \\ \tilde{y}_k \\ \tilde{z}_k \end{Bmatrix} + \frac{1}{2}\zeta h_k \mathbf{v}_k \right) \tag{4}$$

Where $N_k(\xi,\eta)$ is a shape function of the kth node and ζ is a linear coordinate in the thickness direction, h_k is thickness of the shell at the kth node and $\mathbf{v}$ is a unit vector in the direction normal to the mid-surface [13]. The displacements at each node of the degenerated shell are uniquely defined by three components of the mid-surface node displacement and two rotations about orthogonal directions normal to $\mathbf{v}$. To simplify equations, additional degree of freedom (rotation about z axis) is included and constrained [2].

4   Element Connections

The flat structure is assembled of the 4-node degenerated shell elements. Each node belongs to one shell element but the initial coordinates are identical for the nodes which connect two or four neighboring elements, e.g. in Fig. 1 the initial coordinates of nodes 6, 7, 10, 11 (connecting 4 elements) are identical. Moreover, each connection has an indication which describes the direction the elements are connected, e.g. the connection 5-9 has indication 1 which means that elements are connected in the fiber direction of the unidirectional composite and connection 2-3 has indication 2 which means that elements are connected in the transverse direction.

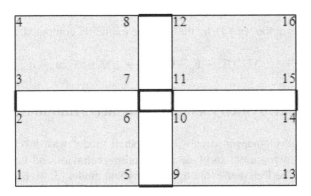

Fig. 1. Element connections and node numbering

Element connections are constrained using Master-Slave or penalty methods. Both methods are described in [6] as methods used for multifreedom constraints. The main idea of both methods is to modify stiffness equations by applying constraints.

4.1   Master – Slave Method

As mentioned above, there are nodes that have identical initial coordinates. One node of this group is chosen as a master node (typically, the one with highest global number) and the other nodes are called slaves. The slave nodes are eliminated and modified equations are used to evaluate displacements at the master nodes. Due to simplicity, it is assumed that constraints are homogeneous, that is the displacements of the one master-slaves group are identical.

The Master-Slave method is implemented by constructing transformation matrix $\mathbf{T}$. First of all, all nodes are classified into independent nodes (nodes 1, 4, 13, 16 in Fig. 1), masters (nodes 3, 9, 11, 12, 15 in Fig. 1) and slaves (others). Matrix $\mathbf{T}$ is a sparse matrix which has $n \times m$ form, where n is a number of degrees of freedom in the structure and m is a number of degrees of freedom of the independent and master nodes. Each row in the matrix $\mathbf{T}$ has only one element that is equal to 1 in the column that corresponds to:

- the degrees of freedom of the independent node if the row corresponds the degrees of freedom of the independent node;
- the degrees of freedom of the master node, if the row corresponds the degrees of freedom of the master node;
- the degrees of freedom of the master node of the group with the slave node, if the row corresponds the degrees of freedom of the slave node.

Matrix $\mathbf{T}$ has $n \times m$ form, where n is a number of degrees of freedom in the structure and m is a number of degrees of freedom of the independent and master nodes.

Then displacements of all nodes $\mathbf{u}$ are written in the matrix form:

$$\mathbf{u} = \mathbf{T}\hat{\mathbf{u}} \qquad (5)$$

Where $\hat{\mathbf{u}}$ is a displacement vector of the modified system which consists of the independent and master nodes. All matrices and vectors in (3) are transformed by the rule:

$$\hat{\mathbf{M}} = \mathbf{T}^T \mathbf{M} \mathbf{T}, \quad \hat{\mathbf{f}} = \mathbf{T}^T \mathbf{f} \qquad (6)$$

Where vectors and matrices with circumflex accent define vectors and matrices of the modified system.

If failure criteria in the specified direction is satisfied and connection between elements is deleted, nodes are re-classified and matrix $\mathbf{T}$ is re-arranged.

4.2   Penalty Function Method

The degenerated shell elements in Fig. 1 are connected at two nodes (ith and jth) by fictitious bar elements called penalty elements. There are 6 degrees of freedom at each node. The length of bar is zero at the initial moment and the axial stiffness of the element is ω and called penalty weight. The stiffness equations for the penalty element are:

$$\omega \begin{bmatrix} \mathbf{I}_{6\times6} & -\mathbf{I}_{6\times6} \\ -\mathbf{I}_{6\times6} & \mathbf{I}_{6\times6} \end{bmatrix} \begin{bmatrix} \mathbf{u}_i \\ \mathbf{u}_j \end{bmatrix} = \begin{bmatrix} \mathbf{0} \\ \mathbf{0} \end{bmatrix} \tag{7}$$

Then the additional equations of penalty elements are added to the initial system of equations. This method is direct (all displacements are computed at once) and no node reduction is used.

However, the basic problem of the method is the penalty weight selection. To maintain the integrity of the structure, we choose the penalty weight equal to Young's modulus in x or y direction respectively to the indication of the degree of freedom.

If failure criteria in the specified direction is satisfied, the penalty weight is changed. In the simplest case, the penalty weight becomes zero. However, more natural case is not considered in this paper when penalty weight decreases if length of the penalty element increases.

5   Failure Criteria

General formulation of failure criteria used to evaluate loads that cause failure of the individual layer of the unidirectional composite is described in [10]. If layer is modeled with the shell elements, it is enough to know stresses in principal material directions. Then failure criteria is described specifying the combination of stresses that cause fracture:

$$F(\sigma_1, \sigma_2, \tau_{12}) = 1 \tag{8}$$

σ_1, σ_2 stresses in principal directions and τ_{12} is shear stress. This means that elements work without failure if $F < 1$, fails if $F = 1$ and is deleted if $F > 1$.

In this article, Hashin failure criteria is employed [12]:

- Tensile fiber mode ($\sigma_1 \geq 0$):

$$\left(\frac{\sigma_1}{X_t}\right)^2 - 1 = \begin{cases} \geq 0, connection\,fails \\ < 0, connection\,remains \end{cases} \tag{9}$$

- Compressive fiber mode ($\sigma_1 < 0$):

$$\left(\frac{\sigma_1}{X_c}\right)^2 - 1 = \begin{cases} \geq 0, connection\,fails \\ < 0, connection\,remains \end{cases} \tag{10}$$

- Tensile matrix mode ($\sigma_2 \geq 0$):

$$\left(\frac{\sigma_2}{Y_t}\right)^2 + \left(\frac{\tau_{12}}{S}\right)^2 - 1 = \begin{cases} \geq 0, connection\,fails \\ < 0, connection\,remains \end{cases} \tag{11}$$

- Compressive matrix mode ($\sigma_2 < 0$):

$$\left(\frac{\sigma_2}{Y_c}\right)^2 + \left(\frac{\tau_{12}}{S}\right)^2 - 1 = \begin{cases} \geq 0, connection\ fails \\ < 0, connection\ remains \end{cases} \tag{12}$$

Where X_t and X_c are respectively longitudinal tension and compression strengths, Y_t and Y_c are respectively transverse tension and compression strengths and S is shear strength.

Failure criteria is evaluated at the node with stresses equal to the average of the stresses of the connecting nodes. Penalty element with indication 1 is deleted if criteria in fiber tensile or compressive mode is satisfied and penalty element with indication 2 is deleted if criteria in matrix tensile or compressive mode is satisfied.

6   Numerical Examples

6.1   Longitudinal Load (Fiber Direction)

The material of the model is orthotropic and the structure is assumed as unidirectional fiber composite where fibers lie along the x axis. Material properties are defined by the parameters listed in Table 1.

Table 1. Material parameters of the degenerated shell model

Young's modulus, E_x	$44.3 \cdot 10^9\ N/m^2$
Young's modulus, E_y	$14.4 \cdot 10^9\ N/m^2$
Poisson's ratio, v_{xy}	0.32
Shear modulus, G_{xy}	$4.43 \cdot 10^9\ N/m^2$
Shear modulus, G_{yz}	$4.05 \cdot 10^9\ N/m^2$
Shear modulus, G_{zx}	$4.94 \cdot 10^9\ N/m^2$
Density, ρ	$1432.7\ kg/m^3$

Penalty weight ω changes in steps and is equal to w - arbitrary value equal to Young's modulus in x or y direction respectively to the indicator of the degree of freedom if failure criteria $F \leq 1$.

$$\omega = \begin{cases} w, F \leq 1 \\ 0, otherwise \end{cases} \tag{13}$$

The flat structure in Fig. 2 is analyzed with linear loads in the x direction. Nodes that lie on the x axis are constrained in the y direction and rotation about the x axis and nodes that lie on the y axis are constrained in the x direction and rotation about the y axis. These constraints are employed in order to simulate only a quarter of the structure and maintain the symmetry of a structure.

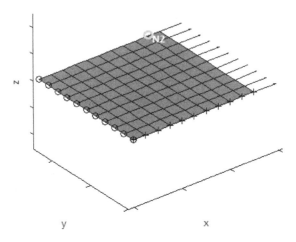

Fig. 2. Shell model used for damage simulation and loads along the x axis

Displacements of the node group N2 (Fig. 3) are compared below. The node group N2 corresponds to nodes 8, 12 in Fig. 1 that are labeled $N2_1$, $N2_2$. Due to the kinematic effects, failure criteria is satisfied for the first row of fictitious elements in the load direction as displayed in Fig. 3. As mentioned above, if failure criteria in tensile fiber mode is satisfied, connection of the elements is deleted and group N2 is disjointed to the nodes $N2_1$ and $N2_2$.

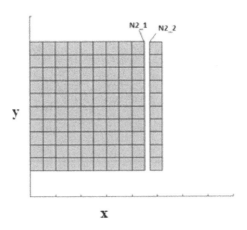

Fig. 3. Damaged structure at the final moment (Displacements multiplied by 10)

The x-displacements at the nodes $N2_1$ and $N2_2$ evaluated by different methods are displayed in Fig. 4. The difference between x-displacements is insignificant and appears because of computational errors. X-Displacements at both nodes are equal for Master-Slave method or differ minutely for penalty method if failure criteria is not satisfied as displayed in Fig. 5. After failure criteria is satisfied, x-displacements at the nodes differ significantly. This is caused by increasing linear load on the edge of the structure.

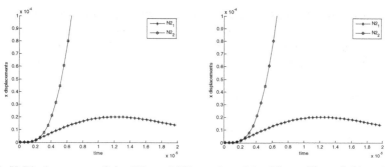

Fig. 4. X-Displacements of the $N2_1$ and $N2_2$ evaluated by Master-Slave (left) and penalty (right) methods

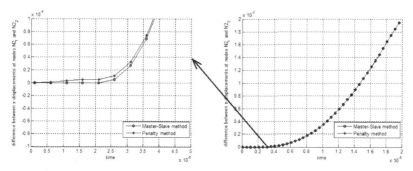

Fig. 5. Difference between displacements at the nodes $N2_1$ and $N2_2$ in the x direction

6.2   Transverse Load

The structure from the previous section is analyzed with linear load of the same magnitude in the transverse direction. Displacements of the node group N1 are compared below. Node group N1 corresponds to nodes 14, 15 in Fig. 1 and are labeled $N1_1$, $N1_2$.

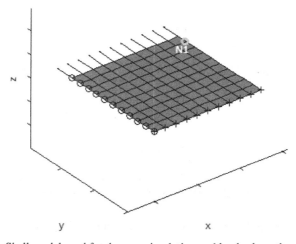

Fig. 6. Shell model used for damage simulation and loads along the y axis

Due to kinematic effects, failure criteria is satisfied for the first row of fictitious elements in the load direction as shown in Fig. 6. If failure criteria in tensile matrix mode is satisfied, connection with indication 2 is deleted and group N1 is disjointed to the nodes $N1_1$ and $N1_2$ (Fig. 7).

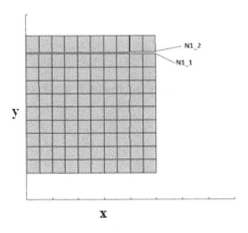

Fig. 7. Damaged structure at the final moment (Displacements multiplied by 10)

As in the previous section, displacements in the load direction (y) of the nodes $N1_1$ and $N1_2$ evaluated by Master-Slave and penalty methods displayed in Fig. 8 differ insignificantly and differences appear due to the computational errors.

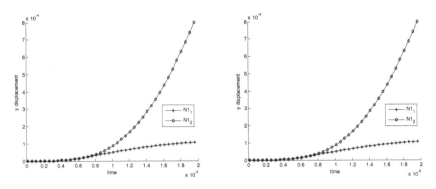

Fig. 8. Y-Displacements of the N1 group evaluated by Master-Slave (left) and penalty (right) methods

Difference between displacements between the nodes $N1_1$ and $N1_2$ also referred as a length of penalty element is zero for Master-Slave method and is small compared with shell element length for penalty method if failure criteria is not satisfied. Like in the previous section, the difference between nodes evolves after failure criteria is satisfied. This is caused by increasing linear load on the edge of the structure.

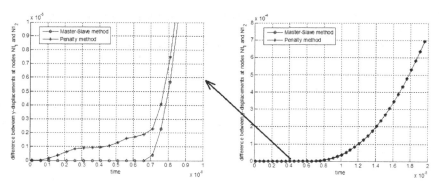

Fig. 9. Difference between displacements at the nodes $N1_1$ and $N1_2$ in the y direction

7 Conclusions

The failure of the flat structure assembled of the degenerated shell elements simulated by Master-Slave and Penalty methods is discussed in this paper. The orthotropic material was used for simulation and penalty weights were selected with respect to material parameters. As expected, for the loads of the same magnitude, structure fails for longitudinal load approximately 3 times faster than for the transverse load because of the orthotropicity of the material.

The obvious advantage of penalty method is a simple implementation. Contrary to the penalty function method, assembling of transformation matrix used in Master-Slave method is rather complex because of the master node selection and rearranging equations if the connection between the elements is deleted. The main advantage of the Master-Slave method is that it reduces the number of unknowns and is similar to the usual assembly process used in FEM. Moreover, all parameters in the Master-Slave method are determined contrary to the penalty method where the main problem is penalty weight selection. The results of the both methods show decent agreement for the considered examples.

References

1. Bathe, K.J.: Finite Element Procedures. Prentice Hall (1996)
2. Benson, D.J., Bazilevs, Y., Hsu, M.C., Hughes, T.J.R.: Isogeometric shell analysis: The Reissner – Mindlin shell. Comput. Methods Appl. Mech. Engrg 19, 276–289 (2010)
3. Carrera, E.: Theories and Finite Elements for Multilayered, Anisotropic, Composite Plates and Shells. Arch. Comput. Meth. Engng 9, 87–140 (2002)
4. Chapelle, D., Bathe, K.J.: The Finite Analysis of Shells – Fundamentals, 2nd edn. Springer (2011)
5. Cui, W.C., Wisnom, M.R., Jones, M.: A comparison of failure criteria to predict delamination of unidirectional glass/epoxy specimens waisted through the thickness. Composites 23, 158–166 (1992)
6. Felippa, C.A.: Introduction to Finite Element Methods (2011)

7. Li, B., Li, Y., Su, J.: A combined interface element to simulate interfacial fracture of laminated shell structures. Composites: Part B 58, 217–227 (2014)
8. Li, M., Zhan, F.: The Finite Deformation Theory for Beam, Plate and Shell. Part IV. The FE Formulation of Mindlin Plate and Shell Based on Green–Lagrangian strain. Comput. Methods Appl. Mech. Engrg. 182, 187–203 (2000)
9. Liu, P.F., Xing, L.J., Zheng, J.Y.: Failure analysis of carbon fiber/epoxy composite cylindrical laminates using explicit finite element method. Composites: Part B 56, 54–61 (2014)
10. Morozov, E.V., Vasiliev, V.V.: Advanced Mechanics of Composite Materials, 2nd edn. Elsevier Science (2007)
11. Spotswood, S.M., Palazotto, A.N.: Progressive failure analysis of a composite shell. Composite Structures 53, 117–131 (2001)
12. Schweizerhof, K., Weimar, K., Munz, T., Rottner, T.: Crashworthiness Analysis with Enhanced Composite Material Models in LS-DYNA – Merits and Limits. In: LS-DYNA World Conference, Detroit, MI, USA (1998)
13. Zienkiewicz, O.C., Taylor, R.L.: The Finite Element Method for Solid and Structural Mechanics. Elsevier (2005)

Security Level versus Energy Consumption in Wireless Protocols for Internet of Things

Algimantas Venčkauskas, Nerijus Jusas, Jevgenijus Toldinas,
and Egidijus Kazanavičius

Kaunas University of Technology, Computer Science Department,
Studentu str. 50, LT-51368, Kaunas, Lithuania
{Algimantas.Venckauskas,Nerijus.Jusas,Eugenijus.Toldinas,
Egidijus.Kazanavicius}@ktu.lt

Abstract. The Internet of Things is a rapidly evolving technology, which creates new challenges to security and energy consumption of devices at the various environmental conditions. Wireless communication technologies are one of the bases of IoT. In this paper, we proposed the security requirements of IoT applications to relate with the operating modes of wireless protocols. In addition, we presented the measurement and analysis of energy consumption and data transfer rates of Wi-Fi and Bluetooth protocols, depending on the security requirements of applications and conditions of environment.

Keywords: Internet of Things, wireless protocol, security, energy consumption.

1   Introduction

Depending on who one talks to, the Internet of Things (IoT) is defined in many different ways, encompassing many aspects of life – from connected homes and cities to connected cars and roads to devices that track an individual's behavior and use the data collection for "push" services [1]. IoT describes technologies where objects become part of the Internet, and all devices have unique identifier and access to the network. The goal of IoT is to enable things to be connected "anytime, anyplace, with anything and anyone ideally using any path/network and any service" [2]. IoT is very rapidly expanding: industry leaders predict that the number of connected devices will surpass 15 billion nodes by 2015 and reach 50 billion by 2020 [3]. Often, devices of IoT (sensors, mobile devices, PDAs, cell phones) operate in an insecure environment, are autonomous, have an independent battery power supply and use wireless Web access. One of the major challenges of IoT is the protection of data and privacy on a limited energy resource [4]. The solution to these problems can be found by using a variety of methods: data encryption, secure communication protocols, VPN, etc. [5].

Wireless communications (Bluetooth, Wi-Fi, RFID, ZigBee and etc.) are mostly used for data transfer in IoT networks. This allows for remote, fixed and mobility object communication without the use of wires. The wireless communications are shown to be less secure than wired connections since an intruder does not require a

G. Dregvaite and R. Damasevicius (Eds.): ICIST 2014, CCIS 465, pp. 419–429, 2014.
© Springer International Publishing Switzerland 2014

physical connection. Because of this, wireless communication protocols adopt numerous encryption technologies, and various protocols provide a different security level with different energy resource requirements. The energy consumption is closely related to a level of security. The better the security, the more extra energy and computation power is required, which in turn increases the cost of the device [6]. Various solutions of IoT are required for different levels of security assurance [7]. Therefore, communication protocols have to be chosen with regard to their security level on a limited energy resource. Other characteristics of the protocol, such as robustness to environmental noise and communication distance, have to be assessed as well. This requires a study of communication protocol energy dependency on security level and environmental conditions.

In this paper we propose a method to evaluate a wireless communication protocol energy consumption depending on level of security and environment conditions, such as noises in urban and rural areas. We experimentally investigate and compare Wi-Fi and Bluetooth protocol energy dependencies on level of security and environment conditions. It is believed that the research presented in this paper would benefit IoT application developers in selecting an appropriate protocol and operation mode.

2   Related Work

Several energy and security measurement techniques have been proposed:

Jin-Shyan Lee, Yu-Wei Su, and Chung-Chou Shen [8] provide a comparative study of wireless communication protocols, where they compare security, data coding efficiency and power consumption. Security comparison is done by using encryption and authentication methods in all protocols. According to the authors, data coding efficiency is defined by the ratio of the data size and message size (the total number of bytes used in the transfer of data. For power consumption, values form various manufacturers of wireless communication modules datasheets are used.

Friedman and Krivolapov [9] describe a study of power and throughput performance of Wi-Fi and Bluetooth in a smartphone. The experiments show power consumption for Wi-Fi to be generally linear with the abstained throughput. Also a dependency in energy consumption and data transmission protocol (UDP and TCP) is observed. Bluetooth is shown to use half the energy for data transmission compared to the Wi-Fi communication protocol.

Prasithsangaree and Krishnamurthy [10] describe an energy measurement framework for wireless communication security protocols. The authors suggest measuring security primitive energy consumption. This can be done in three ways: 1) directly measure the energy consumption of each component of a devices; 2) to assume that an average amount of energy is consumed by normal operations and determine the extra energy consumed by an encryption scheme; 3) by counting the number of computing cycles, which are used by the CPU in computations related to cryptographic operations.

Rice and Hay [11] proposed a power measurement framework for mobile devices. The authors use their setup to measure energy consumption by Wi-Fi data transmission of mobiles devices. The proposed framework measured only the power consumption of the wireless networking hardware.

The authors of analyzed works not have studied a wireless protocol's energy dependence on the security level and environmental conditions.

3   Security Requirements of the Internet of Things and Wireless Protocols

Security for IoT should focus on the protection of the data itself and the network connections between the devices of IoT [8]. Overall, security requirements often vary with IoT application. In IoT we can distinguish the following main requirements of security objectives: confidentiality, integrity and availability. For each security objective a certain number of security levels are introduced. The number and type of data and communication security classification levels will depend on the nature of the IoT solution, e.g., in the business sector, levels, such as Public, Sensitive, Private, and Confidential, in the government sector, labels, such as Unclassified (U), Sensitive But Unclassified (SU), Restricted (R), Confidential (C), Secret (S), and Top Secret (TS) are introduced [7]. For different security objectives, the security levels can be different. Various solutions of IoT are required for different levels of security assurance.

Wireless protocols are commonly used in networks of IoT for communications. Wireless communication protocols (Bluetooth, Wi-Fi, RFID, ZigBee and etc.) operates in different security modes. These security modes provide different levels of security.

Below we will explore the Wi-Fi and Bluetooth protocols and we will associate their operation modes with security levels.

Bluetooth is a short-range radio frequency communication for exchanging data. Bluetooth technology is used in fixed and mobiles devices, building personal are and IoT networks. Nowadays almost all mobile devices have Bluetooth technology. The range for Bluetooth communication is 0.1 - 100 meters, and is power-dependent. Communication between the devices is master-slave based [12]. The master controls all communication and slave cannot communicate directly. A master can communicate ether point-to-point or point-to-multipoint. A group of Bluetooth devices forms a cell called piconet, if several piconets overlap they created "scatternet" network. The same Bluetooth device can depend to several piconets at the same time, thus let expand the coverage area of Bluetooth network.

The Bluetooth protocol defines three security modes: Mode 1 is non-secure (authentication is optional); Mode 2 gives service-level enforced security (the service provided by the application) and Mode 3 is link-level enforced security (both devices must implement security procedures). The main characteristics of Bluetooth protocol are presented in Table 1.

Wi-Fi is a technology that allows an electronic devices to exchange data or connect to the internet by using radio waves [13]. This technology is based on the IEEE 802.11 standards for wireless local area network (WLAN). Many devices, ranging from smartphones to sensors, have Wi-Fi connectivity. These devices can connect to a network or internet by using a wireless network access point. These access points have a range of about 20 meters indoors and a better outdoor range. In addition, wireless communication devices can be connected into ad-hoc network, where devices communicate directly. Wireless devices communicate with each other by using unique identities.

The Wi-Fi protocol defines following security modes: Unprotected; WEP - Wired Equivalent Privacy, WPA - Wi-Fi Protected Access and WPA2 - Wi-Fi Protected Access 2. The main characteristics of the Wi-Fi protocol are presented in Table 1.

Table 1. Comparison of Wi-Fi and Bluetooth protocols

Standard	Bluetooth (classic)	Smart Bluetooth	Wi-Fi	Wi-Fi/n
IEEE spec.	802.15.1	802.15.1	802.11a/b/g	802.11n
Max signal rate	3 Mb/s	1 Mb/s	54Mb/s	100 Mb/s
Nominal range	10 m	10 m	100m	140m
Encryption	E0 stream cipher	AES stream cipher	RC4 stream cipher (WEP), AES block cipher	RC4 stream cipher (WEP), AES block cipher
Authentication	Shared secret	Shared secret	WPA2 (802.11i)	WPA2 (802.11i)
Data Protection	16-bit CRC	24-bit CRC, 32-bit Message integrity check	32-bit CRC	32-bit CRC
Operation (security) mode	Mode 1 (unprotected) Mode 2 (Encrypted), Mode 3 (full encrypted).	Mode 1 (unprotected) Mode 2 (Encrypted), Mode 3 (full encrypted).	Unprotected, WEP_64, WEP_128, WPA_TKIP, WPA_AES, WPA2_TKIP_AES, WPA2_AES.	Unprotected, WEP_64, WEP_128, WPA_TKIP, WPA_AES, WPA2_TKIP_AES, WPA2_AES.

Bluetooth 4.0 single mode (Bluetooth Smart) devices are not inter-operable with classic Bluetooth devices such as Bluetooth 2.1 + EDR devices. Single mode devices are only compliant with other Bluetooth 4.0 devices [16]. However, in IoT applications are still widely used a classic Bluetooth devices, so we will investigate classic Bluetooth protocol.

The IEEE 802.11n takes the spectrally efficient orthogonal frequency division multiplexing physical layer of 802.11 a/g, and adds antennas to take advantage of multiple spatial paths in the radio frequency environment [17]. For example, receiving short packets with a single antenna can be more than twice as energy-efficient as receiving as fast as possible using all three antennas to maximize speed. Because in IoT is important minimization of energy consumption, so we will Investigate Wi-Fi 802.11 a/g protocol.

We have analyzed the operating and security modes of Bluetooth and Wi-Fi protocols, the authentication methods and data encryption algorithms and key lengths used in Bluetooth and Wi-Fi protocols. According to the results of the analysis, we identified relations between the levels of security and operation modes of protocols. In the Table 2 are presented relations between the levels of security and operation modes of Bluetooth and Wi-Fi protocols.

Table 2. Relations between the levels of security and operation modes of Bluetooth and Wi-Fi protocols

Security level	U	SU	SU	R	C	S	TS
Bluetooth	Mode 1	Mode 2	Mode 2	Mode 3	X	X	X
Wi-Fi mode	Unprotected	WEP 64	WEP 128	WPA_ TKIP	WPA_ AES	WPA2_ TKIP_AES	WPA2_ AES

X – not supported security level.

As seen from Table 2, the Wi-Fi protocol supports all our classed levels of security, and protocol Bluetooth supports only the lowest four levels of security.

4   Experimental Setup

The hardware model used in the experiment is based on *.NET Gadgeteer* tools developed by Microsoft and GHIelectronics for the purposes to support small electronic projects [14].

In Fig. 1, we present the model's architecture. The model's architecture is the same for Wi-Fi and Bluetooth protocols. It consists of three components: prototype module (PM), access point (Wi-Fi or Bluetooth) and measurement module (MM). The first is the information source to be transferred, while the second is treated as a sink (user) of this information.

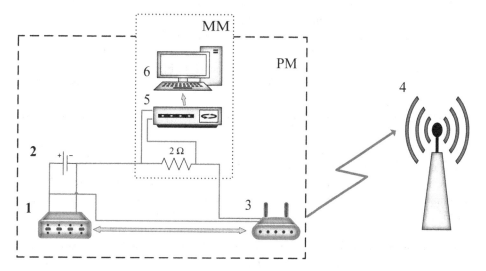

Fig. 1. Architecture of the system. 1. Control and processing module, 2.Power supply , 3. Communication module, 4. Access point, 5. Multimeter, 6. Computer, , PM – prototype module, MM – measurement module.

We performed experiments by simulating the real and the ideal environmental conditions and by changing the length of the data transfer buffer, and the operating modes of the protocols. We have selected the rural location, which we have been identified as an ideal place to provide our experiments because there were no evident radio signals that might make the interference with the measured ones. On contrary, the large organization with the well-developed communication infrastructure within the urban area (city) has been treated as a location to create the real conditions for experiments. Equivalent measurements we performed with Wi-Fi and Bluetooth modules. Internet of Things is typical the small amounts of transferred data at the time of single communication session. We used buffers of 512 bytes and 1024 bytes sizes to transfer data packets of 0.5 MB. In 'ideal' environment was only one communication module and one of the active access point. In 'real' environment were more than 10 active communication modules and the access points. We performed measurements 10 times in each case.

5   Experimental Results

In Fig. 2, we present the measured voltage waveforms recalculated to power units by transferring 0.5 MB of data. Fig. 2(a) shows the signal form for Bluetooth ideal environment, (b) – for Bluetooth real environment, (c) – for Wi-Fi ideal environment and (d), (e), (f) – for Wi-Fi real environment. The waveforms for Bluetooth communication are similar in the ideal and real environmental conditions, that is, energy consumption few depends on the environment noises. The waveforms for Wi-Fi communication are differ significantly in the ideal and real environmental conditions. Practically all 10 trials were different (only 3 variants are given in Fig. 2 (d), (e), (f) to illustrate that); whereas in the real environment each trial practically had the same waveform (it is why we present the only one instance in Fig. 2 (c)). So, in the case of Wi-Fi, energy consumption varies and increases considerably with increasing the environment noise.

Experimental results were obtained using the MATLAB facilities and are presented in following tables and figures.

In the Table 3 and Fig. 3 are presented security level-energy dependencies for Bluetooth and Wi-Fi protocols in ideal and real environments. As can be seen from the results, increasing the level of security from Unclassified (U) to Restricted (R), the consumption of energy increases for Bluetooth protocol by about 30%, and 35% for Wi-Fi. Communication in real (noisy) environment stipulates the increase of 15 % for Bluetooth and 35 – 95% for Wi-Fi in energy consumption. Thus the influence of the security level incrementation for both protocols is similar. Environmental noise level influences the increase of energy consumption for Wi-Fi protocol from 2 to 6 times more than the for Bluetooth protocol.

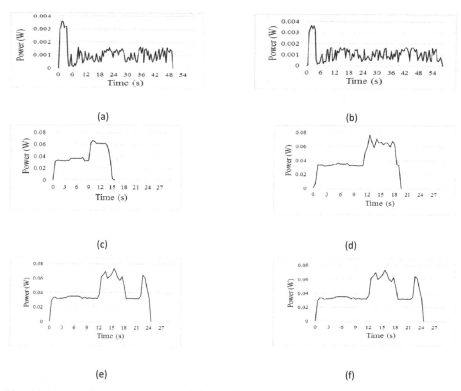

Fig. 2. Data transfer waveforms: (a) – Bluetooth ideal environment; (b) – Bluetooth real environment; (c) – Wi-Fi ideal environment; (d), (e), (f) – real environment

Table 3. Energy-security level dependency in ideal and real modes

Security level	Energy consumption in ideal environment (mJ/kB)		Energy consumption in real environment (mJ/kB)	
	Bluetooth	*Wi-Fi*	*Bluetooth*	*Wi-Fi*
U	0.107	0.928	0.125	1.297
SU	0.116	0.939	0.135	1.561
SU	0.124	0.939	0.133	1.867
R	0.137	1.266	0.155	1.852
C		1.242		1.748
S		1.223		1.770
TS		1.244		1.656

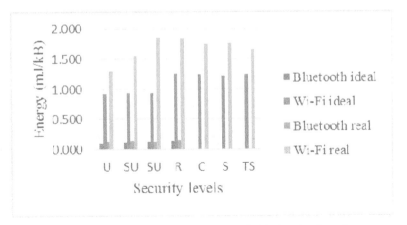

Fig. 3. Energy-security level dependency in ideal and real modes

Table 4. Data transfer rate - security level dependency in ideal and real modes

Security level	Data transfer rate in ideal environment (kB/s)		Data transfer rate in real environment (kB/s)	
	Bluetooth	*Wi-Fi*	*Bluetooth*	*Wi-Fi*
U	9.722	73.438	8.141	57.253
SU	9.796	73.626	7.489	43.900
SU	9.684	76.923	7.184	32.190
R	9.647	73.626	7.001	48.514
C		73.077		45.309
S		73.077		48.279
TS		73.077		45.857

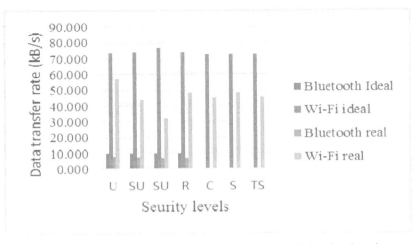

Fig. 4. Data transfer rate - security level dependency in ideal and real modes

Table 5. Energy-security level-environment dependency

Security Level	Energy consumption of session in ideal environment (J)								Energy consumption for session in real environment (J)							
	Bluetooth				Wi-Fi				Bluetooth				Wi-Fi			
	Average	Standard Deviation	Prediction interval		Average	Standard deviation	Prediction interval		Average	Standard Deviation	Prediction interval		average	Standard deviation	Prediction interval	
			min	max			min	max			min	max			min	max
U	0.0547	0.0070	0.0477	0.0617	0.475	0.028	0.473	0.56	0.0641	0.0089	0.0551	0.0730	0.664	0.038	0.67	0.792
SU	0.0594	0.0068	0.0526	0.0662	0.481	0.008	0.479	0.499	0.0691	0.0072	0.0620	0.0763	0.799	0.122	0.728	1.083
SU	0.0635	0.0068	0.0567	0.0703	0.481	0.008	0.479	0.499	0.0682	0.0073	0.0608	0.0755	0.956	0.196	0.804	1.118
R	0.0702	0.0071	0.0631	0.0773	0.648	0.03	0.662	0.762	0.0795	0.0084	0.0711	0.0879	0.948	0.163	0.892	1.346
C					0.636	0.03	0.652	0.75					0.895	0.116	0.872	1.228
S					0.626	0.005	0.622	0.736					0.906	0.104	0.847	1.206
TS					0.637	0.03	0.654	0.752					0.848	0.117	0.747	1.123

In the Table 4 and Fig. 4 are presented security level- data transfer rate dependencies for Bluetooth and Wi-Fi protocols in ideal and real environments. From obtained results we do not observe statistically significant decrease in data transfer rate for Bluetooth protocol when the level of security is increased from Unclassified (U) to Restricted (R). For Wi-Fi increase in security level results in 14% decrease in data transfer rate. The presence of noise decrease data transfer rate by 15 – 25% for Bluetooth and by 35 – 60% for Wi-Fi. While the increase in security level does not provide significant impact for the data transfer rates of either Bluetooth or Wi-Fi protocols, the presence of noise causes the decrease of data transfer rate for Wi-Fi protocol from 2 to 3 times more than the for Bluetooth protocol.

In Table 5, we have provided statically processed results of the experiment, energy consumption for session by transfer 0.5 MB of data. To evaluate the energy consumption dependences on the used security levels, we have calculated the following energy consumption estimates: average, standard deviation and prediction interval [15].

6   Conclusion and Future Work

Measurement and analysis of energy and data transfer rate dependence on security level and the presence of environmental noise for Bluetooth and Wi-Fi communication protocols was performed. From obtained results the following conclusions have been drawn:

1. Operation modes of Wi-Fi and Bluetooth protocols were evaluated and assigned to the specific security levels. The highest recommended security level for individual protocol was defined. Wi-Fi protocol provides a higher level of security than Bluetooth protocol. In accordance with security level classification Bluetooth protocol can be used only in implementation that does not require a higher level of security than R (Restricted).

2. With the increase of security level from Unclassified (U) to Restricted (R), a rise in energy consumption of 30% for Bluetooth, and 35% for Wi-Fi protocols was observed.

3. The comparative influence of noise on energy consumption was observed to be from 2 to 6 times greater for Wi-Fi than for Bluetooth. Energy consumption of Bluetooth protocol increased to 15%, and Wi-Fi – from 35% to 95%.

4. By increasing the security, level from Unclassified (U) to Restricted (R) data transfer rate for protocol Bluetooth practically does not change, and for Wi-Fi - decreases to 14%.

5. The comparative influence of noise on data transfer was observed to be from 1.4 to 3 times greater for Wi-Fi than for Bluetooth. Data transfer rate of Bluetooth protocol decreased up to 25%, and Wi-Fi – from 35% to 60%.

These research results we will use for development of our proposed the energy efficient protocol, which ensures the maximum bandwidth and the required level of security with minimum energy consumption [18]. The proposed adaptive energy efficient protocol composes the Pareto-optimal solutions set, which provides the necessary level of security, maximum bandwidth and minimum energy consumption.

Acknowledgements. This research was funded by the grant No. VP1-3.1-ŠMM-08-K-01-018 financed from the EU SA.

References

1. Karimi, K., Atkinson, G.: What the Internet of Things (IoT) needs to become a reality, `http://www.freescale.com/files/32bit/doc/white_paper/INTOTHN GSWP.pdf`
2. Smith, I.G. (ed.): The Internet of Things 2012: New Horizons. Halifax, UK (2012)
3. Overcoming challenges of connecting intelligent nodes to the Internet of Things. Silicon Laboratories, Inc., `http://www.silabs.com/Support%20Documents/TechnicalDocs/brin ging-the-internet-of-things-to-life.pdf`
4. Webber, R.H.: Internet of Things – new security and privacy challenges. Computer Law & Security Review 26, 23–30 (2010)
5. Kazanavicius, E., Kazanavicius, V., Venckauskas, A., Paskevicius, R.: Securing web application by embedded firewall. Electronics and Electrical Engineering 3(119), 65–68 (2012)
6. Gupta, V., Wurm, M.: The energy cost of SSL in Deeply Embedded Systems, Sun Microsystems Inc. Tech. Rep. SMLI TR-2008-173 (2008)
7. Pastore, M., Emmett, D.: COMPTIA SECURITY+ ST. GUIDE DELUXE. John Wiley & Sons (2006)
8. Lee, J.S., Su, Y.W., Shen, C.C.: A comparative study of wireless protocols. In: The 33rd Annual Conference on Bluetooth, UWB, ZigBee, and Wi-Fi, IEEE Industrial Electronics Society (IECON), Taiwan, ,pp. 46–51 (November 2007)
9. Friedman, R., Krivolapov, Y.: On Power and Throughput Tradeoffs of WiFi and Bluetooth in Smartphones. IEEE Transactions on Mobile Computing 12(7), 1363–1376 (2013)
10. Prasithsangaree, P., Krishnamurthy, P.: On a framework for energy-efficient security protocols in wireless networks. Computer Communications 27(17), 1716–1729 (2004)
11. Rice, A., Hay, S.: Measuring mobile phone energy consumption for 802.11 wireless networking. Pervasive and Mobile Computing Journal 6(6), 595–606 (2010)
12. IEEE 802®: local and metropolitan area network standards, `http://standards. ieee.org/getieee802/download/802.15.1-2005.pdf`
13. EEE 802®: local and metropolitan area network standards, `http://standards. ieee.org/getieee802/download/802.11-2012.pdf`
14. Monk, S.: Getting Started with.NET Gadgeteer. O'Reilly Media (2012)
15. Navidi, W.: Statistics for engineers and scientists. McGraw-Hill, New York (2011)
16. Bluetooth Smart. Bluegiga Technologies (2012)
17. Halperin, D., Greenstein, B., Sheth, A., Wetherall, D.: Demystifying 802.11 n power consumption. In: Proceedings of the 2010 International Conference on Power Aware Computing and Systems. USENIX Association (October 2010)
18. Venčkauskas, A., Jusas, N., Kazanavicius, E., Štuikys, V.: An energy efficient protocol for the internet of things. Journal of Electrical Engineering, 65(xx), pp. xx–xx (2014) (submitted for publication)

Author Index

—